湖北统计年鉴

HUBEI STATISTICAL YEARBOOK

2015

（总第31期）

湖　北　省　统　计　局
国家统计局湖北调查总队　编

中国统计出版社
China Statistics Press

图书在版编目（CIP）数据

湖北统计年鉴.2015 / 湖北省统计局 国家统计局湖北调查总队编
- 北京：中国统计出版社，2015.8
ISBN 978-7-5037-7509-3

Ⅰ. ①湖…
Ⅱ. ①湖…②国…
Ⅲ. ①统计资料-湖北省-2015-年鉴-汉-英
Ⅳ. ①C832.63-54

中国版本图书馆CIP数据核字（2015）第190485号

湖北统计年鉴—2015

作　　者 / 湖北省统计局　国家统计局湖北调查总队
责任编辑 / 佘竞雄　王　道
封面设计 / 刘亚非
出版发行 / 中国统计出版社
地　　址 / 北京市丰台区西三环南路甲6号
邮　　编 / 100073
电　　话 / 邮购（010）63376909　书店（010）68786171
网　　址 / http://csp.stats.gov.cn
印　　刷 / 湖北省统计局印刷厂
经　　销 / 新华书店
开　　本 / 890×1240毫米 1/16
字　　数 / 1240千字
印　　张 / 39.5
印　　数 / 2000册
版　　别 / 2015年8月第1版
版　　次 / 2015年8月第1次印刷
定　　价 / 380元

编 辑 说 明

一、《湖北统计年鉴—2015》是一本信息密集的资料工具书。通过大量数据，全面地分析、记载和反映了湖北省 2014 年经济、社会、科技、文化等方面的发展情况。具有信息量大、权威性强、适用性广等特点。

二、本年鉴包括综合、人口、从业人员和职工工资、固定资产投资、能源生产和消费、物价指数、人民生活、资源和环境、城市概况、农业、工业、建筑业、运输和邮电、国内贸易、对外经济和旅游、财政、金融和保险业、教育、科技和文化、体育、卫生、社会福利、湖北省开发区主要经济指标、武汉城市圈、鄂西生态文化旅游圈、县市概况、附录等 23 个部分。

三、2015 年的湖北统计年鉴，篇章结构与《中国统计年鉴》保持一致，参照执行了国家统计局《省级统计年鉴指标体系目录》，采用了最新的国民经济行业分类标准和指标口径，并对英文注释和指标解释进行了全面修订。

四、本年鉴对过去发表的统计资料重新予以审核，凡与本年鉴资料有出入的，均以本年鉴为准。本年鉴中统计公报的数据为初步数，若与年鉴数据不一致，请以年鉴数据为准。

五、年鉴中指标的使用要结合文中的指标解释，以及注解合理使用，以免发生错误。

六、《湖北统计年鉴》公开出版以来，受到国内外读者的爱护与支持，对本年鉴的内容和编辑工作提出了许多宝贵意见，为此，我们特表谢意。由于水平有限，编辑工作中难免有疏误之处，竭诚欢迎读者批评指正。

COMPLIERS NOTES

I. *Statistical Yearbook of Hubei* 2015 is an information-intensive data reference book. Through a large amount of data, comprehensive analysis, records and reflects the Hubei province 2014 economy, society, science and technology, culture and other aspects of development. With a large amount of information, authoritative, wide applicability and so on.

II. The Yearbook includes comprehensive, population, practitioners and staff salaries, fixed assets investment, energy production and consumption, price index, the life of people and natural resources and the environment, city situation, agriculture, industry, construction, transportation, post and telecommunications, domestic trade, foreign economy and tourism, finance, banking and insurance, education, science and culture, sports, public health, social welfare, Hubei Province Development Zone of main economic norms, Wuhan city circle, ecological cultural tourism circle of Western Hubei, county profiles, Appendix 23 departments, city of part of the Department of city information, not including the city administer county.

III. In the 2015 statistical yearbook of Hubei, discourse structure and "China Statistical Yearbook" remain the same, with reference to the implementation of the "provincial statistics index system directory". The statistic of yearbook adopted the lastest standard and diameter range. And the English version and the interpretation of indicators were revised thoroughy.

IV. The Yearbook of the past published statistical data to examine every and the almanac data discrepancies, refer to this yearbook prevail. The Yearbook of statistics data for the initial count, if the Yearbook text data are not consistent, please refer to the text data is accurate.

V. In the annals of indicators are used to combine the interpretation of indicators, as well as annotations and reasonable use, so as to avoid mistakes.

VI. *Statistical Yearbook of Hubei* published since, by domestic and foreign readers to care and support, the Yearbook content and editorial work put forward a lot of valuable advice, for this, we express our gratitude. Because the level is limited, in the editing work of unavoidable errors, we welcome suggestions and criticisms.

《湖北统计年鉴－2015》

编委会和编辑出版人员

一、编委会

主　　任： 李克勤　王跃新

副 主 任： 郑新华　叶　青　吴中志　张　静　蔡受清　黄承喜　崔永红　李　刚　胡国亮　程良世　梁　冰　陈小清　胡大华　程正华　朱小明

（以姓氏笔划为序）

委　　员： 丁善兵　马泽民　王　博　王建刚　王行刚　尹汉华　叶福生　卢玉廷　卢　薇　龙江舫　乐友来　付晓芳　刘　洪　刘水国　刘国强　刘　荣　许晓红　李团中　李良华　李明星　李昌文　汪　军　陈志明　张　晓　张利阳　张小青　张必洪　张在金　时明国　吴晓秦　明　锋　金　锐　胡先红　贺　宾　夏泽宽　盛少华　龚其民　谢名义　谢余强　蒋宇飞　舒振斌　魏尚平

二、编辑工作人员

总 编 辑： 李团中　许晓红

执行编辑： 邓有成

责任编辑： 周家庆　邓智红　王　道

英文编译： 王　道

Hubei Statistical Yearbook – 2015

EDITORIAL BOARD AND STAFF

目　录

CONTENTS

特　载

SPECIAL LOAD

1　综　合

GENERAL SURVEY

2 人 口

POPULATION

3 就业人员和职工工资

EMPLOYMENT AND WAGES

4　固定资产投资

INVESTMENT IN FIXED ASSETS

6　能　源

ENERGY

7　财政、金融、保险

GOVERNMENT FINANCE， BANKING AND INSURANCE

8 价 格

PRICE

9 居民生活

PEPOLE'S LIVELIHOOD

10　城市概况

CITY OVERVIEW

13 工业

INDUSTRY

14　建筑业

CONSTRUCTION

15 交通运输、邮电

TRANSPORTATION, POSTAL AND TELECOMMUNICATIONS SERVICES

16 国内贸易

DOMESTIC TRADE

17 科技和教育

SCIENCE，TECHNOLOGY AND EDUCATION

18 卫生和社会服务

HEALTH AND SOCIAL SERVICES

19 文化和体育

CULTURE AND SPORTS

20 公共管理及其他

PUBLIC ADMINISTRATION AND OTHER

21 开发区主要经济指标

MAJOR ECONOMIC INDICATORS OF DEVELOPMENT ZONE

22 “两圈”主要经济指标

MAJOR ECONOMIC INDICATORS OF "TWICE"

23 县域经济主要指标

ECONOMY OF CITIES AND COUNTIES

附录 全国分省主要指标

MAJOR INDICATORS BY REGION

2014年湖北省国民经济和社会发展统计公报

湖　北　省　统　计　局
国家统计局湖北调查总队

2014年，面对错综复杂的国内外环境，全省上下在省委、省政府的坚强领导下，以党的十八大、十八届三中、四中全会和习近平总书记系列重要讲话精神为指导，坚持“稳中求进”的总基调和“竞进提质、升级增效”的总要求，践行“绿色决定生死、市场决定取舍、民生决定目的”三维纲要，统筹推进稳增长、促改革、调结构、惠民生，全省经济社会发展保持了“稳中有进、进中向好”的良好态势，延续了“高于全国、中部靠前”的发展势头。

一、综 合

2014年，全省完成生产总值27367.04亿元，按可比价格计算，比上年增长9.7%。其中：第一产业完成增加值3176.89亿元，增长4.8%；第二产业完成增加值12840.22亿元，增长10.1%；第三产业完成增加值11349.93亿元，增长10.5%。三次产业结构由2013年的12.2∶47.6∶40.2调整为11.6∶46.9∶41.5。在第三产业中交通运输仓储和邮政业、批发和零售业、住宿和餐饮业、金融业、房地产业、营利性服务业及非营利性服务业增加值分别增长9.2%、7.6%、6.4%、14.6%、6.6%、12.4%和12.5%。

全省居民消费价格总指数（CPI）为102.0，价格水平上涨2.0%，其中：城市上涨2.0%，农村上涨1.9%。分类别看，食品上涨2.3%，烟酒下降0.3%，衣着上涨2.0%，家庭设备用品及维修服务上涨1.5%，医疗保健及个人用品上涨0.7%，交通和通信价格上涨0.2%，娱乐教育文化用品及服务上涨1.7%，居住上涨3.3%。全年农业生产资料价格下降2.1%。工业生产者出厂价格下降1.6%，工业生产者购进价格下降2.2%。

市场主体发展加快。2014年，全省新登记市场主体87.85万户，其中：新登记私营企业13.9万户，新登记个体工商户71.36万户。

全省城镇新增就业人员81.89万人，增长1.5%。截止12月末，全省城镇登记失业率为3.10%，较上年底回落0.12个百分点。

二、农业

全年粮食种植面积437.03万公顷，比上年增加16.79万公顷；棉花种植面积34.48万公顷，减少10.62万公顷；油料种植面积154.25万公顷，增加2.56万公顷。粮食总产量2584.16万吨，比上年增产82.86万吨，增长3.3%；棉花总产量35.95

万吨，减产 10.02 万吨，下降 21.8%；油料产量 341.9 万吨，增产 8.73 万吨，增长 2.6%（主要农产品产量见表 1）。

2014 年全省主要农产品产量

表 1 单位：万吨

产品名称	产　量	比上年增长%
粮　食	2584.16	3.3%
#夏　粮	505.60	0.9%
秋　粮	2078.56	3. 9%
棉　花	35.95	−21.8%
油　料	341.90	2. 6%
#花　生	69.06	1.4%
油菜籽	257.16	2.7%
茶　叶	25.03	12.8%
水　果(不含果用瓜)	614. 25	7. 9%
蔬　菜	3671. 52	2. 6%

畜牧、水产业稳步增长。全年全省生猪出栏 4475.11 万头，增长 2.7%；水产品产量达到 433 万吨，增长 5.6%。

三、工业和建筑业

工业生产保持稳定增长。2014 年，全省规模以上工业企业达到 14842 家，比上年净增 1463 家，增长 10.9%。完成工业增加值按可比价格计算，比上年增长 10.8%。其中：国有及国有控股企业增长 8.2%；集体企业增长 10.5%；股份合作企业增长 11.0%；外商及港澳台投资企业增长 7.4%；其他经济类型企业增长 12.8%。轻工业增长 12.7%；重工业增长 9.6%（主要工业产品产量见表 2）。

2014 年主要工业产品产量

表 2

产品名称	单位	产　量	比上年增长%
纱	万　吨	335.15	7.8
布	亿　米	82.40	12.1
化学纤维	万　吨	26.15	7.0
卷　烟	亿　支	1407.66	0.7
家用电冰箱	万　台	243.55	7.7
房间空气调节器	万　台	1441.50	21.2
原　煤	万　吨	890. 40	4. 0
原　油	万　吨	79.00	−1.3
发电量	亿千瓦小时	2344.81	6.3
#水电	亿千瓦小时	1375.80	17.1
粗　钢	万　吨	3056.43	2.6
钢　材	万　吨	3429.01	2.5
十种有色金属	万　吨	106.29	−1.1
#精炼铜	万　吨	52.30	3.8
水　泥	万　吨	11669.93	3.1
硫　酸	万　吨	691.31	6.4
纯　碱	万　吨	140.95	6.6
烧　碱	万　吨	103.34	3.5
化　肥（折 100%）	万　吨	1209.02	1.9
发电设备	万千瓦	87.90	−39.7
汽　车	万　辆	174.46	9.4
#轿　车	万　辆	76.12	14.3
移动通信手持机	万　台	2888.35	304.1

工业内部结构改善。高新技术制造业增长较快，全年完成增加值比上年增长 17.0%，占规模以上工业增加值的比重达

7.9%。

工业产销衔接较好，经济效益继续提高。全年全省工业完成主营业务收入40707.96亿元，比上年增长9.6%，其中：农副食品加工业，饮料和精制茶制造业，纺织，化学原料和化学制品制造业，橡胶和塑料制品业，建材，钢铁，有色，金属制造业，通用设备制造业，汽车，电气机械制造业，电子设备制造业，电力等重点行业实现主营业务收入超千亿元。工业产品销售率为97.1%。全年全省工业企业实现利润2174.63元，增长5.9%，其中国有控股工业实现利润674.16亿元，增长7.8%。

建筑业发展步伐加快。全年全省资质以内建筑企业完成施工产值10059.59亿元，比上年增长18.8%；实现利润451.29亿元，增长18.7%；税金480.39亿元，增长15.7%。新开工房屋建筑施工面积3.01亿平方米，增长12.7%。

四、固定资产投资

2014年全省完成固定资产投资(不含农户)24303.05亿元，比上年增长20.4%，其中房地产开发投资完成3983.79亿元，增长21.2%，商品房销售面积5601.98万平方米，增长5.7%，实现商品房销售额3088.31亿元，增长10.7%。按产业划分，全省一、二、三次产业投资分别为536.01亿元、10733.09亿元和13033.94亿元，分别增长32.5%、16.8%、23.1%。全省338个在建重点建设项目全年完成投资2595.36亿元，占全部固定资产投资的比重为10.7%。

五、国内贸易

全年全省实现社会消费品零售总额11806.27亿元，比上年增长12.8%。分城乡看，城镇实现零售额9884.04亿元，增长12.7%；乡村实现零售额1922.23亿元，增长13.2%。其中，限额以上企业（单位）实现消费品零售额7644.28亿元，增长13.6%。

六、对外经济

全年全省实现外贸进出口总额430.64亿美元，比上年增长18.4%，其中：出口266.46亿美元，增长16.7%；进口164.18亿美元，增长21.2%。新批外商直接投资企业301个。全年实际使用外资79.28亿美元，增长15.1%。

七、交通运输、邮电通信和旅游

全年全省完成货物周转量5798.12亿吨公里，比上年增长15.1%；旅客周转量1458.24亿人公里，增长13.0%。

全省邮电业务总量720.35亿元，增长19.3%。长途光缆线路总长度达到3.03万公里；局用交换机达到1197.3万门；固定电话用户907.4万户；移动电话用户达到4606.8万户；全省电话普及率为94.8部/百人；计算机宽带互联网用户869.7万户。

全年全省国内旅游人数4.69亿人次，比上年增长15.5%；国内旅游收入3675.98亿元，增长17.4%。入境旅游人数277.07万人次，增长3.4%。国际旅游外汇收入12.39亿美元，增长1.6%。

八、财政、金融和保险

全年全省完成财政总收入4095.80亿元，比上年增长14.8%，其中地方公共财政预算收入2566.90亿元，增长17.1%。在地方公共财政预算收入中，税收收入1873.11亿元，增长16.7%。全年财政支出5008.85亿元，增长14.6%。

年末全省金融机构本外币各项存款余额36494.82亿元，比年初增加3591.99亿元。其中：个人存款17820.70亿元，增加1840.39亿元。金融机构各项贷款余额25289.82亿元，比年初增加3408.80亿元。其中：短期贷款8613.55亿元，增加

779.18 亿元；中长期贷款 15517.22 亿元，增加 2388.62 亿元。

全年保费收入 700.23 亿元，增长 19.2%。其中，财产险公司实现保费收入 219.37 亿元，增长 20.6%；人身险公司保费收入 480.85 亿元，增长 18.6%。支付各类赔款及给付 230.64 亿元，增长 22.9%，其中，财产险公司赔款 110.29 亿元，增长 21.2%；人身险公司赔付 120.35 亿元，增长 24.6%。

九、教育和科学技术

2014 年末，全省普通高等教育招生 40.03 万人，在校生 141.97 万人，毕业生 39.09 万人；研究生招生 3.97 万人，在校研究生 11.67 万人，毕业生 3.26 万人；各类中等职业教育招生 16.5 万人，在校生 46.6 万人，毕业生 18.2 万人；普通高中招生 29.53 万人，在校生 91.90 万人，毕业生 34.95 万人；普通初中在校生 137.59 万人，小学在校生 321.16 万人，幼儿园在园幼儿 153.82 万人。

科学研究和技术开发取得新的成果。全年全省共登记重大科技成果 1778 项。其中，基础理论成果 13 项，应用技术成果 1728 项，软科学成果 37 项。全年共签订技术合同 21969 项，技术合同成交金额 601.74 亿元，合同金额比上年增长 43.7%。

全省科学研究与实验发展(R＆D)经费支出 510 亿元，增长 15%，占全省生产总值的 1.86%。全年安排“973”计划项目 203 项（课题），经费 2.02 亿元，“863”计划项目 100 项(课题)，经费 1.86 亿元。 全省围绕卫星导航、智能制造装备、生物基材料、生物育种、高技术服务业、移动互联网等领域，加大项目策划和争取力度，共争取国家高技术产业发展项目 20 个，安排国家资金 4.48 亿元。

全省具备向社会出具检测报告的产品质量监督检验机构有 137 个，获得总局批筹的国家产品质量监督检验中心 27 个。全省通过 CNAL 认可的检测/校准实验室 128 家。累计有 10680 家企业通过 ISO9000 体系认证；企业获得强制性认证证书 9501 张。法定计量技术机构有 150 个，强制检定计量器具 145 万台件。

全省天气雷达观测站点有 14 个，卫星云图接受站点 17 个。数字测震台网 52 个，地震台站 3 个。

十、文化、卫生和体育

2014 年末，全省共有国有艺术表演团体 86 个，群艺馆、文化馆 120 个，公共图书馆 112 个，博物馆 139 个。电影放映管理机构 89 个，放映单位 1543 个。广播电台 7 座，电视台 8 座，广播电视台 75 座，有线电视用户 1068.43 万户。全年出版报纸 19.05 亿份，各类期刊 2.92 亿册，图书 2.69 亿册。

全省共有医疗卫生机构 36089 家，其中医院 771 家，基层医疗卫生机构 34506 家，专业公共卫生机构 705 家；全省共有卫生技术人员 33.63 万人，其中执业（助理）医师 12.65 万人，注册护士 14.48 万人；全省共有卫生机构床位 31.87 万张，其中医院床位 22.24 万张，社区卫生服务机构床位 1.23 万张，卫生院床位 6.91 万张。

全年全省运动健儿在国际比赛中共获得冠军 58 项次、亚军 26 项次、季军 28 项次，其中奥运会项目最高水平比赛冠军 17 项次、亚军 5 项次、季军 1 项次；在各类全国比赛中，获冠军 48 项次、亚军 53 项次、第三名 69 项次，其中，全运会项目全国最高水平比赛中冠军 19 项次、亚军 15 项次、第三名 28 项次。全年销售体育彩票 40.87 亿元。

十一、人口、居民生活和社会保障

2014 年末，全省常住人口 5816 万人（指常住本省半年以上人口），其中：城镇 3237.8 万人，乡村 2578.2 万人。城镇化率达到 55.67 %。全年出生人口 68.88 万人，出生率为 11.86‰；死亡人口 40.42 万人，死亡率为 6.96‰，人口自然增长率为 4.9‰。

根据城乡一体化住户调查，全省居民人均可支配收入 18283 元，比上年增长 11.0%。按常住地分，城镇常住居民人均可支配收入 24852 元，比上年增长 9.6%；农村常住居民人均可支配收入 10849 元，比上年增长 11.9%。

社会保障进一步加强。年末全省参加城镇职工基本养老保险人数 1265.3 万人，比上年增加 46 万人，其中：在职职工 846.2 万人，离退休人员 419.1 万人；参加城乡居民基本养老保险人数 2231 万人。参加城镇职工基本医疗保险人数 933 万人，参加城镇居民基本医疗保险人数 1035 万人；参加工伤保险 576 万人；参加生育保险 480 万人；参加失业保险人数 521.4 万人，全年累计领取失业保险金人数 11.7 万人。

全年全省城镇居民最低生活保障对象 107 万人，农村居民最低生活保障人数 221.6 万人，国家抚恤、补助各类优抚对象 50 万人。社会福利事业不断发展。年末全省各类社会福利收养床位 25.6 万张，收养 18.4 万人，城镇社区服务设施共计 5100 个。全年销售社会福利彩票 89.26 亿元。

十二、节能降耗、资源环境

全省继续大力推进节能降耗工作，单位 GDP 能耗继续保持下降态势，可望完成年初确定下降 3%的目标。

长江干流总体水质状况为优。监测的 7 个断面水质符合Ⅱ～Ⅲ类的比例为 71.4%。与上年相比，长江水质总体无明显变化。

全省累计已发现矿种 149 种，累计已查明资源储量的矿种 92 种。

全省自然保护区达到 69 个，其中国家级自然保护区 18 个；省级自然保护区 21 个，自然保护区面积 106.52 万公顷。

注：本公报所列数据为初步统计数。

STATISTICAL COMMUNIQUE OF HUBEI PROVINCE ON THE 2014 NATIONAL ECONOMIC AND SOCIAL DEVELOPMENT

PROVINCIAL STATISTICAL BUREAU OF HUBEI
HUBEI INVESTIGATION TEAM OF NATIONAL STATISTICAL BUREAU

In 2014, facing the intricate environment of international and domestic, people of the whole province in the strong leadership of the provincial Party committee and government, adhere to the spirit of the 18th Party Congress, the third and the forth Plenary Session of the 18th CPC Central Committee, and Xi Jinping's important speeches as guidance, adhere to the "stability" overall tone and the general requirements of " competition, quality and efficiency" and, putting the three-dimensional framework of "green life determine the death, the market determine the choice, people's living determine the destination" to promote co-ordination steady growth, promote reform, adjust structure, benefit people's livelihood. The province's economic and social developments maintain a good momentum of "steady advance into the better" and continue the momentum of "higher than the national level, in the front of the central region".

I. General Outlook

In 2014, the whole province achieves a gross domestic product of 2736.704 billion yuan. In comparable prices, it is an increase of 9.7% over the previous year. Among which, the primary industry completes 317.689 billion yuan, grows by 4.8%; the secondary industry completes 1284.022 billion yuan, grows by 10.1%; the tertiary industry completes 1134.993 billion yuan, grows by 10.5%. The proportion of three industries adjust from 12.2:47.6:40.2 in 2013 to11.6:46.9:41.5. In the tertiary industry, transport and storage and postal services, wholesale and retail, accommodation and catering, finance, real estate, profit and nonprofit services grow by 9.2%, 7.6%, 6.4%, 14.6%, 6.6%, 12.4% and 12.5%, respectively.

The consumer price index is 102.0, a 2.0% increase in the price level. Among which, in city it rises 2.0% and in rural area 1.9%. On details, food rises 2.3%; cigarette and wine falls 0.3%; clothing rises 2.0%; household appliances and services rises 1.5%; medical care and personal items rises 0.7%; transportation and communication rises 0.2%; entertainment and education services rises 1.7%; residence rises 3.3%. The price for agricultural production falls 2.1%. The producer price for industrial products falls 1.6%, the purchasing price for industrial producers falls 2.2%.

Market main body development accelerates. In 2013, the number of provincial new registered market players is 878.5 thousand. Among which, the number of new registered private enterprise is 139.0 thousand; the number of new registered individual businessman is 713.6 thousand.

The increase of the number of provincial registered urban employed persons is 818.9 thousand, grows 1.5%. Till the end of December, the provincial registered urban unemployment rate is 3.10%, which is 0.12% less than the previous year.

II. Agriculture

Grain acreage is 4.37 million hectares, grows 167.9 thousand hectares; cotton planting area is of 344.8 thousand hectares, reduces 106.2 thousand hectares; Oilseed acreage is 1.54 million hectares, grows 25.6 thousand hectares. The total grain output is 25.84 million tons, which is 828.6 thousand tons greater than the previous year, increasing 3.3%; total cotton output is 359.5 thousand tons, reduces 100.2 thousand tons, falls 21.8%; total oilseed output is 3.42 million tons, increases 87.3 thousand tons, grows 2.6%. (Table 1: Major Agricultural Products)

Table 1: Output of Major Agricultural Products, 2014

Item	Output(10,000 tons)	Increased over 2013(%)
Grain	2584.16	3.3
Summer Grain	505.60	0.9
Autumn Grain	2078.56	3.9
Cotton	35.95	-21.8
Oil-bearing Crops	341.90	2.6
Peanuts	69.06	1.4
Rapeseed	257.16	2.7
Tea	25.03	12.8
Fruits (do not contain melon as fruit)	614.25	7.9
Vegetables	3671.52	2.6

Livestock breeding and aquaculture are growing steadily. In this year, live pig output is 44.75 million, grows 2.7%; aquatic product output reaches 4.33 million tons, grows 5.6%.

III. Industry and Construction

Industrial production maintains a steady growth. In 2014, the number of provincial industrial enterprises above designated size reaches 14842, which is 1463 greater than the previous year, grows 10.9%. The industrial added value grows 10.8% in comparable prices. Among which, the state-owned and state-holding enterprises grows 8.2%; collective enterprises increases 10.5%; joint-stock cooperative enterprises increases 11.0%; foreign, Hong Kong and Macao investment enterprises increases 7.4%; other economic enterprises grows 12.8%. Light industrial added value grows 12.7%; heavy industrial added value grows 9.6%. (Table 2: Output of Major Industrial Products)

Table2: Output of Major Industrial Products, 2014

Product	Unit	Output	Increase over 2013(%)
Yarn	10000 tons	335.15	7.8
Cloth	100 million meters	82.40	12.1
Chemical Fiber	10000 tons	26.15	7.0
Cigarettes	100 million units	1407.66	0.7
Household Refrigerators	10000 units	243.55	7.7
Air Conditioner	10000 units	1441.50	21.2
Raw Coal	10000 tons	890.40	4.0
Crude Oil	10000 tons	79.00	-1.3
Electricity	100 million kilowatt-hours	2344.81	6.3
Hydropower	100 million kilowatt-hours	1375.80	17.1
Crude Steel	10000 tons	3056.43	2.6
Rolled Steel	10000 tons	3429.01	2.5
Ten Kinds of Nonferrous Metal	10000 tons	106.29	-1.1
Copper	10000 tons	52.30	3.8
Cement	10000 tons	11669.93	3.1
Sulfuric Acid	10000 tons	691.31	6.4
Sodium Carbonate	10000 tons	140.95	6.6
Caustic Soda	10000 tons	103.34	3.5
Chemical Fertilizer（100% equivalent）	10000 tons	1209.02	1.9
Electricity Generation Equipments	10000 kilowatt-hours	87.90	-39.7
Motor Vehicles	10000 units	174.46	9.4
Automobile	10000 units	76.12	14.3
Mobile Phones	10000 units	2888.35	304.1

The structure of total industrial products improves and high-tech industry is growing rapidly. The province completes high-tech industry added value grows 17.0%, which makes 7.9% of the whole added value of industrial enterprises above designated size.

Industrial production and marketing link well and economic benefit continues to rise. The provincial industrial sales value is 4070.796 billion yuan, grows 9.6%. Among which, Among which, processing of food from agricultural products, manufacture of beverages, manufacture of textile, steel, automobile, petrochemical, electricity, food, electronic information, textile, equipment manufacturing, building materials industry achieve sales value exceeding 100 billion yuan. Industrial product sales rate is 97.1%. The provincial industrial enterprises realizes profits of 217.463 billion yuan, increases 5.9%. Among which, the state-holding industrial enterprises realized profits of 67.416 billion yuan, grows 7.8%.

Development of construction industry accelerates. Qualified construction enterprises together achieve a production value of 1005.959 billion yuan, grows 18.8%; realize profits 45.129 billion yuan, grows 18.7%; pay taxes 48.039 billion yuan, grows 15.7%. New construction area is 301.000 million square meters, grows 12.7%.

IV. Investment in Fixed Assets

The investment in fixed assets (excluding rural households) is 2430.305 billion yuan, increases 20.4%. Among which, real estate investment makes 398.379 billion yuan, grows 21.2%. The total saleable area of commodity house is 56.0198 million square meters, grows 5.7%. The total sales value of commodity house is 308.831 billion yuan, grows 10.7%. Divided by industry, the provincial investment in primary, secondary and tertiary industries are 53.601, 1073.309 and 1303.394 billion yuan, respectively; accordingly grow by 32.5%, 16.8% and 23.1%.

The 338 key provincial construction projects complete investment value 259.536 billion yuan, accounting for 10.7% of the total investment in fixed assets.

V. Domestic Trade

The total retail sales of social consumer goods is 1180.627 billion yuan, grows 12.8%. In terms of urban and rural differences, cities and towns achieve retail sales 988.404 billion yuan, increases 12.7%; the retail sales in rural areas is 192.223 billion yuan, grows 13.2%. In particular, the retail sales by businesses above designated size reaches 764.428 billion yuan, up by 13.6%.

VI. Foreign Economy

Hubei Province achieves a total foreign trade value of 43.064 billion dollars, grows 18.4% than the previous year. Among them, the amount of export is 26.646 billion dollars, grows 16.7%; import amount is 16.418 billion dollars, grows 21.2%. 301 projects of foreign direct investment are approved, and the total amount of FDI is 7.928 billion dollars, grows 15.1%.

VII. Transportation, Post and Telecommunications and Tourism

The provincial annual tonnage mileage is 579.812 billion ton kilometers, grows 15.1%; the volume of passenger transport is 145.824 billion passenger kilometers, grows 13.0%.

The annual income of post and telecommunications industries is 72.035 billion yuan, grows 19.3%. Long distance optical cable lines reach a total length of 30.3 thousand kilometers; the capacity of office telephone exchanges reaches 11.973 million lines. There are 9.074 million fixed phone users and 46.068 million mobile phone users. The provincial telephone penetration rate is 94.8 units/100 people. Broadband Internet users reach 8.697 million.

The number of domestic tourists is 469.0 million person-times, grows 15.5% than last year; domestic tourism income reaches 367.598 billion yuan, grows 17.4%. The number of inbound tourism is 2.7707 million person-times, grows 3.4%. International tourism foreign exchange income reaches 1.239 billion dollars, grows 1.6%.

VIII. Finance, Banking and Insurance

The provincial annual general finance revenue is 409.58 billion yuan, a growth of 14.8% over last year. In particular, the local public finance budget revenue is 256.69 billion yuan, grows 17.1%. In local public finance budget revenue, tax income accounts for 187.311 billion yuan, grows 16.7%. The annual expenditure is 500.885 billion yuan, grows 14.6%.

At the end of 2014, the savings deposit in all items of financial institutions totaled 3649.482 billion yuan, increases 359.199 billion yuan over last year. Among which, personal deposit is 1782.070 billion yuan, an increase of 184.039 billion yuan. Loans in all items of financial institutions reach 2528.982 billion yuan, up 340.880 billion yuan. In particular, short-term loan is 861.355 billion yuan, an increase of 79.918 billion yuan; long-term loan is 1551.722 billion yuan, increases 238.862 billion yuan.

The annual premium income reaches 70.023 billion yuan, grows 19.2%. Among which, property insurance companies achieve a premium income of 21.937 billion yuan, increases 20.6%; personal insurance companies achieve a premium income of 48.085 billion yuan, grows 18.6%. Payment of various claims is 23.064 billion yuan, grows 22.9%. In particular, property insurance companies pay 11.029 billion yuan, increases 21.2%; personal insurance companies pay 12.035 billion yuan, grows 24.6%.

IX. Education, Science and Technology

At the end of 2014, the total number of regular higher education enrollment is 400.3 thousand, the number of students at school is 1.4197 million, and the number of graduated students is 390.9 thousand. Postgraduate enrollment number is 39.7 thousand, in-school graduate students number is 116.7 thousand, and 32.6 thousand graduated. The number of enrollment for vocational education is 165.0 thousand, the number at school is 466.0 thousand, and the number graduated is 182.0 thousand. For regular high school the number of enrollment is 295.3 thousand, the number at school is 0.919 million, and the number graduated is 349.5 thousand. There are 1.3759 million middle school students, 3.2116 million primary school students and 1.5382 million kindergarten pupils.

Scientific research and technology development make new achievements. There are 1778 achievements meet or surpass provincial level. In particular, 13 are about basic theory, 1728 are about application and 37 are about soft science. 21969 technological contracts are signed, which makes an amount of 60.174 billion yuan, grows 43.7%.

The scientific research and experimental development (R&D) expenditure achieves 51.0 billion yuan, grows 15.0%, occupying 1.86% of provincial gross domestic product. The arrangement of '973' projects are 203 tasks, with 202 million yuan of funds; '863' projects make 100 tasks, with 186 million yuan of funds. The province increases project planning and strength for contest in fields of satellite navigation, intelligent manufacturing equipment, bio-based materials, bio-breeding, high-tech services, mobile internet, etc. There are 20 national high technology industry development projects with investment of 4.48 billion from state found.

There are 137 inspection institutions that are capable of issuing quality test report and 27 of them are of national level. 128 detection and calibration laboratories are certified by CNAL. 10680 enterprises receive ISO9000 certification and 9501 China Compulsory Certifications are issued. The number of legal technical institution of metrology is 150 and they complete 1.45 million pieces of compulsory verification.

The number of weather radar observatories is 14. The number of satellite image receiving stations is 17. There are together 52 seismic network and 3 seismic stations.

X. Culture, Public Health and Sports

At the end of 2014, the province has 86 state-owned art troupes, 120 mass art/culture galleries, 112 public libraries and 139 museums. There are 89 film censorship institutions and 1543 showing units. There are 7 broadcasting stations, 8 television stations, 75 radio and television stations, and 10.6843 million cable television subscribers. 1.905 billion national and provincial newspapers copies, 229 million journals and 269 million books are issued.

The province has 36089 health institutions (including village clinic), including 771 hospitals, 34506 health care institutions at grass-root level and 705 specialized public health institutions. There are 336.3 thousand medical technical personnel. Among which, there are 126.5 thousand licensed (assistant) doctors and 144.8 thousand registered nurses. The number of beds of medical and health institutions is 318.7 thousand. Among which, there are 222.4 thousand hospital beds, 12.3 thousand beds of community health service institutions and 69.1 thousand beds of health centers.

In international sports competitions, our athletes win the first, second and third place for 58, 26 and 28 times, respectively. In particular, in Olympic Games it is 17, 5 and 1 times respectively. In all types of nationwide competitions, it is 48, 53 and 69 times respectively, among which, the highest level Championship Games project ,is 19, 15 and 28 times respectively. Annual sales value of sports lottery tickets is 4.087 billion yuan,.

XI. Population, Living Conditions and Social Security

At the end of 2014, the provincial resident population is 58.16 million (refers to the number of people living for more than half a year). In particular, 32.378 million people live in town and 25.782 million people live in the country, reaching a 55.67% urbanization rate. The newly-born population is 688.8 thousand, a birth rate of 11. 86‰. The death population is 404.2 thousand, a death rate of 6.96‰. The natural population growth rate is 4.9‰.

According to the integrated household survey, the disposable income of the provincial residents is 18283 yuan, increases 11.0%. Divided by region, the disposable income of urban residents is 24852 yuan a year, increases 9.6%; the disposable income of rural residents is 10849 yuan a year, increases 11.9%.

Social security is further strengthened. At the end of the year, the number of urban employees basic pension insurance contributors is 12.653 million, grows 460 thousand. In particular, 8.462 million are on-the-job and 4.191 million are retired; there are 22.31 million basic pension insurance contributors for urban and rural residents. There are 9.33 million urban basic medical care insurance contributors for staff and workers; there are 10.35 million urban basic medical care insurance contributors for residents. There are 5.76 million work injury insurance contributors; there are 4.80 million maternity insurance contributors. There are 5.214 million unemployment insurance contributors. The number of person receiving unemployment insurance is 117 thousand.

There are 1.07 million urban lowest social security objects and 2.216 million rural lowest social security objects. 500 thousand people are comforted and compensated by the government. Social welfare continues to develop. At the end of the year, social welfare institutions of various types provided 256 thousand beds for 184 thousand people. There are together 5100 social service center in urban area. The sales value of welfare lottery is 8.926 billion yuan.

XII. Energy-saving and Environment

The province continues to propel energy saving. The energy consumption per GDP maintains a trend of decline, expecting to achieve the goal of a 3% decrease settled at the beginning of this year.

Water quality of the main stream of Yangtze River is generally good. 7 water quality monitoring sections show that 71.4% achieves grade II~III. Compared with 2013,the overall water quality of the Yangtze River does not change much.

Inside the province, 149 types of mineral have been found. 92 kinds are with proven reserves.

The province has 69 natural protection areas. In particular, there are 18 national nature reserves and 21 provincial nature reserves. The total area is 1065.2 thousand hectares.

Note: All figures in the Communiqué are preliminary statistics.

1 综　合

General Survey

资料整理：孙再明　陈福才
朱　江　刘艳丽

综　　合

General　Survey

从数字看2014年的湖北

Statistic about Hubei in 2014

湖　北　的　地　位

Position of Hubei in the Country

地区生产总值27379.22亿元	Gross Domestic Production: billion yuan	占全国的4.30%
#第三产业11349.93亿元	Tertiary Industry: billion yuan	占全国的3.70%
人均地区生产总值47124元	Per Capita Regional GDP: yuan	相当于全国的101.01%
全社会固定资产投资总额25001.77亿元	TotaL Investment in Fixed Assets: billion yuan	占全国的4.88%
社会消费品零售总额12449.3亿元	Total Retail Sales of Social Consumption: billion yuan	占全国的4.58%
进出口总额430.6亿美元	Total Imports and Exports: billion yuan	占全国的1.00%
#出口总额266.50亿美元	Total Exports: billion yuan	占全国的1.14%
实际外商直接投资79.28亿美元	Actual Foreign Direct Investment: billion dollars	占全国的6.63%
粮食产量2584.20万吨	Grain: million tons	占全国的4.26%
钢产量3429.00万吨	Rolled Steel: 28.07 milliom tons	占全国的3.05%
发电量2382.30亿千瓦小时	Electricity: (100 billion kwh)	占全国的4.22%
城镇居民人均可支配收入24852元	Per Capita Disposable Income of Urban Residents: yuan	相当于全国的86.16%
农村居民人均可支配收入10849元	Per Capita Net Incomes of Rural Residents:yuan	相当于全国的103.43%

湖　北　的　人　口

Population of Hubei

常住人口	Population of Permanent Residents	5816万人
从业人员	Employment	3688万人
#在岗职工人数	Staff and Workers	968.77万人
出生人口	Birth Population	68.88万人
死亡人口	Death Population	40.42万人
城镇人口	Urban Population	3237.8万人
乡村人口	Rural Population	2578.2万人
人口密度	Density of Population	313人/平方公里

湖　北　的　经　济　发　展

Economic Development of Hubei

		1979—2014年平均增长(%)
地区生产总值	Regional Gross Production	10.8
第一产业	Primary Industry	4.7
第二产业	Second Industry	12.9
第三产业	Tertiary Industry	12.6
全社会固定资产投资	Investment in Fixed Assets	20.2
财政收入	Government Revenue	13.0
货物运输量	Cargo Transport Volume	7.8
社会消费品零售总额	Total Retail Sales of Social Consumption	16.0
出口总额	Total Exports	15.3

湖　北　的　一　天

One Day in Hubei

地区生产总值	Gross Domestic Product	75.01亿元
第一产业	First Industry	8.7亿元
第二产业	Second Industry	35.21亿元
第三产业	Tertiary Industry	31.1亿元
地方公共财政收入	Local Government Public Finance Income	7.03亿元
货物运输量	Freight Traffic	423.93万吨
竣工房屋面积	Floor Space of Building Completed	58.01万平方米
社会消费品零售总额	Total Retail Sales of Social Consumption	34.11亿元
出口总额	Total Exports	7300.22万美元
出版报纸	Newspapers Published	523.47万份
邮寄函件	Letters and Correspondents Delivered	18.29万件

1—1 土地面积与行政区划
LAND AREA AND ADMINISTRATIVE DIVISION

项目	单位	Item	unit	2000	2005	2010	2012	2013	2014
常住人口	(万人)	Population of the Whole Province	(10 000 persons)	5960	5710	5724	5779	5799	5816
土地面积	(万平方公里)	Land Area	(10 000 sq.km)	18.59	18.59	18.59	18.59	18.59	18.59
耕地面积	(千公顷)	Cultivated Area	(1000 hectares)	3282.96	3161.17	3323.92	3390.06	3409.91	3420.51
行政区划		Adinimisrtative Division							
省辖市	(个)	Municipality	(unit)	12	12	12	12	12	12
自治州	(个)	Autonomous	(unit)	1	1	1	1	1	1
林区	(个)	Forest Zone	(unit)	1	1	1	1	1	1
县级市	(个)	City	(unit)	24	24	24	24	24	24
省辖行政单位	(个)	Adinimistrative Units under the Jurisdiction of Province	(unit)	3	3	3	3	3	3
县	(个)	County	(unit)	41	39	40	40	40	39
乡政府	(个)	Local Government	(unit)	476	217	201	188	175	170
镇政府	(个)	Township Government	(unit)	853	737	742	746	757	761
办事处	(个)	Office	(unit)	145	163	211	298	300	302
村民委员会	(个)	Village Community	(unit)	32400	26678	26018	25991	25955	25606
村民小组	(个)	Village Groups	(unit)	259250	212587	209598	210432	210108	208966

1—2　市、州行政区划
ADMINISTRATIVE DIVISION OF MUNICIPALITIES AND PREFECTURE

单位：个　　(2014年底)(by the End of 2014)　　(unit)

地 区	Region	县级市 Cities	县 Counties	区 Districts	乡政府 Village Government	镇政府 Township Government	村民委员会 Village Community	村民小组 Village Groups
全　省	Total	24	39	39	170	761	25606	208966
武汉市	Wuhan			13	3	5	1957	17346
黄石市	Huangshi	1	1	4	1	27	799	7563
十堰市	Shiyan	1	4	3	35	71	1839	10121
荆州市	Jingzhou	3	3	2	13	89	2418	20414
宜昌市	Yichang	3	5	5	20	67	1386	8215
襄阳市	Xiangyang	3	3	3	4	74	2350	14771
鄂州市	Ezhou			3	3	18	316	4027
荆门市	Jingmen	1	2	2	2	50	1377	9961
孝感市	Xiaogan	3	3	1	23	72	2924	23347
黄冈市	Huanggang	2	7	1	16	99	4285	37321
咸宁市	Xianning	1	4	1	12	52	908	10004
恩施自治州	Enshi	2	6		35	48	2360	23133
随州市	Suizhou	1	1	1		37	850	8369
仙桃市	Xiantao	1				15	626	4482
天门市	Tianmen	1			1	21	754	6455
潜江市	Qianjiang	1				10	390	3105
神农架林区	Shennongjia				2	6	67	332

注：乡政府、镇政府、村民委员会、村民小组数只涉及农村生产经营单位数

Note:The number of village government, township government, village community and village groups only refers to the number of units run by village production operation.

1-3 全省法人、产业活动单位数（2014年）

指标名称	Item	合计 Total
总 计	Total	567794
一、按地区分组	**Grouped by Region**	
武汉市	Wuhan	154305
黄石市	Huangshi	21834
十堰市	Shiyan	34287
宜昌市	Yichang	69749
襄阳市	Xiangyang	64364
鄂州市	Ezhou	11436
荆门市	Jingmen	24190
孝感市	Xiaogan	28866
荆州市	Jingzhou	30124
黄冈市	Huanggang	41993
咸宁市	Xianning	20218
随州市	Suizhou	13632
恩施州	Enshi	27260
仙桃市	Xiantao	8516
潜江市	Qianjiang	7548
天门市	Tianmen	7627
神农架	Shennongjia	1845
二、按国民经济行业门类分组	**Grouped by Sector**	
农、林、牧、渔业	Farming, Forestry, Animal husbandary and Fishery	44612
采矿业	Mining	4757
制造业	Manufacturing	76294
电力、热力、燃气及水生产和供应业	Power, Gas and Water Production and Supply	3553
建筑业	Construction	23630
批发和零售业	Transportaation, Storage and Post	151599
交通运输、仓储和邮政业	Information Transmission, Computer Service and software	14207
住宿和餐饮业	Wholesale and Retail Sale	12083
信息传输、软件和信息技术服务业	Hotel and Catering	10810
金融业	Banking	3192
房地产业	Real Estate	19929
租赁和商务服务业	Leasing and Commerical Service	44965
科学研究和技术服务业	Scietific Research, Polytechnical Service and Geological Prospecting	24724
水利、环境和公共设施管理业	Water Conservancy, Environment and Public Facility Management	5573
居民服务、修理和其他服务业	Resident Service and Others	13000
教育	Education	19842
卫生和社会工作	Health Care, Social Security and Social Welfare	12353
文化、体育和娱乐业	Culture, Sports and Recreation	11787
公共管理、社会保障和社会组织	Public Management and Social Organization	70884

NUMBER OF CORPORATIONS, INDUSTRIAL ACTIVITIES UNITS(2014)

法人单位数（个）Corporation Units			产业活动单位数（个）Number of Economic Activities Units	
单产业法人单位 Single-Industry Corperation Units	多产业法人单位 Multi-Industry Corperation Units	规模、资质或限额以上单位 Unit of Scale, Qualification or Above	合计 Total	多产业法人所属的产业活动单位 Economic Activities Units under Multi-Industry Corperation Units
541467	26327	42752	669226	127759
150233	4072	9397	171323	21090
20629	1205	1995	26135	5506
32083	2204	2916	42231	10148
67331	2418	4216	78889	11558
61982	2382	4770	73976	11994
11045	391	873	13384	2339
22744	1446	2572	28729	5985
26909	1957	2595	36343	9434
27852	2272	3132	37649	9797
39238	2755	3303	54900	15662
19331	887	2067	23978	4647
12703	929	1455	17934	5231
25671	1589	1509	32638	6967
7987	529	786	10125	2138
7242	306	562	9280	2038
6707	920	548	9485	2778
1780	65	56	2227	447
44400	212		46475	2075
4627	130	1131	5045	418
74866	1428	18952	78312	3446
3286	267	424	5311	2025
22759	871	3977	25673	2914
148748	2851	10123	173765	25017
13537	670		18254	4717
11730	353	3194	16128	4398
10607	203		14217	3610
2618	574		13062	10444
18933	996	4951	21773	2840
44223	742		48696	4473
24104	620		26846	2742
5300	273		6852	1552
12829	171		14172	1343
17416	2426		23601	6185
11178	1175		32453	21275
11595	192		12734	1139
58711	12173		85857	27146

1-3 续表1 continued

指 标 名 称	Item	合计 Total
总计	Total	567794
三、按登记注册类型分组	**Grouped by Type of Registration**	
内资	Inner Funded	564594
国有	State-owned	56307
集体	Collective-owned	9171
股份合作	Share Holding Cooperative	1792
联营	Joint Funded	1211
国有联营	State Joint owned	238
集体联营	Collective Joint-owned	545
国有与集体联营	State - owned and Collective Joint-owned	107
其他联营	Other Joint-owned	321
有限责任公司	Co. Ltd	110263
国有独资公司	State-owned Solely Funded Co.	798
其他有限责任公司	Other Co. Ltd	109465
股份有限公司	Share Holding Co.Ltd.	6058
私营	Private - owned Enterprises	251541
私营独资	Private Solely Funded Enterprises	99654
私营合伙	Private Partnership Enterprises	12278
私营有限责任公司	Private Co. Ltd	133377
私营股份有限公司	Private Share Holding Co.Ltd.	6232
其他内资	Others	128251
港澳台商投资	Hongkong, Macao and Taiwan Funded Enterprises	1279
与港澳台商合资经营	Joint Venture with Hongkong, Macao and Taiwan	487
与港澳台商合作经营	Cooperate with Hongkong, Macao and Taiwan Funded	43
港澳台商独资	Enterprises Solely Funded by Hongkong, Macao and Taiwan	664
港澳台商投资股份有限公司	Share Holding Co.Ltd. with Hongkong, Macao and Taiwan Investment	64
其他港、澳、台商投资	Other Hongkong, Macao and Taiwan Investment	21
外商投资	Foreign Funded Enterprises	1921
中外合资经营	Sino - Foreign Joint Funded Enterprises	604
中外合作经营	Sino - Foreign Cooperative Funded Enterprises	36
外资企业	Foreign Solely Funded Enterprises	583
外商投资股份有限公司	Foreign Funded Share Holding Co.Ltd.	50
其他外商投资	Other Foreign Investment	648
四、按机构类型分组	**Grouped by Type**	
企业	Enterprise	429640
事业单位	Public Institution	42640
机关	Government Agency	9874
社会团体	Mass Organization	13447
民办非企业单位	Private Non Enterprise Unit	13366
基金会	Foundation	73
居委会	Neighborhood Committee	4244
村委会	Village Committee	26912
其他组织机构	Others	27598

法人单位数（个） Corporation Units			产业活动单位数（个） Number of Economic Activities Units	
单产业法人单位 Single-Industry Corperation Units	多产业法人单位 Multi-Industry Corperation Units	规模、资质或限额以上单位 Unit of Scale, Qualification or Above	合计 Total	多产业法人所属的产业活动单位 Economic Activities Units under Multi-Industry Corperation Units
541467	26327	42752	669226	127759
538498	26096	41428	664263	125765
48799	7508	910	88272	39473
8599	572	516	18123	9524
1672	120	98	2900	1228
1154	57	37	1973	819
220	18	3	488	268
522	23	14	838	316
99	8	5	190	91
313	8	15	457	144
106836	3427	15040	119987	13151
650	148	290	1029	379
106186	3279	14750	118958	12772
5353	705	1445	13182	7829
247750	3791	22660	265739	17989
99150	504	2226	104246	5096
12153	125	323	13062	909
130404	2973	19071	141521	11117
6043	189	1040	6910	867
118335	9916	722	154087	35752
1165	114	666	2270	1105
451	36	282	869	418
41	2	11	69	28
597	67	347	1061	464
55	9	24	194	139
21	0	2	77	56
1804	117	658	2693	889
547	57	347	759	212
34	2	11	45	11
534	49	269	1071	537
45	5	19	127	82
644	4	12	691	47
419849	9791	42718	482845	62996
37907	4733	3	64312	26405
7562	2312		14869	7307
13305	142		15272	1967
13127	239	2	13127	0
72	1		87	15
3561	683		4350	789
18706	8206		28364	9658
27378	220	29	46000	18622

1-4 国民经济和社会发展总量与速度指标

指　标	Item	总　量　指　标		
		1978	1990	2000
人口与就业	**Population and Employment**			
人口　(万人)	**Population　(10 000 persons)**			
年末人口	Population at Year-end	4574.91	5439.29	5950.89
城镇人口	Urban	690.23	1551.51	2408.49
乡村人口	Rural	3884.68	3887.78	3542.40
就业　(万人)	**Employment　(10 000 persons)**			
就业人数	Employment	1910.37	3040.40	3384.90
职工人数	Staff and Workers	457.34	698.55	677.96
#国有单位	State-owned Units	371.56	524.12	501.11
宏观经济	**Marcoeconomy**			
国民核算　(亿元)	**National Accounting　(100 million yuan)**			
地区生产总值	Gross Domestic Products	151.00	824.38	3545.39
第一产业	First Industry	61.11	289.45	662.30
第二产业	Second Industry	63.71	313.39	1437.38
第三产业	Tertiary Industry	26.18	221.54	1445.71
支出法地区生产总值	Gross Domestic Expenditures			
#最终消费	Final Consumption Expenditures	81.70	535.49	2030.07
居民消费	Resident Consumption	74.70	434.62	1594.08
政府消费	Government Consumption Expenditures	7.00	100.87	436.00
资本形成总额	Gross Capital Formation	43.11	261.95	1882.47
固定资本形成	Fixed Capital Formation	31.40	147.13	1451.85
存货增加	Changes in Stock	11.71	114.82	430.62
固定资产投资　(亿元)	**Investment in Fixed Assets　(100 million yuan)**			
全社会固定资产投资总额	Total Investment in Fixed Assets	33.58	144.44	1421.55
#国有单位	State-Owned Units	33.19	100.35	857.01
集体单位	Collective-owned Units	0.39	15.59	128.32
#房地产开发	Real Estate Development		5.94	134.63
财政　(亿元)	**Public Finance　(100 million yuan)**			
地方公共财政收入	Local Public Financial Revenue	31.38	77.85	214.35
地方公共财政支出	Local Public Financial Expenditures	29.98	84.82	368.77
物价(上年=100)	**Price (preceding year = 100)**			
商品零售价格总指数	General Retail Price Index	100.50	102.90	97.80
居民消费价格指数	General Consumer Price Index	100.30	104.20	99.00
利用外资　(亿美元)	**Utilization of Foreign Capital　(100 million dollars)**			
实际外商直接投资	Actual Foreign Direct Investment		0.29	9.44
产　业	**Industry**			
农业	**Agriculture**			
乡村从业人员　(万人)	Rural Employment　(10 000 persons)	1525.14	1791.30	1781.70
农林牧渔业总产值　(亿元)	Gross Output Value of Farming, Forestry, Animal Husbandry and Fishery　(100 million yuan)	84.46	402.23	1125.64
主要农产品产量　(万吨)	Output of Major Farm Products　(10 000 tons)			
粮食	Grain	1725.63	2475.03	2218.49
棉花	Cotton	36.67	51.73	30.43
油料	Oil-Bearing Crops	23.71	95.75	269.98
糖料	Sugar Crops	8.73	34.66	101.66
蚕茧	Silkworm Cocoons	0.47	0.79	1.22
肉类产量	Output of Meat	64.00	146.85	271.19
水产品	Aquatic Products	11.00	70.98	234.34

注：1.人口数除1982年、1990年、2000年、2010年是以人口普查为基数推算外，1982年及以后为人口抽样调查推算数。
2.2000年以前数据是总人口数，2001年以后数据为常住人口数。

AGGREGATE INDICATORS OF NATIONAL ECNONOMIC AND SOCIAL DEVELOPMENT，THEIR INDICES AND GROWTH RATES

Aggregate Data			速 度 指 标 Indices and Growth Rates								
			2014年比下列各年增长(%) Increases					年平均增长(%) Average Annual Growth Rate			
2010	2013	2014	1978	1990	2000	2010	2013	1979~2014	1991~2014	2001~2014	2011~2014
5723.77	5799.00	5816.00	27.1	6.9	-2.3	1.6	0.3	0.7	0.3	-0.2	0.4
2844.95	3161.03	3237.80	369.1	108.7	34.4	13.8	2.4	4.4	3.1	2.1	3.3
2878.82	2637.97	2578.20	-33.6	-33.7	-27.2	-10.4	-2.3	-1.1	-1.7	-2.2	-2.7
3645.00	3692.00	3687.50	93.0	21.3	8.9	1.2	-0.1	1.8	0.8	0.6	0.3
660.90	939.88	968.77	111.8	38.7	42.9	46.6	3.1	2.1	1.4	2.6	10.0
260.76	251.97	252.43	-32.1	-51.8	-49.6	-3.2	0.2	-1.1	-3.0	-4.8	-0.8
15967.61	24791.83	27379.22	3857.6	1239.4	377.0	53.0	9.7	10.8	11.4	11.8	11.2
2147.00	3030.27	3176.89	428.1	176.6	88.2	19.7	4.8	4.7	4.3	4.6	4.6
7767.24	11786.64	12852.40	7672.2	2169.2	532.7	63.5	10.1	12.9	13.9	14.1	13.1
6053.37	9974.92	11349.93	7124.6	1527.7	375.1	52.2	10.5	12.6	12.3	11.8	11.1
7389.80	11161.21	12562.76	1858.1	851.5	323.0	48.9	10.5	8.6	9.8	10.9	10.5
5136.78	8053.82	9124.48	2366.0	762.0	317.7	66.1	18.9	9.3	9.4	10.8	13.5
2253.02	3107.39	3438.28	12160.1	64.6	436.8	33.8	8.5	14.3	2.1	12.8	7.5
8511.17	14245.35	16109.59	17058.2	2429.8	479.9	72.4	12.0	15.4	14.4	13.4	14.6
8200.40	13701.86	15442.86	4034.2	1568.4	193.0	71.5	11.7	10.9	12.4	8.0	14.4
310.77	543.49	666.73	772.8	89.8	-28.4	104.2	24.5	6.2	2.7	-2.4	19.5
10802.69	20753.91	25001.77	74354.3	17209.5	1658.8	131.4	20.5	20.2	24.0	22.7	23.3
3768.95	5068.42	5829.79	17464.9	5709.5	580.2	54.7	15.0	15.4	18.4	14.7	11.5
602.80	826.51	820.75	210348.7	5164.6	539.6	36.2	-0.7	23.7	18.0	14.2	8.0
1618.24	3286.02	3983.79		66967.2	2859.1	146.2	21.2		31.2	27.4	25.3
1011.20	2191.22	2566.90	8080.1	3197.2	1097.5	153.8	17.1	13.0	15.7	19.4	26.2
2501.40	4371.65	4934.15	16358.1	5717.2	1238.0	97.3	12.9	15.2	18.4	20.4	18.5
103.10	101.80	100.90	372.1	140.7	31.3	11.2	0.9	3.7	1.0	-3.2	-5.9
102.90	102.80	102.00	589.5	233.8	46.1	14.2	2.0	5.1	2.4	-2.1	-5.3
40.50	68.88	79.28		27237.9	739.8	95.8	15.1		26.3	16.4	18.3
2154.44	2280.14	2308.72	51.4	28.9	29.6	7.2	1.3	1.2	1.1	1.9	1.7
3501.99	5161.00	5452.80	6356.1	1255.6	384.4	55.7	5.7	12.3	11.5	11.9	11.7
2315.80	2501.30	2584.16	49.8	4.4	16.5	11.6	3.3	1.1	0.2	1.1	2.8
47.18	45.97	35.95	-2.0	-30.5	18.1	-23.8	-21.8	-0.1	-1.5	1.2	-6.6
311.80	333.17	341.73	1341.3	256.9	26.6	9.6	2.6	7.7	5.4	1.7	2.3
32.36	28.72	30.41	248.3	-12.3	-70.1	-6.0	5.9	3.5	-0.5	-8.3	-1.5
0.71	0.77	0.64	36.2	-19.0	-47.5	-9.9	-16.9	0.9	-0.9	-4.5	-2.6
379.42	430.08	440.44	588.2	199.9	62.4	16.1	2.4	5.5	4.7	3.5	3.8
353.09	410.97	433.30	3839.1	510.5	84.9	22.7	5.4	10.7	7.8	4.5	5.3

Note：a)Data of 1982,1990,2000.and 2010 are based on population census　Data of other years are based on sampling survey
b)Data before 2000 refer to total population. Data after 2001 refer to permanent residents

1-4 续表 1 continued

指 标	单位	Item	unit	总量指标 1978	1990	2000
工业		**Industry**				
主要工业产品产量	(万吨)	Output of Major Industrial Products	(10000 tons)			
钢		Steel		307.97	629.25	895.92
成品钢材		Rolled-Steel		184.63	533.07	811.10
发电量	(亿千瓦小时)	Electricity	100 million kWh)	91.64	340.39	538.11
原煤		Coal		644.01	924.26	389.34
农用化肥(折100%)		Chemical Furtilizers		27.62	132.07	221.11
化学农药		Chemical Pesicide		2.97	1.07	5.18
水泥		Cement		328.65	987.00	2460.92
化学纤维		Chemical Fiber		0.48	2.48	9.82
布	(亿米)	Cloth	100 million meter)	6.70	14.09	17.15
汽车	(万辆)	Automobile	(10000 Units)	0.80	11.38	19.57
建筑业		**Construction**				
建筑业企业职工平均人数	(万人)	Average Number of Employed Persons	(10000 persons)	25.94	41.88	82.76
建筑业总产值	(亿元)	Gross Output Value	100 million yuan)	11.11	49.30	454.35
施工房屋面积	(万平方米)	Floor Space of Building Under Constructio	(10 000 sq.m)	596.00	1684.90	6256.50
竣工房屋面积	(万平方米)	Floor Space of Building Completed	(10 000 sq.m)	297.40	785.90	3150.10
交通运输		**Transportation**				
货运量	(万吨)	Freight Traffic	(10 000 tons)	10199.08	10916.10	9345.19
#铁路		Railway		3342.00	3901.00	3857.00
公路		Highway		3382.00	2941.00	2228.00
水运		Waterway		3096.00	3784.00	3255.00
客运量	(万人)	Passenger Capacity	(10000 persons)	12009.20	32145.93	31593.00
#铁路		Railway		2854.00	2107.00	3469.00
公路		Highway		7429.00	27333.00	27184.00
水运		Waterway		1722.00	2693.00	679.00
港口货物吞吐量	(万吨)	Volume of Freight Handled at Seaports	(10 000 tons)			4113.46
邮电通信业		**Postal Telecommunication Services**				
邮电业务总量	(亿元)	Total Business Revenue	100 million yuan)	0.56	4.80	116.60
函件	(亿件)	Number of Letters Delivered	00 million pieces)	1.18	2.39	3.62
年末移动电话用户	(万户)	Number of Local Telephone Users	(10 000 units)			
国际互联网用户	(万户)	Internet Users	(10 000 units)			
农村电话用户	(万户)	Rural Telephone Users	(10 000 units)	4.13	7.07	180.00
国内商业		**Domestic Commerce**				
社会消费品零售总额	(亿元)	Total Retail Sales of Consumer Goods	100 million yuan)	59.84	326.36	1789.35
对外经济贸易和旅游		**Foreign Trade and Tourism**				
进出口总额	(亿美元)	Total Imports and Exports	00 million dollars)	1.73	11.90	32.10
进口		Imports		0.14	1.18	12.79
出口		Exports		1.59	10.72	19.31
入境旅游人数	(万人次)	Number of Tourists Received	(10 000 persons)	1.01	15.57	45.08
金融保险	**(亿元)**	**Banking and Insurance**	**100 million yuan)**			
金融机构存款		Deposits of Banking System		42.16	406.56	3037.22
金融机构贷款		Loans of Banking System		96.78	732.77	3147.77
国内保险保费收入		Domestic Premium			6.19	60.53

Aggregate Data			速　度　指　标 Indices and Growth Rates								
			2014年比下列各年增长(%) Increases					年平均增长(%) Average Annual Growth Rate			
2010	2013	2014	1978	1990	2000	2010	2013	1979~2014	1991~2014	2001~2014	2011~2014
2498.67	3000.98	3056.43	892.4	385.7	241.1	22.3	1.8	6.6	6.8	9.2	5.2
2894.72	3344.92	3429.01	1757.2	543.3	322.8	18.5	2.5	8.5	8.1	10.8	4.3
2028.67	2118.82	2344.81	2458.7	588.9	335.7	15.6	10.7	9.4	8.4	11.1	3.7
1291.71	855.87	890.40	38.3	-3.7	128.7	-31.1	4.0	0.9	-0.2	6.1	-8.9
899.08	1186.69	1209.02	4277.3	815.4	446.8	34.5	1.9	11.1	9.7	12.9	7.7
19.71	27.25	24.36	720.2	2176.6	370.3	23.6	-10.6	6.0	13.9	11.7	5.4
8982.87	11056.52	11669.93	3450.9	1082.4	374.2	29.9	5.5	10.4	10.8	11.8	6.8
11.66	21.67	26.15	5347.9	954.4	166.3	124.3	20.7	11.7	10.3	7.2	22.4
46.38	79.25	82.4	1129.9	484.8	380.5	77.7	4.0	7.2	7.6	11.9	15.5
172.29	158.70	174.46	21707.5	1433.0	791.5	1.3	9.9	16.1	12.0	16.9	0.3
170.71	174.20	206.37	695.6	392.8	149.4	20.9	18.5	5.9	6.9	6.7	4.9
4344.39	8465.50	10059.60	90445.5	20304.9	2114.1	131.6	18.8	20.8	24.8	24.8	23.4
25046.72	48937.96	62227.88	10340.9	3593.3	894.6	148.4	27.2	13.8	16.2	17.8	25.5
12813.44	22773.70	24867.30	8261.6	3064.2	689.4	94.1	9.2	13.1	15.5	15.9	18.0
97006.94	139740.26	154736.00	1417.2	1317.5	1555.8	59.5	10.7	7.8	11.7	22.2	12.4
10145.60	9010.40	7681.30	129.8	96.9	99.2	-24.3	-14.8	2.3	2.9	5.0	-6.7
71020.00	108824.21	116280.00	3338.2	3853.8	5119.0	63.7	6.9	10.3	16.6	32.6	13.1
15832.00	21897.00	30765.00	893.7	713.0	845.2	94.3	40.5	6.6	9.1	17.4	18.1
105415.50	143100.28	103671.80	763.3	222.5	228.1	-1.7	-27.6	6.2	5.0	8.9	-0.4
7281.30	9010.40	14302.70	401.1	578.8	312.3	96.4	58.7	4.6	8.3	10.6	18.4
96873.00	129533.75	87804.00	1081.9	221.2	223.0	-9.4	-32.2	7.1	5.0	8.7	-2.4
375.80	528.00	533.80	-69.0	-80.2	-21.4	42.0	1.1	-3.2	-6.5	-1.7	9.2
18782.67	26219.00	28969.15			604.3	54.2	10.5			15.0	11.4
1028.09	603.67	720.35	128533.9	14907.3	517.8	-29.9	19.3	22.0	23.2	13.9	-8.5
1.00	1.05	0.67	-43.2	-72.0	-81.5	-33.0	-36.2	-1.6	-5.2	-11.4	-9.5
3454.70	4416.80	4606.80				33.3	4.3				7.5
459.40	813.30	869.70				89.3	6.9				17.3
355.70	321.10	294.40	7028.3	4064.1	63.6	-17.2	-8.3	12.6	16.8	3.6	-4.6
7013.90	11035.94	12449.27	20704.3	3714.6	595.7	77.5	12.8	16.0	16.4	14.9	15.4
259.07	363.89	430.64	24792.5	3518.8	1241.6	66.2	18.3	16.6	16.1	20.4	13.5
114.65	135.52	164.18	117171.4	13813.6	1183.7	43.2	21.1	21.7	22.8	20.0	9.4
144.42	228.38	266.46	16658.5	2385.6	1279.9	84.5	16.7	15.3	14.3	20.6	16.5
181.74	267.96	277.07	27332.7	1679.5	514.6	52.5	3.4	16.9	12.7	13.8	11.1
21568.31	32636.15	36153.65	85653.4	8792.6	1090.4	67.6	10.8	20.6	20.6	19.4	13.8
14136.58	20796.86	24239.96	24946.5	3208.0	670.1	71.5	16.6	16.6	15.7	15.7	14.4
500.33	587.40	700.23		11212.3	1056.8	40.0	19.2		21.8	19.1	8.8

1-4 续表 2 continued

指 标	单位	Item	unit	1978	1990
教育、科技、文化		**Education, Science and Technology,Culture and**			
教育		**Education**			
高等学校本专科在校学生	(万人)	Students Enrollment in Institutions of Higher Eduction	(10 000persons)	4.94	13.04
中等专业学校在校学生	(万人)	Students Enrollment in Specialized Secondary Schools	(10 000persons)	5.36	1458.00
普通中学在校学生	(万人)	Students Enrollment in Regular Secondary Schools	(10 000persons)	372.38	211.56
小学在校学生	(万人)	Students Enrollment in Primary Schools	(10 000persons)	765.73	623.06
文化		**Culture**			
图书出版量	(亿册)	Books Published	(100 million copies)	1.62	4.02
杂志出版量	(亿册)	Magazines Issued	(100 million copies)	0.09	0.73
报纸出版量	(亿份)	Newspaper Issued	(100 million copies)	1.97	6.24
家庭、生活、环境		**Family, People's Livelihood and Environment**			
家庭		**Family**			
城镇居民平均每户家庭人口	(人)	Average Household size in Urban Areas	(person)	4.32	3.47
农村居民平均每户常住人口	(人)	Average Household size in Rural Areas	(person)	6.02	4.67
居住		**Housing**			
城镇居民人均住房建筑面积	(平方米)	Per Capita Net Floor Space of Urban Residents	(sq.m)		9.80
农村居民人均住房面积	(平方米)	Per Capita Net Floor Space of Rural Residents	(sq.m)		25.73
生活		**People's Livelihood**			
城镇居民人均可支配收入	(元)	Per Capita Annual Disposbale Income of Urban Residents	(yuan)	325.00	1427.20
农村居民人均可支配收入	(元)	Per Capita Annual Disposbale Income of Rural Residents	(yuan)	110.52	670.80
居民储蓄存款余额	(亿元)	Saving Deposit	(100 million yuan)	6.96	244.38
工资		**Wages**			
工资总额	(亿元)	Total Wages of Staff and Workers	(100 million yuan)	25.89	131.24
职工平均工资	(元)	Average Wages of Staff and Workers	(yuan)	581.00	1903.00
卫生		**Health Care**			
卫生机构数	(个)	Number of Health Care Organizations	(unit)	5940	10472
#医院		Hospitals		1817	2024
床位数	(万张)	Number of Hospital Beds	(10 000 units)	11.52	16.34
#医院		Hospitals		10.34	13.16
卫生技术人员数	(万人)	Number of Medical Technical Personels	(10 000 persons)	14.06	20.92
#医生		Doctors		5.82	8.68
环境		**Environment**			
污染治理项目本年完成投资	(亿元)	Investment for the Pollusion Treatment projects Completed	(100 million yuan)		1.81
本年施工污染治理项目数	(个)	Number of Pullution Treatment Project Under Construction	(unit)		1545
工业废水排放量	(亿吨)	Volume of Industrial Waste Water Discharged	(100 million tons)		16.23

总量指标 Aggregate Data				速度指标 Indices and Growth Rates								
				2014年比下列各年增长(%) increases					年平均增长(%) Average Annual Growth Rate			
2000	2010	2013	2014	1978	1990	2000	2010	2013	1979~2014	1991~2014	2001~2014	2011~2014
34.66	129.69	142.14	141.97	2773.9	988.7	309.6	9.5	-0.1	9.8	10.5	10.6	2.3
27.86	90.38	41.12	37.26	595.1	-97.4	33.7	-58.8	-9.4	5.5	-14.2	2.1	-19.9
350.93	341.83	247.19	229.49	-38.4	8.5	-34.6	-32.9	-7.2	-1.3	0.3	-3.0	-9.5
667.74	365.55	328.26	321.16	-58.1	-48.5	-51.9	-12.1	-2.2	-2.4	-2.7	-5.1	-3.2
2.88	2.75	2.63	2.72	67.9	-32.3	-5.6	-1.1	3.4	1.4	-1.6	-0.4	-0.3
2.20	3.01	3.09	2.81	3022.2	284.9	27.7	-6.6	-9.1	10.0	5.8	1.8	-1.7
13.42	18.17	19.82	19.11	870.1	206.3	42.4	5.2	-3.6	6.5	4.8	2.6	1.3
3.14	2.93	2.77	2.85	-34.0	-17.9	-9.2	-2.7	2.9	-1.1	-0.8	-0.7	-0.7
4.11	3.98	3.78	2.87	-52.3	-38.5	-30.2	-27.9	-24.1	-2.0	-2.0	-2.5	-7.8
13.90	33.20	38.80	41.90		327.6	201.4	26.2	8.0		6.2	8.2	6.0
30.11	40.99	41.84	54.78		112.9	81.9	33.6	30.9		3.2	4.4	7.5
5524.50	16058.37	22906.40	24852.30	7546.9	1641.3	349.9	54.8	8.5	12.8	12.6	11.3	11.5
2268.50	5832.27	8866.70	10849.06	9716.4	1517.3	378.2	86.0	22.4	13.6	12.3	11.8	16.8
1908.80	9851.00	15972.15	17820.7	255944.5	7192.2	833.6	80.9	11.6	24.4	19.6	17.3	16.0
405.34	1870.51	3588.71	4147.69	15920.4	3060.4	923.3	121.7	15.6	15.1	15.5	18.1	22.0
7565.00	28092.00	38720.00	43217.00	7338.4	2171.0	471.3	53.8	11.6	12.7	13.9	13.3	11.4
11065	10305	35633	36084	507.5	244.6	226.1	250.2	1.3	5.1	5.3	8.8	36.8
2041	603	713	771	-57.6	-61.9	-62.2	27.9	8.1	-2.4	-3.9	-6.7	6.3
14.96	20.07	28.85	31.83	176.3	94.8	112.8	58.6	10.3	2.9	2.8	5.5	12.2
12.99	13.51	20.05	22.20	114.7	68.7	70.9	64.3	10.7	2.1	2.2	3.9	13.2
23.88	25.16	31.16	33.98	141.7	62.4	42.3	35.1	9.1	2.5	2.0	2.6	7.8
10.30	9.69	11.94	12.74	118.9	46.8	23.7	31.5	6.7	2.2	1.6	1.5	7.1
8.52	27.74	25.17	26.29		1352.5	208.6	-5.2	4.4		11.8	8.4	-1.3
851	226	113	127		-91.8	-85.1	-43.8	12.4		-9.9	-12.7	-13.4
10.67	9.46	8.50	8.20		-49.5	-23.1	-13.3	-3.5		-2.8	-1.9	-3.5

1-5 国民经济和社会发展结构指标
STRUCTURAL INDICATORS ON NATIONAL ECONOMIC AND SOCIAL DEVELOPMENT

单位：% (%)

指　标	Item	1978	2000	2005	2010	2012	2013	2014
人口与就业	**Population and Employment**							
人　口	**Population**							
城乡结构	Urban and Rural Structure							
城镇	Urban	14.6	40.2	43.2	49.7	53.5	54.5	55.7
乡村	Rural	85.4	59.8	56.8	50.3	46.5	45.5	44.3
性别结构	Sexual Structure							
男	Male	51.3	52.1	51.8	51.4	51.3	51.3	51.2
女	Female	48.7	47.9	48.2	48.6	48.7	48.7	48.8
就　业	**Employment**							
产业结构	Industrial Structure							
第一产业	First Industry	77.0	48.0	47.7	46.4	44.5	42.9	40.3
第二产业	Second Industry	14.1	20.8	20.5	20.7	21.2	21.5	22.6
第三产业	Tertiary Industry	8.9	31.2	31.8	32.9	34.3	35.7	37.1
经济类型结构	Structrues by Ownership							
城镇单位从业人员	Staff and Workers Employed in Urban Units							
国有单位	State-Owned	81.2	74.7	62.1	40.4	34.6	26.8	26.3
城镇集体单位	Collective-Owned	18.8	14.3	8.0	3.1	2.3	1.5	1.5
其他单位	Others		11.0	29.9	56.5	63.1	71.7	72.2
宏观经济	**Macroeconomy**							
国民核算	**National Accounting**							
地区生产总值产业结构	Industrial Structure							
第一产业	First Industry	40.5	18.7	16.4	13.4	12.8	12.2	11.6
第二产业	Second Industry	42.2	40.5	43.3	48.7	50.3	47.6	46.9
第三产业	Tertiary Industry	17.3	40.8	40.3	37.9	36.9	40.2	41.5
地区生产总值支出结构	Domestic Expenditures							
最终消费	Total Consumption	54.0	54.0	55.9	45.7	44.1	43.9	43.7
居民消费	Residents Consumption	49.4	42.4	42.7	31.7	31.3	31.7	31.8
政府消费	Government Consumption Expenditures	4.6	11.6	13.2	13.9	12.8	12.2	12.0
资本形成总额	Gross Capital Formation	28.5	50.0	45.1	52.6	55.4	56.0	56.1
固定资本	Fixed Capital Formation	20.8	38.6	43.0	50.7	53.2	53.9	53.8
存货增加	Changes in Stock	7.7	11.4	2.1	1.9	2.2	2.1	2.3
净出口	Net Exports	17.4	-4.0	-1.0	1.7	0.5	0.1	0.2
投　资	**Investment**							
经济类型结构	Structrues by Ownership							
国有经济	State-Owned	98.8	60.3	38.7	34.9	25.8	24.4	23.3
集体经济	Collective-Owned	1.2	9.0	2.8	5.6	4.4	4.0	3.3
其他	Others		30.7	58.5	59.5	69.8	71.6	73.4
资金来源结构	Structure of Funded Sources							
国家预算资金	State Budget	77.2	10.0	9.0	8.0	4.8	4.3	4.4
国内贷款	Domestic Loans	0.4	17.2	16.7	16.4	11.9	13.1	11.5
利用外资	Foreign Investment		2.0	2.5	1.4	0.8	0.3	0.3
自筹资金	Fundraising	18.0	54.9	52.7	62.1	71.6	71.4	74.9
其他投资	Others	4.3	15.9	19.1	12.2	11.0	10.9	8.8

1–5 续表 1 continued

指　标	Item	1978	2000	2005	2010	2012	2013	2014
财　政	**Finance**							
地方公共支出结构	Local Public Financial Expenditure Structure							
#一般公共服务	#General Public Service				12.6	12.4	12.5	12.1
教育	Education				14.7	19.5	15.8	15.7
社会保障和就业	Social Security and Employment				14.7	13.3	13.9	14.5
利用外资	**Foreign Investment**							
实际外商直接投资结构	Actual Foreign Direct Investment							
合资经营企业	Joint Venture		63.4	40.8	35.3	45.5	32.5	38.0
合作经营企业	Cooperation		3.0	4.8	1.6	0.1	0.5	0.1
独资经营企业	Sole Proprietorship Business		33.6	34.5	63.1	52.7	64.2	55.6
外商投资股份制企业	Joint-stock Enterprises with Foreign Investment			0.9		1.7	2.8	4.5
产业经济	**Industrial Economy**							
农　业	**Agriculture**							
农林牧渔业产值结构	Agricultural Output Value Structure							
农业	Agriculture	77.3	54.7	52.5	54.9	52.6	51.9	50.6
林业	Forestry	4.9	3.6	2.1	1.9	2.1	2.4	2.9
牧业	Animal Husbandry	12.8	30.1	30.7	26.4	28.2	27.0	26.2
渔业	Fishery	0.8	11.6	13.3	13.1	13.2	14.5	15.5
农林牧渔服务业	Agriculture,Animal Husbandry and Fishery service			1.4	3.8	3.9	4.2	4.8
工　业	**Industry**							
工业产值按经济类型分	Industrial Output by Type							
#国有企业	#State-owned Enterprises	77.3	35.3	25.3	21.0	15.1	9.3	7.5
集体企业	Collective Enterprises	22.7	18.4	1.8	0.9	0.8	0.4	0.3
港澳台商投资企业	Hong Kong, Macao And Taiwan Invested Enterprises		4.2	4.3	5.1	5.7	5.1	4.9
外商投资企业	Foreign-invested Enterprises		6.8	18.3	15.0	11.0	11.3	10.9
工业产值按轻重分	Industrial Output Divided by Weight							
轻工业	Light Industry	47.1	38.4	24.8	27.5	32.7	34.2	35.4
重工业	Heavy Industry	52.9	61.6	75.2	72.5	67.3	65.8	64.6
建筑业	**Building Industry**							
建筑业总产值结构	Gross Output Value Structure							
国有经济	State-owned Economy	88.6	58.6	57.6	52.6	48.7	46.5	47.3
地方	Local	42.8	23.5	19.9	9.5	8.9	8.9	9.2
中央	Central	45.6	35.1	37.7	43.1	39.8	37.5	38.1
城镇集体经济	Urban Collective Economy	11.4	27.2	5.2	1.4	1.9	0.8	0.7
其它经济	Other Economic		14.3	37.3	45.9	49.4	52.7	52.0
运输业	**Transport**							
货运量结构	Cargo Structures							
铁路	Railway	32.8	41.3	17.0	10.5	7.3	6.4	5.0
公路	Highway	33.2	23.8	67.1	73.2	77.0	77.9	75.1
水运	Water Transport	30.3	34.8	15.9	16.3	15.7	15.7	19.9

1-5 续表 2 continued

指 标	Item	1978	2000	2005	2010	2012	2013	2014
国内商业	**Domestic Trade**							
社会消费品零售总额结构	Total Retail Sales of Consumer Goods							
#批发零售贸易业	Wholesale and Retail Sale	85.1	61.9	81.5	85.3	84.1	84.1	85.3
住宿及餐饮业	Hotel and Catering	2.8	10.8	13.1	10.5	12.1	12.0	10.7
其他	Others	12.1	27.3	5.4	4.2	3.8	3.9	4.0
对外经济贸易和国际旅游	**Foreign Trade and Tourism**							
进出口总额	Total Imports and Exports							
#出口	Exports	8.1	39.8	51.1	55.7	60.7	62.8	61.9
进口	Imports	91.9	60.2	48.9	44.3	39.3	37.2	38.1
海外旅游人数结构	Structure of Tourists							
外国人	Foreigners	47.3	79.3	75.9	76.2	72.9	76.4	77.0
港澳台同胞	Compatriots from Hongkong, Macao and Taiwan	52.7	20.7	24.1	23.8	27.1	23.6	23.0
教育、科技、文化	**Education,Science and Culture**							
教　育	**Education**							
在校学生结构	Structure of Students Enrollment							
大学生	College and University Students	0.4	3.3	10.4	15.1	19.0	19.8	19.4
中学生	Secondary School Students	32.6	33.3	45.7	40.6	36.3	34.4	36.5
小学生	Primary School Students	67.0	63.4	43.9	44.3	44.7	45.7	43.9
专任教师结构	Full-Time Teacher by Type							
大学	College and Universities	2.9	11.9	17.5	18.2	16.6	16.9	16.3
中学	Secondary Schools	39.6	38.9	44.5	40.3	43.8	42.4	44.0
小学	Primary Schools	57.5	49.2	38.0	41.5	39.6	40.6	39.2
科　技	**Science and Technology**							
各类专业技术人员结构	Structure of Scientific and Technical Personel							
工程技术人员	Engineering Personel	34.2	18.5	11.1	10.5	10.0		
农业技术人员	Agriculture	5.5	3.4	3.2	2.2	2.1		
科学研究人员	Scientific Research	6.7	0.6	0.8	0.5	0.5		
卫生技术人员	Health Care	32.1	20.9	22.8	24.1	22.3		
教学人员	Teaching	21.5	56.6	62.2	62.6	55.9		
生活、环境	**People's Livelihood and Environment**							
生　活	**People's Livelihood**							
城镇居民消费结构	Consumption Structutre of Urban Residents							
食品	Food		38.3	39.0	38.7	40.3	32.3	32.1
衣着	Clothing		11.4	12.0	12.4	12.3	8.8	9.2
居住	Residence		14.1	10.2	10.4	9.5	21.4	21.7
其他	Others		36.2	38.8	38.5	38.0	37.5	37.1
农村居民消费结构	Consumption Structutre of Rural Residents							
食品	Food	70.8	53.2	49.1	43.1	37.6	32.7	34.7
衣着	Clothing	12.0	4.8	5.1	5.3	5.5	5.3	6.3
居住	Residence	8.9	11.5	12.8	20.0	21.1	23.6	24.8
其他	Others	8.3	30.5	33.0	31.6	35.8	35.2	34.2

1-6　湖北国民经济占全国的比重(2014)
PERCENTAGE OF HUBEI'S NATIONAL ECONOMY IN THE COUNTRY(2014)

指　　标	单位	Item	unit	全　国 Country	湖北 Hubei	湖北占全国的比重(%) Percentage to the Country
土地面积	(万平方公里)	Ground space	(10 000 sq.km.)	960.00	18.59	1.94
年末常住人口	(万人)	Population	(Year-end)	136782	5816	4.25
地区生产总值	(亿元)	Local Gross Production	(100 million yuan)	636463.00	27379.22	4.30
第一产业		First Industry		58332.00	3176.89	5.45
第二产业		Second Industry		271392.00	12852.40	4.74
第三产业		Tertiary Industry		306739.00	11349.93	3.70
人均地区生产总值	(元)	Local Gross Production Per Capita	(yuan)	46652	47124	相当于全国 101.01%
全社会固定资产投资	(亿元)	Total Investment in Fixed Assets	(100 million yuan)	512760.70	25001.77	4.88
#固定资产投资		Investment in Fixed Assets		502004.90	24303.05	4.84
#房地产开发		Development of Real Estate		95035.60	3983.79	4.19
地方公共财政收入	(亿元)	Local Public Financial Revenue		140349.70	2567.00	1.83
社会消费品零售总额	(亿元)	Total Retail Sales of Social Consumption	(100 million yuan)	271896.10	12449.30	4.58
进出口总额	(亿美元)	Total Imports and Exports	(100 million dollars)	43030.40	430.60	1.00
#出口		Exports		23427.50	266.50	1.14
实际外商直接投资	(亿美元)	Actual Foreign Direct Investment	(100 million dollars)	1195.60	79.28	6.63
普通高等学校本专科在校生	(万人)	Students Enrollment in Institutions of Higher Eductioan	(10 000 persons)	2547.70	141.97	5.57
医院卫生院床位数	(万张)	Number of Hospital Beds	(10 000 units)	660.10	31.83	4.82
卫生技术人员	(万人)	Number of Medical Technical Personnels	(10 000 persons)	759.00	33.98	4.48
#执业(助理)医师		Professional (assistant) Doctors		289.30	12.74	4.40
在岗职工平均工资	(元)	Average Wages of Employee		56339	43217	相当于全国 76.71%
城镇居民人均可支配收入	(元)	Per Capita Disposable Income of Urban Residents	(yuan)	28844	24852	相当于全国 86.16%
农村居民人均可支配收入	(元)	Per Capita Net Incomes of Rural Residents	(yuan)	10489	10849	相当于全国 103.43%
居民人均储蓄存款余额	(元)	Deposit Balance Per Capita	(yuan)	35569	30686	相当于全国 86.27%
工农业主要产品产量	(万吨)	Output of Major Products in Argriculture and Industry				
粮食		Grain		60702.60	2584.20	4.26
棉花		Cotton		617.80	36.00	5.83
油料		Oil-Bearing Crops		3507.40	341.70	9.74
粗钢		Crude steel		82269.80	3056.40	3.72
钢材		Steel		112557.20	3429.00	3.05
发电量	(亿千瓦小时)	Electricity	(100 million kWh)	56495.80	2382.30	4.22
原煤		Coal		387400.00	890.40	0.23
农用化肥(折100%)		Chemical Furtilizer		6887.20	1206.00	17.51
水泥		Cement		247613.50	11418.10	4.61
化学纤维		Chemical Fiber		4389.80	26.15	0.60
布	(亿米)	Cloth	(100 million meter)	893.70	84.00	9.40
汽车	(万辆)	Moter Vehicles	(10 000 units)	2372.50	174.5	7.36

1-7 全省人均国民经济主要指标

指 标	单位	Item	unit	1990
地区生产总值	(元)	Gross Domestic Product	(yuan)	1541.00
第一产业		First Industry		541.00
第二产业		Second Industry		586.00
第三产业		Tertiary Industry		414.00
地方公共财政预算收入	(元)	Government Revenue	(yuan)	145.54
地方财政支出	(元)	Government Expenditure	(yuan)	158.57
全社会固定资产投资额	(元)	TotaL Investment in Fixed Assets	(yuan)	270.00
社会消费品零售额	(元)	Total Retail Sales of Consumer Goods	(yuan)	610.00
进出口总额	(美元)	Total Imports and Exports	(US.dollars)	22.24
#出口		Exports	(US.dollars)	20.04
农村居民可支配收入	(元)	Net Income of Rural Residents	(yuan)	671.00
城镇居民可支配收入	(元)	Disposable Income of Urban Residents	(yuan)	1427.00
居民储蓄存款	(元)	Outstanding Amount of Saving Deposits of Urabn And Rural Residents	(yuan)	455.00
在校大学生数	(人/万人)	Number of Students Enrollment in Institutions of Higher Education	(person/10 000 persons)	24.38
医院病床数	(张/万人)	Hospital Beds	(bed/10000 persons)	24.50
卫生技术人员数	(人/万人)	Number of Medical Technical Personnels	(person/10000 persons)	39.11
#医 生		Doctors		16.22
主要工农业产品产量	(千克)	Output of Major Industrial and Agricultural Products	(kg)	
粮 食		Grain		467.10
棉 花		Cotton		9.76
油 料		Oil-Bearing Crops		18.07
钢 材		Steel		100.60
原 煤		Coal		174.43
发电量	(千瓦小时)	Electricity	(kWh)	639.62

MAJOR PER CAPITA INDICATORS OF HUBEI'S NATIONAL ECONOMY

2000	2005	2010	2011	2012	2013	2014
6293.00	11554.00	27906.00	34197.27	38572.33	42825.76	47144.59
1164.00	1897.00	3766.67	4475.44	4938.49	5234.53	5470.32
2525.00	4926.00	13626.74	17098.30	19403.83	20360.41	22130.69
2540.00	4607.00	10619.95	12623.52	14230.01	17230.82	19543.57
376.61	658.36	1767.30	2560.79	3160.35	3785.14	4419.97
1647.93	1368.21	4371.64	5503.96	6517.79	7551.65	8624.80
2498.00	4970.00	18879.60	22525.71	28610.85	35850.60	43050.83
3144.00	5197.00	11743.40	14414.00	16577.10	18804.46	21436.54
56.40	159.40	452.77	583.87	554.03	628.61	741.52
33.93	78.02	252.40	340.28	336.33	394.51	458.82
2268.00	3099.00	5832.27	6898.00	7851.71	8866.95	10849.06
5524.00	8786.00	16058.37	18374.00	20839.59	22906.40	24852.28
3209.00	7929.00	17211.00	19879.00	23589.00	27591.00	29698.80
60.89	177.54	226.66	233.00	240.29	245.53	264.00
21.80	23.10	35.08	38.90	41.00	49.70	54.81
41.96	37.69	43.97	45.31	50.01	53.83	58.51
17.40	14.90	16.93	16.70	17.70	20.63	21.94
372.92	382.00	404.73	416.00	423.30	432.08	444.97
5.12	6.26	8.30	9.20	9.21	7.94	6.20
45.38	51.50	54.50	53.10	55.42	57.55	58.80
136.34	278.04	505.90	626.02	616.87	464.30	590.45
64.45	83.80	225.75	165.93	203.14	147.85	153.32
904.54	2204.00	3545.46	3574.00	3768.87	3660.08	4037.56

1-8 湖北的一天
ONE DAY IN HUBEI

指标	单位	Item	unit	2000	2005	2010	2012	2013	2014
每天创造的财富		**Daily Production**							
地区生产总值	(亿元)	Gross Domestic Products	(100 million yuan)	9.71	17.86	43.75	60.96	67.92	75.01
第一产业		First Industry		1.81	2.96	5.88	7.80	8.30	8.70
第二产业		Second Industry		3.94	7.70	21.28	30.67	32.29	35.21
第三产业		Tertiary Industry		3.96	7.20	16.58	22.49	27.33	31.10
地方公共财政预算收入	(亿元)	Government Revenue	(100 million yuan)	0.59	1.03	2.77	4.99	6.00	7.03
粮食	(万吨)	Grain	(10 000 tons)	6.08	5.97	6.34	6.69	6.85	7.08
肉类产量	(吨)	Meat	(tons)	7430.00	9387.00	10395.07	11295.89	11783.01	12066.85
水产品	(吨)	Aquatic Products	(tons)	6420.00	8718.00	9673.70	10654.79	11259.45	11871.23
钢	(万吨)	Steel	(10 000 tons)	2.45	4.31	6.85	7.69	7.36	8.37
成品钢材	(万吨)	Rolled-Steel	(10 000 tons)	2.22	4.34	7.93	9.75	9.27	9.39
发电量	(亿千瓦小时)	Electricity	(100 million kWh)	1.47	3.44	5.56	5.96	5.80	6.42
水泥	(万吨)	Cement	(10 000 tons)	6.74	12.36	24.61	28.10	30.65	31.97
布	(万米)	Cloth	(10 000 meters)	470.00	573.00	1270.69	1894.79	2176.71	2257.53
每天消费量		**Daily Consumption**							
最终消费	(亿元)	Final Consumption	(100 million yuan)	5.56	9.99	20.25	27.35	30.58	34.42
居民消费	(亿元)	Resident Consumption	(100 million yuan)	4.37	7.63	14.07	19.41	22.07	25.00
城镇居民每人消费性支出	(元)	Per Capita Living Expenditure of Urban Residents	(yuan)	12.72	18.46	31.37	39.71	42.01	45.70
#食品消费		Food Consumption		4.88	7.19	12.14	15.99	13.47	14.77
农村居民每人生活消费支出	(元)	Per Capita Living Expenditure of Rural Residents	(yuan)	4.26	6.66	11.21	15.69	21.51	23.78
#食品消费		Food Consumption		2.27	3.27	4.83	5.90	7.03	7.46
政府消费	(亿元)	Government Consumption Expenditure	(100 million yuan)	1.19	2.36	6.17	7.94	8.51	9.42
社会消费品零售总额	(亿元)	Total Retail Sales of Consumer Goods	(100 million yuan)	4.90	8.12	18.41	26.20	30.24	34.11
每天其他经济活动		**Other Daily Economic Acitivities**							
货物运输量	(万吨)	Freight Traffic	(10 000 tons)	25.60	136.78	265.77	345.74	382.85	423.93
旅客运输量	(万人)	Passenger Traffic	(10 000 persons)	86.56	195.61	288.81	354.82	392.06	284.03
竣工房屋面积	(万平方米)	Floor Space of Housing Completed	(10 000 sq.m)	8.63	18.90	35.11	55.88	62.39	58.01
出版报纸	(万份)	Newspapers Published	(10 000 pieces)	367.67	536.16	497.80	564.66	543.01	523.47
函件	(万件)	Letters Delivered	(10 000 pieces)	99.00	41.64	27.40	35.89	28.77	18.29
进出口总额	(万美元)	Total Imports and Exports	(10 000 USD)	879.45	2490.96	7097.81	8755.89	9969.86	11798.36
#出口		Exports		529.04	1219.18	3956.71	5315.34	6256.99	7300.22
实际外商直接投资	(万美元)	Actual Foreign Direct Investment	(10 000 USD)	258.63	598.63	1109.59	1552.33	1887.12	2172.03
每天人口变动和婚姻		**Daily Population Changes and Marriages**							
出生人数	(人)	Birth	(persons)	1582	1441	1625	1738	1757	1887
死亡人数	(人)	Death	(persons)	979	940	944	967	975	1107
结婚对数	(对)	Marriage	(couple)	969	1080	1564	1687	1769	1704
离婚对数	(对)	Divorce	(couple)	58	146	244	301	350	366

1—9　地区生产总值

GROSS DOMESTIC PRODUCT

本表按当年价格计算 (At current price)

年份 Year	地区生产总值 (亿元) Total Output (100 million yuan)	第一产业 Primary Industry	第二产业 Secondary Industry	工业 Industry	建筑业 Contruction	第三产业 Tertiary Industry	#金融业 Banking	#房地产业 Real Estate	人均地区生产总值 (元) Per Capita GDP (yuan)	人均地区生产总值 (美元) Per Capita GDP (USD)
1952	24.51	13.90	3.83	3.17	0.66	6.78			90.13	34.44
1955	34.05	18.14	7.45	6.25	1.20	8.46			117.88	47.88
1957	48.86	24.33	11.59	9.03	2.56	12.94			162.17	65.87
1962	52.13	29.30	10.63	9.10	1.53	12.20			161.47	65.59
1965	72.43	37.74	21.16	17.36	3.80	13.53			209.26	85.00
1970	88.15	44.41	26.90	21.79	5.11	16.84			221.78	90.09
1975	120.10	53.71	45.48	32.68	12.80	20.91			274.30	139.50
1978	151.00	61.11	63.71	52.17	11.54	26.18	4.54	1.42	332.03	210.53
1980	199.38	71.22	91.67	75.63	16.04	36.49	5.51	2.83	427.98	279.67
1981	219.75	87.00	92.85	78.73	14.12	39.90	6.02	3.19	466.32	273.49
1982	241.55	101.73	94.97	82.69	12.28	44.85	6.50	3.10	506.33	267.53
1983	262.58	105.40	106.50	92.19	14.31	50.68	7.09	2.53	543.27	274.98
1984	328.22	126.36	136.50	120.32	16.18	65.36	9.04	3.89	670.97	288.34
1985	396.26	144.44	174.35	152.88	21.47	77.47	10.71	4.61	800.69	272.66
1986	442.04	163.61	187.96	164.93	23.03	90.47	13.68	5.97	881.61	255.33
1987	517.77	183.99	224.53	197.66	26.87	109.25	17.09	7.39	1018.42	273.61
1988	626.52	214.66	271.25	244.17	27.08	140.61	20.82	8.88	1215.93	326.68
1989	717.08	239.07	300.46	276.47	23.99	177.55	28.14	9.18	1373.22	364.72
1990	824.38	289.45	313.39	284.15	29.24	221.54	33.77	11.36	1541.17	322.20
1991	913.38	279.30	359.86	327.50	32.36	274.22	40.30	13.61	1668.03	313.34
1992	1088.39	303.00	444.61	402.59	42.02	340.78	48.07	17.22	1962.45	355.86
1993	1325.83	346.39	537.60	475.44	62.16	441.84	52.22	25.63	2360.53	409.67
1994	1700.92	501.44	657.63	580.80	76.83	541.85	56.83	37.85	2991.33	347.07
1995	2109.38	619.77	780.18	680.92	99.26	709.43	60.86	42.07	3671.41	439.64
1996	2499.77	716.34	923.68	805.53	118.15	859.75	65.37	62.23	4310.98	811.22
1997	2856.47	767.92	1071.86	929.91	141.95	1016.69	69.68	69.65	4883.80	589.13
1998	3114.02	778.22	1199.08	1041.20	157.88	1136.72	74.14	81.78	5287.03	638.60
1999	3229.29	653.99	1314.44	1139.52	174.92	1260.86	78.81	85.01	5452.46	658.65
2000	3545.39	662.30	1437.38	1243.24	194.14	1445.71	81.49	99.40	6293.41	760.22
2001	3880.53	692.17	1574.39	1360.10	214.29	1613.97	88.48	122.49	6866.99	829.65
2002	4212.82	707.00	1709.89	1473.00	236.89	1795.93	96.95	145.17	7436.58	898.46
2003	4757.45	798.35	1956.02	1682.16	273.86	2003.08	107.31	176.80	8378.01	1012.20
2004	5633.24	1020.09	2320.60	1987.50	333.10	2292.55	118.85	204.80	9897.64	1195.83
2005	6590.19	1082.13	2852.12	2478.66	373.46	2655.94	127.32	217.17	11554.00	1410.45
2006	7617.47	1140.41	3365.08	2929.19	435.89	3111.98	174.99	294.73	13360.00	1710.91
2007	9333.40	1378.00	4143.06	3588.00	555.06	3812.34	337.27	409.65	16386.00	2178.55
2008	11328.92	1780.00	5082.07	4391.23	690.84	4466.85	393.05	526.88	19858.00	2859.57
2009	12961.10	1795.90	6038.08	5183.68	854.40	5127.12	479.11	546.11	22677.00	3317.24
2010	15967.61	2147.00	7767.24	6726.53	1040.71	6053.37	561.27	564.41	27906.00	4122.31
2011	19632.26	2569.30	9815.94	8538.04	1277.90	7247.02	674.57	634.67	34197.27	5294.68
2012	22250.45	2848.77	11193.10	9735.15	1457.95	8208.58	870.36	692.82	38572.33	6110.47
2013	24791.83	3030.27	11786.64	10139.24	1705.95	9974.92	1179.55	972.40	42825.76	6914.96
2014	27379.22	3176.89	12852.40	10992.79	1925.09	11349.93	1372.61	1062.71	47144.60	7674.77

注：从2013年起施行新的三次产业划分方法。

Note:The new classification of three industries has been implemented from 2013.

1－10 地区生产总值指数

INDICES OF GROSS DOMESTIC PRODUCT

按可比价计算，上年=100 (In comparable price, preceding year=100)

年 份 Year	地区生产总值(%) Total Output (%)	第一产业 Primary Industry	第二产业 Secondary Industry			第三产业 Tertiary Industry			人均地区生产总值(%) Per Capita GDP (%)
				工业 Industry	建筑业 Contruction		#金融业 Banking	#房地产业 Real Estate	
1953	114.0	107.4	129.4	141.0	93.3	122.7			111.6
1955	127.1	135.5	104.9	100.2	139.2	127.1			124.8
1957	107.4	106.4	115.3	109.5	146.0	102.6			104.8
1962	100.9	112.3	84.0	92.7	50.5	94.0			99.0
1965	118.1	111.5	132.5	124.5	196.4	114.9			115.4
1970	126.9	112.2	161.2	151.2	222.0	111.3			123.4
1975	111.4	94.5	139.0	135.2	152.5	116.0			110.0
1978	113.5	103.4	128.4	131.9	112.2	107.4			112.2
1980	106.4	86.9	123.5	126.7	107.0	111.0	96.3	160.6	105.1
1981	106.5	113.3	101.5	104.3	87.1	104.9	104.8	108.2	105.3
1982	111.9	115.7	104.7	107.3	88.6	121.6	116.9	105.2	110.6
1983	105.9	99.6	109.9	109.2	115.9	111.5	107.5	80.3	104.6
1984	120.9	114.4	125.0	127.6	106.1	125.2	123.8	149.6	119.5
1985	116.2	108.3	124.7	124.7	124.3	112.4	112.4	112.3	114.8
1986	105.5	103.3	105.2	103.9	116.8	110.2	120.5	122.2	104.1
1987	108.4	103.1	111.3	112.9	99.0	110.7	114.5	113.4	106.9
1988	107.8	94.9	113.7	115.1	101.5	114.3	107.0	105.6	106.4
1989	104.5	105.2	102.1	104.2	81.3	109.3	121.8	93.2	103.1
1990	105.0	107.5	99.0	99.5	92.8	114.8	108.9	109.7	102.5
1991	106.6	95.1	111.1	111.6	106.1	115.4	114.4	114.7	104.2
1992	114.1	108.2	116.6	117.5	107.5	116.9	111.5	117.8	112.6
1993	113.0	105.8	116.7	116.1	123.3	115.2	112.0	119.4	111.6
1994	113.7	107.1	118.8	118.9	117.6	112.4	107.7	127.3	112.3
1995	113.2	108.9	116.1	115.9	118.5	112.5	107.3	121.0	112.0
1996	111.6	104.5	115.5	115.4	116.6	111.3	107.3	116.5	110.5
1997	111.9	106.9	113.4	113.5	112.3	113.5	103.4	110.3	110.9
1998	108.6	99.4	111.2	110.9	113.9	111.5	107.0	117.9	107.9
1999	107.8	101.9	108.2	108.2	107.5	111.0	103.7	106.1	107.2
2000	108.6	102.5	109.1	109.0	110.7	111.5	105.6	116.8	114.2
2001	108.9	102.5	109.9	110.1	108.5	110.8	107.4	122.1	108.5
2002	109.2	102.0	110.1	110.1	110.5	111.4	108.4	114.5	108.9
2003	109.7	105.8	110.2	110.2	110.6	110.8	110.1	119.0	109.5
2004	111.2	106.5	113.6	113.5	114.4	110.6	106.3	114.4	111.0
2005	112.1	104.0	115.2	116.0	109.9	111.8	104.4	103.5	111.8
2006	113.2	105.1	116.0	116.3	115.3	113.5	135.0	129.4	113.2
2007	114.6	104.7	116.7	115.7	123.3	115.9	167.3	132.0	114.7
2008	113.4	106.0	116.6	116.9	114.8	112.4	110.8	115.1	113.2
2009	113.5	105.2	116.8	115.7	123.7	112.3	122.8	111.1	113.3
2010	114.8	104.6	120.2	121.3	112.9	111.3	110.3	103.1	114.7
2011	113.8	104.4	117.9	119.1	110.1	112.0	112.8	104.4	113.5
2012	111.3	104.7	113.2	113.4	111.5	110.8	126.1	105.0	110.7
2013	110.1	104.5	111.3	111.2	111.9	110.1	115.6	110.2	109.7
2014	109.7	104.8	110.1	110.0	110.9	110.5	114.7	106.6	109.3

1－11　地区生产总值指数

INDICES OF GROSS DOMESTIC PRODUCT

按可比价计算，1952=100 (In comparable price, 1952 = 100)

年　份 Year	地区生产总值(%) Total Output (%)	第一产业 Primary Industry	第二产业 Secondary Industry	工业 Industry	建筑业 Contruction	第三产业 Tertiary Industry	#金融业 Banking	#房地产业 Real Estate	人均地区生产总值(%) Per Capita GDP (%)
1953	114.0	107.4	129.4	141.0	93.3	122.7			111.6
1955	121.5	115.8	152.4	168.5	102.2	118.3			114.4
1957	169.6	143.9	280.1	295.3	233.2	172.1			153.0
1962	141.7	130.2	223.9	258.0	116.1	124.2			119.3
1965	205.6	161.5	490.4	538.5	338.9	161.1			161.5
1970	242.6	158.7	705.6	745.9	580.5	202.3			166.0
1975	320.2	185.3	1126.3	1165.1	995.9	259.1			198.9
1978	399.0	204.6	1616.5	1857.1	926.0	314.2			238.6
1980	490.8	211.4	2257.6	2637.6	1173.5	398.9	110.3	181.0	286.5
1981	523.0	239.5	2292.0	2751.0	1021.9	418.4	115.6	195.8	301.8
1982	585.4	277.2	2399.3	2950.6	905.2	508.6	135.1	206.0	333.7
1983	620.1	276.1	2637.8	3220.9	1048.9	567.0	145.2	165.4	348.9
1984	749.7	315.9	3297.0	4111.0	1113.2	709.9	179.8	247.5	416.8
1985	871.1	342.0	4111.1	5128.2	1383.1	797.9	202.1	277.9	478.7
1986	919.1	353.1	4326.3	5327.6	1615.8	879.3	243.5	339.6	498.5
1987	996.7	364.1	4816.5	6017.4	1599.1	973.3	278.8	385.1	533.1
1988	1074.3	345.4	5475.9	6925.0	1623.7	1112.1	298.3	406.7	567.0
1989	1122.7	363.3	5592.5	7218.5	1319.6	1215.1	363.4	379.1	584.7
1990	1178.9	390.6	5536.7	7181.9	1224.3	1394.6	395.7	415.8	599.3
1991	1257.2	371.2	6151.9	8018.2	1298.9	1609.6	452.7	477.0	624.3
1992	1434.3	401.6	7175.3	9419.0	1396.0	1881.8	504.7	561.8	703.3
1993	1621.2	424.7	8372.8	10939.2	1720.9	2166.9	565.3	670.8	784.9
1994	1843.3	454.7	9948.0	13008.9	2024.1	2435.8	608.7	854.0	881.6
1995	2086.5	495.2	11547.9	15073.3	2398.9	2740.9	653.4	1033.2	987.5
1996	2327.5	517.4	13342.9	17402.1	2796.6	3050.0	701.2	1204.1	1091.5
1997	2604.6	553.0	15131.7	19753.3	3139.6	3461.5	725.3	1328.7	1211.0
1998	2829.4	549.4	16822.5	21912.2	3576.3	3858.8	776.3	1566.2	1306.3
1999	3048.8	560.1	18195.4	23713.5	3845.1	4285.0	805.2	1661.6	1399.9
2000	3310.6	574.1	19858.1	25847.7	4254.6	4777.6	850.3	1941.2	1598.1
2001	3604.0	588.5	21828.1	28458.3	4618.0	5291.6	913.2	2370.0	1734.3
2002	3936.2	600.2	24038.5	31332.6	5104.3	5892.2	990.1	2713.0	1889.5
2003	4318.6	634.9	26494.8	34517.7	5643.2	6525.7	1090.1	3229.7	2068.1
2004	4802.5	676.2	30099.5	39171.3	6456.0	7218.6	1158.5	3696.0	2294.6
2005	5383.6	703.2	34674.7	45438.7	7095.2	8070.4	1209.5	3825.4	2565.4
2006	6094.2	739.1	40222.6	52845.2	8180.7	9159.9	1632.8	4948.5	2904.0
2007	6984.0	773.8	46939.8	61141.9	10086.8	10616.3	2731.6	6532.1	3330.9
2008	7919.8	820.3	54731.8	71474.9	11579.7	11932.8	3026.7	7518.4	3770.6
2009	8989.0	862.9	63926.7	82696.4	14324.1	13400.5	3716.7	8353.0	4272.1
2010	10319.4	902.6	76839.9	100310.7	16171.9	14914.8	4099.5	8611.9	4900.1
2011	11746.5	942.3	90571.2	119440.0	17810.1	16701.5	4623.8	8994.3	5561.6
2012	13073.9	986.6	102526.6	135444.9	19858.3	18505.3	5830.7	9444.0	6156.7
2013	14394.4	1031.0	114112.1	150614.7	22221.4	20542.7	6740.3	10407.3	6753.9
2014	15790.7	1080.5	125637.4	165676.2	24643.5	22699.7	7731.1	11094.2	7382.0

注：金融业、房地产业指数以1978年为100。
Note:The indices of banking and real estate are 1978=100

1—12 地区生产总值构成
COMPOSITION OF GROSS DOMESTIC PRODUCT

本表按当年价格计算 (At current prices)

年 份 Year	地区生产总值(%) Total Output (%)	第一产业 Primary Industry	第二产业 Secondary Industry	工业 Industry	建筑业 Contruction	第三产业 Tertiary Industry	#金融业 Banking	#房地产业 Real Estate
1952	100	56.7	15.6	12.9	2.7	27.7		
1955	100	53.3	21.9	18.4	3.5	24.8		
1957	100	49.8	23.7	18.5	5.2	26.5		
1962	100	56.2	20.4	17.5	2.9	23.4		
1965	100	52.1	29.2	24.0	5.2	18.7		
1970	100	50.4	30.5	24.7	5.8	19.1		
1975	100	44.7	37.9	27.2	10.7	17.4		
1978	100	40.5	42.2	34.5	7.6	17.3	3.0	0.9
1980	100	35.7	46.0	37.9	8.0	18.3	2.8	1.4
1981	100	39.6	42.3	35.8	6.4	18.2	2.7	1.5
1982	100	42.1	39.3	34.2	5.1	18.6	2.7	1.3
1983	100	40.1	40.6	35.1	5.4	19.3	2.7	1.0
1984	100	38.5	41.6	36.7	4.9	19.9	2.8	1.2
1985	100	36.5	44.0	38.6	5.4	19.6	2.7	1.2
1986	100	37.0	42.5	37.3	5.2	20.5	3.1	1.4
1987	100	35.5	43.4	38.2	5.2	21.1	3.3	1.4
1988	100	34.3	43.3	39.0	4.3	22.4	3.3	1.4
1989	100	33.3	41.9	38.6	3.3	24.8	3.9	1.3
1990	100	35.1	38.0	34.5	3.5	26.9	4.1	1.4
1991	100	30.6	39.4	35.9	3.5	30.0	4.4	1.5
1992	100	27.8	40.9	37.0	3.9	31.3	4.4	1.6
1993	100	26.1	40.5	35.9	4.7	33.3	3.9	1.9
1994	100	29.5	38.7	34.1	4.5	31.9	3.3	2.2
1995	100	29.4	37.0	32.3	4.7	33.6	2.9	2.0
1996	100	28.7	37.0	32.2	4.7	34.4	2.6	2.5
1997	100	26.9	37.5	32.6	5.0	35.6	2.4	2.4
1998	100	25.0	38.5	33.4	5.1	36.5	2.4	2.6
1999	100	20.3	40.7	35.3	5.4	39.0	2.4	2.6
2000	100	18.7	40.5	35.1	5.5	40.8	2.3	2.8
2001	100	17.8	40.6	35.0	5.5	41.6	2.3	3.2
2002	100	16.8	40.6	35.0	5.6	42.6	2.3	3.4
2003	100	16.8	41.1	35.4	5.8	42.1	2.3	3.7
2004	100	18.1	41.2	35.3	5.9	40.7	2.1	3.6
2005	100	16.4	43.3	37.6	5.7	40.3	1.9	3.3
2006	100	15.0	44.2	38.5	5.7	40.8	2.3	3.9
2007	100	14.8	44.4	38.4	6.0	40.8	3.6	4.4
2008	100	15.7	44.9	38.8	6.1	39.4	3.5	4.7
2009	100	13.8	46.6	40.0	6.6	39.6	3.7	4.2
2010	100	13.5	48.6	42.1	6.5	37.9	3.5	3.5
2011	100	13.1	50.0	43.5	6.5	36.9	3.4	3.2
2012	100	12.8	50.3	43.8	6.5	36.9	3.9	3.1
2013	100	12.2	47.6	40.9	6.7	40.2	4.8	3.9
2014	100	11.6	46.9	40.2	6.7	41.5	5.0	3.9

注：2013年产业结构根据三经普数据进行了调整。

Note:The data of 2013 has been adjusted basing on the files of the 3rd national economics census.

1-13　按支出法计算的地区生产总值

GROSS DOMESTIC PRODUCT BY EXPENDITURE APPROACH

本表按当年价格计算 (At current prices)

年份 Year	地区生产总值（亿元） Gross Domestic Product (100 million yuan)	最终消费 Final Consumption Expenditure	居民消费 Residents Consumption Expenditure	政府消费 Government Consumption Expenditure	资本形成总额 Gross Capital Formation	固定资本形成 Fixed Capital Formation	存货增加 Changes in Inventories	货物和服务净流出 Net Export of Goods and Services
1978	151.20	81.70	74.70	7.00	43.12	31.40	11.72	26.38
1980	200.19	107.79	93.51	14.28	40.10	33.19	6.91	52.30
1985	386.76	240.02	203.23	36.79	135.43	96.71	38.72	11.31
1989	718.07	478.66	398.09	80.57	201.39	115.50	85.89	38.02
1990	818.89	535.49	434.62	100.87	261.95	147.13	114.82	21.45
1991	913.22	597.42	475.85	121.57	281.92	176.32	105.60	33.88
1992	1089.68	689.93	546.61	143.32	355.46	235.63	119.83	44.29
1993	1423.92	876.16	694.49	181.67	512.31	377.95	134.36	35.45
1994	1858.89	1043.25	845.14	198.10	740.13	571.68	168.45	75.51
1995	2364.45	1305.21	1095.97	209.20	973.63	778.25	195.38	85.61
1996	2720.28	1599.74	1346.76	253.00	1191.75	985.03	206.72	-71.21
1997	3107.91	1720.23	1438.12	282.10	1466.81	1102.10	364.71	-79.13
1998	3344.45	1859.97	1518.92	341.10	1614.60	1238.90	375.70	-130.12
1999	3504.01	1887.86	1507.12	380.70	1754.79	1320.10	434.69	-138.64
2000	3760.48	2030.07	1594.08	436.00	1882.47	1451.85	430.62	-152.06
2001	4102.08	2262.67	1767.38	495.30	1884.57	1610.93	273.64	-45.16
2002	4416.88	2499.95	1951.54	548.41	1905.92	1699.78	206.14	11.01
2003	4910.53	2819.24	2188.05	631.20	2037.19	1875.78	161.41	54.10
2004	5633.30	3174.18	2452.62	721.56	2538.77	2325.87	212.90	-79.65
2005	6520.14	3645.71	2785.42	860.29	2943.58	2804.01	139.57	-69.15
2006	7972.33	4245.68	3124.37	1121.31	3634.13	3555.21	78.92	92.52
2007	9550.04	4999.66	3709.69	1289.97	4450.25	4371.14	79.11	100.13
2008	11728.64	5892.03	4225.38	1666.65	5716.36	5368.99	347.37	120.25
2009	13240.42	6325.15	4456.31	1868.84	6827.00	6612.85	214.15	88.27
2010	16182.27	7389.80	5136.78	2253.02	8511.17	8200.40	310.77	281.30
2011	20167.28	8931.48	6241.95	2689.53	11027.27	10597.82	429.45	208.53
2012	22659.38	9982.79	7085.46	2897.33	12554.67	12064.75	489.92	121.92
2013	25431.66	11161.21	8053.82	3107.39	14245.35	13701.86	543.49	25.10
2014	28728.18	12562.76	9124.48	3438.28	16109.59	15442.86	666.73	55.83

1-14 按支出法计算的地区生产总值指数
INDICES OF GROSS DOMESTIC PRODUCT BY EXPENDITURE APPROACH

按可比价计算 1952=100 (In comparable price, 1952=100)

年 份 Year	地区生产总值 (%) Gross Domestic Product (%)	最终消费 Final Consumption Expenditure	居民消费 Residents Consumption Expenditure	政府消费 Government Consumption Expenditure	资本形成总额 Gross Capital Formation	固定资本形成 Fixed Capital Formation	存货增加 Changes in Inventories
1952	100.0	100.0	100.0	100.0	100.0	100.0	100.0
1978	488.3	313.7	308.9	369.3	820.0	1396.6	388.5
1980	605.4	388.8	363.4	706.7	663.9	1270.1	209.7
1985	1007.5	736.7	674.8	1492.5	1962.9	3155.5	1067.1
1990	1337.5	1004.9	897.4	2307.0	2504.8	3460.7	1786.7
1991	1344.2	970.7	850.8	2403.9	2595.0	3955.5	1604.4
1992	1471.9	1023.1	870.3	2819.7	2979.1	4806.0	1670.2
1993	1764.8	1242.1	1045.3	3550.0	3598.7	6218.9	1747.0
1994	2075.4	1379.9	1174.9	3802.1	4530.8	8246.3	1920.0
1995	2339.0	1508.3	1302.9	3950.4	5432.4	9945.0	2261.8
1996	2619.7	1702.8	1467.1	4507.4	6475.4	12520.8	2257.2
1997	2902.6	1776.1	1541.9	4584.0	8120.2	14486.6	3634.1
1998	3140.6	1985.6	1697.7	5418.3	9257.0	16775.4	3961.2
1999	3357.3	2130.6	1765.6	6431.5	10099.4	17966.5	4543.5
2000	3629.3	2260.5	1852.1	7055.4	10927.6	19709.2	4738.9
2001	3930.5	2513.7	2042.9	8057.2	10807.4	21542.2	3028.2
2002	4276.4	2795.3	2281.9	8814.6	11099.2	23093.2	2313.5
2003	4618.5	3072.0	2494.1	9890.0	11443.2	24594.3	1753.6
2004	5052.7	3336.2	2683.6	11086.7	13422.9	28775.3	2121.9
2005	5709.6	3726.5	2976.1	12672.1	15288.7	34041.2	1398.3
2006	6531.8	4326.5	3318.4	16600.0	18315.8	42245.1	465.6
2007	7446.3	4785.1	3680.1	18226.8	21667.6	20102.7	450.2
2008	8399.4	5282.8	3952.4	21653.4	25026.1	22575.3	1848.5
2009	9356.9	5689.6	4177.7	24381.7	30606.9	28151.4	1144.2
2010	11014.0	6423.5	4658.1	28307.2	36758.9	33669.1	1660.3
2011	12886.4	7310.0	5319.6	31902.2	44662.1	40806.9	2148.4
2012	14162.2	7931.3	5862.2	33401.6	50021.5	45662.9	2440.6
2013	15706.9	8653.0	6507.0	34904.7	56574.3	51690.4	2723.7
2014	17513.2	9561.6	7735.8	37871.6	63365.3	57738.2	3391.0

1−15　三次产业贡献率

CONTRIBUTING RATE OF THE THREE INDUSTRIES

单位：%　　本表按可比价格计算 (In comparable price)　　(%)

年　份 Year	地区生产总值 Gross Domestic Product	第一产业 Primary Industry	第二产业 Second Industry	#工　业 Industry	第三产业 Tertiary Industry
1990	100	42.68	-9.84	-4.64	67.16
1991	100	-25.9	65.6	62.7	60.3
1992	100	18.0	48.2	46.4	33.8
1993	100	13.0	53.5	47.7	33.5
1994	100	14.2	59.2	54.7	26.6
1995	100	17.5	54.9	49.8	27.6
1996	100	9.6	62.2	56.7	28.2
1997	100	13.5	53.9	49.8	32.6
1998	100	-1.6	62.8	56.4	38.8
1999	100	5.1	52.2	48.2	42.7
2000	100	5.6	53.0	47.9	41.3
2001	100	5.3	45.2	40.0	49.5
2002	100	3.8	45.1	38.9	51.1
2003	100	9.8	43.4	37.4	46.8
2004	100	9.2	50.4	43.2	40.5
2005	100	6.5	53.5	48.8	40.0
2006	100	6.3	52.4	46.6	41.3
2007	100	4.9	50.9	41.8	44.2
2008	100	6.2	56.0	49.2	37.8
2009	100	5.1	57.9	47.0	37.0
2010	100	3.7	66.1	60.3	30.2
2011	100	4.3	62.9	58.1	32.8
2012	100	5.1	59.1	52.6	35.8
2013	100	7.1	23.4	15.9	69.5
2014	100	5.7	41.2	33.0	53.1

注：产业贡献率指各产业增加值增量与GDP增量之比。

Note:Contribution share of the three components to the increase of the GDP refers to the proportion of the increment of the each component of GDP expenditure approach to the increment of GDP.

1-16 三次产业拉动率

CONTRIBUTION OF THE THREE STRATA OF INDUSTRY TO GDP GROWTH

单位：百分点　　本表按可比价格计算(In comparable price)　　(percentage point)

年 份 Year	地区生产总值 Gross Domestic Product	第一产业 Primary Industry	第二产业 Second Industry	#工 业 Industry	第三产业 Tertiary Industry
1990	5.00	2.1	-0.5	-0.2	3.4
1991	6.6	-1.7	4.3	4.1	4.0
1992	14.1	2.5	6.8	6.5	4.8
1993	13.0	1.7	7.0	6.2	4.4
1994	13.7	1.9	8.1	7.5	3.6
1995	13.2	2.3	7.3	6.6	3.6
1996	11.6	1.1	7.2	6.6	3.3
1997	11.9	1.6	6.4	5.9	3.9
1998	8.6	-0.1	5.4	4.8	3.3
1999	7.8	0.4	4.1	3.8	3.3
2000	8.6	0.5	4.6	4.1	3.6
2001	8.6	0.5	3.9	3.4	4.3
2002	9.2	0.4	4.1	3.6	4.7
2003	9.7	0.9	4.2	3.6	4.5
2004	11.2	1.0	5.6	4.8	4.5
2005	12.1	0.8	6.5	5.9	4.8
2006	13.2	0.8	6.9	6.1	5.5
2007	14.6	0.7	7.4	6.1	6.5
2008	13.4	0.8	7.5	6.6	5.1
2009	13.5	0.7	7.8	6.3	5.0
2010	14.8	0.5	9.8	8.9	4.5
2011	13.8	0.6	8.7	8.0	4.5
2012	11.3	0.6	6.7	5.9	4.0
2013	10.1	0.7	2.4	1.6	7.0
2014	9.7	0.6	4.0	3.2	5.1

注：三次产业对生产总值增长的拉动指GDP增长速度与各产业贡献率之乘积。

Note:Contribution of the three components to GDP growth refers to the growth rate of GDP multiplied by the contribution share of the three components.

1-17　三大需求贡献率

CONTRIBUTING RATE OF THE THREE REQUIREMENTS

单位：%　　本表按可比价格计算 (In comparable price)　　(%)

年　份 Year	地区生产总值 Gross Domestic Product	最终消费支出 Final Consumption Expenditure	资本形成总额 Gross Capital Formation	货物和服务净流出 Net Outflow of Goods and Services
1990	100.0	59.4	111.8	-71.3
1991	100.0	-464.2	238.4	325.8
1992	100.0	35.7	51.8	12.5
1993	100.0	65.2	36.3	-1.5
1994	100.0	38.8	51.3	10.0
1995	100.0	42.5	58.3	-0.8
1996	100.0	60.2	63.5	-23.7
1997	100.0	22.7	99.2	-21.8
1998	100.0	76.6	81.1	-57.6
1999	100.0	58.2	65.9	-24.1
2000	100.0	41.6	51.7	6.8
2001	100.0	72.3	-6.4	34.1
2002	100.0	70.3	13.9	15.8
2003	100.0	70.5	17.0	12.5
2004	100.0	52.6	76.1	-28.6
2005	100.0	50.7	49.0	0.3
2006	100.0	44.3	43.9	11.9
2007	100.0	40.8	58.7	0.5
2008	100.0	35.5	64.4	0.1
2009	100.0	27.4	74.0	-1.4
2010	100.0	27.8	61.6	10.6
2011	100.0	36.9	66.3	-3.2
2012	100.0	38.2	66.2	-4.4
2013	100.0	36.7	67.2	-3.9
2014	100.0	39.0	60.0	1.0

注：贡献率指三大需求增量与支出法地区生产总值增量之比。

Note:Contribution share of the three components to the increase of the GDP refers to the proportion of the increment of the each component of GDP expenditure approach to the increment of GDP.

1-18 三大需求拉动率

CONTRIBUTION OF THE THREE COMPONENTS OF GDP TO THE GROWTH OF GDP

单位：百分点　　本表按可比价格计算 (In comparable price)　　(percentage point)

年　份 Year	地区生产总值 Gross Domestic Product	最终消费支出 Final Consumption Expenditure	资本形成总额 Gross Capital Formation	货物和服务净流出 Net Outflow of Goods and Services
1990	5.0	3.0	5.6	-3.6
1991	6.6	-30.6	15.7	21.5
1992	14.1	5.0	7.3	1.8
1993	13.0	8.5	4.7	-0.2
1994	13.7	5.3	7.0	1.4
1995	13.2	5.6	7.7	-0.1
1996	11.6	7.0	7.4	-2.7
1997	11.9	2.7	11.8	-2.6
1998	8.6	6.6	7.0	-5.0
1999	7.8	4.5	5.1	-1.9
2000	8.6	3.6	4.4	0.6
2001	8.9	6.4	-0.6	3.0
2002	9.2	6.5	1.3	1.5
2003	9.7	6.8	1.6	1.2
2004	11.2	5.9	8.5	-3.2
2005	12.1	6.1	5.9	0.1
2006	13.2	5.8	5.8	1.6
2007	14.6	6.0	8.6	0.1
2008	13.4	4.8	8.6	
2009	13.5	3.7	10.0	-0.2
2010	14.8	4.1	9.1	1.6
2011	13.8	5.1	9.1	-0.4
2012	11.3	4.3	7.5	-0.5
2013	10.9	4.0	7.3	-0.4
2014	11.5	4.5	6.9	0.1

注：1.三大需求指支出法地区生产总值的三大构成项目，即最终消费支出、资本形成总额、货物和服务净流出。
　　2.三大需求对国内生产总值增长的拉动指地区生产总值增长速度与三大需求贡献率的乘积。

Notes：a)Three components of GDP by exoenditure approach are final consumption expenditure, gross capital formation and net exports of goods and services.
　　b)Contribution of the three components to GDP growth refers to the growth refers to the growth rate of GDP multiplied by the contribution share of the three components.

1−19 市、州生产总值(2014)

GROSS DOMESTIC PRODUCT OF CITIES AND PREFECTURES(2014)

单位:亿元 (100 million yuan)

地 区	Regions	地区生产总值 Gross Domestic Product	第一产业 Primary Industry	第二产业 Secondary Industry	第三产业 Tertiary Industry
武 汉	Wuhan	10069.48	350.06	4785.66	4933.76
黄 石	Huangshi	1218.56	105.03	723.45	390.08
十 堰	Shiyan	1200.82	151.19	610.13	439.50
宜 昌	Yichang	3132.21	351.56	1859.78	920.87
襄 阳	Xiangyang	3129.26	401.60	1804.65	923.01
鄂 州	Ezhou	686.64	81.15	407.19	198.30
荆 门	Jingmen	1310.59	198.11	706.52	405.96
孝 感	Xiaogan	1354.72	252.17	664.36	438.19
荆 州	Jingzhou	1480.49	347.00	659.58	473.91
黄 冈	Huanggang	1477.15	375.12	586.10	515.93
咸 宁	Xianning	964.25	172.03	476.59	315.63
随 州	Suizhou	723.45	130.09	350.56	242.80
恩施州	Enshi	612.01	139.03	221.64	251.34
仙 桃	Xiantao	552.27	83.96	295.99	172.32
潜 江	Qianjiang	540.22	68.07	316.86	155.29
天 门	Tianmen	401.86	78.10	209.69	114.07
神农架	Shennongjia	20.24	1.90	8.17	10.18

1-20 市、州生产总值指数(2014)

INDICES OF GROSS DOMESTIC PRODUCT OF CITIES AND PREFECTURES(2014)

(上年=100,单位:%) (preceding year = 100,%)

地 区	Regions	地区生产总值 Gross Domestic Product	第一产业 Primary Industry	第二产业 Secondary Industry	第三产业 Tertiary Industry
武 汉	Wuhan	109.7	105.0	110.2	109.5
黄 石	Huangshi	109.1	105.1	108.7	110.5
十 堰	Shiyan	109.5	105.1	110.2	109.6
宜 昌	Yichang	109.8	105.0	109.9	111.1
襄 阳	Xiangyang	109.8	105.0	110.2	111.0
鄂 州	Ezhou	109.7	105.3	110.1	110.5
荆 门	Jingmen	109.9	105.1	111.0	110.5
孝 感	Xiaogan	109.7	105.1	110.9	110.2
荆 州	Jingzhou	109.8	105.2	110.9	111.4
黄 冈	Huanggang	109.7	105.1	110.6	111.8
咸 宁	Xianning	109.6	105.1	110.9	109.7
随 州	Suizhou	109.7	105.2	110.3	111.2
恩施州	Enshi	109.5	105.2	110.0	111.6
仙 桃	Xiantao	109.7	105.2	109.1	112.6
潜 江	Qianjiang	109.6	105.1	109.6	111.7
天 门	Tianmen	109.6	105.1	110.2	111.6
神农架	Shennongjia	108.0	104.5	107.0	109.6

1-21 市、州支出法生产总值(2014)
GROSS DOMESTIC PRODUCT BY EXPENDITURE APPROACH OF CITIES AND PREFECTURES(2014)

单位:亿元 (100 million yuan)

地区	Regions	Total Gross Domestic Product by Expenditure	最终消费支出 Final Consumption Expenditure	资本形成总额 Gross Capital Formation	货物和服务净流出 Net Export of Goods and Services
武汉	Wuhan	10069.00	4505.00	6672.00	-1108.00
黄石	Huangshi	1202.42	478.10	721.90	2.42
十堰	Shiyan	1202.51	492.80	632.15	77.56
宜昌	Yichang	3132.21	1317.19	1719.09	95.93
襄阳	Xiangyang	3129.00	1435.30	1650.70	43.00
鄂州	Ezhou	686.64	206.00	454.27	26.37
荆门	Jingmen	1310.59	551.64	743.41	15.54
孝感	Xiaogan	1358.40	567.27	778.64	12.49
荆州	Jingzhou	1480.49	684.49	1387.49	-591.49
黄冈	Huanggang	1477.13	755.12	722.01	
咸宁	Xianning	1172.50	349.15	809.47	13.88
随州	Suizhou	722.39	333.25	376.19	12.95
恩施州	Enshi	612.01	471.51	432.03	-291.53
仙桃	Xiantao	552.27	153.19	362.30	36.78
潜江	Qianjiang	538.71	148.22	381.46	9.03
天门	Tianmen	407.90	201.50	194.20	12.20
神农架	Shennongjia	20.24	10.43	11.16	-1.35

1-22 市、州民营经济增加值(2014)
VALUE ADDED OF PRIVATE ECONOMY(2014)

地区	Regions	增加值(亿元) Value-Added (100 million yuan)		占GDP比重(%) Percentage(%)	
		2013	2014	2013	2014
全省	**Total**	**13321.71**	**14905.74**	**54.0**	**54.4**
武汉	Wuhan	3508.87	3950.32	38.8	39.2
黄石	Huangshi	628.34	671.34	55.0	55.1
十堰	Shiyan	476.00	538.39	44.1	44.8
宜昌	Yichang	1671.75	1883.08	59.3	60.1
襄阳	Xiangyang	1458.00	1630.00	51.8	52.1
鄂州	Ezhou	391.26	436.34	62.0	63.5
荆门	Jingmen	679.15	757.46	56.5	57.8
孝感	Xiaogan	781.65	865.62	63.1	63.9
荆州	Jingzhou	616.23	689.18	46.2	46.6
黄冈	Huanggang	833.84	953.38	62.6	64.5
咸宁	Xianning	637.68	712.09	73.1	73.8
随州	Suizhou	456.94	507.54	69.0	70.2
恩施州	Enshi	231.31	257.64	41.9	42.1
仙桃	Xiantao	358.57	400.49	71.1	72.5
潜江	Qianjiang	336.37	372.91	68.3	69.0
天门	Tianmen	248.26	271.74	68.0	67.6
神农架	Shennongjia	7.49	8.21	40.3	40.6

主要统计指标解释

平均增长速度　计算平均增长速度有两种方法：一种是习惯上经常使用的"水平法"，又称几何平均法，是以间隔期最后一年的水平同基期水平对比来计算平均每年增长(或下降)速度；另一种是"累计法"，又称代数平均法或方程法，是以间隔期内各年水平的总和同基期水平对比来计算平均每年增长(或下降)速度。在一般正常情况下，两种方法计算的平均每年增长速度比较接近；但在经济发展不平衡、出现大起大落时，两种方法计算的结果差别较大。

国民经济行业分类　自2003年定期报表开始使用新的《国民经济行业分类》（GB/T4754-2002）该分类是由国家统计局组织修订，经国家质量监督检验检疫总局批准，于2002年5月10日发布实施。这次修订是在1994年分类标准的基础上，参照联合国《全部经济活动的国际标准产业分类》(ISIC/Rev.3)进行的。修订后的《国民经济行业分类》(GB/T4754-2002)共有门类20个，大类95个，中类396个，小类913个。新增门类4个，大类增加3个，中类增加28个，小类增加67个。

企业(单位)登记注册类型　是以在工商行政管理机关登记注册的各类企业为划分对象，以工商行政管理部门对企业登记注册的类型为依据，将企业登记注册类型分为内资企业、港澳台商投资企业和外商投资企业三大类。内资企业包括国有企业、集体企业、股份合作企业、联营企业、有限责任公司、股份有限公司、私营公司和其他企业；港澳台商投资企业和外商投资企业分别包括合资经营企业、合作经营企业、独资经营企业和股份有限公司。对不在工商行政管理部门进行登记注册的行政机关、事业单位和社会团体，主要按其经费来源和管理方式进行划分。

国有企业　指企业全部资产归国家所有，并按《中华人民共和国企业法人登记管理条例》规定登记注册的非公司制的经济组织。不包括有限责任公司中的国有独资公司。

集体企业　指企业资产归集体所有，并按《中华人民共和国企业法人登记管理条例》规定登记注册的经济组织。

股份合作企业　指以合作制为基础，由企业职工共同出资入股，吸收一定比例的社会资产投资组建，实行自主经营，自负盈亏，共同劳动，民主管理，按劳分配与按股分红相结合的一种集体经济组织。

联营企业　指两个及两个以上相同或不同所有制性质的企业法人或事业单位法人，按自愿、平等、互利的原则，共同投资组成的经济组织。联营企业包括国有联营企业、集体联营企业、国有与集体联营企业和其他联营企业。

有限责任公司　指根据《中华人民共和国公司登记管理条例》规定登记注册，由两个以上、五十个以下的股东共同出资，每个股东以其所认缴的出资额对公司承担有限责任，公司以其全部资产对其债务承担责任的经济组织。有限责任公司包括国有独资公司以及其他有限责任公司。

股份有限公司　指根据《中华人民共和国公司登记管理条例》规定登记注册，其全部注册资本由等额股份构成并通过发行股票筹集资本，股东以其认购的股份对公司承担有限责任，公司以其全部资产对其债务承担责任的经济组织。

私营企业　指由自然人投资设立或由自然人控股，以雇佣劳动为基础的营利性经济组织。包括按照《公司法》、《合伙企业法》、《私营企业暂行条例》规定登记注册的私营有限责任公司、私营股份有限公司、私营合伙企业和私营独资企业。

其他企业　指上述企业之外的其他内资经济组织。

与港澳台商合资经营企业　指港澳台地区投资者与内地企业依照《中华人民共和国中外合资经营企业法》及有关法律的规定，按合同规定的比例投资设立、分享利润和分担风险的企业。

与港澳台商合作经营企业　指港澳台地区投资者与内地企业依照《中华人民共和国中外合作经营企业法》及有关法律的规定，依照合作合同的约定进行投资或提供条件设立、分配利润和分担风险的企业。

港澳台商独资经营企业　指依照《中华人民共和国外资企业法》及有关法律的规定，在内地由港澳台地区投资者全额投资设立的企业。

港澳台商投资股份有限公司　指根据国家有关规定，经原外经贸部依法批准设立，其中港、澳、台商的股本占公司注册资本的比例达 25% 以上的股份有限公司。凡其中港、澳、台商的股本占公司注册资本的比例小于 25%的，属于内资企业中的股份有限公司。

中外合资经营企业 指外国企业或外国人与中国内地企业依照《中华人民共和国中外合资经营企业法》及有关法律的规定，按合同规定的比例投资设立、分享利润和分担风险的企业。

中外合作经营企业 指外国企业或外国人与中国内地企业依照《中华人民共和国中外合作经营企业法》及有关法律的规定，依照合作合同的约定进行投资或提供条件设立、分配利润和分担风险的企业。

外资企业 指依照《中华人民共和国外资企业法》及有关法律的规定，在中国内地由外国投资者全额投资设立的企业。

外商投资股份有限公司 指根据国家有关规定，经原外经贸部依法批准设立，其中外资的股本占公司注册资本的比例达 25% 以上的股份有限公司。凡其中外资股本占公司注册资本的比例小于 25%的，属于内资企业中的股份有限公司。

行政机关、事业单位和社会团体 参照企业登记注册类型，主要按其经费来源和管理方式划分。具体规定如下：

⑴行政机关：包括国家机关和政党机关，原则上均列为“国有”。但有特殊规定的，如供销社等，则列为“集体”。

⑵事业单位：包括经国家机构编制部门和有关业务主管部门批准成立的各类事业单位，不包括实行企业化管理的事业单位。事业单位的划分办法如下：

①由国家财政预算拨款或列入财政预算外资金管理以及经费主要来源于国有主管部门或国有上级单位的事业单位，列为“国有”。

②经费主要来源于集体单位的事业单位，列为“集体”。

③公民个人(或个人合伙)开办的事业单位，列为“私营”。

④上述以外的其他事业单位，如果其经费来源不明确，按管理方式进行归类。

⑶社会团体：包括经民政部门批准成立以及未纳入社会团体管理条例范围的工会、妇联等各类社会团体。社会团体的划分办法如下：

①未纳入民政部社会团体管理条例范围的工会、妇联、共青团、青联、工商联、科协、侨联等社会团体，国家拨款设立的基金会或基金管理组织以及经费主要来源于国有业务主管部门或国有上级单位的社会团体，列为“国有”。

②经费主要来源于集体单位的社会团体，列为“集体”。

③公民个人(或个人合伙)开办的社会团体，划为“私营”。

④上述以外的其他社会团体，如果其经费来源不明确，改按管理方式进行归类。

地区生产总值(GDP) 指按市场价格计算的一个地区所有常住单位在一定时期内生产活动的最终成果。地区生产总值有三种表现形态，即价值形态、收入形态和产品形态。从价值形态看，它是所有常住单位在一定时期内生产的全部货物和服务价值超过同期投入的全部非固定资产货物和服务价值的差额，即所有常住单位的增加值之和；从收入形态看，它是所有常住单位在一定时期内创造并分配给常住单位和非常住单位的初次收入之和；从产品形态看，它是所有常住单位在一定时期内最终使用的货物和服务价值减去货物和服务流进价值。在实际核算中，地区生产总值有三种计算方法，即生产法、收入法和支出法。三种方法分别从不同的方面反映地区生产总值及其构成。

国民总收入(GNI) 即国民生产总值，指一个国家(或地区)所有常住单位在一定时期内收入初次分配的最终结果。一国常住单位从事生产活动所创造的增加值在初次分配中主要分配给该国的常住单位，但也有一部分以生产税及进口税(扣除生产和进口补贴)、劳动者报酬和财产收入等形式分配给非常住单位；同时，国外生产所创造的增加值也有一部分以生产税及进口税(扣除生产和进口补贴)、劳动者报酬和财产收入等形式分配给该国的常住单位，从而产生了国民总收入的概念。它等于国内生产总值加上来自国外的净要素收入。与国内生产总值不同，国民总收入是个收入概念，而国内生产总值是个生产概念。

三次产业 三产业的划分是世界上较为常用的产业结构分类，但各国的划分不尽一致。我国的三次产业划分是：

第一产业是指农、林、牧、渔业。

第二产业是指采矿业，制造业，电力、煤气及水的生产和供应业，建筑业。

第三产业是指除第一、二产业以外的其他行业。

劳动者报酬　指劳动者因从事生产活动所获得的全部报酬。包括劳动者获得的各种形式的工资、奖金和津贴，既包括货币形式的，也包括实物形式的，还包括劳动者所享受的公费医疗和医药卫生费、上下班交通补贴、单位支付的社会保险费、住房公积金等。对于个体经济来说，其所有者所获得的劳动报酬和经营利润不易区分，这两部分统一作为劳动者报酬处理。

生产税净额　指生产税减生产补贴后的余额。生产税指政府对生产单位从事生产、销售和经营活动以及因从事生产活动使用某些生产要素(如固定资产、土地、劳动力)所征收的各种税、附加费和规费。生产补贴与生产税相反，指政府对生产单位的单方面转移支出，因此视为负生产税，包括政策亏损补贴、价格补贴等。

固定资产折旧　指一定时期内为弥补固定资产损耗按照规定的固定资产折旧率提取的固定资产折旧，或按国民经济核算统一规定的折旧率虚拟计算的固定资产折旧。它反映了固定资产在当期生产中的转移价值。各类企业和企业化管理的事业单位的固定资产折旧是指实际计提的折旧费；不计提折旧的政府机关、非企业化管理的事业单位和居民住房的固定资产折旧是按照统一规定的折旧率和固定资产原值计算的虚拟折旧。原则上，固定资产折旧应按固定资产当期的重置价值计算，但是目前我国尚不具备对全社会固定资产进行重估价的基础，所以暂时只能采用上述办法。

营业盈余　指常住单位创造的增加值扣除劳动者报酬、生产税净额和固定资产折旧后的余额。它相当于企业的营业利润加上生产补贴，但要扣除从利润中开支的工资和福利等。

支出法地区生产总值　是从最终使用的角度反映一个地区一定时期内生产活动最终成果的一种方法，包括最终消费支出、资本形成总额及货物和服务净流出三部分。计算公式为：

支出法国内生产总值=最终消费支出+资本形成总额+货物和服务净流出

最终消费支出　指常住单位为满足物质、文化和精神生活的需要，从本国经济领土和国外购买的货物和服务的支出。它不包括非常住单位在本国经济领土内的消费支出。最终消费支出分为居民消费支出和政府消费支出。

居民消费支出　指常住住户在一定时期内对于货物和服务的全部最终消费支出。居民消费支出除了直接以货币形式购买的货物和服务的消费支出外，还包括以其他方式获得的货物和服务的消费支出，即所谓的虚拟消费支出。居民虚拟消费支出包括如下几种类型：单位以实物报酬及实物转移的形式提供给劳动者的货物和服务；住户生产并由本住户消费了的货物和服务，其中的服务仅指住户的自有住房服务和付酬的家庭雇员提供的家庭和个人服务；金融机构提供的金融媒介服务；保险公司提供的保险服务。

政府消费支出　指政府部门为全社会提供的公共服务的消费支出和免费或以较低的价格向居民住户提供的货物和服务的净支出，前者等于政府服务的产出价值减去政府单位所获得的经营收入的价值，后者等于政府部门免费或以较低价格向居民住户提供的货物和服务的市场价值减去向住户收取的价值。

资本形成总额　指常住单位在一定时期内获得减去处置的固定资产和存货的净额，包括固定资本形成总额和存货增加两部分。

固定资本形成总额　指生产者在一定时期内获得的固定资产减处置的固定资产的价值总额。固定资产是通过生产活动生产出来的，且其使用年限在一年以上、单位价值在规定标准以上的资产，不包括自然资产。可分为有形固定资本形成总额和无形固定资本形成总额。有形固定资本形成总额包括一定时期内完成的建筑工程、安装工程和设备工器具购置(减处置)价值，以及土地改良、新增役、种、奶、毛、娱乐用牲畜和新增经济林木价值。无形固定资本形成总额包括矿藏的勘探、计算机软件等获得减处置。

存货增加　指常住单位在一定时期内存货实物量变动的市场价值，即期末价值减期初价值的差额，再扣除当期由于价格变动而产生的持有收益。存货增加可以是正值，也可以是负值，正值表示存货上升，负值表示存货下降。存货包括生产单位购进的原材料、燃料和储备物资等存货，以及生产单位生产的产成品、在制品和半成品等存货。

货物和服务净流出　指货物和服务流出减货物和服务流进的差额。流出包括常住单位向非常住单位出售或无偿转让的各种货物和服务的价值；流进包括常住单位从非常住单位购买或无偿得到的各种货物和服务的价值。由于服务活动的提供与使用同时发生，一般把常住单位从非常住单位得到的服务作为流进，非常住单位从常住单位得到的服务作为流出。

Explanatory Notes on Main Statistical Indicators

Average Annual Growth Rate Two methods for calculating average annual growth rate are applied, one is often called level approach, or the method of calculating geometric average, which is derived by comparing the level of the last year of the interval with that of the beginning year; the other is called accumulative approach or algebraic average or equation method, which is derived by the summation of the actual figure of each year in the interval divided by the figure in the base year. Usually the results calculated by the two methods are fairly close, but they differed sharply when uneven economic development occurred with striking fluctuations in growth.

Industrial Classification of the National Economy The new Industrial Classification of the National Economy (GB/T 4754-2002) is introduced starting from the compilation of 2003 annual statistics. The new revision was based on the 1994 classification and organized by the National Bureau of Statistics taking into consideration of the International Standards of the Industrial Classification of All Economic Activities (ISIC/Rev.3) of the United Nations, and the new Classification was promulgated by the National Administration of Quality Supervision, Inspection and Quarantine on May 10, 2002. The revised version of the Industrial Classification of the National Economy (GB/T 4754-2002) is composed of 20 major divisions, 95 divisions, 396 major groups and 913 groups, including 4 new major divisions, 3 new divisions, 28 major groups and 67 groups.

Registration Status of Enterprises Enterprises are classified into 3 categories, namely domestic-funded enterprises, enterprises with investment from Hong Kong, Macau and Taiwan, and enterprises with foreign investment, in the light of the registration status of an enterprise in industrial and commercial administration agencies. Domestic-funded enterprises include state-owned enterprises, collective-owned enterprises, cooperative enterprises, joint ownership enterprises, limited liability corporations, share-holding corporations Ltd., private enterprises and other enterprises. Included in the enterprises with investment from Hong Kong, Macau and Taiwan and enterprises with foreign investment are joint-venture enterprises, cooperative enterprises, sole investment enterprises and share-holding corporations Ltd. For government agencies, institutions and social organizations which are not requested to be registered in industrial and commercial administration agencies, they are classified mainly by their sources of funds and way of management.

State-owned Enterprises refer to non-corporation economic units where the entire assets are owned by the state and which have registered in accordance with the Regulation of the People's Republic of China on the Management of Registration of Corporate Enterprises. Excluded from this category are sole state-funded corporations in the limited liability corporations.

Collective-owned Enterprises refer to economic units where the assets are owned collectively and which have registered in accordance with the Regulation of the People's Republic of China on the Management of Registration of Corporate Enterprises.

Cooperative Enterprises refer to a form of collective economic units (enterprises) where capitals come mainly from employees as their shares, with certain proportion of capital from the outside, where production is organized on the basis of independent operation, independent accounting for profits and losses, joint work, democratic management, and a distribution system that integrates remuneration according to work with dividend according to capital share.

Joint Ownership Enterprises refer to economic units established by two or more corporate enterprises or corporate institutions of the same or different ownership, through joint investment on the basis of equality, voluntary participation and mutual benefits. They include state joint ownership enterprises, collective joint ownership enterprises, joint state-collective enterprises, other joint ownership enterprises.

Limited Liability Corporations refer to economic units established with investment from 2-50 investors and registered in accordance with the Regulation of the People's Republic of China on the Management of Registration of Corporations, each investor bearing limited liability to the corporation depending on its share of investment, and the corporation bearing liability to its debt to the maximum of its total assets. Limited liability corporations include exclusive state-funded limited liability corporations and other limited liability corporations.

Share-holding Corporations Ltd. refer to economic units registered in accordance with the Regulation of the People's Republic of China on the Management of Registration of Corporations, with total registered capitals divided into equal shares and raised through issuing stocks. Each investor bears limited liability to the corporation depending on the holding of shares, and the corporation bears liability to its debt to the maximum of its total assets.

Private Enterprises refer to profit-making economic units invested and established by natural persons, or controlled by natural persons using employed labour. Included in this category are private limited liability corporations, private share-holding corporations Ltd., private partnership enterprises and private-funded enterprises registered in accordance with the Corporation Law, Partnership Enterprises Law and Interim Regulations on Private Enterprises .

Other Domestic-funded Enterprises refer to domestic-funded economic units other than those mentioned above.

Cooperative Enterprises with Funds from Hong Kong Macau and Taiwan established by investors from Hong Kong, Macau and Taiwan with enterprises in the mainland of China in accordance with the Law of the People's Republic of China on Sino-foreign Cooperative Enterprises and other relevant laws, where the investment or provision of facilities, and the share of profits and risks is stipulated in the cooperative contract.

Enterprises with Sole (exclusive) Investment from Hong Kong, Macau and Taiwan refer to enterprises established in the mainland of China with exclusive investment from investors from Hong Kong, Macau and Taiwan in accordance with the Law of the People's Republic of China on Foreign-Funded Enterprises and other relevant laws.

Share-holding Corporations Ltd. with Investment from Hong Kong, Macau and Taiwan refer to share-holding corporations Ltd. established with the approval from the former Ministry of Foreign Trade and Economic Relations in line with relevant state regulations, where the share of investment from Hong Kong, Macau or Taiwan businessmen exceeds 25% of the total registered capital of the corporation. In case the share of investment from Hong Kong, Macau or Taiwan is less than 25% of the total registered capital, the enterprise is to be classified as domestic-funded share-holding corporation Ltd.

Joint-venture Enterprises with Foreign Investment refer to enterprises jointly established by foreign enterprises or foreigners with enterprises in the mainland of China in accordance with the Law of the People's Republic of China on Sino-foreign Joint Venture Enterprises and other relevant laws, where the share of investment, profits and risks is stipulated in the contract.

Cooperation Enterprises with Foreign Investment refer to enterprises jointly established by foreign enterprises or foreigners with enterprises in the mainland of China in accordance with the Law of the People's Republic of China on Sino-foreign Cooperative Enterprises and other relevant laws, where the investment or provision of facilities, and the share of profits and risks is stipulated in the cooperative contract.

Enterprises with Sole (exclusive) Foreign Investment refer to enterprises established in the mainland of China with exclusive investment from foreign investors in accordance with the Law of the People's Republic of China on Foreign-Funded Enterprises and other relevant laws.

Share-holding Corporations Ltd. with Foreign Investment refer to share-holding corporations Ltd. established with the approval from the Ministry of Foreign Trade and Economic Relations in line with relevant state regulations, where the share of investment from foreign investors exceeds 25% of the total registered capital of the corporation. In case the share of foreign investment is less than 25% of the total registered capital, the enterprise is to be classified as domestic-funded share-holding corporation Ltd.

Government Agencies, Institutions and Social Organizations are classified into following categories by source of funds and way of management taking reference of the registration status of enterprises:

(1) Government agencies: include state and party agencies, classified in principle as state-owned. There are exceptions, such as supply and marketing cooperatives which are classified as collective-owned.

(2) Institutions: include institutions of various types established with the approval by organization and staffing departments of the government, but exclude institutions where enterprise management system is introduced. Institutions are further classified as follows:

(a) Institutions whose main budget is listed in the government budget appropriations or extra-budget funds, or allocated from the budget of their competent government agencies. Such institutions are classified as state-owned.

(b) Institutions whose budget mainly comes from collective units. Such institutions are classified as collective-owned.

(c) Institutions other than those mentioned above whose source of budget is not clear. Such institutions are classified by way of management.

(3) Social organizations: include social organizations established with the approval from the Ministry of Civil Affairs, and organizations that are not covered by social organization management regulations such as trade unions, womens federations etc.. Social organizations are further classified as follows:

(a) Social organizations that are not covered by social organization management regulations of the Ministry of Civil Affairs such as trade unions, womens federations, communist youth leagues, youth associations, industrial and commerce associations, scientists associations, overseas Chinese associations, etc., foundations and fund management organizations established with funds from the state, and social organizations whose funds mainly come from the budget of their competent government agencies. Such institutions are classified as state-owned.

(b) Social organizations whose budget mainly comes from collective units. Such institutions are classified as collective-owned.

(c) Social organizations established by individual or a group of citizens, which are classified as private.

(d) Social organizations other than those mentioned above whose source of budget is not clear. Such organizations are classified by way of management.

Gross Domestic Product (GDP) refers to the final products at market prices produced by all resident units in a country (or a region) during a certain period of time. Gross domestic product is expressed in three different forms, i.e. value, income, and products respectively. GDP in its value form refers to the total value of all goods and services produced by all resident units during a certain period of time, minus the total value of input of goods and services of the nature of non-fixed assets; in other term, it is the sum of the value-added of all resident units. GDP in the form of income includes the income created by all resident units and distributed to resident and non-resident units. GDP in the form of products refers to the value of all goods and services for final consumption by all resident units minus the net exports of goods and services during a given period of time. In the practice of national accounting, gross domestic product is calculated with three approaches, i.e. production approach, income approach and expenditure approach, which reflect gross domestic product and its composition from different aspects.

Gross National Income (GNI) also known as gross national product, refers to the final result of the primary distribution of the income created by all the resident units of a country (or a region) during a certain period of time. The value-added created by the resident units of a country engaged in production activities is distributed, during the primary distribution, mainly to the resident units of that country, while part of it is distributed to the non-resident units in the form of production tax and import duties (minus subsidies to production and import), remuneration for the labourers and property income. At the meantime, a part of the value-added created abroad is distributed to the resident units of the country in the form of production tax and import duties (minus subsidies to production and import), remuneration for the labourers and property income. The concept of gross national income is thus developed, which equals to the gross domestic product plus the net factor income from abroad. Unlike the gross domestic product which is a concept of production, the gross national income is a concept of income.

Three Industries Classification of economic activities into three branches of industries is a common practice in the world, although the grouping varies to some extent form country to country. In China economic activities are categorized into following industries:

Primary industry: refers to agriculture, forestry, animal husbandry and fishery.

Secondary industry: refers to mining and quarrying, manufacturing, production and supply of electricity, water and gas, and construction.

Tertiary industry: refers to all other economic activities not included in primary or secondary industry.

Labourers Remuneration refers to the whole payment of various forms earned by the labourers from the productive activities they are engaged in. It includes wages, bonuses and allowances the labourers earned in monetary form and in kind. It also includes the free medical services provided to the labourers and the medicine expenses, traffic subsidies and social insurance, housing fund paid by the employers. As the individual economy is concerned, since the labourers remuneration is not easily distinguished from the operating profit, both are treated as labourers remuneration.

Net Taxes on Production refers to the difference of the taxes on production minus the subsidies on production. The taxes on production refers to the various taxes, extra charges and fees levied on the production units on their production, sale and business activities as well as on the use of some factors of production, such as fixed assets, land and labour force in the production activities they are engaged in. In contrast to the taxes on production, the subsidies on production refer to the unilateral government transfer to the production units and are therefore regarded as negative taxes on production. They include subsidies on the loss due to implementation of government policies, price subsidies, etc.

Depreciation of Fixed Assets refers to the depreciation of fixed assets of a given period, drawn in accordance with the stipulated depreciation rate for the purpose of compensating the wear loss of the fixed assets or the depreciation of fixed assets calculated in a fictitious way in accordance with the stipulated unified depreciation rate in the national economic accounting system. It reflects the value of transfer of the fixed assets in the production of the current period. The depreciation of fixed assets in various enterprises and institutions managed as enterprises refers to the depreciation expenses actually drawn. In government agencies and institutions not managed as enterprises which do not draw the depreciation expenses, as well as for the houses of residents, the depreciation of fixed assets is the imputed depreciation, which is calculated in accordance with the stipulated unified depreciation rate. In principle, the depreciation of fixed assets should be calculated on the basis of the re-purchased value of the fixed assets. However, there is no actual condition to re-evaluate all the fixed assets in China. Therefore, the above-mentioned methods are temporarily adopted at present.

Operating Surplus refers to the balance of the value added created by the resident units deducting the labourers remuneration, net taxes on production and the depreciation of fixed assets. It is equivalent to the business profit of the enterprises plus subsidies on production, but the wages and welfare expenses paid from the profits should be deducted.

GDP by Expenditure Approach refers to the method of measuring the final results of production activities of a country (region) during a given period from the perspective of final use. It includes final consumption expenditure, total capital formation and net export of goods and services, i.e.:

GDP by expenditure approach = final consumption expenditure + total capital formation + net export of goods and services

Final Consumption Expenditure refers to the total expenditure of resident units for purchases of goods and services from domestic economic territory and abroad to meet the requirements of material, cultural and spiritual life. It excludes the expenditure of non-resident units on consumption in the economic territory of the country. The final consumption expenditure is broken down into household consumption expenditure and government consumption expenditure.

Households Consumption Expenditure refers to the total expenditure of resident households on the final consumption of goods and services. In addition to the consumption of goods and services bought by the households directly with money, the households consumption expenditure also includes expenditure on goods and services obtained by the households in other ways, i.e. the so-called imputed consumption expenditure, which includes the following: (a) the goods and services provided to the households by the employer in the form of payment in kind and transfer in kind; (b) goods and services produced and consumed by the households themselves, in which the services refer only to the owner-occupied housing and domestic and individual services provided by the paid household workers; (c) financial intermediate services provided by financial institutions; (d) insurance services provided by insurance companies.

Government Consumption Expenditure refers to the expenditure on the consumption of the public services provided by the government to the whole society and the net expenditure on the goods and services provided by the government to the households free of charge or at low prices. The former equals to the output value of the government services minus the value of operating income obtained by the government departments. The latter equals to the market value of the goods and services provided by the government free of charge or at low prices to the households minus the value received by the government from the households.

Total Capital Formation refers to the fixed assets acquired minus those disposed of and the net value of inventory, including the total fixed capital formation and the increase in inventory.

Total Fixed Capital Formation refers to the value of fixed assets acquired minus those disposed of during a given period. Fixed assets are the assets produced through production activities with specified unit value which could be used for over one year, excluding natural assets. Total fixed capital formation can be categorized into total tangible capital formation and total intangible capital formation. The total tangible capital formation include the value of the construction projects, installation projects completed and the equipment, apparatus and instruments purchased as well as the value of land improved, the value of draught animals, breeding stock, animals for milk, wool and for recreational purpose, and the newly increased forest with economic value during a given period. The total intangible capital formation includes the prospecting of minerals, the acquisition of computer software minus the disposal of them.

Increase in Inventory refers to the market value of the change in inventory of resident units during a given period, i.e. the difference of value between the beginning and the end of the period minus the current gains due to the change in prices. The increase in inventory can be positive or negative. A positive value indicates the increase in inventory while a negative value indicates the decrease in stock. The inventory includes the raw materials, fuels and reserve materials purchased by the production units as well as the inventory of finished products, semi-finished products, work-in-progress, etc.

Outflow of Goods and Services refers to the difference of the exports of goods and services minus the imports of goods and services. The imports include the value of various goods and services sold or gratuitously transferred by the resident units to the non-resident units. The imports include the value of various goods and services purchased or gratuitously acquired by the resident units from the non-resident units. Because the provision of services and the use of them happen simultaneously, the acquisition of services by the resident units from abroad is usually treated as import while the acquisition of services by non-resident units in this country is usually treated as export. The export and import of goods are calculated at FOB.

2 人口

Population

资料整理：章　玲

2-1 总　　人　　口
POPULATION

单位：万人　　(年底数)(number at year-end)　　(10 000 persons)

年份 Year	总人口 Total Population	男 Male	女 Female
1952	2745.0	1414.6	1330.4
1957	3062.4	1579.7	1482.7
1965	3504.5	1793.4	1711.2
1975	4408.2	2261.6	2146.5
1980	4684.5	2401.7	2282.7
1981	4740.3	2430.9	2309.4
1982	4800.9	2464.3	2336.6
1983	4835.3	2485.6	2349.8
1984	4876.1	2510.9	2365.2
1985	4931.0	2540.0	2391.0
1986	4989.0	2573.4	2415.6
1987	5058.1	2608.7	2449.4
1988	5144.2	2652.1	2492.1
1989	5223.9	2694.6	2529.3
1990	5373.5	2771.5	2602.0
1991	5446.8	2805.4	2641.4
1992	5513.6	2841.3	2672.4
1993	5590.5	2880.8	2709.6
1994	5656.8	2915.6	2741.2
1995	5727.1	2952.2	2775.0
1996	5776.3	2979.6	2796.8
1997	5838.8	3014.1	2824.8
1998	5890.6	3039.9	2850.7
1999	5942.5	3061.8	2880.7
2000	5936.0	3066.1	2869.9
2001	5956.6	3073.2	2883.4
2002	5978.2	3086.2	2892.0
2003	6000.5	3109.9	2890.6
2004	6001.3	3107.8	2893.5
2005	5984.1	3102.4	2881.7
2006	6038.3	3129.7	2908.7
2007	6084.9	3154.0	2930.9
2008	6110.8	3167.5	2943.3
2009	6141.9	3185.5	2956.4
2010	6176.0	3202.0	2974.0
2011	6164.1	3194.0	2970.1
2012	6165.4	3193.9	2971.4
2013	6170.6	3199.5	2971.1
2014	6162.3	3198.1	2964.2

注：总人口为户籍总人口，2010年为人口普查户籍人口数。

Note: The total population of the total household population in 2010 census household population.

2-2　人口城乡构成

COMPOSITION OF URBAN AND RURAL POPULATION

单位：万人　　（年底数）(number at year-end)　　(10 000 persons)

年份 Year	Total Population	城镇人口 Urban Population	乡村人口 Rural Population
1952	2687.58	271.41	2416.17
1957	3062.41	411.69	2650.72
1965	3504.54	485.06	3019.48
1975	4408.15	626.22	3781.93
1979	4632.78	747.92	3884.86
1981	4740.35	815.60	3924.75
1982	4800.92	848.76	3952.16
1983	4835.34	873.91	3961.43
1984	4876.07	877.41	3998.66
1985	4930.97	1120.50	3810.47
1986	5047.83	1187.23	3860.60
1987	5120.27	1288.61	3831.66
1988	5184.94	1389.99	3794.95
1989	5258.83	1491.37	3767.46
1990	5439.29	1551.51	3887.78
1991	5512.33	1433.06	4079.27
1992	5579.85	1637.68	3942.17
1993	5653.48	1731.66	3921.82
1994	5718.81	1604.13	4114.68
1995	5772.07	1800.89	3971.18
1996	5825.13	1965.40	3859.73
1997	5872.60	1834.60	4038.00
1998	5907.23	1884.41	4022.82
1999	5938.03	1990.17	3947.86
2000	5646.00	2285.11	3360.89
2001	5658.00	2308.50	3349.50
2002	5672.00	2348.20	3323.80
2003	5685.00	2387.70	3297.30
2004	5698.00	2427.30	2466.70
2005	5710.00	2466.70	3243.30
2006	5693.00	2493.50	3199.50
2007	5699.00	2524.70	3174.30
2008	5711.00	2581.40	3129.60
2009	5720.00	2631.20	3088.80
2010	5723.77	2844.51	2879.26
2011	5758.00	2984.32	2773.68
2012	5779.00	3091.77	2687.23
2013	5799.00	3161.03	2637.97
2014	5816.00	3237.80	2578.20

注：1.人口数除1982年、1990年、2000年是以人口普查为基数推算外，1982年及以后为人口抽样调查推算数。
2.2000年以前数据是总人口数，2010年以后数据为常住人口数,2010年为第六次人口普查数据。

Notes:a) Population than in 1982，1990，2000 census as the base is projected, the population in 1982 and beyond as the number of sample projections.

b) Before2000 the data on total population, since 2010 data for the resident population.

2-3　全省人口自然变动
NATURAL CHANGE OF POLULATION

年　份 Year	人口变动数(万人) Number of Population Changed (10 000 persons)			变动系数(‰) Growth Rates		
	出生数 Number of Birth	死亡数 Number of Death	自然增长数 Number of Nature Growth	出生率 Birth Rate	死亡率 Death Rate	自然增长率 Natural Growth Rate
1965	121.48	34.75	86.73	35.10	10.04	25.06
1975	90.80	34.52	56.28	20.74	7.88	12.86
1980	94.84	32.59	62.25	20.36	7.00	13.36
1985	97.83	37.37	60.46	19.95	7.62	12.33
1986	107.09	39.45	67.64	21.01	7.74	13.27
1987	108.56	36.12	72.44	21.43	7.13	14.30
1988	97.62	32.95	64.67	19.08	6.44	12.64
1989	110.13	36.24	73.89	21.09	6.94	14.15
1990	114.40	38.66	75.74	21.60	7.30	14.30
1991	113.34	40.30	73.04	20.70	7.36	13.34
1992	105.60	38.08	67.52	19.05	6.87	12.18
1993	112.55	38.92	73.63	20.04	6.93	13.11
1994	103.31	37.98	65.33	18.17	6.68	11.49
1995	92.96	39.70	53.26	16.18	6.91	9.27
1996	93.24	40.18	53.06	16.08	6.93	9.15
1997	86.62	39.13	47.49	14.81	6.69	8.12
1998	74.09	39.46	34.63	12.58	6.70	5.88
1999	68.52	37.73	30.79	11.57	6.37	5.20
2000	57.76	35.75	22.01	9.71	6.01	3.70
2001	50.84	36.27	14.57	8.51	6.07	2.44
2002	50.10	36.90	13.20	8.38	6.17	2.21
2003	49.50	35.60	13.90	8.26	5.94	2.32
2004	50.66	36.23	14.43	8.43	6.03	2.40
2005	52.60	34.30	18.30	8.74	5.69	3.05
2006	54.80	35.90	18.90	9.08	5.95	3.13
2007	55.69	36.12	19.57	9.19	5.96	3.23
2008	55.98	39.51	16.47	9.21	6.50	2.71
2009	57.80	36.58	21.22	9.48	6.00	3.48
2010	59.30	34.46	24.84	10.36	6.02	4.34
2011	59.67	34.52	25.15	10.39	6.01	4.38
2012	63.45	35.30	28.15	11.00	6.12	4.88
2013	64.14	35.60	28.54	11.08	6.15	4.93
2014	68.88	40.42	28.46	11.86	6.96	4.90

注：1985年以后人口变动系数为人口抽样调查数，其余为公安年报数。

Note: The data of change of population after 1985 was based on census, the rest were from public security annual report.

2–4 全省市、州、县年底人口数(2014)
POPULATION OF CITIES, TOWNS, AND COUNTIES OF HUBEI AT YEAR-END(2014)

单位:万人 (10 000 persons)

地 区	Region	户籍人口(万人) Total Population	常住人口(万人) Population of Permnant Residents	地 区	Region	户籍人口(万人) Total Population	常住人口(万人) Population of Permnant Residents
全 省	**Province**	**6162.33**	**5816.00**	丹江口市	Danjiangkou	45.99	44.27
武汉市	**Wuhan**	**827.31**	**1033.80**	**宜昌市**	**Yichang**	**400.40**	**410.45**
江岸区	Jiang'an	71.11	93.70	西陵区	Xilin	43.52	53.75
江汉区	Jianghan	47.79	71.90	伍家岗区	Wujiagang	16.50	22.60
硚口区	Qiaokou	53.63	85.63	点军区	Dianjun	10.50	10.48
汉阳区	Hanyang	54.71	62.40	猇亭区	Huting	5.16	6.37
武昌区	Wuchang	111.03	125.51	夷陵区	yiling	52.33	52.29
青山区	Qingshan	43.85	51.70	远安县	Yuan'an	19.42	18.67
洪山区	Hongshan	79.34	149.89	兴山县	xingshan	17.18	17.07
东西湖区	Dongxihu	28.31	50.82	秭归县	Zigui	38.01	36.13
汉南区	Hannan	11.29	12.90	长阳县	Changyang	40.25	38.60
蔡甸区	Caidian	48.43	67.60	五峰县	Wufeng	20.46	18.77
江夏区	Jiangxia	69.81	84.65	宜都市	Yidu	39.68	38.90
黄陂区	Huangpi	112.16	91.10	当阳市	Dangyang	48.35	46.77
新洲区	Xinzhou	95.85	86.00	枝江市	Zhijiang	49.02	50.05
黄石市	**Huangshi**	**265.14**	**244.92**	**襄阳市**	**Xiangyang**	**595.45**	**560.02**
黄石港区	Huangshigang	20.32	23.72	襄城区	Xiangcheng	46.44	48.99
西塞山区	Xisai mountainous	21.46	24.66	樊城区	Fancheng	78.47	88.90
下陆区	Xialu	15.32	18.24	襄州区	Xiangzhou	102.58	91.39
铁山区	Tieshan	5.54	5.83	南漳县	Nanzhang	58.91	53.92
大冶市	Daye	95.90	90.13	谷城县	Gucheng	59.67	52.21
阳新县	Yangxin	106.60	82.34	保康县	Baokang	27.19	25.17
十堰市		**346.97**	**337.27**	老河口市	Laohekou	52.83	48.47
茅箭区	Maojian	28.56	41.59	枣阳市	Zaoyang	112.61	98.95
张湾区	Zhangwan	26.26	38.18	宜城市	Yicheng	56.75	52.02
郧阳区	Yunyang	63.12	56.31	**鄂州市**	**Ezhou**	**110.18**	**105.88**
郧西县	Yunxi	51.71	45.11	梁子湖区	Liangzihu	18.64	14.42
竹山县	Zhushan	46.48	41.29	华容区	Huarong	26.23	23.98
竹溪县	Zhuxi	36.98	31.08	鄂城区	Ercheng	65.31	67.48
房 县	Fang	47.88	39.44				

注：以上数据为第六次人口普查数推算数，常住人口是指常住本地半年以上人口。
Note:The permanent resident population is more than half the local population.

2-4　续表 Continued

单位:万人 (10 000 persons)

地　区	Regions	户籍人口 Total Population	常住人口 Permnant Population	地　区	Regions	户籍人口 Total Population	常住人口 Permnant Population
荆门市	**Jingmen**	**300.29**	**288.91**	蕲春县	Hanchun	101.83	77.36
东宝区	Dongbao	37.24	37.13	黄梅县	Huangmei	105.04	86.37
掇刀区	Zhuodao	33.22	30.14	麻城市	Macheng	115.50	87.54
京山县	Jingshan	64.57	62.71	武穴市	Wuxue	80.52	65.14
沙洋县	Shayang	59.25	57.41	**咸宁市**	**Xianning**	**296.46**	**248.92**
钟祥市	Zhongxiang	106.01	101.52	咸安区	Xian'an	60.94	51.95
孝感市	**Xiaogan**	**525.72**	**486.13**	嘉鱼县	Jiayu	36.70	31.67
孝南区	Xiaonan	96.94	91.77	通城县	Tongcheng	51.17	40.72
孝昌县	Xiaochang	66.79	59.45	崇阳县	Congyang	49.14	39.80
大悟县	Dawu	63.47	61.9	通山县	Tongshan	45.95	36.38
云梦县	Yunmeng	57.41	52.84	赤壁市	Chibi	52.57	48.40
应城市	Yingcheng	66.90	59.81	**随州市**	**Suizhou**	**257.11**	**218.38**
安陆市	Anlu	62.32	57.72	曾都区	Zengdu	64.91	62.67
汉川市	Hanchuan	111.90	102.64	随县	Sui	97.35	79.34
荆州市	**Jingzhou**	**658.45**	**574.42**	广水市	Guangshui	94.85	76.37
沙市区	Shashi	54.76	65.08	**恩施州**	**Enshi Prefecture**	**406.29**	**331.77**
荆州区	Jingzhou	56.51	57.27	恩施市	Enshi	82.09	76.58
公安县	Gong'an	104.20	89.99	利川市	Jianli	91.71	65.95
监利县	Jianli	158.39	107.93	建始县	Jianshi	51.52	41.54
江陵县	Jianglin	40.73	33.25	巴东县	Badong	49.86	42.44
石首市	Shishou	65.80	57.64	宣恩县	Xuan'en	36.37	30.19
洪湖市	Honghu	93.46	85.90	咸丰县	Xianfeng	39.23	30.42
松滋市	Songzi	84.58	77.36	来凤县	Laifeng	33.16	24.50
黄冈市	**Huanggang**	**741.43**	**626.25**	鹤峰县	Hefeng	22.35	20.15
黄州区	Huangzhou	35.10	37.22	**省直管单位**	**Jurisdictional**	**431.13**	**348.88**
团风县	Tuanfeng	37.31	34.06	仙桃市	Xiantao	154.99	116.60
红安县	Hong'an	64.72	60.19	潜江市	Qianjiang	103.97	95.44
罗田县	Luotian	59.47	54.69	天门市	Tianmen	164.24	129.16
英山县	Yingshan	40.20	35.92	神农架林区	Shennongjian	7.92	7.67
浠水县	Xishui	101.73	87.76				

主要统计指标解释

人口数 指一定时点、一定地区范围内有生命的个人总和。

年度统计的年末人口数指每年 12 月 31 日 24 时的人口数。

城镇人口和乡村人口 城镇人口是指居住在城镇范围内的全部常住人口；乡村人口是除上述人口以外的全部人口。

出生率(又称粗出生率) 指在一定时期内(通常为一年)一定地区的出生人数与同期内平均人数(或期中人数)之比，用千分率表示。本资料中的出生率指年出生率，其计算公式为：

$$出生率=\frac{年出生人数}{年平均人数}\times 1000‰$$

式中：出生人数指活产婴儿，即胎儿脱离母体时(不管怀孕月数)，有过呼吸或其他生命现象。年平均人数指年初、年底人口数的平均数，也可用年中人口数代替。

死亡率(又称粗死亡率) 指在一定时期内(通常为一年)一定地区的死亡人数与同期内平均人数(或期中人数)之比，用千分率表示。本资料中的死亡率指年死亡率，其计算公式为：

$$死亡率=\frac{年死亡人数}{年平均人数}\times 1000‰$$

人口自然增长率 指在一定时期内(通常为一年)人口自然增加数(出生人数减死亡人数)与该时期内平均人数(或期中人数)之比，用千分率表示。计算公式为：

$$人口自然增长率=\frac{本年出生人数-本年死亡人数}{年平均人数}\times 1000‰$$

$$=人口出生率-人口死亡率$$

Explanatory Notes on Main Statistical Indicators

Total Population refers to the total number of people alive at a certain point of time within a given area.

The annual statistics on total population is taken at midnight, the 3lst of December.

Urban Population and Rural Population Urban population refer to all people residing in cities and towns, while rural population refer to population other than urban population.

Birth Rate (or Crude Birth Rate) refers to the ratio of the number of births to the average population (or mid-period population) during a certain period of time (usually a year), expressed in ‰. Birth rate in the chapter refers to annual birth rate. The following formula is used:

Birth Rate = (Number of Births/Average Number of Population)×1000‰

Number of births in the formula refers to live births, i.e. when a baby has breathed or showed any vital phenomena regardless of the length of pregnancy.

Annual average number of population is the average of the number of population at the beginning of the year and that at the end of the year. Sometimes it is substituted by the mid-year population.

Death Rate (or Crude Death Rate) refers to the ratio of the number of deaths to the average population (or mid-period population) during a certain period of time (usually a year), expressed in ‰. Death rate in the chapter refers to annual death rate. The following formula is used:

Death Rate= (Number of Deaths/Annual Average Number of Population)×1000‰

Natural Growth Rate of Population refers to the ratio of natural increase in population (number of births minus number of deaths) in a certain period of time (usually a year) to the average population (or mid-period population) of the same period, expressed in ‰. The following formula is applied:

Natural Growth Rate of Population = [(Number of Births-Number of Deaths)/Average Number of Population]×1000‰

Natural Growth Rate of Population = Birth Rate-Death Rate

3 就业人员和职工工资

Employment and Wages

资料整理：张　蔚

3-1　全社会从业人员

NUMBER OF EMPLOYED PERSONS

单位：万人　(10 000 person)

年份 Year	合计 Total	按城乡分 Grouped by Areas		按产业分 Grouped by Industries		
		城镇 Urban	乡村 Rural	第一产业 Primary Industry	第二产业 Secondary Industry	第三产业 Tertiary Industry
1952	1020.30	141.60	878.70			
1965	1404.20	222.70	1181.60			
1970	1618.50	278.00	1340.80			
1975	1802.50	381.70	1420.80			
1978	1910.40	458.00	1452.30	1470.60	269.00	170.80
1980	1986.90	507.20	1479.70	1453.70	286.30	247.00
1985	2238.10	637.60	1600.50	1383.30	485.40	369.50
1990	3040.40	890.80	2149.60	1859.80	628.50	552.10
1991	3082.70	909.40	2173.30	1897.40	623.00	562.30
1992	3118.60	923.10	2195.50	1869.00	650.90	598.70
1993	3157.60	940.90	2216.70	1818.80	684.60	654.20
1994	3196.90	980.10	2216.80	1760.50	717.10	719.30
1995	3232.50	1015.00	2217.50	1697.00	743.50	792.00
1996	3275.50	1050.80	2224.70	1677.10	746.80	851.60
1997	3311.20	1070.50	2240.70	1663.20	752.00	896.00
1998	3328.20	1093.60	2234.60	1612.50	705.60	1010.10
1999	3358.10	1110.50	2247.60	1612.60	697.80	1047.70
2000	3384.90	1123.80	2261.10	1625.10	702.40	1057.40
2001	3414.50	1148.70	2265.80	1639.00	706.80	1068.70
2002	3443.00	1177.00	2266.00	1652.60	704.10	1086.30
2003	3476.00	1211.00	2265.00	1661.50	712.60	1101.90
2004	3507.00	1245.00	2262.00	1672.90	720.30	1113.80
2005	3537.00	1271.00	2266.00	1687.30	725.00	1124.70
2006	3564.00	1297.00	2267.00	1694.70	732.40	1136.90
2007	3584.00	1322.00	2262.00	1697.00	740.10	1146.90
2008	3607.00	1337.00	2270.00	1707.91	730.42	1168.67
2009	3622.00	1357.00	2265.00	1702.30	736.60	1183.10
2010	3645.00	1382.60	2262.40	1691.10	754.70	1199.20
2011	3672.00	1413.00	2259.00	1678.10	771.12	1222.78
2012	3687.00	1430.60	2256.40	1638.90	781.60	1266.50
2013	3692.00	1438.00	2254.00	1582.00	793.80	1316.20
2014	3687.50	1437.60	2249.90	1487.00	834.30	1366.20

3-2　分行业城镇单位从业人员数(2014)

NUMBER OF EMPLOYEES IN URBAN UNITS BY SECTOR (2014)

单位：人　　　　(person)

行业	Sector	城镇全部单位 All the Units In Urban Area	国有经济单位 State Owned Units	城镇集体单位 Urban Collective Owned Units	其他经济单位 Other Units	城镇私营单位 Urban Private Units
总计	**Total**	**10224974**	**2690324**	**148686**	**4228946**	**3157018**
农、林、牧、渔业	Farming, Forest, Herd, Fishery	123230	91082	867	681	30600
采矿业	Mining and Quarrying	179644	11473	4741	61628	101802
制造业	Manufacturing	3368341	189085	23453	1720772	1435031
电力、燃气及水的生产和供应业	Power, Gas and water production and supply	186047	114683	1108	50330	19926
建筑业	Construction	2058090	86923	45668	1308918	616581
批发和零售业	Wholesale and Retail sale	800839	44432	17168	341305	397934
交通运输、仓储和邮政业	Transportation, storage and post	425599	192992	6247	145034	81326
住宿和餐饮业	Hotel and Catering	258487	10431	1505	94126	152425
信息传输、软件和信息技术服务业	Information Transmission, Software and Computer Services	134470	15724	96	89537	29113
金融业	Banking	184698	71042	12632	96195	4829
房地产业	Real Estate	204911	9943	1181	112457	81330
租赁和商务服务业	Leasing and Commerical Services	158753	32697	3909	57125	65022
科学研究、技术服务业	Scietific Research, polytechnical	173239	83898	1584	66223	21534
水利、环境和公共设施管理业	Water Conservance, Environment and Public Facilities Management	112349	87112	7147	9306	8784
居民服务、修理和其他服务业	Resident Service and Others	56291	4582	791	10478	40440
教育	Education	727184	654452	3642	35465	33625
卫生和社会工作	Health, Social Security and	394981	351350	15897	18738	8996
文化、体育和娱乐业	Culture, Sports and Entertainment	84648	45785	674	10469	27720
公共管理、社会保障和社会组织	Public management, social security and social organization	593173	592638	376	159	

注：城镇全部单位统计范围含城镇私营单位。(后表未经特别注明均同此口径)

Note: All Statistics of Units in Urban Areas of 2010 including all the private run unit.

(The following tables if without specific notes are considered the same standard with this one.)

3-3 分行业在岗职工人数(2014)
NUMBER OF STAFF AND WORKERS BY SECTOR(2014)

单位：人 (person)

行业	Sector	城镇全部单位 All the Units In Urban Area	国有经济单位 State Owned Units	城镇集体单位 Urban Collective Owned Units	其他经济单位 Other Units	城镇私营单位 Urban Private Units
总计	**Total**	**9687742**	**2524317**	**135712**	**3870695**	**3157018**
农、林、牧、渔业	Farming, Forest, Herd, Fishery	110300	78266	817	617	30600
采矿业	Mining and Quarrying	173064	9027	4661	57574	101802
制造业	Manufacturing	3326015	182061	22708	1686215	1435031
电力、燃气及水的生产和供应业	Power, Gas and water production and supply	183300	112849	1103	49422	19926
建筑业	Construction	1788965	73708	41487	1057189	616581
批发和零售业	Wholesale and Retail sale	785898	42862	14978	330124	397934
交通运输、仓储和邮政业	Transportation, storage and post	411332	185773	5863	138370	81326
住宿和餐饮业	Hotel and Catering	256186	9973	1400	92388	152425
信息传输、软件和信息技术服务业	Information Transmission, Software and Computer Services	130272	14736	96	86327	29113
金融业	Banking	156199	66456	12365	72549	4829
房地产业	Real Estate	198076	8680	1048	107018	81330
租赁和商务服务业	Leasing and Commerical Services	154643	32268	3754	53599	65022
科学研究、技术服务业	Scietific Research, polytechnical	161455	79041	1439	59441	21534
水利、环境和公共设施 管理业	Water Conservance, Environment and Public Facilities Management	93659	71848	4161	8866	8784
居民服务、修理和其他服务业	Resident Service and Others	54616	3996	628	9552	40440
教育	Education	690660	620161	3389	33485	33625
卫生和社会工作	Health, Social Security and	374859	332553	15072	18238	8996
文化、体育和娱乐业	Culture, Sports and Entertainment	81538	43558	661	9599	27720
公共管理、社会保障和社会组织	Public management, social security and social organization	556705	556501	82	122	

3–4 分行业在岗女职工人数(2014)
NUMBER OF FEMALE STAFF AND WORKERS BY SECTOR(2014)

单位：人 (person)

行业	Sector	城镇全部单位(不含私营单位) All the Units In Urban Area	国有经济单位 State Owned Units	城镇集体单位 Urban Collective Owned Units	其他经济单位 Urban Private Units
总计	**Total**	**2420501**	**1004913**	**49894**	**1365694**
农、林、牧、渔业	Farming, Forest, Herd, Fishery	37998	37652	245	101
采矿业	Mining and Quarrying	17754	4387	311	13056
制造业	Manufacturing	757880	48429	10244	699207
电力、燃气及水的生产和供应业	Power, Gas and water production and supply	50657	33193	376	17088
建筑业	Construction	159694	13597	7929	138168
批发和零售业	Wholesale and Retail sale	219898	15318	10270	194310
交通运输、仓储和邮政业	Transportation, storage and post	94374	53178	1445	39751
住宿和餐饮业	Hotel and Catering	64759	6457	947	57355
信息传输、软件和信息技术服务业	Information Transmission, Software and Computer Services	40665	5757	53	34855
金融业	Banking	89952	35169	5450	49333
房地产业	Real Estate	46347	3626	487	42234
租赁和商务服务业	Leasing and Commerical Services	29467	10258	1043	18166
科学研究、技术服务业	Scietific Research, polytechnical	41792	24434	400	16958
水利、环境和公共设施管理业	Water Conservance, Environment and Public Facilities Management	41109	33954	3010	4145
居民服务、修理和其他服务业	Resident Service and Others	7651	1762	354	5535
教育	Education	306513	286964	1814	17735
卫生和社会工作	Health, Social Security and	226813	208844	5051	12918
文化、体育和娱乐业	Culture, Sports and Entertainment	23470	18542	230	4698
公共管理、社会保障和社会组织	Public Management、social security and Social Organization	163708	163392	235	81

3-5 城镇登记失业人数及失业率
NUMBER OF URBAN UNEMPLOYED PERSONS AND UNEMPLOYMENT RATE

单位：万人 (10 000 person)

年份 Year	年末城镇登记失业人数 The Number of Unemployeed in Urban Areas by the End of Year	年末城镇登记失业率(%) Year End Unemployment registered Rate %
1978	20.03	4.19
1980	15.54	2.97
1990	12.66	1.72
1991	14.20	1.88
1992	16.89	2.17
1993	17.96	2.20
1994	21.06	2.90
1995	24.45	3.10
1996	28.25	3.50
1997	29.83	3.50
1998	31.33	3.30
1999	33.10	3.30
2000	36.64	3.50
2001	42.15	4.00
2002	44.66	4.30
2003	49.34	4.30
2004	49.37	4.20
2005	52.60	4.33
2006	52.56	4.22
2007	46.72	4.21
2008	55.07	4.20
2009	55.25	4.21
2010	55.65	4.18
2011	55.11	4.10
2012	42.26	3.83
2013	40.26	3.49
2014	37.88	3.10

3-6 职工平均工资及指数

年份 Year	平均货币工资(元) Average Money Wages (yuan)					指数(上年=100) Indices(preceding year=100)	
	合计 Total	国有经济单位 State Owned Units	城镇集体经济单位 Urban Collective Owned	其他经济单位 Other Units	城镇私营单位 Urban private units	货币工资 Money Wages	国有经济单位 State Owned Units
1978	581	592	532			104.5	104.5
1980	719	744	619			116.0	115.9
1990	1903	2045	1467	2259		111.7	107.6
1992	2370	2532	1837	2575		113.9	114.4
1993	2933	3141	2183	3248		123.8	124.1
1994	4050	4348	2845	4352		138.1	138.4
1995	4685	4991	3308	5093		115.7	114.8
1996	5099	5411	3590	5754		108.8	108.4
1997	5401	5741	3731	5740		105.9	106.1
1998	6436	6783	4748	6166		108.7	109.1
1999	6991	7381	5001	6681		108.6	108.8
2000	7565	7989	5090	7327		108.2	108.2
2001	8619	9133	5677	8035		113.9	114.3
2002	9611	10403	6534	8180		111.5	113.9
2003	10692	11806	7137	8698		111.2	113.5
2004	11855	13096	7608	10270		110.9	110.9
2005	13330	14774	8663	11572		112.4	112.8
2006	15172	17078	9848	13098		113.8	115.6
2007	17397	21971	12921	16829		114.7	128.7
2008	19597	24756	14840	20293		112.6	112.7
2009	23709	30032	19181	23528	15615	121.0	121.3
2010	28092	35981	24429	28799	18626	118.5	119.8
2011	32050	40345	26988	34354	20788	114.1	112.1
2012	35179	43438	33551	38675	23037	109.8	107.7
2013	38720	46126	34181	43975	25898	110.1	106.2
2014	43217	55071	37599	48163	28534	111.6	119.4

注：1998年以后为在岗职工平均工资。2007年以后统计范围含城镇全部私营单位。

AVERAGE WAGES AND INDICES OF STAFF AND WORKERS

指数(上年=100) Indices(preceding year=100)							
城镇集体经济单位 Urban Collective Owned	其他经济单位 OtherUnits	城镇私营单位 Urban private units	实际工资 Real Wages	国有经济单位 State Owned Units	城镇集体经济单位 Urban Collective Owned	其他经济单位 OtherUnits	城镇私营单位 Urban private units
106.4			104.2	103.9	106.1		
116.4			108.6	108.5	109.0		
107.1	107.1		107.8	108.3	104.4	103.9	
110.5	109.0		103.1	103.5	100.0	98.7	
118.8	126.1		106.6	106.8	102.3	108.6	
130.3	134.0		108.7	109.0	102.6	105.5	
116.3	117.0		96.3	95.6	96.8	97.4	
108.5	113.0		95.1	94.0	95.3	99.9	
103.9	99.8		97.6	96.6	95.9	96.6	
109.2	99.1		110.2	110.2	110.8	100.5	
105.3	108.4		110.0	111.0	107.4	110.6	
101.8	109.7		109.3	109.3	102.7	110.8	
111.5	109.7		113.6	114.0	111.2	109.3	
115.1	101.8		112.0	114.4	115.6	102.2	
109.2	106.3		108.8	111.1	106.8	104.0	
106.6	118.1		105.7	105.7	101.6	112.6	
113.9	112.7		109.2	109.6	110.7	109.5	
113.7	113.2		112.0	113.8	111.9	111.4	
131.2	128.5		109.4	122.8	125.2	122.6	
114.9	120.6		106.0	106.0	108.0	113.4	
129.3	115.9		121.8	122.2	130.2	116.8	
127.4	122.4	119.3	115.1	116.4	123.8	119.0	115.9
110.5	119.3	111.6	107.8	106.0	104.4	112.8	105.5
124.3	112.6	110.8	106.7	104.6	120.8	109.4	107.7
101.9	113.7	112.4	107.1	103.3	99.1	110.6	109.4
110.0	109.5	110.2	109.4	117.1	107.8	107.4	108.0

Notes:Data after 1998 refers to average wages and indices of employed staff and workers.Statistics of 2007 involves all the private run units in urban areas.

3—7　分行业在岗职工平均工资(2014)
AVERAGE WAGES OF STAFF AND WORKER BY SECTOR(2014)

单位：元　(yuan)

行业	Sector	城镇全部单位 All the Units In Urban Area	国有经济单位 State Owned Units	城镇集体单位 Urban Collective Owned Units	其他经济单位 Other Units	城镇私营单位 Urban Private Units
总计	**Total**	**43217**	**55071**	**37599**	**48163**	**28534**
农、林、牧、渔业	Farming, Forest, Herd, Fishery	26209	28176	24412	24479	21156
采矿业	Mining and Quarrying	39797	51602	47840	50491	32087
制造业	Manufacturing	39237	62020	34159	45765	28670
电力、燃气及水的生产 和供应业	Power, Gas and water production and supply	62874	80195	38621	57587	27271
建筑业	Construction	41754	43014	31144	48604	31038
批发和零售业	Wholesale and Retail sale	33148	53344	28740	40867	24519
交通运输、仓储和邮政业	Transportation, storage and post	49674	62855	26406	46832	25780
住宿和餐饮业	Hotel and Catering	28678	32737	35085	33351	25514
信息传输、软件和信息技术服务业	Information Transmission, Software and Computer Services	58560	45647	26537	69239	34907
金融业	Banking	83665	86504	64143	87155	39530
房地产业	Real Estate	42961	42777	36523	48287	35980
租赁和商务服务业	Leasing and Commerical Services	35893	36003	40571	48586	24758
科学研究、技术服务业	Scietific Research, polytechnical	65760	56973	34530	89897	30885
水利、环境和公共设施管理业	Water Conservance, Environment and Public Facilities Management	36385	37719	35295	38106	23698
居民服务、修理和其他服务业	Resident Service and Others	28729	43798	43313	36195	25190
教育	Education	50440	52781	41120	42501	28686
卫生和社会工作	Health, Social Security and	55671	57016	48993	50686	27215
文化、体育和娱乐业	Culture, Sports and Entertainment	43954	51598	43446	61266	24795
公共管理、社会保障和 社会组织	Public Management、social security and Social Organization	51100	52520	24141	41230	

主要统计指标解释

经济活动人口 指在16周岁及以上，有劳动能力，参加或要求参加社会经济活动的人口。包括就业人员和失业人员。

就业人员 指在16周岁及以上，从事一定社会劳动并取得劳动报酬或经营收入的人员。这一指标反映了一定时期内全部劳动力资源的实际利用情况，是研究我国基本国情国力的重要指标。

单位就业人员 指报告期末最后一日24时在各类单位工作，并取得工资或其他形式劳动报酬的人员数。该指标为时点指标，不包括最后一日当天及以前已经与单位解除劳动合同关系的人员，是在岗职工、劳务派遣人员及其他从业人员之和。从业人员不包括：

1.离开本单位仍保留劳动关系，并定期领取生活费的人员；

2.利用课余时间打工的学生及在本单位实习的各类在校学生；

3.本单位因劳务外包而使用的人员。

在岗职工 指在本单位工作且与本单位签订劳动合同，并由单位支付各项工资和社会保险、住房公积金的人员，以及上述人员中由于学习、病伤、产假等原因暂未工作仍由单位支付工资的人员。在岗职工还包括：

1.应订立劳动合同而未订立劳动合同人员（如使用的农村户籍人员）；

2.处于试用期人员；

3.编制外招用的人员，如临时人员；

4.派往外单位工作，但工资仍由本单位发放的人员（如挂职锻炼、外派工作等情况）。

在岗职工平均工资 指单位在岗职工在一定时期内平均每人所得的货币工资。它表明一定时期在岗职工工资收入的高低程度，是反映在岗职工工资水平的主要指标。计算公式为：

$$平均工资=\frac{报告期实际支付的全部在岗职工工资总额}{报告期全部在岗职工平均人数}$$

平均工资指数 指报告期在岗职工平均工资与基期平均工资的比率，是反映不同时期在岗职工货币工资水平变动情况的相对数。计算公式为：

$$平均工资指数=\frac{报告期在岗职工平均工资}{基期在岗职工平均工资}\times 100\%$$

平均实际工资指数 在岗职工平均实际工资指扣除物价变动因素后的在岗职工平均工资。在岗职工平均实际工资指数是反映实际工资变动情况的相对数，表明职工实际工资水平提高或降低的程度。计算公式为：

$$平均实际工资指数=\frac{报告期职工平均工资指数}{报告期城镇居民消费价格指数}\times 100\%$$

城镇登记失业人员 指有非农业户口，在一定的劳动年龄内(16周岁至退休年龄)，有劳动能力，无业而要求就业，并在当地就业服务机构进行求职登记的人员。

城镇登记失业率 城镇登记失业人员与城镇单位就业人员(扣除使用的农村劳动力、聘用的离退休人员、港澳台及外方人员)、城镇单位中的不在岗职工、城镇私营业主、个体户主、城镇私营企业和个体就业人员、城镇登记失业人员之和的比。

$$\text{城镇登记失业率}=\frac{\text{城镇登记失业人数}}{\text{(城镇单位就业人员－使用的农村劳动力－聘用的离退休人员－聘用的港澳台及外方人员)}}\times 100\%$$

Explanatory Notes on Main Statistical Indicators

Economically Active Population refers to the population aged 16 and over who are capable to work, are participating in or willing to participate in economic activities, including employed persons and unemployed persons.

Employed Persons refer to the persons aged 16 and over who are engaged in social working and receive remuneration payment or earn business income. This indicator reflects the actual utilization of total labour force during a certain period of time and is often used for the research on China's economic situation and national power.

Persons Employed in Various Units refer to all the persons working in government agencies of various levels, political and party organizations, social organizations, enterprises and institutions, and receiving wages or other forms of payment. They include fully-employed staff and workers, re-employed retirees, teachers in schools run by the local people, foreigners and Chinese compatriots from Hong Kong, Macao, and Taiwan working in various units, part-time employees, employees of other units working temporarily at current posts, and employees holding the second job, but exclude staff and workers who have left their working units while keeping their labour contract (employment relation) unchanged. This indicator reflects the total number of laborers actually engaged in production or other operations in various units.

Persons Employed in Private Enterprises and Self-Employed Individuals in Urban Areas Persons employed in private enterprises refer to the persons employed in the private enterprises which have been registered at the departments of industrial and commercial administration and are situated at a county town (i.e. a town where the county government is located) for business operation or at urban areas with the level higher than a county town. The self-employed individuals in urban areas refer to persons who hold the certificates of residence in urban areas or have resided in the urban areas for a long time and have been registered at the departments of industrial and commercial administration and approved to be engaged in individual industrial or commercial business, including self-employed persons as well as helpers and hired labourers who work in the individual households engaged in industrial or commercial business.

Registered Urban Unemployed Persons refer to the persons with non-agricultural household registration at certain working ages (16-50 years for male and 16-45 years for females), who are capable of work, unemployed and willing to work, and have been registered at the local employment service agencies to apply for a job.

Registered Urban Unemployment Rate refers to the ratio of the number of the registered unemployed persons to the sum of the number of persons employed in various units (minus the rural labour force, retirees, and Hong Kong, Macao, Taiwan or foreign employees they employ) laid-off workers in urban units, owners and employees in urban private enterprises, urban self-employed individuals and the registered urban unemployed persons. The formula is as follows:

Registered urban unemployment rate = number of registered urban unemployed persons÷(number of persons employed in urban units - rural labour force employed retirees employed - Hong Kong, Macao, Taiwan or foreign employees employ + laid-off workers + owners and employees in urban private enterprises + self-employed individuals in urban areas + registered urban unemployed persons) × 100%.

Staff and Workers refer to persons working in, and receive payment from units of state ownership, collective ownership, joint ownership, share holding ownership, foreign ownership, and ownership by entrepreneurs from Hong Kong, Macao, and Taiwan, and other types of ownership and their affiliated units. They do not include 1) persons employed in township enterprises, 2) persons employed in private enterprises, 3) urban self-employed persons, 4) retirees, 5) re-employed retirees, 6) teachers in the schools run by the local people, 7) foreigners and persons from Hong Kong, Macao and Taiwan who work in urban units, and 8) other persons not to be included by relevant regulations. (Data of 1998 and afterward refer to fully employed staff and workers. Other related statistics such as total wage bill and average wage are adjusted since 1998 accordingly).

State-owned Units refer to economic units whose assets are owned by the state. Included are non-corporation units registered according to Regulation of the People Republic of China on the Registration of Enterprises and Corporations, state organs, institutions and social organizations at the central and local levels.

Collective-Owned Units refer to economic units registered according to Regulation of the People抯 Republic of China on the Registration of Enterprises and Corporations where the means of production are collectively owned.

Units of Other Types of Ownership refer to units registered with other types of ownership, including cooperative units, joint ownership units, limited companies, share holding corporations, units invested by entrepreneurs from Hong Kong, Macao, and Taiwan, and foreign-invested units.

Fully Employed Staff and Workers refer to persons who work in, and receive wages from their working units, as well as persons who have their work posts, but are temporarily absent from work for reasons of study or on sick, injury or maternal leave and still receive wages from their working units.

Total Wages Bill refer to the total remuneration payment to staff and workers in various units during a certain period of time. The calculation of total wages is based on the total remuneration payment to the staff and workers. Therefore, all the wages and salaries and other payments to staff and workers are included in the total wages regardless of their sources, category, and forms (in kind or cash). (Total wages of staff and workers in this yearbook include only total wages of fully employed staff and workers, excluding the living allowances distributed to those who have left their working units while keeping their labour contract/employment relation unchanged).

Average Wage refers to the average wage in money terms per person during a certain period of time for staff and workers in enterprises, institutions, and government agencies, which reflects the general level of wage income during a certain period of time and is calculated as follows:

Average Wage = Total Wages of Staff and Workers at Reference Time /Average Number of Staff and Workers at Reference Time.

Average Wage Indices refers to the ratio of average wage of staff and workers in the report period to that in the base period, which reflects the change of wage of staff and workers at the different period. It is calculated as follows:

Average Wage Indices = Average Wage of Staff and Workers at Reference Time / Average Wage of Staff and Workers at Base Period x 100%

Average Real Wage Indices average real wage of staff and workers refers to the average wage of staff and workers after removing the effects of the price changes and average real wage indices of staff and workers refers to the change of real wage, which reflects the relative increasing or decreasing level of real wage of staff and workers, which is calculated as follows:

Average Real Wage Indices = Average Wage Indices of Staff and Workers at the Reference Time / Urban Consumer Price Indices at Reference Time × 100%

4 固定资产投资

Investment In Fixed Assets

资料整理：柯　超

固定资产投资

INVESTMENT IN FIXED ASSETS

2014

全社会固定资产投资完成额	Total Completed Investment in Fixed Assets	25001.77 亿元
固定资产投资	Urban Investment	24303.05 亿元
#房地产开发	Real Estate Development	3983.79 亿元
#国有经济	State-Owned	5829.79 亿元
集体经济	Collective-Owned	820.75 亿元
房屋施工面积	Floor Space of Building Under Construction	58064.39 万平方米
房屋竣工面积	Floor Space of Building Completed	21175.37 万平方米

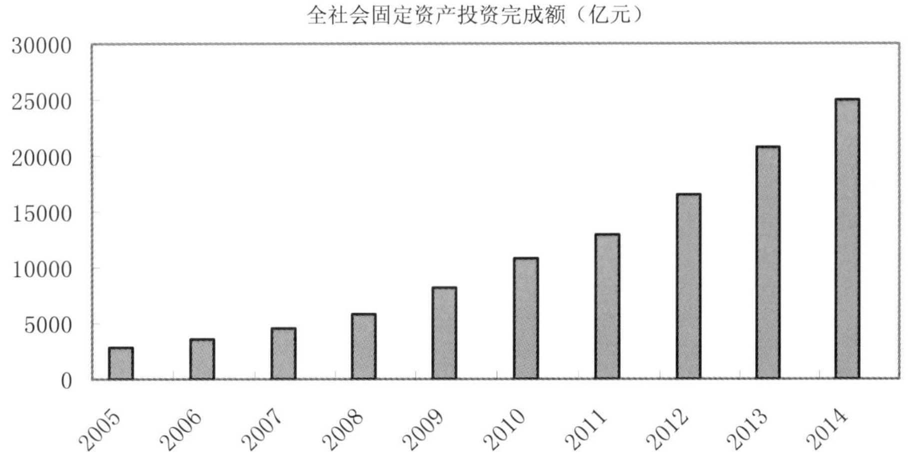

附：全社会固定资产投资完成额构成(%)

		2005	2006	2007	2009	2010	2011	2012	2013	2014
国有投资	State-Owned	38.7	41.2	39.9	38.1	34.9	29.1	25.8	24.4	23.3
集体投资	Collective-Owned	2.8	3.1	3.4	5.0	5.6	5.1	4.4	4.0	3.3
私营个体投资	Individuals	19.6	17.8	19.9	21.6	23.2	25.6	28.6	32.6	34.8
外商港澳台商投资	Foreign, HK, Macao and Taiwan	7.4	6.9	6.8	4.9	4.2	4.5	4.1	3.1	2.7
其他	Others	31.5	31.0	30.0	30.4	32.1	35.7	37.1	35.9	35.9

注：从2011年起固定资产投资统计口径调整为计划总投资500万元及以上项目，取消城镇农村公布口径，其他年份未做相应调整。

Note:Since 2011, the fixed assets investment accounts for investment over 5 million yuan, canceling town and countryside. Other years' statistics do not correspond to this adjustment.

4-1 全社会固定资产投资主要指标

指 标	Item	1990	2000	2005
投资总额(亿元)	**Total Investment (100 million yuan)**	**144.44**	**1421.55**	**2834.75**
按经济类型分	**Grouped by Ownership**			
国有经济	State-owned Units	100.35	857.01	1095.71
集体经济	Collective-owned Units	15.59	128.32	79.47
#农村	Rural Area	9.59	98.95	26.55
私营个体经济	Individuals	28.50	221.43	554.27
#农村	Rural Area	23.62	106.65	135.95
联营经济	Joint-ownership Economic Units		3.94	19.56
股份制经济	Share Holding Co.Ltd.		86.29	232.34
有限责任公司	Limited Liability Corporations		53.33	557.21
港澳台投资经济	Economic Units Funded by Hongkong, Macao and Taiwan		36.57	92.68
外商投资经济	Foreign Funded Enterprise Units		23.90	116.23
其他经济	Others		10.76	87.28
按资金来源分	**Grouped by Source of Finance**			
国家预算内资金	State Budgetary Apporpriations	11.38	141.48	255.76
国内贷款	Domestic Loans	22.22	243.90	474.21
利用外资	Foreign Investment	4.79	28.28	71.34
自筹资金	Fund Raising	92.96	781.50	1492.66
其他资金来源	Others	13.09	226.39	540.78
按构成分	**Grouped by Usage of Funds**			
建筑安装工程	Construction Installation	92.64	814.66	1696.80
设备工器具购置	Purchase of Equipments and Instruments	41.02	371.56	642.86
其他费用	Others	10.78	235.33	495.09
按产业分	**Grouped by Industry**			
#住宅	Residential Housing	39.61	290.24	510.04
第一产业	Primary Industry	12.16	103.05	92.88
第二产业	Second Industry	67.41	521.58	1086.34
第三产业	Tertiary Industry	64.87	796.92	1655.53
房屋建筑面积(万平方米)	**Floor Space of Building (10000 sq.m)**			
施工面积	Floor Space under Construction	5103.48	9920.42	12572.00
#住宅	Residential Housing	3507.53	6831.02	8401.20
竣工面积	Floor Space Completed	4169.12	7508.96	7863.85
#住宅	Residential Housing	3058.40	5417.38	5627.67
商品房销售面积(万平方米)	**Floor Space of Commercial House (sq.m)**	130.53	612.05	1708.02

注：2006年全社会投资(城镇投资)不含城镇工矿区私人建房投资(下同)。由于方法制度调整，按可比口径计算，2005年扣除城镇工矿区私人建房投资基数应为2788.92亿元；从2011年起固定资产投资统计口径调整为计划总投资500万元及以上项目，取消城镇农村公布口径，其他年份未做相应调整。从2012年起，三次产业采用新的划分标准。

MAJOR INDICATORS OF TOTAL INVESTMENT IN FIXED ASSETS

2007	2008	2009	2010	2011	2012	2013	2014
4534.14	**5798.56**	**8211.85**	**10802.69**	**12935.02**	**16504.17**	**20753.91**	**25001.77**
1808.61	2273.83	3124.90	3768.95	3764.22	4265.95	5068.42	5829.79
155.66	253.32	411.18	602.80	660.59	733.92	826.51	820.75
44.10	65.02	77.50	99.23	137.69	118.29	137.45	117.04
900.48	1201.53	1771.61	2510.61	3307.47	4712.60	6763.68	8708.83
186.65	190.19	240.48	301.05	365.51	459.30	576.46	698.73
26.59	15.05	11.32	19.89	22.49	47.70	38.96	11.84
344.51	462.81	659.79	896.87	987.66	1319.31	1487.62	1238.81
872.80	1109.43	1648.26	2221.99	3056.98	3805.18	4692.14	6026.42
145.53	160.62	202.38	207.81	253.89	302.69	245.87	343.93
164.84	178.60	200.79	245.92	328.55	367.76	397.02	333.45
115.12	143.37	181.62	327.85	553.17	949.06	1233.69	1687.95
472.98	570.17	711.98	868.46	663.18	784.27	886.58	1107.45
790.84	894.57	1432.98	1768.79	1707.46	1964.14	2720.19	2874.92
88.37	57.02	68.33	147.03	189.26	131.64	66.82	78.99
2470.28	3677.00	4956.65	6703.61	8800.61	11812.15	14823.15	18732.35
711.66	599.80	1041.91	1314.80	1574.51	1811.96	2257.17	2208.06
2857.31	3568.96	5025.62	6701.91	8056.53	11054.16	14312.25	18185.42
896.36	1245.73	1753.28	2308.73	2812.91	3162.99	3856.68	4292.85
780.47	983.87	1432.95	1792.05	2065.58	2287.02	2584.98	2523.50
709.63	901.26	1127.28	1417.95	1750.16	2198.86	2907.29	3461.65
149.40	231.25	321.59	393.00	440.91	525.45	590.61	799.35
1710.59	2344.36	3097.68	4169.92	5526.40	7281.04	9187.25	10733.09
2674.15	3222.95	4792.58	6239.77	6967.71	8697.68	10976.04	13469.32
13686.34	16417.07	20142.81	25284.83	31388.88	40103.56	51939.51	58064.39
8910.75	9896.66	11762.06	14486.90	16337.96	19154.75	23443.19	27199.41
7557.62	7551.82	9772.28	11802.18	14585.68	16576.18	18828.87	21175.37
5036.19	4679.96	5556.71	6785.61	7375.38	7890.08	8006.06	8702.01
2538.90	1941.62	2718.30	3508.61	4187.62	4037.85	5298.54	5601.98

Note: In 2006 the social investment (town investment) does not contain town private house industrial investment.(same below) Because of method adjustment, according to comparable caliber, 2005's investment base should be 278.892 billion yuan deducting industrial town private house. Since 2011, the fixed assets investment accounts for investment over 5 million yuan, canceling town and countryside. Other years' statistics do not correspond to this adjustment. Since 2012, the division of three industries emploies a new standard.

4-2 全社会固定资产投资额
TOTAL INVESTMENT IN FIXED ASSETS

单位：亿元 (100 million yuan)

年 份 Year	投资额 Investment	#房地产开发 Real Estate Development	#国有经济 State Owned Units	#集体经济 Collective Owned Units	#私营个体 Individuals
"六五"时期 Period of the Six-Year Plan	**315.82**		**207.57**	**49.41**	**58.84**
1981	33.48		29.51	3.69	0.28
1982	48.83		34.46	8.45	5.92
1983	56.13		36.69	8.84	10.60
1984	74.47		45.25	10.99	18.23
1985	102.91		61.66	17.44	23.81
"七五"时期 Peroid of the Seven-Year Plan	**680.12**	**5.94**	**435.32**	**94.17**	**150.64**
1986	111.44		66.42	15.89	29.13
1987	140.08		85.32	22.31	32.46
1988	160.46		102.21	24.60	33.64
1989	123.70		81.02	15.78	26.91
1990	144.44	5.94	100.35	15.59	28.50
"八五"时期 Peroid of the Eight-Year Plan	**2211.67**	**253.77**	**1467.69**	**190.04**	**261.87**
1991	168.19	7.88	119.07	19.49	29.63
1992	240.73	12.55	182.86	22.52	35.35
1993	383.18	37.01	275.84	30.62	40.37
1994	593.07	76.20	401.16	44.83	56.62
1995	826.50	121.13	518.76	72.58	99.90
"九五"时期 Peroid of the Nine-Year Plan	**6022.80**	**334.60**	**3425.23**	**573.74**	**943.77**
1996	984.38	118.40	593.32	96.50	124.78
1997	1083.60	126.47	567.60	107.12	160.56
1998	1231.10	131.23	661.94	116.92	194.52
1999	1302.17	123.87	745.36	124.88	242.48
2000	1421.55	134.63	857.01	128.32	221.43
"十五"时期 Peroid of the Ten-Year Plan	**10321.69**	**1354.15**	**4817.55**	**541.41**	**1806.78**
2001	1551.75	151.24	918.21	126.41	249.59
2002	1695.22	178.64	963.18	121.42	263.00
2003	1883.59	239.04	888.72	109.05	303.90
2004	2356.38	337.28	951.73	105.06	436.02
2005	2834.75	447.95	1095.71	79.47	554.27
"十一五"时期 Peroid of the Eleven-Year Plan	**32919.93**	**4999.84**	**12449.99**	**1533.63**	**7020.48**
2006	3572.69	564.76	1473.70	110.67	636.25
2007	4534.14	723.73	1808.61	155.66	900.48
2008	5798.56	892.67	2273.83	253.32	1201.53
2009	8211.85	1200.44	3124.90	411.18	1771.61
2010	10802.69	1618.24	3768.95	602.80	2510.61
"十二五"时期 Peroid of the Twelve-Year Plan					
2011	12935.02	2066.48	3764.22	660.59	3307.47
2012	16504.17	2539.46	4265.95	733.92	4712.60
2013	20753.91	3286.02	5068.42	826.51	6763.68
2014	25001.77	3983.79	5829.79	820.75	8708.83

注：房地产开发投资统计制度从1990年开始建立。从2011年起固定资产投资统计口径调整为计划总投资500万元及以上项目，取消城镇农村公布口径，其他年份未做相应调整。

Note: The statistical system of real estate development investment is established in 1990. Since 2011, the fixed assets investment accounts for investment over 5 million yuan, canceling town and countryside. Other years' statistics do not correspond to this adjustment.

4—3 按登记注册类型分全社会固定资产投资

TOTAL INVESTMENT IN FIXED ASSETS BY TYPE OF REGISTRATION

单位：亿元

指　　标	Item	2011	2012	2013	2014
总　计	**Total**	**12935.02**	**16504.17**	**20753.91**	**25001.77**
内资企业	Domestic Funded Enterprises	11922.24	15315.74	19497.88	23594.86
国有企业	State-owned Enterprises	3576.83	4117.99	4871.98	5548.96
集体企业	Collective-owned Enterprises	554.48	651.70	677.53	707.76
股份合作企业	Share Holding Cooperative Enterprises	97.38	73.43	131.21	89.71
联营企业	Joint Owned Enterprise	47.30	68.75	78.13	44.09
国有联营	State Joint ownership	16.07	12.27	21.40	8.98
集体联营	Collective Joint Ownership	8.73	8.79	17.77	23.27
国有与集体联营	Joint State-Collective	5.70	12.16	21.23	4.50
其他联营企业	Other Joint Owned Enterprise	16.79	35.54	17.73	7.34
有限责任公司	Co. Ltd	3228.30	3940.87	4867.18	6298.27
国有独资公司	Solely State Funded Co.	171.32	135.69	175.04	271.85
其他有限责任公司	Other Co. Ltd	3056.98	3805.18	4692.14	6026.42
股份有限公司	Share Holding Co.Ltd.	987.66	1319.31	1487.62	1238.81
私营企业	Private - owned enterprises	2877.12	4194.63	6150.55	7979.30
其他企业	Others	553.18	949.05	1233.69	1687.96
港、澳、台商投资企业	Hongkong, Macao and Taiwan Funded	253.89	302.69	245.87	343.93
合资经营企业	Joint Funded Enterprises	138.56	121.23	63.81	102.28
合作经营企业	Cooperative Operation Enterprises	3.50	1.54	1.12	7.56
独资经营企业	Solely Funded Enterprises	87.57	147.23	142.00	187.34
股份有限公司	Share Holding Co.Ltd.	24.26	29.64	35.62	44.38
外商投资企业	Foreign Invested Enterprises	328.55	367.76	397.02	333.45
合资经营企业	Joint Funded Enterprises	156.38	195.14	227.87	104.57
合作经营企业	Cooperative Operation Enterprises	9.74	11.67	8.06	10.60
独资企业	Solely Funded Enterprises	132.90	124.48	116.11	154.10
股份有限公司	Share Holding Co.Ltd.	29.53	14.09	34.38	35.93
个体经营	Individual Investment	430.35	517.97	613.13	729.53
个体户	Individual Self-Employed	406.54	487.04	595.47	717.82
个人合伙	Individual Pattenership	23.81	30.94	17.66	11.71

注：从2011年起固定资产投资统计口径调整为计划总投资500万元及以上项目，取消城镇农村公布口径，其他年份未做相应调整。

Note:Since 2011, the fixed assets investment accounts for investment over 5 million yuan, canceling town and countryside. Other years' statistics do not correspond to this adjustment.

4-4 按构成分固定资产投资(不含农户) (2014)
URBAN INVESTMENT IN FIXED ASSETS BY USAGE OF FUNDS(2014)

单位：亿元 (100 million yuan)

行业	Sector	投资额 Investment	建筑工程 Construction	安装工程 Installation	设备工器具购置 Purchases of Equipments and Instruments	其他 Others
总计	**Total**	**24303.05**	**15569.50**	**2180.53**	**4029.50**	**2523.51**
农、林、牧、渔业	Farming, Forestry, Animal Husbandry and Fishery	688.36	428.41	63.08	118.51	78.36
农业	Farming	221.78	137.70	22.88	36.70	24.50
林业	Forestry	71.57	38.23	4.78	11.38	17.19
畜牧业	Animal Husbandry	188.86	114.68	18.18	35.99	20.00
渔业	Fishery	53.79	35.69	4.96	8.26	4.88
农、林、牧、渔服务业	Farming, Forestry, Animal Husbandry and Fishery Services	152.35	102.12	12.27	26.17	11.79
采矿业	Mining	404.80	223.21	45.00	115.55	21.04
制造业	Manufacturing	9633.97	5202.90	1026.04	2689.61	715.42
农副食品加工业	Food Processing	794.99	441.27	82.26	218.29	53.17
食品制造业	Food Production	322.51	175.31	45.32	76.31	25.58
酒、饮料和精制茶制造业	Beverage Production	305.83	173.17	29.36	81.51	21.79
烟草制品业	Tobacco Processing	28.93	19.58	0.03	7.68	1.63
纺织业	Textile Industry	406.90	210.24	56.07	113.79	26.80
纺织服装、服饰业	Textile Wearing Apparel and Accessaries	253.76	137.63	29.74	68.55	17.84
皮革、毛皮、羽毛及其制品和制鞋业	Leather, Fur, Feather and Related Products	76.70	37.83	4.40	29.03	5.44
木材加工和木、竹、藤、棕、草制品业	Timber Processing and Wood, Bamboo, Rattan, Palm and Straw Products	138.08	75.22	14.88	38.34	9.63
家具制造业	Furniture Manufacturing	137.11	76.51	19.02	31.50	10.07
造纸和纸制品业	Papermaking and Paper Products	186.73	96.98	18.50	55.31	15.94
印刷和记录媒介复制业	Printing and Record Processing	131.93	73.16	15.95	34.83	7.99
文教、工美、体育和娱乐用品制造业	Stationery, Education, Art, Sport and Entertainment Products	104.82	62.20	16.55	20.67	5.40
石油加工、炼焦和核燃料加工业	Petroleum Processing, Coking Products and Nuclear Fuel Processing	67.64	17.33	5.27	22.65	22.39
化学原料和化学制品制造业	Raw Chemical Material and Chemical Products	635.40	312.60	75.24	199.49	48.07
医药制造业	Medical and Pharmaceutical Products	362.42	209.88	33.83	96.00	22.72
化学纤维制造业	Chemical Fibres	22.56	9.58	3.29	6.17	3.52
橡胶和塑料制品业	Rubber Products and Plastic Products	271.24	149.68	27.09	79.31	15.15
非金属矿物制品业	Non-metal Material Products	949.41	461.11	108.16	305.40	74.75
黑色金属冶炼和压延加工业	Smelting and Processing of Ferrous Metals	213.67	100.76	35.45	69.12	8.34
有色金属冶炼和压延加工业	Smelting and Processing of Non-ferrous Metals	142.70	71.51	17.87	37.38	15.93
金属制品业	Metal Products	447.01	232.19	46.52	134.68	33.63
通用设备制造业	General Machinery Manufacturing	493.65	251.68	63.91	139.72	38.33
专用设备制造业	Special Purpose Equipment Manufacturing	617.43	353.06	59.38	160.86	44.12
汽车制造业	Automobile Manufacturing	1036.29	620.33	75.11	296.19	44.66
铁路、船舶、航空航天和其他运输设备制造业	Realway, Ship, Aircraft and Other Transport Equipment Manufacturing	125.69	71.02	13.17	35.34	6.17
电气机械和器材制造业	Electric Machinery and Equipment	540.69	318.87	52.29	140.97	28.56
计算机、通信和其他电子设备制造业	Computers, Communication Equipment and Other Electronic Equipment Manufacturing	538.08	281.43	47.50	123.88	85.27
仪器仪表制造业	Measuring Instruments Manufacturing	94.73	52.64	12.19	19.23	10.67
其他制造业	Other Equipment	87.48	62.86	4.18	13.24	7.19
废弃资源综合利用业	Recycling and Disposal of Waste	77.56	36.82	12.41	25.67	2.65
金属制品、机械和设备修理业	Repairing of Metal and Mechanical Equipment	22.04	10.46	1.10	8.45	2.02
电力、热力、燃气及水生产和供应业	Electric Power, Gas and Water Production and Supply	604.47	301.37	72.72	184.93	45.46
电力、热力生产和供应业	Electric Power and and Heat Power Production and Supply	384.17	160.83	49.23	142.17	31.95
燃气生产和供应业	Gas Production and Supply	72.17	46.29	7.37	15.69	2.82
水的生产和供应业	Water Production and Supply	148.13	94.25	16.12	27.07	10.69

注：从2011年起固定资产投资统计口径调整为计划总投资500万元及以上项目，取消城镇农村公布口径，其他年份未做相应调整。从2012年起执行新的国民经济行业代码（GB/T4754-2011）

Note:Since 2011, the fixed assets investment accounts for investment over 5 million yuan, canceling town and countryside. Other years' statistics do not correspond to this adjustment.Since 2012,a new national economy industry code(GB/T4754-2011)is implemented.

4-4 续表 continued

单位：亿元 (100 million yuan)

行　　业	Sector	投资额 Investment	建筑工程 Construction	安装工程 Installation	设备工器具购置 Purchases of Equipments and Instruments	其他 Others
建筑业	Construction	120.51	67.92	18.19	26.47	7.93
交通运输、仓储和邮政业	Transportation, Storage and Post	2157.93	1650.82	84.80	184.88	237.43
铁路运输业	Railway Transportation	96.59	49.48	2.86	10.40	33.85
道路运输业	Road Transportation	1497.30	1195.98	47.50	97.16	156.67
水上运输业	Waterway Transportation	126.22	96.37	4.93	16.95	7.97
航空运输业	Air Transportation	55.57	44.74	0.98	7.65	2.21
管道运输业	Pipeline Transportation	3.95	2.56	0.62	0.67	0.10
装卸搬运和运输代理业	Load, Unload, and Agency	75.92	43.17	5.62	15.29	11.84
仓储业	Transportation Storage	296.23	214.67	20.86	36.27	24.43
邮政业	Post	6.14	3.86	1.43	0.50	0.35
信息传输、软件和信息技术服务业	Information Transmission, Software and Information Technology Service	104.72	46.34	7.05	46.22	5.11
电信、广播电视和卫星传输服务	Telecom, Radio Tv and Satellite	68.64	25.51	3.35	37.61	2.17
互联网和相关服务	Internet and Related	10.55	5.90	0.78	2.97	0.91
软件和信息技术服务业	Software and Information Technology	25.53	14.93	2.92	5.64	2.04
批发和零售业	Wholesale and Retail	695.08	473.72	73.30	80.02	68.04
住宿和餐饮业	Hotel and Catering Service	320.85	222.56	33.90	34.96	29.43
金融业	Finance	89.11	54.15	5.39	25.25	4.32
货币金融服务	Monetary Financial Service	52.34	27.65	2.56	19.35	2.78
资本市场服务	Monetary Financial Service	30.87	23.81	2.83	2.90	1.32
保险业	Insurance	3.20	0.24		2.81	0.15
其他金融业	Other Financial Acitivities	2.71	2.45		0.18	0.07
房地产业	Real Estate	5287.86	3772.87	444.43	134.39	936.17
租赁和商务服务业	Leasing and Commercial Service	496.70	354.25	50.14	52.13	40.18
租赁业	Leasing Service	14.92	8.91	1.87	3.70	0.44
商务服务业	Commercial Service	481.78	345.34	48.27	48.43	39.73
科学研究和技术服务业	Scientific Research and Technical Services	108.24	77.12	8.71	10.34	12.07
水利、环境和公共设施管理业	Water Conservancy, Environment and Public Facility Management	2212.19	1709.24	135.79	154.75	212.41
水利管理业	Water Conservancy Management	297.63	247.55	13.79	19.81	16.48
生态保护和环境治理业	Environment Management	117.67	85.54	8.02	12.22	11.89
公共设施管理业	Public Facility Management	1796.89	1376.16	113.98	122.72	184.04
居民服务、修理和其他服务业	Resident Service and Others	187.72	142.29	12.59	16.22	16.63
教育	Education	253.54	180.91	13.53	33.93	25.17
卫生和社会工作	Health Care and Social Work	215.48	137.45	18.34	46.98	12.72
卫生	Health Care	165.84	103.65	14.54	41.67	5.99
社会工作	Social Work	49.64	33.79	3.80	5.31	6.73
文化、体育和娱乐业	Culture, Sports and Recreation	280.95	200.75	26.74	31.83	21.63
新闻和出版业	News and Publication	0.92	0.58	0.16	0.16	0.03
广播、电视、电影和影视录音制作业	Radio, Television, Film and Recording	9.04	2.69	1.12	4.95	0.28
文化艺术业	Culture and Arts	102.90	70.69	11.25	14.10	6.86
体育	Sports	59.49	46.15	3.31	4.65	5.38
娱乐业	Receation	108.60	80.64	10.90	7.96	9.09
公共管理、社会保障和社会组织	Public Management and Social Organizations	440.56	323.23	40.79	42.54	34.00

4-5 按建设性质分固定资产投资(不含农户)(2014)
URBAN INVESTMENT IN FIXED ASSETS BY TYPE OF CONSTRUCTION(2014)

单位：亿元 (100 million yuan)

行业	Sector	投资额 Investment	#新建 New Construction	#扩建 Expension	#改建 Replacement
总计	Total	**24303.05**	**17825.59**	**2096.97**	**3871.60**
农、林、牧、渔业	Farming, Forestry, Animal Husbandry and Fishery	688.36	540.95	74.70	64.36
农业	Farming	221.78	181.16	23.35	16.43
林业	Forestry	71.57	59.42	10.65	0.47
畜牧业	Animal Husbandry	188.86	162.23	14.75	10.72
渔业	Fishery	53.79	41.13	6.35	5.65
农、林、牧、渔服务业	Farming, Forestry, Animal Husbandry and Fishery Services	152.35	97.02	19.59	31.10
采矿业	Mining and Qarrying	404.80	146.94	127.38	126.18
制造业	Manufacturing	9633.97	5914.73	824.07	2676.60
农副食品加工业	Food Processing	794.99	469.04	92.16	213.45
食品制造业	Food Production	322.51	173.25	42.83	103.12
酒、饮料和精制茶制造业	Beverage Production	305.83	168.40	26.59	106.08
烟草制品业	Tobacco Processing	28.93	19.21	0.65	9.07
纺织业	Textile Industry	406.90	180.24	47.46	171.41
纺织服装、服饰业	Textile Wearing Apparel and Accessaries	253.76	159.31	31.33	58.87
皮革、毛皮、羽毛及其制品和制鞋业	Leather, Fur, Feather and Related Products	76.70	40.42	10.53	22.11
木材加工和木、竹、藤、棕、草制品业	Timber Processing and Wood, Bamboo, Rattan, Palm and Sraw Works	138.08	88.91	12.11	35.57
家具制造业	Furniture Manufacturing	137.11	103.62	12.19	21.30
造纸和纸制品业	Papermaking and Paper Products	186.73	107.32	27.95	47.91
印刷和记录媒介复制业	Printing and Record Processing	131.93	101.75	9.25	17.69
文教、工美、体育和娱乐用品制造业	Stationery, Education, Art, Sport and Entertainment Products	104.82	87.06	2.61	14.32
石油加工、炼焦和核燃料加工业	Petroleum Processing,Coking products and Nuclear Fuel Processing	67.64	16.82	2.92	44.84
化学原料和化学制品制造业	Raw Chemical Material and Chemical Products	635.40	308.34	51.95	267.59
医药制造业	Medical and pharmaceutical Products	362.42	232.19	31.44	91.75
化学纤维制造业	Chemical Fibers	22.56	7.42	2.65	12.08
橡胶和塑料制品业	Rubber Products and Plastic Products	271.24	143.14	33.93	85.41
非金属矿物制品业	Nonmetal Material Products	949.41	516.11	109.84	302.24
黑色金属冶炼和压延加工业	Smelting and Processing of ferrous Metals	213.67	113.23	18.00	79.32
有色金属冶炼和压延加工业	Smelting and Processing of Nonferrous Metals	142.70	71.52	3.78	65.15
金属制品业	Metal Products	447.01	284.16	52.26	96.99
通用设备制造业	Ordinaryly Machinery Manufacturing	493.65	347.06	16.93	120.36
专用设备制造业	Special Purpose Equipment Manufacturing	617.43	424.69	47.69	134.45
汽车制造业	Automobile Manufacturing	1036.29	700.35	47.65	264.45
铁路、船舶、航空航天和其他运输设备制造业	Realway, Ship, Aircraft and Other Transport Equipment Manufacturing	125.69	81.36	3.25	24.98
电气机械和器材制造业	Electric Machinery and Equipment	540.69	394.53	29.89	103.91
计算机、通信和其他电子设备制造业	Computers, Communication Equipment and Other Electronic Equipment Manufacturing	538.08	385.03	37.88	110.16
仪器仪表制造业	Measuring Instruments Manufacturing	94.73	57.67	15.28	19.60
其他制造业	Other Equipment	87.48	73.13	0.89	11.17
废弃资源综合利用业	Recycling and Disposal of Waste	77.56	45.92	2.17	18.95
金属制品、机械和设备修理业	Repairing of Metal and Mechanical Equipment	22.04	13.54		2.32
电力、热力、燃气及水生产和供应业	Electric Power, Gas and Water Production and Supply	604.47	332.59	45.63	221.06
电力、热力生产和供应业	Electric Power, Steam and Hot Water Production and Supply	384.17	196.48	24.99	159.71
燃气生产和供应业	Gas Production and Supply	72.17	58.27	3.90	9.92
水的生产和供应业	Tap Water Production and Supply	148.13	77.84	16.74	51.44

注：从2011年起固定资产投资统计口径调整为计划总投资500万元及以上项目，取消城镇农村公布口径，其他年份未做相应调整。从2012年起执行新的国民经济行业代码（GB/T4754—2011）

Note:Since 2011, the fixed assets investment accounts for investment over 5 million yuan, canceling town and countryside. Other years' statistics do not correspond to this adjustment.Since 2012,a new national econmy industry code(GB/T4754-2011) is implemanted.

4-5 续表 continued

单位：亿元 (100 million yuan)

行　　业	Sector	投资额 Investment	#新　建 New Construction	#扩　建 Expension	#改　建 Replacement
建筑业	Construction	120.51	98.60	5.54	4.96
交通运输、仓储和邮政业	Transportation, storage and Post	2157.93	1512.66	342.01	251.62
铁路运输业	Railway Transportation	96.59	69.47	0.44	26.69
道路运输业	Road Transportation	1497.30	1011.17	240.11	210.20
水上运输业	Waterway Transportation	126.22	87.70	29.57	4.59
航空运输业	Air Transportation	55.57	41.86	6.37	
管道运输业	Pipeline Transportation	3.95	3.95		
装卸搬运和运输代理业	Load, Unload, and Agency	75.92	61.28	11.78	1.62
仓储业	Transportation Storage	296.23	232.22	52.99	8.14
邮政业	Post	6.14	5.01	0.74	0.38
信息传输、软件和信息技术服务业	Information Transmission, Software and Information Technology Service	104.72	53.62	6.75	15.63
电信、广播电视和卫星传输服务	Telecom, Radio Tv and Satellite	68.64	26.13	4.55	12.01
互联网和相关服务	Internet and Related	10.55	5.29	1.48	3.38
软件和信息技术服务业	Software and Information Technology	25.53	22.20	0.72	0.23
批发和零售业	Wholesale and Retail Trade	695.08	589.48	44.77	51.83
住宿和餐饮业	Hotel and Catering Services	320.85	277.56	21.26	21.95
金融业	Finance	89.11	52.50	11.62	9.29
货币金融服务	Monetary Financial Service	52.34	19.01	11.42	9.02
资本市场服务	Capital Markets Service	30.87	30.60		0.27
保险业	Insurance	3.20	0.38		
其他金融业	Other Financial Acitivities	2.71	2.51	0.20	
房地产业	Real Estate Trade	5287.86	5111.72	79.83	48.17
租赁和商务服务业	Leasing and Commercial Service	496.70	437.47	27.40	25.26
租赁业	Leasing Service	14.92	9.52	2.57	0.28
商务服务业	Commercial Service	481.78	427.95	24.82	24.99
科学研究和技术服务业	Scientific Research, Polytechnical Services	108.24	95.99	5.97	5.20
水利、环境和公共设施管理业	Water Conservancy, Environment and Public Facility Management	2212.19	1640.20	291.76	253.65
水利管理业	Water Conservancy Management	297.63	159.24	62.31	72.12
生态保护和环境治理业	Environment Management	117.67	91.28	6.98	18.13
公共设施管理业	Public Facility Management	1796.89	1389.68	222.47	163.39
居民服务、修理和其他服务业	Resident Service and Others	187.72	162.53	10.20	13.94
教育	Education	253.54	185.68	30.52	16.22
卫生和社会工作	Health Care and Social Work	215.48	139.77	29.42	19.12
卫生	Health Care	165.84	96.73	25.52	17.21
社会工作	Social Work	49.64	43.04	3.89	1.91
文化、体育和娱乐业	Culture, Sports and Recreation	280.95	241.99	16.76	17.94
新闻和出版业	News and Publication	0.92	0.12	0.33	0.47
广播、电视、电影和影视录音制作业	Radio, Television, Film and Recording	9.04	3.87	0.98	3.29
文化艺术业	Culture and Arts	102.90	92.42	5.71	2.74
体育	Sports	59.49	53.57	3.27	2.65
娱乐业	Receation	108.60	92.00	6.47	8.79
公共管理、社会保障和社会组织	Public Management and Social Organizations	440.56	290.62	101.39	28.62

4-6 按控股情况分固定资产投资(不含农户)(2014)
URBAN INVESTMENT IN FIXED ASSETS BY THE SITUATION OF CONTROLLING SHARE HOLDING(2014)

单位：亿元 (100 million yuan)

行业	Sector	投资额 Investment	国有控股 State Share Holding	集体控股 Collective Share Holding	私人控股 Private Share Holding	港澳台商控股 Hongkong, Macao and Taiwan Share Holding	外商控股 Foreign Sgare Holding
总　计	Total	**24303.05**	**6686.88**	**1253.98**	**12772.19**	**225.80**	**285.16**
农、林、牧、渔业	Farming, Forestry, Animal Husbandry and Fishery	688.36	97.53	40.07	463.00	0.70	2.08
农业	Farming	221.78	19.05	16.30	158.37	0.53	
林业	Forestry	71.57	15.96	1.78	40.23		
畜牧业	Animal Husbandry	188.86	3.36	7.07	147.20	0.17	2.08
渔业	Fishery	53.79	2.95	2.76	44.99		
农、林、牧、渔服务业	Farming, Forestry, Animal Husbandry and Fishery Services	152.35	56.22	12.15	72.21		
采矿业	Mining and Qarrying	404.80	100.73	22.16	260.10		
制造业	Manufacturing	9633.97	827.44	286.22	7269.87	79.24	162.59
农副食品加工业	Food Processing	794.99	13.58	25.56	682.33	4.12	6.26
食品制造业	Food Production	322.51	13.60	3.91	268.86	5.12	4.99
酒、饮料和精制茶制造业	Beverage Production	305.83	2.73	0.85	244.02	2.13	1.46
烟草制品业	Tobacco Processing	28.93	20.05		4.82		
纺织业	Textile Industry	406.90	8.22	4.55	362.19	4.52	2.11
纺织服装、服饰业	Textile Wearing Apparel and Accessarie	253.76	1.95	0.59	202.08	0.58	
皮革、毛皮、羽毛及其制品和制鞋业	Leather, Fur, Feather and Related Products	76.70		1.40	70.84	1.03	
木材加工和木、竹、藤、棕、草制品业	Timber Processing and Wwood, Bamboo,Rattan, Palm and Sraw Works	138.08	1.95	0.72	114.47		
家具制造业	Furniture Manufacturing	137.11	0.30	2.24	115.58	0.28	
造纸和纸制品业	Papermaking and Paper Products	186.73	6.05		167.09	1.59	
印刷和记录媒介复制业	Printing and Record Processing	131.93	1.16	10.04	101.28		
文教、工美、体育和娱乐用品制造业	Stationery, Education, Art, Sport and Entertainment Products	104.82		1.97	92.56	4.11	
石油加工、炼焦和核燃料加工业	Petroleum Processing, Coking Products and Nuclear Fuel Processing	67.64	29.72		29.07		
化学原料和化学制品制造业	Raw Chemical Material and Chemical Products	635.40	76.78	8.54	446.83	2.87	5.64
医药制造业	Medical and pharmaceutical Products	362.42	40.47	22.83	256.14	0.94	4.17
化学纤维制造业	Chemical Fibers	22.56			20.43		
橡胶和塑料制品业	Rubber Products and Plastic Products	271.24	6.65	1.27	242.72	0.79	1.68
非金属矿物制品业	Nonmetal Material Products	949.41	24.12	30.41	774.48	0.19	0.19
黑色金属冶炼和压延加工业	Smelting and Processing of ferrous Metals	213.67	49.15	3.31	129.76	0.65	7.78
有色金属冶炼和压延加工业	Smelting and Processing of Nonferrous Metals	142.70	0.34	2.44	124.89	0.79	
金属制品业	Metal Products	447.01	27.58	23.34	330.91	0.95	1.70
通用设备制造业	Ordinaryly Machinery Manufacturing	493.65	50.18	14.18	375.10		5.05
专用设备制造业	Special Purpose Equipment Manufacturing	617.43	63.57	12.13	453.72	1.31	9.15
汽车制造业	Automobile Manufacturing	1036.29	128.19	57.84	677.10	5.47	96.76
铁路、船舶、航空航天和其他运输设备制造业	Realway, Ship, Aircraft and Other Transport Equipment Manufacturing	125.69	31.70	2.08	75.75		0.70
电气机械和器材制造业	Electric Machinery and Equipment	540.69	14.65	12.94	447.66	3.22	11.31
计算机、通信和其他电子设备制造业	Computers, Communication Equipment Other Electronic Equipment Manufactur	538.08	154.07	26.38	281.83	38.57	3.29
仪器仪表制造业	Measuring Instruments Manufacturing	94.73	23.15	14.37	48.05		0.35
其他制造业	Other Equipment	87.48	27.74	0.94	57.62		
废弃资源综合利用业	Recycling and Disposal of Waste	77.56	6.40	1.42	62.27		
金属制品、机械和设备修理业	Repairing of Metal and Mechanical Equipment	22.04	3.38		9.43		
电力、热力、燃气及水生产和供应业	Electric Power, Gas and Water Production and Supply	604.47	402.47	26.87	129.72	3.45	0.32
电力、热力生产和供应业	Electric Power, Steam and Hot Water Production and Supply	384.17	281.37	5.55	74.05	2.60	
燃气生产和供应业	Gas Production and Supply	72.17	26.66	6.49	33.20	0.85	0.32
水的生产和供应业	Tap Water Production and Supply	148.13	94.45	14.83	22.46		

注：从2011年起固定资产投资统计口径调整为计划总投资500万元及以上项目，取消城镇农村公布口径，其他年份未做相应调整。从2012年起执行新的国民经济行业代码（GB/T4754—2011）

Note:Since 2011, the fixed assets investment accounts for investment over 5 million yuan, canceling town and countryside. Other years' statistics do not correspond to this adjustment.Since 2012,a new national econmy industry code(GB/T4754-2011) is implemanted.

4-6 续表 continued

单位：亿元 (100 million yuan)

行业	Sector	投资额 Investment	国有控股 State Share Holding	集体控股 Collective Share Holding	私人控股 Private Share Holding	港澳台商控股 Hongkong, Macao and Taiwan Share Holding	外商控股 Foreign Sgare Holding
建筑业	Construction	120.51	56.37	1.78	42.66	4.08	20.67
交通运输、仓储和邮政业	Transportation, storage and Post	2157.93	1520.20	102.91	401.75		
铁路运输业	Railway Transportation	96.59	87.55		5.98	2.73	17.15
道路运输业	Road Transportation	1497.30	1231.20	78.10	100.62		1.52
水上运输业	Waterway Transportation	126.22	86.80	5.27	20.42		
航空运输业	Air Transportation	55.57	54.43		1.15		
管道运输业	Pipeline Transportation	3.95	3.30				1.63
装卸搬运和运输代理业	Load, Unload, and Agency	75.92	5.12	2.08	58.60	1.35	0.37
仓储业	Transportation Storage	296.23	48.82	17.46	211.84		
邮政业	Post	6.14	2.99		3.15		
信息传输、软件和信息技术服务业	Information Transmission, Software and Information Technology Service	104.72	62.50	6.77	19.13	0.51	
电信、广播电视和卫星传输服务	Telecom, Radio Tv and Satellite	68.64	57.77	5.69	0.52	0.51	
互联网和相关服务	Internet and Related	10.55	3.75	0.09	5.83		
软件和信息技术服务业	Software and Information Technology	25.53	0.98	0.99	12.78		
批发和零售业	Wholesale and Retail Trade	695.08	54.43	59.01	491.90	0.72	10.02
住宿和餐饮业	Hotel and Catering Services	320.85	14.94	4.72	264.24	4.39	5.87
金融业	Finance	89.11	28.49	3.26	49.35		
货币金融服务	Monetary Financial Service	52.34	25.32	3.04	18.24		
资本市场服务	Capital Markets Service	30.87	0.35	0.08	28.16		
保险业	Insurance	3.20	2.81	0.14	0.25		
其他金融业	Other Financial Acitivities	2.71			2.71		
房地产业	Real Estate Trade	5287.86	1025.94	411.49	2319.88	121.06	78.23
租赁和商务服务业	Leasing and Commercial Service	496.70	85.28	22.18	346.68	3.37	1.04
租赁业	Leasing Service	14.92	5.03	0.19	4.49		
商务服务业	Commercial Service	481.78	80.25	21.99	342.19	3.37	1.04
科学研究和技术服务业	Scientific Research, Polytechnical Services	108.24	37.13	2.44	56.40		4.27
水利、环境和公共设施管理业	Water Conservancy, Environment and Public Facility Management	2212.19	1559.11	147.97	334.35	7.18	
水利管理业	Water Conservancy Management	297.63	262.75	23.80	3.72		
生态保护和环境治理业	Environment Management	117.67	75.18	11.69	25.64		
公共设施管理业	Public Facility Management	1796.89	1221.19	112.47	304.99	7.18	
居民服务、修理和其他服务业	Resident Service and Others	187.72	56.08	20.20	61.82		
教育	Education	253.54	197.38	9.85	37.52		
卫生和社会工作	Health Care and Social Work	215.48	156.55	15.78	33.81		
卫生	Health Care	165.84	132.81	11.90	15.63		
社会工作	Social Work	49.64	23.75	3.88	18.18		
文化、体育和娱乐业	Culture, Sports and Recreation	280.95	112.00	12.88	136.24	1.09	0.06
新闻和出版业	News and Publication	0.92	0.45		0.47		
广播、电视、电影和影视录音制作业	Radio, Television, Film and Recording	9.04	3.65	0.28	4.02	1.09	
文化艺术业	Culture and Arts	102.90	50.11	9.57	38.25		0.06
体育	Sports	59.49	38.72	2.22	16.91		
娱乐业	Receation	108.60	19.07	0.82	76.59		
公共管理、社会保障和社会组织	Public Management and Social Organizations	440.56	292.29	57.42	53.77		

4-7 按行业分施工投产项目个数(2014)
NUMBER OF URBAN PROJECTS UNDER CONSTRUCTION AND PUT INTO PRODUCTION BY SECTOR(2014)

行业	Sector	施工项目(个) Number of Projects under Construction (unit)	#新开工 Newly Started	全部建成投产项目(个) Completion and Put into Production of All Projects (unit)	项目建成投产率(%) Rate of Completion and Put into Production (%)
总计	Total	**26893**	**18892**	**17539**	**65.2**
农、林、牧、渔业	Farming, Forestry, Animal Husbandry and Fishery	1665	1254	1125	67.6
农业	Farming	489	379	309	63.2
林业	Forestry	139	88	93	66.9
畜牧业	Animal Husbandry	473	347	340	71.9
渔业	Fishery	139	109	96	69.1
农、林、牧、渔服务业	Farming, Forestry, Animal Husbandry and Fishery Services	425	331	287	67.5
采矿业	Mining and Qarrying	552	353	392	71.0
制造业	Manufacturing	10981	7727	7246	66.0
农副食品加工业	Food Processing	1284	934	877	68.3
食品制造业	Food Production	369	253	244	66.1
酒、饮料和精制茶制造业	Beverage Production	373	244	236	63.3
烟草制品业	Tobacco Processing	12	9	8	66.7
纺织业	Textile Industry	520	378	335	64.4
纺织服装、服饰业	Textile Wearing Apparel and Accessaries	339	264	233	68.7
皮革、毛皮、羽毛及其制品和制鞋业	Leather, Fur, Feather and Related Products	124	84	93	75.0
木材加工和木、竹、藤、棕、草制品业	Timber Processing and Wwood, Bamboo, Rattan, Palm and Sraw Works	209	155	145	69.4
家具制造业	Furniture Manufacturing	191	130	131	68.6
造纸和纸制品业	Papermaking and Paper Products	157	110	102	65.0
印刷和记录媒介复制业	Printing and Record Processing	131	102	91	69.5
文教、工美、体育和娱乐用品制造业	Stationery, Education, Art, Sport and Entertainment Products	80	60	57	71.3
石油加工、炼焦和核燃料加工业	Petroleum Processing, Coking Products and Nuclear Fuel Processing	44	28	21	47.7
化学原料和化学制品制造业	Raw Chemical Material and Chemical Products	756	551	537	71.0
医药制造业	Medical and pharmaceutical Products	380	255	205	53.9
化学纤维制造业	Chemical Fibers	22	18	10	45.5
橡胶和塑料制品业	Rubber Products and Plastic Products	387	293	266	68.7
非金属矿物制品业	Nonmetal Material Products	1507	1123	1081	71.7
黑色金属冶炼和压延加工业	Smelting and Processing of ferrous Metals	202	144	143	70.8
有色金属冶炼和压延加工业	Smelting and Processing of Nonferrous Metals	122	75	92	75.4
金属制品业	Metal Products	459	323	312	68.0
通用设备制造业	Ordinaryly Machinery Manufacturing	570	427	382	67.0
专用设备制造业	Special Purpose Equipment Manufacturing	588	397	387	65.8
汽车制造业	Automobile Manufacturing	973	642	576	59.2
铁路、船舶、航空航天和其他运输设备制造业	Realway, Ship, Aircraft and Other Transport Equipment Manufacturing	100	57	54	54.0
电气机械和器材制造业	Electric Machinery and Equipment	477	299	309	64.8
计算机、通信和其他电子设备制造业	Computers, Communication Equipment and Other Electronic Equipment Manufacturing	342	191	170	49.7
仪器仪表制造业	Measuring Instruments Manufacturing	99	60	43	43.4
其他制造业	Other Equipment	72	55	50	69.4
废弃资源综合利用业	Recycling and Disposal of Waste	78	53	50	64.1
金属制品、机械和设备修理业	Repairing of Metal and Mechanical Equipment	14	13	6	42.9
电力、热力、燃气及水生产和供应业	Electric Power, Gas and Water Production and Supply	1038	683	739	71.2
电力、热力生产和供应业	Electric Power, Steam and Hot Water Production and Supply	543	340	380	70.0
燃气生产和供应业	Gas Production and Supply	116	79	72	62.1
水的生产和供应业	Tap Water Production and Supply	379	264	287	75.7

注：从2011年起固定资产投资统计口径调整为计划总投资500万元及以上项目，取消城镇农村公布口径，其他年份未做相应调整。从2012年起执行新的国民经济行业代码（GB/T4754-2011）

Note:Since 2011, the fixed assets investment accounts for investment over 5 million yuan, canceling town and countryside. Other years' statistics do not correspond to this adjustment.Since 2012,a new national econmy industry code(GB/T4754-2011) is implemanted.

4-7 续表 continued

行　　业	Sector	施工项目(个) Number of Projects under Construction (unit)	#新开工 Newly Started	全部建成投产项目(个) Completion and Put into Production of All Projects (unit)	项目建成投产率(%) Rate of Completion and Put into Production (%)
建筑业	Construction	140	114	104	74.3
交通运输、仓储和邮政业	Transportation, storage and Post	2501	1752	1574	62.9
铁路运输业	Railway Transportation	61	36	16	26.2
道路运输业	Road Transportation	1993	1439	1329	66.7
水上运输业	Waterway Transportation	97	45	43	44.3
航空运输业	Air Transportation	6	1	1	16.7
管道运输业	Pipeline Transportation	4	2	2	50.0
装卸搬运和运输代理业	Load, Unload, and Agency	83	68	43	51.8
仓储业	Transportation Storage	245	151	133	54.3
邮政业	Post	12	10	7	58.3
信息传输、软件和信息技术服务业	Information Transmission, Software and Information Technology Service	142	113	93	65.5
电信、广播电视和卫星传输服务	Telecom, Radio Tv and Satellite	94	81	65	69.1
互联网和相关服务	Internet and Related	19	16	15	78.9
软件和信息技术服务业	Software and Information Technology	29	16	13	44.8
批发和零售业	Wholesale and Retail Trade	995	719	619	62.2
住宿和餐饮业	Hotel and Catering Services	586	433	413	70.5
金融业	Finance	86	54	60	69.8
货币金融服务	Monetary Financial Service	66	41	47	71.2
资本市场服务	Capital Markets Service	15	8	10	66.7
保险业	Insurance	2	2	1	50.0
其他金融业	Other Financial Acitivities	3	3	2	66.7
房地产业	Real Estate Trade	1449	977	795	54.9
租赁和商务服务业	Leasing and Commercial Service	374	204	172	46.0
租赁业	Leasing Service	17	12	12	70.6
商务服务业	Commercial Service	357	192	160	44.8
科学研究和技术服务业	Scientific Research, Polytechnical Services	161	120	111	68.9
水利、环境和公共设施管理业	Water Conservancy, Environment and Public Facility Management	3262	2239	2012	61.7
水利管理业	Water Conservancy Management	847	698	612	72.3
生态保护和环境治理业	Environment Management	170	117	114	67.1
公共设施管理业	Public Facility Management	2245	1424	1286	57.3
居民服务、修理和其他服务业	Resident Service and Others	236	170	160	67.8
教育	Education	838	680	637	76.0
卫生和社会工作	Health Care and Social Work	518	381	370	71.4
卫生	Health Care	347	247	238	68.6
社会工作	Social Work	171	134	132	77.2
文化、体育和娱乐业	Culture, Sports and Recreation	399	282	232	58.1
新闻和出版业	News and Publication	3	2		
广播、电视、电影和影视录音制作业	Radio, Television, Film and Recording	25	21	20	80.0
文化艺术业	Culture and Arts	197	137	116	58.9
体育	Sports	76	53	41	53.9
娱乐业	Receation	98	69	55	56.1
公共管理、社会保障和社会组织	Public Management and Social Organizations	970	637	685	70.6

4-8 按资金来源和构成分全社会固定资产投资
TOTAL INVESTMENT IN FIXED ASSETS BY SOURCE OF FUNDS AND USE OF FUNDS

年 份 Year	按资金来源分 Grouped by Source of Finance					按构成分 Grouped by Use of Funds		
	国家预算内资金 State Budgetary Appropriations	国内贷款 Domestic Loans	利用外资 Foreign Investment	自筹资金 Fund Raising	其他资金来源 Others	建筑安装工程 Construction Installation	设备工器具购置 Purchases of Equipment and Instruments	其他费用 Others
投资额(亿元) Investment(100 million yuan)								
1990	11.38	22.22	4.79	92.96	13.09	92.64	41.02	10.78
1995	58.40	173.47	88.71	422.92	83.00	454.40	248.51	123.59
1996	72.53	206.15	74.86	537.31	93.53	510.52	307.89	165.97
1997	68.08	172.05	51.24	651.08	141.15	600.04	264.16	219.40
1998	85.18	225.95	33.86	703.44	182.66	695.55	323.47	212.08
1999	108.18	207.61	36.57	730.92	218.89	771.24	329.26	201.67
2000	141.48	243.90	28.28	781.50	226.39	814.66	371.56	235.33
2001	174.03	241.96	29.89	874.60	231.27	890.60	419.20	241.95
2002	200.95	280.11	63.22	717.24	433.69	974.73	418.55	301.94
2003	150.20	291.60	57.41	786.40	597.98	1059.98	463.23	360.38
2004	197.03	383.78	64.74	1182.36	528.47	1409.25	537.25	409.88
2005	255.76	474.21	71.34	1492.66	540.78	1696.80	642.86	495.09
2006	378.79	708.39	79.32	1902.71	503.48	2252.72	717.10	602.87
2007	472.98	790.84	88.37	2470.28	711.66	2857.31	896.36	780.47
2008	570.17	894.57	57.02	3677.00	599.80	3568.96	1245.73	983.87
2009	711.93	1432.89	68.32	4956.88	1041.83	5025.62	1753.28	1432.95
2010	868.46	1768.79	147.03	6703.61	1314.80	6701.91	2308.73	1792.05
2011	663.18	1707.46	189.26	8800.61	1574.51	8056.52	2812.91	2065.59
2012	784.27	1964.14	131.64	11812.15	1811.96	11054.16	3162.99	2287.02
2013	886.58	2720.19	66.82	14823.15	2257.17	14312.25	3856.68	2584.98
2014	1107.45	2874.92	78.99	18732.35	2208.06	18185.42	4292.85	2523.50
构成(%) Composition (%)								
1990	7.9	15.4	3.3	64.4	9.0	64.1	28.4	7.5
1995	7.1	21.0	10.7	51.2	10.0	58.6	30.3	11.1
1996	7.4	20.9	7.6	54.6	9.5	62.1	25.9	12.0
1997	6.3	15.9	4.7	60.1	13.0	67.7	22.1	10.2
1998	6.9	18.4	2.8	57.1	14.8	70.2	18.4	11.4
1999	8.3	15.9	2.8	56.1	16.9	63.4	26.5	10.1
2000	10.0	17.2	2.0	55.0	15.8	64.3	23.9	11.8
2001	11.2	15.6	1.9	56.4	14.9	64.8	24.3	10.9
2002	11.9	16.5	3.7	42.3	25.6	64.4	23.6	12.1
2003	8.0	15.5	3.0	41.8	31.7	60.9	23.4	15.7
2004	8.4	16.3	2.7	50.2	22.4	63.9	20.8	15.3
2005	9.0	16.7	2.5	52.7	19.1	59.9	22.7	17.4
2006	10.6	19.8	2.2	53.3	14.1	63.1	20.1	16.8
2007	12.6	19.7	1.3	81.1	13.2	78.7	27.5	21.7
2008	9.8	15.4	1.0	63.4	10.4	61.5	21.5	17.0
2009	8.7	17.4	0.8	60.4	12.7	61.2	21.4	17.4
2010	8.1	16.4	1.4	62.1	12.0	62.0	21.4	16.6
2011	5.1	13.2	1.5	68.0	12.2	62.3	21.7	16.0
2012	4.8	11.9	0.8	71.6	11.0	67.0	19.2	13.9
2013	4.3	13.1	0.3	71.4	10.9	69.0	18.6	12.4
2014	4.4	11.5	0.3	74.9	8.9	72.7	17.2	10.1

注：从2011年起固定资产投资统计口径调整为计划总投资500万元及以上项目，取消城镇农村公布口径，其他年份未做相应调整。
Note:Since 2011,the fixed assets investment statistical adjustment plan for a total investment of 5 million yuan RMB and the above project, cancel the town and countryside,other years did not do corresponding adjustment.

4—9 国有单位固定资产投资

INVESTMENT IN FIXED ASSETS BY STATE OWNED UNITS

指 标	Item	2011		2012		2013		2014	
		合计 Total	#房地产开发 Real Estate Development	合计 Total	#房地产开发 Real Estate Development	合计 Total	#房地产开发 Real Estate Development	合计 Total	#房地产开发 Real Estate Development
建设项目	**Number of Construction Projects**								
施工项目(个)	Projects under Construction (unit)	7889		8311		8861		8747	
全部建成投产项目(个)	Total Projects Completed Put into Operation	5687		5380		5663		5461	
建成项目投产率(%)	Rate of Projects Completed Put into Operation %	72.1		64.7		63.9		62.4	
建设周期(年)	Construction Cycle (year)	1.39		1.54		1.56		1.60	
资金来源(亿元)	**Tatal Financial Allocation and Loans(100 million yuan)**	**3875.10**	**291.90**	**4577.28**	**460.92**	**5248.89**	**467.81**	**5961.19**	**162.88**
国家预算内资金	State Appropriation	591.77		722.06		782.29		959.15	
国内贷款	Domestic Loans	832.92	37.25	761.68	98.62	855.37	111.51	810.50	48.90
利用外资	Foreign Investment	4.66		9.73		16.47		25.57	
自筹资金	Fund Raising	2078.05	126.48	2679.28	126.97	3082.45	123.30	3882.26	66.29
其他资金	Others	367.70	128.17	463.47	235.43	512.32	233.00	283.71	47.69
投资总额(亿元)	**Total Value of Investment (100 million yuan)**	**3764.22**	**213.55**	**4265.95**	**203.98**	**5068.42**	**243.23**	**5829.79**	**126.28**
按构成分	Grouped by Use of Funds								
#建筑工程	Construction Projects	2306.57	105.51	2799.58	150.21	3481.50	164.77	4312.42	89.15
安装工程	Installation Projects	193.12	3.26	269.83	11.87	318.10	15.15	349.58	16.22
设备工具器具购置	Purchase of Equipment, Tools and Instruments	569.86	0.71	577.74	4.55	606.81	8.41	655.97	3.57
按产业分	Grouped by Industry								
第一产业	Primary Industry	103.21		52.51		41.40		40.73	
第二产业	Second Industry	891.80		916.20		1083.13		1117.12	
第三产业	Tertiary Industry	2769.21	213.55	3297.24	203.98	3943.88	243.23	4671.94	126.28
#住宅	Residential Housing	213.99	150.67	239.63	157.97	266.36	171.32	188.42	82.92
按建设性质分	Grouped by Type of Construction								
#新建	New Construction	1963.88	213.55	2425.78	203.98	3168.09	243.23	3836.47	126.28
扩建	Expension	578.63		567.03		613.32		851.17	
改建	Replacement	824.77		860.22		862.82		808.71	
房屋建筑面积(万平方米)	**Floor Space of Building (10000 sq.m)**								
施工面积	Floor Space Under Construction	3807.60	1042.20	5132.23	1087.36	6695.15	1485.48	5872.98	1107.98
#住宅	Residential Buildings	1671.01	940.83	1868.05	935.84	2457.39	1231.75	2199.38	875.67
竣工面积	Floor Spaace Completed	1544.76	247.28	2042.82	285.45	2344.15	276.69	2045.37	165.04
#住宅	Residential Buildings	622.90	232.34	658.05	268.43	757.20	246.64	546.44	146.85

注：建设周期按项目个数计算；本表资金来源均为资金到位数。从2012年起，三次产业采用新的划分标准。

Note: The constructive period is counted by the numbers of project.The sources of capital in this table are the number of achieved funds.Since 2012, the division of three industries emploies a new standard.

4-10 房地产开发投资主要指标

指　　标	Item	1990	1995	2000
企业个数(个)	**Number of Enterprises (unit)**	**129**	**571**	**1052**
内资	Inner Funded	129	404	848
#国有	State - owned	129	292	380
集体	Collective-owned		51	105
港澳台投资	Funded by Enterprises from Hongkong, Macao and Taiwan		68	149
外商投资	Foreign Funded		99	55
投资完成额(亿元)	**Investment Completed This Year**	**5.94**	**121.13**	**134.63**
按构成分	Grouped by Use of Funds			
#建筑安装工程	Construction Projects	5.45	89.56	99.59
设备工器具购置	Installation Projects		4.47	2.83
按工程用途分	Grouped by Use of Projects			
#住宅	Residential Houses	4.70	61.78	93.15
#经济适用房屋	Economical Houses		7.44	23.53
资金来源	Grouped by Source of Finance	5.94	138.88	117.88
国内贷款	Domestic Loans	1.21	39.01	18.08
利用外资	Foreign Investments		16.35	1.15
自筹投资	Fund Raising	3.72	41.26	47.27
其他投资	Others	1.01	42.26	51.38
房屋建筑面积(万平方米)	**Floor Space of Building (10000 sq.m)**			
施工面积	Floor Space Under Construction	390.11	2049.30	2102.86
#住宅	Residential Buildings	325.82	1299.03	1673.84
竣工面积	Floor Spaace Completed	183.91	518.88	843.55
#住宅	Residential Buildings	156.77	427.19	733.27
土地开发及购置(万平方米)	**Land Development and Purchase (10000sq.m)**			
本年土地开发面积	Area of Land development This Year		903.00	469.28
本年土地购置面积	Area of Land Purchased This Year		719.00	838.12
商品房销售情况	**Selling of Commercial Houses**			
房屋销售面积(万平方米)	Floor Psace of Selling Houses (10000sq.m)	130.53	240.00	612.05
#住宅	Residential Buildings	112.67	211.00	571.04
#经济适用房	Economic Houses		40.00	172.99
商品房销售额(亿元)	Sales Value of Commercial House	6.93	31.00	83.74
#住宅				

注：本表资金来源均为资金到位数；从2010年起本年土地开发面积指标取消；从2011年起经济适用房分组指标取消。

MAJOR INDICATORS OF INVESTMENT IN REAL ESTATE DEVELOPMENT

2005	2009	2010	2011	2012	2013	2014
1990	**3460**	**3556**	**3648**	**3785**	**4267**	**4214**
1782	3299	3395	3505	3654	4140	4101
228	191	187	189	184	194	140
74	75	66	66	59	57	19
129	109	106	96	90	87	81
79	52	55	47	41	40	32
447.95	**1200.44**	**1618.24**	**2066.48**	**2539.46**	**3286.02**	**3983.79**
315.15	828.62	1059.26	1407.17	1902.65	2426.17	3092.49
4.68	18.51	29.07	36.29	56.16	75.79	67.78
317.65	804.16	1040.25	1334.42	1698.38	2251.56	2755.42
13.49	74.37	40.33				
513.44	1714.76	2219.50	2864.05	3363.83	4224.48	4322.24
100.41	388.45	415.43	462.25	512.05	796.57	737.54
1.82	15.83	97.29	39.03	1.27		19.63
186.95	577.76	784.39	1195.28	1425.31	1735.33	1971.63
224.26	732.71	922.40	1167.49	1425.20	1692.58	1593.44
4804.35	9536.03	11589.44	13922.07	16819.71	21865.81	26321.99
4012.13	7727.09	9172.43	11013.30	13013.01	16640.27	19610.09
1627.03	2312.11	2541.21	3221.05	3273.71	3040.84	3431.18
1411.67	2007.34	2129.33	2728.39	2795.21	2547.39	2812.35
941.26	1361.67					
1530.64	1000.08	1422.06	1582.27	1303.19	1894.68	1244.99
1708.02	2718.30	3508.61	4187.62	4037.85	5298.54	5601.98
1549.19	2576.32	3236.88	3788.68	3620.10	4765.68	5002.60
111.31	176.99	99.48				
386.57	959.88	1313.20	1878.73	2036.20	2790.32	3088.31
335.19	879.33	1134.94	1569.32	1689.86	2310.04	2543.76

Note: The source of capital in this table are the number of achieved funds; From 2010 the land development indicators of this year had been canceled.From 2011 the group index of affordable housing had been canceled.

4-11 按登记注册类型分房地产开发投资(2014)

单位：亿元

项 目	Item	总计 Total	内资 Inner Funded	国有 State - owned	集体 Collective -owned	股份合作 Share Holding Cooperation	联营 Joint- Owned	国有独资公司 Solely co.	其他有限责任公司 Responsibility Co. Ltd
企业个数(个)	**Number of Enterprises (unit)**	**4214**	**4101**	**87**	**17**	**2**		**53**	**1750**
#亏损企业个数	Loss- Making Enterprises	1868	1809	30	6			24	794
本年完成投资	**Investment Completed This Year**	**3983.79**	**3694.91**	**41.82**	**13.94**	**0.03**		**84.46**	**2027.22**
按构成分	Grouped by Use of Funds								
建筑工程	Construction Projects	2742.34	2552.46	32.90	8.83	0.03		56.25	1387.41
安装工程	Installation Projects	350.16	321.45	3.02	1.06			13.20	140.48
设备工器具购置	Purchase of Equipment, Tools and Instruments	67.78	63.28	0.26	0.19			3.31	26.20
其他费用	Other Funds	823.51	757.72	5.65	3.85			11.70	473.13
#土地购置费	Purchase of Land	509.28	476.81	3.87	3.47			2.28	294.31
按构成用途分	Grouped by Use of Projects								
住宅	Residential Buildings	2755.42	2577.71	37.07	10.19	0.01		45.85	1446.41
#经济适用房	Economical Houses								
别墅、高档公寓	Villa, Top Grade Flat	96.66	61.35					0.01	35.90
办公楼	Office Building	171.65	144.33	0.03	0.05			12.20	84.35
商业营业用房	Business Buildings	639.20	584.03	3.35	1.87	0.02		17.12	303.22
其他	Others	417.52	388.84	1.37	1.83			9.29	193.24
本年新增固定资产	**Newly Increased Fixed Assets This Year**	**1268.16**	**1208.05**	**15.16**	**9.41**			**37.35**	**509.10**
资金来源	**Finance Sources**	**4322.24**	**4082.58**	**50.01**	**13.27**	**0.20**		**112.87**	**2299.84**
国内贷款	Domestic Loans	737.54	691.42	17.29	3.27			31.61	407.24
利用外资	Foreign Investments	19.63							
自筹资金	Fund Raising	1971.63	1903.88	19.75	6.01	0.20		46.55	1006.36
#自有资金	Self Owned	817.62	767.75	4.70	2.23	0.20		33.97	390.01
其他资金来源	Others	1593.44	1487.28	12.98	3.99			34.71	886.24
#定金及预收款	Funds Ordered and Pre-received	852.27	783.45	9.52	2.33			20.25	453.45
土地开发(万平方米)	**Land Development (10000 sq.m)**								
待开发土地面积	Area of Land to be Developed	1717.46	1569.23	0.22				120.78	882.82
本年购置土地面积	Area of Land Purchased This Year	1244.99	1224.67	0.43	10.50			49.43	570.54
本年土地成交价款	Value of Land Transaction	334.87	329.39	0.18	4.03			4.09	208.13

注：本表资金来源均为资金到位数，从2010年起土地开发投资额和本年土地开发面积指标取消。

INVESTMENT IN REAL ESTATE DEVELOPMENT BY TYPE OF REGISTRATION(2014)

(100 million yuan)

股份有限公司 Share Holding Co.Ltd.	私营 Private	其他 Others	港澳台商投资 Hongkong, Macao and Taiwan Funded	合资经营 Joint Venture Corperation	合作经营 Cooperative Corperation	独资 Solely Funded	股份有限公司 Share Holding Co.Ltd.	外商投资 Foreign Investment	合资经营 Joint Venture Corperation	合作经营 Cooperative Corperation	独资 Solely Funded	股份有限公司 Share Holding Co.Ltd.
209	**1978**	**5**	**81**	**37**	**2**	**40**	**2**	**32**	**15**	**1**	**13**	**1**
68	885	2	42	16	1	24	1	17	11		4	
252.57	**1269.61**	**5.26**	**203.48**	**55.95**		**144.46**	**3.06**	**85.40**	**17.77**	**8.28**	**37.87**	**0.09**
162.85	901.27	2.93	139.22	43.64		92.69	2.90	50.65	7.77	5.79	27.97	0.09
31.90	131.66	0.13	20.66	11.72		8.76	0.16	8.05	6.48		1.50	
12.26	20.97	0.08	3.89	0.34		3.55		0.62	0.44		0.13	
45.55	215.71	2.12	39.71	0.25		39.46		26.08	3.08	2.49	8.27	
24.42	147.36	1.11	9.64			9.64		22.83	2.77		7.81	
166.53	866.84	4.81	117.11	53.03		61.03	3.05	60.59	9.15	6.21	24.95	0.09
10.80	14.64		34.56	6.25		28.31		0.74	0.33		0.41	
20.30	27.39	0.01	21.05	0.59		20.47		6.26	5.77			
51.27	207.08	0.10	46.14	1.55		44.58	0.01	9.02	2.07	0.50	5.96	
14.48	168.30	0.34	19.17	0.78		18.39	0.00	9.52	0.78	1.57	6.96	
89.77	**545.56**	**1.70**	**36.78**	**22.14**		**7.01**	**7.63**	**23.33**	**9.65**	**6.82**	**6.87**	
241.48	**1359.64**	**5.27**	**165.12**	**48.35**	**0.08**	**113.80**	**2.88**	**74.55**	**12.87**	**8.56**	**39.90**	**2.06**
45.21	185.93	0.88	27.34	4.19		23.15		18.78	5.23		9.65	
			9.65			9.65		9.97			9.97	
63.62	757.57	3.82	44.93	5.59		36.82	2.52	22.82	1.96		15.65	
29.62	306.34	0.67	35.89	1.67		31.71	2.52	13.98	0.83		13.15	
132.65	416.14	0.57	83.19	38.57	0.08	44.18	0.36	22.98	5.68	8.56	4.62	2.06
77.96	219.67	0.27	52.22	28.60	0.07	23.22	0.34	16.59	2.50	7.95	3.80	1.44
49.82	515.39	0.20	120.97			120.97		27.25	19.60		7.66	
28.55	563.11	2.11	15.16	0.49		14.67		5.16	5.16			
3.24	108.61	1.11	2.74	0.08		2.65		2.74	2.74			

Note: The sources of capital in this table are the number of achieved funds.From 2010,the indicators of investment and area of land development had been canceled.

4-12 市、州全社会固定资产投资

TOTAL INVESTMENT IN FIXED ASSETS IN CITIES AND PREFECTURES

单位：亿元 (100 million yuan)

市、州	Cities and Prefectures	2006	2007	2008	2009	2010	2011	2012	2013	2014
全省	**Total**	**3572.69**	**4534.14**	**5798.56**	**8211.85**	**10802.69**	**12935.02**	**16504.17**	**20753.91**	**25001.77**
武汉市	Wuhan Municipality	1325.29	1732.79	2222.91	3001.10	3752.92	4263.24	5031.25	6001.96	7002.85
黄石市	Huangshi Municipality	138.05	179.85	232.90	343.05	474.06	597.45	750.95	963.50	1168.46
十堰市	Shiyan Municipality	116.61	141.66	185.44	278.35	406.31	522.37	702.72	904.32	1101.51
宜昌市	Yichang Municipality	323.55	390.36	523.46	750.27	949.51	1189.92	1620.98	2106.96	2570.41
襄阳市	Xiangyang Municipality	200.50	265.80	373.77	574.79	835.32	1134.74	1600.09	2086.64	2553.46
鄂州市	Ezhou Municipality	72.05	105.01	150.01	220.60	298.64	336.85	450.01	571.69	698.04
荆门市	Jingmen Municipality	127.74	153.25	210.08	317.18	448.62	590.63	794.40	1014.64	1232.55
孝感市	Xiaogan Municipality	144.82	195.93	270.83	397.26	570.70	729.24	980.82	1260.82	1536.96
荆州市	Jingzhou Municipality	149.67	210.75	291.46	435.16	600.93	771.42	1042.89	1355.60	1651.63
黄冈市	Huanggang Municipality	192.89	258.50	370.85	553.29	736.06	823.71	1102.94	1416.02	1717.39
咸宁市	Xianning Municipality	103.83	138.38	200.83	301.58	436.29	563.08	756.45	971.84	1170.85
随州市	Suizhou Municipality	70.96	101.92	147.07	208.70	291.18	384.48	514.73	654.60	799.33
恩施自治州	Enshi Prefecture	87.53	116.09	139.37	182.21	244.38	314.27	406.19	510.40	613.95
仙桃市	Xiantao Municipality	52.73	64.29	85.24	120.05	167.46	178.11	241.33	314.99	384.55
潜江市	Qianjiang Municipality	52.61	72.37	88.32	123.96	172.92	175.54	237.06	305.88	372.25
天门市	Tianmen Municipality	50.81	67.28	86.07	116.51	153.62	156.07	210.99	272.18	330.65
神农架林区	Shennongjia Forest Zone	5.63	5.63	7.50	10.65	14.15	15.77	20.02	25.56	31.06
不分地区		357.42	334.29	212.43	277.14	249.61	188.13	40.34	16.30	65.86

注：2006年全社会投资(城镇投资)不含城镇工矿区私人建房投资(下同)。由于方法制度调整，按可比口径计算，2005年扣除城镇工矿区私人建房投资基数应为2788.92亿元，各市、州全社会投资未做调整。
从2011年起固定资产投资统计口径调整为计划总投资500万元及以上项目，取消城镇农村公布口径，其他年份未做相应调整。

Note: in 2006 the social investment (town investment) does not contain town private house industrial investment (the same below). Because method system adjustment, the comparable caliber calculation, 2005 deduct industrial town private house should be 278.892 billion yuan investment base; Since 2011,the fixed assets investment statistical adjustment plan for a total investment of 5 million yuan RMB and the above project, cancel the town and countryside,other years did not corresponding adjustment.

4−13　市、州国有单位固定资产投资
INVESTMENT IN FIXED ASSETS BY STATE OWNED UNITS IN CITIES AND PREFECTURES

单位：亿元　　(100 million yuan)

市、州	Cities and Prefectures	2006	2007	2008	2009	2010	2011	2012	2013	2014
全省	**Total**	**1473.70**	**1808.61**	**2273.83**	**3124.16**	**3768.95**	**3764.22**	**4265.95**	**5068.42**	**5829.79**
武汉市	Wuhan	556.09	748.71	1072.32	1312.11	1655.04	1703.62	1676.10	1717.62	1883.46
黄石市	Huangshi	30.74	45.70	57.71	106.17	166.26	126.63	166.27	220.15	227.18
十堰市	Shiyan	55.42	71.51	76.53	136.88	176.18	226.42	344.22	454.68	479.50
宜昌市	Yichang	151.49	163.69	200.93	281.88	279.98	246.92	368.67	474.67	546.80
襄阳市	Xiangyang	58.19	63.70	96.61	111.61	144.10	202.59	300.18	323.20	368.97
鄂州市	Ezhou	28.87	36.40	62.67	112.80	107.33	63.70	102.35	76.26	154.37
荆门市	Jingmen	23.92	37.70	37.64	69.84	113.69	121.27	166.31	203.16	227.23
孝感市	Xiaogan	47.57	54.81	74.62	111.71	119.95	136.08	121.02	214.72	281.76
荆州市	Jingzhou	41.67	59.14	67.44	130.57	144.46	164.24	191.88	291.50	339.64
黄冈市	Huanggang	61.70	79.98	116.76	199.84	236.10	194.99	271.21	399.09	450.68
咸宁市	Xianning	39.15	44.53	59.27	103.42	129.30	155.54	184.16	238.80	291.23
随州市	Suizhou	21.17	25.71	37.99	70.68	77.94	77.30	73.57	124.28	140.37
恩施自治州	Enshi	32.26	45.29	57.47	88.85	111.07	110.16	149.84	193.99	233.63
仙桃市	Xiantao	9.98	9.47	6.54	26.99	12.79	14.48	16.52	25.56	35.45
潜江市	Qianjiang	24.19	38.88	38.82	53.64	68.65	51.62	63.30	60.47	85.85
天门市	Tianmen	11.94	15.78	28.47	30.47	46.30	25.51	15.31	30.16	17.78
神农架林区	Shennongjia	2.61	3.18	4.89	8.69	10.20	13.36	14.79	17.69	18.36
不分地区	Azoanl	276.72	264.43	177.16	168.00	169.60	129.79	40.24	2.40	47.53

4−14 市、州按经济类型分的全社会固定资产投资(2014)
TOTAL INVESTMENT IN FIXED ASSETS BY OWNERSHIP IN CITIES AND PREFECTURES(2014)

单位：亿元　　(100 million yuan)

市、州	Cities and Prefectures	合　计 Total	国有经济单位 State Owned Units	集体经济单位 Collective Owned Units	城乡私人 Private Owned Units	其他经济单位 Others
全省	**Total**	**25001.77**	**5829.79**	**820.75**	**8708.83**	**9642.41**
武汉市	Wuhan	7002.85	1883.46	245.49	1140.98	3732.93
黄石市	Huangshi	1168.46	227.18	39.02	494.47	407.79
十堰市	Shiyan	1101.51	479.50	10.89	450.50	160.62
宜昌市	Yichang	2570.41	546.80	58.48	848.85	1116.28
襄阳市	Xiangyang	2553.46	368.97	53.65	1075.48	1055.36
鄂州市	Ezhou	698.04	154.37	47.83	255.08	240.76
荆门市	Jingmen	1232.55	227.23	51.12	743.46	210.73
孝感市	Xiaogan	1536.96	281.76	84.76	778.45	391.99
荆州市	Jingzhou	1651.63	339.64	37.06	612.11	662.82
黄冈市	Huanggang	1717.39	450.68	108.11	721.35	437.24
咸宁市	Xianning	1170.85	291.23	37.65	524.56	317.40
随州市	Suizhou	799.33	140.37	31.66	261.67	365.63
恩施自治州	Enshi	613.95	233.63	1.23	235.41	143.67
仙桃市	Xiantao	384.55	35.45		249.30	99.79
潜江市	Qianjiang	372.25	85.85	10.19	145.21	131.01
天门市	Tianmen	330.65	17.78	3.44	166.17	143.26
神农架林区	Shennongjia	31.06	18.36	0.15	5.77	6.79
不分地区	Azoanl	65.86	47.53			18.33

4-15 市、州基本建设投资
INVESTMENT IN INFRASTRUCTURE CONSTRUCTION IN CITIES AND PREFECTURES

单位：亿元 (100 million yuan)

市、州	Cities and Prefectures	2006	2007	2008	2009	2010	2011	2012	2013	2014
全省	**Total**	**2059.18**	**2623.06**	**3393.06**	**4955.85**	**6504.20**	**8037.32**	**10715.01**	**13511.09**	**16140.94**
武汉市	Wuhan	665.77	846.72	1132.30	1511.96	1873.82	2312.36	2851.17	3438.78	3676.30
黄石市	Huangshi	80.31	107.58	135.11	214.79	295.51	368.95	550.46	718.40	822.00
十堰市	Shiyan	61.58	78.47	99.94	165.87	266.99	335.23	468.50	641.53	808.56
宜昌市	Yichang	226.79	275.39	371.91	547.86	680.30	854.05	1092.25	1527.28	2028.62
襄阳市	Xiangyang	108.53	133.85	210.13	310.74	428.23	651.27	980.84	1287.08	1707.23
鄂州市	Ezhou	46.04	66.35	84.44	125.34	200.98	266.48	369.63	484.67	608.46
荆门市	Jingmen	68.73	75.34	122.10	207.60	278.03	336.03	519.00	578.07	683.41
孝感市	Xiaogan	76.21	119.52	149.33	226.40	338.58	425.55	619.60	824.23	985.19
荆州市	Jingzhou	67.60	121.12	173.44	290.16	390.92	534.24	750.55	947.60	1181.00
黄冈市	Huanggang	106.56	151.82	245.58	413.73	547.27	567.38	787.85	976.36	1172.58
咸宁市	Xianning	56.29	72.63	117.42	175.98	287.62	395.79	526.46	601.17	718.79
随州市	Suizhou	38.96	65.07	96.23	152.87	206.41	257.42	406.04	466.65	571.49
恩施自治州	Enshi	59.22	76.86	90.74	122.32	158.37	214.65	292.50	365.62	435.87
仙桃市	Xiantao	21.43	39.62	52.62	89.47	135.29	145.69	159.09	238.72	172.70
潜江市	Qianjiang	19.77	26.34	39.40	36.41	66.68	97.11	150.18	167.45	216.79
天门市	Tianmen	29.36	43.09	56.79	75.96	101.33	80.24	130.98	210.89	279.01
神农架林区	Shennongjia	5.13	5.47	7.25	10.40	13.80	15.37	19.56	22.71	27.92
不分地区	Azoanl	320.90	317.81	208.32	277.99	234.06	179.52	40.34	13.90	45.04

4-16 市、州技术改造投资
INVESTMENT IN TECHNOLOGY TRANFER IN CITES AND PREFECTURES

单位：亿元 (100 million yuan)

市、州	Cities and Prefectures	2006	2007	2008	2009	2010	2011	2012	2013	2014
全省	**Total**	**625.43**	**807.56**	**1033.28**	**1301.07**	**1609.33**	**1696.12**	**2032.15**	**2333.72**	**3345.37**
武汉市	Wuhan	216.04	316.90	406.15	410.32	419.75	374.97	331.50	249.30	569.55
黄石市	Huangshi	27.19	38.75	48.91	64.46	83.45	128.33	93.12	119.49	194.82
十堰市	Shiyan	18.96	27.66	31.67	46.87	54.38	35.19	62.66	84.19	123.08
宜昌市	Yichang	46.91	47.67	65.62	86.65	105.96	114.68	257.85	235.32	233.95
襄阳市	Xiangyang	38.80	57.34	70.35	137.43	205.46	229.29	258.40	275.00	313.97
鄂州市	Ezhou	15.82	22.88	38.90	64.77	65.08	31.83	44.37	58.08	58.08
荆门市	Jingmen	32.42	46.26	52.92	60.57	100.51	159.65	165.63	221.70	269.47
孝感市	Xiaogan	35.12	31.16	55.47	79.35	105.82	158.31	190.66	255.04	329.92
荆州市	Jingzhou	41.72	42.15	61.98	75.23	121.84	113.04	131.57	129.36	213.49
黄冈市	Huanggang	31.01	53.16	56.74	61.45	68.45	96.79	142.12	213.75	280.17
咸宁市	Xianning	20.84	25.65	38.68	61.43	62.46	61.96	113.14	177.29	275.99
随州市	Suizhou	10.24	10.87	11.45	12.02	28.86	54.64	45.95	117.72	135.14
恩施自治州	Enshi	10.65	11.33	17.30	21.62	31.96	29.72	37.42	35.71	33.11
仙桃市	Xiantao	8.62	7.99	8.82	4.75	9.10	4.80	54.92	28.60	166.67
潜江市	Qianjiang	29.43	34.02	43.17	81.01	94.07	59.74	73.14	107.68	120.32
天门市	Tianmen	14.53	17.26	21.00	29.68	36.60	34.57	29.69	22.96	5.55
神农架林区	Shennongjia	0.36	0.04	0.05	0.02	0.05			2.35	2.03
不分地区		26.77	16.48	4.11	3.43	15.56	8.60		0.18	20.08

4-17 市、州房地产开发投资
INVESTMENT IN REAL ESTATE DEVELOPMENT IN CITIES AND PREFECTURES

单位：亿元 (100 million yuan)

市、州	Cities and Prefectures	2006	2007	2008	2009	2010	2011	2012	2013	2014
全省	**Total**	**564.76**	**723.73**	**892.67**	**1200.44**	**1618.24**	**2066.48**	**2539.46**	**3286.02**	**3983.79**
武汉市	Wuhan	366.15	459.75	560.36	778.59	1017.40	1282.25	1574.86	1905.60	2353.63
黄石市	Huangshi	16.96	19.66	21.53	25.30	38.36	42.51	56.04	84.68	115.77
十堰市	Shiyan	25.18	26.05	28.99	35.73	41.08	52.00	76.64	101.11	90.80
宜昌市	Yichang	39.18	48.71	56.68	79.33	105.78	135.97	176.59	203.18	194.60
襄阳市	Xiangyang	29.67	36.87	46.21	55.39	106.52	144.97	186.19	301.94	330.94
鄂州市	Ezhou	7.84	9.39	10.79	8.11	11.49	18.82	11.65	22.78	20.39
荆门市	Jingmen	9.07	11.38	16.84	27.19	38.83	55.65	64.31	87.79	123.98
孝感市	Xiaogan	11.26	19.16	28.57	32.40	49.60	56.40	74.95	111.13	136.35
荆州市	Jingzhou	18.14	22.20	26.59	32.87	35.53	55.80	54.89	76.79	134.17
黄冈市	Huanggang	12.17	23.33	27.38	37.33	43.84	62.15	78.57	132.73	174.27
咸宁市	Xianning	7.88	14.60	25.35	39.55	59.57	65.46	84.96	112.06	109.14
随州市	Suizhou	6.83	9.11	15.96	17.05	21.66	24.68	19.79	29.23	33.98
恩施自治州	Enshi	8.29	16.22	16.48	16.97	25.65	35.47	40.28	57.06	91.54
仙桃市	Xiantao	2.39	2.95	3.92	4.79	7.75	16.34	15.66	26.62	24.80
潜江市	Qianjiang	1.32	1.44	2.76	3.57	6.39	5.75	9.15	18.11	22.58
天门市	Tianmen	2.44	2.92	4.27	6.27	8.77	12.26	14.93	15.24	26.84
神农架林区	Shennongjia									

4-18 按国民经济行业分的基本建设投资
ACCORDING TO THE NATIONAL ECONOMIC CONSTRUCTION OF BASIC INDUSTRY INVESTMENT

单位：亿元 (100 million yuan)

行业	sector	全省 2013	全省 2014	#地方 2013	#地方 2014
总 计	**Total**	**13511.09**	**16140.94**	**13220.43**	**15760.07**
农、林、牧、渔业	Farming, Forestry, Animal Husbandry and Fishery	509.11	621.01	507.78	620.73
农业	Farming	146.09	205.36	144.76	205.08
林业	Forestry	47.09	71.10	47.09	71.10
畜牧业	Animal Husbandry	151.81	177.65	151.81	177.65
渔业	Fishery	37.27	47.95	37.27	47.95
农、林、牧、渔服务业	Farming, Forestry, Animal Husbandry and Fishery Services	126.85	118.94	126.85	118.94
采矿业	Mining and Qarrying	186.36	274.33	183.42	208.84
制造业	Manufacturing	6140.72	6812.02	6049.71	6741.83
农副食品加工业	Food Processing	497.73	570.65	497.50	570.65
食品制造业	Food Production	191.00	216.91	191.00	216.91
酒、饮料和精制茶制造业	Beverage Production	178.14	195.42	178.14	194.92
烟草制品业	Tobacco Processing	4.42	19.86	4.42	19.86
纺织业	Textile Industry	213.89	229.40	213.11	229.40
纺织服装、服饰业	Textile Wearing Apparel and Accessaries	152.69	191.75	152.69	191.75
皮革、毛皮、羽毛及其制品和制鞋业	Leather, Fur, Feather and Related Products	59.52	51.45	59.52	51.45
木材加工和木、竹、藤、棕、草制品业	Timber Processing and Wwood, Bamboo,Rattan, Palm and Saw Works	77.43	101.82	76.32	101.17
家具制造业	Furniture Manufacturing	117.90	115.81	117.90	115.81
造纸和纸制品业	Papermaking and Paper Products	117.71	136.41	117.71	136.41
印刷和记录媒介复制业	Printing and Record Processing	55.48	111.89	55.48	111.89
文教、工美、体育和娱乐用品制造业	Stationery, Education, Art, Sport and Entertainment Products	57.43	89.67	57.43	89.67
石油加工、炼焦和核燃料加工业	Petroleum Processing, Coking Products and Nuclear Fuel Processing	22.91	19.79	19.80	19.79
化学原料和化学制品制造业	Raw Chemical Material and Chemical Products	341.40	362.24	324.68	362.24
医药制造业	Medical and pharmaceutical Products	201.51	267.45	200.24	263.34
化学纤维制造业	Chemical Fibers	10.95	10.07	10.95	10.07
橡胶和塑料制品业	Rubber Products and Plastic Products	183.37	180.02	183.37	180.02
非金属矿物制品业	Nonmetal Material Products	545.62	636.61	545.62	636.61
黑色金属冶炼和压延加工业	Smelting and Processing of ferrous Metals	110.06	132.96	110.06	131.99
有色金属冶炼和压延加工业	Smelting and Processing of Nonferrous Metals	92.95	75.80	92.95	75.80
金属制品业	Metal Products	233.39	336.42	233.14	335.77
通用设备制造业	Ordinaryly Machinery Manufacturing	285.46	364.95	275.51	346.50
专用设备制造业	Special Purpose Equipment Manufacturing	469.34	475.38	452.64	456.92
汽车制造业	Automobile Manufacturing	825.36	751.75	808.09	737.33
铁路、船舶、航空航天和其他运输设备制造业	Realway, Ship, Aircraft and Other Transport Equipment Manufacturing	106.79	95.46	105.01	94.74
电气机械和器材制造业	Electric Machinery and Equipment	454.29	426.83	441.01	426.83
计算机、通信和其他电子设备制造业	Computers, Communication Equipment and Other Electronic Equipment Manufacturing	337.50	424.98	329.38	417.22
仪器仪表制造业	Measuring Instruments Manufacturing	81.28	72.95	80.95	70.75
其他制造业	Other Equipment	43.58	74.66	43.48	73.35
废弃资源综合利用业	Recycling and Disposal of Waste	64.70	58.54	64.70	58.54
金属制品、机械和设备修理业	Repairing of Metal and Mechanical Equipment	6.92	14.15	6.92	14.15
电力、热力、燃气及水生产和供应业	Electric Power, Gas and Water Production and Supply	335.57	380.41	298.50	342.36
电力、热力生产和供应业	Electric Power, Steam and Hot Water Production and Supply	194.88	221.71	158.80	186.76
燃气生产和供应业	Gas Production and Supply	43.48	62.25	42.49	59.15
水的生产和供应业	Tap Water Production and Supply	97.21	96.44	97.21	96.44

注：从2012年起执行新的国民经济行业代码（GB/T4754-2011）

Note:Since 2012,a new national economy industry code(GB/T4754-2011)is implemented.

4-18 续表 continued

单位：亿元 (100 million yuan)

行业	sector	全省		#地方	
		2013	2014	2013	2014
建筑业	Construction	89.75	104.15	89.75	102.79
交通运输、仓储和邮政业	Transportation, storage and Post	1492.42	1871.58	1435.04	1804.02
铁路运输业	Railway Transportation	66.51	69.91	16.27	15.26
道路运输业	Road Transportation	1007.73	1267.18	1001.04	1256.46
水上运输业	Waterway Transportation	88.37	117.66	88.37	117.66
航空运输业	Air Transportation	43.84	48.23	43.84	48.23
管道运输业	Pipeline Transportation	2.72	3.95	2.72	3.95
装卸搬运和运输代理业	Load, Unload, and Agency	43.30	73.06	43.30	73.06
仓储业	Transportation Storage	235.62	285.83	235.17	283.64
邮政业	Post	4.33	5.76	4.33	5.76
信息传输、软件和信息技术服务业	Information Transmission, Software and Information Technology Service	59.83	60.45	47.59	57.00
电信、广播电视和卫星传输服务	Telecom, Radio Tv and Satellite	27.01	30.76	14.77	27.31
互联网和相关服务	Internet and Related	5.42	6.77	5.42	6.77
软件和信息技术服务业	Software and Information Technology	27.40	22.92	27.40	22.92
批发和零售业	Wholesale and Retail Trade	472.61	639.70	450.97	635.85
住宿和餐饮业	Hotel and Catering Services	243.99	298.90	243.99	298.90
金融业	Finance	66.83	64.12	64.84	62.27
货币金融服务	Monetary Financial Service	34.33	30.43	32.34	28.59
资本市场服务	Capital Markets Service	14.55	30.60	14.55	30.60
保险业	Insurance	1.66	0.38	1.66	0.38
其他金融业	Other Financial Acitivities	16.29	2.71	16.29	2.71
房地产业	Real Estate Trade	979.12	1255.75	971.12	1252.23
租赁和商务服务业	Leasing and Commercial Service	291.88	464.88	291.88	464.88
租赁业	Leasing Service	5.40	12.11	5.40	12.11
商务服务业	Commercial Service	286.47	452.78	286.47	452.78
科学研究和技术服务业	Scientific Research, Polytechnical Services	78.08	102.76	75.16	95.76
水利、环境和公共设施管理业	Water Conservancy, Environment and Public Facility Management	1594.42	1956.30	1567.35	1905.89
水利管理业	Water Conservancy Management	175.29	224.21	155.57	204.22
生态保护和环境治理业	Environment Management	54.59	99.29	54.59	99.29
公共设施管理业	Public Facility Management	1364.54	1632.80	1357.19	1602.38
居民服务、修理和其他服务业	Resident Service and Others	105.22	173.25	105.22	173.25
教育	Education	174.80	223.98	157.82	190.90
卫生和社会工作	Health Care and Social Work	139.06	174.73	135.36	163.30
卫生	Health Care	105.89	127.00	102.24	115.57
社会工作	Social Work	33.17	47.73	33.11	47.73
文化、体育和娱乐业	Culture, Sports and Recreation	173.43	261.18	170.51	248.56
新闻和出版业	News and Publication	4.01	0.45	4.01	0.45
广播、电视、电影和影视录音制作业	Radio, Television, Film and Recording	3.93	4.85	3.93	4.85
文化艺术业	Culture and Arts	66.12	100.15	66.10	98.63
体育	Sports	30.48	56.84	27.58	48.37
娱乐业	Receation	68.89	98.88	68.89	96.26
公共管理、社会保障和社会组织	Public Management and Social Organizations	377.91	401.46	374.45	390.67

4—19 按国民经济行业分的技术改造投资
ACCORDING TO THE NATIONAL ECONOMIC INDUSTRY TECHNICAL TRANSFORMATION INVESTMENT

单位：亿元 (100 million yuan)

行业	sector	全省		#地方	
		2013	2014	2013	2014
总　计	Total	**2333.72**	**3345.37**	**2165.12**	**3207.10**
农、林、牧、渔业	Farming, Forestry, Animal Husbandry and Fishery	29.34	48.89	29.34	48.89
农业	Farming	10.83	15.44	10.83	15.44
林业	Forestry	1.80		1.80	
畜牧业	Animal Husbandry	0.68	5.27	0.68	5.27
渔业	Fishery	1.44	5.13	1.44	5.13
农、林、牧、渔服务业	Farming, Forestry, Animal Husbandry and Fishery Services	14.60	23.06	14.60	23.06
采矿业	Mining and Qarrying	171.36	118.61	124.99	118.61
制造业	Manufacturing	1604.71	2501.57	1535.72	2451.13
农副食品加工业	Food Processing	161.80	201.00	161.80	201.00
食品制造业	Food Production	46.61	96.99	46.61	96.99
酒、饮料和精制茶制造业	Beverage Production	52.00	94.58	52.00	94.58
烟草制品业	Tobacco Processing	6.76	9.07	6.76	9.07
纺织业	Textile Industry	102.35	161.62	102.35	159.47
纺织服装、服饰业	Textile Wearing Apparel and Accessaries	35.06	55.51	35.06	55.51
皮革、毛皮、羽毛及其制品和制鞋业	Leather, Fur, Feather and Related Products	9.07	22.11	9.07	22.11
木材加工和木、竹、藤、棕、草制品业	Timber Processing and Wwood, Bamboo,Rattan, Palm and Sraw Works	15.71	32.22	15.71	32.22
家具制造业	Furniture Manufacturing	8.83	20.30	8.83	20.30
造纸和纸制品业	Papermaking and Paper Products	25.43	42.96	25.43	42.96
印刷和记录媒介复制业	Printing and Record Processing	9.60	15.95	9.60	15.95
文教、工美、体育和娱乐用品制造业	Stationery, Education, Art, Sport and Entertainment Products	6.55	14.32	6.55	14.32
石油加工、炼焦和核燃料加工业	Petroleum Processing, Coking Products and Nuclear Fuel Processing	32.96	42.87	10.60	18.95
化学原料和化学制品制造业	Raw Chemical Material and Chemical Products	206.83	253.53	205.56	253.03
医药制造业	Medical and pharmaceutical Products	50.44	83.42	48.06	82.96
化学纤维制造业	Chemical Fibers	4.27	12.08	4.27	12.08
橡胶和塑料制品业	Rubber Products and Plastic Products	58.30	85.27	58.30	85.27
非金属矿物制品业	Nonmetal Material Products	218.53	276.67	218.31	275.37
黑色金属冶炼和压延加工业	Smelting and Processing of ferrous Metals	66.99	76.65	52.89	74.65
有色金属冶炼和压延加工业	Smelting and Processing of Nonferrous Metals	22.00	60.74	19.82	60.74
金属制品业	Metal Products	74.92	89.45	74.92	89.45
通用设备制造业	Ordinaryly Machinery Manufacturing	80.60	114.05	71.55	114.05
专用设备制造业	Special Purpose Equipment Manufacturing	53.74	117.33	49.92	117.32
汽车制造业	Automobile Manufacturing	116.55	241.83	114.85	232.10
铁路、船舶、航空航天和其他运输设备制造业	Realway, Ship, Aircraft and Other Transport Equipment Manufacturing	12.52	24.76	5.91	15.75
电气机械和器材制造业	Electric Machinery and Equipment	53.26	99.36	53.26	99.36
计算机、通信和其他电子设备制造业	Computers, Communication Equipment and Other Electronic Equipment Manufacturing	50.83	107.09	45.73	105.76
仪器仪表制造业	Measuring Instruments Manufacturing	10.81	18.40	10.61	18.39
其他制造业	Other Equipment	3.32	10.17	3.32	10.17
废弃资源综合利用业	Recycling and Disposal of Waste	3.14	18.95	3.14	18.95
金属制品、机械和设备修理业	Repairing of Metal and Mechanical Equipment	4.95	2.32	4.95	2.32
电力、热力、燃气及水生产和供应业	Electric Power, Gas and Water Production and Supply	154.93	199.47	110.30	144.86
电力、热力生产和供应业	Electric Power, Steam and Hot Water Production and Supply	124.35	155.21	79.72	101.07
燃气生产和供应业	Gas Production and Supply	2.36	4.11	2.36	4.11
水的生产和供应业	Tap Water Production and Supply	28.22	40.15	28.22	39.67

4—19 续表 continued

单位：亿元 (100 million yuan)

行业	sector	全省 2013	全省 2014	#地方 2013	#地方 2014
建筑业	Construction	6.68	2.96	6.68	2.96
交通运输、仓储和邮政业	Transportation, storage and Post	124.46	157.52	123.97	133.34
铁路运输业	Railway Transportation	0.89	24.93	0.64	1.00
道路运输业	Road Transportation	95.78	119.35	95.55	119.35
水上运输业	Waterway Transportation	1.37	4.47	1.37	4.47
航空运输业	Air Transportation				
管道运输业	Pipeline Transportation	0.24		0.24	
装卸搬运和运输代理业	Load, Unload, and Agency	1.81	1.11	1.81	1.11
仓储业	Transportation Storage	24.17	7.49	24.17	7.24
邮政业	Post	0.20	0.18	0.20	0.18
信息传输、软件和信息技术服务业	Information Transmission, Software and Information Technology Service	20.65	14.59	14.64	9.02
电信、广播电视和卫星传输服务	Telecom, Radio Tv and Satellite	16.56	10.97	10.76	5.41
互联网和相关服务	Internet and Related	2.18	3.38	1.97	3.38
软件和信息技术服务业	Software and Information Technology	1.91	0.23	1.91	0.23
批发和零售业	Wholesale and Retail Trade	13.45	37.99	13.25	37.34
住宿和餐饮业	Hotel and Catering Services	6.60	15.04	6.60	15.04
金融业	Finance	2.83	3.62	1.81	2.83
货币金融服务	Monetary Financial Service	2.59	3.62	1.81	2.83
资本市场服务	Monetary Financial Service				
保险业	Insurance	0.24			
其他金融业	Other Financial Acitivities				
房地产业	Real Estate Trade	21.48	20.16	21.48	20.16
租赁和商务服务业	Leasing and Commercial Service	4.49	5.77	4.49	5.77
租赁业	Leasing Service		0.28		0.28
商务服务业	Commercial Service	4.49	5.50	4.49	5.50
科学研究和技术服务业	Scientific Research, Polytechnical Services	6.40	4.46	6.40	4.46
水利、环境和公共设施管理业	Water Conservancy, Environment and Public Facility Management	121.53	142.45	120.73	141.49
水利管理业	Water Conservancy Management	46.07	45.03	46.07	45.03
生态保护和环境治理业	Environment Management	11.89	10.40	11.89	10.40
公共设施管理业	Public Facility Management	63.57	87.02	62.77	86.07
居民服务、修理和其他服务业	Resident Service and Others	0.49	9.23	0.49	9.23
教育	Education	10.93	12.03	10.93	12.03
卫生和社会工作	Health Care and Social Work	9.53	16.10	9.53	15.25
卫生	Health Care	8.77	15.06	8.77	14.21
社会工作	Social Work	0.75	1.04	0.75	1.04
文化、体育和娱乐业	Culture, Sports and Recreation	13.51	13.01	13.51	12.81
新闻和出版业	News and Publication		0.47		0.47
广播、电视、电影和影视录音制作业	Radio, Television, Film and Recording	3.06	1.47	3.06	1.47
文化艺术业	Culture and Arts	1.34	1.58	1.34	1.38
体育	Sports	3.37	2.23	3.37	2.23
娱乐业	Receation	5.75	7.26	5.75	7.26
公共管理、社会保障和社会组织	Public Management and Social Organizations	10.35	21.88	10.25	21.88

4-20 全社会按构成分的投资额
ACCORDING TO THE COMPOSITION OF SOCIAL CAPITAL

单位:亿元 (100 million yuan)

年 份 In copies	全省 建筑安装工程 Building installation	全省 设备工具器具购置 Equipment tools, equipment purchase	全省 其他费用 Other expenses	#地方 建筑安装工程 Building installation	#地方 设备工具器具购置 Equipment tools, equipment purchase	#地方 其他费用 expenses Other
1978	20.30	9.98	3.30	9.89	4.51	0.48
1980	23.85	9.76	1.89	14.01	4.55	0.97
"六五"时期	**216.19**	**83.11**	**16.52**	**155.63**	**59.71**	**7.43**
1985	67.53	28.67	6.71	54.64	23.00	3.39
"七五"时期	**434.43**	**195.59**	**50.10**	**352.24**	**152.75**	**32.96**
1986	72.40	31.24	7.84	60.18	23.91	4.81
1987	86.83	40.54	12.71	71.79	32.83	7.83
1988	100.58	49.28	10.60	82.40	41.51	7.35
1989	81.98	33.51	8.21	64.30	25.19	5.86
1990	92.64	41.02	10.78	73.58	29.31	7.11
"八五"时期	**1300.95**	**606.68**	**304.04**	**972.09**	**429.78**	**178.69**
1991	108.07	45.11	15.01	86.74	33.68	10.64
1992	149.34	68.03	23.36	119.61	51.46	15.94
1993	227.25	98.91	57.02	174.02	74.17	39.83
1994	361.89	146.12	85.06	261.27	99.72	49.60
1995	454.40	248.51	123.59	330.45	170.75	62.68
"九五"时期	**3392.01**	**1596.34**	**1034.45**	**2593.68**	**1108.81**	**598.32**
1996	510.52	307.89	165.97	392.06	218.14	82.28
1997	600.04	264.16	219.40	405.69	171.97	201.38
1998	695.55	323.47	212.08	556.36	230.59	101.48
1999	771.24	329.26	201.67	594.41	248.78	94.54
2000	814.66	371.56	235.33	645.16	239.33	118.64
"十五"时期	**6031.36**	**2481.09**	**1809.24**	**5317.08**	**1883.69**	**1216.75**
2001	890.60	419.20	241.95	739.97	276.93	124.89
2002	974.73	418.55	301.94	829.11	303.57	155.49
2003	1059.98	463.23	360.38	945.58	363.78	243.47
2004	1409.25	537.25	409.88	1282.71	416.98	307.87
2005	1696.80	642.86	495.09	1519.71	522.43	385.03
"十一五"时期	**20406.53**	**6921.20**	**5592.20**	**18649.08**	**5890.61**	**4859.93**
2006	2252.72	717.10	602.87	1918.63	601.90	477.07
2007	2857.31	896.36	780.47	2492.24	756.58	660.27
2008	3568.97	1245.73	983.86	3226.13	971.37	819.50
2009	5025.62	1753.28	1432.95	4683.30	1472.52	1243.52
2010	6701.91	2308.73	1792.05	6328.78	2088.24	1659.57
"十二五"时期						
2011	8056.52	2812.91	2065.59	7626.28	2520.40	1950.61
2012	11054.16	3162.99	2287.02	10609.45	2942.10	2192.00
2013	14312.25	3856.68	2584.98	13934.73	3702.30	2508.97
2014	18185.42	4292.85	2523.50	17765.47	4160.35	2425.92

4-21 全社会按国民经济行业分的固定资产投资

ACCORDING TO THE NATIONAL ECONOMY SOCIETY OF FIXED ASSETS INVESTMENT

单位：亿元 (100 million yuan)

行业	sector	全省		#地方	
		2013	2014	2013	2014
总　计	Total	**20753.91**	**25001.77**	**20146.00**	**24351.75**
农、林、牧、渔业	Farming, Forestry, Animal Husbandry and Fishery	748.53	951.70	747.19	951.42
农业	Farming	345.85	485.12	344.51	484.85
林业	Forestry	50.14	71.57	50.14	71.57
畜牧业	Animal Husbandry	155.48	188.86	155.48	188.86
渔业	Fishery	39.14	53.79	39.14	53.79
农、林、牧、渔服务业	Farming, Forestry, Animal Husbandry and Fishery	157.92	152.35	157.92	152.35
采矿业	Mining and Qarrying	369.67	404.80	320.36	339.31
制造业	Manufacturing	8219.26	9633.97	8055.16	9505.59
农副食品加工业	Food Processing	684.86	794.99	684.63	794.99
食品制造业	Food Production	243.04	322.51	243.04	322.51
酒、饮料和精制茶制造业	Beverage Production	244.96	305.83	244.96	305.33
烟草制品业	Tobacco Processing	11.51	28.93	11.51	28.93
纺织业	Textile Industry	329.08	406.90	328.30	404.74
纺织服装、服饰业	Textile Wearing Apparel and Accessaries	194.71	253.76	194.71	253.76
皮革、毛皮、羽毛及其制品和制鞋业	Leather, Fur, Feather and Related Products	69.10	76.70	69.10	76.70
木材加工和木、竹、藤、棕、草制品业	Timber Processing and Wwood, Bamboo,Rattan, F	99.89	138.08	98.78	137.43
家具制造业	Furniture Manufacturing	132.09	137.11	132.09	137.11
造纸和纸制品业	Papermaking and Paper Products	149.27	186.73	149.27	186.73
印刷和记录媒介复制业	Printing and Record Processing	80.75	131.93	80.75	131.93
文教、工美、体育和娱乐用品制造业	Stationery, Education, Art, Sport and Entertainment Products	64.75	104.82	64.75	104.82
石油加工、炼焦和核燃料加工业	Petroleum Processing, Coking Products and Nucle	58.36	67.64	32.90	41.00
化学原料和化学制品制造业	Raw Chemical Material and Chemical Products	605.09	635.40	587.09	634.90
医药制造业	Medical and pharmaceutical Products	267.54	362.42	263.89	357.84
化学纤维制造业	Chemical Fibers	15.22	22.56	15.22	22.56
橡胶和塑料制品业	Rubber Products and Plastic Products	250.32	271.24	250.32	271.24
非金属矿物制品业	Nonmetal Material Products	818.85	949.41	818.05	948.11
黑色金属冶炼和压延加工业	Smelting and Processing of ferrous Metals	192.16	213.67	177.96	210.64
有色金属冶炼和压延加工业	Smelting and Processing of Nonferrous Metals	126.18	142.70	124.00	142.70
金属制品业	Metal Products	323.24	447.01	322.99	446.36
通用设备制造业	Ordinaryly Machinery Manufacturing	386.23	493.65	367.23	474.78
专用设备制造业	Special Purpose Equipment Manufacturing	550.85	617.43	530.34	598.76
汽车制造业	Automobile Manufacturing	1017.94	1036.29	998.97	1012.14
铁路、船舶、航空航天和其他运输设备制造业	Realway, Ship, Aircraft and Other Transport Equipment Manufacturing	151.88	125.69	142.06	112.58
电气机械和器材制造业	Electric Machinery and Equipment	522.99	540.69	509.71	540.69
计算机、通信和其他电子设备制造业	Computers, Communication Equipment and Other Electronic Equipment Manufacturing	401.94	538.08	387.86	528.02
仪器仪表制造业	Measuring Instruments Manufacturing	94.39	94.73	93.86	92.52
其他制造业	Other Equipment	48.13	87.48	48.03	86.17
废弃资源综合利用业	Recycling and Disposal of Waste	69.24	77.56	69.24	77.56
金属制品、机械和设备修理业	Repairing of Metal and Mechanical Equipment	14.71	22.04	13.58	22.04
电力、热力、燃气及水生产和供应业	Electric Power, Gas and Water Production and Supply	531.71	604.47	444.99	508.74
电力、热力生产和供应业	Electric Power, Steam and Hot Water Production a	343.14	384.17	257.97	293.17
燃气生产和供应业	Gas Production and Supply	51.25	72.17	50.26	69.07
水的生产和供应业	Tap Water Production and Supply	137.31	148.13	136.76	146.51

注：从2012年起执行新的国民经济行业代码（GB/T4754-2011）

4−21 续表 continued

单位：亿元 (100 million yuan)

行业	sector	全省		#地方	
		2013	2014	2013	2014
建筑业	Construction	104.63	120.51	99.97	109.01
交通运输、仓储和邮政业	Transportation, storage and Post	1733.95	2157.93	1671.03	2063.15
铁路运输业	Railway Transportation	70.08	96.59	16.98	16.26
道路运输业	Road Transportation	1205.69	1497.30	1198.77	1486.58
水上运输业	Waterway Transportation	94.11	126.22	91.70	124.93
航空运输业	Air Transportation	48.43	55.57	48.38	55.57
管道运输业	Pipeline Transportation	2.96	3.95	2.96	3.95
装卸搬运和运输代理业	Load, Unload, and Agency	46.98	75.92	46.98	75.92
仓储业	Transportation Storage	260.50	296.23	260.05	293.78
邮政业	Post	5.20	6.14	5.20	6.14
信息传输、软件和信息技术服务业	Information Transmission, Software and Information Technology Service	114.95	104.72	90.48	95.10
电信、广播电视和卫星传输服务	Telecom, Radio Tv and Satellite	70.34	68.64	52.30	59.31
互联网和相关服务	Internet and Related	14.77	10.55	8.34	10.55
软件和信息技术服务业	Software and Information Technology	29.84	25.53	29.84	25.25
批发和零售业	Wholesale and Retail Trade	520.65	695.08	497.89	690.59
住宿和餐饮业	Hotel and Catering Services	270.24	320.85	270.24	320.85
金融业	Finance	81.53	89.11	73.71	85.21
货币金融服务	Monetary Financial Service	48.52	52.34	41.15	48.44
资本市场服务	Monetary Financial Service	14.61	30.87	14.61	30.87
保险业	Insurance	2.11	3.20	1.66	3.20
其他金融业	Other Financial Acitivities	16.29	2.71	16.29	2.71
房地产业	Real Estate Trade	4708.01	5723.24	4592.16	5627.90
租赁和商务服务业	Leasing and Commercial Service	307.23	496.70	307.23	496.70
租赁业	Leasing Service	7.20	14.92	7.20	14.92
商务服务业	Commercial Service	300.03	481.78	300.03	481.78
科学研究和技术服务业	Scientific Research, Polytechnical Services	93.62	108.24	90.30	101.24
水利、环境和公共设施管理业	Water Conservancy, Environment and Public Facility Management	1853.06	2212.19	1824.38	2158.90
水利管理业	Water Conservancy Management	247.98	297.63	228.26	275.73
生态保护和环境治理业	Environment Management	72.58	117.67	72.58	117.67
公共设施管理业	Public Facility Management	1532.49	1796.89	1523.54	1765.51
居民服务、修理和其他服务业	Resident Service and Others	108.69	187.72	108.69	187.72
教育	Education	203.36	253.54	177.85	210.49
卫生和社会工作	Health Care and Social Work	177.35	215.48	173.19	202.12
卫生	Health Care	142.44	165.84	138.33	152.48
社会工作	Social Work	34.91	49.64	34.85	49.64
文化、体育和娱乐业	Culture, Sports and Recreation	194.01	280.95	191.09	268.14
新闻和出版业	News and Publication	4.01	0.92	4.01	0.92
广播、电视、电影和影视录音制作业	Radio, Television, Film and Recording	7.47	9.04	7.47	9.04
文化艺术业	Culture and Arts	69.96	102.90	69.94	101.18
体育	Sports	34.04	59.49	31.14	51.02
娱乐业	Receation	78.54	108.60	78.54	105.98
公共管理、社会保障和社会组织	Public Management and Social Organizations	413.64	440.56	410.08	429.55

4-22 全社会按三次产业划分的投资额
ACCORDING TO THE THREE INDUSTRIES OF WHOLE SOCIETY OF INVESTMENT

单位：亿元 (100 million yuan)

年 份 In copies	全省 第一产业 The first industry	全省 第二产业 The second industry	全省 第三产业 The third industry	#地方 第一产业 The first industry	#地方 第二产业 The second industry	#地方 第三产业 The third industry
1978	**2.24**	**25.28**	**6.06**	**2.24**	**8.80**	**3.85**
1980	2.11	22.75	10.64	2.03	9.98	7.52
"六五"时期	**24.77**	**155.02**	**136.03**	**24.05**	**83.83**	**114.89**
1985	8.37	47.42	47.12	8.09	31.48	41.46
"七五"时期	**49.76**	**335.53**	**294.83**	**47.24**	**245.00**	**245.71**
1986	7.89	50.33	53.22	7.40	34.88	46.62
1987	9.52	70.17	60.39	9.07	52.40	50.98
1988	11.11	85.76	63.59	10.53	67.14	53.59
1989	9.08	61.86	52.76	8.63	44.28	42.43
1990	12.16	67.41	64.87	11.61	46.30	52.09
"八五"时期	**78.98**	**1074.06**	**1058.63**	**73.97**	**674.84**	**831.75**
1991	12.48	77.95	77.76	12.12	55.25	63.69
1992	12.42	121.00	107.31	11.04	87.18	88.79
1993	11.89	170.93	200.36	10.10	114.05	163.87
1994	14.97	302.49	275.61	14.38	173.32	222.89
1995	27.22	401.69	397.59	26.11	220.95	316.82
"九五"时期	**272.08**	**2298.38**	**3452.34**	**271.69**	**1265.99**	**2763.13**
1996	29.76	451.28	503.34	29.73	272.79	389.96
1997	41.02	436.04	606.54	41.02	269.87	468.15
1998	59.48	450.16	721.46	59.48	234.94	594.01
1999	71.22	439.32	791.63	71.22	227.20	639.31
2000	70.60	521.58	829.37	70.24	261.19	671.70
"十五"时期	**416.79**	**3952.90**	**5969.82**	**414.74**	**2724.92**	**5277.86**
2001	77.48	590.01	902.08	77.33	323.55	740.91
2002	80.08	648.81	966.33	79.02	375.77	833.38
2003	88.80	714.81	1079.98	88.35	489.49	974.99
2004	77.55	912.93	1365.90	77.16	684.54	1245.86
2005	92.88	1086.34	1655.53	92.88	851.57	1482.72
"十一五"时期	**1202.88**	**12641.78**	**19075.27**	**1197.58**	**10748.83**	**17471.71**
2006	107.64	1317.12	2147.93	107.56	1044.17	1845.87
2007	149.40	1710.74	2674.00	148.72	1395.28	2365.09
2008	231.25	2346.32	3220.99	230.95	1859.42	2926.62
2009	321.59	3097.68	4792.58	319.58	2656.02	4442.25
2010	393.00	4169.92	6239.77	390.77	3793.94	5891.88
"十二五"时期						
2011	440.91	5526.40	6967.71	440.51	5032.88	6623.90
2012	525.45	7281.04	8697.68	525.13	6891.67	8326.75
2013	590.61	9187.25	10976.04	589.28	8883.83	10672.89
2014	799.35	10733.09	13469.32	799.07	10432.00	13120.68

注：从2012年起，三次产业采用新的划分标准。

4–23 全社会竣工房屋建筑面积及竣工率

THE FLOOR SPACE OF BUILDINGS COMPLETED ALL SOCIAL AND COMPLETION RATE

年 份	施工面积(万平方米)		竣工面积(万平方米)		竣工率(%)	
In copies	Construction area (million square meters)	#住宅 # residential	Completion of (million square meters)	#住宅 # residential	Completion rate (%)	#住宅 # residential
1978	**1343.27**	**513.20**	**666.76**	**280.16**	**49.6**	**54.6**
1980	1951.16	1004.17	1024.51	586.27	52.5	58.4
"六五"时期			**25700.97**	**19626.87**		
1985	8079.90	5965.71	6899.59	5434.20	85.4	91.1
"七五"时期			**29202.17**	**22387.23**		
1986	8760.15	6686.78	7754.53	6308.96	88.5	94.3
1987	7922.23	5684.88	6803.61	5233.59	85.9	92.1
1988	7225.98	4892.04	6060.44	4484.69	83.9	91.7
1989	5250.24	3590.22	4414.47	3301.59	84.1	92.0
1990	5103.48	3507.53	4169.12	3058.40	81.7	87.2
"八五"时期			**23403.26**	**16559.28**		
1991	5300.98	3652.67	4211.39	3157.13	79.4	86.4
1992	5954.84	4066.51	4621.87	3383.72	77.6	83.2
1993	5807.24	3540.57	4050.56	2798.42	69.8	79.0
1994	7158.68	4476.46	4916.24	3482.20	68.7	77.8
1995	8294.84	5304.79	5603.20	3737.81	67.6	70.5
"九五"时期			**35861.86**	**26378.48**		
1996	8749.65	5581.32	6073.43	4485.82	69.4	80.4
1997	8963.28	5976.86	6430.48	4790.34	71.7	80.1
1998	10485.86	7179.25	7897.96	5792.97	75.3	80.7
1999	10228.93	7219.06	7951.03	5891.97	77.7	81.6
2000	9920.42	6831.02	7508.96	5417.38	75.7	79.3
"十五"时期			**40164.49**	**29588.06**		
2001	10040.11	7273.21	7716.37	5850.27	76.9	80.4
2002	10301.00	7019.76	7796.76	5583.27	75.7	79.5
2003	10667.78	7276.62	7469.17	5457.42	70.0	75.0
2004	13152.08	9285.64	9318.34	7069.45	70.6	75.9
2005	12572.00	8401.20	7863.85	5627.67	62.6	67.0
"十一五"时期			**43810.54**	**26870.86**		
2006	12346.48	8039.75	7126.64	4812.39	57.7	59.9
2007	13686.34	8910.75	7557.62	5036.19	55.2	56.5
2008	16417.07	9896.66	7551.82	4679.96	46.0	47.3
2009	20142.81	11762.06	9772.28	5556.71	48.5	47.2
2010	25284.83	14486.90	11802.18	6785.61	46.7	46.8
"十二五"时期						
2011	31388.88	16337.96	14585.68	7375.38	46.5	45.1
2012	40103.56	19154.75	16576.18	7890.08	41.3	41.2
2013	51939.51	23443.19	18828.87	8006.06	36.3	34.2
2014	58064.39	27199.41	21175.37	8702.01	36.5	32.0

主要统计指标解释

全社会固定资产投资　是以货币形式表现的在一定时期内全社会建造和购置固定资产的工作量以及与此有关的费用的总称。该指标是反映固定资产投资规模、结构和发展速度的综合性指标，又是观察工程进度和考核投资效果的重要依据。全社会固定资产投资按登记注册类型可分为国有、集体、个体、联营、股份制、外商、港澳台商、其他等。

固定资产投资　指各种登记注册类型的企业、事业、行政单位及个体户进行的计划总投资500万元及500万元以上的建设项目投资、房地产开发投资、城镇和工矿区私人建房投资。

房地产开发投资　指各种登记注册类型的房地产开发公司、商品房建设公司及其他房地产开发法人单位和附属于其他法人单位实际从事房地产开发或经营活动的单位统一开发的包括统代建、拆迁还建的住宅、厂房、仓库、饭店、宾馆、度假村、写字楼、办公楼等房屋建筑物和配套的服务设施，土地开发工程（如道路、给水、排水、供电、供热、通讯、平整场地等基础设施工程）的投资；不包括单纯的土地交易活动。

城镇和工矿区私人建房投资　包括市、县城、城关镇、工矿区所辖范围内的全部私人建房，不论其房主是否系本地的常住户口均应包括。

农村投资　包括在农村区域范围内进行固定资产投资活动的企业、事业、行政单位及农村个人投资。

固定资产投资的资金来源　根据固定资产投资的资金来源不同，分为国家预算内资金、国内贷款、利用外资、自筹资金和其他资金。

(1)国家预算内资金：分为财政拨款和财政安排的贷款两部分。包括中央财政的基本建设基金(分经营性基金和非经营性基金两部分)、专项支出(如煤代油专项等)、收回再贷、贴息资金，财政安排的挖潜改造和新产品试制支出、城建支出、商业部门简易建筑支出、不发达地区发展基金等资金中用于固定资产投资的资金；地方财政中由国家统筹安排的资金等。

(2)国内贷款：指报告期固定资产投资单位向银行及非银行金融机构借入的用于固定资产投资的各种国内借款，包括银行利用自有资金及吸收的存款发放的贷款、上级主管部门拨入的国内贷款、国家专项贷款(包括煤代油贷款、劳改煤矿专项贷款等)、地方财政专项资金安排的贷款、国内储备贷款、周转贷款等。

(3)利用外资：指报告期收到的用于固定资产建造和购置的国外资金(包括设备、材料、技术在内)。包括对外借款(外国政府、国际金融组织贷款、出口信贷、外国银行商业贷款、对外发行债券和股票)、外商直接投资及外商其他投资。不包括我国自有外汇资金(国家外汇、地方外汇、留成外汇、调剂外汇和中国银行自有资金发行的外汇贷款等)。计算利用外资时，需要折算成人民币，折算中所使用的外汇汇率按现汇计算，即按使用外汇时的汇率计算。

(4)自筹资金：指固定资产投资单位报告期收到的，由各地区、各部门及企、事业单位筹集用于固定资产投资的预算外资金，包括中央各部门、各级地方和企、事业单位的自筹资金。

(5)其他资金：指在报告期收到的除以上各种资金之外其他用于固定资产投资的资金，包括企业或金融机构通过发行各种债券筹集到的资金、群众集资、个人资金、无偿捐赠的资金及其他单位拨入的资金等。

固定资产投资按国民经济行业分　根据建设项目建成投产后的主要产品或主要用途及社会经济活动性质来确定国民经济行业。一般情况下，一个建设项目或一个企业、事业单位只能属于一种国民经济行业。

固定资产投资按隶属关系分　是按建设单位或企业、事业、行政单位的主管上级机关确定的。

（1）中央：是指中共中央、人大常委会和国务院各部、委、局、总公司以及直属机构直接领导的建设项目和企业、事业、行政单位。这些单位的固定资产投资计划由国务院各部门直接编制和下达，建设中所需物资、主要设备以及建设中的问题都由中央有关部门安排和解决。

（2）地方：是由省（自治区、直辖市）、地区（州、盟、省辖市）、县（旗、县级市）三级政府及业务主管部门直接领导和管理的建设项目、企业、事业、行政单位。地方项目还包括不隶属以上各级政府及主管部门的建设项目和企业、事业单位，如外商投资企业和无主管部门的企业等。

固定资产投资按建设性质分　根据整个建设项目情况来确定。建设项目的性质一般分为新建、扩建、改建和技术改造、迁建、恢复。房地产开发单位、农村投资、城镇工矿区私人建房投资不划分建设性质。

(1)新建：一般指从无到有“平地起家”开始建设的企业、事业和行政单位或建设项目。现有企业、事业、行政单位一般不属于新建。但如有的单位原有基础很小，经过建设后新增的固定资产价值超过该企、事业、行政单位原有固定资产价值(原值)三倍以上的也应作为新建。

(2)扩建：指在厂内或其他地点，为扩大原有产品的生产能力(或效益)或增加新的产品生产能力，而增建主要的生产车间(或主要工程)、分厂、独立的生产线。行政、事业单位在原单位增建业务用房(如学校增建教学用房、医院增建门诊部、病房等)也作为扩建。

现有企、事业单位为扩大原有主要产品生产能力或增加新的产品生产能力，增建一个或几个主要生产车间(或主要工程)、分厂，同时进行一些更新改造工程的，也应作为扩建。

(3)改建和技术改造：指现有企业、事业单位，对原有设施进行技术改造或更新(包括相应配套的辅助性生产、生活福利设施) 的建设项目。现有企业、事业单位为适应市场变化的需要，而改变企业的主要产品种类(如军工企业转产民用品等) 的建设项目，应作为改建。原有产品生产作业线由于各工序(车间)之间能力不平衡，为填平补齐充分发挥原有生产能力而增建不增加本企业主要产品设计能力的车间，也应作为改建。技术改造是指企业、事业单位在现有基础上，用先进的技术代替落后的技术，用先进的工艺和装备代替落后的工艺和装备，以改变企业落后的技术经济面貌，实现以内涵为主的扩大再生产，达到提高产品质量、促进产品更新换代、节约能源、降低消耗、扩大生产规模、全面提高社会经济效益的目的。技术改造具体包括以下内容：机器设备和工具的更新改造；生产工艺改革、节约能源和原材料的改造；厂房建筑和公共设施的改造；劳动条件和生产环境的改造等。

固定资产投资按构成分　固定资产投资活动按其工作内容和实现方式分为建筑安装工程，设备、工具、器具购置，其他费用三个部分。

(1)建筑安装工程(建筑安装工作量)：指各种房屋、建筑物的建造工程和各种设备、装置的安装工程。包括各种房屋建造工程；各种用途设备基础和各种工业窑炉的砌筑工程及金属结构工程；为施工而进行的各种准备工作和临时工程以及完工后的清理工作等；铁路、道路的铺设，矿井的开凿及石油管道的架设等；水利工程；防空地下建筑等特殊工程；列入房屋工程预算内的暖气、卫生、通风、照明、煤气等设备的价值及装设油饰工程；列入建筑工程预算内的各种管道(蒸汽、压缩空气、石油、给排水等管道)、电力、电讯电缆导线等的敷设工程；以及各种机械设备的安装工程；为测定安装工程质量，对设备进行的试运工作；房地产开发单位进行的商品房屋开发建设工程、土地开发工程。

在安装工程中，不包括被安装设备本身的价值。

(2)设备、工具、器具购置：指建设单位或企、事业单位购置或自制的，达到固定资产标准的设备、工具、器具的价值。新建单位及扩建单位的新建车间，按照设计或计划要求购置或自制的全部设备、工具、器具，不论是否达到固定资产标准均计入“设备、工具、器具购置”中。

(3)其他费用：指在固定资产建造和购置过程中发生的，除上述几项内容以外的各种应分摊计入固定资产的费用。

施工项目　指报告期内进行过建筑或安装施工活动的项目。凡是报告期内施过工的建设项目，不论施工时间长短，均作为施工项目统计。施工项目个数可以反映一定时期固定资产投资的实际规模，与同期全部建成投产项目个数相比，可以从建设速度的角度反映固定资产投资的效果。根据建设项目施工活动的不同性质，施工项目又分为：本年正式施工项目、本年收尾项目和以前年度全部停缓建项目。

全部建成投产项目　工业项目指设计文件规定形成生产能力的主体工程及其相应配套的辅助设施全部建成，经负荷试运转，证明具备生产设计规定合格产品的条件，并经过验收鉴定合格或达到竣工验收标准，与生产性工程配套的生活福利设施可以满足近期正常生产的需要，正式移交生产的建设项目。非工业项目指设计文件规定的主体工程和相应的配套工程全部建成，能够发挥设计规定的全部效益，经验收鉴定合格或达到竣工验收标准，正式移交使用的建设项目。

新增生产能力(或工程效益)　指通过固定资产投资活动而增加的设计能力(或工程效益)，该指标是以实物形态表现的反映固定资产投资成果的指标，也是考核投资经济效果的重要依据之一。

房屋建筑面积　指房屋建筑物勒脚以上外墙外围的水平截面面积，包括房屋建筑物的有效面积和结构面积。该指标是从实物形态上反映建设规模和建设成果的重要指标之一，也是检查工程形象进度、计算工程造价、分析投资效果、研究施工任务和建筑材料之间平衡情况的重要依据。

住宅建筑面积　指施工和竣工房屋建筑面积中供居住用的房屋建筑面积。

施工面积　指报告期内施工的全部房屋建筑面积。包括本期新开工的面积和上期开工跨入本期继续施工的房屋面积，以及上期已停建在本期恢复施工的房屋面积。本期竣工和本期施工后又停缓建的房屋，其建筑面积仍计入本期房屋施工面积中。

竣工面积　指在报告期内房屋建筑按照设计要求已经全部完工，达到住人和使用条件，经验收鉴定合格(或达到竣工验收标准)，正式移交使用单位的各栋房屋建筑面积的总和。

房屋建筑面积竣工率　指一定时期内房屋竣工面积占同期房屋施工面积的比率。是从房屋建筑施工速度的角度反映投资效果的指标。

新增固定资产　指报告期内已经完成建造和购置过程，并已交付生产或使用单位的固定资产价值。该指标是表示固定资产投资成果的价值指标，也是反映建设进度，计算固定资产投资效果的重要指标。

项目建设投产率　指一定时期内全部建成投产项目个数与同期施工项目个数的比率。该指标是从建设单位建设速度的角度反映投资效果的指标。

固定资产交付使用率　指一定时期新增固定资产与同期完成投资额的比率。该指标是反映固定资产动用速度，衡量建设过程中宏观投资效果的综合指标。由于新增固定资产是较长时期内形成的结果，而投资额则是当年完成的，因此，该指标一般适宜于反映较长时期内固定资产的动用情况。

商品房销售面积　指报告期内出售商品房屋的合同总面积(即双方签署的正式买卖合同中所确定的建筑面积)。由现房销售建筑面积和期房销售建筑面积两部分组成。

商品房销售额　指报告期内出售商品房屋的合同总价款(即双方签署的正式买卖合同中所确定的合同总价)。该指标与商品房销售面积同口径，由现房销售额和期房销售额两部分组成。

经济适用房　指根据地方经济适用房计划安排建设的政策性住宅。经济是指房屋建筑造价和销售价格低于一般商品住宅；适用是指适合中低收入家庭购买使用。经济适用房主要是由国家统一下达投资计划，房地产公司开发，对外销售；用地一般采用行政划拨或招标投标方式，免收土地出让金；对各种经批准的收费减半征收，开发利润不超过 3%；销售价格实行政府指导价。该指标可以分析房地产投资结构，反映中低收入家庭商品住宅的供求平衡情况。

Explanatory Notes on Main Statistical Indicators

Total Investment in Fixed Assets in the Whole Country refers to the volume of activities in construction and purchases of fixed assets and related fees, expressed in monetary terms. It is a comprehensive indicator which shows the size, structure and growth of the investment in fixed assets, providing basis for observing the progress of construction projects and evaluating results of investment. Total investment in fixed assets in the whole country includes, by type of ownership, the investment by the state-owned units, collective units, individuals, joint ownership units, share-holding units, as well as investment by businessmen from foreign countries and from Hong Kong, Macao and Taiwan, and by other units.

Investment in Fixed Assets refers to construction projects involving a total planned investment of 500,000 yuan and over by enterprises and institutions of various types of ownership, by administrative units and by individuals, investment in real estate development, and housing investment by individuals in urban areas and in industrial and mining areas.

Investment in Real Estate Development refers to the investment by the real estate development companies, commercial buildings construction companies and other real estate development units of various types of ownership in the construction of house buildings, such as residential buildings, factory buildings, warehouses, hotels, guesthouses, holiday villages, office buildings, and the complementary service facilities and land development projects, such as roads, water supply, water drainage, power supply, heating, telecommunications, land leveling and other projects of infrastructure. It excludes the activities in pure land transactions.

Investment in Housing Construction in Urban Areas and in Industrial and Mining Areas refers to all private housing construction under the jurisdiction of cities, county towns and industrial and mining areas, no matter whether the owner of the house is registered as the permanent resident in the locality or not.

Investment in Rural Areas refers to investment in fixed assets by enterprises, institutions and individuals in rural areas.

Sources of Funds for Investment in Fixed Assets include fund from state budget, domestic loans, foreign investment, self-raised funds, and others depending on the source of investment.

(1) Fund from state budget consists of budgetary appropriation and loans from state budget. More specifically, it includes, from the budget of the central government, capital construction fund (operation fund and non-operational fund), special expenses (e.g. expenses on substituting petroleum with coal), loans from repayment, discount fund, expenses on innovation and trial production of new products, expenses on urban construction, expenses on temporary construction by trade departments, development fund for less developed areas, as well as local budgetary fund transferred from the central budget.

(2) Domestic loans refer to loans of various forms borrowed by investing units from banks and non-bank financial institutions during the reference period for the purpose of investment in fixed assets, including loans issued by banks from their self-owned funds and deposit, loans appropriated by higher responsible authorities, special loans by government (including loan for substituting petroleum with coal, special loan for reform-through-labour coal mines), loans arranged by local government from special funds, domestic reserve loan, and working loan, etc..

(3) Foreign Investment refers to foreign funds received during the reference period for the construction and purchase of investment in fixed assets (covering equipment, materials and technology), including foreign borrowings (loans from foreign governments and international financial institutions, export credit, commercial loans from foreign banks, issue of bonds and stocks overseas), foreign direct investment and other foreign investment. Excluded in this category are capitals in foreign exchanges owned by China (foreign exchanges owned by the central and local governments, foreign exchanges retained by enterprises, foreign exchanges by enterprises through regulating mechanism, loans in foreign exchanges issued by the Bank of China with its own fund, etc.). In calculating the utilization of foreign capitals, foreign currencies are converted into Chinese Renminbi applying the current exchange rate when the foreign capitals are actually used.

(4) Self-raised funds refer to extra-budgetary funds for investment in fixed assets received by investing units from central government ministries, local governments, enterprises and institutions, including their self-raised funds.

(5) Others refer to funds for investment in fixed assets received from the sources other than those listed above, including capitals raised through issuing bonds by enterprises or financial institutions, funds raised from individuals and through donations, and funds transferred from other units.

Investment in Fixed Assets by Sector The classification of construction projects by sector is determined by the major products or the purpose of the projects when they are put into production or use, and by the nature of their social economic activities. In general, one project or one enterprise or institution can only be classified into one sector.

Investment in Fixed Assets by Jurisdiction of Management refers to the classification of investment by the competent authorities under which investment is made by construction units, enterprises, institutions or administrative units.

(1) Central investment refers to the investment in projects or by enterprises, institutions or administrative units which are under the direct leadership and management of the CPC Central Committee, the NPC Standing Committee, the State Council and of the national commissions, ministries, agencies and state-owned large corporations. Various ministries and departments of the State Council prepare and implement plans for investment in fixed assets by those departments, and arrange and ensure the supply of materials and key equipment required for the projects.

(2) Local investment refers to the investment in projects or by enterprises, institutions or administrative units which are under the direct leadership and management of departments under the provincial, prefecture and county governments. Also included are projects

by foreign-invested enterprises and enterprises without competent managing authorities.

Investment in Fixed Assets by Type of Construction The construction projects in general can be classified, by the type of construction, into new construction, expansion, reconstruction and technical transformation, moving and restoration. However, investment by type of construction is not applied to investment by real-estate development units, investment in rural areas and investment in housing by urban individuals.

(1) New construction in general refers to newly constructed enterprises, institutions, administrative agencies or independent projects from scratch. Construction in the existing enterprises, institutions or agencies is not considered as new construction. In case the assets of the existing unit is quite small, and the value of newly added fixed assets exceeds the original value of assets by three times, the expansion will be considered as new construction.

(2) Expansion refers to construction of new major production workshop, branch factory or independent production line within a factory or in other locations, for the purpose of increasing the production capacity (or improving efficiency) of the original products. Newly constructed houses for the operation of institutions and administrative organizations (such as the newly constructed buildings for teaching in schools, buildings for clinics or wards in hospitals, etc.) are also classified as expansion.

Also included in the expansion are investments by existing enterprises or institutions in building major production line(s) or branch factory(ies) along with some work on innovation, for the purpose of expending the production capacity of original products or producing new products.

(3) Reconstruction refers to construction projects by existing enterprises or institutions in innovation or technical transformation of the old facilities (including auxiliary production equipment and welfare facilities). Also considered as reconstruction is the construction of new workshops by the existing enterprises or institutions to change the variety of products to meet the market demand (such as the production of civil products by defence industries), or to bring the designed production capacity into full play through a more balanced production process on production lines. Technical transformation refers to replacement of old technology or equipment by new technology or equipment, in order to expand the reproduction through improvement of technology contents in production, to improve product quality, to promote new products, to save energy and reduce consumption and to improve overall social-economic efficiency. Contents of technical transformation include: updating of machinery, equipment and tools; reforming production process by using energy or materials saving technology; construction of factory workshops and transformation of public facilities; improvement of working conditions and environment, etc.

Investment in Fixed Assets by Structure By their contents, investment activities are classified into 3 categories, i.e. construction and installation, purchase of equipment and instrument, and other expenses.

(1) Construction and installation (work volume of construction and installation) refers to the construction of various houses and buildings and installation of various kinds of equipment and instruments. They include construction of various houses; equipment foundations, industrial kilns and stoves, and metal structure work; preparation works for project construction, and clearing up works post project construction; pavement of railways and roads, drilling of mines and putting up of oil pipes; construction of projects of water conservancy; construction of underground air-raid shelters and construction of other special projects; value of equipment for heating, sanitation, ventilation, lighting, gas, painting, etc. that are covered by the budget of housing projects; laying out of various pipelines (for steam, compressed air, petroleum, tap water and sewage) and lines for electric power and for communications; installation of various machinery equipment, testing operation for pre-testing the quality of installation projects, and land and other development work conducted by real estate developers for commercial housing. The value of equipment installed is not included in the value of installation projects.

(2) Purchase of equipment and instruments refers to the total value of equipment, tools, and instruments purchased or self-produced which come up to standards for fixed assets by the construction units or investing enterprises or institutions. Equipment, tools and instruments purchased or self-produced for new workshops by newly established or expanded units are categorized as "purchase of equipment and instruments" no matter whether they come up to the standards for fixed assets.

(3) Other expenses refer to expenses occurring during the construction or purchase of fixed assets other than those mentioned above.

Projects under Construction refer to projects with construction and installation activities undertaken in the reference period. All projects that have construction activities undertaken during the reference period are reported as projects under construction irrespective of the length of construction work. The number of projects under construction can reflect the actual size of investment in fixed assets during a given period, and when compared with the number of projects completed and put into use during the same period, it demonstrates the results of investment in fixed assets. Depending on the nature of construction activities, projects under construction can also be classified into projects under construction in current year, winding-up projects in current year and stopped or suspended projects in previous years (with preservation work in current year).

Projects Completed and Put into Use Industrial projects refer to the major projects and accessory facilities completed which result in forming production capacity and have been checked and accepted while the living and welfare facilities have been completed and can ensure normal production and formally put into production. Non-industrial projects refer to the major projects and accessory facilities completed which possess the designed capacity and have been checked, accepted and formally put into production.

Newly Increased Production Capacity (or Project Efficiency) refers to the increase of designed capacity (or project efficiency) through investment in fixed assets, which reflects the accomplishment of investment in fixed assets in kind and serves as important basis for evaluating the economic efficiency of investment.

Floor Space of Buildings under Construction refers to total floor space of the horizontal section of outer walls above the plinth of the building, including the effective area and the area occupied by the structure. This indicator is one of the important indicators in physical terms to reflect the scale and accomplishment of the construction industry, and important basis for monitoring the progress, calculating the cost, analyzing the efficiency and studying the supply of building materials in relation with the construction projects.

Floor Space of Residential Buildings refers to the floor space of the residential buildings among the total space of buildings under construction or completed.

Floor Space under Construction refers to total floor space of all buildings under construction during the reference period, including floor space of newly started buildings during the reference period, floor space of construction extended from the previous period to the current period, and floor space of construction suspended during the previous period and resumed in the current period. Floor space of construction completed in the current period, and floor space of construction started and then suspended in the current period are also included in the floor space under construction of the current year.

Floor Space of Buildings Completed refers to the floor space of all buildings completed in the reference period, which have been appraised and accepted (or come up to the designed standards) and have been transferred to the owners for use.

Completion Rate of Floor Space of Buildings refers to the ratio of the floor space of buildings completed in certain period of time to the floor space of buildings under construction in the same period. This indicator reflects the investment result from the perspective of the speed of construction.

Newly Increased Fixed Assets refer to the newly increased value of fixed assets, constructed or purchased, that have been transferred to the investors. This is an indicator that demonstrates the results of investment in fixed assets in monetary terms, and an important indicator to reflect the speed of construction and to calculate the efficiency of investment.

Rate of Construction Projects Completed and Put into Use refers to the ratio of the number of construction projects completed and put into use in certain period of time to the number of projects under construction in the same period. This reflects the investment efficiency from the perspective of the speed of projects construction.

Rate of Projects of Fixed Assets Completed and Put into Operation refers to the ratio of the newly increased fixed assets to the total investment made in the same period. This is a comprehensive indicator reflecting the speed of the employment of fixed assets and the investment efficiency at the macro-level. As the newly increase fixed assets is the result of a long period while the investment is completed in the current year, this indicator is expected to be used to reflect the employment of fixed assets over a long period of time.

Area of Commercial Housing Sold refers to total contracted area of commercial housing (i.e. area of floor space as designated in the formal contracts signed by both sides) during the reference time. It constitutes floor space of completed housing and floor space of future housing.

Value of Commercial Housing Sold refer to total value of contracts (i.e. value of sales/purchase for selling/purchase of commercial housing as designated in the contracts signed by both sides) during the reference time. It has the same coverage as the area of commercial housing sold, constituting completed housing and floor space of future housing

Economically Affordable Housing refers to housing constructed according to the state plan for economically affordable housing. Houses of this category featured in low cost in construction and low prices, and therefore are affordable to mid-income or low income households. Economically affordable housing projects are developed by real estate companies under the state investment plan, with the land provided through government allocation or tendering procedures. Developers are exempted from land utilization fees and enjoy another 50% exemption of all other legitimate fees, while their profits are limited to less than 3%, and the completed houses are sold under the government-guided prices. This indicator helps to analyze the investment structure of the real estate industry and the demand and supply of housing for mid or low income households.

5 对外经济贸易和旅游

Foreign Economic, Trade and Tourism

资料整理：陈彬彬

5-1 对外经济主要指标

MAJOR INDICATORS OF FOREIGN TRADE AND ECONOMIC COOPERATION

单位：万美元 (USD 10 000)

指　标	Item	1995	2000	2005	2009	2010	2011	2012	2013	2014
进出口总额	**Total Imports and Exports**	**340920**	**320249**	**905475**	**1725102**	**2593211**	**3358693**	**3196409**	**3638928**	**4306401**
进口总额	Total Imports	142484	127369	462607	727222	1149031	1405233	1256525	1355160	1641821
出口总额	Total Exports	198435	192880	442868	997880	1444180	1953460	1939884	2283768	2664580
合同外商直接投资项目(个)	**Contracted Projets of Foreign Direct Investment (uint)**	**881**	**331**	**520**	**268**	**306**	**339**	**271**	**297**	**301**
合同外商直接投资	**Contracted Value of Foreign Direct Investment**	**108847**	**106583**	**211023**	**204916**	**278627**	**497130**	**363927**	**485467**	**629624**
实际外商直接投资	**Actual Value of Foreign Direct Investment**	**62253**	**94368**	**218475**	**365766**	**405015**	**465503**	**566591**	**688847**	**792792**
对外经济合作	**Economic and Technical Cooperation with Foreign Countries**									
合同金额	Contracted Value	7300	36706	35953	532879	776945	639273	737945	1033540	
#对外承包工程	#Contracted Projects			27952	526671	765547	631308	726900	1015084	1269954
对外劳务合作	Labor Services			5568	6208	11398	7965	11045	12286	
完成营业额	Value of Business Fulfilled	4100	15815	31843	263356	327164	415002	465863	538927	
#对外承包工程	#Contracted Projects			28852	256368	319979	406741	456194	520733	579636
对外劳务合作	Labor Services			2601	6988	7186	8261	9669	18194	

5-2 对外贸易进出口总额

TOTAL IMPORTS AND EXPORTS

单位：万美元 (USD 10 000)

年　份 Year	合　计 Total	进　口 Imports	出　口 Exports
1991	152188	39185	113003
1992	174533	58696	115837
1993	222912	100170	122743
1994	274880	103035	171845
1995	340920	142484	198435
1996	286287	133684	152603
1997	320668	128583	192084
1998	283189	112478	170711
1999	268107	116729	151378
2000	320249	127369	192880
2001	357720	178041	179679
2002	395314	185488	209826
2003	510930	245393	265537
2004	676581	338361	338219
2005	905475	462607	442868
2006	1176219	550157	626063
2007	1489647	669593	820054
2008	2070567	899676	1170891
2009	1725102	727222	997880
2010	2593211	1149031	1444180
2011	3358693	1405233	1953460
2012	3196409	1256525	1939884
2013	3638928	1355160	2283768
2014	4306401	1641821	2664580

注：根据海关统计有关文件规定2008年年终数据部分调整。

Note:According to the provisions of the relevant documents to customs statistics data portion of the 2008 year-end adjustments.

5-3 按贸易方式和经济类型分的进出口总额

单位：万美元

项 目	Item	2000		2005	
		进 口 Imports	出 口 Exports	进 口 Imports	出 口 Exports
总 计	**Total**	**127369**	**192880**	**462607**	**442868**
按贸易方式分	**Grouped by Type of Trade**				
一般贸易	General Trade	91576	138907	340768	350354
来料加工装配贸易	Processing and Assembling Trade	20136	13265	15428	22381
进料加工贸易	Raw Material Input Processing Trade	32803	14154	54328	71920
来料加工装配进口的设备	Processing and Assembling Import Equipment Provided With Material	6		18	
外商作为投资进口的设备	Goods as Invested for Import Equipments	8602		45087	
租赁贸易	Leasing Trade			114	
出料加工贸易	Raw Material Output Processing Trade				
易货贸易	Repalce Goods with Goods				
保税仓库进出境货物	Import and Export Goods of Protcetive Tariff Storage	105		8028	33
按经济类型分	**Grouped by Ownership**				
#国有企业	#State-Owned Enterprises	64805	140826	221963	213955
集体企业	Collective-Owned Enterprises	1255	9124	5719	20033
外商投资企业	Foreign-funded Enterprises	61691	42901	190170	130579
民营企业	Private-Owned Enterprises	111	240	45839	80397

(USD 10 000)

2010		2011		2012		2013		2014	
进 口 Imports	出 口 Exports	进 口 Imports	出 口 Exports	进 口 Imports	出 口 Exports	进 口 Imports	出 口 Exports	进 口 Imports	出 口 Exports
1149031	**1444180**	**1405233**	**1953460**	**1256525**	**1939884**	**1355160**	**2283768**	**1641821**	**2664580**
841306	829994	1029457	1104728	947733	1152839	1000601	1520152	1164862	1845637
28304	32269	27162	39859	21218	39039	18128	38854	14331	54818
210483	518911	261048	687508	208043	622969	281413	593316	430709	704313
348		37				230		38	
43809		42713		24772		13487		12775	
5	144	5		7	92	5	150	96	70
320	212	568	319	187	322	729	532	822	729
20511	16794	33697	29981	50275	41619	32427	38794	9389	17789
513134	472230	633360	618532	500014	540497	452200	527257	481941	545399
4021	16161	4729	18140	3802	18511	2427	19933	1746	19684
534565	569501	647416	760098	618044	762022	665555	732420	682190	772107
93032	386177	108581	556609	130133	618934	190004	1002635	455332	1326652

5-4 进出口商品主要国别和地区

IMPORTS AND EXPORTS VALUE BY COUNTRIES AND REGIONS

单位：万美元 (USD 10 000)

国家(地区)	Countries (Regions)	2013			2014		
		进出口 Imports and Exports	进口 Imports	出口 Exports	进出口 Imports and Exports	进口 Imports	出口 Exports
亚 洲	**Asia**	**1712629**	**577203**	**1135426**	**2230534**	**838644**	**1391889**
#香港	#Hongkong	253776	36060	217716	430030	92164	337866
印度	India	125416	10559	114858	126569	11965	114604
日本	Japan	252613	165265	87348	291864	187856	104008
新加坡	Singapore	78360	17076	61283	105161	25775	79385
韩国	Korea, Rep.	130304	65879	64425	182928	95983	86945
台湾省	Taiwan Province	98249	67967	30282	184491	134034	50457
非 洲	**Afria**	**184190**	**81650**	**102540**	**208550**	**82662**	**125888**
#南非	#South Africa	68052	53971	14082			
欧 洲	**European**	**719755**	**254663**	**465092**	**826684**	**290948**	**535737**
#比利时	#Belgium	33141	11789	21352			
英国	United Kingdom	64776	11375	53401			
德国	Germany	124615	60687	63927	138948	74270	64678
法国	France	121266	98233	23033	132127	109297	22830
意大利	Italy	43530	15861	27669			
荷兰	Netherland	53581	7260	46321			
西班牙	Spanish	26658	6045	20613			
芬兰	Finland	6655	3862	2792			
拉丁美洲	**Latin America**	**333673**	**116670**	**217003**	**326200**	**102367**	**223833**
#巴西	#Brazil	63730	25784	37946	65939	28862	37077
智利	Chile	54384	36128	18256			
北美洲	**North America**	**454298**	**150429**	**303870**	**489994**	**154774**	**335219**
#加拿大	#Canada	79062	62226	16836	76071	57561	18509
美国	United States of America	375226	88202	287024	413902	97213	316690
大洋洲	**Oceania**	**234351**	**174491**	**59861**	**224404**	**177526**	**52014**
#澳大利亚	#Australia	213046	173897	39149	214661	172128	42533
附：东南亚国家联盟	**Association of Southeast-Asia Nations**	**533251**	**123524**	**409727**	**598448**	**177526**	**420922**
欧洲联盟	**European Union**	**638111**	**242190**	**395921**	**70972**	**275711**	**434002**
亚太经济合作组织	**Asia-Pacific Economic Cooperation**	**2258220**	**954830**	**1303390**	**2715725**	**1146844**	**1568881**

5-5　合同外商直接投资项目

NUMBER OF CONTRACTED PROJECTS OF FOREIGN DIRECT INVESTMENT

单位：个　　(unit)

指　标	Item	1990	1995	2000	2005	2009	2010	2011	2012	2013	2014
合　计	**Total**	**99**	**881**	**331**	**520**	**268**	**306**	**339**	**271**	**297**	**301**
合资经营企业	Joint Venture	17	577	156	203	86	108	138	102	116	127
合作经营企业	Cooperative Operation	75	44	16	29	16	5	8	5	8	3
独资经营企业	Foreign Solely Funded Enterprises	7	260	158	285	165	193	193	164	173	169
外商投资股份制企业	Share Holding Enterprises With Foreign Investment			1	3	1					2

5-6　合同外商直接投资金额

VALUE OF CONTRACTED PROJECTS OF FOREIGN DIRECT INVESTMENT

单位：万美元　　(USD 10 000)

指　标	Item	1990	1995	2000	2005	2009	2010	2011	2012	2013	2014
合　计	**Total**	**3947**	**108847**	**106583**	**211023**	**204916**	**278627**	**497130**	**363927**	**485467**	**629624**
合资经营企业	Joint Venture	1364	68923	27936	51010	122227	132679	253542	93573	135618	262121
合作经营企业	Cooperative Operation	2464	7899	48711	24480	21117	3319	11217	7315	15924	13424
独资经营企业	Foreign Solely Funded	119	32025	29936	132897	198474	235498	224344	252964	334151	345271
外商投资股份制企业	Share Holding Enterprises With Foreign Investment				2636	23948	33519	8027	10075	-226	8808

5-7 实际外商直接投资金额

ACTUAL VALUE OF FOREIGN DIRECT INVESTMENT

单位：万美元 (USD 10 000)

指 标	Item	1990	1995	2000	2003	2004	2005
合 计	**Total**	**2900**	**62253**	**94368**	**155702**	**207126**	**218475**
合资经营企业	Joint Venture	2492	40259	59879	104622	130048	65472
合作经营企业	Cooperative Operation	85	5012	2789	5513	11741	5089
独资经营企业	Foreign Solely Funded	323	16982	31700	45139	62155	75305
外商投资股份制企业	Share Holding With Foreign Investment						2739

5-7 续表 continued

单位：万美元 (USD 10 000)

指 标	Item	2007	2008	2009	2010	2011	2012	2013	2014
合 计	**Total**	**276622**	**324481**	**365766**	**405015**	**465503**	**566591**	**688847**	**792792**
合资经营企业	Joint Venture	43946	101474	122227	132679	202268	257765	223950	300982
合作经营企业	Cooperative Operation	6077	16665	21117	3319	2992	647	3758	759
独资经营企业	Foreign Solely Funded	81762	180960	198474	235498	231847	298393	442107	440949
外商投资股份制企业	Share Holding Enterprises With Foreign Investment	1650	25382	23948	33519	28396	9786	19032	35969

5–8 按行业分外商直接投资(2014)
FOREIGN DIRECT INVESTMENT GROUPED BY SECTOR (2014)

行 业	Item	项目(个) Number of Projects (unit)	合同外资 (万美元) Contracted Foreign Capital (USD 10 000)	实际投资 (万美元) Actual Foreign Investment (USD 10 000)
总 计	**Total**	**301**	**629624**	**792792**
农、林、牧、渔业	Farming, Forestry, Animal Husbandry and Fishery	19	41607	21082
采矿业	Mining and Quarrying		-1379	543
制造业	Manufactruring	122	312971	400108
电力、燃气及水的生产和供应业	Power, Gas and Water Production and Supply	8	23561	62877
建筑业	Construction	3	18374	598
交通运输、仓储和邮政业	Transportation, Storage and Post	7	23542	15475
信息传输、计算机服务和软件业	Information Transmmision, Computer Service and software	6	698	12081
批发和零售业	Wholesale and Retail sale	49	29071	43910
住宿和餐饮业	Hotel and Catering	8	3373	1650
金融业	Finance	3	3425	11250
房地产业	Real Estate	12	124539	182052
租赁和商务服务业	Leasing and Commerical Service	29	23227	19117
科学研究、技术服务和地质勘查业	Scietific research, Polytechnical Service and Geological Prospecting	26	8277	5571
水利、环境和公共设施管理业	Water Conservancy, Environment and Public Facility Management	1	6341	11295
居民服务和其他服务业	Resident Service and Others	3	5302	2449
教育	Education	2	9	
卫生、社会保障和社会福利业	Health Care, Social Security and Social Welfare	1	6080	
文化、体育和娱乐业	Culture, Sports and Recreation	2	606	2734

5–9 年末登记外商投资企业行业分布情况(2014)
SECTOR DISTRIBUTION REGISTERED OF FOREIGN-FUNDED ENTERPRISES AT THE YEAR-END(2014)

单位：个 (unit)

行 业	Item	企业数 Number of Enterprises
总 计	**Total**	**301**
农、林、牧、渔业	Farming, Forestry, Animal Husbandry and Fishery	19
采矿业	Mining and Quarrying	
制造业	Manufactruring	122
电力、燃气及水的生产和供应业	Power, Gas and Water Production and Supply	8
建筑业	Construction	3
交通运输、仓储和邮政业	Transportation, Storage and Post	7
信息传输、计算机服务和软件业	Information Transmmision, Computer Service and software	6
批发和零售业	Wholesale and Retail sale	49
住宿和餐饮业	Hotel and Catering	8
金融业	Finance	3
房地产业	Real Estate	12
租赁和商务服务业	Leasing and Commerical Service	29
科学研究、技术服务和地质勘查业	Scietific research, Polytechnical Service and Geological Prospecting	26
水利、环境和公共设施管理业	Water Conservancy, Environment and Public Facility Management	1
居民服务和其他服务业	Resident Service and Others	3
教育	Education	2
卫生、社会保障和社会福利业	Health Care, Social Security and Social Welfare	1
文化、体育和娱乐业	Culture, Sports and Recreation	2

5−10 对外承包工程和劳务合作

CONTRACTED PROJECTS AND LABOR SERVICES CO-OPERATION WITH FOREIGN COUNTRIES

年 份 Year		合同金额 (万美元) Contracted Value (USD 10 000)	实际完成营业额 (万美元) Value of Business Fulfilled (USD 10 000)	年末在外人数(人) Number of Persons Working Abroad at Year-end (person)
1997		18100	6800	4338
1998		17400	9500	4933
1999		18100	12200	5718
2000		36706	15815	6584
2001		12019	14653	7058
2002		29469	15863	7102
2003		29882	20333	4923
2004		31141	27384	5854
2005		35953	31843	7599
2006		63704	41097	10363
2007		195692	62267	15115
2008		331419	152116	15406
2009		532879	263356	15148
2010		776945	327164	22372
2011		639273	415002	17386
2012		737945	465863	24662
2013		1033540	538927	29097
2014				
对外承包工程	**Contracted Projects**			
2003		17900	28552	1759
2004		28027	25334	2199
2005		27952	28852	2365
2006		56930	36266	2671
2007		183749	54416	5950
2008		318872	142456	9145
2009		526671	256368	10546
2010		765547	319978	17655
2011		631308	406741	13961
2012		726900	456194	16404
2013		1021254	520733	20801
2014		1269954	579636	
对外劳务合作	**Labor Cooperation**			
2003		823	1783	3136
2004		1565	1597	3583
2005		5568	2601	5143
2006		6331	4379	7602
2007		6520	5340	8704
2008		6016	6856	6239
2009		6208	6988	4602
2010		11398	7186	4717
2011		7965	8261	3425
2012		11045	9669	8258
2013		12286	18194	8296
2014				
对外设计咨询	**Design Consulting**			
2002		541	267	42
2003		507	650	28
2004		475	1517	72
2005		390	2433	91
2006		983	452	90
2007		5423	2511	461
2008		6531	2804	22

注:2009年起“对外设计咨询”指标数并入“对外承包工程”中;“年末在外人数(人)”修订为“劳务外派人数(人)”

Note:From 2009, "design and consultation," index number into the "International Contractors" in; "at the end of outer (person)" to "manning (person)".

5−11 湖北旅游主要指标
MAJOR INDICATORS OF HUBEI TOURISM

年 份 Year	旅游总收入 (亿元) Total Earnings of Tourism (100 million yuan)	国内旅游收入 (亿元) Earnings from Domestic Tourism (100 million yuan)	国内旅游人数 (万人次) Number of Domestic Tourists (10 000 persons-time)	外汇收入 (万美元) Foreign Exchange Earnings (USD 10 000)	入境旅游人数 (万人次) Number of Tourists Received (10 000 persons-time)
1982				299.60	2.00
1983				355.30	2.40
1984				731.30	5.40
1985				1008.60	8.50
1986	3.47	2.50	1262	1166.00	10.50
1987	3.67	2.40	1184	1545.00	12.20
1988	3.56	2.40	1208	1411.80	11.30
1989	3.99	3.10	1034	1085.50	8.20
1990	4.56	2.70	890	2263.20	15.60
1991	5.83	3.90	984	2350.00	17.00
1992	9.03	5.40	1071	4432.20	26.30
1993	13.26	9.50	1350	4588.90	23.10
1994	18.09	13.00	1500	6211.40	24.70
1995	24.00	18.00	1700	7316.90	27.10
1996	163.28	153.00	3152	12545.60	36.90
1997	193.92	180.00	3600	16977.50	58.00
1998	217.24	210.00	4044	8831.40	29.60
1999	247.11	238.50	4659	10498.50	30.50
2000	282.26	270.30	5478	14572.10	45.10
2001	353.66	337.20	6064	20075.20	66.80
2002	407.48	384.20	6670	28390.90	102.40
2003	342.77	331.60	5684	13626.90	40.50
2004	410.00	394.20	6849	19240.40	61.20
2005	473.15	450.80	7630	27636.30	82.60
2006	539.74	514.24	8459.78	32000.38	105.57
2007	640.87	609.40	10135.00	41264.00	131.81
2008	744.19	713.43	11678.00	44255.31	118.75
2009	1004.48	969.63	15065.18	51020.22	133.46
2010	1460.53	1409.48	20946.00	75116.49	181.74
2011	1992.89	1931.80	27154.87	94018.00	213.52
2012	2629.54	2553.55	34230.00	120296.72	264.72
2013	3205.61	3130.13	40621.04	121892.18	267.96
2014	3752.11	3675.98	46900.00	123851.30	277.07

5—12 接待入境旅游人数
NUMBER OF ENTRANCE TOURISTS

单位：人次 (person-times)

年 份 Year	总计 Total	外国人 Foreigners	港澳台同胞 Compatroits from Hongkong, Maco and Taiwan	#港澳同胞 #Compatroits from Hongkong, Macao	#台湾同胞 #Compatroits from Taiwan
1982	19775	15126	4649		
1983	24200	18903	5297		
1984	53800	40496	13304		
1985	84598	68103	16495		
1986	105300	83570	21730		
1987	122390	82029	40361		
1988	113051	78206	34845	19725	15120
1989	81781	49511	32270	13908	18362
1990	155734	36374	119360	11560	107800
1991	170121	53055	117066	12645	104421
1992	263401	72691	190323	14054	176269
1993	230883	84552	146331	28460	117871
1994	247212	133343	113869	56417	57452
1995	270890	172869	98021	42785	55236
1996	368877	243595	125282	58949	66333
1997	580223	359700	220523	64466	156057
1998	295643	209402	86241	30337	55904
1999	305408	224748	80660	30935	49725
2000	450805	357352	93453	42928	53162
2001	667818	542737	125081	48417	76664
2002	1024312	755718	268594	49113	219481
2003	405214	323151	82063	40294	41769
2004	611859	501873	109986	57086	52900
2005	825700	626805	198895	107141	91754
2006	1055752	857028	198724	110246	88478
2007	1318179	1077189	240990	140384	100606
2008	1187549	926625	260924	152631	108293
2009	1334634	1017620	317014	182616	134398
2010	1817416	1385457	431959	241430	190529
2011	2135247	1601129	534118	291487	242631
2012	2647163	1929571	717592	410921	306671
2013	2679623	2047316	632307	365184	267123
2014	2770689	2132562	638127	363810	274317

5−13 入境旅游外汇收入

FOREIGN EXCHANGE REVENUE OF ENTRANCE TOURISTS

年 份 Year	外汇收入(万美元) Foreign Exchange Earnings (USD 10 000)	发展指数(1978年为100) Development Index (year1978=100)	同比 Comparision Percentage (±%)	人均天花费(美元) Expenditures Per Capita (USD)	
				全国 The Whole Nation	湖北 Hubei
1982	299.64	129.85	82.00		
1983	355.30	153.98	18.58		
1984	731.30	316.92	105.83		
1985	1008.58	327.69	37.92		
1986	1166.00	505.31	15.61		
1987	1545.00	669.56	32.50		
1988	1411.75	611.81	-8.62		
1989	1085.45	470.40	-23.11		
1990	2263.18	980.79	108.50		
1991	2350.00	1018.42	3.84		
1992	4432.16	1920.76	88.60		
1993	4588.88	1988.68	3.54		
1994	6211.42	2691.84	35.36	125.10	125.10
1995	7316.86	3170.90	17.80	141.10	155.70
1996	12545.60	5436.88	71.46	131.16	167.04
1997	16977.51	7357.53	35.33	135.11	168.52
1998	8831.43	3827.27	-47.98	133.87	162.87
1999	10498.49	4549.72	18.88	135.00	166.31
2000	14572.13	6315.12	38.80	136.85	166.58
2001	20075.16	8699.96	37.76	138.76	164.25
2002	28390.95	12303.77	41.42	140.09	160.57
2003	13626.93	5905.50	-52.00	140.09	160.57
2004	19240.41	8338.21	51.00	156.84	169.92
2005	27636.30	11976.73	43.64	154.16	170.14
2006	32000.38	13867.99	15.79	164.29	177.16
2007	41264.00	17882.56	28.95	179.79	181.68
2008	44255.31	19178.90	7.25	186.18	197.56
2009	51020.22	22110.60	15.29	180.77	193.43
2010	75116.49	32553.20	47.23	184.01	192.84
2011	94018.00	40744.53	25.16	195.38	195.36
2012	120296.72	52132.92	27.95	195.53	193.04
2013	121892.18	52824.35	1.33	200.17	194.44
2014	123851.30	53675.70	1.61		

5-14 接待入境旅游者天数
NUMBER OF DAYS THE ENTRANCE TOURISTS STAYED IN HUBEI

单位：人天 (person/day)

年 份 Year	总计 Total	外国人 Foreigners	港澳台同胞 Compatroits from Hongkong, Maco and Taiwan	#港澳同胞 #Compatroits from Hongkong, Macao	#台湾同胞 #Compatroits from Taiwan
1981	22946	15282	7664		
1982	29016	24188	4828		
1983	29830	25298	4532		
1984	107600	37806	69794		
1985	143815	115774	28041		
1986	186379	139677	46702		
1987	167035	115219	51816		
1988	190486	132301	58185	35505	22680
1989	127891	79217	48674	20862	27812
1990	178737	49487	129250	11960	117290
1991	235595	74913	160682	17450	143232
1992	351591	101878	249713	18973	230740
1993	324350	142240	182110	49959	132151
1994	472467	231716	240751	117889	122862
1995	501038	317246	183792	86910	96882
1996	729968	477152	252816	131993	120823
1997	949661	591127	358534	111291	247243
1998	513569	366348	147221	61491	85730
1999	622037	478486	143551	57765	85786
2000	852455	676130	176325	81432	94893
2001	1208938	891787	317151	93376	223775
2002	1712230	1232818	479412	86427	392985
2003	799824	603001	196823	98230	98593
2004	1069442	849071	220371	118234	102137
2005	1513678	1135995	377683	194122	183561
2006	1824387	1502277	322110	176901	145209
2007	2342786	1926484	416302	233946	182356
2008	2217172	1734211	482961	243638	239323
2009	2640362	2025972	614390	338898	275492
2010	3750746	2868024	882722	481484	401238
2011	4596252	3494098	1102154	581193	520961
2012	5934359	4424239	1510060	822210	687850
2013	6009111	4581165	1427946	802642	625304
2014	6370867	4926991	1443876	805502	638374

注：2000年国家不再设“华侨”指标，“华侨”人数含在“外国人”中。
Note:The item of "overseas Chinese" is cancled by state since 2000, The number of "Overseas Chinese" is included in the number of "Foreigner".

5−15 湖北国内旅游接待人数及收入

TOATL NUMBER OF DOMESTIC TOURISTS AND EARNINGS FORM DOMESTIC TORUISM

年份 Year	接待人数(万人次) Number of Tourists Received (10 000person-times)	同比(±%) Comparision Percentage (±%)	旅游收入(亿元) Earnings (100 million yuan)	同比(±%) Comparision Percentage (±%)	人均天花费(元) Expenditures Per Capita a day (yuan) 全国 The Whole Nation	湖北 Hubei
1987	1184	-6.18	2.37	-6.0		
1988	1208	2.03	2.42	2.1		
1989	1034	-14.40	3.10	28.1		
1990	890	-13.92	2.67	-13.9		
1991	984	10.56	3.93	47.2		
1992	1071	8.84	5.36	36.4		
1993	1350	26.05	9.50	77.2		
1994	1500	11.11	13.00	36.8		
1995	1700	13.33	18.00	38.5		
1996	3152	85.41	152.95		256	485
1997	3600	14.21	180.00	17.7	328	500
1998	4044	12.33	210.03	16.7	344	519
1999	4659	15.21	238.50	13.6	394	511
2000	5478	17.58	270.31	13.3	427	493
2001	6064	10.70	337.18	24.7	450	556
2002	6670	9.99	384.24	14.0	441	576
2003	5684	-14.78	331.60	-13.7	395	583
2004	6849	20.50	394.22	18.9	550	576
2005	7630	11.40	450.76	14.3	436	591
2006	8460	10.88	514.24	14.1	447	607
2007	10135	19.80	609.40	18.5	482	601
2008	11678	15.2	713.43	17.1	511	610
2009	15065	29.0	969.63	35.9	535	644
2010	20946	39.0	1409.48	45.4	598	673
2011	27155	29.6	1931.80	37.1	731	711
2012	34230	26.1	2553.55	32.2	766	746
2013	40621	18.6	3130.13	22.6	806	771
2014	46900	15.5	3752.11	17.1		782

注：表中所列是人均花费(元)。

Note: The table is a list of per capita spending ($).

5-16 湖北旅游总收入及占全省GDP比重
THE RATIO OF TOTAL EARNINGS OF HUBEI TOURISM IN PROVINCIAL GDP

年 份 Year	旅游总收入 Total Earnings of Tourism		占GDP及第三产业比重 Percentage in GDP and Three Industries	
	绝对额(亿元) (100 million yuan)	同比(±%) Comparision Percentage (±%)	占GDP比重(%) GDP(%)	占第三产业增加值比重(%) Proportion of total added value of tertiary industry (%)
1997	193.92	18.8	5.6	18.0
1998	217.27	12.0	5.9	18.1
1999	247.11	13.7	6.4	18.8
2000	282.26	14.2	6.6	18.9
2001	353.64	24.9	7.6	21.4
2002	407.52	15.2	8.2	22.4
2003	342.77	-15.9	6.4	17.0
2004	410.00	19.6	6.5	17.8
2005	473.15	15.5	7.3	20.6
2006	539.74	14.1	7.2	18.0
2007	640.87	18.7	7.0	17.6
2008	744.19	16.1	6.6	16.2
2009	1004.48	35.0	7.8	20.1
2010	1460.53	45.4	9.2	24.8
2011	1992.89	36.5	10.2	27.7
2012	2629.54	32.0	11.8	32.0
2013	3205.61	21.9	13.0	34.1
2014	3752.11	17.1	13.7	33.1

主要统计指标解释

进出口总额 指实际进出我国国境的货物总金额。包括对外贸易实际进出口货物，来料加工装配进出口货物，国家间、联合国及国际组织无偿援助物资和赠送品，华侨、港澳台同胞和外籍华人捐赠品，租赁期满归承租人所有的租赁货物，进料加工进出口货物，边境地方贸易及边境地区小额贸易进出口货物(边民互市贸易除外)，中外合资企业、中外合作经营企业、外商独资经营企业进出口货物和公用物品，到、离岸价格在规定限额以上的进出口货样和广告品(无商业价值、无使用价值和免费提供出口的除外)，从保税仓库提取在中国境内销售的进口货物，以及其他进出口货物。该指标可以观察一个国家在对外贸易方面的总规模。我国规定出口货物按离岸价格统计，进口货物按到岸价格统计。

商品经营单位所在地进、出口额 指所在地海关注册登记的有进出口经营权的企业实际进、出口额。

商品目的地进口额和商品货源地出口额 目的地进口额指进口货物的消费、使用或最终抵运地的实际进口额；货源地出口额指出口货物的产地或原始发货地的实际出口额。

利用外资 指我国各级政府、部门、企业和其他经济组织通过对外借款、吸收外商直接投资以及用其他方式筹措的境外现汇、设备、技术等。

对外借款 指通过对外正式签订借款协议，从境外筹措的资金，包括外国政府贷款、国际金融组织贷款、外国银行商业贷款、出口信贷以及对外发行债券等。1996 年及以前还包括对外发行股票。该指标是我国利用外资的重要部分。

外商直接投资 指外国企业和经济组织或个人(包括华侨、港澳台胞以及我国在境外注册的企业)按我国有关政策、法规，用现汇、实物、技术等在我国境内开办外商独资企业、与我国境内的企业或经济组织共同举办中外合资经营企业、合作经营企业或合作开发资源的投资(包括外商投资收益的再投资)，以及经政府有关部门批准的项目投资总额内企业从境外借入的资金。

外商其他投资 指除对外借款和外商直接投资以外的各种利用外资的形式。包括企业在境内外股票市场公开发行的以外币计价的股票（目前主要是在香港证券市场发行的H股和在境内证券市场发行的B股）发行价总额，国际租赁进口设备的应付款，补偿贸易中外商提供的进口设备、技术、物料的价款，加工装配贸易中外商提供的进口设备、物料的价款。

对外直接投资 指我国国内投资者以现金、实物、无形资产等方式在国外及港澳台地区设立、购买国（境）外企业，并以控制该企业的经营管理权为核心的经济活动。

对外承包工程 指各对外承包公司以招标议标承包方式承揽的下列业务：(1)承包国外工程建设项目；(2)承包我国对外经援项目；(3)承包我国驻外机构的工程建设项目；(4)承包我国境内利用外资进行建设的工程项目；(5)与外国承包公司合营或联合承包工程项目时我国公司分包部分；(6)对外承包兼营的房屋开发业务。对外承包工程的营业额是以货币表现的本期内完成的对外承包工程的工作量，包括以前年度签订的合同和本年度新签订的合同在报告期内完成的工作量。

对外劳务合作 指以收取工资的形式向业主或承包商提供技术和劳动服务的活动。我国对外承包公司在境外开办的合营企业，中国公司同时又提供劳务的，其劳务部分也纳入劳务合作统计。劳务合作营业额按报告期内向雇主提交的结算数(包括工资、加班费和奖金等)统计。

对外设计咨询 指以服务成果向业主收费的技术服务项目。包括承担地形地貌测绘，地质资源勘探与普查，建设区域规划，提供设计文件、图纸、生产工艺技术资料和工程技术经济咨询，工程项目的可行性考察、研究和评估，进行技术指导和培训人员等；也包括承担国(境)内利用外资建设工程项目中的设计咨询项目内收取外币部分。

旅游者人数

(1)入境国际旅游者人数：指来中国参观、访问、旅行、探亲、访友、休养、考察、参加会议和从事经济、科技、文化、教育、宗教等活动的外国人、华侨、港澳同胞和台湾同胞的人数。不包括外国在我国的常驻机构，如使领馆、通讯社、企业办事处的工作人员；来我国常住的外国专家、留学生以及在岸逗留不过夜人员。

(2)出境居民人数：指大陆居民因公务活动或私人事务短期出境的人数。公务活动出境居民人数包括在国际交通工具上的中国服务员工，因私出境居民人数不包括在国际交通工具上的中国服务员工。

(3)国内旅游者人数：指我国大陆居民和在我国常住 1 年以上的外国人、华侨、港澳台同胞离开常住地在境内其他地方的旅游设施内至少停留一夜，最长不超过 6 个月的人数。

国际旅游(外汇)收入　指入境旅游的外国人、华侨、港澳同胞和台湾同胞在中国大陆旅游过程中发生的一切旅游支出，其对于国家来说就是国际旅游(外汇)收入。

国际旅行社　指经营对外招徕并接待外国人、华侨、港澳同胞和台湾同胞来中国、归国或回内地旅游业务的旅行社。

国内旅行社　指负责经营招徕、组团、接待国内旅客的旅游业务，以及不对外招徕，负责经营接待国际旅行社或其它涉外部门组织的外国人、华侨、港澳同胞和台湾同胞来中国、归国或回内地的旅游业务的旅行社。

星级饭店　指已评定星级的饭店。

Explanatory Notes on Main Statistical Indicators

Total Imports and Exports at Customs refer to the real value of commodities imported into and exported from the boundary of China. They include the actual imports and exports through foreign trade, imported and exported goods under the processing and assembling trades and materials, supplies and gifts as aid given gratis between governments and by the United Nations and other international organizations, and contributions donated by overseas Chinese, compatriots in Hong Kong and Macao and Chinese with foreign citizenship, leasing commodities owned by tenant at the expiration of leasing period, the imported and exported commodities processed with imported materials, commodities trading in border areas (excluding mutual exchange goods), the imported and exported commodities and articles for public use of the Sino-foreign joint ventures, cooperative enterprises and ventures exclusively with foreign own investment. Also included are import or export of samples and advertising goods for whose CIF or FOB value are beyond the permitted ceiling (excluding goods of no trading or use value and free commodities for export), imported goods sold in China from bonded warehouses and other imported or exported goods. The indicator of the total imports and exports at customs can be used to observe the total size of external trade in a country. In accordance with the stipulation of the Chinese government, imports are calculated at CIF, while exports are calculated at FOB.

Import Export Value by Location of China' s Foreign Trade Managing Units refers to actual value of imports and exports carried out by corporations which have been registered by the local customhouse and are vested with right to run import export business.

Import Value of Commodities by the Places of their Destination and Export Value of Commodities by the Places of their Origin in China The former indicator refers to the value of import commodities of the places of their consumption, utilization or the places of their final destination. The latter indicator refers to the value of export commodities of the places of their origin or the places of the commodities dispatched.

Utilization of Foreign Capitals refers to remittance, equipment and technology financed from abroad, by loans, foreign direct investment and other forms undertaken by the Chinese governments at all levels, by various departments, enterprises and other economic units.

Foreign Borrowings refer to funds borrowed from abroad through formal signing of borrowing agreements with foreign institutions, including loans of foreign governments, loans of international financial institutions, commercial loans of foreign banks, export credit, and funds raised by Chinese bonds (and shares before 1996) issued abroad. It is an important part of China's utilization of foreign capitals.

Foreign Direct Investment refers to the investments inside China by foreign enterprises and economic organizations or individuals (including overseas Chinese, compatriots from Hong Kong, Macao and Taiwan, and Chinese enterprises registered abroad), following the relevant policies and laws of China, for the establishment of ventures exclusively with foreign own investment, Sino-foreign joint ventures and cooperative enterprises or for co-operative exploration of resources with enterprises or economic organizations in China. It includes the re investment of the foreign entrepreneurs with the profits gained from the investment and the funds that enterprises borrow from abroad in the total investment of projects which are approved by the relevant department of the government.

Overseas Direct Investment refers to enterprises set up or bought by domestic investors in foreign countries and in Hong Kong, Macao and Taiwan, and the economic activities centering on operation and management of those enterprises are under the control of domestic investors. The statistical scope covers various corporation type enterprises and non-corporation type enterprises receiving direct investment from domestic investment entities.

Other Investment by Foreign Entrepreneurs refers to all forms of utilization of foreign capitals other than foreign borrowings and foreign direct investment. It includes the total value of stock shares in foreign currencies issued by enterprises at domestic or foreign stock exchanges (now mainly consisting of H shares issued at Hong Kong Security Market and B shares issued at domestic security markets), rent payable for the imported equipment through international leasing arrangement, cost of imported equipment, technology and materials provided by foreign counterparts in compensation trade and processing and assembly trade.

Contracted Projects with Foreign Countries refer to projects undertaken by Chinese contractors (project contracting companies) through bidding process. They include: (1) overseas civil engineering construction projects financed by foreign investors; (2) overseas projects financed by the Chinese government through its foreign aid programs; (3) construction projects of Chinese diplomatic missions, trade offices and other institutions stationed abroad; (4) construction projects in China financed by foreign investment; (5) sub-contracted projects to be taken by Chinese contractors through a joint umbrella project with foreign contractor(s); (6) housing development projects. The business income from international contracted projects is the work volume of contracted projects completed during the reference period, expressed in monetary terms, including completed work on projects signed in previous years.

Service Cooperation with Foreign Countries refers to the activities of providing technology and labor services to employers or contractors in the forms of receiving salaries and wages. Labor services providing by contractual joint ventures of Chinese international contracting corporations should be included in the statistics of service co-operation with foreign countries. The business income of labor service cooperation is the income in the form of wages and salaries, overtime pay, bonuses and other remuneration received from the employers during the reference period.

Overseas Design and Consultation Service refers to projects with charges for technical services from overseas operators. It includes geographic and topographic mapping, geological resource prospecting and survey, planning of construction areas, provision of design documents, blueprints, materials on production process and techniques, as well as engineering, technical and economic consultation, and feasibility study, research and evaluation of projects. Also included under this category are the above-mentioned services of foreign-financed projects in China that are paid in foreign currencies.

Number of Tourists

(1) International tourists refer to foreigners, overseas Chinese, Chinese compatriots from Hong Kong, Macao and Taiwan coming to China for sight-seeing, visits, tours, family reunions, vacations, study tours, conferences and other activities of a business, scientific and technological, cultural, educational and religious nature. It does not include representatives and employees of resident institutions of foreign countries in China such as embassies, consulates, news agencies and offices of foreign companies and organizations, nor does it include long-term foreign experts or students residing in China, or persons in transition without spending a night in China.

(2) Chinese residents going abroad refer to Chinese residents going abroad for short terms for either public business or private purposes. Chinese employees working on international transport carriers are included in those going abroad for public business purpose, not in those for private purpose.

(3) Domestic tourists refer to residents of the mainland of China who stay for one night at least but no more than 6 months at tourist facilities in other places than their permanent residence within the territory of the mainland China, including foreigners, overseas Chinese and Chinese compatriots from Hong Kong, Macao and Taiwan who have resided in China for over one year.

Foreign Exchange Earnings from International Tourism refer to the total expenditures of foreigners, overseas Chinese, Chinese compatriots from Hong Kong, Macao and Taiwan during their stay in the mainland of China, which are earnings of foreign exchange from international tourism from the point of view from China.

International Travel Agencies refer to travel agencies engaged in the promotion, solicitation, organization and reception of tours to the mainland of China by foreigners, overseas Chinese, Chinese compatriots from Hong Kong, Macao and Taiwan.

Domestic Travel Agencies refer to travel agencies engaged in the promotion, solicitation, organization and reception of domestic tourists, and in the reception of foreigners, overseas Chinese, Chinese compatriots from Hong Kong, Macao and Taiwan organized by international travel agencies or other departments concerned, without their own promotion and solicitation programmes.

Star-Hotels refer to hotels rated with stars.

6 能　源

Energy

资料整理：李　川　汪文华

6—1　工业能源生产量

OUTPUT OF ENERGY PRODUCTION OF INDUSTRY

产品	单位	Item	Unit	2011	2012	2013	2014
一次能源生产量	（万吨标煤）	Primary Energy Output	10 000 tons standardized coal)	4719.90	5582.98	5165.45	5708.76
原煤	（万吨）	Coal	(10 000 ton)	952.60	887.44	885.42	890.40
原油	（万吨）	Crude Oil	(10 000 ton)	88.00	78.90	80.08	79.00
天然气	（亿立方米）	Natural Gas	(100 million cu.m)	1.55	1.65	3.09	1.45
水电	（亿千瓦时）	Water and Electricity	(100 million KW/h)	1166.72	1379.59	1175.95	1375.80

说明：1.一次能源生产量为全部工业一次能源生产量；原煤、原油、天然气以及水电产量为规模以上工业生产量。
2.按照国家统计局统一部署和要求，2013年、2014年数据为根据第三次全国经济普查资料进行调整后的数据（下同）。
Note:1.Primary energy production is the entire industrial primary energy production, raw coal, crude oil, natural gas and hydropower output are the above scale industrial production.
2.According to the requirements of the NBS, the data in 2013 and 2014 have been adjusted basing on the files of the third national economic census.

6—2　规模以上工业能源消费量

ENERGY CONSUMPTION OF INDUSTRY ABOVE DESIGNATED SIZE

产品	计量单位	Item	Unit	2011	2012	2013	2014
能源消费量合计	（万吨标煤）	Total	（10000 tons standardized coal）	12328.80	12083.97	13310.45	13766.37
原煤	（万吨）	Coal	（10000 ton）	8077.16	7674.12	8270.13	7984.97
洗精煤	（万吨）	Cleaned Coal	（10000 ton）	1427.61	1340.05	1382.42	1346.53
其他洗煤	（万吨）	Other Washed Coal	（10000 ton）	11.48	10.72	13.04	11.16
煤制品	（万吨）	Moulded Coal	（10000 ton）	6.88	8.69	11.35	10.92
焦炭	（万吨）	Coke	（10000 ton）	1172.72	1113.90	1114.39	1124.40
其他焦化产品	（万吨）	Other Coked Products	（10000 ton）	5.38	3.96	1.34	1.93
焦炉煤气	（亿立方米）	Coke-oven Gas	（100 million cu.m）	42.39	39.18	38.59	38.23
高炉煤气	（亿立方米）	Bblast Furnace Gas	（100 million cu.m）	360.83	344.72	345.87	342.73
其他煤气	（亿立方米）	Other Gases	（100 million cu.m）	24.47	22.80	24.04	21.07
天然气	（亿立方米）	Natural Gas	（100 million cu.m）	11.79	13.56	18.10	17.42
原油	（万吨）	Crude Oil	（10000 ton）	1025.83	946.99	1176.30	1290.47
汽油	（万吨）	Gasoline	（10000 ton）	11.65	14.62	13.48	12.09
煤油	（万吨）	Kerasene	（10000 ton）	1.02	0.93	1.08	1.34
柴油	（万吨）	Diesel Oil	（10000 ton）	45.49	48.30	49.72	58.52
燃料油	（万吨）	Fuel Oil	（10000 ton）	8.89	8.55	6.74	6.87
液化石油气	（万吨）	LPG	（10000 ton）	3.46	2.47	8.95	31.30
炼厂干气	（万吨）	Dry Gas	（10000 ton）	33.18	29.62	34.68	38.47
其他石油制品	（万吨）	Other Petroleum Products	（10000 ton）	120.50	110.13	176.62	280.52
热力	（万百万千焦）	Heat	（10 billion kilo-joule）	7388.78	7916.47	7744.13	7626.11
电力	（亿千瓦时）	Electricity	（100 million kW/h）	1162.64	1215.06	1281.29	1317.88
其他燃料	（万吨标准煤）	Other Fuels	（10000 tons standardized coal）	23.52	18.20	22.97	24.69

注：能源消费量包括加工转换投入量，且为当量值。
Note: The conversion of energy consumption, including processing input, and when the money is.

6-3 规模以上工业分行业能源消费量（2014）

ENERGY CONSUMPTION OF INDUSTRY ABOVE DESGINATED SIZE(2014)

行业	Item	原煤消费量(万吨) Coal Consumption (10000 tons)	汽油消费量(万吨) Gasoline Consumption (10000tons)	柴油消费量(万吨) Diesel Consumption (10000tons)	电力消费量(亿千瓦小时) Electricity Consumption (100million kw/h)
总消费量	**Total Consumption**	**7984.97**	**12.09**	**58.52**	**1317.88**
采矿业	**Mining**	**138.21**	**0.92**	**18.56**	**41.99**
煤炭开采和洗选业	Mining and Washing of Coal	59.74	0.08	0.25	3.57
石油和天然气开采业	Extraction of Petroleum and Natural Gas	12.12	0.20	1.06	9.36
黑色金属矿采选业	Mining and Processing of Ferrous Metal Ores	8.83	0.09	1.39	12.81
有色金属矿采选业	Mining and Processing of Non-Ferrous Metal Ores	0.66	0.01	0.08	3.08
非金属矿采选业	Mining and Processing of Non-metal Ores	45.30	0.32	4.83	12.31
开采辅助活动	Mining Auxiliary	11.55	0.22	10.94	0.85
其他采矿业	Mining of Other Ores	0.00	0.00	0.00	0.03
制造业	**Manufacturing**	**4191.94**	**10.91**	**38.68**	**1116.41**
农副食品加工业	Processing of Food from Agricultural Products	119.45	0.68	2.64	47.82
食品制造业	Manufacture of Foods	94.50	0.23	0.37	16.05
酒、饮料和精制茶制造业	Manufacture of Wine, Beverages and Tea	63.38	0.28	0.39	13.43
烟草制品业	Manufacture of Tobacco	1.20	0.01	0.02	1.36
纺织业	Manufacture of Textile	37.86	0.46	0.58	70.85
纺织服装、服饰业	Manufacture of Textile Wearing Apparel	6.31	0.27	0.49	7.12
皮革、毛皮、羽毛及其制品和制鞋业	Manufacture of Leather, Fur, Feather and Related and Footware	0.98	0.05	0.04	2.72
木材加工和木、竹、藤、棕、草制品业	Processing of Timber, Manufacture of Wood, Bamboo, Rattan, Palm, and Straw Products	6.71	0.06	0.40	12.30
家具制造业	Manufacture of Furniture	0.84	0.04	0.27	1.41
造纸和纸制品业	Manufacture of Paper and Paper Products	69.93	0.05	0.67	17.35
印刷和记录媒介复制业	Printing and Reproduction of Recording Media	2.65	0.15	0.13	5.05
文教、工美、体育和娱乐用品制造业	Manufacture of Articles for Culture, Education, Art, Sport and Entertainment	4.13	0.02	0.01	1.54
石油加工、炼焦和核燃料加工业	Processing of Petroleum, Coking and Nuclear Fuel	9.56	0.06	0.11	12.65
化学原料和化学制品制造业	Manufacture of Raw Chemical Materials and Chemical Products	1657.97	1.65	2.76	261.68
医药制造业	Manufacture of Medicines	115.64	0.61	1.82	20.33
化学纤维制造业	Manufacture of Chemical Fibres	25.36	0.01	0.03	3.34
橡胶和塑料制品业	Manufacture of Rubber and Plastics	16.69	0.41	0.93	26.47
非金属矿物制品业	Manufacture of Non-metal Mineral Products	1173.21	0.92	8.92	157.05
黑色金属冶炼和压延加工业	Smelting an Processing of Ferrous Metals	560.61	0.35	3.08	200.89
有色金属冶炼和压延加工业	Smelting an Processing of Non-ferrous Metals	62.61	0.07	0.85	46.10
金属制品业	Manufacture of Metal Products	14.99	0.52	1.21	28.61
通用设备制造业	Manufacture of General Purpose Machinery	7.86	0.57	3.98	19.27
专用设备制造业	Manufacture of Special Purpose Machinery	6.19	0.55	2.90	16.00
汽车制造业	Manufacture of Automobile	125.39	1.91	4.00	79.49
铁路、船舶、航空航天和其他运输设备制造业	Manufacture of Realway, Ship, Aircraft and Other Transport Equipment	0.15	0.24	0.52	4.28
电气机械和器材制造业	Manufacture of Electrical Machinery and Equipment	3.87	0.42	0.36	26.33
计算机、通信和其他电子设备制造业	Manufacture of Computers, Communication Equipment and Other Electronic Equipment	0.31	0.12	0.05	12.25
仪器仪表制造业	Manufacture of Measuring Instruments	0.30	0.10	0.03	1.55
其他制造业	Manufacture of Other Products	2.58	0.01	0.01	2.10
废弃资源综合利用业	Recycling and Disposal of Waste	0.71	0.03	0.29	0.78
金属制品、机械和设备修理业	Repairing of Metal Products and Mechanical Equipment	0.00	0.06	0.81	0.22
电力、燃气及水生产和供应业	**Electric Power, Gas and Water Production and Supply**	**3654.82**	**0.26**	**1.28**	**159.47**
电力、热力生产和供应业	Production and Supply of Electric Power and Heat Power	3654.82	0.10	1.17	150.26
燃气生产和供应业	Production and Supply of Gas	0.00	0.05	0.06	1.68
水的生产和供应业	Production and Supply of Water	0.01	0.11	0.05	7.54

6-4 全社会综合能源平衡表(等价值)
BALANCE SHEET OF DOMESTIC ENERGY (EQIVALENCE PRICE)

单位:万吨标准煤 (10000 tons standardized coal)

项 目	Item	2013	2014
一、可供量	**Quantity Available**	**15703**	**16320**
一次能源生产量	Primary Energy Production	5165	5709
外省(区、市)调入量	Engery moblized from other Province	13011	13606
进 口 量	Import Volume		
我轮、机在外国加油量	Volume of Fuel Charged Abroad		
本省(区、市)调出量(-)	Engery moblized to other Province	2444	2892
出 口 量(-)	Output Volume		
外轮、机在我国加油量(-)	Volume of Fuel Charged at Home		
年初年末库存差额	Storage Balance Difference between the Beginning and the End of the Year	-29	-102
年初库存量	Storage Volume at the Beginning of the Year	589	624
年末库存量(-)	Storage Volume by the End of the Year	618	726
二、消费量	**Consumption**	**15703**	**16320**
消费量分组一	Consumption Group 1.	15703	16320
1.农.林.牧.渔业	Agriculture, Forestry, Animal Husbandary, Fishing	494	507
2.工 业	Industry	10121	10570
3.建 筑 业	Construction	400	417
4.交通运输.仓储和邮政业	Transport communication, Storage, Post Service	1502	1552
5.批发、零售业和住宿、餐饮业	Wholesale,Retail Sale, Hotel and Catering Industry	799	749
6.其他	Others	626	683
7.生活消费	Living Consumption	1761	1843
消费量分组二	Consumption Group 2.	15703	16320
1. 终端消费	Terminal Consumption	15491	16172
#工业	Industry	9909	10422
2. 加工转换损失	Loss in Processing	-114	-179
火力发电损失	Loss in Thermal Power Generation		
供热损失	Loss in Heating	265	234
洗选煤损失	Loss in Coal Seperation	1	1
炼焦损失	Loss in Coke Making	51	33
炼油及煤制油损失	Loss in Oil Refining	10	2
制气损失	Loss in Gas Drying	2	
天然气液化损失	Loss in Natural gas liquefaction		1
煤制品加工损失	Loss in Coal Products Processing	1	1
回收能	Recuperated Energy	-443	-449
3. 损 失 量	Loss in Processing	326	327
三、平衡差额	**Balance**		

6-5 全社会煤炭平衡表
BALANCE SHEET OF DOMESTIC COAL CONSUMPTION

单位：万吨 (10 000 tons)

项　目	Item	2013	2014
一、可供量	**Quantity Available**	**12167**	**11888**
生产量	Production Capacity	1096	1057
外省(区、市)调入量	Engery moblized from other Province	11089	10968
进口量	Import Volume		
本省(区、市)调出量(-)	Engery moblized to other Province		
出口量(-)	Output Volume		
年初年末库存差额	Storage Balance Difference between the Beginning and the End of the Year	-18	-137
年初库存量	Storage Volume at the Beginning of the Year	704	724
年末库存量(-)	Storage Volume by the End of the Year	723	861
二、消费量	**Consumption**	**12167**	**11888**
消费量分组一	Consumption Group 1.	12167	11888
1.农.林.牧.渔业	Agriculture, Forestry, Animal Husbandary, Fishing	220	232
2.工　业	Industry	10698	10381
3.建 筑 业	Construction	131	129
4.交通运输.仓储和邮政业	Transport communication, Storage, Post Service	70	67
5.批发、零售业和住宿、餐饮业	Wholesale,Retail Sale, Hotel and Catering Industry	279	263
6.其　他	Others	230	235
7.生活消费	Living Consumption	538	582
消费量分组二	Consumption Group 2.	12167	11888
1. 终端消费	Terminal Consumption	6445	6466
#工业	Industry	4976	4959
2. 用于加工转换	Coal Used for Processing	5722	5422
火力发电	Thermal Power Generation	3875	3646
供　热	Heating	475	447
洗煤损耗	Loss in Washing Coal	10	13
炼　焦	Coke Making	1349	1316
炼油及煤制油	Oil Refining and Coal Preparation		
制　气	Air Drying	12.49	
型煤加工损耗	Loss in Standardlized Coal Processing	0.08	0.03
3. 损 失 量	Loss		
三、平衡差额	**Balance**		

6-6　全社会石油平衡表

BALANCE SHEET OF DOMESTIC PETROLEUM

单位:万吨　　(10 000 tons)

项　目	Item	2013	2014
一、可供量	**Quantity Available**	**2268**	**2505**
生产量	Production Capacity	80	79
外省(区、市)调入量	Engery moblized from other Province	2200	2457
进 口 量	Import Volume		
我轮、机在外国加油量	Volume of Fuel Charged Abroad		
本省(区、市)调出量(-)	Engery moblized to other Province	6	25
出 口 量(-)	Output Volume		
外轮、机在我国加油量(-)	Volume of Fuel Charged at Home		
年初年末库存差额	Storage Balance Difference between the Beginning and the End of the Year	-6	-5
年初库存量	Storage Volume at the Beginning of the Year	30	35
年末库存量(-)	Storage Volume by the End of the Year	35	40
二、消费量	**Consumption**	**2268**	**2505**
消费量分组一	Consumption Group 1.	2268	2505
1.农.林.牧.渔业	Agriculture, Forestry, Animal Husbandary, Fishing	158	162
2.工　业	Industry	490	740
3.建 筑 业	Construction	162	168
4.交通运输.仓储和邮政业	Transport communication, Storage, Post Service	889	882
5.批发、零售业和住宿、餐饮业	Wholesale,Retail Sale, Hotel and Catering Industry	206	157
6.其他	Others	109	96
7.生活消费	Living Consumption	254	299
消费量分组二	Consumption Group 2.	2268	2505
1. 终端消费	Terminal Consumption	2318	2541
#工业	Industry	540	776
2. 加工转换损失	Coal Used for Processing	-50	-36
火力发电	Thermal Power Generation	2	2
供　热	Heating	5	3
炼油损耗	Loss in Oil Refining	-56	-40
制　气	Gas Making		
3. 损 失 量	Loss		
三、平衡差额	**Balance**		

6-7 全社会电力平衡表
BALANCE SHEET OF DOMESTIC ELECTRICITY

单位:亿千瓦时 (100 million kw/h)

项　目	Item	2013	2014
一、可供量	**Quantity Available**	**1814**	**1854**
生产量	Production Capacity	2237	2383
火力发电	Thermal Power Generation	1022	962
水力发电、核发电、其它发电	Hydroelectricity Generation, Nuclearpower Generation, and others	1216	1421
外省(区、市)调入量	Engery moblized from other Province	331	383
进 口 量	Import Volume		
本省(区、市)调出量(－)	Engery moblized to other Province	753	913
出 口 量(–)	Output Volume		
二、消费量	**Consumption**	**1814**	**1854**
消费量分组一	Consumption Group 1.	1814	1854
1.农.林.牧.渔业	Agriculture, Forestry, Animal Husbandary, Fishing	30	30
2.工　　业	Industry	1282	1318
3.建 筑 业	Construction	22	25
4.交通运输.仓储和邮政业	Transport communication, Storage, Post Service	35	38
5.批发、零售业和住宿、餐饮业	Wholesale,Retail Sale, Hotel and Catering Industry	79	80
6.其他	Others	95	101
7.生活消费	Living Consumption	271	262
消费量分组二	Consumption Group 2.	1814	1854
1. 终端消费	Terminal Consumption	1711	1749
#工业	Industry	1179	1213
2. 输配电损失量	Distribution Loss	103	104
三、平衡差额	**Balance**		

6–8 分市州单位GDP能耗降低率

UNIT GDP ENERGY CONSUMPTION OF SUB-CITY(2014)

地　区　Regions	2010年单位GDP能耗比2005年降低(±%) 2010year Unit GDP energy consumption lower than in 2005	2013年单位GDP能耗比2012年降低(±%) 2013year Unit GDP energy consumption lower than in 2012	2014年单位GDP能耗比2013年降低(±%) 2014year Unit GDP energy consumption lower than in 2013
全　省　Total	**-21.67**	**-4.13**	**-5.24**
武汉市　Wuhan	-21.85	-3.51	-2.88
黄石市　Huangshi	-21.71	-6.06	-6.83
十堰市　Shiyan	-20.13	-5.99	-9.91
宜昌市　Yichang	-20.87	-5.50	-5.78
襄阳市　Xiangyang	-21.40	-3.77	-3.53
鄂州市　Ezhou	-22.83	-3.96	-3.91
荆门市　Jingmen	-21.15	-5.34	-6.48
孝感市　Xiaogan	-22.55	-5.69	-5.98
荆州市　Jingzhou	-21.93	-3.92	-3.91
黄冈市　Huanggang	-22.02	-4.03	-6.98
咸宁市　Xianning	-22.10	-3.72	-4.72
随州市　Suizhou	-20.04	-3.19	-3.12
恩施州　Enshi	-20.20	-3.33	-3.66
仙桃市　Xiantao	-20.03	-2.75	-5.25
潜江市　Qianjiang	-20.91	-3.65	-3.60
天门市　Tianmen	-20.99	-2.77	-3.86
神农架　Shennongjia	-19.35	-2.48	-2.42

主要统计指标解释

能源生产总量 指一定时期内，一次能源生产量的总和。该指标是观察能源生产水平、规模、构成和发展速度的总量指标。一次能源生产量包括原煤、原油、天然气、水电、核能及其他动力能(如风能、地热能等)发电量，不包括低热值燃料生产量、生物质能、太阳能等的利用和由一次能源加工转换而成的二次能源产量。

能源消费总量 指一定区域内（国家或地区）国民经济各行业和居民家庭在一定时期消费的各种能源的总和。能源消费总量分为三部分，即终端能源消费量、能源加工转换损失量和能源损失量。

(1)终端能源消费量：指一定时期内地区各行业和居民生活消费的各种能源在扣除了用于加工转换二次能源消费量和损失量以后的数量。

(2)能源加工转换损失量：指一定时期内地区投入加工转换的各种能源数量之和与产出各种能源产品之和的差额。该指标是观察能源在加工转换过程中损失量变化的指标。

(3)能源损失量：指一定时期内，能源在输送、分配、储存过程中发生的损失和由客观原因造成的各种损失量，不包括各种气体能源放空、放散量。

单位国内生产总值能耗 指一定时期内，一个国家或地区每生产一个单位的国内生产总值所消耗的能源。计算公式为：

$$单位国内生产总值能耗=\frac{能源消费总量}{国内生产总值}$$

Explanatory Notes on Main Statistical Indicators

Total Energy Production refers to the total production of primary energy by all energy producing enterprises in a given period of time. It is a comprehensive indicator to show the capacity, scale, composition and development of energy production. The production of primary energy includes that of coal, crude oil, natural gas, hydro-power and electricity generated by nuclear energy and other means such as wind power and geothermal power. However, it excludes the production of fuels of low calorific value, bio-energy, solar energy and the secondary energy converted from the primary energy.

Total Domestic Energy Consumption refers to the total consumption of energy of various kinds by material production sectors, non material production sectors and households in a given period of time. It is a comprehensive indicator to show the scale, composition and development of energy consumption. The total energy consumption includes that of coal, crude oil and their products, natural gas and electricity, However, it excludes the consumption of fuel of low calorific value, bio-energy and solar energy. Total domestic energy consumption can be divided into three parts: final energy consumption, loss during the process of energy conversion, and energy loss.

(1)Final Energy Consumption: It refers to the total energy consumption by material production sectors, non material production sectors and households in a given period of time, but excludes the consumption in conversion of the primary energy into the secondary energy and the loss in the process of energy conversion.

(2)Loss During the Process of Energy Conversion: It refers to the total input of various kinds of energy for conversion, minus the total output of various kinds of energy in a given period of time. It is an indicator to show the loss that occurs during the process of energy conversion.

(3)Energy Loss: It refers to the total of the loss of energy during the course of energy transport, distribution and storage and the loss caused by any objective reason in a given period of time. The loss of various kinds of gas due to gas discharges and stocktaking is excluded.

Energy Consumption per Unit of GDP refers to the energy consumption per unit of gross domestic production in a country or the gross region production in a region in the same reference period. The formula is:

Energy Consumption per Unit of GDP = Total Energy Consumption / Gross Domestic Production

7 财政、金融、保险

Government Finance, Banking and Insurance

资料整理：陈福才

财政、金融、保险
GOVERNMENT FINANCE, BANKING AND INSURANCE
2014

地方公共财政收入	Local Public Financial Revenue(100 million yuan)	2567 (亿元)
地方公共财政支出	Local Public Financial Expenditure(100 million yuan)	4934 (亿元)
金融机构(含外资)人民币存款年末余额	Balance of RMB Deposits of Financial Organizations (including Foreign Funded Enterprises) By the End of the year(100 million yuan)	36495 (亿元)
#个人存款	#People's Savings Deposit	17821 (亿元)
金融机构(含外资)人民币贷款年末余额	Balance of RMB Loans of Financial Organizations (including Foreign Funded Enterprises) By the End of the year(100 million yuan)	25290 (亿元)

地方公共财政收入与地方公共财政支出(亿元)

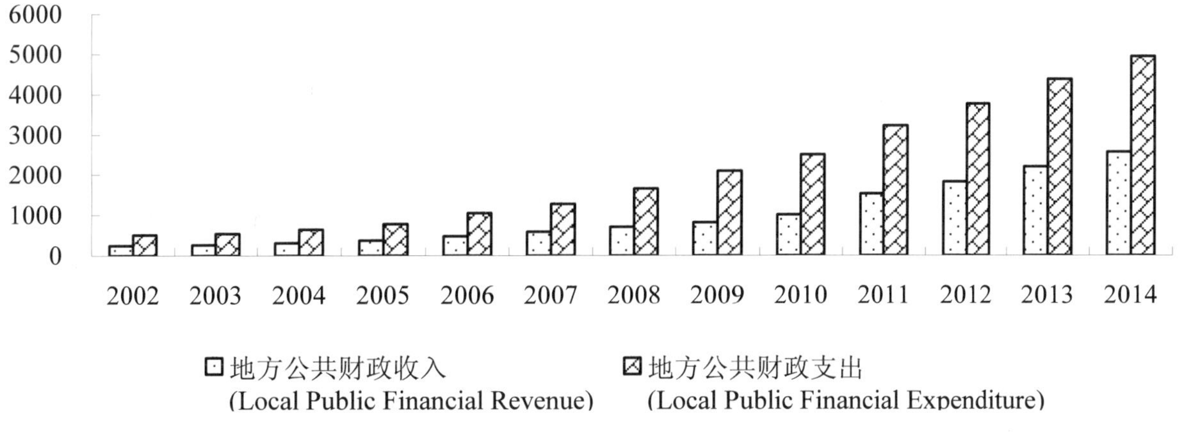

地方公共财政收入与地方公共财政支出(亿元)

Local Budgetary Revenue and Expenditure(100 million yuan)

年份(Year)	2002	2003	2004	2005	2006	2007	2008	2009	2010	2011	2012	2013	2014
地方公共财政收入 (Local Public Financial Revenue)	243	260	311	376	476	590	711	815	1011	1527	1823	2191	2567
地方公共财政支出 (Local Public Financial Expenditure)	511	540	646	779	1047	1274	1650	2091	2501	3215	3760	4372	4934

7-1 历年地方财政收支额及指数

AMOVNT AND INDICES OF FINANCIAL REVENUE AND EXPENDITURE OVER THE YEARS

单位:亿元 (100 million yuan)

年份 Year	财政总收入 Total fiscal revenue	地方公共财政收入 Local Public Financial Revenue	地方公共财政支出 Local Public Financial Expenditure	指数(上年=100) Index (previous year=100)	
				收入 Revenue	支出 Expenditure
1952	3.81	3.81	1.96	100.0	100.0
1957	6.27	6.27	3.55	109.8	96.7
1965	11.26	11.26	6.85	97.4	105.2
1970	15.20	15.20	15.73	170.6	158.1
1975	24.05	24.05	17.52	139.5	103.9
1978	31.38	31.38	29.98	149.0	148.6
1980	34.01	34.01	26.53	107.6	94.5
1985	50.26	50.26	43.60	119.3	137.5
1990	77.85	77.85	84.82	100.8	106.1
1993	115.07	115.07	114.58	122.2	115.8
1994	149.64	77.46	137.20		119.7
1995	180.57	99.69	162.43	128.7	118.4
1996	216.68	124.51	197.44	124.9	121.6
1997	246.35	139.89	223.70	112.4	113.3
1998	284.44	168.95	280.12	120.8	125.2
1999	314.91	194.44	336.46	115.1	120.1
2000	343.98	214.35	368.77	110.2	109.6
2001	374.15	231.94	484.40	108.2	131.4
2002	435.50	243.44	511.39	105.0	105.6
2003	483.90	259.76	540.44	106.7	105.7
2004	589.65	310.45	646.29	119.5	119.6
2005	727.61	375.52	778.72	121.0	120.5
2006	901.17	476.08	1047.00	126.8	134.5
2007	1115.47	590.36	1274.27	124.0	121.7
2008	1338.75	710.85	1650.28	120.4	129.5
2009	1541.55	814.87	2090.92	114.6	126.7
2010	1918.94	1011.23	2501.40	124.1	119.7
2011	2639.81	1526.91	3214.74	151.0	128.5
2012	3115.63	1823.05	3759.79	119.4	117.0
2013	3566.89	2191.22	4371.65	120.2	116.3
2014	4096.00	2566.90	4934.15	117.1	112.9

7-2 财政收支

FINANCIAL REVENUE AND EXPENDITURE

单位：亿元　　(100 million yuan)

指标	Item	2011	2012	2013	2014
地方公共财政收入	**Local Public Financial Revenue**	**1526.91**	**1823.05**	**2191.22**	**2566.90**
#税收收入	Revenue	1067.11	1324.44	1604.85	1856.53
#增值税25%	#25% Taxes on Value Added	148.36	162.39	225.68	254.92
营业税	Run Taxes	366.77	472.36	526.43	593.27
企业所得税	Enterprise Income Taxes	155.51	196.87	215.23	250.45
个人所得税	Individual Income Taxes	48.85	48.55	57.74	64.50
城市维护建设税	Taxes on City Maintenance and Construction	77.83	92.50	109.04	121.34
房产税	Real Estate Taxews	22.37	29.28	34.70	42.28
耕地占用税	Taxes on Use of Cultivated Land	50.63	69.29	80.39	99.66
地方公共财政支出	**Local Public Financial Expenditure**	**3214.74**	**3759.79**	**4371.65**	**4934.15**
1.一般公共服务	General Public Service	394.95	466.51	546.49	598.45
2.外交	Foreign Affairs				
3.国防	National Defence	2.51	2.99	4.12	4.18
4.公共安全	Public Security	188.40	204.53	227.04	259.05
5.教育	Education	488.16	732.37	690.63	773.35
6.科学技术	Science and Technology	44.19	54.39	77.21	134.46
7.文化体育与传媒	Culture, Sports and Media	47.09	62.47	72.44	76.65
8.社会保障和就业	Social Security and Employment	449.29	501.13	605.70	717.63
9.医疗卫生	Medical Care	247.30	267.99	322.08	410.31
10.节能环保	Environmental Protecction	101.11	95.63	109.72	103.78
11.城乡社区事务	Community Service in Urban and Rural Community	161.33	201.73	320.36	364.31
12.农林水事务	Water Affairs of Agriculture and Forestry	376.23	419.02	465.34	483.80
13.交通运输	Transportation	255.18	212.68	308.82	396.04
14.其他支出	Others	459.00	538.35	621.70	612.14

7–3 财政收入占地区生产总值的比重
FINANCIAL REVENUE AS PERCENTAGE TO GROSS DOMESTIC PRODUCT

年 份 Year	地方公共财政收入(亿元) Local Public Financial Revenue (100 million yuan)	地区生产总值(亿元) Gross Domestic Product (100 million yuan)	地方公共财政收入占地区生产总值的比重(%) Percentage of Local Financial Revenue to GDP (%)
1980	26.53	199.38	13.31
1981	23.60	219.75	10.74
1982	25.47	241.55	10.54
1983	28.32	262.58	10.79
1984	31.72	328.22	9.66
1985	43.50	396.26	10.98
1986	58.04	442.04	13.13
1987	60.98	517.77	11.78
1988	68.66	626.52	10.96
1989	79.07	717.08	11.03
1990	84.82	824.38	10.29
1991	95.09	913.38	10.41
1992	94.14	1088.39	8.65
1993	115.07	1325.83	8.68
1994	77.46	1700.92	4.55
1995	99.69	2109.38	4.73
1996	124.51	2499.77	4.98
1997	139.89	2856.47	4.90
1998	168.95	3114.02	5.43
1999	194.44	3229.29	6.02
2000	214.35	3545.39	6.05
2001	231.94	3880.53	5.98
2002	243.44	4212.82	5.78
2003	259.76	4757.45	5.46
2004	310.45	5633.24	5.51
2005	375.52	6590.19	5.70
2006	476.08	7617.47	6.25
2007	590.36	9333.40	6.33
2008	710.85	11328.92	6.27
2009	814.87	12961.10	6.29
2010	1011.23	15967.61	6.33
2011	1526.91	19632.26	7.78
2012	1823.05	22250.45	8.19
2013	2191.22	24668.49	8.88
2014	2566.90	27379.22	9.38

7-4 市州地方公共财政收入

FINANCIAL REVENUE OF CITIES AND PREFECTURE

单位：亿元 (100 million yuan)

市、州	Municipalities and Prefecrure	2004	2005	2006	2007	2008	2009	2010	2011	2012	2013	2014
全　省	**The Total**	**310.45**	**375.52**	**476.08**	**590.36**	**710.85**	**814.87**	**1011.23**	**1526.91**	**1823.05**	**2191.22**	**2566.90**
省　级	Provinial	72.71	94.59	131.60	161.83	174.37	184.06	206.78	188.67	130.07	126.27	133.16
武汉市	Wuhan	104.02	138.82	178.60	221.68	277.32	316.07	390.19	673.26	828.58	978.52	1101.02
黄石市	Huangshi	9.72	11.96	15.33	19.71	24.09	26.03	34.10	53.84	65.64	78.36	89.38
十堰市	Shiyan	10.17	11.37	13.20	15.59	19.89	25.76	43.77	66.71	76.93	73.53	85.77
荆州市	Jingzhou	13.45	12.05	12.86	15.24	18.71	22.36	27.60	44.33	56.76	71.95	88.17
宜昌市	Yichang	19.13	22.53	27.37	35.57	44.27	54.94	70.24	113.98	153.25	206.31	271.51
襄阳市	Xiangyang	17.85	18.40	20.62	24.02	30.06	37.02	51.01	97.41	139.85	191.53	249.24
鄂州市	Ezhou	3.97	4.93	6.46	8.51	10.70	13.02	15.66	26.31	33.02	38.43	42.74
荆门市	Jingmen	9.29	9.34	10.17	12.06	14.92	18.14	23.25	39.39	50.69	59.84	69.82
孝感市	Xiaogan	10.13	10.78	12.73	16.63	21.46	26.97	34.20	51.58	69.50	89.05	107.22
黄冈市	Huanggang	13.11	13.14	15.35	19.93	26.21	32.17	38.98	51.61	62.92	79.98	96.04
咸宁市	Xianning	6.40	7.43	8.71	11.10	14.33	18.14	23.34	35.56	45.82	58.71	70.76
恩施自治州	Enshi	7.85	8.35	10.03	13.05	15.40	18.28	22.16	31.89	40.43	50.05	57.82
随州市	Suizhou	4.48	4.25	4.76	5.47	6.68	7.60	9.53	17.07	22.99	29.67	36.68
仙桃市	Xiantao	3.18	2.81	2.80	3.31	4.21	5.05	7.35	13.13	17.14	21.00	24.16
天门市	Tianmen	1.82	1.37	1.67	2.18	2.80	3.53	4.71	7.90	11.00	15.02	17.35
潜江市	Qianjiang	2.94	3.02	3.29	3.85	4.71	4.86	7.25	12.50	16.02	20.00	22.69
神农架林区	Shennongjia	0.25	0.42	0.50	0.60	0.73	0.87	1.10	1.77	2.44	3.00	3.37

7-5 市州地方公共财政支出

FINANCIAL EXPENDITURE OF CITIES AND PREFECTURES

单位：亿元 (100 million yuan)

市、州	Municipalities and Prefecrure	2004	2005	2006	2007	2008	2009	2010	2011	2012	2013	2014
全　省	**The Total**	**646.29**	**778.73**	**1047.00**	**1274.27**	**1650.28**	**2090.92**	**2501.40**	**3214.74**	**3759.79**	**4371.65**	**4934.15**
省　级	Provinial	183.98	205.75	284.30	312.94	388.90	258.00	273.40	378.50	449.69	484.45	661.60
武汉市	Wuhan	142.62	176.88	257.81	307.23	377.88	503.64	583.55	765.04	885.55	1122.88	1175.10
黄石市	Huangshi	18.34	23.47	31.43	40.90	53.06	80.85	102.56	128.69	140.43	150.79	152.97
十堰市	Shiyan	26.90	33.42	42.83	54.24	73.97	118.50	146.98	185.09	207.75	231.42	258.87
荆州市	Jingzhou	34.14	39.51	52.57	65.80	90.41	130.35	163.15	197.18	226.83	255.92	276.29
宜昌市	Yichang	38.92	47.63	62.76	79.78	105.86	156.50	196.51	241.13	297.45	364.44	439.92
襄阳市	Xiangyang	36.38	49.19	56.78	71.52	96.64	148.16	184.92	248.14	313.97	364.87	437.93
鄂州市	Ezhou	7.98	10.38	13.55	17.85	23.97	35.67	43.01	56.66	62.69	70.87	75.65
荆门市	Jingmen	19.47	24.58	29.33	38.65	49.18	81.66	95.46	125.34	142.20	158.79	178.96
孝感市	Xiaogan	26.23	32.50	41.89	54.60	74.64	109.79	133.58	172.61	201.79	227.90	253.18
黄冈市	Huanggang	37.10	44.40	57.13	76.23	104.47	155.09	188.13	225.54	278.92	305.16	344.66
咸宁市	Xianning	17.33	21.41	27.72	37.87	56.50	84.97	100.02	127.07	143.03	158.14	176.97
恩施自治州	Enshi	26.19	32.12	41.92	54.89	71.04	102.25	129.79	160.14	179.69	216.69	216.32
随州市	Suizhou	11.45	14.11	18.08	23.10	31.73	46.11	57.23	72.32	85.55	100.04	103.70
仙桃市	Xiantao	7.44	8.29	9.81	13.30	17.03	26.25	32.91	42.34	47.71	50.08	59.56
天门市	Tianmen	5.18	6.22	8.11	10.79	15.14	23.44	28.27	38.51	41.84	46.53	54.36
潜江市	Qianjiang	5.34	6.99	8.62	11.43	15.36	23.03	28.60	37.68	42.01	46.80	51.27
神农架林区	Shennongjia	1.32	1.86	2.37	3.13	4.26	6.66	13.33	12.76	12.69	15.88	16.84

7-6 金融机构(含外资)人民币存款年末余额

BALANCE OF RMB DEPOSITS IN FINANCIAL ORGANIZATIONS (INCLUDING FOREIGN FUNDED ENTERPRISES) BY THE END

单位：亿元 (100 million yuan)

指 标	Item	2013	2014
各项存款	**Deposits**	**32636.15**	**36153.65**
1.单位存款	Corporate Deposits	14569.65	15786.85
其中：活期存款	Demand Deposits	7286.91	7646.86
定期存款	Time Deposits	2997.64	3480.78
通知存款	Notice Deposits	315.46	305.47
保证金存款	Margin Deposits	1858.25	1950.75
2.个人存款	Personal Deposits	15905.45	17744.95
储蓄存款	Saving Deposits	15507.03	17247.58
保证金存款	Margin Deposits	34.72	59.04
结构性存款	Structured Deposits	363.70	438.32
3.财政性存款	Public Financial Deposits	1696.23	2049.20
4.临时性存款	Temporary Deposits	42.55	33.64
5.委托存款	Entrusted Deposits	71.23	104.29
6.其他存款	Others	351.04	434.72

7-7 金融机构(含外资)人民币贷款年末余额

BALANCE OF RMB LOANS OF FINANCIAL ORGANIZTIONS (INCLUDING FOREIGN FUNDED ENTERPISES) BY THE END

单位：亿元 (100 million yuan)

指 标	Item	2013	2014
各项贷款	**Loans**	**20796.86**	**24239.96**
(一)境内贷款	**Domestil Loans**	**20794.32**	**24237.66**
1.短期贷款	Short-term Loans	7479.38	8286.23
个人贷款及透支	Individual Loans	1424.89	1743.06
单位普通贷款及透支	Commercial Loans	5122.86	5646.86
普通并购贷款	Construction Loans		
银团贷款	Agricnltural Loan	73.57	81.25
贸易融资	Loans to Township Enterprises	858.06	815.07
境外筹资转贷款	On-lending of Overseas Borrowing		
2.中长期贷款	Medium-term and Long-term Loans	12820.21	15263.83
个人贷款	Individual Loans	3789.81	4561.18
单位普通贷款	Commercial Loans	7737.74	9151.95
普通并购贷款	Construction Loans	35.13	51.96
银团贷款	Agricnltural Loan	1133.30	1399.09
贸易融资	Loans to Township Enterprises	122.15	98.02
境外筹资转贷款	On-lending of Overseas Borrowing	2.08	1.63
3.融资租赁	Loans for Accomodation and Rent	190.51	247.62
4.票据融资	Bill Financing	291.65	369.46
5.各项垫款	Money Advanced Payment for Others	12.57	70.51
(二)境外贷款	**Foreign Loans**	**2.54**	**2.30**

7-8　保险业务主要指标

MAJOR INDICATORS OF INSURANCE BUSINESS

项　　目		Item		2011	2012	2013	2014
一、保险密度	(元/人)	Density of Insurance	(yuan/person)	871.52	922.84	1012.94	1204.00
二、保险深度	(%)	Depth of Insurance	(%)	2.56	2.40	2.38	2.56
三、保费收入	(亿元)	Premium	(100 million yuan)	501.82	533.31	587.40	700.23
(一)财产保险		Property Insurnce		114.71	135.26	169.35	204.55
1.财产险		Property Insurnce		7.04	10.13	11.04	12.29
2.机动车辆保险		Machine Driving Cars Insurnce		87.28	103.31	128.98	161.27
3.责任险		Responsibility Insurance		4.32	5.46	6.63	7.84
4.信用保证险		Credit Guarantee Insurance		3.26	4.60	8.40	9.05
5.其它		Others		12.81	11.76	14.29	14.10
(二)人身保险		Life Insurance		387.11	398.05	418.07	495.67
1.人身意外伤害保险		Accident Insurance		11.24	13.06	15.79	18.52
团体保险		Group Insurance		5.81	6.74	8.06	9.35
个人保险		Individual Insurance		5.43	6.32	7.73	9.17
2.健康险		Healthy Insurance		22.59	27.70	39.47	55.64
团体保险		Group Insurance		5.45	6.82	14.69	21.24
个人保险		Individual Insurance		17.14	20.88	24.78	34.40
3.寿险		Personal Insurance		353.28	357.29	362.81	421.51
团体保险		Group Insurance		1.65	3.99	1.80	2.77
个人保险		Individual Insurance		351.63	353.30	361.01	418.78
四、各项赔款和给付	(亿元)	Claim and Payment	(100 million yuan)	101.09	128.55	187.61	230.59
(一)财产保险		Property Insurnce		52.92	68.34	86.32	100.90
1.财产险		Property Insurnce		3.08	3.53	4.01	4.51
2.机动车辆保险		Machine Driving Cars Insurnce		42.86	56.10	71.60	83.82
3.责任险		Responsibility Insurance		2.07	2.42	3.00	3.69
4.信用保证险		Credit Guarantee Insurance		0.60	0.46	0.50	1.17
5.其它		Others		4.31	5.83	7.21	7.71
(二)人身保险		Life Insurance		48.17	60.21	101.28	129.69
1.人身意外伤害保险		Accident Insurance		2.68	3.42	3.93	4.67
团体保险		Group Insurance		1.02	1.43	1.61	2.03
个人保险		Individual Insurance		1.66	1.99	2.32	2.64
2.健康险		Healthy Insurance		9.57	10.29	14.43	26.73
团体保险		Group Insurance		3.56	4.47	7.49	18.54
个人保险		Individual Insurance		6.01	5.82	6.94	8.19
3.寿险		Personal Insurance		35.93	46.50	82.92	98.29
团体保险		Group Insurance		6.56	7.57	7.69	8.10
个人保险		Individual Insurance		29.37	38.93	75.23	90.19

注：本表采用数据均为保险业新口径数据。

Note:Data from this table are based on the new standard.

主要统计指标解释

财政总收入 指地方一般预算收入与上划中央税收收入之和。

公共财政收入 是指各级政府为履行职能，按照国家法律、法规规定收取的纳入一般预算管理的各项税收及非税收入总和。主要包括：

（1）各项税收：包括国内增值税、国内消费税、进口货物增值税和消费税、出口货物退增值税和消费税、营业税、企业所得税、个人所得税、资源税、城市维护建设税、房产税、印花税、城镇土地使用税、土地增值税、车船税、船舶吨税、车辆购置税、关税、耕地占用税、契税、烟叶税等。

（2）非税收入：包括专项收入、行政事业性收费、罚没收入和其他收入。

公共财政支出 国家财政将筹集起来的资金进行分配使用，以满足经济建设和各项事业的需要。主要包括：

（1）一般公共服务：指政府提供基本公共管理与服务的支出，包括人大事务、政协事务、政府办公厅（室）及相关机构事务、发展与改革事务、统计信息事务、财政事务、税收事务、审计事务、海关事务、人力资源事务、纪检监察事务、人口与计划生育事务、商贸事务、知识产权事务、工商行政管理事务、国土资源事务、海洋管理事务、测绘事务、地震事务、气象事务、民族事务、宗教事务、港澳台侨事务、档案事务、共产党事务、民主党派事务及工商联事务、群众团体事务、彩票事务等。

（2）外交：指政府外交事务支出，包括外交行政管理、驻外机构、对外援助、国际组织、对外合作与交流、边界勘界联检等方面的支出。

（3）国防：指政府用于国防方面的支出，包括用于现役部队、预备役部队、民兵、国防科研事业、专项工程、国防动员等方面的支出。

（4）公共安全：指政府维护社会公共安全方面的支出，包括武装警察、公安、国家安全、检察、法院、司法行政、监狱、劳教、国家保密、缉私警察等。

（5）教育：指政府教育事务支出，包括教育行政管理、学前教育、小学教育、初中教育、普通高中教育、普通高等教育、初等职业教育、中专教育、技校教育、职业高中教育、高等职业教育、广播电视教育、留学生教育、特殊教育、干部继续教育、教育机关服务等。

（6）科学技术：指用于科学技术方面的支出，包括科学技术管理事务、基础研究、应用研究、技术研究与开发、科技条件与服务、社会科学、科学技术普及、科技交流与合作等。

（7）文化教育与传媒：指政府在文化、文物、体育、广播影视、新闻出版等方面的支出。

（8）社会保障和就业：指政府在社会保障与就业方面的支出，包括社会保障和就业管理事务、民政管理事务、财政对社会保险基金的补助、补充全国社会保障基金、行政事业单位离退休、企业改革补助、就业补助、抚恤、退役安置、社会福利、残疾人事业、城市居民最低生活保障、其他城镇社会救济、农村社会救济、自然灾害生活救助、红十字事务等。

（9）医疗卫生：指政府医疗卫生方面的支出，包括医疗卫生管理事务支出、医疗服务支出、医疗保障支出、疾病预防控制支出、卫生监督支出、妇幼保健支出、农村卫生支出等。

（10）节能环保：指政府环境保护支出，包括环境保护管理事务支出、环境监测与监察支出、污染治理支出、自然生态保护支出、天然林保护工程支出、退耕还林支出、风沙荒漠治理支出、退牧还草支出、已垦草原退耕还草、能源节约利用、污染减排、可再生能源和资源综合利用等支出。

（11）城乡社区事务：指政府城乡社区事务支出，包括城乡社区管理事务支出、城乡社区规划与管理支出、城乡社区公共设施支出、城乡社区住宅支出、城乡社区环境卫生支出、建设市场管理与监督支出等。

（12）农林水事务：指政府农林水事务支出，包括农业支出、林业支出、水利支出、扶贫支出、农业综合开发支出等。

（13）交通运输：指政府交通运输和邮政业方面的支出，包括公路运输支出、水路运输支出、铁路运输支出、民用航空运输支出、邮政业支出等。

信贷资金 指金融机构以信用方式积聚和分配的货币资金。金融机构信贷资金的来源有各项存款、金融债券发行、应付及暂收款、对国际金融机构负债、流通中货币、各项准备、所有者权益和其他项目等；信贷资金的运用有各项贷款、有价证券及投资、应收及预付款、委托投资、金银占款、外汇占款、库存现金、财政借款及在国际金融机构中的资产等。

存款 指企业、机关、团体或居民根据资金必须收回的原则，把货币资金存入银行或其他信贷机构保管并取得一定利息的一种信用活动形式。根据存款对象或性质的不同可划分为企业存款、财政存款、机关团体存款、基本建设存款、储蓄存款、农村存款、委托存款、其他存款等科目。它是银行信贷资金的主要来源。

贷款 指银行或其他信贷机构根据资金必须归还的原则，按一定利率，为企业、个人等提供资金的一种信用活动形式。我国银行贷款分为短期贷款、中期流动资金贷款、中长期贷款、信托贷款、融资租赁、委托贷款、票据融资、各项垫款等。

保险公司 在中国境内的、经过保险监督管理部门批准设立，并依法登记注册的各类商业保险公司。

保险金额 指保险人承担赔偿或者给付保险金责任的最高限额。

保费 指投保人为取得保险人在约定范围内所承担赔偿责任而支付给保险人的费用。

赔款 指保险人根据保险合同的规定，向被保险人支付的赔偿保险责任损失的金额。

给付 包括死伤医疗给付和满期给付。死伤医疗给付是指保险人根据人寿保险及长期健康保险合同的规定，因被保险人在保险期内发生保险责任范围内的保险事故支付给被保险人(或受益人)的金额。满期给付是指被保险人生存期满，保险人按人寿保险合同规定支付给被保险人的满期保险金额。

Explanatory Notes on Main Statistical Indicators

Total income refers to the local fiscal revenue and the general budget tax revenue and central planning.

Public Financial revenue is to perform its functions in accordance with national laws and regulations collected into the general budget of the revenue management and non-tax revenues combined.

Public Financial Expenditure refers to the distribution and use of the funds the government finances has risen, so as to meet the needs of economic construction and various causes. It includes the following main items:

(1) Expenditure for general public services: It refers to the spending on the basic public management and services which provided by governments, including the expense on affairs of People's Congress, affairs of People's Political Consultative Conference, affairs of government general office and relative institutions, affairs of development and reform, affairs of statistics, affairs of finance, affairs of taxation, affairs of audit, affairs of customs, affairs of human resources and social security, affairs of discipline inspection and supervision, affairs of population and family planning, affairs of commerce and trade, affairs of intellectual property, affairs of administration for industry and commerce, affairs of land and resources, affairs of oceanic administration, affairs of surveying and mapping, affairs of earthquake, ethnic affairs, religious affairs, affairs of Hong Kong, Macao, Taiwan, and Overseas Chinese, affairs of archives administration, affairs of Chinese Communist Party, affairs of democratic parties and federation of industry and commerce, affairs of mass organization, and affairs of lottery, etc.

(2) Expenditure for foreign affairs: It refers to the spending of government on foreign affairs, including the expense on administration of foreign affairs, missions overseas, external assistance, international organizations, foreign cooperation and

communication, surveying and joint inspection on borderline, etc.

(3) Expenditure for national defence: It refers to the spending of government on national defence, including the expense on active force, reserve force, militia, scientific research on national defence, special projects, mobilization of national defence, etc.

(4) Expenditure for public security: It refers to the spending of government on maintaining social and public security, including the expense on armed police force, public security, state security, prosecution, courts, justice, prison, labour education and rehabilitation, protection of state secrecy, anti-smuggling police, etc.

(5) Expenditure for education: It refers to the spending of government on education, including the expense on the administration of education, pre-primary education, primary education, secondary education, high school education, regular higher education, primary vocational education, secondary vocational education, technical school education, vocational high school education and higher vocational education, radio and television education, student abroad education, special education, on the job training of cadres, education authorities services, etc.

(6) Expenditure for science and technology: It refers to the spending of government on science and technology (S&T), including the expense on the administration of S&T, basic research, applied research, research and development, conditions and services of S&T, popularization of social science, science and technology, exchanges and cooperation of S&T, etc.

(7) Expenditure for culture, sport and media: It refers to the spending of government on culture, cultural heritage, sports, radio, film, television, press and publication, etc.

(8) Expenditure for social safety net and employment effort: It refers to the spending of government on social safety net and employment, including the expense on administration of social safety net and employment, civil affairs, budgetary subsidy on the social insurance funds, subsidy on National Social Security Fund, retirees of administrative units and institutions, subsidy on enterprise reform, subsidy on employment effort, pension, placement of ex-serviceman, social welfare, the handicapped undertakings, the system of cost of living allowances for urban residents, other urban social relief, rural social relief, living relief of natural disasters, affairs of Red Cross Society, etc.

(9) Expenditure for medical and health care: It refers to the spending of government on medical and health care, including the expense on administration of medical and health care, medical services, health care, disease prevention and control, health inspection and supervision, women and children's health, rural health care, etc.

(10) Expenditure for environment protection: It refers to the spending of government on environment protection, including the expense on administration of environment protection, environment monitoring and supervision, pollution control, natural ecology protection, project of virgin forests protection, reforesting farmland, controlling the sources of dust storms, returning pastureland to grassland, returning pastureland to grassland, returning cultivated land to grassland, energy conservation, emissions reduction, comprehensive utilization of renewable energy and resources, etc.

(11) Expenditure for urban and rural community affairs: It refers to the spending of government on urban and rural community affairs, including the expense on administration of urban and rural community, planning and management of urban and rural community, public facilities of urban and rural community, housing of urban and rural community, sanitation of urban and rural community, management and supervision on the construction market, etc.

(12) Expenditure for agriculture, forestry and water conservancy: It refers to the spending of government on agriculture, forestry

and water conservancy, including the expense on agriculture, forestry, water conservancy, poverty alleviation, comprehensive agricultural development, etc.

(13) Expenditure for transportation: It refers to the spending of government on transportation and postal services, including the expense on road transportation, waterway transportation, railway transportation, civil aviation transportation, and postal services.

Credit Funds refer to the funds issued as loans by banking institutions. The sources of credit funds of the banking institutions included deposits, issue of financial bonds, account-payable and temporary gathering, liabilities to international financial institutions, currency in circulation, various reserves, owners' rights and interests and other items. The credit funds can be used in forms of loans, securities and investment, account receivable and advance payment, entrusted investment, gold, foreign exchange, cash on hand, government debt and assets in the international financial institutions.

Deposit is a form of credit by which enterprises, institutions, organizations or households can put money into banks and other credit institutions for safekeeping and interest earning under the principle of free withdrawal. According to different depositors, deposits are divided into enterprise deposits, treasury deposits, deposits of government agencies and organizations, capital construction deposits, savings deposits, rural saving deposits, entrusted deposits and other deposits. Deposits are major sources of the credit funds of banks.

Loan is a form of credit by which banks and other credit institutions provide funds at certain interest rate to enterprises and individuals in the light of the principle of unconditional repayment. Loans from Chinese banks include circulating capital loans, fixed assets loans, loans to urban and rural individuals engaged in industrial and commercial business and agricultural loans.

Insurance Companies refer to commercial insurance companies of various forms registered by law and established in China with the approval of insurance regulatory agencies.

Amount Insured refers to the maximum that the insurant will get for the claim of the case insured.

Premium is the fee paid by the insurant to the insurer to obtain the obligation of compensation from the insurance within the agreed terms.

Settled Claim is the compensation paid by the insurer to the insurant in accordance with the insurance contract.

Payment includes payment for death, injury or medical treatment and mature payment. Payment for death, injury or medical treatment refers to the money paid to the insurant (or the beneficiary) in accordance with the life or health insurance contract when the insurant encounters accidents within the insured period covered in the contract. Mature payment refers to the mature payment to the insurant in accordance with the life insurance contract at the end of the insured period.

8 价格

Price

资料整理：董胜男

8-1　物 价 总 指 数 (2014)

GENERAL PRICE INDICES(2014)

基　　期	Base Period	商品零售价格总指数 General Rtail Price Index	居民消费价格总指数 General Consumption Price Index
以1950年价格为100	The Price of 1950 Equals 100	655.4	1014.9
以1952年价格为100	The Price of 1952 Equals 100	581.2	892.8
以1957年价格为100	The Price of 1957 Equals 100	526.2	791.4
以1965年价格为100	The Price of 1965 Equals 100	471.5	696.3
以1970年价格为100	The Price of 1970 Equals 100	475.2	698.9
以1975年价格为100	The Price of 1975 Equals 100	475.9	692.1
以1978年价格为100	The Price of 1978 Equals 100	472.1	689.5
以1980年价格为100	The Price of 1980 Equals 100	445.1	629.6
以1985年价格为100	The Price of 1985 Equals 100	388.0	529.3
以1990年价格为100	The Price of 1990 Equals 100	240.7	333.8
以1995年价格为100	The Price of 1995 Equals 100	129.0	157.0
以2000年价格为100	The Price of 2000 Equals 100	131.3	146.1
以2005年价格为100	The Price of 2005 Equals 100	126.6	132.4
以2010年价格为100	The Price of 2010 Equals 100	111.2	114.2
以上年价格为100	The Price of Last Year Equals 100	100.9	102.0

8-2　各市、县物价指数(2014)

GENERAL PRICE INDICES(2014)

(上年=100) (preceding year = 100)

地　区	Region	居民消费价格指数 Consumer Price Index	商品零售价格指数 Retail Price Index	农业生产资料价格指数 Agricultural Production Material Price Index
湖北省	**Hubei**	**102.0**	**100.9**	**97.9**
武汉市	Wuhan	101.9	100.5	
黄石市	Huangshi	102.2	101.3	
十堰市	Shiyan	101.5	100.5	
竹山县	zhushan	102.3	101.6	100.3
宜昌市	Yichang	102.2	101.0	
宜都市	Yidu	102.0	100.6	96.3
襄阳市	Xiangyang	101.5	101.2	
老河口市	Laohekou	102.0	100.7	96.4
鄂州市	Ezhou	102.0	101.1	
荆门市	Jingmen	101.9	101.3	
孝感市	Xiaogan	102.0	101.2	
大悟县	Dawu	102.3	100.9	96.7
荆州市	Jingzhou	102.1	100.7	
洪湖市	Honghu	102.6	102.4	97.4
黄冈市	Huanggang	101.3	100.6	
浠水县	Xishui	101.2	100.7	97.8
麻城市	Macheng	101.0	100.6	102.8
咸宁市	Xianning	101.8	100.9	97.6
崇阳县	Chongyang	102.1	101.4	99.6
恩施市	Enshi	102.6	100.9	92.4
随州市	Suizhou	101.9	100.7	
天门市	Tianmen	101.5	100.6	100.7

8-3 全省居民消费、商品零售价格分类指数(2014)
RETAIL PRICE INDICES BY CATEGORY OF COMMODITIES(2014)

(上年=100) (preceding year=100)

类　　别	Item	全　省 Provincial Indices	城　市 Urban Indices	农　村 Rural Indices
居民消费价格总指数	**General Consumer Price Index**	**102.0**	**102.0**	**101.9**
*服务项目价格指数	Service Price Index	103.3	103.2	103.3
一、食品	Foods	102.3	102.4	102.2
二、烟酒及用品	Tobacco,Liquor and Articles	99.7	99.9	99.4
三、衣着	Clothing	102.0	102.2	101.5
四、家庭设备用品及维修服务	Household Facilities and Articles	101.5	101.8	101.0
五、医疗保健和个人用品	Medicine and Medical Articles	100.7	100.1	102.3
六、交通和通讯	Transportation and Communication	100.2	100.2	100.3
七、娱乐教育文化用品及服务	Receation, Education and Culture Articles and Services	101.7	101.5	102.0
八、居住	Housing Condition	103.3	103.4	102.9
商品零售价格总指数	**General Price Index**	**100.9**	**100.8**	**101.0**
一、食品	Foods	102.3	102.4	102.1
二、饮料、烟酒	Beverage, Tobacco and Liquor	100.2	99.9	100.5
三、服装、鞋帽	Garments, Shoes and Hats	101.9	102.3	101.4
四、纺织品	Texiles	102.2	103.1	101.2
五、家用电器及音像器材	Household Electric Appliance and Stereo	98.2	97.4	99.4
六、文化办公用品	Stationery and Business Articles	98.8	98.1	100.0
七、日用品	Daily Use Articles	100.9	100.5	101.3
八、体育娱乐用品	Sports and Receation Articles	100.1	100.1	100.1
九、交通、通信用品	Transportation and Communication Articles	96.3	96.5	96.1
十、家具	Furniture	101.1	101.3	100.7
十一、化妆品	Cosmetics	100.5	100.2	100.9
十二、金银珠宝	Gold, Silver and Pearls Jewelery	91.8	92.6	91.0
十三、中西药品及医疗保健用品	Chinese Traditional Medicine, Western Medicines and Health Care Appliances	101.6	100.4	103.1
十四、书报杂志及电子出版物	Books, Newspaper, Magzines and Electronic Publications	100.8	100.2	101.6
十五、燃料类	Fuels	99.7	99.8	99.5
十六、建筑材料及五金电料	Building and Decoration Materials	101.1	101.4	100.9
农业生产资料价格指数	**General Price Index of Means of Agricultural Production**	**97.9**		**97.9**

8-4　工业生产者出厂价格指数
EX-FACTORY PRICE INDICES OF INDUSTRIAL PRODUCTS

分　类	Group Name	上年=100 preceding year=100	1990年=100 1990=100	
		2014	2013	2014
总指数	General Indices	98.40	280.96	276.46
一、按轻重工业分	Grouped by Light Industry and Heavy Industry			
1.轻工业	Light Industry	99.90	225.57	225.34
以农产品为原料	Using Farm Products as Raw Material	100.00	257.73	257.73
以非农产品为原料	Using Non-Farm Products as Raw Material	99.50	148.67	147.93
2.重工业	Heavy Industry	97.90	333.56	326.56
采　掘	Mining and Quarrying	96.00	742.81	713.10
原　料	Raw Material	96.60	497.89	480.96
加　工	Processing	98.70	195.29	192.75
二、按两大部类分	Grouped by Two Sectors			
1.生产资料	Means of Production	97.80	325.08	317.93
采　掘	Mining and Quarrying	96.00	742.21	712.52
原　料	Raw Material	96.50	410.01	395.66
加　工	Processing	98.50	205.59	202.51
2.生活资料	Consumer Goods	100.10	203.99	204.19
食　品	Foods	100.40	275.31	276.41
衣　着	Clothing	100.90	225.64	227.67
一般日用品	Daily Use Articles	99.00	194.74	192.79
耐用消费品	Durable Consumer Goods	100.00	62.53	62.53

8–5 原材料、燃料、动力购进价格指数

RAW MATERIAL, FUEL, POWER PURCHASE PRICE INDICES

分　　类	Group Name	上年=100 preceding year=100	1990年=100 1990=100	
		2014	2013	2014
总指数	General Index	97.80	424.23	414.90
燃料、动力类	Fuel Powers	96.80	699.02	676.65
黑色金属材料类	Ferrous Metal	95.90	318.25	305.20
有色金属材料类	Non-ferrous Metal	95.20	333.31	317.31
化工原材料类	Chemical Materials	98.90	221.33	218.90
木材及纸浆类	Timber and Pulp	99.60	184.23	183.49
建筑材料及非金属矿类	Construction Materials and Non-Metal Mining Industry	97.50	324.84	316.72
其它工业原材料及半成品类	Other Industrial Raw Materials and Semi-Finished Products	98.80	193.29	190.97
农副产品类	Farm and Sideline Products	102.40	420.75	430.85
纺织原料类	Textile Raw Materials	99.30	213.27	211.78

8–6 固定资产投资价格指数

PRICE INDICES OF INVESTMENT IN FIXED ASSETS

分类	Name of Group	上年=100 preceding year=100	1990年=100 1990=100
		2014	2014
总指数	Total Indices	101.0	293.4
建筑安装工程	Construction and Installation	101.1	332.0
设备、工器具	Equipment and Devices	99.5	177.9
其他费用	Others	102.6	368.7

主要统计指标解释

居民消费价格指数　是反映一定时期内城乡居民所购买的生活消费品价格和服务项目价格变动趋势和程度的相对数，是对城市居民消费价格指数和农村居民消费价格指数进行综合汇总计算的结果。该指数可以观察和分析消费品的零售价格和服务价格变动对城乡居民实际生活费支出的影响程度。

城市居民消费价格指数　是反映一定时期内城市居民家庭所购买的生活消费品价格和服务项目价格变动趋势和程度的相对数。该指数可以观察和分析消费品的零售价格和服务项目价格变动对城镇职工货币工资的影响，作为研究职工生活和确定工资政策的依据。

农村居民消费价格指数　是反映一定时期内农村居民家庭所购买的生活消费品价格和服务项目价格变动趋势和程度的相对数。该指数可以观察农村消费品的零售价格和服务项目价格变动对农村居民生活消费支出的影响，直接反映农民生活水平的实际变化情况，为分析和研究农村居民生活问题提供依据。

商品零售价格指数　是反映一定时期内城乡商品零售价格变动趋势和程度的相对数。商品零售价格的变动直接影响到城乡居民的生活支出和国家的财政收入，影响居民购买力和市场供需的平衡，影响到消费与积累的比例关系。因此，该指数可以从一个侧面对上述经济活动进行观察和分析。

农业生产资料价格指数　指反映一定时期内农业生产资料价格变动趋势和程度的相对数。农业生产资料价格指数分为小农具、饲料、产品畜、役畜、半机械化农具、机械化农具、化学肥料、农药及农药械、农机用油、其他农业生产资料十大类。其编制目的是了解农业生产中物质资料投入价格的变动状况，服务于国民经济核算。1994 年以前，农业生产资料价格指数仅仅是商品零售价格指数的一个类别，此后，从商品零售价格指数中分离出来，单独编制。

农产品生产价格指数　是反映一定时期内，农产品生产者出售农产品价格水平变动趋势及幅度的相对数。该指数可以客观反映全国农产品生产价格水平和结构变动情况，满足农业与国民经济核算需要。其中某代表品生产价格指数是通过对全部有出售该产品行为的调查单位的个体指数进行几何平均求得的，类价格指数是通过对其所属的类（或代表品）的价格指数进行加权平均求得的。季度累计价格指数的计算方法与分季指数的计算方法相同。

工业生产者出厂价格指数　是反映一定时期内全部工业产品出厂价格总水平的变动趋势和程度的相对数，包括工业企业售给本企业以外所有单位的各种产品和直接售给居民用于生活消费的产品。该指数可以观察出厂价格变动对工业总产值及增加值的影响。

工业生产者购进价格指数　是反映工业企业作为生产投入，而从物资交易市场和能源、原材料生产企业购买原材料、燃料和动力产品时，所支付的价格水平变动趋势和程度的统计指标，是扣除工业企业物质消耗成本中的价格变动影响的重要依据。

目前，我国编制的原材料、燃料和动力购进价格指数所调查的产品包括燃料动力、黑色金属、有色金属、化工、建材等九大类的近 1800 种产品。

固定资产投资价格指数　是反映一定时期内固定资产投资品及项目的价格变动趋势和程度的相对数。固定资产投资额是由建筑安装工程投资完成额、设备工器具购置投资完成额和其他费用投资完成额三部分组成的。编制固定资产投资价格指数应首先分别编制上述三部分投资的价格指数，然后采用加权算术平均法求出固定资产投资价格总指数。

该指数可以准确地反映固定资产投资中涉及的各类投资品和取费项目价格变动趋势和变动幅度，消除按现价计算的固定资产投资指标中的价格变动因素，真实地反映固定资产投资的规模、速度、结构和效益，为国家科学地制定、检查固定资产投资计划并提高宏观调控水平，为完善国民经济核算体系提供科学的、可靠的依据。

房地产价格指数　是反映一定时期内房地产价格变动趋势和程度的相对数，包括房屋销售价格指数、房屋租赁价格指数、土地交易价格指数和物业管理价格指数。这四套指数的计算方法相似，均采用由下到上逐级汇总的方法。

Explanatory Notes on Main Statistical Indicators

Urban Consumer Price Indices reflect the trend and degree of changes in prices of consumer goods and services purchased by urban households during a given period. It can be used to observe and analyze the impact of price changes in consumer goods and services on wages (in monetary terms) of urban staff and workers, and provide basis for policy-making concerning the living cost and wages of staff and workers.

Rural Consumer Price Indices reflect the trend and degree of changes in prices of consumer goods and services purchased by rural households during a given period. It can be used to observe the impact of change in retail prices of consumer goods and service prices in rural areas on living expenditure of rural households, and to show the changes in the living standard of peasants. It provides basis for analysis and research on condition of life in rural areas.

Retail Price Indices reflect the trend and degree of change in retail prices of commodities during a given period. The change in retail prices of commodities directly affect the living expenditure of urban and rural residents, government revenue, purchasing power of residents and the equilibrium of market supply and demand, and the ratio of consumption to accumulation. Therefore, the retail price indices are useful to analyze the changes of the above economic activities.

Price Indices of Means of Agricultural Production reflect the trend and degree of changes in prices of means of agricultural production during a given period. Price indices of means of agricultural production are composed of 10 categories including small farm tools, feeds, domestic animals for meat, draught domestic animals, semi-mechanized farm machinery, mechanized farm machinery, chemical fertilizers, pesticides and spraying machinery, fuels for farm machinery and other means of agricultural production. Compilation of these indices helps to understand the changes in prices of input into agricultural production and facilitate the compilation of national account statistics. Before 1994, price indices of means of agricultural production was a sub-category in the in the retail price indices of commodities, and it has been compiled separately since 1994.

Indices of Producers' Prices for Farm Products reflect the trend and degree of changes in producers' prices received by farmers when they sell farm products during a given period. These indices depict the change in the level and structure of producers' prices of farm products of the country and meet the needs of agriculture statistics and national account statistics. The producers' price index of a given product is calculated through geometrical mean of individual indices of all surveyed units who sell such product, and the indices of a product category is obtained through weighted mean of price indices of all products in the category. Method for calculating accumulative quarterly indices is the same as for calculating the distinctive quarterly indices.

Ex-factory Price Indices of Industrial Products reflect the trend and degree of changes in general ex-factory prices of all industrial products during a given period, including sales of industrial products by an industrial enterprise to all units outside the enterprise, as well as sales of consumer goods to residents. It can be used to analyze the impact of ex-factory prices on gross output value and value-added of the industrial sector.

Indices of Purchasing Prices of Raw Materials, Fuels and Power reflect changes in the level and degree of prices paid by industrial enterprises when they purchase production input such as raw materials, fuels and power from the market or from other energy or raw materials producing enterprises. These indices provide important basis for measuring the material consumption of industrial enterprises after removing influence of price changes.

At present, close to 1,800 products in 9 categories, including fuels and power, ferrous metals, non-ferrous metals, chemicals, building materials, are covered in China for the survey to produce indices of purchasing prices of raw materials, fuels and power.

Price Indices of Investment in Fixed Assets reflect the trend and degree of changes in prices of investment goods and projects in fixed assets during a given period. The investment in fixed assets consists of three components, namely the investment in construction and installation, the investment in purchases of equipment and instrument, and the investment in other items. Price indices of investment in fixed assets are calculated as the weighted arithmetic mean of the price indices of the three components of investment in fixed assets.

Removing the factor of price change in the aggregates of investment at current prices, this indicator shows the changes in the prices of commodities and fees involved in the investment of fixed assets, and can be used to observe the actual size, growth, structure, and efficiency of investment in fixed assets and provides reliable and scientific data for government planning, management, decision-making, and further improving the current national accounting system.

Price Indices for Real Estate reflect the trend and degree of changes in prices of real estate during a given period, including price indices for selling houses and buildings, price indices for leasing houses and buildings and price indices for land transaction. The methods for the compilation of the three sets of indices are similar in that they all use bottom-up approach under which data are reported from lower level to higher level.

9 居民生活

People's Livelihood

资料整理：徐　菁　黄　蓉
　　　　　孙再明　陈福才

9-1 居民生活水平情况
PEOPLE'S LIVING STANDARD

项　目	Item	单位	unit	2000	2005	2010	2012	2013	2014
一、城乡就业	Employment								
每一农村劳动力负担人数	Average Person Supported by a Rural Laborer	人	person	1.49	1.34	1.27	1.28	1.31	1.41
每一城镇就业者负担人数	Average Person Supported by a Urban Laborer	人	person	1.73	1.96	2.01	1.95	1.81	1.79
城镇登记失业率	The Rate of Registered Unemployment	%	ercentage	3.50	4.33	4.18	3.83	3.49	3.10
二、城乡居民收入	Revenue								
农村居民人均可支配收入	Net Income of Rural Residents Per Capita	元	yuan	2267.00	3099.00	5832.00	7852.00	8866.95	10849.06
农村居民人均可支配收入指数(1990=100)	Indices of Net Income of Rural Residents Per Capita (1990=100)	%	ercentage	338.20	461.80	869.24	1170.22	1321.48	1617.33
城镇居民人均可支配收入	Annual Disposable Income of Urban Residents	元	yuan	5525.00	8786.00	16058.00	20839.59	22906.40	24852.28
城镇居民人均可支配收入指数(1990=100)	Indices of Net Annual Disposable Income of Urban Residents (1990=100)	%	ercentage	387.10	615.80	1125.45	1459.92	1604.71	1741.33
国有职工平均工资	Average Wages of Staff and Workers in State-Owned Units	元	yuan	7989	14774	35981	43438	46126	55071
三、城乡居民人平消费水平	Consumption Level								
农村居民	Rural Residents	元	yuan	1302	2503	4758	6705	7755	8608
城镇居民	Urban Residents	元	yuan	6250	8051	13576	17296	19156	21854
四、储　蓄	Savings								
城乡居民人平储蓄存款余额	Balance of Saving Deposits of Rural and Urban Residents Per Capita	元	yuan	3209	7929	17216	23589	27591	30686
五、平均每人居住面积	Floor Area of Housing Per Capita								
城　市(大、中)	Municipalities (Large and Medium-sized)	平方米	sq.m	13.90	29.90	33.20	35.79	38.82	41.90
农　村	Rural Areas	平方米	sq.m	30.11	36.05	40.99	44.98	41.84	54.78
六、交　通	Transportations								
城镇每百户拥有汽车	Cars Ouned Per 100	辆	set			5.53	12.48	13.28	13.65
七、文　化	Culture								
每百人每天有报纸	Newspaper Owned Per 100 Persons Every Day	份	unit	6.17	8.89	8.70	9.77	9.36	9.01
每人每年有图书、杂志	Books and Magazines Owned Per Capita Anuually	册	unit	8.54	8.99	9.90	10.40	9.87	9.52
八、教　育	Education								
学龄儿童入学率	Emrollment Ratio of School-Age Children	%	ercentsge	99.53	99.65	99.96	99.97	99.98	99.99
每万人口有大学生数	Number of University Students Per 10000 Persons	人	person	57.49	167.91	226.58	239.85	245.12	244.10
九、卫　生	Health Care								
每千人有医院病床数	Number of Hospital-Beds Owned By Per 1000 Person	张	unit	2.18	2.31	3.26	4.10	4.97	5.47
每千人有医生	Number of Doctors Owned By Per 1000 Persons	人	person	1.74	1.49	1.62	1.77	2.06	2.19

注：平均每人居住面积中，城市(大、中)从2002年起为建筑面积，以前年份为居住面积。

Notes: Of Average Housing Areas, it refers to Construction Area of Municipalities (large and medium-sized)areas.since 2002, before2002, it refers to living areas.

9–2 居民消费水平

PEOPLE'S CONSUMPTION LEVEL

年 份 year	居民消费 (亿元) People's Censurption (100 million yuan)	农村居民 rural residernts	城镇居民 wrban residernts	居民消费水平 (元) level of consumption	农村居民 rural residernts	城镇居民 wrban residernts
1982	126.75	90.67	36.08	266	227	462
1983	141.49	101.17	40.32	293	251	502
1984	172.19	120.41	51.78	352	300	592
1985	203.23	129.78	73.45	411	328	738
1986	247.13	158.31	88.82	493	402	825
1987	271.22	172.47	98.75	533	434	891
1988	328.82	204.21	124.61	638	509	1092
1989	398.09	255.09	143.00	762	630	1218
1990	434.62	273.27	161.35	813	659	1341
1991	475.85	286.08	189.77	869	674	1541
1992	546.61	301.60	245.01	986	706	1926
1993	694.49	357.10	337.35	1236	831	2554
1994	845.14	413.40	431.75	1486	964	3086
1995	1095.97	504.10	591.85	1908	1183	3989
1996	1346.76	594.80	751.99	2323	1396	4892
1997	1438.12	614.90	823.26	2459	1441	5208
1998	1518.92	610.20	908.68	2579	1427	5632
1999	1507.12	558.40	948.69	2545	1302	5802
2000	1594.08	559.10	1034.96	2680	1302	6250
2001	1767.38	585.40	1181.96	2962	1365	7042
2002	1951.54	606.80	1344.70	3263	1418	7899
2003	2188.05	637.70	1550.36	3853	1926	6547
2004	2452.62	700.80	1751.85	4309	2134	7277
2005	2785.42	815.32	1970.10	4883	2503	8051
2006	3124.37	906.15	2218.22	5480	2813	8944
2007	3709.69	1051.82	2657.87	6513	3300	10593
2008	4225.38	1217.95	3007.43	7406	3864	11780
2009	4456.31	1277.72	3178.59	7791	4137	12080
2010	5136.78	1419.65	3717.13	8977	4758	13576
2011	6241.95	1597.69	4644.26	10873	5653	15935
2012	7085.46	1830.83	5254.63	12283	6705	17296
2013	8053.82	2064.74	5989.08	13912	7755	19156
2014	9124.48	2292.06	6832.42	15762	8608	21854

9–3 居民消费水平指数

INDICES OF PEOPLE'S CONSUMPTION LEVEL

(1978年=100)

年 份 year	居民消费 (%) People's Censurption (%)	农村居民 rural residernts	城镇居民 wrban residernts	居民消费水平 (%) level of consumption(%)	农村居民 rural residernts	城镇居民 wrban residernts
1982	156.2	169.2	132.3	149.0	164.2	111.5
1983	172.2	186.6	145.4	162.1	179.7	119.0
1984	196.6	205.4	181.4	183.3	198.7	136.6
1985	218.4	212.2	233.3	201.1	208.2	154.2
1986	253.2	247.7	267.4	229.7	244.3	163.5
1987	263.0	255.1	282.4	235.4	249.4	167.4
1988	268.8	257.1	295.6	237.8	248.6	170.4
1989	278.8	273.6	292.7	243.0	262.6	163.9
1990	290.5	281.2	312.9	247.6	263.3	170.8
1991	275.4	257.6	314.1	229.3	235.7	167.6
1992	281.7	254.0	339.6	231.8	230.5	175.3
1993	338.3	276.9	460.8	274.7	250.1	229.1
1994	380.3	292.4	553.4	304.9	264.6	259.6
1995	421.7	303.5	653.0	334.8	276.3	288.9
1996	474.9	340.2	737.9	373.6	310.0	315.2
1997	499.1	342.9	802.9	389.3	311.8	333.1
1998	549.5	354.6	927.3	425.5	321.8	377.1
1999	571.5	356.0	989.4	440.0	322.1	397.1
2000	599.5	361.0	1062.6	459.8	326.0	420.9
2001	661.3	377.2	1206.1	505.8	341.3	471.0
2002	738.6	391.9	1394.3	564.0	355.3	537.0
2003	807.3	393.9	1578.3	614.7	359.2	595.0
2004	868.7	405.3	1726.7	659.6	372.5	640.2
2005	963.4	458.4	1899.3	729.5	425.0	692.7
2006	1074.2	502.9	2132.9	826.5	480.7	777.9
2007	1191.3	557.2	2365.4	917.4	538.4	853.4
2008	1279.5	599.5	2540.4	984.4	585.8	900.3
2009	1352.4	631.3	2690.3	1038.5	625.0	935.4
2010	1507.9	676.1	3045.4	1156.9	693.1	1017.7
2011	1722.0	710.6	3584.4	1316.6	768.6	1125.6
2012	1897.6	785.9	3946.4	1444.3	880.0	1188.6
2013	2106.3	863.7	4396.3	1597.4	991.8	1286.1
2014	2342.2	941.4	4919.5	1769.9	1107.8	1399.3

注：2003年以前数据根据2004年第一次经济普查资料修订。
Notes:Data before 2003 is Gmended accordity to ecorymic survey 2004.

9–4 城镇居民家庭基本情况

年份 Year	调查户数 (户) Number of Households Surveyed (household)	平均每户家庭人口 (人) Average Number of people Per Household (person)	平均每户就业人口 (人) Number of Employees Per Household (person)	每一就业者负担人数 (人) Average Persons Supported by a Labor (person)
1963	240	5.30	1.63	3.25
1964	299	5.36	1.61	3.33
1965	370	5.22	1.60	3.26
1980	571	4.20	2.32	1.81
1985	1658	3.84	2.15	1.79
1986	1910	3.76	2.13	1.77
1987	1900	3.73	2.12	1.76
1988	1950	3.61	2.07	1.74
1989	1990	3.52	2.05	1.72
1990	1990	3.47	2.04	1.70
1991	1990	3.45	2.04	1.69
1992	1940	3.36	2.02	1.66
1993	1890	3.29	1.98	1.66
1994	1330	3.23	1.95	1.66
1995	1330	3.22	1.92	1.68
1996	1390	3.24	1.95	1.66
1997	1790	3.23	1.89	1.71
1998	1640	3.19	1.90	1.68
1999	1540	3.15	1.86	1.69
2000	1540	3.14	1.81	1.73
2001	1540	3.10	1.77	1.75
2002	1600	3.07	1.64	1.87
2003	1600	3.06	1.68	1.82
2004	1700	3.03	1.65	1.83
2005	1800	2.98	1.52	1.96
2006	1800	2.96	1.55	1.91
2007	1850	2.95	1.59	1.86
2008	1900	2.96	1.50	1.97
2009	1900	2.94	1.48	1.99
2010	1900	2.93	1.46	2.01
2011	1900	2.90	1.47	1.97
2012	1900	2.89	1.48	1.95
2013	1718	2.77	1.53	1.81
2014	3060	2.85	1.59	1.79

注：①2002年方法制度重新修订，部分指标有所变化：原“平均每人居住面积”改为“平均每人建筑总面积”；原“平均每人实际收入”改为“平均每人总收入”；原“平均每人实际支出”改为“平均每人总支出”。
②2014年起使用城乡一体化住户收支与生活状况调查数据，与之前的分城镇和农村住户调查的范围、方法、指标口径有所不同(此后相关表同)。
③2014年为城镇常住居民人均可支配收入，与2014年以前不同。

BASIC CONDITIONS OF URBAN HOUSEHOLDS

平均每户就业面 (%) Percentage of Employed Persons Per Household (%)	平均每人 Per Capita 总收入 (元) Actual Income (yuan)	#可支配收入 (元) Disposable Income (yuan)	平均每人 Per Capita 总支出 (元) Actual Expenditures (yuan)	消费性支出 Living Expenditures	#食品 Food	平均每人建筑面积 (平方米) Average Living Floor Space Per Cappita (sq.m)
30.75	238.1	238.1	237.2	218.4	133.9	
30.04	232.9	232.9	228.3	211.7	122.7	
30.65	224.3	224.3	218.8	204.4	118.0	3.3
55.24	413.7	413.7	394.2	369.3	210.6	5.1
55.99	713.3	704.2	693.1	644.2	324.5	7.9
56.65	861.5	851.3	815.5	751.5	387.5	8.2
56.84	960.6	951.8	919.1	836.1	443.2	8.4
57.34	1136.4	1128.1	1153.1	1058.8	538.9	8.9
58.24	1271.6	1262.6	1250.0	1130.7	607.0	9.1
58.79	1437.1	1427.2	1349.4	1220.3	652.4	9.8
59.13	1603.7	1592.9	1538.2	1380.2	717.4	9.6
60.12	1886.4	1874.2	1799.9	1577.7	799.0	9.9
60.18	2453.5	2438.7	2358.1	2097.6	941.5	10.5
60.37	3360.0	3346.0	3588.6	2733.1	1307.1	11.1
59.63	4031.9	4016.7	3977.3	3433.8	1680.6	11.9
60.19	4367.0	4350.2	4290.6	3713.5	1731.4	11.8
58.51	4693.8	4673.2	4549.7	3855.6	1773.6	12.8
59.56	4849.4	4826.4	4903.1	4074.4	1787.7	12.7
59.04	5234.5	5212.8	5333.8	4340.6	1783.4	13.2
57.64	5542.6	5524.5	5643.6	4644.5	1779.4	13.9
57.10	5888.7	5856.0	5774.8	4804.8	1799.4	15.2
53.42	7142.2	6789.0	7159.7	5608.9	2087.8	26.2
54.90	7745.8	7322.0	7551.1	5963.3	2279.6	26.3
54.46	8522.1	8022.8	8076.1	6398.5	2516.2	27.3
51.01	9395.1	8786.0	8582.8	6737.0	2625.4	29.9
52.36	10533.3	9803.0	9839.7	7397.0	2868.4	31.0
53.90	12421.8	11485.0	11476.7	8701.0	3456.0	32.3
50.68	14174.3	13153.0	12471.0	9478.0	3996.0	32.0
50.34	15698.0	14367.0	13868.0	10294.0	4160.5	32.8
49.83	17572.8	16058.4	15612.3	11451.0	4429.3	33.2
50.69	20193.3	18373.9	18123.4	13163.8	5363.7	35.5
51.21	22903.9	20839.6	20107.1	14496.0	5837.9	35.8
55.23	25180.5	22906.4	20419.5	15749.5	6259.2	38.8
55.73	27538.9	24852.3	23175.1	16681.4	3688.3	41.9

Note:①" Per Capita Living Space (sq.m)" in the above table was changed into "Per Capita Living Floor Space(sq.m)";"Per Capita Actual Income(yuan)"into; "Per Capita Actual Expenditures(yuan)" into "Per Capita Total Expenditures(yuan)';owing to the changes of items in the reversion of 2002 mearurement system.

② The integrated household income and expenditure survey has been used since 2014, including both urban and rural households. The coverage ,methodology and definitions used in the survey are different from those used for the separate urban and rural household survey prior to 2014(…).

③ The concept is Per Capita Disposable Income of Rural Permanent Residents in 2014 ,different from that before 2014.

9-5 城镇居民家庭收支情况(2014)

单位：元

项　　目	Item	总　计 Total
调查户数(户)	Households Surveyed	3059.92
比　重(%)	Ratio	100.00
平均每户家庭人口(人)	Average Number of Residents Per Household	2.85
平均每户离退休人口(人)	Average Number of Retirees Per Household	0.41
平均每一就业者负担人数(人)	Average Persons supported by a Urban Labor	1.79
平均每户就业面(%)	Average Employment Rate Per Household	55.73
平均每人总收入	Per Capita Total Income	27538.89
#可支配收入	Disposable Income	24852.28
平均每人借贷收入	Income of Loans Per Capita	1279.24
#提取储蓄存款	Savings Withdrawn	929.24
平均每人借贷支出	Expenditures of Loans Per Capita	1128.48
#存入储蓄款	Money Saved	662.06
平均每人总支出	Total Expenditure Per Capita	23175.07
#消费性支出	Consumption Expenditure	16681.41
一、食品烟酒	Food Cigarettes and Wine	5390.63
食品	Food	3688.32
谷物	Grain	582.54
薯类	Patato	25.77
豆类	Bean	65.23
食用油	Edible Oil	194.18
蔬菜和食用菌	Vegetable and Edible Fungi	633.49
肉类	Meat	803.60
禽类	Poultry	151.74
水产品	Aquatic Products	287.33
蛋类	Egg	99.29
奶类	Milk	181.62
干鲜瓜果类	Fruits and Processed Products	315.54
糖果糕点类	Sweet	116.75
其他食品	Others	231.25
烟酒	Cigarettes and Wine	573.81
饮料	Drink	87.55
饮食服务	Food Service	1040.95
二、衣　着	Clothing	1463.90
衣类	Clothing	1153.01
鞋类	Shoes	310.89
三、居　住	Residence	3575.10
租赁房房租	Rent	188.69
住房维修及管理	Management	376.52
水电燃料及其他	Water and Power	805.96
自有住房折算租金	Converted Rent of Zts Own	2203.93
四、生活用品及服务	Household Facilities Articles and Services	1024.67
家具及室内装饰品	Furniture	101.22
家用器具	Appliances	287.14
家用纺织品	Drygoods	81.66
家庭日用杂品	Commodity	350.92
个人用品	Personal Helongings	147.31
家庭服务	Households Service	56.40
五、交通通信	Transport and Communication	1802.35
交通	Transport	1071.02
通信	Communication	731.33
六、教育文化娱乐	Education Culture and Recreation	1894.84
教　育	Education	1139.92
文化娱乐用品	Cultural Recreation Articals	215.12
文化娱乐服务	Cultural Recreation Services	539.79
七、医疗保健	Medicine and Medical Service	1187.81
医疗器具及药品	medical apparatus and instruments	388.03
医疗服务	Medical Service	799.78
八、其他用品和服务	Miscellaneous Goods and Services	342.11
其他用品	Goods	191.62
其他服务	Services	150.50

注：2014年城镇居民消费居住支出中自有住房折算租金指现住房为自有住房的住户为自身消费提供住房服务的折算价值，属于实物消费，不包括在现金消费支出中。

PER CAPITA INCOME AND EXPENDITURE OF URBAN HOUSEHOLDS(2014)

(yuan)

低收入户 Low Income Households	中低收入户 Lower Middle Income Households	中等收入户 Middle Income Households	中高收入户 Upper Middle Income Households	高收入户 High Income Households
612.17	612.58	614.17	614.50	606.50
20.01	20.02	20.07	20.08	19.82
3.24	3.20	2.95	2.65	2.19
0.19	0.35	0.45	0.52	0.56
1.92	1.79	1.78	1.77	1.67
52.00	55.79	56.17	56.36	59.80
13520.18	20224.02	26361.75	34947.59	52962.39
10642.96	18232.43	24321.02	32043.68	48879.38
1184.47	917.45	1601.51	1357.68	1437.49
892.28	573.12	1176.83	855.55	1283.96
689.82	917.23	1001.80	1455.96	1901.18
472.55	464.42	513.06	858.42	1221.46
14683.94	18482.88	22596.42	27387.50	39136.50
9562.83	13232.83	16381.57	19861.64	29500.91
3449.84	4535.63	5340.13	6516.81	8384.74
2581.24	3216.17	3666.48	4348.41	5340.33
416.51	446.68	516.79	689.11	1007.69
21.77	20.97	25.11	30.60	34.26
50.27	60.43	64.87	77.55	80.91
164.58	179.92	193.55	205.92	248.35
468.39	577.65	643.39	733.16	837.60
576.29	734.19	814.09	939.99	1078.52
102.29	140.55	150.56	185.04	205.79
183.13	250.75	288.56	347.16	429.01
74.86	91.95	98.51	113.65	131.64
126.69	165.26	171.52	216.38	262.69
171.95	259.26	326.63	391.04	515.56
60.35	86.33	111.89	152.16	213.66
164.15	202.22	261.01	266.65	294.64
345.70	481.69	619.75	670.69	885.46
53.98	69.34	83.57	114.31	139.75
468.92	768.42	970.33	1383.40	2019.19
696.02	1120.97	1539.89	1792.68	2669.47
539.19	881.35	1202.17	1417.88	2126.42
156.83	239.62	337.72	374.80	543.05
1939.82	2625.77	3375.79	4222.10	7048.32
74.27	93.76	188.86	270.27	410.23
202.99	331.84	474.51	347.53	616.27
565.06	643.41	747.92	866.81	1435.78
1097.50	1556.77	1964.49	2737.49	4586.04
527.27	699.48	1022.69	1221.58	2055.56
42.21	70.02	93.31	113.22	237.16
138.14	174.76	275.83	359.31	617.31
49.29	55.09	91.14	104.32	131.33
215.07	286.82	372.98	412.12	553.70
55.61	98.37	147.79	197.61	301.61
26.95	14.41	41.65	34.99	214.45
780.60	1486.60	1804.46	2128.93	3467.31
376.73	890.26	1061.70	1251.10	2217.99
403.87	596.34	742.77	877.82	1249.32
1264.11	1656.93	1795.85	2339.53	2821.95
994.49	1147.63	1074.26	1285.44	1262.76
108.22	152.45	201.29	273.36	424.18
161.41	356.85	520.31	780.74	1135.01
744.13	881.28	1166.33	1272.24	2275.03
236.99	326.10	368.02	461.50	654.17
507.14	555.18	798.31	810.74	1620.86
161.03	226.19	336.40	367.78	778.53
97.65	135.00	186.60	180.04	446.83
63.38	91.19	149.80	187.74	331.70

Note : Home ownership conversion in urban household residence consumption expenditure in 2014,refers to a resident who lives on a self-owned house now, provides housing service the conversion value for their own consumption. It belongs to material consumption, not included in cash consumption expenditure.

9-6 城镇居民家庭平均每百户年末耐用品拥有量(2014)

品名		Item		总平均 Total Average	低收入户 Low Income Households
摩托车	(辆)	Motorcycles	unit	31.64	47.83
助力车	(辆)	Auxiliary Drving Bikes	unit	22.83	20.50
家用汽车	(辆)	Cars for Household Use	unit	13.65	7.91
洗衣机	(台)	Washing Machins	unit	88.04	79.12
电冰箱	(台)	Refrigerators	unit	93.24	85.08
彩色电视机	(台)	Color TV Sets	unit	116.59	111.25
家用电脑	(台)	Computers	unit	69.95	43.82
组合音响	(套)	Hi-Fi Stereo Systems	unit	11.75	9.08
摄像机	(台)	TV Cameras	unit	6.24	1.54
照相机	(架)	Cameras	unit	28.35	9.67
中高档乐器	(件)	Medium and High-Grade Musical Instruments	unit	2.81	0.05
微波炉	(台)	Microwave Stove	unit	44.98	19.53
空调器	(台)	Air Conditioners	unit	119.26	71.93
热水器	(台)	Showers	unit	84.27	69.21
消毒碗柜	(台)	Disinfection cabinet	unit	8.91	2.60
洗碗机	(台)	Dishwasher	unit	2.03	1.10
健身器材	(件)	Health Care Instruments	unit	3.33	0.52
固定电话	(部)	Fixed telephone	set	41.71	32.80
移动电话	(部)	Mobile Phones	set	212.26	212.45

NUMBER OF DURABLE CONSUMER GOODS OWNED PER 100 URBAN HOUSEHOLDS AT THE YEAR-END BY INCOME LEVEL(2014)

中低收入户 Lower Middle Income Households	中等收入户 Middle Income Households	中高收入户 Upper Middle Income Households	高收入户 High Income Households
39.98	30.51	24.86	15.07
31.06	26.90	19.95	15.75
9.18	14.46	15.07	21.63
88.08	89.03	92.15	91.78
97.69	95.12	95.32	93.00
120.45	115.22	118.62	117.40
67.01	72.53	76.71	89.66
10.80	13.25	11.55	14.09
4.30	6.57	7.90	10.91
19.92	26.86	37.78	47.51
0.96	4.17	3.64	5.23
35.74	45.15	61.23	63.21
105.49	125.58	135.05	158.19
82.92	87.21	87.22	94.76
6.90	8.82	12.53	13.70
0.98	3.37	2.75	1.96
3.03	4.80	3.88	4.42
41.52	45.06	46.15	42.99
227.93	223.96	207.21	189.77

9—7 城镇居民家庭房屋居住分布情况
URABN HOUSEHOLDS HOUSING CONDITIONS

分组	Group	各组户数占总户数比重(%) Percentage of Household in Each Group of the Total Households				
		2010	2011	2012	2013	2014
总计	Total	1900	1900	1900	1718	3060
一、房屋产权	Building Property Right					
租赁公房	Leased Pubilc Houses	7.2	6.0	5.5	3.6	5.3
租赁私房	Leased Private Houses	2.9	1.9	1.9	7.5	7.7
原有私房	Original Private Houses	15.5	15.2	14.1	24.4	28.9
房改私房	Private Houses	50.9	44.5	44.1	28.3	24.5
商品房	Commercial Houses	21.6	30.1	32.4	32.8	26.1
借用房	Borrowed				1.4	1.1
其他	Others	1.9	2.4	1.0	1.9	6.3
二、住宅样式	Housing Pattens					
单栋住宅	Sole-Unit Houses	8.0	10.9	10.5	23.1	35.7
四居室	Four-Room Houses	4.1	4.6	4.9	3.8	3.2
三居室	Three-Room Houses	25.3	28.1	28.7	25.3	25.5
二居室	Two-Room Houses	42.4	42.9	43.6	35.2	27.0
一居室	One-Room Houses	4.7	3.9	4.2	5.8	6.3
普通楼房	Ordinary Houses	11.9	7.7	6.4	2.1	-
平房及其他	Bungalow and Others	3.6	1.9	1.7	4.6	2.2
三、用水情况	Waters					
独用自来水	Private Tap Water	99.5	99.8	99.8	97.8	94.7
公用自来水	Public Tap Water	0.2	0.2	0.2		-
井、河水	Water from Rivers and Wells	0.3			1.5	3.9
其他	Others				0.7	1.4
四、卫生设备	Sanitary Faciities					
无卫生设备	Have not	2.1	0.9	0.7	3.5	3.0
独立卫生设备	Independent Health Facilities	95.1	97.8	98.3	93.8	89.2
公用卫生设备	Public Health Facilities	2.9	1.3	1.0	2.6	7.8
五、取暖设备	Warming Facilities					
无取暖设备	Have not	36.0	24.7	22.5	29.5	33.8
空调设备	Air Conditioner	56.7	65.9	66.7		-
暖气	Heater	5.8	4.0	5.2		-
其他	Others	1.5	5.4	5.6	70.4	66.2
六、燃料使用情况	Fuel Material Usage Conditions					
煤	Coal	10.2	5.9	5.1	2.3	2.1
罐装液化石油气	LPG cylinders	55.7	43.4	43.0	47.5	30.6
管道液化石油气	LPG Pipeline	1.8	2.0	1.6	2.6	1.3
管道煤气	Piped Coal Gas	6.4	5.2	4.0	6.9	2.3
管道天然气	Gas pipeline	25.7	42.7	45.5	31.1	18.6
其他	Others	0.3	0.9	0.8	9.2	45.1
七、通信设备使用情况	Telecommunication Facilities Usage Conditions					
1.每百户固定电话	Per 100 fixed telephone	71.9	61.2	59.3	39.2	41.7
2.每百户移动电话	Mobile Phones Per 100 Households	166.0	193.8	204.4	207.6	212.3

注：2014年住宅样式为四居室的数据包含四居室及以上单元房的占比。
Note:The data refers to four bedroom and above for four bedroom units in 2014.

9-8 农民家庭基本情况
BASIC CONDITIONS OF RURAL HOUSEHOLDS

年 份	调查户数 Number of Households Surveyed	常住人口(人) Permanent Residents (person)	平均每户常住人口(人) Average Permanent Residents Per Households (person)	平均每户整半劳动力(人) Average Full-Time and Part-Time Labors Per Household (person)	平均每个劳动力负担人口(人) Average Person Supported by Each Labor (person)
1981	954	5497	5.76	2.67	2.16
1982	948	5364	5.66	2.73	2.08
1983	1470	8267	5.62	2.99	1.88
1984	1510	8317	5.51	3.02	1.83
1985	3300	16473	5.07	2.98	1.71
1986	3300	16432	4.98	2.96	1.68
1987	3300	16195	4.91	2.94	1.67
1988	3300	15966	4.84	2.93	1.65
1989	3300	15567	4.72	2.86	1.65
1990	3300	15411	4.67	2.84	1.65
1991	3300	15094	4.57	2.66	1.72
1992	3300	14900	4.52	2.63	1.71
1993	3300	14651	4.44	2.65	1.67
1994	3300	14466	4.38	2.72	1.61
1995	3300	14447	4.38	2.77	1.58
1996	3300	14053	4.26	2.75	1.55
1997	3200	13453	4.20	2.64	1.60
1998	3200	13239	4.14	2.62	1.58
1999	3200	13082	4.09	2.63	1.55
2000	3300	13557	4.11	2.76	1.49
2001	3300	13490	4.09	2.75	1.49
2002	3300	13420	4.07	2.78	1.46
2003	3300	13385	4.06	2.86	1.42
2004	3300	13356	4.05	2.92	1.39
2005	3300	13228	4.01	2.99	1.34
2006	3300	13259	4.02	3.03	1.34
2007	3300	13186	4.00	3.06	1.30
2008	3300	13163	3.99	3.08	1.29
2009	3300	13151	3.99	3.12	1.28
2010	3300	13123	3.98	3.14	1.27
2011	3300	13120	3.98	3.12	1.27
2012	3300	13140	3.98	3.12	1.28
2013	2096	7921	3.78	2.88	1.31
2014	2522	7233	2.87	2.03	1.41

注:①2014年起使用城乡一体化住户收支与生活状况调查数据,与之前的分城镇和农村住户调查的范围、方法、指标口径有所不同(此后相关表同)。

②2014年起农民人均纯收入改为农村常住居民人均可支配收入。

Note: ①The integrated household income and expenditure survey has been used since 2014 , including both urban and rural households. The coverage , methodology and definitions used in the survey are different from those used for the separate urban and rural household survey prior to 2014.(Related tables the same ever since).

② Per Capita Income of Rural Households has been changed into Per Capita Disposable Income of Rural Permanent Residents since 2014.

9–8 续表 1 continued

年 份 year	平均每户经营耕地面积(亩) Space of Cultivation land Per Household (mu)	平均每户年末拥有生产性固定资产原值(元) Value of Production Fixed Assets Per Household (yuan)	平均每户年内新建购房屋面积(平方米) Floor Space of Rooms Newly Built Per Household (sq.m)	平均每人年末使用房屋面积(平方米) Lving Space Per Capita (sq.m)
1981	0.52		6.51	15.31
1982	0.57	159.20	5.36	16.45
1983	8.95	389.97	5.65	18.04
1984	8.66	530.20	6.70	19.03
1985	7.60	557.86	8.24	21.18
1986	7.48	610.47	8.45	22.63
1987	7.31	672.87	7.79	23.50
1988	7.04	759.61	4.90	24.15
1989	6.95	819.53	5.50	25.10
1990	6.79	861.91	6.20	25.73
1991	6.58	1068.45	4.56	27.33
1992	6.47	1146.94	4.07	27.94
1993	6.36	1281.66	3.75	25.80
1994	6.69	1542.58	3.91	25.22
1995	6.73	1775.57	4.66	25.92
1996	6.82	2291.60	4.25	26.58
1997	6.56	2688.67	4.98	27.99
1998	6.08	2604.21	4.74	28.38
1999	6.08	2543.61	4.19	29.87
2000	5.93	2482.02	3.48	30.11
2001	5.94	2773.52	2.98	31.19
2002	6.01	2953.37	4.65	31.55
2003	6.03	2989.82	4.01	32.44
2004	6.15	3046.47	2.82	33.68
2005	6.15	4121.20	3.88	36.05
2006	6.12	4297.19	4.22	36.77
2007	6.41	4996.00	3.36	37.96
2008	6.36	5434.99	5.90	39.04
2009	6.51	6368.83	4.40	40.11
2010	6.73	7078.46	5.05	40.99
2011	6.44	9636.11	7.88	44.24
2012	6.80	10813.13	5.46	44.98
2013	7.08	13839.73	6.06	41.84
2014	6.97	12048.41	5.81	54.78

9-8 续表 2 continued

年 份	平均每户年末使用房屋价值(元) Value of Per Households Living Space (yuan)	平均每人总收入(元) Total Income Per Capita (yuan)	平均每人纯收入(元) Net Income Per Capita (yuan)	平均每人生活消费支出(元) Living Expenditures Per Capita (yuan)
1981	1249.13	232.64	217.44	183.78
1982	1261.51	311.51	286.07	226.96
1983	1688.93	405.14	299.24	252.47
1984	1786.54	525.86	392.29	305.03
1985	2068.78	569.74	421.24	334.63
1986	2319.44	605.67	445.13	373.53
1987	2514.22	638.64	460.66	408.69
1988	2751.40	710.47	497.84	450.62
1989	3095.15	820.70	571.84	540.13
1990	3545.50	957.01	670.80	607.58
1991	4661.58	936.57	626.92	615.40
1992	4885.77	1015.62	677.82	611.84
1993	5004.02	1135.77	783.18	722.09
1994	5887.81	1690.49	1170.06	1012.95
1995	6729.46	2184.20	1511.22	1245.10
1996	10050.26	2642.45	1863.62	1630.41
1997	11432.61	2913.16	2102.20	1660.13
1998	12966.45	2917.66	2172.24	1699.43
1999	13654.80	2871.62	2217.08	1572.90
2000	13717.28	3008.13	2268.50	1555.61
2001	16007.50	3124.10	2352.16	1649.18
2002	16581.94	3239.81	2444.06	1745.63
2003	19010.48	3378.80	2566.76	1801.63
2004	20254.50	3826.27	2890.01	2088.98
2005	24815.99	4221.81	3099.20	2430.19
2006	27772.00	4580.79	3419.35	2732.46
2007	31696.83	5365.78	3997.48	3090.00
2008	36250.27	6266.27	4656.38	3652.57
2009	41493.01	6663.13	5035.26	3725.40
2010	47606.56	7699.27	5832.27	4090.78
2011	61870.37	9387.20	6897.92	5010.74
2012	77338.15	10525.66	7851.71	5726.73
2013	101314.51	11896.06	8866.95	6279.52
2014	110492.00	14836.14	10849.06	8680.93

9-9 农民家庭年人均纯收入（可支配收入）及构成
PER CAPITA DISPOSABLE INCOME OF RURAL HOUSEHOLDS PER CAPITA AND COMPOSITION

单位：元 (yuan)

指 标	Item	2004	2005	2006	2007	2008	2009	2010	2011	2012	2013	2014
全年总收入	Total Revenue	3826.27	4221.81	4580.79	5365.78	6266.27	6663.13	7699.27	9387.20	10525.66	11896.06	14836.14
全年纯收入	Annual Net Income	2890.01	3099.20	3419.35	3997.48	4656.38	5035.26	5832.27	6897.92	7851.71	8866.95	10849.06
工资性收入	Money Wage	755.23	941.64	1199.16	1454.50	1742.33	1900.54	2186.11	2703.05	3189.84	3648.20	3298.61
家庭经营纯收入	House Business Revenue	2051.62	2049.04	2095.15	2379.82	2690.83	2828.53	3234.94	3731.34	4123.49	4616.55	5009.34
转移性收入	Transfer Income	66.96	91.71	99.13	125.46	182.40	247.81	304.30	379.08	472.51	518.07	2415.66
财产性收入	Property Income	16.19	16.81	25.91	37.70	40.82	58.37	106.92	84.45	65.87	84.13	125.44
比重(纯收入=100)	Ratio (net income = 100)											
工资性收入	Money Wage	26.13	30.38	35.07	36.39	37.42	37.74	37.48	39.19	40.63	41.14	30.40
家庭经营纯收入	House Business Revenue	70.99	66.12	61.27	59.53	57.79	56.17	55.47	54.09	52.52	52.06	46.17
转移性收入	Transfer Income	2.32	2.96	2.90	3.14	3.92	4.92	5.22	5.50	6.02	5.84	22.27
财产性收入	Property Income	0.56	0.54	0.76	0.94	0.88	1.16	1.83	1.22	0.84	0.95	1.16

注：2014年起为农村常住居民人均可支配收入、工资性收入、家庭经营净收入、财产净收入、转移净收入。
Note: It has been Per Capita Disposable Income of Rural Permanent Residents, Money Wage, House Business Revenue. Property Income, Transfer Income since 2014.

9-10 农民家庭年人均纯收入（可支配收入）分组
RURAL HOUSEHOLDS GROUPED BY PER CAPITA DISPOSABLE INCOME

单位：户 (household)

指 标	Item	2003	2004	2005	2006	2007	2008	2009	2010	2011	2012	2013	2014
调查户总计	Total Households Surveyed	3300	3300	3300	3300	3300	3300	3300	3300	3300	3300	2096	2522
2000元以下	Below 2000 yuan	1265	935	888	710	508	414	411	257	233	155	48	70
2000–3000元	2000-3000 yuan	1007	1034	840	787	659	519	478	365	295	197	83	57
3000–4000元	3000-4000 yuan	513	611	702	684	660	559	492	419	313	289	127	118
4000–5000元	4000-5000 yuan	255	339	413	479	510	510	460	469	373	286	170	139
5000元以上	5000 yuan and Over	260	381	457	640	969	1298	1459	1790	2086	2373	1668	
5000–10000元	5000-10000 yuan												814
10000–15000元	10000-15000 yuan												661
15000–20000元	15000-20000 yuan												353
20000元以上	20000 yuan and Over												311

注：2014年起为农村常住居民人均可支配收入分组。
Note: It has been Rural Permanent Grouped by Per Capita Disposable Income since 2014.

9-11 农民家庭年人均经营总收入
ANNUAL TOTAL INCME OF RURAL HOUSEHOLDS PER CAPITA

单位：元 (yuan)

指 标	Item	2007	2008	2009	2010	2011	2012	2013	2014
家庭经营总收入	Total Income of Family Business	3743.44	4287.96	4435.68	5077.04	6134.62	6718.36	7022.00	8699.22
农业收入	Farming	2316.71	2546.31	2638.00	3115.06	3682.89	4056.77	4049.41	4663.10
林业收入	Forestry	60.37	61.54	59.33	65.63	79.26	88.49	140.80	272.35
牧业收入	Animal Husbandry	741.27	946.28	863.14	869.13	1013.07	1044.46	1077.50	1610.39
渔业收入	Fishery	212.64	271.92	311.80	329.55	389.88	423.50	403.93	476.41
工业收入	Industry	46.53	53.95	58.65	69.15	135.22	144.59	60.66	204.82
建筑业收入	Construction	83.83	99.12	133.29	154.25	167.18	177.49	307.83	188.27
交通运输邮电业收入	Transportation, Post Services	106.20	116.66	127.96	155.76	277.54	322.49	328.76	353.50
批零贸易餐饮业收入	Wholesales, Retail Sales and Catering	118.82	133.06	164.99	220.55	273.17	317.95	401.46	572.30
社会服务和文教卫生业收入	Social Services and Public Health Services	44.40	44.70	63.47	78.53	91.43	113.54	177.96	211.73
农林牧渔服务业收入	Agriculture and forestry services								133.44
其他家庭经营收入	Other Family Revenue	12.22	13.23	14.14	18.79	23.55	26.87	10.54	12.93

9-12 农民家庭年人均生产支出
ANNUAL PRODUCTION EXPENDITURES OF RURAL HOUSEHOLDS PER CAPITA

单位：元 (yuan)

指 标	Item	2007	2008	2009	2010	2011	2012	2013	2014
一、家庭经营费用支出	Expenditures of Family Business	1262.04	1493.00	1489.40	1713.15	2199.08	2402.73	2408.72	3413.49
农业生产支出	Agricultural Expenditures	663.21	759.00	746.68	866.74	1029.67	1076.28	1049.49	1329.35
林业生产支出	Forestry Expenditures	8.56	6.14	6.69	7.74	16.65	16.33	19.52	27.68
牧业生产支出	Animal Husbandary Expenditures	369.78	493.71	463.78	470.43	593.09	693.65	753.88	1279.08
渔业生产支出	Fishery Expenditures	77.58	86.30	104.37	125.68	216.01	230.50	174.04	217.63
工业生产支出	Industrial Expenditures	19.20	14.56	16.37	18.89	54.66	84.17	28.31	78.83
建筑业支出	Construction Expenditures	32.56	37.45	45.15	54.95	61.78	54.28	120.30	158.47
交通运输邮电业支出	Expenditures of Transportation and Post Services	36.01	35.09	38.14	60.29	107.32	120.00	81.99	74.77
批零贸易餐饮业支出	Expenditures of Wholesales, Retail Sales and Catering	42.36	46.38	51.96	88.76	90.88	100.13	82.03	166.42
社会服务和文教卫生业支出	Expenditures of Social Services and Public Health Services	9.50	10.76	13.73	14.89	19.82	20.52	69.33	39.98
农林牧渔服务业支出	Agriculture and forestry services								36.77
其他家庭经营支出	Other Family Expenditures	3.28	3.60	2.53	4.78	9.22	6.85	2.19	4.51
二、购置住房、生产性固定资产支出	Purchase of Housing, the Productive Expenditure of Fixed Assets	75.47	99.92	148.69	142.67	231.28	240.00	315.23	876.97
三、税费支出	Expenditures of Taxation	18.22	13.30	11.21	10.28	9.28	11.09		

9–13 农民家庭年人均生活消费支出
LIVING EXPENDITURES OF RURAL HOUSEHOLDS PER CAPITA

单位：元 (yuan)

指 标	Item	2007	2008	2009	2010	2011	2012	2013	2014
全年总支出	Total Annual Expenditures	4565.40	5402.06	5537.59	6131.23	7971.52	8923.73	9477.33	16775.27
生活消费支出	Living Expenditures	3090.00	3652.57	3725.40	4090.78	5010.74	5726.73	6279.52	8680.93
一、食品消费	Food Consumption	1479.04	1711.34	1668.35	1763.05	1954.62	2154.01	2308.45	2724.10
主 食	Grain	305.79	323.50	320.19	329.34	334.56	350.86	334.10	440.21
副 食	Non-Staple Food	625.66	771.94	695.66	744.85	859.31	969.20	1037.53	1401.57
其他食品	Others	329.14	369.51	392.37	413.46	480.38	542.32	514.98	691.15
在外饮食	Travelling Catering Service	209.62	237.24	249.14	264.06	273.91	282.94	393.63	191.17
二、衣着消费	Clothing Consumption	168.64	187.07	195.45	217.61	272.12	316.41	347.67	495.73
三、居住消费	Residence Consumption	434.91	651.50	702.62	816.42	1086.86	1206.16	1415.73	1944.56
住 房	Housing	292.43	508.63	572.69	655.39	918.61	973.60	1013.20	1523.05
电 费	Electricity Fees	46.43	58.77	70.08	80.50	85.04	112.57	138.37	209.40
燃 料	Fuel	70.34	63.96	39.16	50.14	55.28	91.16	197.33	115.15
四、家庭设备用品及服务	Famlty facilities and Services	166.25	234.92	229.32	262.26	359.57	397.86	425.00	574.31
耐用消费品	Durable Consumer Goods	90.40	117.85	133.42	158.37	230.49	238.55	249.85	298.95
日用杂品	Daily Necessities	69.58	110.17	88.20	94.33	116.88	142.41	164.10	260.06
五、交通通讯消费	Transportation and Telecommunication Fees	281.12	290.44	307.22	331.35	414.36	496.10	605.95	816.43
交通工具	Transportation	92.97	97.88	108.82	124.59	186.09	235.85	324.51	378.07
通讯工具	Telecommunication	29.48	26.17	23.71	34.86	33.04	39.84	45.85	76.43
交通、邮电服务费	Transport, Postal Services	158.66	166.38	174.70	171.90	195.23	220.41	235.48	361.94
六、教育文化娱乐	Culture, Education and Receation	284.13	267.13	281.68	288.12	341.87	394.63	407.42	1010.19
文教娱乐用品	Cultural, Educational and Receational Articles	53.97	53.40	61.71	62.30	94.96	107.87	104.20	122.61
学杂费	School Fees	185.74	156.51	146.81	102.61	139.02	136.21	159.18	98.51
技术培训费	Technical Training	5.30	5.23	5.44	7.19	10.43	12.85	28.88	20.89
一揽子教育服务费	Education Service Charge								661.05
文体休闲娱乐费	Sports Recreation Fee	7.52	11.03	9.92	13.81	17.44	23.05	35.58	62.47
七、医疗保健消费	Medicine and Medical Services Fees	178.77	210.36	236.31	295.24	438.20	591.87	624.40	907.33
医疗保健用品	Health Care Supplies	60.17	64.34	71.18	71.61	102.19	117.28	127.71	200.10
医疗保健服务费	Health Care Service Fees	118.60	146.02	165.13	223.63	336.01	474.59	496.69	707.22
八、其他商品和服务	Other Commdities and Services	97.13	99.80	104.29	116.73	143.14	169.68	144.90	208.28

9-14 农民家庭年人均现金收支
ANNUAL CASH REVENUE AND EXPENDITURE OF RURAL HOUSEHOLDS PER CAPITA

单位：元 (yuan)

指 标	Item	2007	2008	2009	2010	2011	2012	2013	2014
期内现金收入合计	Total Cash Income at Year-End	4498.98	5256.32	5718.37	6664.44	8232.92	9337.04	10819.88	13243.58
一、工资性现金收入	Cash Income By Wages	1454.46	1742.25	1898.93	2185.60	2696.32	3186.99	3858.97	3282.57
二、家庭经营现金收入	Cash Income By Family Business	2888.24	3289.11	3509.20	4063.37	5011.97	5546.68	5959.60	7328.03
农业	Farm Products	1655.22	1782.47	1924.84	2306.34	2807.96	3096.78	3179.27	3614.71
林业	Forestry Products	56.01	55.94	55.54	60.38	80.14	88.34	142.91	163.40
牧业	Animal husbandary Products	557.71	722.03	658.16	675.22	773.47	837.81	891.19	1404.35
渔业	Fishery Products	206.85	266.99	307.25	323.77	380.89	418.62	395.83	468.59
工业	Industry Products	46.53	53.95	58.65	69.15	135.22	144.59	60.66	204.82
建筑业	Building Industry	83.83	98.93	133.29	154.25	167.18	177.49	307.83	188.27
交通运输邮电业	Transportation and Post Service	106.20	116.66	127.96	155.76	277.54	322.49	328.76	353.50
批零贸易餐饮业	Retail Sales and Catering	118.82	133.06	164.99	220.55	273.17	317.95	401.46	572.30
社会服务和文教卫生业	Social services and educational sector	44.40	44.70	63.47	78.53	91.43	113.54	177.96	211.73
农林牧渔服务业	Agriculture and forestry services								133.44
其他家庭经营收入	Cash Income of Other	12.67	14.38	14.14	19.42	23.55	26.87	10.54	12.93
三、转移性现金收入	Transfer Cash Income	126.97	194.68	264.72	328.92	460.73	544.46	902.05	2497.66
四、财产性现金收入	Property Cash Income	29.31	30.29	45.52	86.55	63.91	58.91	99.26	135.33
期内现金支出合计	Total Cash Expenditures at Year-End	3740.56	4496.87	4723.52	5294.37	7194.75	8149.22	8563.81	14688.88
一、家庭经营费用现金支出	Cash Expenditures By Family Business	1159.13	1383.60	1368.00	1562.32	2051.67	2285.75	2243.66	3249.87
购买化肥	Fertilizers Purchases	255.96	340.71	313.95	320.80	377.07	374.44	396.06	456.72
购买农药	Purchases of Farm Chemical	81.13	94.78	87.72	94.03	125.52	129.82	112.80	140.48
购买农用薄膜	Purchase of Agricultural Film	5.18	5.42	3.40	5.07	6.80	6.31	4.80	7.94
二、购买住房、生产性固定资产支出	Purchase of Housing, the Productive Expenditure	75.47	99.92	148.38	142.17	231.28	240.00	315.23	876.97
三、税费现金支出	Cash Expenditures of Taxations	18.22	13.29	11.20	10.28	9.28	10.85		
四、生活消费现金支出	Cash Expenditures of Living Consumption	2368.68	2857.78	3033.37	3406.12	4382.95	5070.68	5531.07	6738.17
五、转移性现金支出	Transfer Cash Expenditures	113.88	133.30	153.91	162.25	511.12	530.85	471.72	287.31
六、财产性现金支出	Property Cash Expenditures	5.17	8.97	8.33	10.74	8.45	11.10	2.13	8.67

9–15 农民家庭年人均出售主要农副产品情况
ANNUAL SELLING OF FARM AND SIDELINE PRODUCTS OF RURL HOUSEHOLDS PER CAPITA

单位：千克

品 名	Item	2004	2005	2006	2007	2008	2009	2010	2011	2012	2013	2014
粮 食	Grain	303.46	383.48	391.24	386.98	390.60	422.65	447.78	451.98	489.22	591.56	770.96
小 麦	Wheat	40.06	54.25	77.67	94.39	76.73	62.01	75.44	86.70	91.93	79.55	111.05
稻 谷	Paddy	234.53	302.70	288.86	268.94	292.78	320.27	331.71	302.69	329.15	432.85	528.86
棉 花	Cotton	55.99	55.95	69.22	81.48	70.09	76.43	55.03	88.30	93.94	72.29	48.98
油 料	Oil Producer	79.72	77.73	62.04	61.27	65.14	77.04	72.15	60.91	58.57	73.99	77.34
糖 料	Sugar	3.99	5.47	6.28	9.16	4.31	4.48	6.43	0.16	0.17	2.16	2.08
烟 草	Tobacco	1.30	2.34	2.07	1.55	2.11	2.92	2.77	2.97	3.82	7.89	7.07
蔬 菜	Vegetable	148.96	135.09	133.11	138.89	136.45	133.11	139.41	137.62	143.53	99.54	134.68
瓜 类	Melon	26.75	14.21	26.56	16.20	14.80	19.07	19.69	17.40	17.60	40.74	33.63
水 果	Fruits	66.57	69.54	76.41	82.72	90.38	99.70	78.09	66.13	109.87	62.86	111.30
茶 叶	Tea	0.80	1.24	1.25	1.56	1.56	1.29	1.95	4.17	8.08	5.02	5.01
猪 肉	Pork	26.67	29.70	30.80	26.03	26.38	28.70	30.92	22.91	25.68	28.51	58.86
家 禽	Poultry	1.63	4.47	5.19	4.44	7.16	7.29	8.38	2.28	2.80	1.65	8.63
蛋 类	Eggs	8.10	11.98	10.69	8.99	8.25	10.94	11.19	10.33	13.01	16.54	29.12
水产品	Aquatic Produc	25.59	28.59	33.06	35.66	37.26	42.12	38.70	43.09	43.25	39.61	40.65

9–16 农民家庭主要生活用品购买量
ANNUAL PURCHASES OF ARTICLES FOR BAILY USE OF RURAL HOUSEHOLDS PER CAPITA

品 名		Item		2005	2006	2007	2008	2009	2010	2011	2012	2013	2014
粮 食	(千克/人)	Grain	(Kg/person)	26.55	26.28	25.72	26.56	27.45	29.46	42.35	44.45	38.34	44.06
植物油	(千克/人)	Edible Vegetable	(Kg/person)	2.89	2.85	3.21	3.55	3.35	3.61	5.20	5.70	5.11	7.41
动物油	(千克/人)	Edible Animal O	(Kg/person)	0.73	0.63	0.50	0.47	0.38	0.33	0.43	0.39	0.27	0.47
蔬菜	(千克/人)	Vegetables	(Kg/person)	16.33	16.33	16.44	17.85	16.21	17.73	19.40	18.27	16.51	25.95
猪肉	(千克/人)	Pork	(Kg/person)	6.93	7.46	6.27	6.22	7.04	7.43	8.38	8.71	8.76	13.13
牛羊肉	(千克/人)	Beef and Mutton	(Kg/person)	0.37	0.42	0.49	0.41	0.41	0.51	0.56	0.47	0.54	0.85
家禽	(千克/人)	Poultry	(Kg/person)	0.79	0.79	1.08	1.21	1.16	1.17	1.26	1.24	0.97	2.40
鲜蛋	(千克/人)	Fresh Eggs	(Kg/person)	0.93	0.97	0.97	1.33	1.55	1.30	1.85	2.20		2.83
鲜活鱼类	(千克/人)	Fresh Fish	(Kg/person)	6.64	7.07	7.69	7.29	6.97	6.99	7.11	7.06		9.58
卷烟	(盒/人)	Tobacco	(pack/person)	30.53	30.98	29.06	28.88	27.51	27.50	31.12	31.42	26.93	41.00
酒	(千克/人)	Wine	(Kg/person)	10.13	11.90	12.30	11.70	11.35	10.72	11.37	11.06	10.06	16.23
水 果	(千克/人)	Fruits	(Kg/person)	6.84	6.34	6.87	6.80	6.72	6.22	6.87	8.27		17.63
服 装	(件/人)	Clothing	(piece/person	1.81	1.82	1.82	1.99	2.94	1.95	2.46	2.52		
鞋 类	(双/人)	Footwear	(Two/person)	1.42	1.45	1.35	1.43	1.28	1.36	1.39	1.80		2.10
水 泥	(千克/人)	Cement	(Kg/person)	70.67	108.80	85.93	134.97	137.25	150.72	236.88	149.81		
钢 材	(千克/人)	Steel	(Kg/person)	4.52	6.66	5.84	10.45	10.11	10.21	13.85	9.72		
生活用煤	(千克/人)	Coal	(Kg/person)	52.97	52.65	49.44	32.82	20.22	19.70	14.77	13.18		14.84
电视机	(台/百户)	TV Sets	(set/100 hous	6.88	6.79	5.79	4.95	3.97	3.70	6.67	6.48	5.76	5.31
洗衣机	(台/百户)	Washing Machin	(set/100 hous	1.85	1.79	1.92	2.73	2.67	3.21	6.09	5.09	4.44	4.93
电风扇	(台/百户)	Electric Fans	(set/100 hous	8.21	9.73	8.85	9.73	11.45	10.52	10.79	13.67		
电冰箱	(台/百户)	Refrigerators	(set/100 hous	1.66	2.67	4.18	5.64	7.06	7.00	8.30	7.12	6.16	6.03
自行车	(辆/百户)	Bycicle	(set/100 hous	5.29	4.50	3.91	4.83	5.29	2.42	3.73	3.09	2.39	3.16
摩托车	(辆/百户)	Motocycle	(set/100 hous	4.39	5.00	5.28	4.73	4.26	3.88	6.09	5.30	3.91	3.65
热水器	(台/百户)	Shower	(set/100 hous	1.24	1.67	2.06	3.11	3.79	4.36	6.18	5.70	3.58	2.75
电话机	(部/百户)	Telephone Sets	(set/100 hous	5.09	6.15	4.52	4.33	4.37	3.36	3.41	2.76	1.86	1.03
手 机	(部/百户)	Mobile Phones	(set/100 hous	9.64	8.30	12.97	13.82	14.42	18.92	25.39	28.00	33.40	39.75

9-17 农民家庭年人均主要食品消费量
RURAL HOUSEHOLD ANNUAL CONSUMPTION ON MAJOR FOOD PER CAPITA

单位：千克 (Kg)

品　名		2005	2006	2007	2008	2009	2010	2011	2012	2013	2014
一、粮 食	Grain	215.68	213.71	208.29	193.60	192.22	178.37	162.86	151.06	125.59	153.08
#小 麦	Wheat	22.58	23.11	21.80	22.02	19.87	17.60	17.41	15.55	10.17	16.74
稻 谷	Paddy	171.47	170.17	168.61	155.37	155.18	146.13	135.87	126.67	104.27	121.21
豆类	Bean	3.64	3.65	3.82	3.30	3.27	3.22	2.53	1.97	3.85	7.25
二、蔬菜及菜制品	Fresh Vegetables and	152.47	143.75	143.57	132.58	137.04	137.51	131.68	119.33	88.16	118.03
鲜 菜	Fresh Vegetables	147.06	138.12	140.57	130.05	134.69	136.22	130.67	118.25	86.56	116.30
三、油脂类	Oil and Fats	3.70	3.56	3.77	4.11	3.85	5.49	8.17	10.39	11.05	29.71
植物油	Edible Vegetable Oil	2.98	2.89	3.23	3.58	3.39	5.13	7.71	9.93	10.61	29.02
动物油	Edible Animal Oil	0.73	0.67	0.53	0.53	0.47	0.36	0.46	0.47	0.43	0.70
四、肉禽及其制品	Meat and Processed Products	24.79	25.27	22.70	22.21	22.99	22.79	22.90	22.80	22.91	29.82
猪 肉	Pork	20.63	20.91	17.83	17.51	18.14	17.98	17.40	17.63	18.11	23.12
牛羊肉	Beef and Mutton	0.44	0.53	0.52	0.50	0.48	0.57	0.65	0.53	0.63	0.93
家 禽	Poultry	3.02	2.91	3.30	3.23	3.22	2.91	3.23	2.94	2.87	4.19
五、蛋类及蛋制品	Eggs and Processed Products	4.14	4.15	4.17	4.69	4.93	4.47	5.03	5.02	4.68	6.65
六、奶及奶制品	Milk and Dariy Products	0.23	0.33	0.50	0.81	1.11	1.22	1.55	1.67	2.11	3.53
七、水产品	Aquatic Products	8.11	8.51	9.38	8.71	8.34	8.33	8.38	8.54	7.93	11.10
鱼 类	Fish	7.81	8.18	9.03	8.40	7.97	7.93	8.03	8.09	7.58	10.55
八、干鲜瓜果	Fresh and Dry	16.17	19.75	18.66	16.01	16.84	15.70	16.38	16.83	13.33	20.74
九、酒 类	Liquor and Drinks	10.17	11.93	12.35	11.76	11.41	10.77	11.40	11.12	10.08	14.25
白 酒	Wine Spirit	3.91	4.06	3.87	3.85	3.94	3.70	3.69	3.52	3.65	5.82
啤 酒	Beer	6.21	7.83	8.42	7.84	7.40	7.01	7.67	7.53	6.41	8.41

9—18 农民家庭每百户主要耐用消费品拥有量

POSSESSTION OF URABLE CONSUMER GOODS PER 100 RURAL HOUSEHOLDS

品 名		Item		2005	2006	2007	2008	2009	2010	2011	2012	2013	2014
彩电	(台)	Color TV Set	(unit)	83.18	92.12	98.82	102.24	105.42	109.18	114.36	116.24	114.35	116.50
照相机	(架)	Camera	(unit)	1.88	1.76	1.82	2.06	2.58	2.64	3.55	3.64	5.24	4.89
洗衣机	(台)	Washing Machine	(unit)	26.39	30.12	34.68	37.12	41.70	47.97	57.09	62.42	53.79	57.94
电冰箱	(台)	Refrigerator	(unit)	14.82	19.18	26.18	30.52	41.36	51.48	73.73	80.18	75.82	79.53
摩托车	(辆)	Motocycle	(unit)	39.15	45.00	51.45	55.52	59.76	64.12	72.33	74.76	68.84	76.52
摄像机	(台)	Videorecorder	(unit)	0.55	0.76	1.06	0.91	0.52	0.70	1.42	1.52	0.62	0.50
抽油烟机	(台)	Ventilator	(unit)	3.12	3.72	5.03	6.10	7.70	10.03	13.70	15.82	10.94	13.59
空调机	(台)	Air Conditioner	(unit)	3.79	5.39	7.61	9.91	12.45	18.36	28.58	33.15	33.05	37.79
热水器	(台)	Shower	(unit)	6.21	8.79	12.21	16.03	22.73	32.00	48.24	55.91	52.16	58.01
电话机	(部)	Telephone Set	(set)	51.64	57.20	58.36	59.33	55.61	55.70	41.94	40.06	31.44	37.15
移动电话	(部)	Moblile Phone	(set)	71.18	90.10	104.67	117.88	134.21	152.27	204.82	215.06	211.52	223.46
家用计算机	(台)	PC	(unit)	1.09	2.33	2.00	3.00	5.15	7.39	15.58	19.73	22.14	25.72

9—19 市、州农民年人均纯收入(可支配收入)

ANAUAL NET INCOME OF RURAL HOUCEHOLD PER CAPITA IN CITIES AND PREFERCTURES

单位：元 (yuan)

地 区	Item	农村居民人均纯收入									农村常住居民人均可支配收入	
		2005	2006	2007	2008	2009	2010	2011	2012	2013	2013	2014
全 省	Province	3099	3419	3997	4656	5035	5832	6898	7852	8867	9692	10849
武 汉 市	Wuhan	4341	4748	5371	6349	7161	8295	9814	11190	12713	14390	16160
黄 石 市	Huangshi	2810	3182	3742	4374	4811	5524	6487	7477	8492	9781	10957
十 堰 市	Shiyan	1990	2191	2490	2841	3110	3499	4044	4566	5226	6212	7046
宜 昌 市	Yichang	3108	3433	4022	4686	5186	5980	7055	8046	9121	10458	11837
襄 阳 市	Xiangyang	3191	3519	4114	4880	5440	6365	7549	8684	9785	11176	12534
鄂 州 市	Ezhou	3495	3799	4393	5096	5718	6645	7909	9072	10210	11309	12692
荆 门 市	Jingmen	3738	4059	4652	5332	5956	6951	8248	9387	10615	12082	13481
孝 感 市	Xiaogan	3028	3336	3915	4636	5131	5943	7029	7988	9023	10360	11597
荆 州 市	Jingzhou	3108	3502	4140	4889	5464	6453	7664	8710	9909	11280	12625
黄 冈 市	Huanggang	2644	2861	3295	3744	4130	4634	5438	6142	6966	8385	9388
咸 宁 市	Xianning	2911	3213	3737	4411	4873	5606	6588	7505	8480	9709	10891
随 州 市	Suizhou	3223	3581	4177	4967	5457	6279	7427	8419	9490	10702	11984
恩施自治州	Enshi	1643	1848	2143	2519	2810	3255	3939	4571	5235	6364	7194
仙 桃 市	Xiantao	3818	4190	4695	5248	5856	6807	8006	9076	10365	11809	13193
天 门 市	Tianmen	3273	3658	4207	4761	5326	6207	7407	8507	9608	10809	12086
潜 江 市	Qianjiang	3398	3813	4378	4929	5531	6486	7684	8785	10017	11448	12862
神农架林区	Shennongjia	2164	2394	2850	3330	3707	4083	4640	5110	5677	6305	6920

注：2013年前分城镇和农村开展住户调查，指标为农民人均纯收入。2014年起使用城乡一体化住户收支与生活状况调查数据，指标改为农村常住居民人均可支配收入。

Note: Urban and rural household surveys are separate prior to 2013,the concept is Per Capita Net Income of Rural Households, The data from an integrated household income and expenditure survey has been used since 2014 , the concept was changed into Per Capita Disposable Income of Rural Permanent Residents.

主要统计指标解释

一、 城镇住户调查（到 2012 年）

城镇家庭人口 指居住在一起，经济上合在一起共同生活的家庭成员。凡计算为家庭人口的成员其全部收支都包括在本家庭中。

城镇就业面 指就业人口占家庭人口的百分比。

城镇就业者负担人数 指家庭人口与就业人口之比。

城镇家庭总收入 指家庭成员得到的工资性收入、经营净收入、财产性收入、转移性收入之和，不包括出售财物收入和借贷收入。

城镇居民家庭可支配收入 指家庭成员得到可用于最终消费支出和其它非义务性支出以及储蓄的总和，即居民家庭可以用来自由支配的收入。它是家庭总收入扣除交纳的个人所得税、个人交纳的社会保障支出以及记账补贴后的收入。计算公式为：

城镇居民家庭可支配收入=家庭总收入−交纳所得税−个人交纳的社会保障支出−记帐补贴

城镇家庭总支出 指家庭除借贷支出以外的全部实际支出。包括现金消费支出、财产性支出、转移性支出、社会保障支出、购房与建房支出。

城镇家庭现金消费支出 指家庭用于日常生活的全部现金支出，包括食品、衣着、家庭设备及用品、交通通信、文教娱乐、医疗保健、其他等八大类支出。

城镇家庭服务性消费支出 指家庭用于支付社会提供的各种文化和生活方面的非商品性服务费用。

城镇家庭收入分组方法 是将所有调查户依户人均可支配收入由低到高排队，按 10%，10%，20%，20%，20%，10%，10%的比例依次分成：最低收入户、较低收入户、中等偏下收入户、中等收入户、中等偏上收入户、高收入户、最高收入户等七组。总体中最低 5%的户为困难户。

恩格尔系数 指食品支出在现金消费支出中所占的比例。计算公式为：

$$恩格尔系数=\frac{食品支出}{现金消费支出}\times 100\%$$

二、农村住户调查（到 2012 年）

农村住户 指农村常住户。农村常住户指长期(一年以上)居住在乡镇(不包括城关镇)行政管理区域内的住户，以及长期居住在城关镇所辖行政村范围内的农村住户。户口不在本地而在本地居住一年及以上的住户也包括在本地农村常住户范围内；有本地户口，但举家外出谋生一年以上的住户，无论是否保留承包耕地都不包括在本地农村住户范围内。

常住人口 指全年经常在家或在家居住 6 个月以上，而且经济和生活与本户连成一体的人口。外出从业人员在外居住时间虽然在 6 个月以上，但收入主要带回家中，经济与本户连为一体，仍视为家庭常住人口；在家居住，生活和本户连成一体的国家职工、退休人员也为家庭常住人口。但是现役军人、中专及以上(走读生除外)的在校学生、以及常年在外(不包括探亲、看病等)且已有稳定的职业与居住场所的外出从业人员，不算家庭常住人口。家庭常住人口主要作为计算农村住户平均每人收入、消费和积累水平及分析家庭人口状况的依据。

整、半劳动力 整劳动力指男子 18 周岁到 50 周岁，女子 18 周岁到 45 周岁；半劳动力指男子 16 周岁到 17 周岁，51

周岁到60周岁；女子16周岁到17周岁，46周岁到55周岁，同时具有劳动能力的人。虽然在劳动年龄之内，但已丧失劳动能力的人，不应算为劳动力；超过劳动年龄，但能经常参加劳动，计入半劳动力数内。常住人口中的职工，若这些职工为劳动力，就包括在本户的整半劳动力中。

总收入 指调查期内农村住户和住户成员从各种来源渠道得到的收入总和。按收入的性质划分为工资性收入、家庭经营收入、财产性收入和转移性收入。

工资性收入 指农村住户成员受雇于单位或个人，靠出卖劳动而获得的收入。

家庭经营收入 指农村住户以家庭为生产经营单位进行生产筹划和管理而获得的收入。农村住户家庭经营活动按行业划分为农业、林业、牧业、渔业、工业、建筑业、交通运输业邮电业、批发和零售贸易餐饮业、社会服务业、文教卫生业和其他家庭经营。

财产性收入 指金融资产或有形非生产性资产的所有者向其他机构单位提供资金或将有形非生产性资产供其支配，作为回报而从中获得的收入。

转移性收入 指农村住户和住户成员无须付出任何对应物而获得的货物、服务、资金或资产所有权等，不包括无偿提供的用于固定资本形成的资金。一般情况下，是指农村住户在二次分配中的所有收入。

现金收入 指农村住户和住户成员在调查期内得到以现金形态表现的收入。按来源分成工资性收入、家庭经营现金收入、财产性收入、转移性收入。

农村居民家庭纯收入 指农村住户当年从各个来源得到的总收入相应地扣除所发生的费用后的收入总和。计算方法：

农村居民家庭纯收入=总收入-家庭经营费用支出-税费支出-生产性固定资产折旧-赠送农村内部亲支

纯收入主要用于再生产投入和当年生活消费支出，也可用于储蓄和各种非义务性支出。“农民人均纯收入”按人口平均的纯收入水平，反映的是一个地区农村居民的平均收入水平。

总支出 指农村住户用于生产、生活和再分配的全部支出。包括家庭经营费用支出、购置生产性固定资产支出、税费支出、消费支出、财产性支出和转移性支出。

三、一体化住户调查

从2012年四季度起，国家统计局对分别进行的城乡住户调查实施了一体化改革，统一了城乡居民收入指标名称、分类和统计标准，建立了城乡统一的一体化住户调查《住户收支与生活状况调查》，并据此获得全国居民有关数据。

居民可支配收入 居民可支配收入指居民可用于最终消费支出和储蓄的总和，即居民可用于自由支配的收入。既包括现金收入、也包括实物收入。按照收入的来源，可支配收入包含四项，分别为：工资性收入、经营性净收入、转移性净收入和财产性净收入。

居民消费支出 居民消费支出是指居民用于满足家庭日常生活消费需要的全部支出，既包括现金消费支出，也包括实物消费支出。消费支出可划分为食品烟酒、衣着、居住、生活用品及服务、交通和通信、教育文化和娱乐、医疗保健以及其他用品及服务八大类。

Explanatory Notes on Main Statistical Indicators

Ⅰ.Urban Households(to the year of 2012)

Population of Urban Households refer to members of the household living and sharing economically together. All income and expenditure of the population of the household are included in the income and expenditure of the household.

Proportion of Urban Employment refer to the proportion of employed population to the population of urban households.

Number of Dependents per Urban Employee refers to the ratio between number of persons in urban households and the number of dependents.

Total Income of Urban Households refers to the sum of wage and salary, net business income, income from properties, and income from transfers of members of the households, excluding income from selling of properties and income from borrowings.

Disposable Income of Urban Households refers to the actual income at the disposal of members of the households which can be used for final consumption, other non-compulsory expenditure and savings. This equals to total income minus income tax, personal contribution to social security and sample household subsidy for keeping diaries. Following formula is used:

Disposable income = total household income - income tax - personal contribution to social security - sample household subsidy for keeping diaries

Total Expenditure of Urban Households refer to all expenditure of the households except expenditure on leading. It includes expenditure on consumption, on purchasing or building houses, on transfers, on properties and on social security.

Consumption Expenditure of Urban Households refers to total expenditure of the sample households for consumption in daily life, including expenditure on eight categories such as food, clothing, household appliances and services, health care and medical services, transport and communications, recreation, education and cultural services, housing, miscellaneous goods and services.

Expenditure of Urban Households on Consumption of Services refers to expenditure of households on services of various kinds provided by the society.

Urban Households by Income Group All households in the sample are grouped, by per capita disposable income of the household, into groups of lowest income, low income, lower middle income, middle income, upper middle income, high income and highest income, each group consisting of 10%, 10%, 20%, 20%, 20%, 10% and 10% of all households respectively. The lowest 5% of households are also referred to as poor households.

Engel Coefficient refers to the percentage of expenditure on food in the total consumption expenditure, using the following formula:

Engel Coefficient = (expenditure on food / total living consumption expenditure) x 100%

Ⅱ. Rural Households(to the year of 2012)

Rural Households refer to resident households in rural areas. Resident households in rural areas are the households residing for more than one year in the areas under the jurisdiction of administration of township governments (excluding county towns), and in the areas under the jurisdiction of administration of villages in county towns. Migrated households residing in the current addresses for over one year with their household registration in other places are included in the resident households of their current addresses. For households with their household registration in one place but all members of the households moving away for living in another place for over one year, they will not be included in the rural households of the area where they are registered, irrespective of whether they still keep their contracted land.

Resident Population refers to population staying at home permanently or for over 6 months during a year and sharing life economically with the household. Members of the household staying away from the household for over 6 months but keeping a close economic relation with the household by sending the majority of income to the household are regarded as resident population of the household. Government staff and workers or retirees living as close members of the household are also considered as resident population. However, servicemen, students of secondary technical schools or schools of higher education and persons with stable jobs and residence outside the household (excluding those visiting relatives or seeking medical service) are not included as resident population of the household. Resident population is used in calculating income, consumption, accumulation on per capita basis of rural households and in analyzing composition of rural households.

Full/Semi Labor Force Full labor force refers to persons capable of work, aged 18-50 for males and 18-45 for females. Semi labor force refers to persons capable of work, aged 16-17 and 51-60 for males and 16-17 and 46-55 for females. Persons at their working ages but not capable of work are not to be included as labor force. Persons not at working ages but participating regularly in work are included in semi labor force. For staff and workers as resident population of the household, they are included as full or semi labor force of the household if they are in the labor force.

Total Income refers to the sum of income earned from various sources by the rural households and their members during the reference period, and is classified as income from wages and salaries, income from household operations, income from properties and income from transfers.

Income from Wages and Salaries refers to income from labor earned by the members of rural households employed by other units or individuals.

Income from Household Operations refers to income by the rural households as units of production and operations. Operations by rural households are classified by economic activities as agriculture, forestry, animal husbandry, fishery, manufacturing, construction, transportation, post and telecommunications, wholesale, retail and catering, social service, culture, education, health, and other household operations.

Income from Properties refers to the income received as returns by owners of financial assets or tangible non-productive assets by providing capitals or tangible non-productive assets to other institutional units.

Income from Transfers refers to the receipt by rural households and their members of goods, services, capitals or rights of assets without giving or repaying accordingly, excluding capitals provided to them for the formation of fixed assets. In general, it refers to all income received by rural households through redistribution.

Cash Income refers to income received by rural households and their members in the form of cash during the reference period. It is classified, by source of income, into income from wages and salaries, cash income from household operations, income from properties and income from transfers.

Net Income refers to the total income of rural households from all sources minus all corresponding expenses. The formula for calculation is as follows:

Net income = total income - taxes and fees paid - household operation expenses - taxes and fees depreciation of fixed assets for production - subsidy for participating in household survey - gifts to non-rural relatives

Net income is mainly used as input for reproduction and as consumption expenditure of the year, and also used for savings and non-compulsory expenses of various forms. "Per capital net income of farmers" is the level of net income averaged by population which reflects the average income level of rural households in a given area.

Total Expenditure refers to total expenses of rural households on production, consumption and redistribution, including expenditure on household operations, on purchase of productive fixed assets, depreciation of productive fixed assets, taxes and fees, expenses on household consumption, expenses on properties and expenses on transfers.

Ⅲ. Integrated Household Survey

In the fourth quarter of 2012，the NBS launched its reform on the household survey program in order to produce aggregates with the same concepts and definitions for urban and rural population. This new survey program is an integrated one whereas there had existed two separate household surveys for the urban and rural households. The reform took a number of measures，including the integration of concepts，classifications and standards，which provided a basis for producing data covering all households. The new survey includes the following indicators：

Disposable Income of Households has a national coverage comparable between urban and rural households，and refers to the kind of income that households call have at them disposal. It includes income both in cash and in kind from four categories: income from wages and salaries, cash income from household operations, income from properties and income from transfers.

Consumption Expenditure of Households has a national coverage comparable between urban and rural households, and refers to the all the expenditures of households for consumption in daily life. It includes expenditure in cash and in kind on eight categories: food; clothing; housing; household appliances and services; transport and communications; education, cultural and recreational activities; and medical care. The expenditure on housing also includes rents, water, electricity, fuels and imputed rents Of owner—occupied dwellings.

10 城市概况

City Overview

资料整理：程文懿

10-1　主要城市土地面积、人口情况(2014)
LAND AREA AND PULATION OF MAJOR MUNICIPALITIES (2014)

城市	Municipalities	土地面积(平方公里) Land Area (sq.km)	常住人口(万人) Resident Population (10 000 persons)	当年出生人口(人) Births (persons)	当年死亡人口(人) Deaths (persons)	人口密度(人/平方公里) Population Desity (person/sq.km)
武 汉	Wuhan Municipality	8494	1033.80	100784	41007	1217.09
黄 石	Huangshi Municipality	4586	244.92	54422	10224	534.06
十 堰	Shiyan Municipality	23680	337.27	46607	23689	142.43
宜 昌	Yichang Municipality	21084	410.45	36610	27748	194.67
襄 阳	Xiangyang Municipality	19724	560.02	73455	69518	283.93
鄂 州	Ezhou Municipality	1596	105.88	13524	5588	663.41
荆 门	Jingmen Municipality	12404	288.91	30356	14015	232.92
孝 感	Xiaogan Municipality	8910	486.13	67021	27190	545.60
荆 州	Jingzhou Municipality	14067	574.42	71342	50900	408.35
黄 冈	Huanggang Municipality	17457	626.25	107984	34126	358.74
咸 宁	Xianning Municipality	10049	248.92	52889	15121	247.71
随 州	Suizhou Municipality	9636	218.38	32715	9507	226.63

10-2　主要城市就业情况(2014)
EMPLOYMENT OF MAJOR MUNICIPALITIES (2014)

单位：人　　(persons)

城市	Municipalities	年末单位从业人数 Employment (year-end)	从业人员按三次产业分 Employment Grouped by Type of Industry			#城镇私营和个体人数 #Employment in Private Enterprises and Self-employed Individuals of Urban Areas
			第一产业 Primary Industry	第二产业 Secondary Industry	第三产业 Tertiary Industry	
武 汉	Wuhan Municipality	2023435	3571	1039720	980144	2155600
黄 石	Huangshi Municipality	333700	1400	208900	123400	362300
十 堰	Shiyan Municipality	624000	7100	313700	303200	682714
宜 昌	Yichang Municipality	877800	3400	488100	386300	1876500
襄 阳	Xiangyang Municipality	666900	3800	353000	310100	649111
鄂 州	Ezhou Municipality	208196	95	141631	66470	101033
荆 门	Jingmen Municipality	382962	6998	211991	163973	369910
孝 感	Xiaogan Municipality	806182	8019	470744	327419	644877
荆 州	Jingzhou Municipality	432695	14839	199096	218760	967800
黄 冈	Huanggang Municipality	656600	22000	382800	251800	170506
咸 宁	Xianning Municipality	234783	658	95520	138605	226300
随 州	Suizhou Municipality	144160	650	69500	74010	543671

10–3 主要城市地区生产总值及指数(2014)
GROSS DOMESTIC PRODUCTS OF MAJOR MUNICIPALITIES (2014)

城 市	Municipalities	地区生产总值 (亿元) Gross Domestic Product (100 million yuan)	(当年价格) 第一产业 Primary Industry	第二产业 Secondary Industry	第三产业 Tertiary Industry	人均地区生产总值 (元) Per Capita GDP(yuan)
武 汉	Wuhan Municipality	10069.48	350.06	4785.66	4933.76	98000
黄 石	Huangshi Municipality	1218.56	105.03	723.45	390.08	49796
十 堰	Shiyan Municipality	1200.82	151.19	610.13	439.50	35604
宜 昌	Yichang Municipality	3132.21	351.56	1857.56	923.09	76369
襄 阳	Xiangyang Municipality	3129.26	401.60	1804.65	923.01	55924
鄂 州	Ezhou Municipality	686.64	81.15	407.19	198.30	64851
荆 门	Jingmen Municipality	1310.59	198.11	706.52	405.96	45378
孝 感	Xiaogan Municipality	1354.72	252.17	664.36	438.19	27891
荆 州	Jingzhou Municipality	1480.49	347.00	659.58	473.91	25774
黄 冈	Huanggang Municipality	1459.15	357.12	586.10	515.93	23128
咸 宁	Xianning Municipality	964.25	172.03	476.59	315.63	38770
随 州	Suizhou Municipality	723.45	130.09	350.56	242.80	33156

10–4 主要城市固定资产投资(2014)
INVESTMENT IN FIXED ASSETS OF MAJOR MUNICIPALITIES (2014)

单位：亿元 (100 million yuan)

城市	Municipalities	固定资产投资 Investment in Fixed Assets	房地产开发投资 Investment in Real Estate	#住宅 #Residential Buildings	新增固定资产 Newly Increased Fixed Assets	商品房屋销售建筑面积(万平方米) Construction Floor Space of Commercial House Sold (10 000 sq.km)	#住宅 #Residential Buildings
武 汉	Wuhan Municipality	6962.53	2353.63	1560.55	2584.92	2273.16	1978.96
黄 石	Huangshi Municipality	1149.50	115.77	78.12	835.43	205.16	196.24
十 堰	Shiyan Municipality	1040.32	90.80	59.71	620.56	145.13	133.83
宜 昌	Yichang Municipality	2471.04	194.60	152.20	1888.71	477.88	439.28
襄 阳	Xiangyang Municipality	2448.29	330.94	221.86	1342.16	578.16	474.67
鄂 州	Ezhou Municipality	687.08	19.91	15.55	303.30	57.35	55.55
荆 门	Jingmen Municipality	1190.15	123.98	83.53	928.71	217.29	200.47
孝 感	Xiaogan Municipality	1482.93	136.35	111.61	1171.18	245.06	237.81
荆 州	Jingzhou Municipality	1571.09	134.17	112.48	1025.19	162.50	150.93
黄 冈	Huanggang Municipality	1657.59	174.27	135.50	1165.96	432.70	406.80
咸 宁	Xianning Municipality	1148.75	109.14	82.96	805.02	299.16	263.15
随 州	Suizhou Municipality	768.81	33.98	25.99	628.28	98.96	94.57

10-5 主要城市规上工业基本情况(2014)
BASIC STATISTICS ON INDUSTRY OF MAJOR MUNICIPALITIES (2014)

单位：亿元 (100 million yuan)

城市	Municipalities	工业企业单位数(个) Number of Industrial Enterprises (unit)	主营业务收入 Major Business Income	利润总额 Total Profits
武 汉	Wuhan Municipality	2442	11265.31	468.17
黄 石	Huangshi Municipality	730	2602.74	95.63
十 堰	Shiyan Municipality	973	1703.76	157.39
宜 昌	Yichang Municipality	1464	4738.59	415.24
襄 阳	Xiangyang Municipality	1773	4691.00	480.40
鄂 州	Ezhou Municipality	492	1304.37	38.57
荆 门	Jingmen Municipality	1097	2851.63	138.23
孝 感	Xiaogan Municipality	1242	2349.43	114.52
荆 州	Jingzhou Municipality	1149	2050.06	127.09
黄 冈	Huanggang Municipality	1413	1525.63	83.68
咸 宁	Xianning Municipality	896	1577.22	106.24
随 州	Suizhou Municipality	679	1190.90	80.76

10-6 主要城市规上工业总产值(2014)
GROSS OUTPUT VALUE OF INDUSTRY OF MAJOR MUNICIPALITIES (2014)

单位：亿元 (100 million yuan)

城市	Municipalities	工业总产值(当年价) Total Value of Industry	内资企业 Inner Funded Enterprises	外商港澳台投资企业 Foreign, Hongkong, Macao and Taiwan Funded Enterprises	#国有企业 #State-owned Enterprise
武 汉	Wuhan Municipality	11947.87	8378.84	3569.03	2412.05
黄 石	Huangshi Municipality	2190.61	1734.37	456.24	2.68
十 堰	Shiyan Municipality	1871.07	1322.02	549.05	26.87
宜 昌	Yichang Municipality	4970.41	4594.30	376.11	274.56
襄 阳	Xiangyang Municipality	5120.40	4600.20	520.20	14.90
鄂 州	Ezhou Municipality	1362.38	1254.10	108.28	89.28
荆 门	Jingmen Municipality	2925.13	2765.59	159.54	2.95
孝 感	Xiaogan Municipality	2438.71	2237.89	200.82	8.73
荆 州	Jingzhou Municipality	2183.50	2032.31	151.19	38.13
黄 冈	Huanggang Municipality	1757.46	1635.79	121.67	10.10
咸 宁	Xianning Municipality	1701.34	1537.15	164.19	2.58
随 州	Suizhou Municipality	1237.47	1159.87	77.60	16.30

10-7 主要城市财政收支(2014)
GOVERNMENT REVENUE AND EXPENDITURES OF MAJOR MUNICIPALITIES (2014)

单位：亿元 (100 million yuan)

城市	Municipalities	公共财政收入 The public finance income	#各项税收 #Taxes	公共财政支出 The public finance expenditures	#社会保障和就业支出 #Subsides Expenditures for Social Security	#城乡社区事务支出 #Expenditures for City Maintenance
武 汉	Wuhan Municipality	1101.02	906.76	1175.10	166.47	144.22
黄 石	Huangshi Municipality	89.38	63.75	167.14	28.96	9.76
十 堰	Shiyan Municipality	85.77	65.03	258.17	39.72	8.32
宜 昌	Yichang Municipality	271.52	181.51	442.82	42.36	34.03
襄 阳	Xiangyang Municipality	249.23	177.55	437.93	59.74	29.95
鄂 州	Ezhou Municipality	42.74	28.41	75.61	8.42	9.34
荆 门	Jingmen Municipality	69.82	49.76	178.96	25.07	9.18
孝 感	Xiaogan Municipality	107.32	69.15	253.18	38.09	10.67
荆 州	Jingzhou Municipality	88.17	65.56	276.29	50.97	7.79
黄 冈	Huanggang Municipality	96.04	64.70	345.40	52.59	8.19
咸 宁	Xianning Municipality	70.76	48.99	178.08	20.64	5.60
随 州	Suizhou Municipality	36.68	27.02	103.71	16.44	3.21

10-8 主要城市金融机构存贷款余额(2014)
DEPOSITS AND LOANS BALANCE OF BANKING INSTITUTIONS OF MAJOR MUNICIPALITIES (2014)

单位：亿元 (100 million yuan)

城市	Municipalities	年末金融机构人民币各项存款余额 Deposit Balance	#居民储蓄存款 #Savings Deposits from Residents	年末金融机构人民币各项贷款余额 Loans Balance
武 汉	Wuhan Municipality	16268.71	5352.13	14463.40
黄 石	Huangshi Municipality	1245.52	661.03	838.96
十 堰	Shiyan Municipality	1651.80	894.42	882.21
宜 昌	Yichang Municipality	2583.25	1323.07	1967.51
襄 阳	Xiangyang Municipality	2483.96	1541.39	1507.60
鄂 州	Ezhou Municipality	449.20	267.60	303.51
荆 门	Jingmen Municipality	1257.01	836.25	653.25
孝 感	Xiaogan Municipality	1613.55	1083.16	785.56
荆 州	Jingzhou Municipality	1967.02	1345.24	954.50
黄 冈	Huanggang Municipality	1994.05	1404.99	811.10
咸 宁	Xianning Municipality	891.72	516.34	533.30
随 州	Suizhou Municipality	845.87	585.73	396.58

10—9 主要城市贸易、外经(2014)
DOMESTIC TRADE AND FOREIGN ECONOMY OF MAJOR MUNICIPALITIES (2014)

城市	Municipalities	社会消费品零售总额(亿元) Total Retail Sales of consumer Goods (100 million yuan)	进出口总额(亿美元) Total Import and Export (USD 100 million)	进口 Imports	出口 Exports	当年实际使用外资金额(亿美元) ActualForeign Direct Investment (USD 100 million)
武 汉	Wuhan Municipality	4369.32	264.29	126.38	137.91	61.99
黄 石	Huangshi Municipality	519.70	28.55	14.08	14.47	5.50
十 堰	Shiyan Municipality	548.65	5.66	0.24	5.41	1.80
宜 昌	Yichang Municipality	964.53	26.97	4.41	22.56	3.12
襄 阳	Xiangyang Municipality	1030.57	11.70	6.23	5.46	5.69
鄂 州	Ezhou Municipality	230.28	5.19	3.15	2.04	2.11
荆 门	Jingmen Municipality	451.78	9.67	1.99	7.68	2.96
孝 感	Xiaogan Municipality	689.33	11.96	2.57	9.39	3.11
荆 州	Jingzhou Municipality	831.44	16.51	3.55	12.96	1.22
黄 冈	Huanggang Municipality	715.65	6.12	0.78	5.34	0.87
咸 宁	Xianning Municipality	361.77	4.67	0.70	3.97	0.59
随 州	Suizhou Municipality	354.37	14.31	1.56	12.74	1.00

10—10 主要城市邮电、电力(2014)
POST SERVICE AND POWER IN MAJOR MUNICIPALITIES（2014）

城市	Municipalities	邮电业务收入(全市)(亿元) Revenue from Posts and Telecommunication Services(100 million yuan)	固定电话用户(万户) Telephones (10 000 Subscribers)	移动电话用户(万户) Mobile Telephones (10 000 Subscribers)	国际互联网用户(万户) Internet Service (10 000 Subscribers)	全年用电量(亿千瓦小时) Power Consumption (100 million kWh)	#城乡居民生活用电 #Urban and Rural Residents Power Consumption
武 汉	Wuhan Municipality	185.28	255.00	1644.00	390.00	445.22	76.26
黄 石	Huangshi Municipality	21.78	38.70	233.64	42.85	110.41	11.65
十 堰	Shiyan Municipality	21.71	49.00	301.00	63.00	86.56	12.65
宜 昌	Yichang Municipality	31.13	57.50	384.24	72.00	216.51	18.26
襄 阳	Xiangyang Municipality	30.76	61.90	441.90	47.80	126.28	21.78
鄂 州	Ezhou Municipality	10.19	22.39	100.23	17.24	64.10	5.06
荆 门	Jingmen Municipality	19.48	36.25	212.28	34.68	82.71	10.75
孝 感	Xiaogan Municipality	24.82	47.48	307.77	44.39	105.70	18.31
荆 州	Jingzhou Municipality	35.15	63.03	386.41	82.81	98.37	22.64
黄 冈	Huanggang Municipality	31.45	84.61	377.92	64.90	91.49	20.70
咸 宁	Xianning Municipality	16.41	43.22	248.06	43.31	56.56	11.61
随 州	Suizhou Municipality	13.22	37.54	258.55	33.88	30.96	7.76

10-11 主要城市环境保护(2014)
ENVIRONMENTAL PROTECTION OF MAJOR MUNICIPALITIES(2014)

城市	Municipalities	工业废水排放量(万吨) Industrial Waste Water Discharged (10,000 tons)	工业二氧化硫排放量(万吨) Industrial Sulphur Dioxide Emission (100 million tons)	工业固体废物综合利用率(%) Ratio of Industrial Solid Wastes Vtilized (%)	污水处理厂集中处理率(%) Ratio of Central Sewage Treatment (%)	生活垃圾无害化处理率(%) Ratio of Consumption Treated
武汉	Wuhan Municipality	17097	8.5	98.7	93.0	100.0
黄石	Huangshi Municipality	5812	6.6	93.4	90.6	100.0
十堰	Shiyan Municipality	2112	1.8	39.8	90.8	100.0
宜昌	Yichang Municipality	17763	7.2	62.9	90.7	92.9
襄阳	Xiangyang Municipality	8412	3.7	97.7	75.9	99.1
鄂州	Ezhou Municipality	1710	3.3	88.8	82.0	100.0
荆门	Jingmen Municipality	3825	3.5	91.1	84.9	100.0
孝感	Xiaogan Municipality	4900	4.0	61.8	80.9	77.6
荆州	Jingzhou Municipality	9923	4.7	38.2	88.4	42.0
黄冈	Huanggang Municipality	3011	1.5	91.4	85.0	
咸宁	Xianning Municipality	1918	2.4	54.7	91.0	100.0
随州	Suizhou Municipality	1700	0.4	99.9	61.5	99.8

10-12 主要城市居民收支情况(2014)
INCOME AND EXPENDITURE OF MAJOR URBAN HOUSEHOLDS (2014)

单位：元 (yuan)

城市	Municipalities	城镇常住居民人均可支配收入 Per Capita Disposable Income of Urban Residents	城镇常住居民人均消费性支出 Per Capita Living Expenditure of Urban Residents	人均住房建筑面积(平方米) Per Capita Utility Floor Space of Residential Buildings (sq.m)
武汉	Wuhan Municipality	33270	22002	35.8
黄石	Huangshi Municipality	25208	15459	32.4
十堰	Shiyan Municipality	22143	12508	32.8
宜昌	Yichang Municipality	25025	15516	47.7
襄阳	Xiangyang Municipality	25863	15433	53.7
鄂州	Ezhou Municipality	22763	14545	53.5
荆门	Jingmen Municipality	26498	19669	43.1
孝感	Xiaogan Municipality	22912	15380	40.8
荆州	Jingzhou Municipality	25930	15484	45.0
黄冈	Huanggang Municipality	23242	18566	49.7
咸宁	Xianning Municipality	23758	15525	44.9
随州	Suizhou Municipality	22939	16285	42.9

10−13 主要城市居民消费支出、价格(2014)

LIVING EXPENDITURES AND PRICE OF MAJOR URBAN HOUSEHOLDS (2014)

单位：元 (yuan)

城 市	Municipalities	城镇常住居民人均消费性支出 Per Capita Living Expenditures for Consumption of Urban Residents				市辖区居民消费价格指数(上年=100) Consumer Price Index (preceding year=100)
		#医疗保健 #Medicine and Medicine and Medical Service	#交通和通讯 #Transport and Telecom-munication	#娱乐、教育、文化服务 #Recreation,Education and Cultural Services	#居住 #Residence	
武 汉	Wuhan Municipality	1445	2264	2130	5669	101.9
黄 石	Huangshi Municipality	1123	1605	1982	2443	102.2
十 堰	Shiyan Municipality	832	1765	1404	2160	101.5
宜 昌	Yichang Municipality	1319	1771	1552	3674	102.2
襄 阳	Xiangyang Municipality	1469	1360	1722	2495	101.5
鄂 州	Ezhou Municipality	1396	1107	1177	2321	102.1
荆 门	Jingmen Municipality	1542	1875	1956	4215	101.9
孝 感	Xiaogan Municipality	946	1395	1663	1540	102.0
荆 州	Jingzhou Municipality	1076	1655	1725	1821	102.1
黄 冈	Huanggang Municipality	2114	1294	1655	2018	101.3
咸 宁	Xianning Municipality	1408	1987	1824	3571	101.8
随 州	Suizhou Municipality	941	2100	2115	2225	101.9

10−14 主要城市文教、科技、卫生(2014)

CULTURE, EDUCATION, SCIENCE AND TECHNOLOGY AND PUBLIC HEALTH OF MAJOR MUNICIPALITIES (2014)

城 市	Municipalities	高等学校在校学生数(万人) Number of Students Enrolled in Institutions of Higher Education (10 000 persons)	从事科技活动人员数(人) Number of Scientific and technical Personel (person)	公共图书馆图书总藏量(万册) Total Volume of Collection of Public Libraries (10 000 volumes)	医院、卫生院数(个) Number of Health Care Institutions (unit)	医院、卫生院数床位数(万张) Number of Beds In Health Care Intitutions (10 000 units)	执业(助理)医师(万人) Practioner Doctors (Assitant) (10 000 persons)
武 汉	Wuhan Municipality	96.21		1274.62	266	6.42	2.95
黄 石	Huangshi Municipality	3.69	13267	128.50	74	1.26	0.50
十 堰	Shiyan Municipality	4.97	14476	118.60	173	2.51	0.87
宜 昌	Yichang Municipality	5.92	27818	207.52	170	2.31	0.98
襄 阳	Xiangyang Municipality	5.26	29721	174.05	211	2.86	1.14
鄂 州	Ezhou Municipality	1.48	3213	41.00	464	0.51	0.18
荆 门	Jingmen Municipality	2.04	7255	114.10	102	1.45	0.67
孝 感	Xiaogan Municipality	3.92	58116	81.00	159	1.71	0.78
荆 州	Jingzhou Municipality	11.18	10082	117.20	167	2.32	1.02
黄 冈	Huanggang Municipality	4.64	9261	173.00	286	2.77	2.89
咸 宁	Xianning Municipality	4.02	18000	90.13	93	1.10	0.64
随 州	Suizhou Municipality	0.62	6685	232.62	103	0.92	0.36

主要统计指标解释

供水综合生产能力 指按供水设施取水、净化、送水、出厂输水干管等环节设计能力计算的综合生产能力。包括在原设计能力的基础上，经挖、革、改增加的生产能力。计算时，以四个环节中最薄弱的环节为主确定能力。

年末供水管道长度 指从送水泵至用户水表之间所有管道的长度。不包括新安装尚未使用的管道。

全年供水总量 指报告期供水企业(单位)供出的全部水量。包括有效供水量和漏损水量。

生活用水量 包括公共服务用水和居民家庭用水。公共服务用水指为城市社会公共生活服务的用水。包括行政事业单位、部队营区和公共设施服务、社会服务业、批发零售贸易业、旅馆饮食业以及其他公共服务业等单位的用水。居民家庭用水指城市范围内所有居民家庭的日常生活用水。包括城市居民、农民家庭、公共供水站用水。

用水普及率 指城市用水人口数与城市人口总数的比率。计算公式：

$$用水普及率=\frac{城市用水人口数}{城市人口总数}\times 100\%$$

供气管道长度 指报告期末从气源厂压缩机的出口或门站出口至各类用户引入管之间的全部已经通气投入使用的管道长度。不包括煤气生产厂、输配站、液化气储存站、灌瓶站、储配站、气化站、混气站、供应站等厂(站)内的管道。

全年供气总量 指全年燃气企业(单位)向用户供应的燃气数量。包括销售量和损失量。

用气普及率 指报告期末使用燃气的城市人口数与城市人口总数的比率。计算公式为：

$$用气普及率=\frac{城市用气人口数}{城市人口总数}\times 100\%$$

城市供热能力 指供热企业(单位)向城市热用户输送热能的设计能力。

城市供热总量 指在报告期供热企业(单位)向城市热用户输送全部蒸汽和热水的总热量。

城市供热管道长度 指从各类热源到热用户建筑物接入口之间的全部蒸汽和热水的管道长度。不包括各类热源厂内部的管道长度。

年末道路长度 指年末道路长度和与道路相通的广场、桥梁、隧道的长度，按车行道中心线计算。在统计时只统计路面宽度在3.5米(含3.5米)以上的各种铺装道路，包括开放型工业区和住宅区道路在内。

城市桥梁 指为跨越天然或人工障碍物而修建的构筑物。包括跨河桥、立交桥、人行天桥以及人行地下通道等。包括永久性桥和半永久性桥。

城市排水管道长度 指所有排水总管、干管、支管、检查井及连接井进出口等长度之和。

城市污水日处理能力 指污水处理厂(或处理装置)每昼夜处理污水量的设计能力。

年末运营车数 指年末公交企业(单位)用于运营业务的全部车辆数。以企业(单位)固定资产台帐中已投入运营的车辆数为准。

城市园林绿地面积 指报告期末用作园林和绿化的各种绿地面积。包括公共绿地、居住区绿地、单位附属绿地、防护绿地、生产绿地、道路绿地和风景林地面积。不包括：

1.屋顶绿化、垂直绿化、阳台绿化和室内绿化。

2.以物质生产为主的林地、耕地、牧草地、果园和竹园等。

3.城市总体规划中不列入绿地的水域。

公共绿地　指向公众开放的市级、区级、居住区级各类公园、街旁游园，包括其范围内的水域。其中居住区级公园应不小于 1 万平方米，街旁游园的宽度不小于 8 米，面积不小于 400 平方米。

Explanatory Notes on Main Statistical Indicators

Production Capacity of Water Supply refers to the designed comprehensive production capacity of water facilities, covering the 4 links of water collection, purification, conveyance, and outflow through trunk pipelines. Increase capacity through transformation and innovation projects are included as well. The capacity is determined mainly on the weakest of the above-mentioned 4 links.

Length of Water Supply Pipelines at the Year-end refers to the total length of all the pipelines between the water pumps and the user 抯 water meters, excluding pipelines newly installed but not used yet.

Annual Volume of Water Supply refers to the total volume of water supplied by water-works (units) during the reference period, including both the effective water supply and loss during the water supply.

Consumption of Water for Residential Use refers to the water consumption of households for daily life and the water consumption of public service facilities. The latter refers to water consumption for urban public services, including the consumption of government agencies and public institutions, military barracks, public facilities, wholesale and retail outlets, restaurants, hotels, and other units providing public services. Household water consumption refers to consumption of water for daily life of all households in the boundary of cities, including households of urban residents and farmers, and public water supply stations.

Percentage of Urban Population with Access to Tap Water refers to the ratio of the urban population with access to tap water to the total urban population. The formula is:

Percentage of population with access to tap water= (Urban population with access to tap water) / (Urban population)×100%

Length of Gas Pipelines refers to the total length of pipelines in use between the outlet of the compressor of gas-work or outlet of gas stations and the leading pipe of users, excluding pipelines within gasworks, delivery stations, LPG storage stations, refilling stations, gas-mixing stations and supply stations.

Volume of Gas Supply refers to the total volume of gas provided to users by gas-producing enterprises (units) in a year, including the volume sold and the volume lost.

Percentage of Urban Population with Access to Gas refers to the ratio of the urban population with access to gas to the total urban population at the end of the reference period. The formula is:

Percentage of population with access to gas = (Urban population with access to gas / Urban population) x 100%

Heating Capacity in Urban Area refers to the designed capacity of heating enterprises (units) in supplying heating energy to urban users during the reference period.

Quantity of Heat Supplied in Urban Area refers to the total quantity of heat from steam and hot water supplied to urban users by heating enterprises (units) during the reference period.

Length of Heating Pipelines refers to the total length of steam or hot water pipelines for sources of heat to the leading pipelines of the buildings of the users, excluding internal pipelines in heat generating enterprises.

Length of Paved Roads at the Year-end refers to the length of roads with paved surface including squares bridges and tunnels connected with roads by the end of the year. Length of the roads is measured by the central lines for vehicles for paved roads with a width of 3.5 meters and over, including roads in open-ended factory compounds and residential quarters.

Urban Bridges refer to bridges built to cross over natural or man-made barriers, including bridges over rivers, overpasses for traffic and for pedestrian, underpasses for pedestrian, etc. Both permanent and semi-permanent bridges are included.

Length of Urban Sewage Pipes refers to the total length of general drainage, trunks. branch and inspection wells, connection wells, inlets and outlets, etc.

Daily Disposal Capacity of Urban Sewage refers to the designed 24 hour capacity of sewage disposal by the sewage treatment works or facilities.

Number of Vehicles under Operation at the Year-end refers to the total number of vehicles under operation by public transport enterprises (units) at the end of the year, based on the records of operational vehicles by the enterprises (units).

Area of Urban Gardens and Green Areas refers to the total area occupied for green projects at the end of the reference period, including public green land, green land in residential quarters, green land attached to institutions, protection green land, production green land, roadside green land and forest in scenic spots. It does not include the following:

(1) Greenery and plants on roofs, balconies, indoors and vertical green areas;

(2) Forest, cultivated land, grassland, orchards and bamboo grooves that are for production purpose; and

(3) Water areas that are not included in urban master plan as green land.

Public Green Area refers to green areas open to the public such as municipal, community and neighborhood parks and roadside parks, including waters within parks. Neighborhood parks should occupy an area larger than 10,000 square meters, and the width of roadside parks should occupy an area larger than 400 square meters, with a width of more that 8 meters.

11 资源和环境

Resources and Environment

资料整理：苏　畅

11-1 “三废”排放和处理综合利用情况

"THREE WASTES" DISCHARGE AND TREATMENT UTILIZATION SITUATION

分　　类	Item	2011	2012	2013	2014
一、废水排放总量　（万吨）	Total Volume of Waste Water Discharged　(10 000 ton)	293064	290200	294054	301703
工业废水排放总量	Total Volume of Industrial Waste Water Discharged	104434	91609	84993	81657
二、废气排放总量　（亿标立方米）	Total Volume of Waste Gas Discharged　(100 million cu.m)	22840	19512	19986	21702
三、废气中污染物排放量　（万吨）	Pollutants Discharged in Waste Gas　(10 000 ton)				
二氧化硫	Sulfur Dioxide	66.56	62.24	59.94	58.38
#工业二氧化硫	#Industrial Sulfur Dioxide	59.50	54.86	52.40	50.62
烟粉尘	Soot and Dust	30.74	34.97	35.95	50.40
四、工业固体废物产生量　（万吨）	Volume of Industrial Solid Wastes Producced　(10 000 ton)	7596	7611	8181	8006
已处置的	Teated	1424	1561	1646	1701
已综合利用的	Utilized In a Comprehensive Way	6007	5737	6196	6139
已贮存的	Stored	268	377	412	221
工业固体废物排放量	Volume of Industrial Solid Wastes Emission	16.64	1.06	0.80	0.46
五、锅炉总数　（台）	Total Number of Boiler　(unit)	2339	2451	2413	2617
锅炉蒸吨数　（蒸吨）	Steam Tons of Boiler　(steam ton)	60862	72444	75469	87176
六、工业炉窑　（座）	Number of Industrial Kiln Stove　(unit)	2494	2475	2298	2262

11−2 工业污染治理情况

项　　目		Item	Unit	1990	1995	2000
一、汇总工业企业单位数	(个)	Total Number of Industrial Enterprises	(unit)	991	613	583
二、污染治理项目本年投资来源合计	(万元)	Total Resource of Investment in Pollutant Treatment Projects	(10 000 yuan)	18051	27433	85238
国家预算内资金		State Budgetary Funds		5568	3540	962
环境保护补助资金		Environmental Protection Subsidy Funds		2531	5430	1282
环保贷款		Environmental Protection Loans		2149	3143	7579
其　　他		Others		1372	7966	61881
三、污染治理项目本年完成投资合计	(万元)	Total Investment in Pollutant Treatment Projects	(10 000 yuan)			85238
治理废水		Waste Water		5637	12042	45653
治理废气		Waste Gas		9891	9164	26668
治理固体废物		Solid Waste		1371	5293	6072
治理噪声		Noise Abatement		534	583	644
其　　他		Others		618	351	6201
四、本年施工项目数	(个)	Projects Carried Out in This Year	(unit)	1545	939	851
治理废水		Waste Water		450	305	384
治理废气		Waste Gas		758	367	361
治理固体废物		Solid Waste		119	121	27
治理噪声		Noise Abatement		139	109	31
其　　他		Others		79	37	48
五、本年竣工项目	(个)	Projects Completed in This Year	(unit)	1312	832	692
治理废水		Waste Water		353	256	316
治理废气		Waste Gas		662	339	286
治理固体废物		Solid Waste		99	96	22
治理噪声		Noise Abatement		126	106	26
其　　他		Others		72	35	42

STATISTICS ON TREATMENT OF INDUSTRIAL POLLUTION

2005	2006	2007	2008	2009	2010	2011	2012	2013	2014
336	354	342	307	225	159	232	171	147	152
148097	148873	169405	161453	281332	277416	153812	154496	251745	262884
7591	9040	4434	4244	5602	3892	7216	4128	3667	1890
7385	2942	5543	3713	4092	1894	1290	676	210	2177
	9574		3487			2950			
133121	127318	159428	153497	271638	271631	145306	149693	247868	258817
148097	148873	169405	161453	281332	277416	153812	154496	251745	262884
48068	59632	78246	82635	54002	35627	84573	35868	15873	18409
40008	65822	74455	60834	213918	197293	47920	80510	216673	230712
11408	10241	2004	3960	5970	9580	10505	3565	1720	2762
440	13179	1411	1041	675	867	1081	1114	52	104
48173	650	13288	12983	6768	34050	9734	33439	17427	10896
473	447	504	406	318	226	364	136	113	127
191	199	224	178	126	98	158	43	28	38
176	188	188	139	132	74	122	56	59	78
15	29	21	23	11	13	17	7	3	2
20	17	21	15	11	12	18	8	1	4
71	44	50	51	38	29	49	22	22	5
428	403	442	345	273	195	331	117	148	134
174	165	197	152	108	84	143	42	42	37
160	167	168	115	111	64	112	49	83	88
11	22	18	19	10	10	16	7	3	1
18	15	20	14	9	10	18	6		3
65	34	39	45	35	27	42	13	20	5

11–3 排污费征收、使用和污染赔(罚)款情况
STATISTICS ON COLLECTION, REPARATIONS AND FINES ON POLLUTION DSICHARGES

项 目	Item	1990	1995	2000	2008	2009	2010	2011	2012	2013	2014
交纳排污费单位（个）	Number of Enterprises Charged (unit)	4072	9409	32581	19607	15584	12017	10581	10895	7269	7566
本年征收排污费数(万元)	Amount of Pollutant Fees (10 000 yuan)	7823	13870	20092	40600	38176	40300	44975	50587	60161	65626

11–4 工业企业废水处理设施情况
STATISTICS ON INDUSTRIAL WASTE WATER TREATMENT FACILITES

项 目	Item	2000	2005	2009	2010	2011	2012	2013	2014
汇总企业单位数 （个）	Total Number of Enterprises (unit)	2172	2313	2552	2643	3911	3699	3590	3911
治理设施数量 （套）	Number of Treatment Facilities	2120	2163	2068	2093	5296	2110	2084	2238
处理能力 （万吨/日）	Treatment Capacity(10 000 ton/day)		912	951	1037	1322	1023	1029	1043
运行费用 （万元）	Operation Fees (10 000 yuan)	46651	77931	134207	137920	344256	176058	168277	232869

11-5　全省当年建成投产的建设项目“三同时”执行情况

STATISTICS ON IMPLEMENTATION OF "THREE MEANWHILE" OF CONSTRUCTION PROJECTS IN HUBEI PROVINCE

项　　目	Item	1990	1995	2000	2005	2008	2009	2010	2011	2012	2013	2014
一、建设项目　（个）	Numberof Construction Projects (unit)	306	245	359	1437	1498	2150	2107	3078	4912	3267	3250
二、建设项目投资总额（亿元）	Total investmentin Construction Projects (100 million yuan)	12.72	33.60	69.61	1603.13	315.73	2085.81	624.86	1099.26	3913.09	1180.10	1889.70
#环保工程投资(亿元)	#Investment in Environmental Protection Projects (100 million yuan)	0.32	1.5	2.37	11.22	25.65	51.89	29.16	53.06	117.40	73.00	71.40
三、“三同时”执行情况	Implementation of "Three Meanwhile"											
实际执行项目数　（个）	Number of Projects Actually Being Implemented (unit)	221	227	356	1336	1491	2148	2107	3078	2076	3267	3250
执行项目中合格的（个）	Qualified (unit)	217	211	356	1191	1481	2135	2087	2977	2032	3138	3154

主要统计指标解释

工业废水排放量 指经过企业厂区所有排放口排到企业外部的工业废水量。包括生产废水、外排的直接冷却水、超标排放的矿井地下水和与工业废水混排的厂区生活污水，不包括外排的间接冷却水(清污不分流的间接冷却水应计算在内)。

工业废水排放达标量 指报告期内废水中各项污染物指标都达到国家或地方排放标准的外排工业废水量，包括未经处理外排达标的，经废水处理设施处理后达标排放的，以及经污水处理厂处理后达标排放的。

工业废水排放达标率 指工业废水排放达标量占工业废水排放量的百分率，计算公式为：

$$\text{工业废水排放达标率}=\frac{\text{工业废水排放达标量}}{\text{工业废水排放量}}\times 100\%$$

工业废气排放量 指报告期内企业厂区内燃料燃烧和生产工艺过程中产生的各种排入大气的含有污染物的气体的总量，以标准状态(273K，101325Pa)计算。测算公式为：

工业废气排放量 ＝ 燃料燃烧过程中废气排放量 ＋ 生产工艺过程中废气排放量

工业烟尘排放量 指企业厂区内燃料燃烧过程中产生的烟气中夹带的颗粒物排放量。

工业粉尘排放量 指企业在生产工艺过程中排放的能在空气中悬浮一定时间的固体颗粒物排放量。如钢铁企业的耐火材料粉尘、焦化企业的筛焦系统粉尘、烧结机的粉尘、石灰窑的粉尘、建材企业的水泥粉尘等。不包括电厂排入大气的烟尘。

工业固体废物产生量 指报告期内企业在生产过程中产生的固体状、半固体状和高浓度液体状废弃物的总量，包括危险废物、冶炼废渣、粉煤灰、炉渣、煤矸石、尾矿、放射性废物和其他废物等；不包括矿山开采的剥离废石和掘进废石(煤矸石和呈酸性或碱性的废石除外)。酸性或碱性废石指采掘的废石其流经水、雨淋水的pH值小于4或pH值大于10.5者。

工业固体废物综合利用量 指报告期内企业通过回收、加工、循环、交换等方式，从固体废物中提取或者使其转化为可以利用的资源、能源和其他原材料的固体废物量(包括当年利用往年的工业固体废物贮存量)，如用作农业肥料、生产建筑材料、筑路等。综合利用量由原产生固体废物的单位统计。

工业固体废物综合利用率 指工业固体废物综合利用量占工业固体废物产生量(包括综合利用往年贮存量)的百分率。计算公式为：

$$\text{工业固体废物综合利用率}=\frac{\text{工业固体废物综合利用量}}{\text{工业固体废物产生量}+\text{综合利用往年贮存量}}\times 100\%$$

生活垃圾无害化处理率 指报告期生活垃圾无害化处理量与生活垃圾产生量比率。在统计上，由于生活垃圾产生量不易取得，可用清运量代替。计算公式为：

$$\text{生活垃圾无害化处理率}=\frac{\text{生活垃圾无害化处理量}}{\text{生活垃圾产生量}}\times 100\%$$

Explanatory Notes on Main Statistical Indicators

Waste Water Discharged by Industry refers to the volume of waste water discharged by industrial enterprises through all their outlets, including waste water from production process, directly cooled water, groundwater from mining wells which does not meet discharge standards and sewage from households mixed with waste water produced by industrial activities, but excluding indirectly cooled water discharged (It should be included if the discharge is not separated with waste water).

Industrial Waste Water Meeting Discharge Standards refers to volume of industrial waste water discharge which, with or without treatment, reaches national or local standards with regard to all pollutants.

Ratio of Industrial Waste Water Meeting Discharge Standards refers to percentage of industrial waste water meeting discharge standards over total industrial waste water discharge. It is calculated as:

Ratio of industrial waste water meeting discharge standards = industrial waste water meeting discharge standards / total industrial waste water discharge

Industrial Waste Air Emission refers to discharge into atmosphere of waste air containing pollutants generated from fuel burning and production process in enterprises within a given period of time. It is calculated at standard status (273K, 101325Pa) as:

Industrial waste air emission = emission through fuel burning + emission through production process

Industrial Soot Emission refers to volume of soot in smoke emitted in process of fuel burning in premises of enterprises.

Industrial Dust Emission refers to volume of dust emitted by production process of enterprises and suspended in the air for a given period of time, including dust from refractory material of iron and steel works, dust from coke-screening systems and sintering machines of coke plants, dust from lime kilns and dust from cement production in building material enterprises, but excluding soot and dust emitted from power plants.

Industrial Solid Wastes Produced refers to total volume of solid, semi-solid and high concentration liquid residues produced by industrial enterprises from production process in a given period of time, including hazardous wastes, slag, coal ash, gangue, tailings, radioactive residues and other wastes, but excluding stones stripped or dug out in mining (gangue and acid or alkaline stones not included). A stone is acid or alkaline depending on the pH value of the water below 4 or above 10.5 when the stone is in, or soaked by, the water.

Industrial Solid Wastes Utilized refers to volume of solid wastes from which useful materials can be extracted or which can be converted into usable resources, energy or other materials by means of reclamation, processing, recycling and exchange (including utilizing in the year the stocks of industrial solid wastes of the previous year). Examples of such utilizations include fertilizers, building materials and road materials. The information shall be collected by the producing units of the wastes.

Ratio of Industrial Solid Wastes Utilized refers to the percentage of industrial solid wastes utilized over industrial solid wastes produced (including stocks of the previous years). It is calculated as:

Ratio of industrial solid wastes utilized = volume of industrial solid wastes utilized / (industrial solid wastes produced + stock of previous years) ×100%

Ratio of Consumption Wastes Treated refers to consumption wastes treated over that produced. In practical statistics, as it is difficult to estimate, the volume of consumption wastes produced is replaced with that transported. It is calculated as:

Ratio of consumption wastes treated = consumption wastes treated / consumption wastes produced×100%

12 农业

Agriculture

资料整理：朱　江

12-1 农村基层组织和农业基本情况

BASIC CONDITIONS OF RURAL GRASSROOTS UNITS AND AGRICULTURE

指 标	Item	1995	2000	2005	2010	2011	2012	2013	2014
农村组织情况 (个)	**Rural Units (unit)**								
乡个数	Township	1040	476	217	201	194	188	175	170
镇个数	Town Governments	861	853	737	742	742	746	757	761
村委会个数	Village Committees	32802	32400	26678	26018	26025	25991	25452	25606
村民小组个数	Villager Group	260641	259250	212587	209598	206848	210432	210108	208966
乡村户数、人口	**Rural Households,Population**								
乡村户数 (万户)	Rural Households (10 000 units)	1004.21	983.94	1015.72	1062.14	1071.75	1084.79	1088.01	1094.98
乡村人口 (万人)	Rural Population (10 000 persons)	4041.67	3947.26	3991.47	4031.73	4057.10	4089.38	4092.19	4110.29
乡村从业人员 (万人)	**Rural Employment (10 000 persons)**	**1810.44**	**1781.70**	**1931.15**	**2154.44**	**2665.02**	**2259.91**	**2280.14**	**2308.72**
按性别分	Grouped by Sex								
男	Male	955.74	937.67	1026.48	1154.45	1422.55	1208.63	1217.97	1238.01
女	Female	854.70	844.03	904.67	999.99	1242.47	1051.28	1062.17	1070.71
按行业分	Grouped by Sector								
农林牧渔业	Farming, Forestry, Animal husbandary and Fishery	1329.18	1159.13	1101.29	900.14	885.63	863.49	869.79	865.21
国营农林牧渔场从业人员	Employees in State-run Agriculture, forestry,animal husbandry, fishery Farm	59.05	54.94	55.73	54.31	58.25	50.89	47.38	51.69
农业从业人员	Agriculture Employees	35.59	34.08	35.27	31.56	34.35	30.04	27.93	28.96
非农业从业人员	Non-agriculture Employees	23.46	20.86	20.46	22.37	23.90	20.85	19.45	22.73
年末实有耕地面积(千公顷	**Cultivated Areas (Year-End) (1 000 hectares)**	**3358.01**	**3282.96**	**3161.17**	**3323.92**	**3361.86**	**3390.00**	**3409.91**	**3420.51**
农业机械总动力(万千瓦)	Total Agricultural Machinery Power (10 000 kW)	1174.34	1414.00	2057.37	2796.99	3571.23	3842.00	4081.05	4292.90
化肥施用量 (万吨)	Consumption of Chemical Fertilizers (10 000 tons)	228.41	247.08	285.83	350.77	354.89	357.66	351.93	348.27
农村用电量(亿千瓦小时)	Electricity Consumed in Rural Areas (100 million kWh)	47.36	60.86	70.09	109.78	112.26	121.23	130.14	142.23
农作物总播种面积(千公顷)	Total Sown Area (1 000 hectares)	7413.71	7584.07	7391.30	7997.57	8009.57	8105.69	8106.19	8112.26
#粮食	Grain Crops	4776.65	4156.20	4068.15	4068.37	4122.07	4180.05	4258.40	4370.34
主要农产品产量(万吨)	**Volume of Major Agricultural Products (10 000 tons)**								
粮食	Grain Crops	2463.84	2218.49	2177.38	2315.80	2388.53	2442.00	2501.30	2584.16
棉花	Cotton Crops	58.60	30.43	37.50	47.18	52.58	53.15	45.97	35.95
油料	Oil-Bearing Crops	189.44	269.98	293.90	311.80	304.72	319.70	333.17	341.73
肉类产量	Output of Meat	279.40	271.19	342.63	379.42	381.87	412.30	430.08	440.44
水产品产量	Output of Aquatic Products	150.91	234.34	318.21	353.09	356.22	388.90	410.37	433.30

注:主要生产品产量2006、2007年数据按农业普查数据进行衔接、调整。
Note:Statistics of output of major farm products of 2006,2007 is adusted according to Second Agriculture Survey.

12-2 耕地面积
AREAS UNDER CULTIVATION

单位：千公顷 (1 000 hectares)

年 份 Year	年末实有耕地面积 Cultivated Areas (Year-End)	水 田 Paddy Fields	旱 地 Dry Fields	年内减少 Dereased in Cultivated Areas in This Year	#国家基建占地 Capital Construction	人均占有耕地(公顷) Per Capita Cultivated Area (sq.m) 按乡村人口计算 By Rural Population	按农林牧渔业劳动力计算 By Farming, Forestry, Animal husbandry and Fishery Laborers
1949	2742.58	1765.11	1977.47			0.12	0.29
1952	4015.90	1876.62	2139.28			0.16	0.39
1957	4172.31	1945.05	2227.26			0.16	0.37
1962	4271.33	1847.19	2424.56			0.15	0.39
1965	4239.93	1966.38	2273.55			0.14	0.37
1970	3964.01	1982.20	1981.81			0.11	0.31
1975	3823.00	1996.10	1826.77	54.10		0.10	0.28
1978	3768.07	1959.63	1808.43	30.77	7.75	0.10	0.28
1979	3754.51	1940.27	1814.24	29.13	5.50	0.10	0.27
1980	3738.51	1929.50	1809.01	35.82	4.69	0.10	0.27
1981	3730.20	1924.66	1805.73	23.64	3.23	0.09	0.26
1982	3718.20	1916.53	1801.67	22.53	2.68	0.09	0.26
1983	3698.74	1907.51	1791.23	28.83	4.93	0.09	0.25
1984	3643.68	1892.89	1750.79	65.23	8.18	0.09	0.25
1985	3584.61	1864.15	1720.46	71.70	8.56	0.09	0.27
1986	3545.00	1847.63	1697.37	49.30	7.30	0.09	0.27
1987	3517.99	1845.17	1672.82	36.16	7.13	0.09	0.26
1988	3498.47	1838.37	1660.10	25.98	4.55	0.09	0.25
1989	3486.57	1858.25	1628.33	17.47	1.83	0.09	0.25
1990	3476.77	1871.77	1605.00	15.60	2.73	0.08	0.24
1991	3458.46	1869.19	1589.27	24.11	4.03	0.08	0.24
1992	3421.57	1845.31	1576.26	41.67	4.95	0.08	0.24
1993	3392.74	1815.75	1576.99	32.84	6.11	0.08	0.24
1994	3375.60	1805.42	1570.18	21.21	3.77	0.08	0.24
1995	3358.01	1780.40	1577.61	21.36	4.23	0.08	0.25
1996	3349.25	1800.00	1549.25	13.80	2.85	0.08	0.26
1997	3342.45	1796.07	1546.38	12.24	2.43	0.08	0.26
1998	3327.16	1788.95	1538.21	19.95	3.83	0.08	0.27
1999	3310.40	1786.34	1524.06	23.08	5.13	0.08	0.27
2000	3282.96	1757.63	1525.33	34.15	5.18	0.08	0.28
2001	3242.85	1742.69	1500.16	46.26	7.76	0.08	0.27
2002	3094.03	1708.58	1385.45	110.10	12.04	0.08	0.27
2003	3033.45	1665.49	1367.96	181.18	7.51	0.08	0.27
2004	3091.75	1789.10	1302.65	39.81	5.36	0.08	0.28
2005	3131.17	1856.17	1305.00	40.70	4.93	0.08	0.28
2006	3201.66	1881.74	1319.92	20.65	5.49	0.08	0.29
2007	3226.62	1890.04	1336.58	21.08	5.67	0.08	0.31
2008	3289.33	1914.07	1375.26	10.68	4.29	0.08	0.33
2009	3308.35	1928.67	1379.68	15.06	5.61	0.08	0.34
2010	3323.92	1932.05	1391.87	14.90	9.44	0.08	0.37
2011	3361.86	1954.61	1407.25	14.09	5.15	0.08	0.38
2012	3390.06	1963.13	1426.93	14.82	6.93	0.08	0.39
2013	3409.91	1976.12	1433.79	16.33	6.75	0.08	0.39
2014	3420.51	1986.01	1434.50	12.69	4.69	0.08	0.40

注：1996年及以后为农业普查接轨数(下同)。

Notes:Since 1996,the relative targers were in line with the data of agricultural gereral survey (the same as the following tables).

12-3　农林牧渔业总产值

GROSS OUTPUT VALUE OF FARMING, FORESTRY, ANIMAL HUSBANDRY AND FISHERY

单位：亿元　　　　当年价格　　　　(At current price, 100 million yuan)

年　份 Year	农林牧渔业总产值 Gross Output Value of FFAF	农业 Farming	林业 Foresty	畜牧业 Animal Husbandry	渔业 Fishery	农林牧渔服务业 Service Industry for Farming, Forestry, Animal husbandry and Fishery
1949	10.72	7.22	0.69	0.97	0.10	
1952	16.59	12.08	0.79	1.48	0.18	
1957	28.59	20.55	1.46	3.81	0.46	
1962	33.66	26.52	1.71	3.61	0.46	
1965	47.48	37.44	1.98	6.02	0.51	
1970	51.27	40.62	2.07	6.41	0.92	
1975	74.68					
1978	84.46					
1979	109.85					
1980	94.95	64.70	7.28	17.29	1.46	
1981	111.68	82.78	6.47	14.88	1.61	
1982	128.35	95.32	7.24	17.97	2.12	
1983	134.09	97.53	7.29	20.05	2.96	
1984	169.20	123.09	7.54	26.51	4.79	
1985	192.32	129.61	8.15	39.08	8.18	
1986	219.10	146.79	8.75	43.86	10.77	
1987	249.68	160.13	9.97	54.86	14.19	
1988	297.51	175.12	10.98	80.80	18.83	
1989	335.04	198.56	11.75	91.47	20.66	
1990	402.23	252.92	14.15	98.04	23.88	
1991	405.04	247.01	16.81	102.19	25.06	
1992	435.42	265.53	17.36	110.37	27.59	
1993	501.17	301.99	22.39	134.02	42.77	
1994	786.84	481.82	26.47	219.53	59.01	
1995	988.53	612.12	28.33	268.09	79.98	
1996	1140.76	670.27	33.62	337.02	99.86	
1997	1243.68	711.91	37.33	381.40	113.04	
1998	1222.58	688.06	41.29	371.37	121.86	
1999	1126.10	645.98	40.86	311.43	127.83	
2000	1125.64	615.74	40.24	338.77	130.89	
2001	1172.82	658.26	27.11	352.63	134.82	
2002	1203.30	671.20	28.33	354.84	148.93	
2003	1342.09	733.36	34.78	383.71	170.43	
2004	1695.44	921.59	31.78	514.52	205.68	21.87
2005	1775.58	932.15	37.30	545.40	236.49	24.24
2006	1842.20	995.46	40.50	487.09	221.42	97.73
2007	2296.84	1152.09	41.86	686.19	310.83	105.87
2008	2940.47	1395.76	49.69	1008.65	372.98	113.39
2009	2985.19	1511.49	57.67	881.78	413.14	121.11
2010	3501.99	1921.67	65.37	925.04	458.58	131.33
2011	4252.90	2299.30	86.10	1205.80	508.80	152.90
2012	4732.10	2488.10	100.10	1334.00	626.20	183.70
2013	5161.00	2678.10	122.00	1395.40	748.40	216.70
2014	5452.80	2761.70	157.00	1427.60	844.20	262.30

12-4 农、林、牧、渔业总产值指数
INDICES OF GROSS OUTPUT VALUE OF FARMING, FORESTRY, ANIMAL HUSBANDRY AND FISHERY

单位：% 上年=100 (preceding year=100)

年份 Year	合计 Total	农业 Farming	林业 Forestry	畜牧业 Animal Husbandry	渔业 Fishery	农林牧渔服务业 Service Industry for Farming, Forestry, Animal husbandry and Fishery
1978	104.00	103.10	104.90	107.60	94.20	
1980	88.80	83.70	102.80	108.10	111.30	
1985	106.30	101.70	103.00	127.80	133.30	
1986	103.40	100.60	98.50	107.30	129.80	
1987	102.70	101.20	104.50	101.00	120.10	
1988	97.20	93.90	90.60	105.40	105.60	
1989	105.00	104.50	101.60	105.20	108.30	
1990	107.10	108.40	106.00	104.90	106.70	
1991	100.70	97.66	118.80	104.23	104.94	
1992	107.50	107.50	103.27	108.00	110.10	
1993	115.10	113.73	128.97	121.43	155.02	
1994	157.00	159.55	118.27	163.80	137.93	
1995	125.63	127.04	106.99	122.12	135.54	
1996	115.40	109.50	118.67	125.71	124.87	
1997	109.02	106.21	111.04	113.17	113.20	
1998	98.30	96.65	110.61	97.37	107.80	
1999	92.11	93.88	98.95	83.86	104.90	
2000	99.96	95.32	98.48	108.78	102.39	
2001	104.19	106.91	67.37	104.09	103.00	
2002	102.60	101.97	104.50	100.63	110.47	
2003	111.53	109.26	122.77	108.14	114.44	
2004	126.33	125.67	91.37	134.09	120.68	
2005	104.73	101.15	117.37	106.00	114.98	110.84
2006	105.37	109.29	108.58	96.04	109.87	116.05
2007	124.68	115.73	103.36	140.88	140.38	108.33
2008	128.02	121.15	118.17	146.99	119.99	107.10
2009	101.52	108.29	116.10	87.42	110.77	106.81
2010	109.95	121.28	113.35	94.12	106.86	100.16
2011	121.40	119.70	137.70	130.40	110.90	116.40
2012	111.30	108.20	116.30	110.60	123.10	120.10
2013	109.06	107.64	121.88	104.60	119.51	117.96
2014	105.70	103.10	128.70	102.30	112.80	121.00

注:2009年畜牧业数据变动原因为与农普数衔接。
Note: 2009 data changes due to livestock and agricultural census data convergence.

12–5 农、林、牧、渔业总产值指数
INDICES OF GROSS OUTPUT VALUE OF FARMING, FORESTRY, ANIMAL HUSBANDRY AND FISHERY

单位：%　　1978年=100　　(year 1978 =100)

年 份 Year	合 计 Total	农 业 Farming	林 业 Forestry	牧 业 Animal Husbandry	渔 业 Fishery
1980	97.3	91.4	104.7	127.9	121.5
1981	108.2	102.4	95.4	138.2	134.1
1982	122.6	116.5	104.1	135.6	156.8
1983	122.7	115.9	105.3	160.5	181.2
1984	148.4	140.0	110.6	164.7	254.0
1985	157.7	142.4	114.0	206.2	338.6
1986	163.1	143.3	112.3	263.5	439.5
1987	167.5	145.0	117.3	282.7	527.8
1988	162.9	136.1	106.3	285.5	557.3
1989	171.0	142.3	108.0	301.0	603.6
1990	183.1	154.2	114.5	315.7	644.0
1991	181.7	147.7	125.9	334.0	631.8
1992	194.4	158.7	120.1	360.7	689.3
1993	207.4	168.0	129.5	410.9	936.1
1994	227.8	175.0	152.0	461.7	1203.0
1995	259.9	195.3	156.0	535.1	1530.2
1996	277.6	198.0	168.5	611.1	1732.0
1997	304.0	213.4	179.3	671.6	2007.4
1998	307.3	209.1	204.6	682.3	2164.0
1999	309.5	220.2	196.7	627.9	2270.0
2000	318.1	226.3	194.2	650.4	2324.5
2001	327.6	238.7	141.6	669.6	2382.4
2002	334.2	233.1	145.9	700.2	2677.3
2003	351.8	237.2	167.2	730.8	2824.4
2004	374.7	257.9	153.9	760.8	2979.6
2005	392.4	260.9	180.6	806.4	3425.9
2006	171.8	137.9	58.7	502.2	2214.2
2007	214.3	159.6	60.7	707.4	3108.3
2008	274.3	193.3	72.0	1039.8	3729.8
2009	278.5	209.3	83.6	909.1	4131.4
2010	326.7	266.2	94.7	953.6	4585.8
2011	396.7	318.5	124.8	1243.1	5088.0
2012	441.4	344.6	145.1	1375.3	6262.0
2013	481.4	370.9	176.8	1438.6	7484.0
2014	508.6	382.5	227.6	1471.8	8442.0

12–6 农、林、牧、渔业增加值(2014)
VALUE ADDED OF FARMING, FORESTRY, ANIMAL HUSBANDRY AND FISHERY(2014)

单位：亿元　　(100 million yuan)

项 目	Item	合 计 Total	农 业 Farming	林 业 Forestry	牧 业 Animal Husbandry	渔 业 Fishery	农林牧渔服务业 Service Industry for Farming, Forestry,Animal husbandry and Fishery
一、总产值(现价)	Gross Output Value(current price)	5452.80	2761.70	157.00	1427.60	844.20	262.30
二、中间消耗	Intermedium-Consumption	2196.80	988.70	86.00	606.60	332.20	183.30
三、增加值	Value-Added	3256.00	1773.00	71.00	821.00	512.00	79.00

12-7 农作物播种面积

单位：千公顷

年 份 Year	总播种面积 Total Sown Areas	粮食作物 Grain Crops	小麦 Wheat	稻谷 Rice	薯类 Tubers	玉米 Corn	大豆 Soybean	经济作物 Economic Crops
1978	7931.05	5544.78	1122.28	2894.63	427.23	403.14	173.43	971.53
1980	7477.06	5352.04	1292.29	2708.22	387.46	406.91	138.94	977.58
1985	7331.71	5108.25	1331.42	2538.57	354.01	374.17	134.64	1280.89
1990	7361.14	5200.01	1352.10	2636.47	391.90	386.11	164.65	1343.23
1991	7423.92	5194.50	1347.53	2622.79	402.38	395.19	150.61	1414.37
1992	7183.83	4955.35	1287.91	2537.49	392.59	376.18	140.23	1405.87
1993	7125.47	4812.05	1271.23	2377.82	384.33	365.96	181.69	1381.64
1994	7181.43	4797.95	1225.60	2373.26	203.39	373.02	201.52	1456.00
1995	7431.71	4776.65	1179.93	2408.66	397.65	393.77	188.01	1683.56
1996	7579.01	4880.28	1230.14	2448.58	419.53	405.07	174.71	1676.71
1997	7739.21	4944.66	1276.52	2467.51	415.74	400.30	182.51	1689.03
1998	7695.98	4737.15	1212.08	2244.74	431.02	442.84	201.32	1703.80
1999	7788.66	4673.11	1074.43	2284.98	448.72	460.82	207.01	1739.07
2000	7584.07	4156.20	845.10	1995.29	467.61	424.10	224.75	1984.76
2001	7488.99	4015.73	735.85	1953.77	237.75	401.11	218.01	1972.36
2002	7281.61	3816.08	679.02	1888.75	430.61	384.04	217.82	1981.04
2003	7153.24	3572.74	603.43	1808.75	208.56	349.81	196.47	2083.26
2004	7225.13	3817.89	605.08	2084.02	403.79	357.49	186.05	2079.51
2005	7391.30	4068.05	730.61	2162.39	397.75	428.79	179.79	1974.56
2006	7100.59	3902.27	1016.93	1975.07	218.67	431.93	118.40	1825.40
2007	7130.01	3981.43	1096.25	1978.82	219.19	436.34	114.75	1787.79
2008	7272.33	3906.69	1000.57	1978.94	216.09	470.37	206.79	1973.85
2009	7527.50	4012.53	993.36	2045.08	237.93	507.28	195.76	2018.78
2010	7997.57	4068.37	1000.11	2038.17	274.29	531.38	104.76	2116.92
2011	8009.57	4122.07	1013.61	2036.17	303.64	549.66	152.97	2127.49
2012	8105.69	4180.05	1065.50	2017.88	299.65	593.34	95.31	2204.36
2013	8106.19	4258.40	1094.80	2101.15	303.27	573.47	86.67	2159.12
2014	8112.26	4370.34	1074.33	2143.95	308.81	642.38	98.90	2102.34

注:2006、2007年度农业普查衔接数据。

TOTAL SOWN AREAS OF FARM CROPS

(1 000 hectares)

棉花 Cotton	油菜籽 Rape-Seed	花生 Peanuts	芝麻 Sesame	黄红麻 Jute and Ambary	甘蔗 Sugar-cane	甜菜 Beet-Roots	烤烟 Flue-Cured Tobacco	其他作物 Others
593.19	165.27	34.14	102.71	8.39	2.31	0.13	24.75	1414.73
591.67	175.75	40.76	113.51	12.17	1.49	0.12	9.69	1147.44
464.97	361.42	65.94	173.31	94.17	7.85	0.08	37.67	942.56
455.92	744.31	63.75	126.85	27.33	8.07	0.01	46.35	817.90
461.55	610.10	61.59	128.17	20.42	8.47	0.02	56.83	815.05
507.19	534.41	64.73	126.32	18.15	10.64	0.02	72.76	822.61
486.06	522.14	79.70	127.24	22.41	15.00	0.03	64.32	931.78
497.58	615.87	86.97	114.77	11.70	15.73		38.69	927.48
502.03	838.82	91.91	110.04	10.83	15.97	0.03	41.16	953.50
474.38	855.26	90.82	107.72	8.59	16.59		51.92	1022.02
480.56	829.80	95.20	107.35	10.10	18.00		70.99	1105.52
431.58	887.01	121.48	113.62	7.94	19.97		48.47	1255.03
310.70	1003.64	143.87	127.14	4.30	23.34		48.32	1376.48
318.07	1158.94	193.42	143.82	3.14	22.17		48.10	1443.11
346.65	1118.06	210.06	129.93	2.65	18.88		40.43	1500.90
286.37	1155.25	206.04	138.88	5.13	19.18		42.90	1484.49
355.02	1174.63	201.11	124.00	2.97	17.24		39.45	1497.24
408.30	1186.10	173.03	111.20	1.36	10.01		39.94	1327.73
360.95	1178.65	171.71	102.52	0.98	9.95		43.68	1348.69
496.40	1001.20	140.10	97.24	0.69	3.70		32.13	1372.92
514.22	927.10	137.80	94.67	0.59	3.60		32.70	1360.79
542.96	1089.61	142.26	92.18	0.50	6.62		46.78	1391.79
460.08	1165.88	183.73	99.64	0.35	10.35		55.87	1496.19
480.05	1159.88	189.26	92.46	0.11	8.05		40.76	1812.28
488.66	1141.38	192.17	89.16	0.10	7.80		47.65	1760.01
472.87	1167.33	239.80	88.19	0.09	7.75	0.03	52.06	1721.28
415.59	1226.30	200.35	84.37	0.08	7.50	0.02	49.64	1688.67
344.81	1248.70	198.52	89.88	0.05	7.56	0.02	39.17	1639.58

Note:Statistics of 2006 and 2007 are linkage data of Second Agricluture Survey.

12–8 主要农作物播种面积和产量(2014)
TOTAL SOWN AREAS AND OUTPUT OF FARM CROPS(2014)

指 标	Item	播种面积(千公顷) Sown Areas (1 000 hectares)	总产量(万吨) Total Output(10000 ton)
农作物总播种面积	**Total Sown Areas of Farm Crops**	**8112.26**	
粮食作物总计	**Total Grain**	**4370.34**	**2584.16**
夏粮	Summer Grain	1380.85	505.6
小麦	Wheat	1074.33	421.6
大麦	Barley	24.99	8.91
蚕豌豆	Broad and Dea Bean	63.67	11.19
秋粮	Autumn Grain	2989.49	2078.56
稻谷	Rice	2143.95	1729.47
#中稻	#Semilate Rice	1258.64	1167.89
双季晚稻	Late Double- crop Rice	472.91	322.91
秋薯	Tubers	91.47	29.51
玉米	Corn	642.38	293.65
高粱	Sorghum	1.71	0.7
大豆	Soybeans	98.90	23.93
绿豆	#Green Beans	9.03	1.19
经济作物（全口径）	**Economic Crops**	**3741.92**	
棉花	Cotton	344.81	35.95
油料	Oil-Bearing Crops	1542.46	341.73
#花生	#Peanuts	198.52	69.06
油菜籽	Rapeseed	1248.70	257.16
芝麻	Sesame	89.88	14.53
麻类	Hemp Crops	10.10	2.53
#黄麻	#Jute	0.05	0.01
苎麻	Ramie	10.05	2.51
糖类	Sugar Crops	7.61	30.41
#甘蔗	#Sugarcane	7.59	30.41
烟叶	Tobacco Crops	46.11	8.81
药材	Crude Drugs	151.25	
#蔬菜(含菜用瓜)	#Vegetable	1173.52	3671.52
瓜果类	Melon and Fruits	103.62	358.09
花卉种植面积	**Flower Gardening**	**41.87**	
其他农作物	**Others**	**362.44**	
绿肥	Organic Fertilizer	76.23	

12-9 主要农产品产量

OUTPUT OF MAJOR FARM CROPS

单位：万吨 (10 000 ton)

年 份 Year	粮 食 Grain	夏 粮 Summer Grain	秋 粮 Autumn Grain	棉 花 Cotton	油 料 Oil Bearing Crops	#花 生 Peanuts	#油菜籽 Rapeseed
1949	578.13	101.85	476.28	5.74	13.37	3.17	4.12
1952	747.54	148.81	598.73	12.17	22.34	4.56	7.09
1957	986.08	180.87	805.21	21.02	25.26	11.23	4.86
1962	960.41	246.34	714.07	14.22	18.30	3.81	4.29
1965	1241.34	255.01	986.33	38.29	22.32	5.15	6.76
1970	1268.67	187.06	1081.62	29.64	14.93	4.82	3.94
1975	1561.51	230.10	1331.41	40.61	21.44	5.12	10.65
1978	1725.60	315.04	1410.56	36.67	23.71	4.90	10.72
1980	1536.43	341.32	1195.11	31.63	20.58	5.85	11.59
1985	2216.13	429.58	1786.56	49.22	72.98	13.52	41.14
1990	2475.03	474.96	2000.07	51.73	95.75	12.79	70.90
1991	2244.10	476.20	1767.90	49.11	106.29	11.44	83.75
1992	2426.60	450.90	2022.83	60.99	99.74	15.72	70.86
1993	2325.70	471.87	1853.85	42.50	111.74	20.68	78.35
1994	2422.10	472.70	1949.40	45.00	137.77	24.81	98.07
1995	2463.84	447.20	2016.64	58.60	189.44	27.28	146.24
1996	2484.40	465.24	2019.16	43.01	181.82	30.77	134.88
1997	2634.40	542.60	2091.80	58.09	195.47	31.24	147.53
1998	2475.79	501.69	1974.10	32.50	216.69	42.87	154.76
1999	2451.88	392.71	2059.17	28.15	228.27	48.15	159.97
2000	2218.49	322.39	1896.10	30.43	269.98	53.46	192.40
2001	2138.49	319.14	1819.35	37.35	279.45	63.99	194.79
2002	2047.00	232.27	1841.73	32.26	245.29	72.25	151.40
2003	1921.02	255.65	1665.37	32.50	272.72	68.37	187.10
2004	2100.12	271.24	1828.96	39.54	314.38	63.19	235.12
2005	2177.38	302.49	1874.89	37.50	293.90	60.19	219.15
2006	2099.10	369.08	1730.02	55.20	254.45	48.40	191.83
2007	2185.44	406.44	1779.00	55.73	254.75	48.60	193.30
2008	2227.23	386.24	1840.99	51.30	283.56	49.41	214.89
2009	2309.10	398.45	1910.65	48.05	314.05	62.62	236.51
2010	2315.80	420.60	1895.18	47.18	311.80	64.45	232.57
2011	2388.53	425.83	1962.70	52.58	304.72	68.74	220.39
2012	2441.81	447.44	1994.37	53.15	319.66	74.34	230.03
2013	2501.30	501.00	2000.30	45.97	333.17	68.11	250.47
2014	2584.16	505.60	2078.56	35.95	341.73	69.06	257.16

注：2006、2007年为农业普查衔接数据。

Note:Statistics 2006 and 2007 are linkage data of Second Agriculture Survey.

12-10 人均占有主要农产品产量

PER CAPITA OUTPUT OF MAJOR FARM PRODUCTS

单位：千克/人 (kg/person)

年 份 Year	粮 食 Grain	棉 花 Cotton	油 料 Oil Bearing Crops	猪、牛、羊肉 Output of Pork, Beef and Mutton	水产品 Output of Aquatic Products
1952	275	4.5	8.2		2.9
1957	327	7.0	8.4		4.0
1962	302	4.4	5.8		2.3
1965	359	11.1	6.4		3.3
1970	319	7.5	3.8		2.8
1975	357	9.3	4.9		2.6
1978	379	8.1	5.2		2.4
1980	330	6.8	4.4	11.9	2.9
1985	452	10.0	14.9	20.7	7.6
1990	467	9.8	18.1	27.7	13.4
1991	415	8.9	19.6	29.0	12.9
1992	443	11.1	18.2	31.9	14.9
1993	416	7.6	20.0	35.3	18.1
1994	431	8.0	24.5	41.8	23.0
1995	429	10.2	33.0	48.6	26.3
1996	428	7.4	31.4	40.4	30.1
1997	450	9.9	33.4	44.4	34.6
1998	419	5.5	36.7	44.2	37.0
1999	413	5.0	38.4	44.8	38.6
2000	372	5.1	45.3	45.5	39.3
2001	358	6.3	46.8	48.3	40.5
2002	342	5.4	41.0	49.4	45.4
2003	316	6.5	45.5	51.4	47.8
2004	349	6.6	52.3	54.1	50.2
2005	361	6.2	48.7	56.8	52.8
2006	365	7.4	46.2	42.0	46.7
2007	360	9.2	42.0	42.5	49.1
2008	390	9.0	49.7	49.8	54.9
2009	404	8.4	54.9	53.5	59.1
2010	405	8.2	54.5	54.6	61.7
2011	416	9.2	53.1	55.2	62.1
2012	423	9.2	55.4	59.7	67.4
2013	431	7.9	57.5	61.9	70.8
2014	445	6.2	58.8	63.7	74.6

注:按全省常住人口计算的人均占有量。

Notes:The data is caculated by resident population.

12-11 蚕、茶、果生产情况
STATISTICS ON SILKWORM COCOONS, TEA AND FRUITS

指 标	Item	1995	2000	2005	2010	2011	2012	2013	2014
蚕茧产量 (万吨)	Silkworm Cocoons (10 000 tons)	2.24	1.22	1.07	0.71	0.84	0.82	0.77	0.64
茶叶产量 (万吨)	Tea (10 000 tons)	3.90	6.37	8.50	16.57	18.42	20.70	22.20	25.03
红茶	Red Tea	0.12		0.65	1.54	1.94	2.17	2.38	2.75
绿茶	Green Tea	3.05	5.15	6.72	13.71	14.85	16.50	17.04	18.65
其他茶	Others			0.18	0.33	0.37	0.46	0.44	0.39
园林水果产量 (万吨)	Garden fruit production (10 000 tons)	114.70	215.68	260.79	437.13	521.78	541.72	569.42	614.25
#苹果	#Apples	3.21	3.02	1.24	0.97	0.99	1.06	1.02	0.99
柑桔	Citrus	58.14	94.62	146.26	301.04	330.97	385.31	400.39	437.12
梨	Pears	26.02		46.80	48.05	46.29	53.64	56.31	54.63
葡萄	Grapes			4.97	13.12	15.19	20.49	23.68	27.15
桃子	Peaches	14.59	30.87	46.88	60.75	69.02	67.42	72.49	77.81
猕猴桃	Kiwi fruit			0.85	1.06	1.33	1.95	2.10	2.32
红枣	Dates			2.02	2.91	3.13	3.21	3.39	3.62
柿子	Persimmons			4.77	5.05	5.74	5.83	6.61	6.78
茶园面积 (千公顷)	Area of Tea Plantations (1 000 hectares)	113.39	121.02	138.43	214.61	242.98	260.13	291.77	303.80
#当年采摘面积	#Pick Area	7.42		101.62	155.92	174.70	189.36	205.39	218.90
果园 (千公顷)	Area of Orchards (1 000 hectares)	199.80	233.93	265.05	376.77	398.84	400.75	403.55	423.26
#苹果园	#Apples	13.66	8.98	3.30	0.17	1.94	2.01	1.63	1.33
柑桔园	Citrus	98.39	99.13	143.15	229.19	244.48	243.59	239.66	245.58
梨园	Pears	35.42	33.49	35.90	36.60	48.83	37.35	39.35	41.75
葡萄园	Grapes			4.77	5.57	8.45	10.21	10.01	12.65

12–12　林业生产情况
STATISTICS ON FORESTRY

单位：公顷　　(hectare)

指标名称	Item	2013	2014
造林面积	Build Forestry Areas	246858	243799
用材林	Material Forests	83439	85622
经济林	Economic Forests	58163	51338
防护林	Windbreak Forests	103083	105254
薪炭林	Firewood Forests	112	13
特种用途林	Forests for Soecial Puppse	2061	1572
更新造林	Updateing Areas	2952	3589
四旁（零星）植树	Planting	12014	13786
育苗面积	Raise Seedlings Areas	39353	39658
本年新增	The Nw Seedlings	8181	9938
主要林产品产量（吨）	Output of Forestry Products (ton)		
生漆	Lacquer	6897	6298
油桐籽	Tung-Oil Seeds	25290	24895
乌桕籽	Tea-oil Seeds	18344	18503
油茶籽	Tallow Seeds	87483	127419
五倍子	Gallnut	3710	3241
棕片	palm pieces	3656	3714
松脂	Turpentine	39867	44994
竹笋干	Bamboo Shoots	8428	12299
核桃	Walnut	93987	94241
板栗	Chestnut	410983	414049
花椒	Pepper	3324	3475
八角	Star anise	18	23
香菇	Mushroom	95996	105849
黑木耳	Jew's-ear	23784	25624
木材采伐量（万立方米）	Output of Timber Cut(10 000 cu.m)	388.98	333
竹材采伐量（万根）	Output of Bamboo Cut (10 000 cu.m)	3297.30	3414

12-13　畜牧业生产情况
STATISTICS ON LIVESTOCK

指　标	Item	1995	2000	2005	2010	2011	2012	2013	2014
牲畜年末存栏头数（万头）	(10 000 heads)								
大牲畜	Large Animals	413.86	431.50	384.32	327.54	321.80	334.90	345.29	353.19
牛	Cattles and Buffalloes	409.45	428.38	382.14	326.00	320.50	333.60	344.07	352.25
#良种及改良乳牛	Fine Improved Variety Cows	2.20		4.69	4.97	9.05	6.30	6.34	6.49
马	Horses	2.52	1.83	1.58	0.92	0.76	0.75	0.61	0.59
驴	Donkeys	1.60	0.98	0.44	0.46	0.39	0.36	0.41	0.26
骡	Mules	0.29	0.30	0.16	0.16	0.14	0.11	0.18	0.07
猪	Hogs	2449.11	2132.79	2289.05	2476.10	2533.10	2543.20	2566.07	2550.67
羊	Sheep (10 000 heads)	263.23	224.80	337.66	401.70	422.00	435.10	462.91	469.89
山羊	Goats	260.04	223.55	336.97	401.23	421.50	434.50	462.75	469.73
绵羊	Sheep	3.19	1.25	0.69	0.47	0.50	0.60	0.15	0.16
畜产品产量	**Livestock Products**								
猪牛羊出栏头数（万头）	Hogs, Sheep and Goats (10 000heads)	3246.34	3023.96	3841.82	4459.80	4499.70	4823.50	5011.74	5169.09
当年肉猪出栏头数	Hogs	2981.48	2714.44	3345.18	3827.40	3871.40	4180.80	4356.43	4475.11
当年出售和自宰的肉用牛	Ox by Sold and Killed	67.40	104.26	115.49	123.10	126.40	131.70	140.28	152.11
当年出售和自宰的肉用羊(万只	Sheep by Slod and Killed (10 000heads)	197.46	205.26	381.15	509.30	501.90	511.00	515.03	541.87
肉类产量（万吨）	Output of Meat (10 000 tons)	279.40	271.19	342.63	379.42	381.87	412.30	430.08	440.44
猪肉	Pork	239.60	215.84	271.23	287.00	290.50	317.30	330.60	339.60
牛肉	Beef	8.33	13.80	16.91	17.70	18.20	18.90	20.17	21.87
羊肉	Mutton	2.78	3.04	6.00	8.10	8.00	8.20	8.22	8.61
禽肉	Poultry	28.69	38.51	48.49	65.80	64.30	67.00	70.11	69.20
其他禽产品产量（吨）	Others (tons)								
牛奶产量	Milk Cow	38214	56400	122223	140000	142000	153000	154048	161000
绵羊毛产量	Sheep's Wool	14.16	34.57	4.00			3.30	3.56	4.00
山羊毛产量	Goats' Wool	11.01	52.17	16.00	13.73	8.40	74.90	73.82	74.00
蜂蜜	Cashmere	1077	9187	7890	10182	17695	20071	23289	26504
禽蛋（万吨）	Poultry Eggs (10 000 tons)	87.92	102.56	121.25	132.60	137.00	139.40	145.05	155.06

12–14 水产品产量
OUTPUT OF AQUATIC PRODUCTS

指　标	Item	1995	2000	2005	2010	2011	2012	2013	2014
水产品产量　（万吨）	**Output of Aquatic Products　(10 000 tons)**	**150.91**	**234.34**	**318.03**	**353.00**	**356.22**	**388.94**	**410.37**	**433.30**
鱼类产量	Fish	141.44	219.88	277.82	308.42	308.67	331.46	349.18	359.68
虾蟹产量	Shrimp, Prawn and Crab	3.52	7.51	7.71	35.93	40.03	46.25	51.00	56.83
贝类产量	Shell Fish	3.39	5.38	1.13	4.32	4.12	5.91	5.47	4.08
其它类产量	Others	2.56	1.58		3.66	3.40	5.32	4.72	5.62
养殖产量	Artificially Cultivated	131.69	194.84	274.45	321.56	335.62	350.23	371.06	399.64
捕捞产量	Captured	19.22	39.50	43.58	31.44	20.60	38.71	39.32	33.66
养殖按水面分类产量(万吨)	Grouped by waters　(10 000 tons)	131.69	193.92	274.45	321.56	335.62	350.23	371.06	399.64
湖　　泊	Lakes	15.24	20.84	28.44	33.03	31.38	33.17	32.96	33.77
水　　库	Reservoir	6.51	8.15	12.52	19.96	19.24	19.58	19.56	20.66
塘　　堰	Pools	31.26	33.05	38.87	26.61	29.07	31.03	32.60	35.07
精 养 池	Fine Cultivated Pools	73.10	122.96	177.54	224.86	239.98	264.23	283.98	297.99
河　　沟	Rivers	2.25	2.90	6.03	2.03	1.74	1.84	1.78	1.71
其　　它	Others	3.33	6.02	8.03	1.33	1.19	1.26	1.32	1.31
鱼苗产量　（亿尾）	Young Fry　(100 million tons)	373.84	444.01	521.39	750.00	697.00	773.00	901.00	1050
鱼种产量　（万吨）	Advanced Fry　(10 000 tons)	25.58	38.79	54.04	82.03	86.00	94.30	100.26	110.37
投放鱼种量　（万吨）	Volume of Advanced Fry　(10 000 tons)	25.55	40.16	57.08	80.74	84.00	92.31	97.54	104.38
水产养殖面积　（千公顷）	**Aquatic Raised Areas　(1 000 hectares)**								
湖　　泊	Lakes	229.64	196.46	175.34	196.17	209.36	212.73	207.66	190.07
水　　库	Reservoir	144.92	166.07	102.18	110.77	127.52	140.35	150.53	106.64
塘　　堰	Pools	141.09	134.79	119.20	87.44	91.36	92.36	97.36	99.66
精 养 池	Fine Cultivated Pools	125.88	156.33	220.37	252.96	263.00	275.13	275.15	284.75
河　　沟	Rivers	18.67	20.86	21.89	5.71	22.91	23.56	22.91	22.40
其　　它	Others	19.00	32.92	34.56	3.67	23.58	25.40	28.91	21.68

注：2008年为国家核定数据。
Note:Data for 2008 approved a number of countries.

12-15　农业现代化情况
STATISTICS ON AGRICULTURAL MODERNIZATION

单位：千公顷

指　标	Item	1995	2000	2005	2010	2011	2012	2013	2014
农业机械化情况	**Statistics on Agricultural Machinery**								
机耕面积	Areas Ploughed by Tractors	1247.00	1969.55	2015.93	4517.14	4732.21	5118.70	5459.02	5847.00
机播面积	Seeded Areas by Tractors	83.38	255.69	233.66	815.61	1107.84	1419.31	1821.53	2091.28
机械植保面积	Plant Protection Area by Tractors	1783.65	2426.95	2848.66	4074.38	4260.10	4430.36	4611.68	4792.82
机械收获面积	Harvest Area by Tractors	130.95	643.65	1407.62	2780.52	3135.31	3461.33	3746.95	4179.37
农村电气化情况	**Electrification of Rural Area**								
农村用电量　(亿千瓦小时)	Electricity Consumed in Rural Area (100 million kWh)	47.36	60.86	70.09	109.78	112.26	121.23	130.14	142.23
农用物资使用情况	**Used Agricultural Product Material**								
化肥施用量(折纯量)　(万吨)	Consumption of Chemical Fertilizers (10 000 tons)	228.41	247.08	285.83	350.77	354.89	357.66	351.93	348.27
每亩耕地施用化肥(折纯量)(千克)	Per Mu Consumption of Chemical Fertilizers (kg)	45.35	50.17	60.28	70.35	70.38	70.34	68.81	67.88
农用塑料薄膜使用量　(万吨)	Used Plastic Film (10 000 tons)			5.46	6.38	6.50	6.98	6.63	6.92
农用柴油使用量　(万吨)	Used Diesel Oil (10 000 tons)		107.81	41.31	58.29	61.84	66.48	65.73	67.33
农药使用量　(万吨)	Used Agricultural Chemical Insecticides (10 000 tons)	11.24	11.54	11.02	14.00	13.95	13.59	12.72	12.61
农田水利情况	**Irrigation and Water Conservancy**								
有效灌溉面积	Effective Irrigation Area	2172.08	2072.53	2064.59	2187.17	2227.63	2252.91	2291.17	2325.84
#机电排灌面积	#Electrical Well	1257.70		1236.11	1320.53	1314.67	1339.66	1357.19	1416.82
占有效灌溉面积的比重 (%	Rate in Effective Irrigation Area (%)	57.9		59.9	60.4	59.0	59.5	59.2	60.9

12-16 主要农业机械和农产品加工机械拥有量

年 份 Year	农业机械总动力（万千瓦） Total Power of Agricultural Machinery(1000 kW)	农用大中型拖拉机（万台） Large and Medium Agricultural Tractors(10 000 units)	农用小型及手扶拖拉机(万台) Mini and Walking Agricultural Tractors (10 000 units)	农用排灌动力机械（万千瓦） Machinery for Machinery for Agricultural Drainage and Irrigation (1000 kW)	农用水泵（万台） Agricultual Water Pump(10 000 units)
1978	616.07	2.80	7.75		21.22
1980	772.53	3.60	10.90		23.70
1985	910.94	5.72	14.62	55.22	21.06
1990	1099.62	8.60	17.70	99.28	24.30
1991	1120.92	8.60	18.30	362.88	24.10
1992	1120.90	8.45	17.92	368.46	23.98
1993	1108.99	7.89	16.99	360.75	23.95
1994	1136.13	7.38	15.72	368.55	24.37
1995	1174.34	7.12	15.47	384.48	26.56
1996	1222.20	7.03	16.47	401.49	27.62
1997	1276.04	7.11	18.50	408.09	28.76
1998	1325.90	7.13	20.60	410.77	29.59
1999	1363.70	7.03	22.67	419.83	32.57
2000	1414.00	6.82	23.63	434.49	35.47
2001	1469.24	6.58	24.88	450.40	40.46
2002	1557.40	6.64	26.68	461.86	43.89
2003	1661.70	6.59	28.23	469.45	45.63
2004	1768.60	6.83	32.09	484.71	50.82
2005	2057.37	7.66	48.39	518.49	55.92
2006	2263.15	8.50	55.69	531.33	71.42
2007	2551.08	9.30	74.12	541.33	82.70
2008	2796.99	10.42	85.23	559.24	87.73
2009	3057.24	11.85	90.84	594.17	87.70
2010	3371.00	12.71	99.10	663.92	85.40
2011	3571.23	13.08	106.48	673.50	89.48
2012	3842.16	13.84	111.56	668.19	103.30
2013	4081.05	14.94	114.12	714.05	105.63
2014	4292.90	15.85	112.98	732.89	110.60

NUMBER OF AGRICULTURAL MACHINERY AND MACHINERY FOR PROCESSING FARM PRODUCTS OWNED AT YEAR-END

喷灌机械 (万套) Machinery for Sprinkling (10 000 units)	联合收割机 (台) Combine Hearvesters (unit)	机动脱粒机 (万台) Motorized Huller (10 000 units)	机动喷雾(粉)器 (万部) Motorized Duster (10 000 units)	饲料粉碎机 (万台) Fodder Grinder (10 000 units)	大中型拖拉机配套农具 (万部) Large and Medium Tractors Towing Farm Machinery (10 000 units)	小型拖拉机配套农具 (万部) Mini Tractors Towing Farm Machinery (10 000 units)
0.30	425	15.00	0.78	7.78	4.66	4.92
1.08	602	17.40	1.00	8.20	4.99	7.20
0.73	479	15.22	0.60	5.90	2.39	4.95
0.31	2335	12.60	3.70	5.60	2.70	10.14
0.34	455	12.50	4.60	5.55	3.00	11.87
0.60	390	12.35	4.70	5.32	3.86	12.30
0.48	345	11.97	4.77	5.12	3.05	11.64
0.47	346	11.39	5.29	5.50	2.91	12.38
0.72	312	11.25	6.44	5.32	2.85	15.48
0.72	553	12.33	6.74	8.70	3.05	23.02
7.75	1521	11.11	7.36	8.79	3.63	29.46
0.80	2338	11.56	8.27	9.65	4.33	37.75
0.71	2559	11.56	8.00	10.48	4.80	42.84
0.85	2704	12.25	8.70	10.73	4.81	37.48
1.01	3363	12.79	9.07	12.60	5.22	41.12
1.08	5722	12.81	9.72	9.59	5.97	46.44
1.17	6708	12.62	10.26	12.33	6.21	49.03
1.20	10585	12.88	11.86	15.01	7.45	59.31
1.55	16085	14.33	15.98	23.88	9.36	96.69
1.75	22407	12.54	25.44	26.37	11.18	111.02
1.81	29803	13.14	30.58	27.04	12.96	149.08
2.23	34983	12.99	35.41	29.94	15.49	169.69
2.21	41904	15.37	38.40	33.46	20.37	178.55
2.52	50509	18.09	43.56	35.50	21.49	204.66
2.88	58398	23.33	48.73	36.23	24.01	211.97
4.77	66860	24.28	55.07	32.30	25.74	214.51
10.73	73808	26.43	60.41	32.87	28.00	215.42
11.04	81410	32.03	72.26	33.09	31.80	223.01

12-17 市、州乡村从业人员
RURAL EMPLOYMENT IN CITIES AND PREFECTURES

单位：万人

市、州	Municipalities and Prefecrures	2013	农林牧渔业从业人员 Employment in Farming, Forestry, Animal Husbandry and Fishery	2014	农林牧渔业从业人员 Employment in Farming, Forestry, Animal Husbandry and Fishery
全　省	**Province**	**2280.14**	**869.49**	**2308.72**	**865.21**
武汉市	Wuhan	145.32	47.05	145.83	49.91
黄石市	Huangshi	87.79	19.97	92.74	20.82
十堰市	Shiyan	136.76	47.20	137.78	52.83
荆州市	Jingzhou	235.37	101.16	240.36	100.68
宜昌市	Yichang	162.96	69.47	164.89	69.30
襄阳市	Xiangyang	220.47	83.47	221.32	77.58
鄂州市	Ezhou	40.30	19.03	39.96	18.56
荆门市	Jingmen	107.57	37.96	108.46	36.64
孝感市	Xiaogan	246.23	84.59	244.87	79.72
黄冈市	Huanggang	322.26	130.93	328.67	127.65
咸宁市	Xianning	108.60	40.21	111.84	41.11
随州市	Suizhou	106.28	39.79	107.17	40.66
恩施自治州	Enshi	192.77	92.12	195.23	91.16
仙桃市	Xiantao	65.73	23.18	66.88	24.26
天门市	Tianmen	60.32	18.12	60.67	17.50
潜江市	Qianjiang	38.70	13.92	39.35	14.14
神农架林区	Shennongjia	2.71	1.32	2.70	2.69

12-18 市、州耕地面积

CULTIVATED AREA OF CITIES AND PREFECTURES

市、州	Municipalities and Prefecrures	2000		2010		2013		2014	
		年末耕地面积（千公顷）Cultivated Area at Year-end(1 000 hectares)	人平耕地（亩）Cultivated Area Per Capita(Mu)	年末耕地面积（千公顷）Cultivated Area at Year-end(1000 hectares)	人平耕地（亩）Cultivated Area Per Capita(Mu)	年末耕地面积（千公顷）Cultivated Area at Year-end(1000 hectares)	人平耕地（亩）Cultivated Area Per Capita(Mu)	年末耕地面积（千公顷）Cultivated Area at Year-end(1000 hectares)	人平耕地（亩）Cultivated Area Per Capita(Mu)
全省	**Province**	**3282.96**	**0.83**	**3323.92**	**0.87**	**3409.91**	**0.88**	**3420.51**	**0.88**
武汉市	Wuhan	217.84	0.40	204.79	0.31	197.64	0.29	197.25	0.29
黄石市	Huangshi	79.32	0.48	89.80	0.55	89.39	0.55	89.24	0.55
十堰市	Shiyan	181.54	0.79	169.91	0.76	177.05	0.79	175.54	0.78
宜昌市	Yichang	257.71	0.94	230.14	0.85	266.44	0.98	267.80	0.98
襄阳市	Xiangyang	412.96	1.09	436.91	1.19	452.20	1.21	451.58	1.21
鄂州市	Ezhou	40.28	0.59	41.05	0.59	40.41	0.57	40.40	0.57
荆门市	Jingmen	256.53	1.29	255.69	1.33	266.69	1.39	266.92	1.39
孝感市	Xiaogan	247.10	0.74	261.27	0.81	266.84	0.82	267.88	0.83
荆州市	Jingzhou	432.58	1.03	464.80	1.22	468.71	1.22	469.39	1.23
黄冈市	Huanggang	312.36	0.65	337.52	0.82	343.63	0.82	344.21	0.83
咸宁市	Xianning	145.94	0.81	155.85	0.95	158.65	0.96	167.90	1.01
随州市	Suizhou	136.58	0.85	144.94	1.00	143.35	0.99	143.39	0.99
恩施自治州	Enshi	280.59	1.11	255.89	1.17	260.29	1.18	261.33	1.18
仙桃市	Xiantao	98.68	1.01	90.59	1.16	90.54	1.15	90.54	1.16
潜江市	Qianjiang	66.99	1.01	70.22	1.11	72.10	1.14	72.18	1.14
天门市	Tianmen	107.62	1.00	108.36	1.15	109.66	1.28	110.16	1.28
神农架林区	Shennongjia	8.35	1.54	6.19	1.22	6.32	1.24	4.80	0.94

12-19 市、州农、林、牧、渔业总产值及指数

GROSS OUTPUT VALUE AND ITS INDICES OF FARMING, FORESTRY, ANIMAL HUSBANDRY AND FISHERY OF CITIES AND PREFECTURES

市、州	Municipalities and Prefecrures	绝对数(亿元) Absolute Number (100 milion yuan)					指数(%) Indices (%)				
		2000	2010	2012	2013	2014	2000	2010	2012	2013	2014
全 省	**Province**	**1125.64**	**3501.99**	**4732.12**	**5161.00**	**5452.80**	**102.8**	**110.0**	**111.3**	**109.1**	**105.7**
武汉市	Wuhan	126.94	281.09	410.67	530.27	559.44	105.3	111.6	124.6	129.1	105.5
黄石市	Huangshi	27.63	83.91	122.85	133.76	147.01	104.2	115.3	120.3	108.9	109.9
十堰市	Shiyan	44.65	133.19	212.57	250.15	273.11	111.1	119.0	126.6	117.7	109.2
荆州市	Jingzhou	147.69	423.79	534.97	578.34	616.16	91.0	110.1	110.5	108.1	106.5
宜昌市	Yichang	97.19	294.05	502.96	555.63	581.45	102.6	117.4	125.6	110.5	104.6
襄阳市	Xiangyang	158.15	409.04	624.55	678.91	704.46	93.5	111.8	124.1	108.7	103.8
鄂州市	Ezhou	13.92	92.82	126.68	138.50	143.13	106.7	115.8	116.5	109.3	103.3
荆门市	Jingmen	100.13	253.14	316.65	337.93	351.67	103.0	109.2	108.5	106.7	104.1
孝感市	Xiaogan	111.63	306.61	417.57	452.40	470.53	90.7	117.7	117.3	108.3	104.0
黄冈市	Huanggang	127.48	374.79	505.72	532.22	559.63	102.4	115.0	109.0	105.2	105.2
咸宁市	Xianning	52.87	168.52	237.64	264.70	280.29	104.5	120.2	121.1	111.4	105.9
随州市	Suizhou	58.06	150.29	195.33	216.72	225.93	141.5	113.9	110.6	111.0	104.2
恩施自治州	Enshi	76.78	174.25	209.20	227.22	237.01	102.3	114.3	108.3	108.6	104.3
仙桃市	Xiaotao	39.01	94.41	127.85	136.29	142.59	102.2	113.2	112.8	106.6	104.6
天门市	Tianmen	33.15	80.94	101.23	108.58	113.73	100.4	111.6	108.7	107.3	104.7
潜江市	Qianjiang	30.58	85.55	101.34	109.28	114.24	101.9	122.2	108.2	107.8	104.5
神农架林区	Shennongjia	0.99	2.59	3.16	3.56	3.77	87.1	112.6	111.0	112.4	106.1

注：本表产值按当年价格计算，指数按不变价格计算；全省合计数为调整数，故市、州相加不等于合计数。
Notes:The data of in this table is caculated at current prices of output valul,and the data of indices is calulaled at constort prices therefore,the total of provice is an adiusted number,and that of municipalities and prefecture if added are not egual to the total number.

12–20 市、州农、林、牧、渔业产值(现价)(2014)

GROSS OUTPUT VALUE OF FARMING, FORESTRY, ANIMAL HUSBANDRY AND FISHERY OF CITIES AND PREFECTURES (AT CURRENT PRICES)(2014)

单位：亿元 (100 million yuan)

市、州	Municipalities and Prefecrures	合计 Total	农业 Farming	林业 Forestry	牧业 nimal Husband	渔业 Fishery	农林牧渔服务业 Service Industry for Farming, Forestry, Animal Husbandry and Fishery
全省	**Province**	**5452.80**	**2761.70**	**157.00**	**1427.60**	**844.20**	**262.30**
武汉市	Wuhan	559.44	316.27	8.71	126.99	87.40	20.06
黄石市	Huangshi	147.01	56.81	1.80	44.60	42.09	1.70
十堰市	Shiyan	273.11	156.95	11.80	87.97	15.02	1.38
荆州市	Jingzhou	616.16	262.74	7.02	142.40	196.18	7.83
宜昌市	Yichang	581.45	303.49	6.87	215.40	41.04	14.65
襄阳市	Xiangyang	704.46	325.53	8.32	312.36	29.69	28.55
鄂州市	Ezhou	143.13	40.97	2.31	34.65	64.80	0.40
荆门市	Jingmen	351.67	153.89	5.72	116.69	66.64	8.73
孝感市	Xiaogan	470.53	199.14	10.79	170.24	81.47	8.89
黄冈市	Huanggang	559.63	269.36	7.66	203.34	67.78	11.50
咸宁市	Xianning	280.29	144.98	12.50	67.24	53.60	1.97
随州市	Suizhou	225.93	120.07	5.21	83.42	11.07	6.16
恩施自治州	Enshi	237.01	133.58	9.66	90.73	1.22	1.82
仙桃市	Xiaotao	142.59	51.22	1.34	31.61	55.86	2.56
天门市	Tianmen	113.73	51.69	0.58	27.85	29.05	4.56
潜江市	Qianjiang	114.24	46.94	3.40	32.55	29.07	2.28
神农架林区	Shennongjia	3.77	2.24	0.32	1.14	0.03	0.04

12-21 市、州农、林、牧、渔业中间消耗(2014)
INTERMEDIATE-CONSUMPTION OF OF FARMING, FORESTRY, ANIMAL HUSBANDRY AND FISHERY OF CITIES AND PREFECTURES(2014)

单位：亿元 (100 million yuan)

市、州	Municipalities and Prefecrures	合计 Total	农业 Farming	林业 Forestry	牧业 Animal Husbandry	渔业 Fishery	农林牧渔服务业 Service Industry for Farming, Forestry, Animal Husbandry and Fishery
全省	**Province**	**2196.80**	**988.70**	**86.00**	**606.60**	**332.20**	**183.30**
武汉市	Wuhan	209.38	110.96	3.89	54.57	33.83	6.12
黄石市	Huangshi	41.98	14.89	0.42	15.59	10.56	0.52
十堰市	Shiyan	121.92	66.37	6.09	43.07	5.77	0.62
荆州市	Jingzhou	269.15	105.00	1.78	68.43	90.18	3.76
宜昌市	Yichang	229.89	116.97	2.86	87.18	16.38	6.50
襄阳市	Xiangyang	302.90	133.43	3.01	139.60	14.11	12.74
鄂州市	Ezhou	61.98	20.65	1.70	13.09	26.29	0.25
荆门市	Jingmen	153.56	59.46	2.05	60.60	28.23	3.22
孝感市	Xiaogan	218.37	85.45	4.83	82.79	41.01	4.29
黄冈市	Huanggang	184.52	83.89	4.25	74.15	18.73	3.49
咸宁市	Xianning	108.26	56.75	4.66	26.46	19.75	0.64
随州市	Suizhou	94.87	54.88	1.97	33.74	3.31	0.95
恩施自治州	Enshi	97.98	55.52	4.31	37.14	0.34	0.68
仙桃市	Xiaotao	58.63	17.13	1.06	14.52	24.92	1.00
天门市	Tianmen	35.63	18.91	0.16	8.50	6.69	1.37
潜江市	Qianjiang	46.18	15.80	0.55	21.83	6.87	1.12
神农架林区	Shennongjia	1.88	1.16	0.11	0.56	0.02	0.02

注：全省中间消耗为省级核算数，故市、州相加不等于合计数。
Note:The statistics of Intermedium Consumption is checked by Provincial Statistical Burea,thus the total of municipalities and prefecture do not equal to the total of the whole province.

12-22 市、州农、林、牧、渔业增加值(2014)

VALUE ADDED OF FARMING, FORESTRY, ANIMAL HUSBANDRY AND FISHERY OF CITIES AND PREFECTURES(2014)

单位：亿元 (100 million yuan)

市、州	Municipalities and Prefecrures	合计 Total	农业 Farming	林业 Forestry	牧业 Animal Husbandry	渔业 Fishery	农林牧渔服务业 Service Industry for Farming, Forestry, Animal Husbandry and Fishery
全省	**Province**	**3256.00**	**1773.00**	**71.00**	**821.00**	**512.00**	**79.00**
武汉市	Wuhan	350.06	205.31	4.82	72.42	53.58	13.93
黄石市	Huangshi	105.03	41.92	1.37	29.02	31.53	1.18
十堰市	Shiyan	151.19	90.59	5.71	44.90	9.25	0.75
荆州市	Jingzhou	347.00	157.74	5.23	73.96	106.00	4.07
宜昌市	Yichang	351.56	186.53	4.01	128.21	24.67	8.14
襄阳市	Xiangyang	401.56	192.09	5.31	172.76	15.58	15.81
鄂州市	Ezhou	81.15	20.32	0.61	21.56	38.51	0.15
荆门市	Jingmen	198.11	94.43	3.67	56.09	38.40	5.51
孝感市	Xiaogan	252.17	113.69	5.96	87.45	40.46	4.60
黄冈市	Huanggang	375.12	185.47	3.42	129.19	49.05	8.00
咸宁市	Xianning	172.03	88.23	7.84	40.77	33.85	1.33
随州市	Suizhou	131.06	65.19	3.24	49.68	7.75	5.21
恩施自治州	Enshi	139.03	78.06	5.35	53.59	0.89	1.14
仙桃市	Xiaotao	83.96	34.09	0.28	17.10	30.93	1.56
天门市	Tianmen	78.10	32.78	0.42	19.35	22.36	3.19
潜江市	Qianjiang	68.07	31.14	2.84	10.72	22.20	1.17
神农架林区	Shennongjia	1.90	1.08	0.20	0.58	0.01	0.02

注：全省数为省级核算数，故分市州汇总不等于全省。

Note:The statistics of the whole province is checked by Provincial Statistical Burea, thus the total of municipalities and prefecture do not equal to the total of the whole province.

12—23 市、州主要农作物产量(2014)

单位：万吨

市、州	Municipalities and Prefecrures	粮食 Grain	稻谷 Rice	小麦 Wheat	玉米 Corn	薯类 Tubers	大豆 Soybean	棉花 Cotton
全省	**Province**	**2584.16**	**1729.47**	**421.60**	**293.65**	**93.22**	**23.93**	**35.95**
武汉市	Wuhan	127.13	101.46	6.47	10.45	3.92	2.91	2.05
黄石市	Huangshi	64.98	49.51	3.88	4.74	4.93	0.85	0.55
十堰市	Shiyan	117.89	26.85	24.44	37.82	21.42	4.77	0.01
荆州市	Jingzhou	400.02	334.08	42.31	10.45	5.41	4.65	9.64
宜昌市	Yichang	167.77	70.89	15.38	51.46	25.55	2.27	2.04
襄阳市	Xiangyang	503.72	186.09	215.13	78.94	18.28	1.70	3.01
鄂州市	Ezhou	36.39	30.44	1.22	0.54	2.64	0.61	0.48
荆门市	Jingmen	272.93	189.25	50.55	19.94	7.33	4.61	3.05
孝感市	Xiaogan	227.41	181.45	32.06	2.33	7.51	1.87	3.13
黄冈市	Huanggang	325.75	269.86	18.73	5.61	26.72	2.31	5.00
咸宁市	Xianning	107.22	85.24	2.73	9.08	7.43	1.30	0.36
随州市	Suizhou	160.92	99.41	42.80	6.83	9.01	0.73	1.04
恩施自治州	Enshi	164.85	37.77	1.45	68.68	50.21	4.38	0.00
仙桃市	Xiaotao	82.58	63.86	8.52	6.38	0.95	1.80	2.29
天门市	Tianmen	73.42	50.89	14.80	1.80	2.61	3.07	3.05
潜江市	Qianjiang	53.27	38.15	10.51	2.56	0.78	1.13	2.09
神农架林区	Shennongjia	2.21	0.05	0.10	0.93	0.93	0.07	

OUTPUT OF MAJOR FARM CROPS OF CITIES AND PREFECTURES(2014)

(10 000tons)

油料 Oil Bearing Crops	花生 Peanuts	油菜籽 Rapeseed	芝麻 Sesame	麻类 Hemp Crops	苎麻 Ramie	糖类 Sugar Crops	甘蔗 Crane	烟叶 Tobacoo Crops	烤烟 Tobacco
341.73	**69.06**	**257.16**	**14.53**	**2.53**	**2.51**	**30.41**	**30.41**	**8.81**	**7.20**
18.55	4.40	12.00	2.12	0.24	0.24	4.72	4.72		
9.46	0.99	7.21	1.27	0.80	0.80	0.16	0.16		
13.37	4.38	7.20	1.61			1.49	1.48	1.94	1.65
62.33	0.65	60.10	1.58	0.01		5.18	5.18		
23.82	3.48	19.74	0.51			0.17	0.17	1.02	0.55
24.87	13.26	10.49	1.10	0.02	0.02	0.72	0.72	0.84	0.84
6.16	0.41	5.14	0.61	0.03	0.03	0.85	0.85		
39.56	8.40	30.17	0.99			3.11	3.11		
23.93	7.74	15.28	0.91	0.01	0.01	2.09	2.06		
55.61	15.20	38.95	1.45	0.56	0.56	3.45	3.45		
10.45	1.68	8.15	0.61	0.85	0.85	5.45	5.43		
6.97	3.50	2.69	0.78			0.51	0.51		
10.26	2.11	7.41	0.06			0.02	0.02	5.01	4.16
13.46	0.24	12.75	0.47			1.83	1.83		
11.74	2.14	9.38	0.21			0.43	0.43		
10.96	0.48	10.27	0.20			0.24	0.24		
0.04	0.00	0.03	0.00						

12–24 市、州大牲畜、羊、猪年末存栏、出栏、肉产量(2014)

市、州	Municipalities and Prefecrures	牛存栏（万只） Cattles and Bufflaoes	羊存栏（万只） Sheep in Stock (10 000 heads)	山羊 Goats	年末生猪存栏（万头） Hogs in Stock at Year-end(10 000 heads)
全省	**Province**	**352.25**	**469.89**	**469.70**	**2550.70**
武汉市	Wuhan	20.17	5.54	5.46	215.53
黄石市	Huangshi	8.74	7.52	7.52	93.28
十堰市	Shiyan	44.13	123.64	123.64	198.97
荆州市	Jingzhou	8.28	15.01	15.01	357.83
宜昌市	Yichang	17.04	143.50	143.50	506.02
襄阳市	Xiangyang	103.35	144.77	143.85	526.24
鄂州市	Ezhou	3.91	2.40	2.40	77.78
荆门市	Jingmen	23.61	48.93	48.90	285.26
孝感市	Xiaogan	47.97	29.79	29.79	302.44
黄冈市	Huanggang	105.05	102.70	102.67	451.70
咸宁市	Xianning	16.29	18.03	18.03	203.66
随州市	Suizhou	21.95	51.99	51.99	162.52
恩施自治州	Enshi	43.29	97.34	97.34	433.17
仙桃市	Xiaotao	0.86	0.30	0.29	64.19
天门市	Tianmen	7.78	1.74	1.74	72.80
潜江市	Qianjiang	3.24	2.01	2.00	59.31
神农架林区	Shennongjia	0.70	2.79	2.79	4.20

STATISTICS ON LIVE ANIMALS, SHEEP, HOGS IN STOCK AND OUT OF STOCK AT YEAR-END AND OUTPUT OF MEAT OF CITIES AND PREFECTURES(2014)

年内出栏肉猪 (万头) Hogs out of Stock at Year-end(10 000 heads)	年内出栏羊 (万只) Sheep out of Stock at Year-end(10 000 heads)	出笼禽 (万只) Poultry out of Stock at Year-end(10 000 heads)	猪肉产量 (万吨) Output of pork Meat (10 000 tons)	牛肉产量 beef	羊　肉 muttom	禽蛋产量 (万吨) Output of Eggs (10 000 tons)
4475.10	**541.90**	**51635.80**	**339.60**	**21.90**	**8.60**	**155.10**
317.02	5.01	5500.37	23.52	0.87	0.10	22.04
124.12	5.48	2985.00	9.33	0.30	0.11	4.35
205.52	107.22	3330.00	15.38	1.85	1.61	5.39
513.58	18.16	8000.00	39.28	0.81	0.24	19.55
629.68	163.11	3750.00	51.48	1.19	3.42	6.66
644.75	174.08	8780.00	53.03	10.68	4.18	27.04
123.00	2.46	1540.00	1.09		0.06	5.66
422.15	61.04	4950.02	32.36	2.75	1.46	16.50
406.73	26.02	12430.99	31.30	2.31	0.60	39.06
524.58	79.04	5950.00	46.82	7.14	1.76	61.16
288.90	18.46	4002.33	21.67	0.41	0.45	3.14
249.38	60.47	8850.00	19.05	2.06	1.03	8.21
510.74	88.13	1298.00	42.22	2.22	1.71	3.13
115.24	0.74	905.00	8.87	0.24	0.01	4.80
106.26	1.24	1200.30	7.97	0.45	0.02	5.29
113.34	2.52	1760.00	8.50	0.49	0.04	4.12
5.00	1.73	34.00	0.50	0.03	0.04	0.03

12–25 市、州主要土特产品产量(2014)
OUTPUT OF LOCAL SPECIALITY OF CITIES AND PREFECTURES(2014)

市、州	Municipalities and Prefecrures	茶叶 (万吨) Tea (10 000 tons)	绿毛茶 Green Tea	蚕茧 (吨) Silkworm Coccons (ton)	桑蚕茧 Mulbeery Silkworm Coccons	园林水果 (万吨) Fruits (10 000 tons)	桃子 Peaches	柑桔 Citrus	苹果 Apples	黑木耳 (吨) Jew's Ear (ton)
全省	**Province**	**25.03**	**18.65**	**6438.00**	**6317.00**	**614.25**	**77.81**	**437.12**	**1.00**	**25624**
武汉市	Wuhan	0.29	0.29			11.02	3.02	4.15		160.00
黄石市	Huangshi	0.05	0.04	36.00	36.00	4.43	0.17	3.58	0.01	28.00
十堰市	Shiyan	1.43	1.33	850.00	850.00	38.87	0.87	35.01	0.08	2563.00
荆州市	Jingzhou	0.01	0.01	6.00	6.00	47.52	0.91	29.44		65.00
宜昌市	Yichang	6.27	5.12	972.00	972.00	313.72	3.36	306.56	0.04	637.00
襄阳市	Xiangyang	1.24	1.11	888.00	888.00	63.95	42.67	6.14	0.21	3225.00
鄂州市	Ezhou	0.01	0.01			4.22	0.37	3.17		
荆门市	Jingmen	0.02	0.02			43.20	2.86	15.39	0.03	1740.00
孝感市	Xiaogan	0.97	0.90			17.99	8.92	2.37	0.06	679.00
黄冈市	Huanggang	3.50	3.37	3475.00	3475.00	11.77	3.18	5.65	0.10	697.00
咸宁市	Xianning	3.42	1.18			7.10	0.71	4.03		1477.00
随州市	Suizhou	0.28	0.27	121.00		15.12	9.00	0.79	0.17	14278.00
恩施自治州	Enshi	7.53	4.98	90.00	90.00	27.05	0.53	19.00	0.29	22.00
仙桃市	Xiaotao					2.93	0.45	1.13		
天门市	Tianmen					1.75	0.11	0.54		
潜江市	Qianjiang					3.57	0.68	0.17		
神农架林区	Shennongjia	0.01				0.02	0.01			53.00

注：根据国家报表制度变化，取消白木耳统计

12−26 市、州人平粮、棉、油、肉、水产品生产水平(2014)
PER CAPITA PRODUCTION LEVEL OF GRAIN,COTTON,OIL,MEAT AND AQUATIC PRODUCTS OF CITIES AND PREFECTURES(2014)

单位:千克 (kg)

市、州	Municipalities and Prefecrures	粮食 Grain	棉花 Cotton	油料 Oil Bearing Crops	猪肉 Pork	水产品 Aquatic Products	禽蛋 Eggs
按常住人口平均	**Average of Total Population**						
全省	**Province**	**444.97**	**6.19**	**58.84**	**58.48**	**74.61**	**26.70**
武汉市	Wuhan	123.68	1.99	18.04	22.88	49.18	21.44
黄石市	Huangshi	265.56	2.25	38.66	38.13	88.09	17.78
十堰市	Shiyan	349.85	0.04	39.67	45.64	21.61	16.00
宜昌市	Yichang	409.07	4.96	58.08	125.51	47.95	16.24
襄阳市	Xiangyang	900.19	5.38	44.45	94.77	35.43	48.32
鄂州市	Ezhou	343.95	4.57	58.20	10.28	428.80	53.49
荆门市	Jingmen	945.01	10.57	136.98	112.04	179.83	57.13
孝感市	Xiaogan	468.20	6.43	49.26	64.44	90.82	80.43
荆州市	Jingzhou	696.68	16.78	108.55	68.41	225.68	34.04
黄冈市	Huanggang	520.60	8.00	88.87	74.83	80.74	97.75
咸宁市	Xianning	431.12	1.44	42.01	87.13	102.07	12.64
随州市	Suizhou	737.48	4.75	31.95	87.31	41.72	37.61
恩施自治州	Enshi	497.31	0.00	30.96	127.37	2.28	9.44
仙桃市	Xiaotao	702.58	19.45	114.49	75.46	290.04	40.80
潜江市	Qianjiang	558.73	21.89	114.90	89.15	125.93	43.20
天门市	Tianmen	569.02	23.68	90.95	61.77	102.80	41.01
神农架林区	Shennongjia	288.26		5.19	65.22	3.12	3.81
按乡村人口平均	**Average of Country Population**						
全省	**Province**	**628.71**	**8.75**	**83.14**	**82.62**	**105.42**	**37.72**
武汉市	Wuhan	502.99	8.09	73.39	93.06	200.01	87.21
黄石市	Huangshi	372.51	3.15	54.24	53.48	123.57	24.94
十堰市	Shiyan	478.51	0.05	54.26	62.42	29.56	21.88
宜昌市	Yichang	616.91	7.49	87.59	189.29	72.31	24.49
襄阳市	Xiangyang	1346.66	8.05	66.49	141.77	53.00	72.29
鄂州市	Ezhou	472.19	6.27	79.89	14.11	588.66	73.44
荆门市	Jingmen	1422.79	15.92	206.24	168.69	270.76	86.02
孝感市	Xiaogan	544.29	7.48	57.27	74.91	105.58	93.50
荆州市	Jingzhou	911.21	21.95	141.97	89.48	295.17	44.52
黄冈市	Huanggang	557.72	8.57	95.20	80.16	86.50	104.72
咸宁市	Xianning	494.10	1.65	48.15	99.86	116.98	14.49
随州市	Suizhou	813.11	5.23	35.22	96.26	46.00	41.47
恩施自治州	Enshi	476.42	0.00	29.66	122.02	2.18	9.05
仙桃市	Xiaotao	713.66	19.75	116.29	76.65	294.62	41.44
潜江市	Qianjiang	739.76	28.99	152.13	118.04	166.73	57.20
天门市	Tianmen	575.58	23.95	92.00	62.48	103.99	41.48
神农架林区	Shennongjia	470.21		8.47	106.38	5.09	6.21

12−27　市、州农业机械、用电、化肥、水利情况(2014)
AGRICULTURAL MACHINERY, ELECTRICITY CONSUMPTION, CHEMICAL FERTILIZERS AND IRRAGATION IN CITIES AND PREFECTURES(2014)

市、州	Municipalities and Prefecrures	农业机械总动力(万千瓦特) Total Power of Agricultural Machinery (10 000kW)	当年实际机耕面积(千公顷) Actual Sown Areas (1 000 hectares)	农村用电量(万千瓦小时) Rural Electricity Consumption (1 000kW/h)	化肥施用量(折纯量)(万吨) Consumption of Chemical Fertilizers (pure) (10 000tons)	有效灌溉面积(千公顷) Effective Irrigation Area (1 000 hectares)
全省	**Province**	**4292.90**	**5847.00**	**1422300.00**	**348.27**	**2325.84**
武汉市	Wuhan	274.05	287.44	146764.00	14.32	151.81
黄石市	Huangshi	98.51	150.17	120425.00	5.58	55.92
十堰市	Shiyan	207.48	165.62	55959.84	13.46	36.20
荆州市	Jingzhou	590.76	813.97	158630.00	35.75	419.31
宜昌市	Yichang	305.44	384.18	107190.00	36.83	115.59
襄阳市	Xiangyang	608.50	890.76	96905.99	60.61	268.97
鄂州市	Ezhou	64.44	66.96	47850.00	9.15	27.73
荆门市	Jingmen	444.08	558.36	104729.30	32.45	212.48
孝感市	Xiaogan	251.97	403.82	124146.00	21.26	238.94
黄冈市	Huanggang	347.24	770.26	219495.90	39.77	253.84
咸宁市	Xianning	192.05	251.77	45839.83	12.48	93.90
随州市	Suizhou	208.67	284.08	45725.00	17.08	125.13
恩施自治州	Enshi	252.78	214.98	46423.52	28.37	68.51
仙桃市	Xiaotao	140.57	227.33	55894.00	6.46	85.99
天门市	Tianmen	175.00	224.83	29883.10	7.58	110.16
潜江市	Qianjiang	120.22	149.86	14976.92	7.09	61.12
神农架林区	Shennongjia	11.16	2.60	1450.00	0.03	0.24

主要统计指标解释

农林牧渔业总产值　指以货币表现的农、林、牧、渔业全部产品和对农林牧渔业生产活动进行的各种支持性服务活动的价值总量，它反映一定时期内农林牧渔业生产总规模和总成果。1957 年以前的农林牧渔业总产值中包括了厩肥和农民自给性手工业(如农民自制衣服、鞋、袜，自己从事粮食初步加工等)。1958 年及以后，林业中增加了村及村以下竹木采伐产值；牧业中取消了厩肥产值；副业中取消了农民自给性手工业产值，增加了村及村以下办的工业产值；渔业中增加了海洋捕捞水产品产值。1980 年及以后，在副业中增加了农民家庭兼营工业商品部分的产值。从 1984 年起村及村以下工业产值划归工业。从 1993 年起取消副业，将野生动物的捕猎划入牧业，野生植物采集和农民家庭兼营商品性工业划归农业。从 2003 年起，执行新的国民经济行业分类标准，农林牧渔业总产值中包括了农林牧渔服务业产值。林业中增加了森林采运业产值。农业中取消了家庭兼营商品性工业产值，将野生林产品的采集划归林业。第一次农业普查以后，由于畜牧业产品年报数据与普查数据之间存在一定的差距，国家统计局农调总队对畜牧业年报数据与普查数据进行衔接，对畜牧业产值进行相应调整。

农林牧渔业总产值的计算方法通常是按农、林、牧、渔业产品及其副产品的产量分别乘以各自单位产品价格求得；少数生产周期较长，当年没有产品或产品产量不易统计的，则采用间接方法匡算其产值；然后将四业产品产值相加即为农林牧渔业总产值。

粮食产量　指全社会的产量。包括国有经济经营的、集体统一经营的和农民家庭经营的粮食产量，还包括工矿企业办的农场和其他生产单位的产量。粮食除包括稻谷、小麦、玉米、高粱、谷子及其他杂粮外，还包括薯类和豆类。其产量计算方法，豆类按去豆荚后的干豆计算；薯类(包括甘薯和马铃薯，不包括芋头和木薯)1963 年以前按每 4 公斤鲜薯折 1 公斤粮食计算，从 1964 年开始改为按 5 公斤鲜薯折 1 公斤粮食计算。城市郊区作为蔬菜的薯类(如马铃薯等)按鲜品计算，并且不作粮食统计。其他粮食一律按脱粒后的原粮计算。1989 年以前全国粮食产量数据主要靠全面报表取得，1989 年开始使用抽样调查数据。

棉花产量　指全社会的产量。包括春播棉和夏播棉。产量按皮棉计算。不包括木棉。

油料产量　指全部油料作物的生产量。包括花生、油菜籽、芝麻、向日葵籽、胡麻籽（亚麻籽）和其他油料。不包括大豆、木本油料和野生油料。花生以带壳干花生计算。

水产品产量　指人工养殖的水产品和天然生长的水产品的捕捞量。包括海水的鱼类、虾蟹类、贝类和藻类以及内陆水域的鱼类、虾蟹类和贝类，不包括淡水生植物。水产品产量是通过各级水产和统计部门逐级上报取得数据。1995 年及以前，贝类中牡蛎按鲜肉计算；蚶、蛤、蛙按 5 斤鲜品折 1 斤计算。1996 年以后则统一按鲜品计算。

猪、牛、羊肉产量　指当年出栏并已屠宰、除去头蹄下水后带骨肉(即胴体重)的重量。包括全社会范围内的产量。1996 年前为各级逐级上报数据。1996 年第一次农业普查以后，由于畜牧业产品年报数据与普查数据之间存在一定的差距，国家统计局农调总队对畜牧业年报数据与普查数据进行衔接。1999 年以后，国家统计局开展了猪、牛、羊、禽等主要畜禽品种的抽样调查，并用抽样数据作为国家定案数据使用。未开展抽样调查的品种，仍使用各级统计部门逐级上报数据。

期初(末)畜禽存栏头(只)数　指报告期初(末)农村各种合作经济组织和国营农场、农民个人、机关、团体、学校、工矿企业、部队等单位以及城镇居民饲养的大牲畜、猪、羊、家禽等畜禽的存栏数。数据上报方式及数据调整情况同猪、牛、羊肉产量。

常用耕地　是指耕地总资源中专门种植农作物并经常进行耕种、能够正常收获的土地。包括当年实际耕种的熟地；弃耕、休闲不满三年，随时可以复耕的地；开荒利用三年以上的土地。在统计口径上包括南方小于 1 米、北方小于 2 米宽的沟、渠、路和田埂。不包括临时种植农作物的坡度在 25 度以上的陡坡地；在河套、湖畔、库区临时开发的成片或零星土地；也不包括已列为国家和省（区、市）退耕计划但临时耕种的土地。常用耕地是国家需要重点保护的耕地，是反映我国农业综合生产能力的一个重要指标。

农作物播种面积 指实际播种或移植有农作物的面积。凡是实际种植有农作物的面积，不论种植在耕地上还是种植在非耕地上，均包括在农作物播种面积中。在播种季节基本结束后，因遭灾而重新改种和补种的农作物面积，也包括在内。它是反映我国耕地面积利用情况的一个重要指标。目前，农作物播种面积主要包括粮食、棉花、油料、糖料、麻类、烟叶、蔬菜和瓜类、药材和其他农作物九大类。

有效灌溉面积 指具有一定的水源，地块比较平整，灌溉工程或设备已经配套，在一般年景下，当年能够进行正常灌溉的耕地面积。在一般情况下，有效灌溉面积应等于灌溉工程或设备已经配备，能够进行正常灌溉的水田和水浇地面积之和。它是反映我国耕地抗旱能力的一个重要指标。

农用化肥施用量 指本年内实际用于农业生产的化肥数量，包括氮肥、磷肥、钾肥和复合肥。化肥施用量要求按折纯量计算数量。折纯量是指把氮肥、磷肥、钾肥分别按含氮、含五氧化二磷、含氧化钾的百分之百成份进行折算后的数量。复合肥按其所含主要成分折算。公式为：

折纯量=实物量×某种化肥有效成份含量的百分比

农业机械总动力 指主要用于农、林、牧、渔业的各种动力机械的动力总和。包括耕作机械、排灌机械、收获机械、农用运输机械、植物保护机械、牧业机械、林业机械、渔业机械和其他农业机械〔内燃机按引擎马力折成瓦(特)计算、电动机按功率折成瓦(特)计算〕。不包括专门用于乡、镇、村、组办工业、基本建设、非农业运输、科学试验和教学等非农业生产方面用的动力机械与作业机械。这个指标的统计数据主要来源于农机部门。

乡村从业人员 指乡村人口中劳动年龄在 16 周岁以上实际参加生产经营活动并取得实物或货币收入的人员，包括劳动年龄内经常参加劳动的人员，也包括超过劳动年龄但经常参加劳动的人员，但不包括户口在家的在外学生、现役军人和丧失劳动能力的人，也不包括待业人员和家务劳动者。从业人员按从事主业时间最长（时间相同按收入）分为农林牧渔业从业人员、工业从业人员、建筑业从业人员、交通运输业、仓储及邮电通信业从业人员、批零贸易业、餐饮业从业人员、其他非农行业从业人员。

Explanatory Notes on Main Statistical Indicators

Gross Output Value of Farming, Forestry, Animal Husbandry and Fishery refers to the total value of products of farming, forestry, animal husbandry and fishery, and total value of services rendered to support farming, forestry, animal husbandry and fishery activities. It reflects the total scale and results of agricultural production during a given period. Prior to 1957, Chinas gross agricultural output value included barnyard manure and handicraft products for self-consumption (clothes, shoes, stockings, and initial grain processing undertaken by peasants). Since 1958, cutting and felling of bamboo and trees by villages and other cooperative organizations under villages have been included in forestry; value of barnyard manure has been excluded from animal husbandry; self consumed handicrafts has been excluded from sideline occupations, while the output value of industries run by villages and cooperative organizations under village had been included in sideline occupations and the output value of fish catches by motor fishing boats has been added to fishery. Since 1980, the value of handicraft products made for sale by individuals in households had been added to sideline occupations. Since 1984, industries run by villages and under villages have been included in the sector of industry. Since 1993, the subdivision of sideline occupations has been canceled, and the hunting of wild animals has been classified into animal husbandry, and the gathering of wild plants and commodity industry run by rural household have been included in farming. A new industrial classification of economic activities was introduced in 2003. Under the new classification, value of services to farming, forestry, animal husbandry and fishery is included in the gross output value of agriculture, value of wood felling and transport is included in forestry, value of industrial output by rural households is not included in agriculture, and the collection of wild forest products is taken from agriculture and included in the forestry. The first agriculture census of China revealed some discrepancy between the production of animal products from the annual reports and that from the census. Efforts were made by the Rural Socio-economic Survey Organization of NBS to adjust the output value of animal husbandry to make the figures from the annual reports consistent with the census data.

Gross output value of agriculture is obtained by first multiplying the output of each product or by product by its price, resulting in the output value of each single item. For a small number of products, annual output of which is not available or difficult to get due to the long production (growing) process involved, the output value is estimated through an indirect approach. The sum of output value of all products of farming, forestry, animal husbandry and fishery is then equal to the gross output value of agriculture.

Grain Output refers to the total output in the whole country including grains produced by state farms, collective units, rural households, as well as by farms affiliated to industrial and mining enterprises and other production units. Grain includes rice, wheat, corn, sorghum, millet and other miscellaneous grains as well as tubers and bean. Output of beans refers to dry beans without pods. The output of tubers (sweet potatoes and potatoes, not including taros and cassava) was converted into that of grain at the ratio 4:1, i.e. 4 kilograms of fresh tubers was equivalent to 1 kilogram of grain up to 1963. Since 1964 the ratio for conversion has been 5:1. Tubers supplied as vegetables (such as potatoes) in cities and suburbs are calculated as fresh vegetables and their output is not included in the output of grain. Output of all other grains refers to husked grain. Data on grain production before 1989 were obtained through Comprehensive Statistical Reporting System. Since 1989, data from sample surveys are used.

Cotton Output refers to the cotton production in the whole country including cotton sown in spring and in autumn. Output is measured as the weight of ginned cotton. Ceiba is not included.

Output of Oil-bearing Crops refers to the total production of oil-bearing crops of various kinds, including peanuts, (dry, in shell) rapeseeds, sesame, sunflower seeds, flax seeds, and other oil-bearing crops. Soybeans, oil-bearing woody plants, and wild oil-bearing crops are not included.

Output of Aquatic Products refers to catches of both artificially cultured and naturally grown aquatic products, including fish, shrimps, crabs and shellfish in sea and inland water as well as seaweed. Freshwater plants are not included. Data on output of aquatic products are reported by aquatic product and statistical agencies level by level. Before 1995, among the shellfish, the oyster was counted as fresh meat; 5 kilograms of ark shell, clams and frogs are equivalent to 1 kilogram of fresh aquatic products; they are all counted as fresh aquatic products since 1996.

Output of Pork, Beef, and Mutton refers to the meat of slaughtered hogs, cattle, sheep and goats with head, feet, and offal taken away. Data refers to the production of the whole country. The first agriculture census of China in 1996 revealed some discrepancy between the production of animal products from the annual reports and that from the census. Efforts were made by the Rural Socio-economic Survey Organization of NBS to adjust the output value of animal husbandry to make the figures from the annual reports consistent with the census data. Since 1999, NBS conducted sample survey for the major animal husbandry products, such as hogs, cattle, sheep and goats and fowls, and the data from sample surveys are used as national finalized data. Those products, which are not covered by the sample survey, are still reported by statistical agencies level by level.

Number of Livestock or Poultry in Stock at Beginning (or End) refers to the total number of large animals, pigs, sheep, fowls, etc. raised by rural cooperative organizations, state farms, rural individuals, government agencies, schools, industrial and mining enterprises, army, and urban residents at the beginning (or end) of the reference period. Data reporting system and data adjustment are the same as that in the output of pork, beef and mutton.

Regularly Cultivated Land refers to farmland among the total land resources, which is exclusively used for farming and is under regular cultivation with harvest in normal years. Included are currently cultivated land, land that has been abandoned or put in idle for less than 3 years and could be re-used for cultivation at any time, and new-claimed land that has been put into cultivation for more than 3 years. According to statistical coverage, it includes the gouges, dykes, roads and ridges of field with 1 meter wide in Southern areas and 2 meters wide in Northern areas. Excluded under this category are steep slope land over 25 degrees under temporary cultivation, land (large or small plots) that is claimed along river bends, lake sides or banks of reservoirs, as well as land that has been designated under the "Green for Grain" programme of the state and provincial governments but is still temporarily under cultivation. The regularly cultivated land is the key protection land of the nation, an important indicator reflecting the comprehensive productivity of agriculture of China.

Sown Area of Crops refers to area of land sown or transplanted with crops regardless of being in cultivated area or non-cultivated area. Area of land re-sown due to natural disasters is also included. This is an important indicator that can reflect the utilization condition of the cultivated land in China. At present, the sown area of crops mainly include the following 9 categories of crops: grain, cotton, oil-bearing crops, sugar crops, fiber crops, Tobacco, Vegetables and melons, medicinal materials and other farm crops.

Irrigated Area refers to areas that are effectively irrigated, i.e. level land, which has water source and complete sets of irrigation facilities to lift and move adequate water for irrigation purpose under normal conditions. Under normal conditions, irrigated area is the sum of watered fields and irrigated fields where irrigation systems or equipment have been installed for regular irrigation purpose. This important indicator reflects drought resistance capacity of the cultivated land in China.

Consumption of Chemical Fertilizers in Agriculture refers to the quantity of chemical fertilizers applied in agriculture in the year, including nitrogenous fertilizer, phosphate fertilizer, potash fertilizer, and compound fertilizer. The consumption of chemical fertilizers is required in calculation to convert the gross weight into weight containing 100% effective component (e.g. 100% nitrogen content in nitrogenous fertilizer, 100% phosphorous pent oxide contents in phosphate fertilizer, 100% potassium oxide contents in potash fertilizer). Compound fertilizer is converted with its major component. The formula is :

Volume of effective component= physical quantity x effective component of certain chemical fertilizer (%)

Total Power of Farm Machinery refers to total mechanical power of machinery used in farming, forestry, animal husbandry, and fishery, including ploughing, irrigation and drainage, harvesting, transport, plant protection, stock breeding, forestry and fishery. The power of internal combustion engines is required to convert horsepower into watts and the power of electric motors is required to be converted into watts. Machinery employed for non-agricultural purposes, such as the machines used in township run and village-run industry, construction, non-agricultural transport, scientific experiments and teaching, is excluded. Data are mainly from agricultural machinery agencies.

Rural Employed Persons refer to rural labor forces aged over 16 years old who are engaged in real production and management activities and receive payment in kind or wages, including those covered within the age frame and regularly participating in production activities, and those who are out of the range of age frame and also participating in production activities regularly. Excluding students studying in other places with their permanent residence registered in local areas, servicemen and persons incapable of working; also excluding those who are waiting for jobs and those engaged in household work. Persons employed are classified as persons engaged in agriculture, forestry, animal husbandry or fishery activities; persons engaged in industrial activities; persons engaged in construction activities; persons engaged in transport, storage and telecommunications activities; persons engaged in whole sales and retail sales trade and catering activities; and persons engaged in other non-agriculture activities, depending upon the longest period of employment in major activities (or using income indicator when period of employment is the same).

13 工业

Industry

资料整理：何良伟　陶　禹

工　业

INDUSTRY

2014

规模以上工业企业	Industrial Enterprises Above Designated Size		
工业总产值(现价)	Total Output Value (at current price)	43393.87	(亿元)
#轻工业	Light Industry	15378.14	(亿元)
重工业	Heavy Industry	28015.73	(亿元)
#大型企业	Large Scale Enterprises	16117.49	(亿元)
中型企业	Medium Scale Enterprises	9722.07	(亿元)
资产总计	Total Assets	32940.84	(亿元)
负债合计	Total Liability	18193.00	(亿元)
主营业务收入	Income from Major Business	41401.49	(亿元)
利税总额	Total Revenue	4465.72	(亿元)
从业人员年平均人数	Annually Average number of Employment	359.45	(万人)

规模以上工业总产值构成（%）
Composition of Industry above desginated size

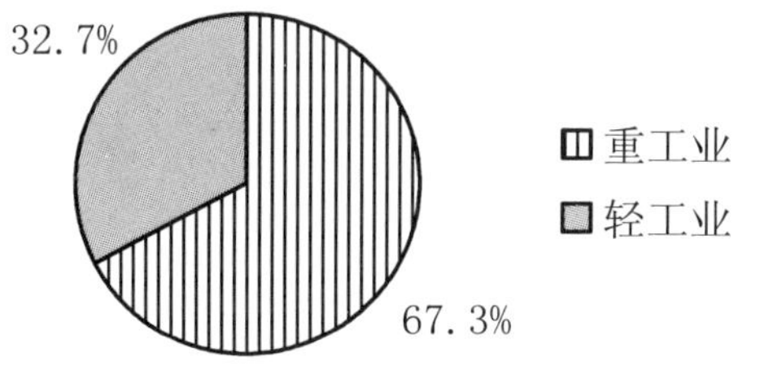

2013

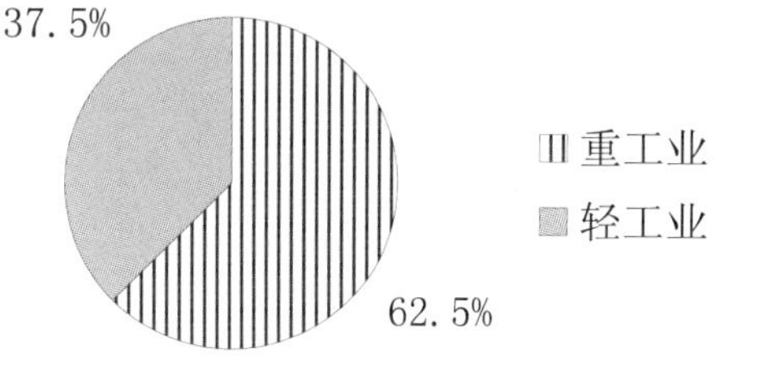

2014

规模以上工业增加值（上年＝100）

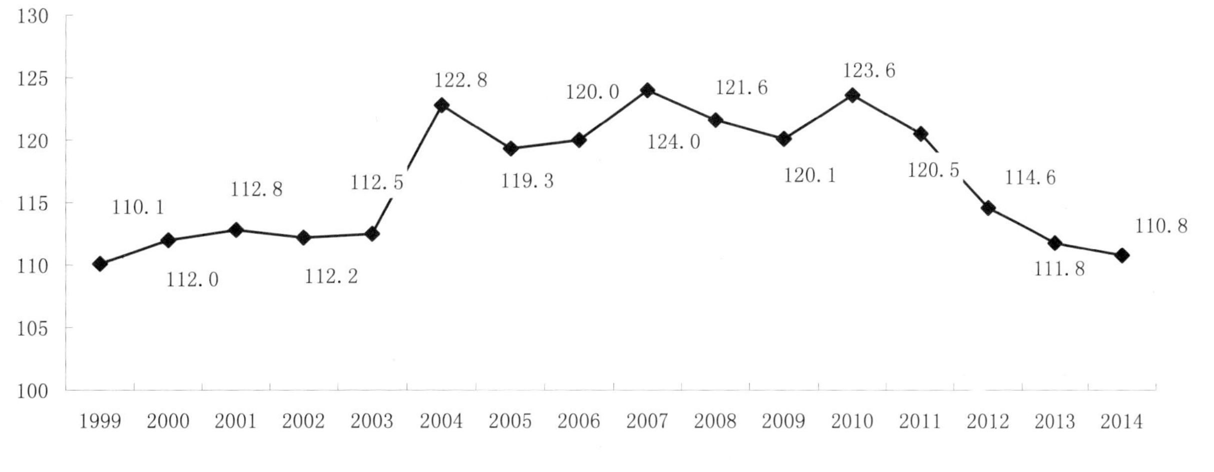

13−1 工业发展基本情况

THE BASIC SITUATION OF INDUSTRIAL DEVELOPMENT

年份 Year	工业企业单位数(个) Number of Industrial Enterprises (unit)	轻工业 Light industry	重工业 Heavy industry	工业总产值(当年价)(亿元) Total Output Value(currentprice) (100 million yuan)	轻工业 Light industry	重工业 Heavy industry
1979	16073	10100	5973	220.82	93.45	107.37
1981	17032	11192	5840	249.72	131.13	118.59
1982	18066	11960	6106	272.08	137.66	134.42
1983	18926	12325	6637	319.21	157.33	161.88
1984	22713	14664	8049	371.93	182.57	189.36
1985	25011	15309	9702	467.22	216.47	250.75
1986	27697	16890	10807	538.28	256.06	282.22
1987	26294	15528	10766	659.19	315.49	343.70
1988	26016	15279	10737	834.84	405.13	429.71
1989	25999	15035	10964	976.93	463.35	513.58
1990	25913	14885	11028	1008.20	476.76	531.44
1991	25204	14317	10887	1136.02	531.26	604.76
1992	23985	13428	10557	1373.66	605.11	768.55
1993	22600	11958	10642	1992.31	770.20	1222.11
1994	23275	12096	11179	3024.72	1360.78	1663.94
1995	27815	14827	12988	3697.91	1870.12	1827.79
1996	25986	13618	12368	4836.33	2470.90	2365.43
1997	24498	12723	11775	5977.00	3158.47	2818.53
1998	7399	3581	3818	6731.31	3534.67	3196.64
1999	6874	3308	3566	2831.70	1109.92	1721.78
2000	6282	3026	3256	3064.43	1177.24	1887.18
2001	6197	2981	3216	3239.51	1194.90	2044.61
2002	6183	2947	3236	3589.26	1184.78	2404.48
2003	6271	2789	3482	3631.29	1192.46	2438.82
2004	6232	2632	3600	4960.25	1180.07	3780.17
2005	6813	2953	3860	6066.96	1503.00	4563.95
2006	7546	3272	4274	7454.07	1898.34	5555.73
2007	8996	3808	5188	9601.52	2492.88	7108.64
2008	12067	4806	7261	13454.94	3344.80	10110.14
2009	14027	5515	8512	15567.02	4234.52	11332.50
2010	16106	6326	9780	21623.12	5935.78	15687.33
2011	10633	4347	6286	28072.73	8370.27	19702.45
2012	12441	5012	7429	33450.66	10941.70	22508.95
2013	14650	5855	8795	39208.98	13405.24	25803.74
2014	15957	6453	9504	43393.87	15378.14	28015.73

注：1.本表规模以上工业1997年及以前统计范围为乡及乡以上工业。1998—2006年为全部国有工业及年销售收入500万元以上非国有工业企业;2007年—2010年为主营业务收入500万元以上工业企业。2011年起为主营业务收入2000万元及以上的工业法人企业。(下表同)

2."国有及国有控股经济"一栏，1998年以前统计范围为国有工业。

3.2011年行业小类码按照《国民经济行业分类》(GB/T4754—2011)填写。(下表同)

Note:1.The scopes of industrial statistics are all township and above town industrial enterprises before 1998.The scopes are all state-owned industrial enterprises and non-state-owned industrial enterprise with revenue from principal business over 5 million yuan from 1998 to 2006.For 2007 to 2010,the scopes are all industrial enterprices with revenue from principal business over 5 million yuan.From 2011,the scopes are all industrial enterprises with revenue from principal business over 20 millon yuan.The same applies to the talbe following.

2."State-owned and state-controlled economy"a column,prior to 1998 statistics the range of state-owned industries.

3.Accordring to GB/T4754-2011,the small classes code of industries are filled in the table from 2011.The same applies to the talbe following.

13−1 续表　continued

单位:亿元　(100 million yuan)

年份 Year	主营业务收入 (亿元) Main business income (100 million yuan)	利润总额 (亿元) Total profit (100 million yuan)	利税总额 (亿元) Total profits and taxes (100 million yuan)	职工人数 (万人) Number of employees (1000 persons)
1979	163.52	20.70	34.19	161.98
1981	210.15	25.71	43.53	185.80
1982	239.64	27.50	47.82	197.62
1983	268.98	31.77	53.46	202.80
1984	308.66	37.33	62.38	292.49
1985	381.43	43.64	80.82	306.83
1986	438.95	40.22	82.14	333.63
1987	526.95	48.54	96.16	343.43
1988	654.72	58.85	117.28	356.43
1989	706.99	50.99	112.12	360.88
1990	705.97	26.73	88.40	358.65
1991	800.01	31.79	103.46	367.41
1992	1041.66	43.19	127.15	357.74
1993	1500.71	67.00	167.92	357.97
1994	1690.94	74.06	190.29	381.45
1995	2066.38	52.26	181.57	379.84
1996	2305.57	43.93	181.41	369.80
1997	2681.36	57.71	221.53	362.50
1998	2433.92	44.71	195.96	274.43
1999	2602.26	68.82	232.24	250.07
2000	2870.36	106.47	29.36	230.36
2001	3043.82	134.49	335.36	212.48
2002	3378.31	175.60	404.23	205.82
2003	3993.99	194.40	444.96	198.60
2004	4832.43	270.98	559.28	176.70
2005	5962.54	371.84	727.48	188.30
2006	7314.81	454.00	897.19	190.85
2007	9390.43	647.85	1229.16	200.35
2008	13081.90	909.03	1761.47	235.90
2009	15331.62	1092.47	1987.88	272.39
2010	21151.56	1668.55	2950.08	294.97
2011	27072.02	1864.46	3093.57	279.59
2012	32325.95	2046.28	3528.80	311.13
2013	38183.39	2475.07	4451.87	346.29
2014	41401.49	2402.63	4465.72	359.45

13-2 规模以上工业企业单位数和产销总值 (2014)

单位:亿元

项 目	Item	企业单位数(个) Number of Enterprises (unit)
总 计	**Total**	**15957**
一、按登记注册类型分组:	**Grouped by Type of Registration**	
内资企业	Inner Funded Enterprises	15092
国有企业	State Owned Enterprises	160
中央企业	Central Enterprises	41
地方企业	Local Enterprises	119
集体企业	Collective-owned Enterprise	107
股份合作企业	Share Holding Cooperative Enterprises	19
联营企业	Joint Owned Enterprise	5
国有联营企业	State Joint Ownership	
集体联营企业	Collective Joint Ownership	1
国有与集体联营企业	Joint State- Collective Ownership	1
其他联营企业	Other Joint Owned Enterprise	3
有限责任公司	Responsibility Co. Ltd	5495
国有独资公司	State Solely Funded Co.	113
其他有限责任公司	Others	5382
股份有限公司	Share Holding Co.Ltd.	630
私营企业	Private - owned enterprises	8586
私营独资企业	Solely Private - owned enterprises	309
私营合伙企业	Private Joint Venture	63
私营有限责任公司	Private Responsibility Co. Ltd	7754
私营股份有限公司	Private Share Holding Co.Ltd.	460
其他企业	Others	90
港、澳、台商投资企业	Hongkong, Macao and Taiwan Funded Enterprises	382
合资经营企业(港或澳、台资)	Joint Venture with Hongkong, Macao and Taiwan	173
合作经营企业(港或澳、台资)	Cooperate with Hongkong, Macao and Taiwan Funded	4
港澳台商独资经营企业	Enterprises Solely Funded by Hongkong, Macao and Taiwan Businessmen	188
港澳台商投资股份有限公司	Share Holding Co.Ltd. With Hongkong, Macao and Taiwan Investment	15
外商投资企业	Foreign Funded Enterprises	483
中外合资经营企业	Sino - Foreign Joint Funded Enterprises	261
中外合作经营企业	Sino - Foreign Cooperative Funded Enterprises	10
外资企业	Foreign Solely Funded Enterprises	197
外商投资股份有限公司	Foreign Funded Share Holding Co.Ltd.	12
二、在总计中:亏损企业	**Of the Total: enterprises running under deficit**	**1274**
在总计中:国有控股企业	Of the Total: State-Owned Share Holding Enterprises	742
在总计中:农村工业	Of the Total: Rural Industry	114
在总计中:轻工业	Of the Total: Light Industry	6453
重工业	Heavy Industry	9504
在总计中:大型企业	Of the Total: Large Scale Enterprises	349
中型企业	Medium Scale Enterprises	1933
小型企业	Small Enterprises	13675

THE NUMBER OF UNITS OF INDUSTRIAL ENTERPRISES ABOVE DESIGNATED SIZE AND GROSS SALES(2014)

工业总产值 （当年价格） Total Output Value (current price)	工业销售产值 （当年价格） Output Value of Industrial Products Sales(current price)	出口交货值 Delivery Value for Export
43393.87	**42012.20**	**1456.40**
36533.55	35451.80	1092.55
3273.86	3245.21	139.05
3073.57	3049.40	119.70
200.29	195.81	19.35
140.03	136.98	
20.38	18.75	
16.85	16.47	
2.23	2.08	
0.81	0.83	
13.81	13.56	
14148.58	13637.31	365.70
1955.37	1889.81	43.49
12193.21	11747.51	322.21
4353.12	4243.50	181.59
14430.52	14005.81	404.16
411.80	403.11	6.66
89.64	87.77	
12797.19	12429.79	364.05
1131.89	1085.13	33.45
150.21	147.77	2.05
2120.50	1983.56	209.66
1302.52	1190.58	115.81
8.67	6.45	
739.93	718.54	79.67
56.89	55.79	14.19
4739.82	4576.83	154.19
3661.47	3521.19	76.86
46.54	46.00	1.22
797.02	774.08	75.78
232.99	233.87	
3475.85	**3334.34**	**115.10**
11494.30	11198.49	358.58
206.81	200.37	
15378.14	14814.99	741.29
28015.72	27197.21	715.11
16117.49	15656.00	736.58
9722.07	9352.23	400.93
17554.30	17003.97	318.89

13-2 续表 continued

单位:亿元

项 目	Item	企业单位数(个) Number of Enterprises(unit)
按行业分	**Grouped by sector**	**15957**
采矿业	**Mining and Qarrying**	
煤炭开采和洗选业	Coal Mining and Processing	147
石油和天然气开采业	Petroleum and Natural Gas Extraction	1
黑色金属矿采选业	Ferrous Metals Mining and Processing	128
有色金属矿采选业	Non-ferrous Metals Mining and Processing	43
非金属矿采选业	Non-metal Minerals Mining and Processing	423
开采辅助活动	Mining Auxiliary Activities	5
其他采矿业	Other Minerals Mining and Processing	2
制造业	**Manufacturing**	
农副食品加工业	Food Processing	1745
食品制造业	Food Production	404
酒、饮料和精制茶制造业	Wine,Beverage and Refined Tea Production	436
烟草制品业	Tobacco Processing	7
纺织业	Textile Industry	1041
纺织服装、服饰业	Textile,Garments, and Fashion Industry	549
皮革、毛皮、羽毛及其制品和制鞋业	Leather, Furs,Down and Related Products	161
木材加工和木、竹、藤、棕、草制品业	Timber Processing, Wood, Bamboo, Cane, Palm and Sraw Products	266
家具制造业	Furniture Manufacturing	124
造纸和纸制品业	Papermaking and Paper Products	272
印刷和记录媒介复制业	Printing and Record Processing	221
文教、工美、体育和娱乐用品制造业	Stationery, Education and Sports Goods	104
石油加工、炼焦和核燃料加工业	Petroleum Processing, Coking Products and Nuclear Fuel Processing	49
化学原料和化学制品制造业	Raw Chemical Material and Chemical Products	1098
医药制造业	Medical and pharmaceutical Products	393
化学纤维制造业	Chemical Fibers	22
橡胶和塑料制品业	Rubber and plastic products	618
非金属矿物制品业	Nonmetal Material Products	1920
黑色金属冶炼和压延加工业	Smelting and Pressing of Ferrous Metals	353
有色金属冶炼和压延加工业	Smelting and Pressing of Nonferrous Metals	168
金属制品业	Metal Products	765
通用设备制造业	Ordinary Machinery Manufacturing	723
专用设备制造业	Special Purpose Equipment Manufacturing	631
汽车制造业	Motor manufacturing	1423
铁路、船舶、航空航天和其他运输设备制造业	Railway,Watercraft,Aviation and other Transporlation Equipment manufacturing	166
电气机械和器材制造业	Electric Machinery and Equipment	651
计算机、通信和其他电子设备制造业	Telecommunication Computer,Equipment and Other Electronic Equipment Manufacturing	308
仪器仪表制造业	Instruments and Meters, Manufacturing	123
其他制造业	Other Manufacturing	87
废弃资源综合利用业	Waste Comprehensive Vtilization of Resources Industry	51
金属制品、机械和设备修理业	Metal products,Machinery and Equipment Repairing	21
电力、燃气及水的生产和供应业	**Electric Power, Gas and Water Production and Supply**	
电力、热力生产和供应业	Electric Power, Steam and Hot Water Production and Supply	160
燃气生产和供应业	Gas Production and Supply	63
水的生产和供应业	Tap Water Production and Supply	85

(100 million Yuan)

工业总产值 (当年价格) Total Output Value(current price)	工业销售产值 (当年价格) Output Value of Industrial Products Sales(current price)	出口交货值 Delivery Value for Export
43393.87	**42012.20**	**1456.40**
121.52	120.29	
75.74	75.82	0.62
427.47	414.63	
52.98	51.32	
571.66	556.70	
68.62	68.68	0.10
1.55	1.55	
4582.01	4425.31	138.71
982.86	949.86	66.69
1532.31	1480.60	7.57
612.91	573.62	1.26
2210.95	2147.77	141.33
911.38	882.26	123.86
184.01	180.02	59.90
428.40	409.07	2.51
154.96	148.76	0.18
530.14	504.99	0.47
336.03	317.34	2.11
144.65	140.43	19.33
927.29	909.67	
3923.94	3824.90	144.42
1010.37	956.59	95.03
82.39	80.98	4.19
1119.89	1092.06	9.86
3037.32	2953.68	29.04
2582.00	2549.18	74.85
932.99	920.63	33.71
1464.43	1413.60	20.29
1367.06	1325.63	21.98
1091.97	1045.89	35.70
5414.38	5292.93	82.03
646.56	616.19	62.11
1786.12	1721.96	65.77
1836.49	1655.53	203.54
160.06	152.47	4.85
168.30	158.63	3.50
131.27	128.28	0.14
36.86	33.47	0.73
1560.71	1550.98	
125.63	124.45	
57.73	55.47	0.01

13−3 规模以上工业企业主要经济指标（2014）

单位:亿元

项 目	Item	企业单位数(个) Number of Enterprises (unit)
总 计	**Total**	**19597**
一、按登记注册类型分组:	**Grouped by Type of Registration**	
内资企业	Inner Funded Enterprises	15092
国有企业	State Owned Enterprises	160
中央企业	Central Enterprises	41
地方企业	Local Enterprises	119
集体企业	Collective-owned Enterprise	107
股份合作企业	Share Holding Cooperative Enterprises	19
联营企业	Joint Owned Enterprise	5
国有联营企业	State Joint Ownership	
集体联营企业	Collective Joint Ownership	1
国有与集体联营企业	Joint State- Collective Ownership	1
其他联营企业	Other Joint Owned Enterprise	3
有限责任公司	Responsibility Co. Ltd	5495
国有独资公司	State Solely Funded Co.	113
其他有限责任公司	Others	5382
股份有限公司	Share Holding Co.Ltd.	630
私营企业	Private - owned enterprises	8586
私营独资企业	Solely Private - owned enterprises	309
私营合伙企业	Private Joint Venture	63
私营有限责任公司	Private Responsibility Co. Ltd	7754
私营股份有限公司	Private Share Holding Co.Ltd.	460
其他企业	Others	90
港、澳、台商投资企业	Hongkong, Macao and Taiwan Funded Enterprises	382
合资经营企业(港或澳、台资)	Joint Venture with Hongkong, Macao and Taiwan	173
合作经营企业(港或澳、台资)	Cooperate with Hongkong, Macao and Taiwan Funded	4
港澳台商独资经营企业	Enterprises Solely Funded by Hongkong, Macao and Taiwan Businessmen	188
港澳台商投资股份有限公司	Share Holding Co.Ltd. With Hongkong, Macao and Taiwan Investment	15
外商投资企业	Foreign Funded Enterprises	483
中外合资经营企业	Sino - Foreign Joint Funded Enterprises	261
中外合作经营企业	Sino - Foreign Cooperative Funded Enterprises	10
外资企业	Foreign Solely Funded Enterprises	197
外商投资股份有限公司	Foreign Funded Share Holding Co.Ltd.	12
二、在总计中:亏损企业	**Of the Total: enterprises running under deficit**	**1274**
在总计中:国有控股企业	Of the Total: State-Owned Share Holding Enterprises	742
在总计中:农村工业	Of the Total: Rural Industry	114
在总计中:轻工业	Of the Total: Light Industry	6453
重工业	Heavy Industry	9504
在总计中:大型企业	Of the Total: Large Scale Enterprises	349
中型企业	Medium Scale Enterprises	1933
小型企业	Small Enterprises	13675

MAJOR ECONOMIC INDICATORS OF INDUSTRIAL ENTERPRISES ABOVE DESIGNATED SCALE (2014)

(100 million Yuan)

资产总计 Total Assets	流动资产合计 Circulating Funds	应收帐款净额 Net Value of Account Received	固定资产合计 Total Fixed Assets
32940.84	**14798.24**	**3443.76**	**12605.10**
27926.54	12260.70	2875.35	10746.86
5676.39	1398.97	280.40	3242.64
5417.81	1263.26	257.86	3151.59
258.59	135.70	22.54	91.05
56.90	32.89	13.06	17.94
8.47	5.84	2.86	2.18
2.18	1.34	0.60	0.34
0.43	0.05	0.01	
0.96	0.79	0.54	0.14
0.79	0.51	0.05	0.20
10700.17	5303.35	1338.31	3839.55
2027.45	1002.03	188.63	667.70
8672.72	4301.32	1149.68	3171.85
5138.84	2427.09	517.78	1236.08
6298.20	3071.59	718.23	2387.49
102.81	45.15	10.62	44.10
24.65	10.88	3.24	9.69
5721.34	2802.23	657.91	2164.30
449.40	213.33	46.46	169.40
45.38	19.63	4.11	20.64
1343.10	615.16	163.10	591.12
810.84	385.64	80.84	352.75
9.79	2.83	0.84	1.89
458.04	194.59	72.28	214.54
59.98	29.46	8.58	20.78
3671.21	1922.38	405.32	1267.12
2630.31	1427.84	264.34	858.37
32.16	8.36	2.14	22.05
710.00	405.08	125.11	222.96
296.29	79.28	12.66	163.45
3793.57	**1813.00**	**436.96**	**1286.53**
14805.00	5592.96	1105.75	6374.69
89.58	49.17	15.35	25.44
7938.18	4094.89	785.00	2665.59
25002.66	10703.36	2658.77	9939.51
16801.15	6931.27	1389.96	6730.48
6485.11	3285.35	775.20	2257.95
9654.58	4581.63	1278.60	3616.67

13-3 续表 1 continued

单位:亿元

项 目	Item	企业单位数(个) Number of Enterprises(unit)
按行业分	**Grouped by sector**	**15957**
采矿业	**Mining and Qarrying**	
煤炭开采和洗选业	Coal Mining and Processing	147
石油和天然气开采业	Petroleum and Natural Gas Extraction	1
黑色金属矿采选业	Ferrous Metals Mining and Processing	128
有色金属矿采选业	Non-ferrous Metals Mining and Processing	43
非金属矿采选业	Non-metal Minerals Mining and Processing	423
开采辅助活动	Mining Auxiliary Activities	5
其他采矿业	Other Minerals Mining and Processing	2
制造业	**Manufacturing**	
农副食品加工业	Food Processing	1745
食品制造业	Food Production	404
酒、饮料和精制茶制造业	Wine,Beverage and Refined Tea Production	436
烟草制品业	Tobacco Processing	7
纺织业	Textile Industry	1041
纺织服装、服饰业	Textile,Garments, and Fashion Industry	549
皮革、毛皮、羽毛及其制品和制鞋业	Leather, Furs,Down and Related Products	161
木材加工和木、竹、藤、棕、草制品业	Timber Processing, Wood, Bamboo, Cane, Palm and Sraw Products	266
家具制造业	Furniture Manufacturing	124
造纸和纸制品业	Papermaking and Paper Products	272
印刷和记录媒介复制业	Printing and Record Processing	221
文教、工美、体育和娱乐用品制造业	Stationery, Education and Sports Goods	104
石油加工、炼焦和核燃料加工业	Petroleum Processing, Coking Products and Nuclear Fuel Processing	49
化学原料和化学制品制造业	Raw Chemical Material and Chemical Products	1098
医药制造业	Medical and pharmaceutical Products	393
化学纤维制造业	Chemical Fibers	22
橡胶和塑料制品业	Rubber and Plastic Products	618
非金属矿物制品业	Nonmetal Material Products	1920
黑色金属冶炼和压延加工业	Smelting and Pressing of Ferrous Metals	353
有色金属冶炼和压延加工业	Smelting and Pressing of Nonferrous Metals	168
金属制品业	Metal Products	765
通用设备制造业	Ordinary Machinery Manufacturing	723
专用设备制造业	Special Purpose Equipment Manufacturing	631
汽车制造业	Motor manufacturing	1423
铁路、船舶、航空航天和其他运输设备制造业	Railway,Watercraft,Aviation and other Transporlation Equipment manufacturing	166
电气机械和器材制造业	Electric Machinery and Equipment	651
计算机、通信和其他电子设备制造业	Telecommunication Computer,Equipment and Other Electronic Equipment Manufacturing	308
仪器仪表制造业	Instruments and Meters, Manufacturing	123
其他制造业	Other Manufacturing	87
废弃资源综合利用业	Waste Comprehensive Vtilization of Resources Industry	51
金属制品、机械和设备修理业	Metal products,Machinery and Equipment Repairing	21
电力、燃气及水的生产和供应业	**Electric Power, Gas and Water Production and Supply**	
电力、热力生产和供应业	Electric Power, Steam and Hot Water Production and Supply	160
燃气生产和供应业	Gas Production and Supply	63
水的生产和供应业	Tap Water Production and Supply	85

(100 million Yuan)

资产总计 Total Assets	流动资产合计 Circulating Funds	应收帐款净额 Net Value of Account Received	固定资产合计 Total Fixed Assets
32940.84	**14798.24**	**3443.76**	**12605.10**
77.66	27.93	3.78	34.31
117.12	5.78		103.43
147.34	65.83	17.90	65.85
41.45	17.39	3.48	13.44
357.79	176.68	36.26	104.43
79.11	33.19	25.20	35.22
0.96	0.57	0.01	0.24
1668.43	774.54	137.64	690.05
471.19	208.36	46.51	187.09
1026.41	628.12	57.44	255.84
408.47	319.37	20.09	31.91
877.36	408.16	75.50	367.92
461.73	275.67	42.65	136.45
89.20	44.37	10.25	32.41
228.32	102.66	14.03	85.38
88.87	38.69	7.45	31.77
310.72	152.03	37.04	116.37
191.59	105.40	31.42	60.46
74.96	41.22	6.05	19.90
229.13	95.04	11.09	124.56
2828.20	1107.30	190.75	1230.21
819.55	385.80	91.58	283.51
53.49	20.75	4.52	17.97
535.87	281.89	72.47	187.52
1850.44	746.47	192.10	800.35
3112.93	998.00	162.61	1236.33
542.77	293.05	35.99	158.54
975.66	570.41	140.78	293.91
1399.17	723.73	218.83	352.48
1028.02	657.81	187.11	276.85
4823.36	2615.91	599.16	1065.21
749.21	444.95	137.34	188.02
1154.66	694.87	269.37	349.92
1497.18	1069.40	399.69	263.93
164.65	88.08	30.65	52.68
150.89	81.91	22.02	39.36
74.00	48.41	11.57	15.06
20.48	14.07	5.09	4.79
3737.20	288.93	69.74	3128.64
179.83	53.95	7.05	69.71
295.51	91.56	11.55	93.08

13-3 续表 2 continued

单位:亿元

项目	Item	固定资产原价 Original Price of Fixed Assets
总计	**Total**	**22424.03**
一、按登记注册类型分组:	**Grouped by Type of Registration**	
内资企业	Inner Funded Enterprises	19438.51
国有企业	State Owned Enterprises	5204.86
中央企业	Central Enterprises	5067.22
地方企业	Local Enterprises	137.64
集体企业	Collective-owned Enterprise	33.53
股份合作企业	Share Holding Cooperative Enterprises	3.10
联营企业	Joint Owned Enterprise	0.64
国有联营企业	State Joint Ownership	
集体联营企业	Collective Joint Ownership	
国有与集体联营企业	Joint State- Collective Ownership	0.38
其他联营企业	Other Joint Owned Enterprise	0.26
有限责任公司	Responsibility Co. Ltd	6281.82
国有独资公司	State Solely Funded Co.	1061.16
其他有限责任公司	Others	5220.65
股份有限公司	Share Holding Co.Ltd.	2207.86
私营企业	Private - owned enterprises	5675.99
私营独资企业	Solely Private - owned enterprises	86.69
私营合伙企业	Private Joint Venture	12.78
私营有限责任公司	Private Responsibility Co. Ltd	5229.84
私营股份有限公司	Private Share Holding Co.Ltd.	346.68
其他企业	Others	30.72
港、澳、台商投资企业	Hongkong, Macao and Taiwan Funded Enterprises	976.28
合资经营企业(港或澳、台资)	Joint Venture with Hongkong, Macao and Taiwan	604.87
合作经营企业(港或澳、台资)	Cooperate with Hongkong, Macao and Taiwan Funded	5.03
港澳台商独资经营企业	Enterprises Solely Funded by Hongkong, Macao and Taiwan Businessmen	336.88
港澳台商投资股份有限公司	Share Holding Co.Ltd. With Hongkong, Macao and Taiwan Investment	28.11
外商投资企业	Foreign Funded Enterprises	2009.24
中外合资经营企业	Sino - Foreign Joint Funded Enterprises	1379.90
中外合作经营企业	Sino - Foreign Cooperative Funded Enterprises	38.46
外资企业	Foreign Solely Funded Enterprises	339.77
外商投资股份有限公司	Foreign Funded Share Holding Co.Ltd.	250.72
二、在总计中:亏损企业	**Of the Total: enterprises running under deficit**	**2231.94**
在总计中:国有控股企业	Of the Total: State-Owned Share Holding Enterprises	10076.67
在总计中:农村工业	Of the Total: Rural Industry	112.21
在总计中:轻工业	Of the Total: Light Industry	5775.78
重工业	Heavy Industry	16648.25
在总计中:大型企业	Of the Total: Large Scale Enterprises	11438.02
中型企业	Medium Scale Enterprises	4411.07
小型企业	Small Enterprises	6574.94

(100 million Yuan)

资产总计 Total Assets		负债合计	流动负债合计	应付账款
累计折旧 Accumulated Depreciation	在建工程 Construction in process	Total Liability	Total Circulating Liability	Account Payable
10751.20	**1637.17**	**18193.00**	**13668.54**	**3679.72**
9525.26	1410.77	15197.98	11216.77	2773.68
2135.94	368.98	3318.05	2403.34	575.90
2075.44	355.87	3157.53	2307.62	553.18
60.50	13.10	160.52	95.72	22.72
18.38	1.43	33.38	26.94	11.43
1.27	0.09	4.95	4.29	1.36
0.31	0.03	1.44	0.95	0.36
		0.37		
0.25	0.03	0.68	0.68	0.33
0.06		0.39	0.26	0.03
2763.46	668.46	6484.44	5048.65	1299.40
425.24	126.32	1248.19	981.72	306.87
2338.22	542.14	5236.25	4066.94	992.53
1114.03	159.63	2573.62	1665.07	401.70
3479.86	211.66	2764.60	2053.21	479.52
46.18	1.70	37.36	25.40	5.17
4.68	0.48	9.88	5.70	1.43
3238.75	197.40	2507.93	1859.05	439.15
190.26	12.08	209.43	163.06	33.78
12.00	0.49	17.49	14.33	4.00
400.39	28.07	717.83	557.75	202.04
260.48	18.29	462.73	362.23	141.80
3.15	0.01	2.65	2.07	0.88
127.42	7.01	221.62	168.20	51.30
9.09	2.72	27.41	21.83	7.83
825.56	198.33	2277.19	1894.02	704.00
595.98	161.31	1671.10	1456.49	556.70
18.70	2.03	20.88	11.16	3.55
124.45	24.29	391.65	312.40	105.42
86.33	10.54	192.26	112.68	37.71
1042.21	**275.76**	**2733.21**	**1993.57**	**538.73**
4078.54	849.01	8779.13	6711.67	1806.43
90.91	1.80	47.33	34.21	5.01
3405.16	304.01	3823.02	3009.31	682.31
7346.04	1333.16	14369.98	10659.23	2997.40
5141.60	897.89	9744.73	7374.59	1963.57
2307.53	288.00	3624.71	2844.27	827.97
3302.08	451.28	4823.56	3449.69	888.17

13-3 续表 3 continued

单位:亿元

项 目	Item	固定资产原价 Original Price of Fixed Assets
按行业分	**Grouped by sector**	**22424.03**
采矿业	**Mining and Qarrying**	
煤炭开采和洗选业	Coal Mining and Processing	41.38
石油和天然气开采业	Petroleum and Natural Gas Extraction	299.39
黑色金属矿采选业	Ferrous Metals Mining and Processing	103.68
有色金属矿采选业	Non-ferrous Metals Mining and Processing	25.18
非金属矿采选业	Non-metal Minerals Mining and Processing	346.05
开采辅助活动	Mining Auxiliary Activities	52.98
其他采矿业	Other Minerals Mining and Processing	0.35
制造业	**Manufacturing**	
农副食品加工业	Food Processing	2071.22
食品制造业	Food Production	439.43
酒、饮料和精制茶制造业	Wine,Beverage and Refined Tea Production	432.19
烟草制品业	Tobacco Processing	87.59
纺织业	Textile Industry	741.98
纺织服装、服饰业	Textile,Garments, and Fashion Industry	252.52
皮革、毛皮、羽毛及其制品和制鞋业	Leather, Furs,Down and Related Products	61.42
木材加工和木、竹、藤、棕、草制品业	Timber Processing, Wood, Bamboo, Cane, Palm and Sraw Products	161.49
家具制造业	Furniture Manufacturing	53.25
造纸和纸制品业	Papermaking and Paper Products	330.67
印刷和记录媒介复制业	Printing and Record Processing	124.53
文教、工美、体育和娱乐用品制造业	Stationery, Education and Sports Goods	62.19
石油加工、炼焦和核燃料加工业	Petroleum Processing, Coking Products and Nuclear Fuel Processing	198.57
化学原料和化学制品制造业	Raw Chemical Material and Chemical Products	2282.47
医药制造业	Medical and pharmaceutical Products	386.25
化学纤维制造业	Chemical Fibers	36.77
橡胶和塑料制品业	Rubber and Plastic Products	405.30
非金属矿物制品业	Nonmetal Material Products	1252.46
黑色金属冶炼和压延加工业	Smelting and Pressing of Ferrous Metals	2370.71
有色金属冶炼和压延加工业	Smelting and Pressing of Nonferrous Metals	236.50
金属制品业	Metal Products	509.08
通用设备制造业	Ordinary Machinery Manufacturing	576.41
专用设备制造业	Special Purpose Equipment Manufacturing	574.63
汽车制造业	Motor manufacturing	1693.68
铁路、船舶、航空航天和其他运输设备制造业	Railway,Watercraft,Aviation and other Transporlation Equipment manufacturing	246.41
电气机械和器材制造业	Electric Machinery and Equipment	517.25
计算机、通信和其他电子设备制造业	Telecommunication Computer,Equipment and Other Electronic Equipment Manufacturing	467.47
仪器仪表制造业	Instruments and Meters, Manufacturing	75.52
其他制造业	Other Manufacturing	59.07
废弃资源综合利用业	Waste Comprehensive Vtilization of Resources Industry	20.11
金属制品、机械和设备修理业	Metal products,Machinery and Equipment Repairing	8.50
电力、燃气及水的生产和供应业	**Electric Power, Gas and Water Production and Supply**	
电力、热力生产和供应业	Electric Power, Steam and Hot Water Production and Supply	4589.78
燃气生产和供应业	Gas Production and Supply	85.02
水的生产和供应业	Tap Water Production and Supply	144.60

(100 million Yuan)

资产总计 Total Assets		负债合计	流动负债合计	应付账款
累计折旧 Accumulated Depreciation	在建工程 Construction in process	Total Liability	Total Circulating Liability	Account Payable
10751.20	**1637.17**	**18193.00**	**13668.54**	**3679.72**
9.83	4.37	35.73	30.57	4.96
168.48	7.42	20.50	9.17	8.45
44.12	8.41	82.52	65.91	24.90
13.20	4.48	21.72	18.15	1.96
258.41	12.38	189.29	143.02	21.50
20.42	7.83	61.48	61.35	17.64
0.10		0.54	0.01	
1504.81	59.85	710.66	542.09	102.46
263.30	17.09	202.34	161.41	39.63
208.98	48.35	601.71	533.97	79.07
55.68	9.28	149.49	148.86	43.58
404.19	23.88	407.41	308.55	59.96
125.59	10.53	197.08	161.84	28.54
31.13	1.06	48.09	28.71	7.71
80.27	12.82	85.71	55.27	10.43
26.01	2.48	38.74	25.33	4.90
219.73	10.85	168.95	131.31	28.85
67.22	7.71	94.88	72.67	20.76
44.84	3.14	40.71	29.04	5.01
91.93	14.47	124.83	111.32	18.36
1103.84	171.65	1755.59	1251.98	250.74
137.00	43.45	405.61	299.83	61.56
19.16	1.31	26.36	22.97	4.46
233.80	15.93	246.54	191.92	49.40
490.82	63.46	912.20	636.94	172.11
1152.72	194.78	1974.00	1568.02	283.80
87.26	38.52	367.81	297.53	39.64
240.32	50.82	570.75	464.35	149.28
264.39	37.73	907.36	403.10	114.65
306.65	17.52	499.33	409.39	99.58
744.43	330.28	2544.77	2264.05	907.17
78.63	44.47	513.11	417.38	171.63
206.60	56.12	647.06	538.71	210.95
225.61	41.22	890.99	780.41	334.43
29.56	6.82	96.50	80.05	20.05
23.78	4.45	97.59	55.16	24.88
7.45	6.60	50.82	30.48	7.76
3.79	0.42	11.09	10.28	4.66
1674.55	181.15	2117.79	1114.46	214.66
19.41	35.33	121.76	94.26	20.74
63.19	28.72	153.57	98.71	8.93

13-3 续表 4 continued

单位:亿元

项 目	Item	非流动负债合计	所有者权益合计 Total Rights of Owners
总 计	**Total**	**3077.12**	**14624.35**
一、按登记注册类型分组:	**Grouped by Type of Registration**		
内资企业	Inner Funded Enterprises	2678.16	12553.80
国有企业	State Owned Enterprises	893.54	2356.69
中央企业	Central Enterprises	851.41	2259.04
地方企业	Local Enterprises	42.13	97.65
集体企业	Collective-owned Enterprise	4.75	23.27
股份合作企业	Share Holding Cooperative Enterprises	0.05	3.44
联营企业	Joint Owned Enterprise	0.13	0.74
国有联营企业	State Joint Ownership		
集体联营企业	Collective Joint Ownership		0.06
国有与集体联营企业	Joint State- Collective Ownership		0.28
其他联营企业	Other Joint Owned Enterprise	0.13	0.40
有限责任公司	Responsibility Co. Ltd	1070.96	4169.57
国有独资公司	State Solely Funded Co.	256.12	778.32
其他有限责任公司	Others	814.84	3391.25
股份有限公司	Share Holding Co.Ltd.	375.22	2527.32
私营企业	Private - owned enterprises	332.68	3445.58
私营独资企业	Solely Private - owned enterprises	2.83	61.53
私营合伙企业	Private Joint Venture	1.33	13.74
私营有限责任公司	Private Responsibility Co. Ltd	304.17	3136.18
私营股份有限公司	Private Share Holding Co.Ltd.	24.35	234.13
其他企业	Others	0.83	27.18
港、澳、台商投资企业	Hongkong, Macao and Taiwan Funded Enterprises	145.19	615.65
合资经营企业(港或澳、台资)	Joint Venture with Hongkong, Macao and Taiwan	92.41	343.64
合作经营企业(港或澳、台资)	Cooperate with Hongkong, Macao and Taiwan Funded	0.11	7.13
港澳台商独资经营企业	Enterprises Solely Funded by Hongkong, Macao and Taiwan Businessmen	47.97	231.36
港澳台商投资股份有限公司	Share Holding Co.Ltd. With Hongkong, Macao and Taiwan Investment	4.70	32.48
外商投资企业	Foreign Funded Enterprises	253.76	1454.90
中外合资经营企业	Sino - Foreign Joint Funded Enterprises	130.28	1020.43
中外合作经营企业	Sino - Foreign Cooperative Funded Enterprises	6.86	13.01
外资企业	Foreign Solely Funded Enterprises	41.09	316.76
外商投资股份有限公司	Foreign Funded Share Holding Co.Ltd.	75.53	103.54
二、在总计中:亏损企业	**Of the Total: enterprises running under deficit**	**371.38**	**1018.58**
在总计中:国有控股企业	Of the Total: State-Owned Share Holding Enterprises	1908.20	6102.11
在总计中:农村工业	Of the Total: Rural Industry	7.18	39.96
在总计中:轻工业	Of the Total: Light Industry	501.44	4046.41
重工业	Heavy Industry	2575.68	10577.94
在总计中:大型企业	Of the Total: Large Scale Enterprises	1881.37	7115.99
中型企业	Medium Scale Enterprises	523.35	2849.20
小型企业	Small Enterprises	672.39	4659.16

(100 million Yuan)

实收资本 Assets Recevied	国家资本 National Assets	所有者权益合计 Total Rights of Owners 集体资本 Collective Assets	法人资本 Corperative Assets	个人资本 Individual Assets	港澳台资本 Assets from Hongkong, Maco and Taiwan Funded Enterprises
7327.76	**1607.76**	**111.04**	**2367.96**	**2655.51**	**149.76**
6254.80	1389.13	102.02	2094.75	2623.50	5.23
522.57	452.27	1.61	18.12	48.26	
486.35	429.49	0.84	13.38	42.64	
36.22	22.78	0.77	4.74	5.62	
9.15	0.66	4.20	2.30	1.90	
1.78		0.05	1.48	0.26	
0.28		0.08	0.05	0.14	
0.06				0.06	
0.14		0.08	0.05		
0.08				0.08	
3257.06	650.45	62.51	1063.47	1465.20	2.94
384.92	306.17	2.30	78.46	1.68	
2872.14	344.29	60.21	985.01	1463.51	2.94
718.54	279.43	11.05	188.75	228.87	0.22
1737.10	6.31	22.51	818.37	872.86	2.07
40.92			8.83	22.83	
5.92		0.33	2.58	3.65	
1590.60	5.72	21.41	763.70	792.83	1.48
99.66	0.59	0.77	43.26	53.55	0.59
8.31		0.01	2.20	6.00	
325.10	12.29	4.07	100.25	13.23	115.75
199.21	10.68	4.07	76.26	7.48	50.86
5.38			3.75	0.23	1.40
108.55	1.38		14.24	2.91	60.69
10.67	0.22		6.00	1.83	2.31
747.86	206.35	4.96	172.96	18.78	28.78
527.01	195.28	4.76	143.83	13.41	10.90
11.62		0.20	5.58	0.11	
187.59	8.83		7.39	5.21	17.88
21.10	2.23		15.67	0.05	
903.58	**350.79**	**15.03**	**304.27**	**123.96**	**22.34**
2211.23	1532.30	20.34	445.91	106.99	4.23
16.61	0.19	2.43	4.01	8.99	0.12
2763.63	107.77	28.35	802.43	1642.19	61.63
4564.13	1499.99	82.69	1565.53	1013.32	88.13
2171.84	1234.89	8.73	457.30	245.15	59.85
1347.82	188.72	33.42	653.98	316.22	32.98
3808.10	184.15	68.90	1256.68	2094.14	56.93

13-3 续表 5 continued

单位:亿元

项 目	Item	非流动负债合计	所有者权益合计 Total Rights of Owners
按行业分	**Grouped by sector**	**3077.12**	**14624.35**
采矿业	**Mining and Qarrying**		
煤炭开采和洗选业	Coal Mining and Processing	3.66	40.67
石油和天然气开采业	Petroleum and Natural Gas Extraction	11.33	96.62
黑色金属矿采选业	Ferrous Metals Mining and Processing	10.35	63.50
有色金属矿采选业	Non-ferrous Metals Mining and Processing	2.42	19.61
非金属矿采选业	Non-metal Minerals Mining and Processing	28.35	164.42
开采辅助活动	Mining Auxiliary Activities	0.14	17.62
其他采矿业	Other Minerals Mining and Processing		0.41
制造业	**Manufacturing**		
农副食品加工业	Food Processing	92.04	936.76
食品制造业	Food Production	19.01	262.05
酒、饮料和精制茶制造业	Wine,Beverage and Refined Tea Production	54.57	421.24
烟草制品业	Tobacco Processing	0.64	258.98
纺织业	Textile Industry	52.59	457.31
纺织服装、服饰业	Textile,Garments, and Fashion Industry	18.38	260.04
皮革、毛皮、羽毛及其制品和制鞋业	Leather, Furs,Down and Related Products	9.69	40.00
木材加工和木、竹、藤、棕、草制品业	Timber Processing, Wood, Bamboo, Cane, Palm and Sraw Products	19.36	138.50
家具制造业	Furniture Manufacturing	5.02	48.46
造纸和纸制品业	Papermaking and Paper Products	17.60	137.32
印刷和记录媒介复制业	Printing and Record Processing	12.48	94.88
文教、工美、体育和娱乐用品制造业	Stationery, Education and Sports Goods	4.66	33.80
石油加工、炼焦和核燃料加工业	Petroleum Processing, Coking Products and Nuclear Fuel Processing	12.46	104.10
化学原料和化学制品制造业	Raw Chemical Material and Chemical Products	342.51	1065.86
医药制造业	Medical and pharmaceutical Products	91.92	411.78
化学纤维制造业	Chemical Fibers	2.92	26.64
橡胶和塑料制品业	Rubber and plastic products	29.11	284.69
非金属矿物制品业	Nonmetal Material Products	166.80	914.27
黑色金属冶炼和压延加工业	Smelting and Pressing of Ferrous Metals	223.74	1099.60
有色金属冶炼和压延加工业	Smelting and Pressing of Nonferrous Metals	62.77	173.30
金属制品业	Metal Products	75.77	412.90
通用设备制造业	Ordinary Machinery Manufacturing	127.85	548.95
专用设备制造业	Special Purpose Equipment Manufacturing	53.58	525.20
汽车制造业	Motor manufacturing	198.16	2264.38
铁路、船舶、航空航天和其他运输设备制造业	Railway,Watercraft,Aviation and other Transporlation Equipment manufacturing	78.59	232.73
电气机械和器材制造业	Electric Machinery and Equipment	84.59	497.31
计算机、通信和其他电子设备制造业	Telecommunication Computer,Equipment and Other Electronic Equipment Manufacturing	96.98	602.15
仪器仪表制造业	Instruments and Meters, Manufacturing	9.80	67.51
其他制造业	Other Manufacturing	20.26	53.37
废弃资源综合利用业	Waste Comprehensive Vtilization of Resources Industry	3.15	22.65
金属制品、机械和设备修理业	Metal products,Machinery and Equipment Repairing	0.02	9.38
电力、燃气及水的生产和供应业	**Electric Power, Gas and Water Production and Supply**		
电力、热力生产和供应业	Electric Power, Steam and Hot Water Production and Supply	971.87	1617.63
燃气生产和供应业	Gas Production and Supply	18.02	56.90
水的生产和供应业	Tap Water Production and Supply	43.96	140.81

(100 million Yuan)

实收资本 Assets Recevied	国家资本 National Assets	所有者权益合计 Total Rights of Owners			
		集体资本 Collective Assets	法人资本 Corperative Assets	个人资本 Individual Assets	港澳台资本 Assets from Hongkong, Maco and Taiwan Funded Enterprises
7327.76	**1607.76**	**111.04**	**2367.96**	**2655.51**	**149.76**
19.28	1.33	1.19	5.52	10.47	0.39
35.20	14.15	2.12	11.85	7.07	
8.34	4.46	0.06	1.41	2.41	
74.56	1.05	4.68	33.45	35.11	
10.02	4.82		5.09	0.11	
0.26	0.04	0.06		0.17	
348.35	13.97	7.97	122.19	176.27	6.04
123.83	5.22	0.54	70.56	38.97	4.87
170.24	3.82	5.78	42.14	74.66	14.70
35.01	3.52	1.05	30.44		
313.03	5.29	2.39	195.91	97.89	3.85
168.31	0.43	0.48	121.32	40.17	3.52
24.70		0.04	6.75	8.40	5.31
67.26	3.72	0.24	42.43	20.66	0.07
16.03	0.04	0.01	7.12	8.53	0.16
71.52	0.81	1.66	36.07	22.77	2.40
37.28	4.40	0.69	12.79	17.43	1.72
19.32	1.28	0.17	7.37	4.75	1.65
132.42	114.92	0.30	3.20	4.06	
497.08	72.20	12.28	245.13	116.31	5.77
1161.95	15.26	3.64	75.53	1051.84	12.14
18.86	0.12		6.06	4.42	
124.26	3.17	3.54	46.38	66.69	1.76
407.59	17.47	9.82	199.50	151.37	1.64
359.08	210.65	1.42	66.04	40.31	2.13
94.30	58.75	3.43	12.19	17.85	
215.69	41.12	4.29	77.54	83.99	5.64
194.77	40.62	5.62	64.32	66.53	4.80
325.24	56.30	2.49	110.74	144.98	1.36
904.95	331.78	13.02	299.94	124.52	6.88
152.18	88.08	1.37	46.39	14.72	0.65
245.58	19.45	4.91	89.55	88.51	13.02
242.48	36.45	5.20	136.76	32.13	26.65
31.49	2.45	0.99	15.76	9.71	0.75
23.59	14.27	0.05	2.98	5.50	0.20
17.52	0.47	0.74	10.77	4.75	0.78
6.61	0.80	0.96	3.90	0.93	
552.00	380.45	4.14	90.19	48.55	16.33
28.94	5.79	3.09	6.89	6.16	4.57
48.65	28.84	0.58	5.78	5.84	

13-3 续表 6 continued

单位:亿元

项 目	Item	所有者权益合计 Total owner 外商资本 Total Rights of the Owners Foreign Assets
总 计	**Total**	**406.46**
一、按登记注册类型分组:	**Grouped by Type of Registration**	
内资企业	Inner Funded Enterprises	19.34
国有企业	State Owned Enterprises	2.30
中央企业	Central Enterprises	
地方企业	Local Enterprises	2.30
集体企业	Collective-owned Enterprise	
股份合作企业	Share Holding Cooperative Enterprises	
联营企业	Joint Owned Enterprise	
国有联营企业	State Joint Ownership	
集体联营企业	Collective Joint Ownership	
国有与集体联营企业	Joint State- Collective Ownership	
其他联营企业	Other Joint Owned Enterprise	
有限责任公司	Responsibility Co. Ltd	14.54
国有独资公司	State Solely Funded Co.	
其他有限责任公司	Others	14.54
股份有限公司	Share Holding Co.Ltd.	1.47
私营企业	Private - owned enterprises	1.02
私营独资企业	Solely Private - owned enterprises	
私营合伙企业	Private Joint Venture	
私营有限责任公司	Private Responsibility Co. Ltd	1.02
私营股份有限公司	Private Share Holding Co.Ltd.	
其他企业	Others	
港、澳、台商投资企业	Hongkong, Macao and Taiwan Funded Enterprises	75.80
合资经营企业(港或澳、台资)	Joint Venture with Hongkong, Macao and Taiwan	46.45
合作经营企业(港或澳、台资)	Cooperate with Hongkong, Macao and Taiwan Funded	
港澳台商独资经营企业	Enterprises Solely Funded by Hongkong, Macao and Taiwan Businessmen	29.04
港澳台商投资股份有限公司	Share Holding Co.Ltd. With Hongkong, Macao and Taiwan Investment	0.31
外商投资企业	Foreign Funded Enterprises	311.32
中外合资经营企业	Sino - Foreign Joint Funded Enterprises	157.80
中外合作经营企业	Sino - Foreign Cooperative Funded Enterprises	5.73
外资企业	Foreign Solely Funded Enterprises	144.58
外商投资股份有限公司	Foreign Funded Share Holding Co.Ltd.	3.14
二、在总计中:亏损企业	**Of the Total: enterprises running under deficit**	**81.31**
在总计中:国有控股企业	Of the Total: State-Owned Share Holding Enterprises	100.90
在总计中:农村工业	Of the Total: Rural Industry	0.58
在总计中:轻工业	Of the Total: Light Industry	99.05
重工业	Heavy Industry	307.40
在总计中:大型企业	Of the Total: Large Scale Enterprises	167.19
中型企业	Medium Scale Enterprises	126.55
小型企业	Small Enterprises	112.71

(100 million Yuan)

营业收入 Proceeds Of Business	主营业务收入 Revenue of Major Business	营业成本 Operating Costs	主营业务成本 Cost of Major Business	营业税金及附加 Tax of Major Business	主营业务税金及附加 Tax of Major Business	其他业务收入 Revenue of Other Business	其他业务利润 Profit from Other Business	销售费用 Selling Expenses
42182.06	**41401.49**	**35615.63**	**34843.30**	**845.85**	**829.79**	**780.57**	**86.13**	**1269.28**
35584.25	35039.18	30277.12	29748.70	696.59	681.69	545.07	52.82	989.97
3406.40	3328.96	2957.35	2867.58	16.23	10.31	77.44	3.05	42.63
3200.80	3139.20	2786.31	2716.00	15.38	9.49	61.60	2.35	37.43
205.59	189.75	171.04	151.58	0.86	0.82	15.84	0.70	5.20
138.45	136.65	118.79	116.95	2.01	2.00	1.80	0.19	3.32
18.37	18.33	14.90	14.85	0.10	0.10	0.05		0.72
14.24	14.24	12.82	12.82	0.05	0.05			0.13
0.18	0.18	0.16	0.16					
0.83	0.83	0.73	0.73	0.01	0.01			0.01
13.23	13.23	11.93	11.93	0.04	0.04			0.12
14159.85	13828.81	11996.34	11677.70	469.52	467.18	331.04	27.44	376.48
2130.63	1942.70	1530.17	1335.17	391.69	391.31	187.92	2.87	32.06
12029.22	11886.10	10466.17	10342.53	77.83	75.88	143.12	24.57	344.42
4084.57	4006.67	3327.24	3276.80	82.64	81.99	77.90	18.53	187.71
13620.14	13563.39	11724.46	11656.87	124.97	118.99	56.75	3.62	376.52
395.45	394.74	339.72	338.81	4.34	4.27	0.71	-0.01	10.24
87.18	87.04	74.73	74.62	0.85	0.85	0.14		2.23
12108.24	12071.72	10433.28	10385.53	110.60	104.78	36.51	3.27	330.29
1029.28	1009.89	876.73	857.91	9.18	9.08	19.39	0.36	33.76
142.22	142.13	125.23	125.12	1.06	1.06	0.09		2.47
1986.45	1882.16	1713.63	1614.40	8.77	8.39	104.29	3.60	64.12
1215.77	1143.61	1054.76	984.98	3.99	3.99	72.15	2.47	34.01
8.19	8.17	7.40	7.39	0.03	0.03	0.02	0.01	0.39
695.94	666.89	596.74	570.50	4.08	3.75	29.05	1.13	27.72
56.67	54.82	45.17	43.55	0.65	0.60	1.86		1.71
4611.36	4480.15	3624.88	3480.20	140.48	139.72	131.21	29.70	215.18
3557.80	3441.15	2785.41	2655.07	131.65	131.30	116.66	26.62	162.53
45.85	45.44	37.05	36.73	0.21	0.21	0.41	0.09	0.89
789.06	776.97	633.24	624.19	6.10	5.69	12.09	2.73	38.56
216.91	214.92	167.95	163.03	2.50	2.50	1.99	0.25	13.18
3199.74	**3085.06**	**2927.17**	**2819.01**	**123.29**	**122.73**	**114.68**	**4.87**	**100.93**
12317.97	11852.84	10090.72	9610.92	595.61	588.27	465.13	39.97	317.72
193.41	193.13	165.61	165.46	1.65	1.61	0.28	-0.13	4.73
14539.65	14325.87	11991.29	11797.64	452.27	450.28	213.79	32.38	554.75
27642.40	27075.62	23624.34	23045.66	393.57	379.51	566.78	53.75	714.52
16503.41	15963.28	13681.96	13128.19	631.69	624.30	540.13	63.70	523.77
9233.41	9076.63	7804.98	7663.54	73.48	70.26	156.78	13.85	275.06
16445.24	16361.58	14128.69	14051.57	140.68	135.24	83.66	8.59	470.44

13-3 续表 7 continued

单位：亿元

项 目	Item	所有者权益合计 Total owner 外商资本 Total Rights of the Owners Foreign Assets
按行业分	**Grouped by sector**	**406.46**
采矿业	**Mining and Qarrying**	
煤炭开采和洗选业	Coal Mining and Processing	
石油和天然气开采业	Petroleum and Natural Gas Extraction	
黑色金属矿采选业	Ferrous Metals Mining and Processing	
有色金属矿采选业	Non-ferrous Metals Mining and Processing	
非金属矿采选业	Non-metal Minerals Mining and Processing	0.02
开采辅助活动	Mining Auxiliary Activities	
其他采矿业	Other Minerals Mining and Processing	
制造业	**Manufacturing**	
农副食品加工业	Food Processing	11.92
食品制造业	Food Production	3.76
酒、饮料和精制茶制造业	Wine,Beverage and Refined Tea Production	25.75
烟草制品业	Tobacco Processing	
纺织业	Textile Industry	6.09
纺织服装、服饰业	Textile,Garments, and Fashion Industry	1.78
皮革、毛皮、羽毛及其制品和制鞋业	Leather, Furs,Down and Related Products	4.20
木材加工和木、竹、藤、棕、草制品业	Timber Processing, Wood, Bamboo, Cane, Palm and Saw Products	0.14
家具制造业	Furniture Manufacturing	0.16
造纸和纸制品业	Papermaking and Paper Products	7.20
印刷和记录媒介复制业	Printing and Record Processing	0.22
文教、工美、体育和娱乐用品制造业	Stationery, Education and Sports Goods	0.62
石油加工、炼焦和核燃料加工业	Petroleum Processing, Coking Products and Nuclear Fuel Processing	9.91
化学原料和化学制品制造业	Raw Chemical Material and Chemical Products	44.97
医药制造业	Medical and pharmaceutical Products	3.16
化学纤维制造业	Chemical Fibers	8.26
橡胶和塑料制品业	Rubber and plastic products	1.70
非金属矿物制品业	Nonmetal Material Products	27.07
黑色金属冶炼和压延加工业	Smelting and Pressing of Ferrous Metals	38.15
有色金属冶炼和压延加工业	Smelting and Pressing of Nonferrous Metals	2.08
金属制品业	Metal Products	3.92
通用设备制造业	Ordinary Machinery Manufacturing	8.66
专用设备制造业	Special Purpose Equipment Manufacturing	9.26
汽车制造业	Motor manufacturing	129.16
铁路、船舶、航空航天和其他运输设备制造业	Railway,Watercraft,Aviation and other Transporlation Equipment manufacturing	0.66
电气机械和器材制造业	Electric Machinery and Equipment	28.79
计算机、通信和其他电子设备制造业	Telecommunication Computer,Equipment and Other Electronic Equipment Manufacturing	6.95
仪器仪表制造业	Instruments and Meters, Manufacturing	1.04
其他制造业	Other Manufacturing	0.01
废弃资源综合利用业	Waste Comprehensive Vtilization of Resources Industry	
金属制品、机械和设备修理业	Metal products,Machinery and Equipment Repairing	
电力、燃气及水的生产和供应业	**Electric Power, Gas and Water Production and Supply**	
电力、热力生产和供应业	Electric Power, Steam and Hot Water Production and Supply	11.04
燃气生产和供应业	Gas Production and Supply	2.43
水的生产和供应业	Tap Water Production and Supply	7.40

(100 million Yuan)

营业收入 Proceeds Of Business	主营业务收入 Revenue of Major Business	营业成本 Operating Costs	主营业务成本 Cost of Major Business	营业税金及附加 Tax of Major Business	主营业务税金及附加 Tax of Major Business	其他业务收入 Revenue of Other Business	其他业务利润 Profit from Other Business	销售费用 Selling Expenses
42182.06	**41401.49**	**35615.63**	**34843.30**	**845.85**	**829.79**	**780.57**	**86.13**	**1269.28**
116.81	116.49	93.51	93.22	2.61	2.54	0.32	0.01	3.07
98.31	75.97	71.04	48.68	13.78	13.67	22.34		0.94
409.70	409.67	349.27	349.18	3.90	3.89	0.03	0.03	14.20
49.18	48.09	35.48	34.59	0.87	0.87	1.09	-0.01	0.72
535.59	521.14	426.58	413.80	14.04	13.85	14.46	0.39	18.92
74.81	73.98	68.05	67.17	0.45	0.44	0.83		0.08
1.01	1.01	0.78	0.78					0.02
4299.57	4280.41	3846.33	3830.88	20.13	19.14	19.17	3.25	102.73
947.73	943.54	783.94	778.92	6.77	6.60	4.19	0.25	50.50
1437.54	1411.95	1061.68	1049.19	31.69	31.47	25.59	20.28	122.99
657.21	559.04	216.56	117.60	336.78	336.78	98.17	-0.86	12.28
2119.99	2109.70	1843.81	1836.31	17.33	17.31	10.30	0.54	53.71
848.26	847.24	728.15	725.41	7.89	7.86	1.02	0.34	26.80
172.47	172.22	151.63	151.24	1.17	1.17	0.25		3.42
394.62	394.32	336.18	335.48	4.99	4.71	0.31	0.06	10.77
144.05	143.82	122.08	121.90	1.22	1.22	0.22	0.08	4.82
491.48	488.22	433.77	430.87	2.86	2.84	3.27	0.23	15.25
306.63	305.48	251.26	250.55	2.62	2.60	1.15	0.59	9.74
137.61	136.91	117.33	116.65	0.94	0.91	0.70	0.19	3.83
922.69	896.76	815.93	789.74	97.64	97.63	25.93	0.13	3.15
3833.72	3792.76	3331.06	3301.80	22.15	21.97	40.96	4.61	106.58
950.31	946.29	732.26	729.86	7.00	6.79	4.02	0.50	74.12
82.94	80.14	74.87	72.63	0.54	0.54	2.80	0.26	1.21
1071.19	1065.49	906.30	901.47	8.36	8.00	5.70	0.69	28.77
2815.06	2809.28	2334.78	2326.98	32.83	30.62	5.78	1.23	96.87
2775.88	2627.63	2547.48	2384.92	11.52	6.12	148.25	2.05	38.06
1524.68	1504.84	1459.92	1440.69	2.36	2.30	19.84	0.61	7.54
1376.83	1336.23	1195.31	1156.52	10.55	10.36	40.60	0.85	40.81
1210.98	1205.12	968.30	958.51	17.74	15.22	5.86	0.41	36.02
962.70	957.02	806.01	802.26	6.92	6.82	5.68	0.80	29.36
5310.49	5148.98	4316.36	4145.93	122.40	121.51	161.51	32.82	206.20
576.15	561.21	521.35	502.63	3.49	3.47	14.94	1.40	9.60
1659.85	1623.97	1429.09	1392.35	9.25	8.82	35.88	5.70	48.09
1627.04	1606.38	1423.14	1406.61	6.32	5.93	20.66	2.84	66.46
146.89	146.00	115.46	114.62	1.07	1.02	0.89	0.21	6.45
157.09	155.54	131.53	128.31	1.38	1.37	1.54	0.10	4.38
128.74	128.34	118.20	117.10	0.41	0.41	0.40		1.11
32.89	32.86	28.50	28.49	0.29	0.29	0.02		0.53
1580.03	1550.55	1263.62	1238.52	12.06	11.26	29.47	4.04	1.31
132.20	130.34	107.47	106.27	0.96	0.92	1.86	0.72	4.47
61.14	56.56	51.28	44.69	0.56	0.51	4.58	0.80	3.39

13-3 续表 8 continued

单位:亿元

项 目	Item	管理费用 Management Expense
总 计	**Total**	**1704.51**
一、按登记注册类型分组:	**Grouped by Type of Registration**	
内资企业	Inner Funded Enterprises	1402.91
国有企业	State Owned Enterprises	136.98
中央企业	Central Enterprises	122.01
地方企业	Local Enterprises	14.97
集体企业	Collective-owned Enterprise	9.23
股份合作企业	Share Holding Cooperative Enterprises	0.66
联营企业	Joint Owned Enterprise	0.26
国有联营企业	State Joint Ownership	
集体联营企业	Collective Joint Ownership	
国有与集体联营企业	Joint State- Collective Ownership	0.11
其他联营企业	Other Joint Owned Enterprise	0.15
有限责任公司	Responsibility Co. Ltd	530.17
国有独资公司	State Solely Funded Co.	73.66
其他有限责任公司	Others	456.51
股份有限公司	Share Holding Co.Ltd.	240.49
私营企业	Private - owned enterprises	481.83
私营独资企业	Solely Private - owned enterprises	10.76
私营合伙企业	Private Joint Venture	2.80
私营有限责任公司	Private Responsibility Co. Ltd	433.68
私营股份有限公司	Private Share Holding Co.Ltd.	34.59
其他企业	Others	3.30
港、澳、台商投资企业	Hongkong, Macao and Taiwan Funded Enterprises	98.12
合资经营企业(港或澳、台资)	Joint Venture with Hongkong, Macao and Taiwan	70.35
合作经营企业(港或澳、台资)	Cooperate with Hongkong, Macao and Taiwan Funded	0.30
港澳台商独资经营企业	Enterprises Solely Funded by Hongkong, Macao and Taiwan Businessmen	24.02
港澳台商投资股份有限公司	Share Holding Co.Ltd. With Hongkong,	3.26
外商投资企业	Foreign Funded Enterprises	203.49
中外合资经营企业	Sino - Foreign Joint Funded Enterprises	150.73
中外合作经营企业	Sino - Foreign Cooperative Funded Enterprises	0.68
外资企业	Foreign Solely Funded Enterprises	40.47
外商投资股份有限公司	Foreign Funded Share Holding Co.Ltd.	11.52
二、在总计中:亏损企业	**Of the Total: enterprises running under deficit**	**154.15**
在总计中:国有控股企业	Of the Total: State-Owned Share Holding Enterprises	520.89
在总计中:农村工业	Of the Total: Rural Industry	7.40
在总计中:轻工业	Of the Total: Light Industry	585.91
重工业	Heavy Industry	1118.60
在总计中:大型企业	Of the Total: Large Scale Enterprises	650.99
中型企业	Medium Scale Enterprises	425.55
小型企业	Small Enterprises	627.97

(100 million Yuan)

税金 Tax	财务费用 Financial Expense	利息收入 Interest Income	利息支出 Interest Expense
99.66	**522.40**	**37.45**	**490.65**
86.14	489.98	35.93	439.18
7.69	97.92	9.21	99.20
7.01	95.51	9.07	96.92
0.68	2.41	0.14	2.28
0.46	0.70	0.02	0.56
0.01	0.13		0.07
0.01	0.03		0.01
0.01	0.03		
31.26	182.90	13.21	171.03
2.70	27.49	3.55	29.93
28.56	155.41	9.66	141.10
16.94	53.68	10.04	58.60
29.59	153.82	3.44	109.20
0.89	4.44	0.04	2.66
0.07	0.84	0.01	0.56
26.38	137.86	2.94	97.50
2.26	10.67	0.45	8.48
0.18	0.79	0.02	0.51
4.04	15.31	2.76	15.93
2.27	8.48	2.60	10.00
0.03	0.06		0.06
1.60	5.49	0.14	5.02
0.12	1.24	0.01	0.80
9.47	17.11	-1.24	35.54
6.10	4.28	-2.84	22.09
0.02	0.60	0.03	0.61
2.52	4.58	1.38	5.92
0.83	7.64	0.19	6.91
6.91	**56.53**	**6.44**	**54.44**
23.22	196.32	21.26	223.18
0.31	1.95	-0.01	1.59
49.45	148.34	8.48	120.25
50.20	374.06	28.97	370.40
40.35	216.26	24.89	244.69
22.93	113.34	7.52	99.68
36.38	192.80	5.05	146.28

13-3 续表 9 continued

单位:亿元

项 目	Item	管理费用 Management Expense
按行业分	**Grouped by sector**	**1704.51**
采矿业	**Mining and Qarrying**	
煤炭开采和洗选业	Coal Mining and Processing	6.54
石油和天然气开采业	Petroleum and Natural Gas Extraction	9.31
黑色金属矿采选业	Ferrous Metals Mining and Processing	15.25
有色金属矿采选业	Non-ferrous Metals Mining and Processing	3.57
非金属矿采选业	Non-metal Minerals Mining and Processing	22.78
开采辅助活动	Mining Auxiliary Activities	4.98
其他采矿业	Other Minerals Mining and Processing	0.12
制造业	**Manufacturing**	
农副食品加工业	Food Processing	109.51
食品制造业	Food Production	49.78
酒、饮料和精制茶制造业	Wine,Beverage and Refined Tea Production	78.65
烟草制品业	Tobacco Processing	22.54
纺织业	Textile Industry	75.72
纺织服装、服饰业	Textile,Garments, and Fashion Industry	34.66
皮革、毛皮、羽毛及其制品和制鞋业	Leather, Furs,Down and Related Products	7.46
木材加工和木、竹、藤、棕、草制品业	Timber Processing, Wood, Bamboo, Cane, Palm and Sraw Products	12.78
家具制造业	Furniture Manufacturing	5.87
造纸和纸制品业	Papermaking and Paper Products	15.46
印刷和记录媒介复制业	Printing and Record Processing	20.74
文教、工美、体育和娱乐用品制造业	Stationery, Education and Sports Goods	5.94
石油加工、炼焦和核燃料加工业	Petroleum Processing, Coking Products and Nuclear Fuel Processing	12.44
化学原料和化学制品制造业	Raw Chemical Material and Chemical Products	127.90
医药制造业	Medical and pharmaceutical Products	59.58
化学纤维制造业	Chemical Fibers	1.83
橡胶和塑料制品业	Rubber and plastic products	39.27
非金属矿物制品业	Nonmetal Material Products	111.57
黑色金属冶炼和压延加工业	Smelting and Pressing of Ferrous Metals	105.34
有色金属冶炼和压延加工业	Smelting and Pressing of Nonferrous Metals	35.14
金属制品业	Metal Products	65.92
通用设备制造业	Ordinary Machinery Manufacturing	59.35
专用设备制造业	Special Purpose Equipment Manufacturing	50.47
汽车制造业	Motor manufacturing	264.04
铁路、船舶、航空航天和其他运输设备制造业	Railway,Watercraft,Aviation and other Transporlation Equipment manufacturing	29.58
电气机械和器材制造业	Electric Machinery and Equipment	79.68
计算机、通信和其他电子设备制造业	Telecommunication Computer,Equipment and Other Electronic Equipment Manufacturing	93.45
仪器仪表制造业	Instruments and Meters, Manufacturing	11.97
其他制造业	Other Manufacturing	9.46
废弃资源综合利用业	Waste Comprehensive Vtilization of Resources Industry	10.13
金属制品、机械和设备修理业	Metal products,Machinery and Equipment Repairing	2.19
电力、燃气及水的生产和供应业	**Electric Power, Gas and Water Production and Supply**	
电力、热力生产和供应业	Electric Power, Steam and Hot Water Production and Supply	22.68
燃气生产和供应业	Gas Production and Supply	4.21
水的生产和供应业	Tap Water Production and Supply	6.63

(100 million Yuan)

税金 Tax	财务费用 Financial Expense	利息收入 Interest Income	利息支出 Interest Expense
99.66	**522.4**	**37.45**	**490.65**
0.19	0.86	0.01	0.70
0.12	0.54	0.17	0.70
0.81	3.81	0.04	2.89
0.11	0.39	0.03	0.34
0.96	8.67	0.10	6.30
0.04	0.96	0.07	0.69
0.06			
7.81	38.18	1.31	30.62
5.82	8.95	0.99	8.12
12.39	14.66	1.69	14.25
0.70	1.25	0.28	1.86
7.07	32.67	0.66	20.52
3.14	8.74	0.64	6.59
0.45	1.85	0.03	1.27
1.20	4.95	0.06	3.46
0.19	1.31	0.01	1.17
1.33	5.73	0.79	5.77
1.30	2.82	0.13	1.97
0.26	1.56	0.02	0.99
0.31	2.12	0.41	2.39
6.93	65.33	2.10	60.80
3.78	11.73	0.92	10.86
0.09	1.19	0.12	1.18
2.47	11.89	0.55	9.48
6.87	40.63	1.18	37.05
7.15	60.01	6.90	58.63
1.33	9.77	3.06	9.39
2.26	17.18	0.68	14.21
2.33	15.07	1.60	13.84
1.57	13.63	1.11	11.36
10.65	13.31	2.19	31.19
0.96	7.00	1.06	7.66
3.44	12.69	1.56	11.31
1.63	7.71	3.99	9.41
0.41	1.56	0.10	1.43
0.32	2.00	0.10	1.58
0.21	1.39	0.04	1.14
0.03	0.43		0.42
2.20	86.20	2.41	85.61
0.23	1.17	0.29	1.27
0.56	2.49	0.06	2.22

13-3 续表 10 continued

单位:亿元

项 目	Item	营业利润 Operating Profit
总 计	**Total**	**2357.20**
一、按登记注册类型分组:	**Grouped by Type of Registration**	
内资企业	Inner Funded Enterprises	1924.62
国有企业	State Owned Enterprises	177.08
中央企业	Central Enterprises	164.92
地方企业	Local Enterprises	12.16
集体企业	Collective-owned Enterprise	6.14
股份合作企业	Share Holding Cooperative Enterprises	0.80
联营企业	Joint Owned Enterprise	0.28
国有联营企业	State Joint Ownership	
集体联营企业	Collective Joint Ownership	0.01
国有与集体联营企业	Joint State- Collective Ownership	-0.03
其他联营企业	Other Joint Owned Enterprise	0.30
有限责任公司	Responsibility Co. Ltd	675.51
国有独资公司	State Solely Funded Co.	89.73
其他有限责任公司	Others	585.79
股份有限公司	Share Holding Co.Ltd.	261.32
私营企业	Private - owned enterprises	794.23
私营独资企业	Solely Private - owned enterprises	24.09
私营合伙企业	Private Joint Venture	4.56
私营有限责任公司	Private Responsibility Co. Ltd	687.03
私营股份有限公司	Private Share Holding Co.Ltd.	78.55
其他企业	Others	9.25
港、澳、台商投资企业	Hongkong, Macao and Taiwan Funded Enterprises	96.81
合资经营企业(港或澳、台资)	Joint Venture with Hongkong, Macao and Taiwan	51.08
合作经营企业(港或澳、台资)	Cooperate with Hongkong, Macao and Taiwan Funded	0.12
港澳台商独资经营企业	Enterprises Solely Funded by Hongkong, Macao and Taiwan Businessmen	41.36
港澳台商投资股份有限公司	Share Holding Co.Ltd. With Hongkong, Macao and Taiwan Investment	4.47
外商投资企业	Foreign Funded Enterprises	335.77
中外合资经营企业	Sino - Foreign Joint Funded Enterprises	262.39
中外合作经营企业	Sino - Foreign Cooperative Funded Enterprises	6.25
外资企业	Foreign Solely Funded Enterprises	47.74
外商投资股份有限公司	Foreign Funded Share Holding Co.Ltd.	19.03
二、在总计中:亏损企业	**Of the Total: enterprises running under deficit**	**-205.09**
在总计中:国有控股企业	Of the Total: State-Owned Share Holding Enterprises	677.57
在总计中:农村工业	Of the Total: Rural Industry	12.09
在总计中:轻工业	Of the Total: Light Industry	886.07
重工业	Heavy Industry	1471.13
在总计中:大型企业	Of the Total: Large Scale Enterprises	842.39
中型企业	Medium Scale Enterprises	612.25
小型企业	Small Enterprises	902.55

(100 million Yuan)

补贴收入 Income from subsidy	营业外收入 Non-operating Income	营业外支出 Non-operating Expense	利润总额 Total Profit	应交所得税 Income Tax	亏损企业亏损总额 Total Loss of Enterprises Running under Deficit
85.16	**180.08**	**59.97**	**2402.63**	**335.33**	**195.53**
69.58	153.25	52.66	1992.33	243.99	163.29
23.89	43.67	4.08	216.73	42.48	14.40
23.64	43.10	3.70	204.37	40.38	13.32
0.25	0.56	0.37	12.35	2.10	1.08
0.11	0.26	0.16	6.18	0.66	1.76
	0.03	0.05	0.76	0.06	0.01
0.05	0.05		0.33		
			0.01		
0.05	0.05		0.01		
			0.30		
31.32	64.23	21.96	697.41	103.77	77.02
8.59	15.02	3.24	92.57	22.93	26.08
22.73	49.21	18.72	604.84	80.84	50.94
7.46	27.49	8.27	273.38	31.00	47.73
6.76	17.49	17.55	788.99	65.12	22.31
0.07	0.39	0.73	23.64	1.77	0.04
		0.18	4.34	0.44	0.09
5.91	15.04	13.31	683.93	58.27	20.27
0.78	2.06	3.34	77.09	4.64	1.91
	0.04	0.59	8.56	0.90	0.06
2.85	7.67	2.29	101.90	16.96	5.25
2.23	5.72	1.72	54.74	9.51	2.42
	0.01		0.13	-0.01	0.01
0.59	1.34	0.54	42.15	6.62	2.74
0.01	0.20	0.02	4.71	0.85	0.04
12.73	19.16	5.02	308.40	74.38	26.99
7.67	12.05	3.81	229.91	54.90	14.52
	0.01	0.29	5.97	1.65	0.06
1.92	3.75	0.67	50.04	12.33	12.04
3.11	3.30	0.25	22.09	5.49	0.37
6.35	**17.84**	**6.50**	**-195.53**	**-3.16**	**195.53**
57.32	107.57	17.19	702.36	133.78	97.75
0.01	0.38	2.83	9.68	0.87	0.27
12.21	29.80	22.75	872.40	111.46	41.51
72.95	150.27	37.22	1530.23	223.86	154.02
55.03	100.65	19.99	873.79	161.39	90.58
15.98	44.90	12.77	627.03	86.12	47.46
14.16	34.53	27.21	901.81	87.82	57.49

13-3 续表 11 continued

单位:亿元

项 目	Item	营业利润 Operating Profit
按行业分	**Grouped by sector**	**2357.20**
采矿业	**Mining and Qarrying**	
煤炭开采和洗选业	Coal Mining and Processing	10.64
石油和天然气开采业	Petroleum and Natural Gas Extraction	-20.81
黑色金属矿采选业	Ferrous Metals Mining and Processing	18.88
有色金属矿采选业	Non-ferrous Metals Mining and Processing	8.36
非金属矿采选业	Non-metal Minerals Mining and Processing	43.85
开采辅助活动	Mining Auxiliary Activities	0.18
其他采矿业	Other Minerals Mining and Processing	0.08
制造业	**Manufacturing**	
农副食品加工业	Food Processing	238.16
食品制造业	Food Production	60.52
酒、饮料和精制茶制造业	Wine,Beverage and Refined Tea Production	103.37
烟草制品业	Tobacco Processing	68.76
纺织业	Textile Industry	106.56
纺织服装、服饰业	Textile,Garments, and Fashion Industry	43.19
皮革、毛皮、羽毛及其制品和制鞋业	Leather, Furs,Down and Related Products	6.80
木材加工和木、竹、藤、棕、草制品业	Timber Processing, Wood, Bamboo, Cane, Palm and Sraw Products	22.54
家具制造业	Furniture Manufacturing	7.99
造纸和纸制品业	Papermaking and Paper Products	21.05
印刷和记录媒介复制业	Printing and Record Processing	20.33
文教、工美、体育和娱乐用品制造业	Stationery, Education and Sports Goods	7.57
石油加工、炼焦和核燃料加工业	Petroleum Processing, Coking Products and Nuclear Fuel Processing	-8.79
化学原料和化学制品制造业	Raw Chemical Material and Chemical Products	193.42
医药制造业	Medical and pharmaceutical Products	68.55
化学纤维制造业	Chemical Fibers	4.53
橡胶和塑料制品业	Rubber and plastic products	70.59
非金属矿物制品业	Nonmetal Material Products	207.31
黑色金属冶炼和压延加工业	Smelting and Pressing of Ferrous Metals	20.62
有色金属冶炼和压延加工业	Smelting and Pressing of Nonferrous Metals	12.36
金属制品业	Metal Products	58.06
通用设备制造业	Ordinary Machinery Manufacturing	70.08
专用设备制造业	Special Purpose Equipment Manufacturing	45.68
汽车制造业	Motor manufacturing	464.25
铁路、船舶、航空航天和其他运输设备制造业	Railway,Watercraft,Aviation and other Transporlation Equipment manufacturing	7.22
电气机械和器材制造业	Electric Machinery and Equipment	95.56
计算机、通信和其他电子设备制造业	Telecommunication Computer,Equipment and Other Electronic Equipment Manufacturing	27.17
仪器仪表制造业	Instruments and Meters, Manufacturing	10.22
其他制造业	Other Manufacturing	9.30
废弃资源综合利用业	Waste Comprehensive Vtilization of Resources Industry	-0.34
金属制品、机械和设备修理业	Metal products,Machinery and Equipment Repairing	1.00
电力、燃气及水的生产和供应业	**Electric Power, Gas and Water Production and Supply**	
电力、热力生产和供应业	Electric Power, Steam and Hot Water Production and Supply	213.84
燃气生产和供应业	Gas Production and Supply	14.31
水的生产和供应业	Tap Water Production and Supply	4.25

(100 million Yuan)

补贴收入 Income from subsidy	营业外收入 Non-operating Income	营业外支出 Non-operating Expense	利润总额 Total Profit	应交所得税 Income Tax	亏损企业亏损总额 Total Loss of Enterprises Running
85.16	**180.08**	**59.97**	**2402.63**	**335.33**	**195.53**
0.01	0.04	0.16	10.51	0.98	1.32
	0.88	0.60	-20.53	-1.51	20.53
0.01	0.16	0.21	18.83	2.84	1.11
0.04	0.09	0.05	8.50	1.78	0.19
0.11	0.44	1.90	42.27	3.31	1.08
0.59	0.62	0.04	0.76	0.28	0.52
			0.08		
2.48	6.25	3.65	231.45	16.31	9.03
0.35	0.86	1.44	59.80	7.57	3.05
1.11	3.04	3.92	103.10	19.42	3.82
0.01	0.29	1.25	67.80	18.33	
0.77	3.15	4.13	105.36	10.92	7.19
0.24	0.72	0.92	42.88	4.22	1.36
0.12	0.38	0.15	7.03	0.39	0.34
0.64	1.36	0.39	23.50	2.05	1.28
0.02	0.05	0.08	7.96	0.61	0.40
0.84	1.57	1.85	19.82	2.56	2.32
0.72	1.00	0.10	21.25	2.50	0.87
	0.16	0.18	7.56	0.67	0.40
0.16	0.93	0.66	-9.07	-1.18	13.03
4.02	8.56	4.91	196.80	24.17	11.23
3.29	6.15	2.19	72.61	9.76	3.29
0.07	0.36	0.13	5.07	0.92	0.96
1.13	1.96	2.71	69.84	9.30	1.19
8.23	13.66	5.93	212.00	25.01	7.84
3.11	16.95	1.98	35.35	3.69	8.03
1.80	2.61	0.67	14.21	1.12	5.95
2.19	3.73	1.19	61.22	7.56	5.15
4.51	10.34	1.23	74.31	6.46	4.19
0.95	3.92	0.95	48.35	5.21	3.11
11.32	20.79	6.10	441.24	69.92	26.02
1.46	7.33	0.35	13.79	4.86	14.34
1.44	5.49	2.41	88.69	12.92	6.09
6.24	15.99	1.80	41.29	6.93	15.06
1.90	3.26	0.14	12.64	1.12	0.40
0.08	0.17	0.04	9.44	0.29	0.17
1.48	1.88	0.01	0.93	0.24	2.92
0.14	0.14	0.01	1.14	0.13	0.09
23.12	33.32	4.83	235.59	50.10	9.10
0.08	0.38	0.55	14.13	3.28	0.33
0.37	1.10	0.19	5.15	0.29	2.25

13-3 续表 12 continued

单位:亿元 (100 million Yuan)

项目	Item	利税总额 Total Profit	本年应付职工薪酬 Wages Welfarism payable This Year
总计	**Total**	**4465.72**	**1916.98**
一、按登记注册类型分组:	**Grouped by Type of Registration**		
内资企业	Inner Funded Enterprises	3641.07	1612.71
国有企业	State Owned Enterprises	357.47	303.14
中央企业	Central Enterprises	340.86	285.89
地方企业	Local Enterprises	16.60	17.25
集体企业	Collective-owned Enterprise	12.48	8.98
股份合作企业	Share Holding Cooperative Enterprises	1.35	0.66
联营企业	Joint Owned Enterprise	0.48	0.26
国有联营企业	State Joint Ownership		
集体联营企业	Collective Joint Ownership	0.05	0.03
国有与集体联营企业	Joint State- Collective Ownership	0.06	0.04
其他联营企业	Other Joint Owned Enterprise	0.37	0.20
有限责任公司	Responsibility Co. Ltd	1549.62	601.27
国有独资公司	State Solely Funded Co.	591.43	84.11
其他有限责任公司	Others	958.18	517.15
股份有限公司	Share Holding Co.Ltd.	462.82	220.37
私营企业	Private - owned enterprises	1242.55	473.34
私营独资企业	Solely Private - owned enterprises	35.79	11.57
私营合伙企业	Private Joint Venture	6.69	2.13
私营有限责任公司	Private Responsibility Co. Ltd	1086.19	424.97
私营股份有限公司	Private Share Holding Co.Ltd.	113.88	34.67
其他企业	Others	14.32	4.69
港、澳、台商投资企业	Hongkong, Macao and Taiwan Funded Enterprises	158.69	91.97
合资经营企业(港或澳、台资)	Joint Venture with Hongkong, Macao and Taiwan	84.61	55.05
合作经营企业(港或澳、台资)	Cooperate with Hongkong, Macao and Taiwan Funded	0.37	0.47
港澳台商独资经营企业	Enterprises Solely Funded by Hongkong, Macao and Taiwan Businessmen	66.32	32.81
港澳台商投资股份有限公司	Share Holding Co.Ltd. With Hongkong, Macao and Taiwan Investment	7.09	3.56
外商投资企业	Foreign Funded Enterprises	665.96	212.30
中外合资经营企业	Sino - Foreign Joint Funded Enterprises	543.79	153.00
中外合作经营企业	Sino - Foreign Cooperative Funded Enterprises	8.52	1.84
外资企业	Foreign Solely Funded Enterprises	77.21	43.47
外商投资股份有限公司	Foreign Funded Share Holding Co.Ltd.	35.91	13.89
二、在总计中:亏损企业	**Of the Total: enterprises running under deficit**	**-4.86**	**183.27**
在总计中:国有控股企业	Of the Total: State-Owned Share Holding Enterprises	1785.47	735.61
在总计中:农村工业	Of the Total: Rural Industry	14.95	6.39
在总计中:轻工业	Of the Total: Light Industry	1741.55	589.05
重工业	Heavy Industry	2724.18	1327.93
在总计中:大型企业	Of the Total: Large Scale Enterprises	2072.03	910.44
中型企业	Medium Scale Enterprises	963.97	466.59
小型企业	Small Enterprises	1429.72	539.96

13—3 续表 13 continued

单位:亿元

项 目	Item	利税总额 Total Profit	本年应付职工薪酬 Wages Welfarism Payable this year
按行业分	Grouped by sector	**4465.72**	**1916.98**
采矿业	**Mining and Qarrying**		
煤炭开采和洗选业	Coal Mining and Processing	19.88	15.44
石油和天然气开采业	Petroleum and Natural Gas Extraction	1.02	18.92
黑色金属矿采选业	Ferrous Metals Mining and Processing	32.10	10.41
有色金属矿采选业	Non-ferrous Metals Mining and Processing	12.68	3.87
非金属矿采选业	Non-metal Minerals Mining and Processing	76.47	19.12
开采辅助活动	Mining Auxiliary Activities	6.55	11.14
其他采矿业	Other Minerals Mining and Processing	0.13	0.13
制造业	**Manufacturing**		
农副食品加工业	Food Processing	325.03	103.18
食品制造业	Food Production	94.69	37.90
酒、饮料和精制茶制造业	Wine,Beverage and Refined Tea Production	176.51	46.04
烟草制品业	Tobacco Processing	479.67	12.46
纺织业	Textile Industry	176.96	110.48
纺织服装、服饰业	Textile,Garments, and Fashion Industry	71.57	61.85
皮革、毛皮、羽毛及其制品和制鞋业	Leather, Furs,Down and Related Products	11.76	12.59
木材加工和木、竹、藤、棕、草制品业	Timber Processing, Wood, Bamboo, Cane, Palm and Sraw Products	38.46	18.05
家具制造业	Furniture Manufacturing	12.37	7.04
造纸和纸制品业	Papermaking and Paper Products	35.43	17.99
印刷和记录媒介复制业	Printing and Record Processing	32.78	14.59
文教、工美、体育和娱乐用品制造业	Stationery, Education and Sports Goods	11.11	6.82
石油加工、炼焦和核燃料加工业	Petroleum Processing, Coking Products and Nuclear Fuel Processing	107.02	10.39
化学原料和化学制品制造业	Raw Chemical Material and Chemical Products	296.03	108.52
医药制造业	Medical and pharmaceutical Products	118.80	53.96
化学纤维制造业	Chemical Fibers	7.74	4.06
橡胶和塑料制品业	Rubber and plastic products	108.27	46.10
非金属矿物制品业	Nonmetal Material Products	334.67	116.89
黑色金属冶炼和压延加工业	Smelting and Pressing of Ferrous Metals	107.61	161.81
有色金属冶炼和压延加工业	Smelting and Pressing of Nonferrous Metals	27.48	24.99
金属制品业	Metal Products	103.32	55.91
通用设备制造业	Ordinary Machinery Manufacturing	118.83	58.95
专用设备制造业	Special Purpose Equipment Manufacturing	79.73	50.89
汽车制造业	Motor manufacturing	783.91	280.70
铁路、船舶、航空航天和其他运输设备制造业	Railway,Watercraft,Aviation and other Transporlation Equipment manufacturing	28.40	52.25
电气机械和器材制造业	Electric Machinery and Equipment	134.04	80.81
计算机、通信和其他电子设备制造业	Telecommunication Computer,Equipment and Other Electronic Equipment Manufacturing	73.12	104.26
仪器仪表制造业	Instruments and Meters, Manufacturing	17.64	14.24
其他制造业	Other Manufacturing	13.57	10.21
废弃资源综合利用业	Waste Comprehensive Vtilization of Resources Industry	4.51	3.59
金属制品、机械和设备修理业	Metal products,Machinery and Equipment Repairing	2.82	3.18
电力、燃气及水的生产和供应业	**Electric Power, Gas and Water Production and Supply**		
电力、热力生产和供应业	Electric Power, Steam and Hot Water Production and Supply	357.40	131.54
燃气生产和供应业	Gas Production and Supply	18.01	5.61
水的生产和供应业	Tap Water Production and Supply	7.63	10.11

13-3 续表 14 continued

单位:亿元 (100 million Yuan)

项 目	Item	应交税金及附加 Tax and Extra Charges	本年应交增值税 Value Added Payable of the Current Year	全部从业人员年平均人数(万人) Average Number of Empolyment of the Current Year (10000 persons)
总 计	**Total**	**2498.08**	**1217.24**	**359.45**
一、按登记注册类型分组:	**Grouped by Type of Registration**			
内资企业	Inner Funded Enterprises	1978.88	952.15	312.77
国有企业	State Owned Enterprises	190.91	124.51	31.02
中央企业	Central Enterprises	183.88	121.12	27.32
地方企业	Local Enterprises	7.03	3.39	3.69
集体企业	Collective-owned Enterprise	7.42	4.29	2.08
股份合作企业	Share Holding Cooperative Enterprises	0.66	0.49	0.18
联营企业	Joint Owned Enterprise	0.16	0.10	0.12
国有联营企业	State Joint Ownership			
集体联营企业	Collective Joint Ownership	0.04	0.03	0.01
国有与集体联营企业	Joint State- Collective Ownership	0.05	0.04	0.04
其他联营企业	Other Joint Owned Enterprise	0.07	0.02	0.07
有限责任公司	Responsibility Co. Ltd	987.25	382.69	120.31
国有独资公司	State Solely Funded Co.	524.5	107.17	11.54
其他有限责任公司	Others	462.75	275.52	108.77
股份有限公司	Share Holding Co.Ltd.	237.38	106.79	37.62
私营企业	Private - owned enterprises	548.26	328.58	120.34
私营独资企业	Solely Private - owned enterprises	14.82	7.82	3.50
私营合伙企业	Private Joint Venture	2.85	1.50	0.65
私营有限责任公司	Private Responsibility Co. Ltd	486.9	291.67	107.32
私营股份有限公司	Private Share Holding Co.Ltd.	43.69	27.60	8.87
其他企业	Others	6.84	4.70	1.11
港、澳、台商投资企业	Hongkong, Macao and Taiwan Funded Enterprises	77.8	48.02	18.33
合资经营企业(港或澳、台资)	Joint Venture with Hongkong, Macao and Taiwan	41.65	25.88	9.70
合作经营企业(港或澳、台资)	Cooperate with Hongkong, Macao and Taiwan Funded	0.26	0.21	0.10
港澳台商独资经营企业	Enterprises Solely Funded by Hongkong, Macao and Taiwan Businessmen	32.39	20.09	7.86
港澳台商投资股份有限公司	Share Holding Co.Ltd. With Hongkong, Macao and Taiwan Investment	3.35	1.72	0.65
外商投资企业	Foreign Funded Enterprises	441.4	217.07	28.35
中外合资经营企业	Sino - Foreign Joint Funded Enterprises	374.88	182.24	17.63
中外合作经营企业	Sino - Foreign Cooperative Funded Enterprises	4.23	2.35	0.23
外资企业	Foreign Solely Funded Enterprises	42.01	21.06	8.66
外商投资股份有限公司	Foreign Funded Share Holding Co.Ltd.	20.14	11.32	1.81
二、在总计中:亏损企业	**Of the Total: enterprises running under deficit**	**194.42**	**67.38**	**36.61**
在总计中:国有控股企业	Of the Total: State-Owned Share Holding Enterprises	1240.12	487.50	83.27
在总计中:农村工业	Of the Total: Rural Industry	6.44	3.62	1.68
在总计中:轻工业	Of the Total: Light Industry	1030.07	416.88	142.07
重工业	Heavy Industry	1468.01	800.37	217.38
在总计中:大型企业	Of the Total: Large Scale Enterprises	1399.97	566.55	122.93
中型企业	Medium Scale Enterprises	445.99	263.46	99.90
小型企业	Small Enterprises	652.11	387.23	136.62

13-3 续表 15 continued

单位:亿元 (100 million Yuan)

项 目	Item	应交税金及附加 Tax and Extra Charges	本年应交增值税 Value Added Payable of the Current Year	全部从业人员年平均人数(万人) Average Number of Empolyment of the Current Year (10000 persons)
按行业分	Grouped by sector	**2498.08**	**1217.24**	**359.45**
采矿业	**Mining and Qarrying**			
煤炭开采和洗选业	Coal Mining and Processing	10.54	6.77	3.23
石油和天然气开采业	Petroleum and Natural Gas Extraction	20.16	7.77	1.82
黑色金属矿采选业	Ferrous Metals Mining and Processing	16.92	9.37	2.61
有色金属矿采选业	Non-ferrous Metals Mining and Processing	6.07	3.32	0.65
非金属矿采选业	Non-metal Minerals Mining and Processing	38.47	20.15	4.85
开采辅助活动	Mining Auxiliary Activities	6.11	5.34	1.83
其他采矿业	Other Minerals Mining and Processing	0.11	0.05	0.04
制造业	**Manufacturing**			
农副食品加工业	Food Processing	117.69	73.45	24.82
食品制造业	Food Production	48.27	28.12	9.60
酒、饮料和精制茶制造业	Wine,Beverage and Refined Tea Production	105.21	41.71	11.46
烟草制品业	Tobacco Processing	430.90	75.09	0.88
纺织业	Textile Industry	89.59	54.27	28.24
纺织服装、服饰业	Textile,Garments, and Fashion Industry	36.06	20.81	17.20
皮革、毛皮、羽毛及其制品和制鞋业	Leather, Furs,Down and Related Products	5.57	3.56	4.08
木材加工和木、竹、藤、棕、草制品业	Timber Processing, Wood, Bamboo, Cane, Palm and Sraw Products	18.22	9.98	4.07
家具制造业	Furniture Manufacturing	5.21	3.20	1.75
造纸和纸制品业	Papermaking and Paper Products	19.50	12.75	4.55
印刷和记录媒介复制业	Printing and Record Processing	15.33	8.91	3.46
文教、工美、体育和娱乐用品制造业	Stationery, Education and Sports Goods	4.48	2.61	1.92
石油加工、炼焦和核燃料加工业	Petroleum Processing, Coking Products and Nuclear Fuel Processing	115.22	18.45	1.21
化学原料和化学制品制造业	Raw Chemical Material and Chemical Products	130.33	77.08	22.44
医药制造业	Medical and pharmaceutical Products	59.73	39.19	11.36
化学纤维制造业	Chemical Fibers	3.69	2.13	0.88
橡胶和塑料制品业	Rubber and plastic products	50.19	30.07	10.40
非金属矿物制品业	Nonmetal Material Products	154.55	89.84	26.77
黑色金属冶炼和压延加工业	Smelting and Pressing of Ferrous Metals	83.10	60.74	18.11
有色金属冶炼和压延加工业	Smelting and Pressing of Nonferrous Metals	15.72	10.90	4.84
金属制品业	Metal Products	51.92	31.55	12.13
通用设备制造业	Ordinary Machinery Manufacturing	53.32	26.79	12.46
专用设备制造业	Special Purpose Equipment Manufacturing	38.16	24.46	10.90
汽车制造业	Motor manufacturing	423.23	220.26	41.11
铁路、船舶、航空航天和其他运输设备制造业	Railway,Watercraft,Aviation and other Transporlation Equipment manufacturing	20.43	11.11	7.65
电气机械和器材制造业	Electric Machinery and Equipment	61.72	36.10	15.61
计算机、通信和其他电子设备制造业	Telecommunication Computer,Equipment and Other Electronic Equipment Manufacturing	40.39	25.51	14.88
仪器仪表制造业	Instruments and Meters, Manufacturing	6.53	3.93	2.67
其他制造业	Other Manufacturing	4.74	2.76	2.25
废弃资源综合利用业	Waste Comprehensive Vtilization of Resources Industry	4.03	3.17	0.77
金属制品、机械和设备修理业	Metal products,Machinery and Equipment Repairing	1.85	1.40	0.83
电力、燃气及水的生产和供应业	**Electric Power, Gas and Water Production and Supply**			
电力、热力生产和供应业	Electric Power, Steam and Hot Water Production and Supply	174.11	109.75	12.15
燃气生产和供应业	Gas Production and Supply	7.38	2.92	0.90
水的生产和供应业	Tap Water Production and Supply	3.32	1.91	2.07

13-4 国有控股工业企业单位数和主要经济指标（2014）

单位：亿元

项 目	Item	企业单位数(个) Number of Enterprises(unit)	工业总产值(当年价格) Total Output Value(current price)
总 计	**Total**	**742**	**11494.30**
在总计中：	Of the Total		
亏损企业	Enterprises running under Deficit	145	1391.31
在总计中：	Of the Total:		
中央企业	Central Enterprises	41	3073.57
地方企业	Local Enterprises	112	166.67
在总计中：	Of the Total:		
轻工业	Light Industry	209	1359.92
重工业	Heavy Industry	533	10134.38
在总计中：	Of the Total:		
大型企业	Large Scale Enterprises	115	9706.51
中型企业	Medium Scale Enterprises	203	1070.39
小型企业	Small Enterprises	424	717.40
按行业分	Grouped by sector		
采矿业	**Mining and Qarrying**		
煤炭开采和洗选业	Coal Mining and Processing	7	6.08
石油和天然气开采业	Petroleum and Natural Gas Extraction	1	75.74
黑色金属矿采选业	Ferrous Metals Mining and Processing	3	53.43
有色金属矿采选业	Non-ferrous Metals Mining and Processing	3	11.74
非金属矿采选业	Non-metal Minerals Mining and Processing	13	11.70
开采辅助活动	Mining Auxiliary Activities	3	67.05
其他采矿业	Other Minerals Mining and Processing		
制造业	**Manufacturing**		
农副食品加工业	Food Processing	51	188.08
食品制造业	Food Production	10	37.01
酒、饮料和精制茶制造业	Wine,Beverage and Refined Tea Production	11	48.77
烟草制品业	Tobacco Processing	5	610.62
纺织业	Textile Industry	18	62.82
纺织服装、服饰业	Textile,Garments, and Fashion Industry	8	21.47
皮革、毛皮、羽毛及其制品和制鞋业	Leather, Furs,Down and Related Products	1	2.63
木材加工和木、竹、藤、棕、草制品业	Timber Processing, Wood, Bamboo, Cane, Palm and Sraw Products	5	13.42
家具制造业	Furniture Manufacturing	1	0.79
造纸和纸制品业	Papermaking and Paper Products	2	10.20
印刷和记录媒介复制业	Printing and Record Processing	14	32.10
文教、工美、体育和娱乐用品制造业	Stationery, Education and Sports Goods	2	0.82
石油加工、炼焦和核燃料加工业	Petroleum Processing, Coking Products and Nuclear Fuel Processing	6	748.17
化学原料和化学制品制造业	Raw Chemical Material and Chemical Products	49	1096.92
医药制造业	Medical and pharmaceutical Products	16	58.97
化学纤维制造业	Chemical Fibers	1	0.83
橡胶和塑料制品业	Rubber and plastic products	10	77.09
非金属矿物制品业	Nonmetal Material Products	60	160.70
黑色金属冶炼和压延加工业	Smelting and Pressing of Ferrous Metals	15	1495.66
有色金属冶炼和压延加工业	Smelting and Pressing of Nonferrous Metals	5	369.19
金属制品业	Metal Products	29	160.16
通用设备制造业	Ordinary Machinery Manufacturing	37	283.24
专用设备制造业	Special Purpose Equipment Manufacturing	28	189.26
汽车制造业	Motor manufacturing	78	2744.64
铁路、船舶、航空航天和其他运输设备制造业	Railway,Watercraft,Aviation and other Transporlation Equipment manufacturing	28	429.73
电气机械和器材制造业	Electric Machinery and Equipment	26	296.69
计算机、通信和其他电子设备制造业	Telecommunication Computer,Equipment and Other Electronic Equipment Manufacturing	30	564.82
仪器仪表制造业	Instruments and Meters, Manufacturing	15	31.31
其他制造业	Other Manufacturing	4	25.60
废弃资源综合利用业	Waste Comprehensive Vtilization of Resources Industry	3	10.01
金属制品、机械和设备修理业	Metal products,Machinery and Equipment Repairing	3	4.37
电力、燃气及水的生产和供应业	**Electric Power, Gas and Water Production and Supply**		
电力、热力生产和供应业	Electric Power, Steam and Hot Water Production and Supply	83	1402.15
燃气生产和供应业	Gas Production and Supply	10	52.06
水的生产和供应业	Tap Water Production and Supply	48	38.26

THE NUMBER OF STATE-OWNED SHARE HOLDING INDUSTRIAL ENTERPRISES AND THEIR TOTAL OUTPUT OF PRODUCTION AND SALES (2014)

(100 million yuan)

工业销售产值(当年价格) Output Value of Industrial Products Sales (current price)	出口交货值 Delivery Value for Export	资产总计 Total Assets	流动资产合计 Circulating Funds	固定资产合计 Total Fined Assets	固定资产原价 Original Value of Fixed Assets	主营业务收入 Revenue of Major Business	全部从业人员年平均人数(万人) Average Number of Empolyment of the Curreat Year(10 000 Bersons)
11198.49	**358.58**	**14805.00**	**5592.96**	**6374.69**	**10076.67**	**11852.84**	**83.27**
1365.23	34.86	1339.38	497.40	600.99	1099.36	1279.57	13.39
3049.40	119.70	5417.81	1263.26	3151.59	5067.22	3139.20	27.32
162.51	19.28	199.43	99.46	71.33	115.13	156.60	2.89
1289.59	24.65	1216.83	720.29	266.97	466.47	1242.51	10.13
9908.90	333.93	13588.17	4872.66	6107.73	9610.20	10610.33	73.13
9488.39	333.80	12234.42	4538.58	5241.11	8480.50	10117.24	65.26
1024.63	19.57	1549.55	715.55	559.40	883.24	1056.06	12.10
685.47	5.21	1021.03	338.82	574.18	712.93	679.55	5.91
5.86		12.93	8.20	4.16	5.20	4.52	0.58
75.82	0.62	117.12	5.78	103.43	299.39	75.97	1.82
52.01		30.35	10.07	15.38	31.96	52.31	0.35
11.39		18.02	4.65	3.66	10.17	11.50	0.23
11.72		26.84	12.33	6.17	3.83	11.31	0.18
67.11	0.10	78.81	32.99	35.13	52.88	72.48	1.82
184.34	0.21	57.70	37.58	16.82	28.00	177.34	0.71
35.36	5.38	68.68	33.46	17.78	41.02	50.94	0.56
47.46		30.06	16.40	10.82	19.90	36.95	0.70
570.91	1.26	393.44	308.96	29.03	80.80	555.69	0.70
58.76	2.30	44.34	25.19	14.75	34.52	61.51	1.03
17.67	4.77	54.02	42.67	5.78	6.07	17.54	0.94
2.36		0.04	0.03	0.01	0.02	2.60	0.01
13.09		8.19	4.04	2.14	2.62	12.98	0.11
0.79		0.85	0.65	0.18	0.12	0.79	0.01
10.21		29.40	15.90	11.17	15.60	9.39	0.08
28.97		29.89	19.10	8.07	18.07	24.08	0.36
0.76		0.72	0.50	0.11	0.16	0.76	0.02
739.68		151.99	60.12	91.82	155.96	750.85	0.75
1066.39	68.98	1324.69	391.56	665.23	886.62	1107.04	5.03
55.77	3.08	86.96	41.44	27.74	34.88	66.00	0.96
0.83		5.49	3.20	0.56	1.54	0.99	0.06
76.10	0.16	64.09	47.39	13.86	20.53	69.67	0.55
154.00	1.89	170.77	59.92	75.22	108.15	148.85	1.44
1487.35	41.22	2412.68	667.58	1035.26	1929.29	1631.39	12.09
369.56	27.52	354.07	198.73	89.51	136.00	976.54	1.78
152.41	8.04	291.63	212.25	48.90	73.53	154.76	1.85
282.11	8.03	332.15	173.99	127.32	152.98	246.62	2.83
171.47	21.30	203.37	142.19	52.18	75.43	152.43	2.13
2658.85	28.09	2875.11	1531.64	469.61	840.19	2647.38	15.46
408.52	60.56	626.55	376.86	147.27	188.74	364.44	5.20
295.74	12.02	286.07	184.40	82.21	109.23	292.70	2.37
537.86	62.12	773.22	557.18	130.09	266.34	509.65	5.78
30.20	0.91	65.16	27.49	28.19	31.51	28.15	0.64
20.50		26.63	17.73	5.32	9.97	20.40	0.52
9.97		4.22	3.53	0.27	0.47	9.35	0.05
4.22		1.63	0.97	0.60	0.95	4.37	0.11
1394.07		3402.79	218.78	2888.99	4243.29	1397.81	11.38
51.54		89.84	18.30	35.05	45.36	57.68	0.36
36.76	0.01	254.49	79.18	74.91	115.40	37.10	1.69

13–5 集体工业企业单位数和主要经济指标（2014）

单位：亿元

项 目	Item	企业单位数(个) Number of Enterprises (unit)	工业总产值(当年价格 Total Output Value (current price)
总 计	**Total**	**337**	**988.99**
在总计中：	Of the Total:		
亏损企业	Enterprises running under Deficit	46	122.83
在总计中：	Of the Total:		
农村工业	Rural Industry	25	83.03
在总计中：	Of the Total:		
轻工业	Light Industry	74	361.31
重工业	Heavy Industry	263	627.68
在总计中：	Of the Total:		
大型企业	Large Scale Enterprises	16	443.71
中型企业	Medium Scale Enterprises	70	249.31
小型企业	Small Enterprises	251	295.97
按行业分	Grouped by sector		
采矿业	**Mining and Qarrying**		
煤炭开采和洗选业	Coal Mining and Processing	7	16.10
石油和天然气开采业	Petroleum and Natural Gas Extraction		
黑色金属矿采选业	Ferrous Metals Mining and Processing	11	105.42
有色金属矿采选业	Non-ferrous Metals Mining and Processing	1	0.59
非金属矿采选业	Non-metal Minerals Mining and Processing	34	70.16
开采辅助活动	Mining Auxiliary Activities		
其他采矿业	Other Minerals Mining and Processing	1	0.63
制造业	**Manufacturing**		
农副食品加工业	Food Processing	9	72.72
食品制造业	Food Production	4	4.50
酒、饮料和精制茶制造业	Wine,Beverage and Refined Tea Production	9	30.20
烟草制品业	Tobacco Processing		
纺织业	Textile Industry	8	23.18
纺织服装、服饰业	Textile,Garments, and Fashion Industry	8	13.50
皮革、毛皮、羽毛及其制品和制鞋业	Leather, Furs,Down and Related Products		
木材加工和木、竹、藤、棕、草制品业	Timber Processing, Wood, Bamboo, Cane, Palm and Sraw Products	1	11.48
家具制造业	Furniture Manufacturing	1	0.32
造纸和纸制品业	Papermaking and Paper Products	5	72.44
印刷和记录媒介复制业	Printing and Record Processing	5	4.76
文教、工美、体育和娱乐用品制造业	Stationery, Education and Sports Goods	1	0.31
石油加工、炼焦和核燃料加工业	Petroleum Processing, Coking Products and Nuclear Fuel Processing	1	1.00
化学原料和化学制品制造业	Raw Chemical Material and Chemical Products	20	34.44
医药制造业	Medical and pharmaceutical Products	6	23.72
化学纤维制造业	Chemical Fibers		
橡胶和塑料制品业	Rubber and plastic products	13	12.41
非金属矿物制品业	Nonmetal Material Products	32	57.37
黑色金属冶炼和压延加工业	Smelting and Pressing of Ferrous Metals	12	12.48
有色金属冶炼和压延加工业	Smelting and Pressing of Nonferrous Metals	9	7.68
金属制品业	Metal Products	18	14.05
通用设备制造业	Ordinary Machinery Manufacturing	19	26.82
专用设备制造业	Special Purpose Equipment Manufacturing	9	51.93
汽车制造业	Motor manufacturing	30	148.01
铁路、船舶、航空航天和其他运输设备制造业	Railway,Watercraft,Aviation and other Transporlation Equipment manufacturing	4	6.15
电气机械和器材制造业	Electric Machinery and Equipment	21	117.23
计算机、通信和其他电子设备制造业	Telecommunication Computer,Equipment and Other Electronic Equipment Manufacturing	4	4.41
仪器仪表制造业	Instruments and Meters, Manufacturing	3	0.82
其他制造业	Other Manufacturing	4	26.19
废弃资源综合利用业	Waste Comprehensive Vtilization of Resources Industry	10	6.67
金属制品、机械和设备修理业	Metal products,Machinery and Equipment Repairing	6	5.09
电力、燃气及水的生产和供应业	**Electric Power, Gas and Water Production and Supply**		
电力、热力生产和供应业	Electric Power, Steam and Hot Water Production and Supply	4	1.92
燃气生产和供应业	Gas Production and Supply	1	1.22
水的生产和供应业	Tap Water Production and Supply	6	3.08

THE NUMBER OF COLLECTIVE-OWNED INDUSTRIAL ENTERPRISES(2014)

(100 million yuan)

工业销售产值(当年价格) Output Value of Industrial Products Sales (current price)	出口交货值 Delivery Value for Export	资产总计 Total Assets	流动资产合计 Circulating Funds	固定资产合计 Total Fined Assets	固定资产原价 Original Value of Fixed Assets	主营业务收入 Revenue of Major Business	全部从业人员年平均人数(万人) Average Number of Empolyment of the Curreat Year (10 000 Bersons)
977.62	**41.94**	**638.11**	**385.27**	**168.51**	**559.16**	**934.43**	**11.32**
119.51	10.77	134.18	82.30	32.86	49.67	116.67	2.19
79.72		35.71	17.57	9.39	65.83	79.44	0.72
342.64	14.73	196.41	108.40	66.88	342.61	318.40	3.35
634.98	27.22	441.70	276.87	101.63	216.55	616.03	7.97
452.26	30.39	288.74	187.93	63.44	308.13	424.06	3.66
240.19	5.17	158.65	87.51	49.83	171.00	238.26	4.39
285.17	6.38	190.72	109.84	55.24	80.03	272.11	3.27
16.11		4.77	1.82	2.95	3.80	16.11	0.31
103.04		21.89	14.60	6.92	20.51	103.32	0.78
0.59		0.08	0.05	0.01	0.03	0.55	0.01
69.17		49.39	22.48	13.13	13.67	64.66	0.71
0.63		0.69	0.52	0.16	0.23	0.33	0.02
70.28	0.58	10.62	5.67	3.74	132.86	69.44	0.38
4.35		1.91	0.92	0.68	1.06	3.83	0.06
29.78		8.34	4.47	3.25	4.77	28.63	0.16
22.44	0.35	21.35	9.75	9.28	12.78	20.60	0.58
13.45		4.83	3.22	1.28	0.70	13.50	0.17
11.45		3.65	1.21	2.45	4.29	11.47	0.19
0.26		0.58	0.11	0.44	0.44	0.29	0.03
66.31		9.52	5.81	3.67	137.39	63.44	0.25
4.67		6.43	2.18	1.74	3.56	5.42	0.11
0.26	0.01	0.33	0.19	0.11	0.10	0.26	0.01
1.00		1.35	0.58	0.31	0.44	0.46	0.02
33.17	5.92	18.21	11.08	5.46	8.83	31.12	0.39
21.94	11.26	18.66	7.41	10.70	14.52	21.29	0.32
11.81		8.47	4.85	2.19	2.92	11.24	0.25
56.31	0.61	20.12	10.44	8.47	11.22	56.37	0.63
12.10		9.31	4.23	2.57	12.24	12.11	0.39
7.67		6.16	3.97	1.66	1.70	8.29	0.17
13.69	0.24	10.84	8.78	1.29	2.59	13.39	0.43
25.86		18.80	10.40	4.62	6.55	24.36	0.42
48.97	0.61	62.45	46.45	10.02	66.42	42.35	0.42
167.29	19.42	152.61	105.10	24.22	42.32	158.58	1.50
5.88		2.60	1.65	0.89	1.12	4.15	0.14
110.52	2.95	82.16	50.94	18.35	19.48	93.35	0.93
4.01		9.37	4.50	1.22	1.59	4.08	0.11
0.82		0.95	0.79	0.11	0.23	0.80	0.05
26.14		47.75	28.90	16.57	18.19	26.02	0.53
6.59		7.87	4.97	2.42	3.23	13.32	0.36
4.89		5.44	4.73	0.20	0.57	4.73	0.43
1.91		7.46	1.72	5.38	6.14	2.34	0.05
1.22		1.36	0.47	0.89	1.05	1.22	0.01
3.02		1.79	0.30	1.17	1.62	2.98	0.03

13-6 外商投资和港澳台商投资工业企业单位数和主要经济指标（2014）

单位：亿元

项 目	Item	企业单位数(个) Number of Enterprises (unit)
总计		**626**
在总计中：	Of the Total:	
亏损企业	Enterprises running under Deficit	113
在总计中：	Of the Total:	
港、澳、台商投资企业	Hongkong, Macao and Taiwan Funded Enterprises	284
合资经营企业(港或澳、台资)	Joint Venture with Hongkong, Macao and Taiwan	77
合作经营企业(港或澳、台资)	Cooperate with Hongkong, Macao and Taiwan Funded	2
港澳台商独资经营企业	Enterprises Solely Funded by Hongkong, Macao and Taiwan Businessmen	188
港澳台商投资股份有限公司	Share Holding Co.Ltd.With Hongkong,Macao and Taiwan Businessmen	15
其他港澳台投资	Othes	2
外商投资企业	Foreign Funded Enterprises	327
中外合资经营企业	Sino - Foreign Joint Funded Enterprises	113
中外合作经营企业	Sino - Foreign Cooperative Funded Enterprises	3
外资企业	Foreign Solely Funded Enterprises	197
外商投资股份有限公司	Foreign Funded Share Holding Co.Ltd.	12
其他外商投资	Othes	2
在总计中：	Of the Total:	
国有控股企业	State-Owned Share Holding Enterprises	
在总计中：	Of the Total:	
农村工业	Rural Industry	1
在总计中：	Of the Total:	
轻工业	Light Industry	275
重工业	Heavy Industry	351
在总计中：	Of the Total:	
大型企业	Large Scale Enterprises	
中型企业	Medium Scale Enterprises	54
小型企业	Small Enterprises	167
按行业分	Grouped by sector	405
采矿业	**Mining and Oarrying**	
煤炭开采和洗选业	Coal Mining and Processing	1
石油和天然气开采业	Petroleum and Natural Gas Extraction	
黑色金属矿采选业	Ferrous Metals Mining and Processing	
有色金属矿采选业	Non-ferrous Metals Mining and Processing	
非金属矿采选业	Non-metal Minerals Mining and Processing	2
开采辅助活动	Mining Auxiliary Activities	
其他采矿业	Other Minerals Mining and Processing	
制造业	**Manufacturing**	
农副食品加工业	Food Processing	31
食品制造业	Food Production	25
酒、饮料和精制茶制造业	Wine,Beverage and Refined Tea Production	25
烟草制品业	Tobacco Processing	
纺织业	Textile Industry	39
纺织服装、服饰业	Textile,Garments, and Fashion Industry	34
皮革、毛皮、羽毛及其制品和制鞋业	Leather, Furs,Down and Related Products	12
木材加工和木、竹、藤、棕、草制品业	Timber Processing, Wood, Bamboo, Cane, Palm and Sraw Products	4
家具制造业	Furniture Manufacturing	4
造纸和纸制品业	Papermaking and Paper Products	18
印刷和记录媒介复制业	Printing and Record Processing	7
文教、工美、体育和娱乐用品制造业	Stationery, Education and Sports Goods	7
石油加工、炼焦和核燃料加工业	Petroleum Processing, Coking Products and Nuclear Fuel Processing	3
化学原料和化学制品制造业	Raw Chemical Material and Chemical Products	33
医药制造业	Medical and pharmaceutical Products	26
化学纤维制造业	Chemical Fibers	2
橡胶和塑料制品业	Rubber and plastic products	24
非金属矿物制品业	Nonmetal Material Products	32
黑色金属冶炼和压延加工业	Smelting and Pressing of Ferrous Metals	5
有色金属冶炼和压延加工业	Smelting and Pressing of Nonferrous Metals	2
金属制品业	Metal Products	18
通用设备制造业	Ordinary Machinery Manufacturing	25
专用设备制造业	Special Purpose Equipment Manufacturing	13
汽车制造业	Motor manufacturing	122
铁路、船舶、航空航天和其他运输设备制	Railway,Watercraft,Aviation and other Transporlation Equipment manufacturing	3
电气机械和器材制造业	Electric Machinery and Equipment	43
计算机、通信和其他电子设备制造业	Telecommunication Computer,Equipment and Other Electronic Equipment Manufacturing	29
仪器仪表制造业	Instruments and Meters, Manufacturing	7
其他制造业	Other Manufacturing	1
废弃资源综合利用业	Waste Comprehensive Vtilization of Resources Industry	1
金属制品、机械和设备修理业	Metal products,Machinery and Equipment Repairing	
电力、燃气及水的生产和供应业	**Electric Power, Gas and Water Production and Supply**	
电力、热力生产和供应业	Electric Power, Steam and Hot Water Production and Supply	8
燃气生产和供应业	Gas Production and Supply	17
水的生产和供应业	Tap Water Production and Supply	3

THE NUMBER OF FOREIGN FUNDED AND HONGKONG MACO AND TAIWAN FUNDED INDUSTRIAL ENTERPRISES AND THEIR TOTAL OUTPUT OF PRODUCTION AND SALES (2014)

(100 million yuan)

工业总产值(当年价格) Total Output Value (current price)	工业销售产值(当年价格) Output Value of Industrial Products Sales (current price)	出口交货值 Delivery Value for Export	资产总计 Total Assets	流动资产合计 Circulating Funds	固定资产合计 Total Fined Assets	固定资产原价 Original Value of Fixed Assets	主营业务收入 Revenue of Major Business	全部从业人员年平均人数(万人) Average Number of Empolyment of the Curreat Year (10 000 Bersons)
3357.18	**3145.99**	**252.21**	**2551.19**	**1219.56**	**1051.81**	**1597.90**	**3021.24**	**30.63**
297.38	277.28	16.52	319.44	143.05	139.77	204.19	267.61	4.66
1609.72	1464.99	154.57	1025.88	472.08	459.66	682.92	1383.53	14.64
798.00	676.39	60.71	502.95	245.11	223.01	316.34	651.07	6.08
2.40	2.07		0.45	0.28	0.17	0.20	2.08	0.02
739.93	718.54	79.67	458.04	194.59	214.54	336.88	666.89	7.86
56.89	55.79	14.19	59.98	29.46	20.78	28.11	54.82	0.65
12.50	12.21		4.45	2.64	1.16	1.39	8.68	0.02
1729.90	1663.57	96.65	1500.15	737.88	579.67	897.30	1620.81	15.78
670.36	626.66	20.55	486.96	250.58	190.54	300.45	600.34	5.15
28.62	28.15		5.45	1.87	2.50	6.05	27.77	0.13
797.02	774.08	75.78	710.00	405.08	222.96	339.77	776.97	8.66
232.99	233.87		296.29	79.28	163.45	250.72	214.92	1.81
0.92	0.81	0.32	1.45	1.08	0.21	0.31	0.81	0.02
5.90	4.93		3.68	3.37	0.31	0.68	6.64	0.02
1224.40	1154.00	109.67	737.20	382.25	264.92	430.22	1090.33	14.37
2132.78	1991.99	142.54	1813.99	837.30	786.89	1167.68	1930.91	16.25
1477.96	1343.64	142.87	1086.28	485.28	477.14	711.10	1304.07	15.71
1167.28	1111.39	68.77	859.93	444.94	331.03	543.30	1063.12	9.94
711.94	690.95	40.57	604.99	289.33	243.65	343.50	654.06	4.98
0.26	0.26		0.72	0.38	0.34	0.39	0.26	0.05
0.73	0.72		0.70	0.57	0.11	0.02	0.52	0.01
217.33	193.82	3.18	81.49	42.38	28.87	42.51	168.07	0.85
163.67	158.13	4.00	77.24	27.87	31.36	66.20	149.36	1.23
247.94	227.10		202.80	114.20	65.48	114.93	221.69	1.85
102.65	98.50	22.11	57.27	24.20	26.37	39.77	94.93	1.49
95.08	91.11	28.54	38.07	22.72	11.55	15.50	87.45	2.02
26.29	26.25	10.81	18.01	5.54	10.42	12.12	21.98	1.82
4.34	4.15		2.46	1.11	1.19	1.48	2.80	0.12
7.06	6.79		2.81	1.67	0.92	1.17	5.34	0.08
49.26	46.62	0.07	37.38	19.49	14.58	19.39	47.28	0.53
17.48	16.07		16.59	11.36	4.00	11.03	15.61	0.19
11.78	11.50	1.23	12.09	7.43	3.29	9.75	11.70	0.33
51.94	51.27		23.93	5.79	15.45	20.47	19.07	0.07
93.51	87.16	12.91	87.24	35.71	40.57	54.73	91.84	1.00
122.05	117.70	19.08	92.13	44.05	38.95	49.11	111.29	2.28
13.14	12.79	1.22	10.41	3.75	6.25	10.25	11.88	0.08
43.78	42.62	0.07	48.62	26.80	12.13	17.61	40.56	0.50
247.10	250.11	1.81	365.00	105.82	203.82	304.87	234.01	2.12
182.02	181.82	28.31	148.10	56.85	81.75	133.47	171.08	0.76
30.20	29.97	0.29	13.03	3.87	5.40	6.13	23.17	0.15
72.17	71.03	0.52	56.89	19.05	33.84	51.11	67.50	0.27
56.70	55.79	4.42	62.10	36.95	16.63	21.99	53.34	0.58
31.63	31.11	8.37	39.16	19.36	7.79	11.76	33.64	0.76
564.03	549.03	12.47	464.94	291.49	124.83	195.09	550.14	5.00
4.57	4.52	0.28	5.27	4.59	0.61	1.32	5.44	0.04
250.24	244.88	21.49	176.43	94.76	73.94	118.60	237.88	2.17
511.11	396.88	68.88	198.46	141.17	45.11	69.59	404.33	3.40
11.78	11.48	2.15	5.77	3.10	1.95	2.66	11.12	0.39
			0.45	0.09	0.24	0.25	0.04	0.01
16.77	16.29		4.94	4.17	0.14	0.16	14.28	
76.30	76.30		147.68	24.50	119.87	166.34	75.77	0.11
32.27	32.20		37.89	13.93	18.96	21.52	35.81	0.27
2.02	2.02		15.11	4.83	5.09	6.64	2.06	0.08

13-7 私营工业企业单位数和主要经济指标（2014）

单位：亿元

项 目	Item	企业单位数(个) Number of Enterprises (unit)	工业总产值(当年价格) Total Output Value (current price)
总计		**13367**	**25057.24**
在总计中：	Of the Total:		
亏损企业	Enterprises running under Deficit	869	1174.01
在总计中：	Of the Total:		
轻工业	Light Industry	5554	11637.13
重工业	Heavy Industry	7813	13420.11
在总计中：	Of the Total:		
大型企业	Large Scale Enterprises		
中型企业	Medium Scale Enterprises	142	3603.40
小型企业	Small Enterprises	1341	6439.24
按行业分	Grouped by Sector	11884	15014.60
采矿业	**Mining and Qarrying**		
煤炭开采和洗选业	Coal Mining and Processing	118	84.09
石油和天然气开采业	Petroleum and Natural Gas Extraction		
黑色金属矿采选业	Ferrous Metals Mining and Processing	110	254.27
有色金属矿采选业	Non-ferrous Metals Mining and Processing	38	40.41
非金属矿采选业	Non-metal Minerals Mining and Processing	361	466.71
开采辅助活动	Mining Auxiliary Activities	2	1.57
其他采矿业	Other Minerals Mining and Processing	1	0.93
制造业	**Manufacturing**		
农副食品加工业	Food Processing	1582	3900.57
食品制造业	Food Production	341	746.56
酒、饮料和精制茶制造业	Wine,Beverage and Refined Tea Production	377	1186.37
烟草制品业	Tobacco Processing	1	1.83
纺织业	Textile Industry	928	1897.84
纺织服装、服饰业	Textile,Garments, and Fashion Industry	469	734.77
皮革、毛皮、羽毛及其制品和制鞋业	Leather, Furs,Down and Related Products	145	151.12
木材加工和木、竹、藤、棕、草制品业	Timber Processing, Wood, Bamboo, Cane, Palm and Sraw Products	243	374.69
家具制造业	Furniture Manufacturing	114	143.93
造纸和纸制品业	Papermaking and Paper Products	229	364.35
印刷和记录媒介复制业	Printing and Record Processing	182	273.84
文教、工美、体育和娱乐用品制造业	Stationery, Education and Sports Goods	90	126.74
石油加工、炼焦和核燃料加工业	Petroleum Processing, Coking Products and Nuclear Fuel Processing	34	124.06
化学原料和化学制品制造业	Raw Chemical Material and Chemical Products	933	2449.59
医药制造业	Medical and pharmaceutical Products	302	645.41
化学纤维制造业	Chemical Fibers	16	60.15
橡胶和塑料制品业	Rubber and plastic products	534	912.04
非金属矿物制品业	Nonmetal Material Products	1728	2420.22
黑色金属冶炼和压延加工业	Smelting and Pressing of Ferrous Metals	300	819.10
有色金属冶炼和压延加工业	Smelting and Pressing of Nonferrous Metals	141	497.33
金属制品业	Metal Products	649	1125.13
通用设备制造业	Ordinary Machinery Manufacturing	589	805.60
专用设备制造业	Special Purpose Equipment Manufacturing	544	758.65
汽车制造业	Motor manufacturing	1102	1652.68
铁路、船舶、航空航天和其他运输设备制造业	Railway,Watercraft,Aviation and other Transporlation Equipment manufacturing	123	203.21
电气机械和器材制造业	Electric Machinery and Equipment	517	989.71
计算机、通信和其他电子设备制造业	Telecommunication Computer,Equipment and Other Electronic Equipment Manufacturing	217	415.32
仪器仪表制造业	Instruments and Meters, Manufacturing	88	107.91
其他制造业	Other Manufacturing	69	107.67
废弃资源综合利用业	Waste Comprehensive Vtilization of Resources Industry	35	93.94
金属制品、机械和设备修理业	Metal products,Machinery and Equipment Repairing	12	27.41
电力、燃气及水的生产和供应业	**Electric Power, Gas and Water Production and Supply**		
电力、热力生产和供应业	Electric Power, Steam and Hot Water Production and Su	54	50.50
燃气生产和供应业	Gas Production and Supply	25	28.53
水的生产和供应业	Tap Water Production and Supply	24	12.52

THE NUMBER OF PRIVATE-OWNED INDUSTRIAL ENTERPRISES AND THEIR MAJOR ECONOMIC INDICATORS (2014)

(100 million yuan)

工业销售产值(当年价格) Output Value of Industrial Products Sales(current price)	出口交货值 Delivery Value for Export	资产总计 Total Assets	流动资产合计 Circulating Funds	固定资产合计 Total Fined Assets	固定资产原价 Original Value of Fixed Assets	主营业务收入 Revenue of Major Business	全部从业人员年平均人数(万人) Average Number of Empolyment of the Curreat Year (10 000 Bersons)
24291.44	**662.16**	**12579.55**	**6389.56**	**4339.95**	**9007.56**	**23312.98**	**211.94**
1112.16	22.46	1560.44	812.98	447.58	708.07	965.15	13.87
11272.37	524.15	5112.10	2596.38	1764.30	4092.89	10930.96	104.95
13019.07	138.01	7467.45	3793.18	2575.65	4914.67	12382.03	106.99
3526.00	161.42	2127.45	1175.79	673.95	1592.02	3316.39	31.63
6212.02	257.83	3247.35	1728.76	1098.68	2277.75	5981.37	65.02
14553.42	242.91	7204.75	3485.01	2567.31	5137.79	14015.22	115.29
82.90		55.01	16.50	23.95	28.50	80.96	2.07
245.54		89.54	37.23	41.93	49.60	240.01	1.36
39.12		23.22	12.61	9.75	14.94	35.83	0.39
453.77		266.71	134.12	80.85	169.23	425.46	3.72
1.57		0.30	0.20	0.10	0.11	1.50	0.01
0.93		0.27	0.05	0.09	0.12	0.68	0.02
3781.79	117.03	1329.71	646.02	502.26	1676.59	3682.03	21.60
722.48	52.20	300.73	134.48	128.46	319.17	713.26	7.50
1158.86	7.56	762.17	477.39	171.60	288.26	1106.70	8.52
2.23		12.75	9.12	2.67	5.98	2.74	0.15
1846.87	108.40	702.35	320.52	298.75	613.19	1811.30	23.35
715.39	84.73	343.07	195.43	109.84	218.43	685.61	13.17
147.48	46.11	68.51	37.18	21.14	48.60	143.77	2.14
357.03	2.51	177.58	67.29	73.47	146.29	345.21	3.49
138.47	0.18	82.13	35.23	29.44	50.81	135.04	1.55
351.19	0.26	182.22	84.65	73.38	139.40	338.97	3.28
259.89	2.11	133.79	69.40	45.27	88.84	252.49	2.61
123.30	18.07	57.53	31.63	13.57	44.46	119.59	1.47
115.59		50.80	28.04	16.51	21.50	124.68	0.35
2397.82	35.10	1275.02	612.97	468.65	1226.12	2326.17	14.61
607.94	43.87	456.13	224.37	139.27	196.19	598.86	6.19
58.86	0.17	20.68	9.74	6.66	13.80	58.81	0.44
889.03	5.61	373.18	183.37	140.38	335.80	880.84	8.39
2345.62	24.68	1182.63	527.58	461.32	749.34	2229.75	21.25
803.70	4.61	498.67	243.93	102.10	275.18	752.09	4.59
485.58	2.69	158.37	78.81	59.12	88.65	468.65	2.58
1082.93	7.37	575.07	309.77	194.26	346.02	1012.63	8.84
773.66	7.15	440.30	241.15	143.94	329.03	739.50	7.10
736.61	3.46	606.21	361.28	188.33	371.46	671.11	6.89
1617.52	12.44	1021.54	521.53	381.78	505.77	1507.79	14.76
194.30	1.27	110.87	58.57	38.70	54.43	184.26	2.16
952.92	22.16	508.15	297.87	149.63	234.63	872.41	8.55
390.20	46.87	336.40	211.83	70.39	109.50	363.69	4.80
101.87	1.36	86.99	52.63	21.26	39.65	98.29	1.50
103.60	3.44	68.25	31.34	15.48	27.79	101.18	1.00
91.56		48.81	33.39	10.90	14.67	89.16	0.32
24.37	0.73	13.41	8.36	3.99	6.99	23.76	0.30
49.14		112.90	25.66	78.92	128.44	46.40	0.46
28.00		31.65	13.77	12.34	14.20	29.24	0.22
11.81		15.92	4.54	9.52	15.91	12.57	0.23

13-8 大中型工业企业单位数和产销总值（2014）

单位:亿元

项　目	Item	企业单位数(个) Number of Enterprises (unit)
总　　计	**Total**	**2282**
一、按登记注册类型分组:	**Grouped by Type of Registration**	
内资企业	Inner Funded Enterprises	1963
国有企业	State Owned Enterprises	65
中央企业	Central Enterprises	29
地方企业	Local Enterprises	36
集体企业	Collective-owned Enterprise	18
股份合作企业	Share Holding Cooperative Enterprises	
联营企业	Joint Owned Enterprise	2
国有联营企业	State Joint Ownership	
集体联营企业	Collective Joint Ownership	
国有与集体联营企业	Joint State- Collective Ownership	1
其他联营企业	Other Joint Owned Enterprise	1
有限责任公司	Responsibility Co. Ltd	843
国有独资公司	State Solely Funded Co.	60
其他有限责任公司	Others	783
股份有限公司	Share Holding Co.Ltd.	218
私营企业	Private - owned enterprises	813
私营独资企业	Solely Private - owned enterprises	16
私营合作企业	Private Joint Venture	3
私营有限责任公司	Private Responsibility Co. Ltd	725
私营股份有限公司	Private Share Holding Co.Ltd.	69
其他企业	Others	4
港、澳、台商投资企业	Hongkong, Macao and Taiwan Funded Enterprises	139
合资经营企业(港或澳、台资)	Joint Venture with Hongkong, Macao and Taiwan	70
合作经营企业(港或澳、台资)	Cooperate with Hongkong, Macao and Taiwan Funded	1
港澳台商独资经营企业	Enterprises Solely Funded by Hongkong, Macao and Taiwan Businessmen	63
港澳台商投资股份有限公司	Share Holding Co.Ltd. With Hongkong, Macao and Taiwan Investment	5
其他港澳台投资	Others	
外商投资企业	Foreign Funded Enterprises	180
中外合资经营企业	Sino - Foreign Joint Funded Enterprises	100
中外合作经营企业	Sino - Foreign Cooperative Funded Enterprises	3
外资企业	Foreign Solely Funded Enterprises	70
外商投资股份有限公司	Foreign Funded Share Holding Co.Ltd.	7
其他外商投资	Others	
二、在总计中:亏损企业	**Of the Total: enterprises running under deficit**	**250**
在总计中:国有控股企业	Of the Total: State-Owned Share Holding Enterprises	318
在总计中:农村工业	Of the Total: Rural Industry	11
在总计中:轻工业	Of the Total: Light Industry	1117
重工业	Heavy Industry	1165
在总计中:大型企业	Of the Total: Large Scale Enterprises	349
中型企业	Medium Scale Enterprises	1933
按行业分	Grouped by Sector	
采矿业	**Mining and Qarrying**	

NUMBER OF LARGE AND MEDIUM SCALE INDUSTRIAL ENTERPRISES AND THEIR TOTAL VALUE OF PRODUCTION AND SALES (2014)

(100 million yuan)

工业总产值(当年价格) Total Output Value (current price)	工业销售产值(当年价格) Output Value of Industrial Products Sales (current price)	出口交货值 Delivery Value for Export
25839.56	**25008.23**	**1137.51**
19941.85	19402.90	843.33
3177.94	3151.24	139.05
3053.42	3029.03	119.70
124.52	122.21	19.35
37.91	37.24	
10.73	10.64	
0.81	0.83	
9.92	9.81	
8306.71	8014.14	311.04
1880.51	1816.94	43.49
6426.20	6197.20	267.55
3637.88	3559.09	161.57
4745.95	4606.00	231.67
56.45	55.72	6.66
15.23	15.10	
4152.58	4035.91	206.87
521.68	499.27	18.14
24.75	24.56	
1689.02	1542.32	184.69
1064.39	936.72	100.75
4.26	4.18	
581.93	563.48	70.99
38.44	37.94	12.96
4208.69	4063.01	109.49
3365.11	3234.23	50.36
29.14	28.71	
590.17	574.57	59.12
224.27	225.50	
2624.78	**2532.19**	86.05
10776.90	10513.02	353.37
99.82	96.28	
8355.80	8009.96	526.86
17483.76	16998.27	610.65
16117.49	15656.00	736.58
9722.07	9352.23	400.93

13-8 续表1 continued

单位:亿元

项 目	Item	企业单位数(个) Number of Enterprises(unit)
煤炭开采和洗选业	Coal Mining and Processing	20
石油和天然气开采业	Petroleum and Natural Gas Extraction	1
黑色金属矿采选业	Ferrous Metals Mining and Processing	15
有色金属矿采选业	Non-ferrous Metals Mining and Processing	4
非金属矿采选业	Non-metal Minerals Mining and Processing	21
开采辅助活动	Mining Auxiliary Activities	3
其他采矿业	Other Minerals Mining and Processing	
制造业	**Manufacturing**	
农副食品加工业	Food Processing	158
食品制造业	Food Production	79
酒、饮料和精制茶制造业	Wine,Beverage and Refined Tea Production	59
烟草制品业	Tobacco Processing	2
纺织业	Textile Industry	289
纺织服装、服饰业	Textile,Garments, and Fashion Industry	170
皮革、毛皮、羽毛及其制品和制鞋业	Leather, Furs,Down and Related Products	19
木材加工和木、竹、藤、棕、草制品业	Timber Processing, Wood, Bamboo, Cane, Palm and Sraw Products	25
家具制造业	Furniture Manufacturing	10
造纸和纸制品业	Papermaking and Paper Products	36
印刷和记录媒介复制业	Printing and Record Processing	32
文教、工美、体育和娱乐用品制造业	Stationery, Education and Sports Goods	17
石油加工、炼焦和核燃料加工业	Petroleum Processing, Coking Products and Nuclear Fuel Processing	7
化学原料和化学制品制造业	Raw Chemical Material and Chemical Products	146
医药制造业	Medical and pharmaceutical Products	73
化学纤维制造业	Chemical Fibers	8
橡胶和塑料制品业	Rubber and plastic products	80
非金属矿物制品业	Nonmetal Material Products	177
黑色金属冶炼和压延加工业	Smelting and Pressing of Ferrous Metals	47
有色金属冶炼和压延加工业	Smelting and Pressing of Nonferrous Metals	38
金属制品业	Metal Products	72
通用设备制造业	Ordinary Machinery Manufacturing	75
专用设备制造业	Special Purpose Equipment Manufacturing	64
汽车制造业	Motor manufacturing	230
铁路、船舶、航空航天和其他运输设备制造业	Railway,Watercraft,Aviation and other Transporlation Equipment manufacturing	35
电气机械和器材制造业	Electric Machinery and Equipment	100
计算机、通信和其他电子设备制造业	Telecommunication Computer,Equipment and Other Electronic Equipment Manufacturing	71
仪器仪表制造业	Instruments and Meters, Manufacturing	18
其他制造业	Other Manufacturing	17
废弃资源综合利用业	Waste Comprehensive Vtilization of Resources Industry	6
金属制品、机械和设备修理业	Metal products,Machinery and Equipment Repairing	7
电力、燃气及水的生产和供应业	**Electric Power, Gas and Water Production and Supply**	
电力、热力生产和供应业	Electric Power, Steam and Hot Water Production and Supply	30
燃气生产和供应业	Gas Production and Supply	6
水的生产和供应业	Tap Water Production and Supply	15

(100 million yuan)

工业总产值(当年价格) Total Output Value	工业销售产值(当年价格) Output Value of Industrial Products Sales(current price)	出口交货值 Delivery Value for Export
33.31	32.88	
75.74	75.82	0.62
188.39	184.24	
13.69	13.57	
102.46	99.41	
67.05	67.11	0.10
1828.73	1747.20	86.09
531.14	510.57	55.16
1120.30	1085.16	0.12
600.37	560.54	1.26
1294.13	1262.20	115.99
545.08	526.68	109.23
56.36	55.92	14.45
135.73	128.32	
46.82	44.55	
270.02	253.87	0.13
137.67	124.49	2.11
52.38	50.27	10.08
858.52	848.38	
2368.88	2312.16	118.23
577.21	544.24	78.03
49.53	48.46	2.03
479.24	470.83	5.15
1030.04	1005.96	13.93
2154.59	2140.75	70.24
697.00	689.68	29.24
591.53	568.95	12.76
612.32	600.18	17.42
489.94	466.33	30.64
4037.77	3941.95	67.14
497.02	475.14	59.51
1126.68	1088.36	56.06
1527.98	1361.73	175.96
65.34	62.50	4.34
110.61	102.65	0.60
11.46	11.44	0.14
18.67	18.52	0.73
1363.00	1354.94	
50.70	50.71	
22.17	21.54	0.01

13-8 续表2 continued

单位:亿元

项 目	Item	资产总计 Total Assets
总 计	**Total**	**23286.26**
一、按登记注册类型分组:	Grouped by Type of Registration	
内资企业	Inner Funded Enterprises	19091.27
国有企业	State Owned Enterprises	5593.24
中央企业	Central Enterprises	5396.60
地方企业	Local Enterprises	196.64
集体企业	Collective-owned Enterprise	19.33
股份合作企业	Share Holding Cooperative Enterprises	
联营企业	Joint Owned Enterprise	1.40
国有联营企业	State Joint Ownership	
集体联营企业	Collective Joint Ownership	
国有与集体联营企业	Joint State- Collective Ownership	0.96
其他联营企业	Other Joint Owned Enterprise	0.44
有限责任公司	Responsibility Co. Ltd	6928.39
国有独资公司	State Solely Funded Co.	1912.04
其他有限责任公司	Others	5016.35
股份有限公司	Share Holding Co.Ltd.	4366.31
私营企业	Private - owned enterprises	2174.76
私营独资企业	Solely Private - owned enterprises	15.88
私营合作企业	Private Joint Venture	2.19
私营有限责任公司	Private Responsibility Co. Ltd	1942.54
私营股份有限公司	Private Share Holding Co.Ltd.	214.15
其他企业	Others	7.84
港、澳、台商投资企业	Hongkong, Macao and Taiwan Funded Enterprises	993.48
合资经营企业(港或澳、台资)	Joint Venture with Hongkong, Macao and Taiwan	627.87
合作经营企业(港或澳、台资)	Cooperate with Hongkong, Macao and Taiwan Funded	8.45
港澳台商独资经营企业	Enterprises Solely Funded by Hongkong, Macao and Taiwan Businessmen	306.86
港澳台商投资股份有限公司	Share Holding Co.Ltd. With Hongkong, Macao and Taiwan Investment	50.30
其他港澳台投资	Others	
外商投资企业	Foreign Funded Enterprises	3201.51
中外合资经营企业	Sino - Foreign Joint Funded Enterprises	2373.95
中外合作经营企业	Sino - Foreign Cooperative Funded Enterprises	4.96
外资企业	Foreign Solely Funded Enterprises	528.06
外商投资股份有限公司	Foreign Funded Share Holding Co.Ltd.	294.54
其他外商投资	Others	
二、在总计中:亏损企业	**Of the Total: enterprises running under deficit**	2433.27
在总计中:国有控股企业	Of the Total: State-Owned Share Holding Enterprises	13783.98
在总计中:农村工业	Of the Total: Rural Industry	35.02
在总计中:轻工业	Of the Total: Light Industry	4884.98
重工业	Heavy Industry	18401.28
在总计中:大型企业	Of the Total: Large Scale Enterprises	16801.15
中型企业	Medium Scale Enterprises	6485.11
按行业分	Grouped by Sector	
采矿业	**Mining and Qarrying**	

(100 million yuan)

流动资产合计 Circulating Funds	固定资产合计 Total Fined Assets	固定资产原价 Original Value of Fixed Assets	主营业务收入 Revenue of Major Business	全部从业人员年平均人数（万人） Average Number of Empolyment of the Curreat Year (10 000 Bersons)
10216.62	**8988.43**	**15849.10**	**25039.92**	**222.83**
8062.61	7475.11	13377.31	19585.49	182.91
1354.17	3212.12	5152.95	3239.85	29.76
1249.40	3144.44	5054.91	3121.36	27.14
104.78	67.69	98.04	118.49	2.62
9.79	6.44	17.23	39.49	1.04
1.16	0.20	0.46	10.31	0.09
0.79	0.14	0.38	0.83	0.04
0.37	0.06	0.07	9.48	0.05
3528.68	2375.78	4129.00	8475.30	74.01
964.52	599.74	967.96	1866.01	10.85
2564.16	1776.03	3161.04	6609.30	63.16
2041.88	1055.42	1951.87	3347.28	32.35
1121.94	822.45	2122.65	4448.70	45.53
9.61	5.34	9.36	56.41	0.80
1.33	0.84	1.16	15.08	0.11
1004.87	733.35	1970.25	3937.07	40.00
106.14	82.91	141.88	440.14	4.61
4.98	2.71	3.17	24.56	0.14
474.34	419.94	737.93	1483.87	15.55
318.01	253.89	459.97	925.79	8.47
2.23	1.59	4.38	4.18	0.06
127.26	148.47	250.50	515.95	6.48
26.85	15.99	23.08	37.96	0.54
1679.67	1093.38	1733.85	3970.56	24.38
1295.15	761.61	1215.60	3160.50	15.49
2.28	2.66	6.50	28.28	0.15
303.86	166.06	261.87	574.92	6.94
78.37	163.05	249.88	206.85	1.79
1171.95	879.12	1721.85	2345.50	26.04
5254.13	5800.51	9363.74	11173.29	77.36
20.11	9.06	87.49	93.67	0.74
2646.18	1531.66	3451.91	7747.79	85.09
7570.44	7456.77	12397.19	17292.12	137.74
6931.27	6730.48	11438.02	15963.28	122.93
3285.35	2257.95	4411.07	9076.63	99.90

13-8 续表3 continued

单位:亿元

项 目	Item	资产总计 Total Assets
煤炭开采和洗选业	Coal Mining and Processing	21.39
石油和天然气开采业	Petroleum and Natural Gas Extraction	117.12
黑色金属矿采选业	Ferrous Metals Mining and Processing	65.51
有色金属矿采选业	Non-ferrous Metals Mining and Processing	18.73
非金属矿采选业	Non-metal Minerals Mining and Processing	65.90
开采辅助活动	Mining Auxiliary Activities	78.81
其他采矿业	Other Minerals Mining and Processing	
制造业	**Manufacturing**	
农副食品加工业	Food Processing	691.77
食品制造业	Food Production	270.78
酒、饮料和精制茶制造业	Wine,Beverage and Refined Tea Production	808.95
烟草制品业	Tobacco Processing	390.02
纺织业	Textile Industry	530.44
纺织服装、服饰业	Textile,Garments, and Fashion Industry	351.02
皮革、毛皮、羽毛及其制品和制鞋业	Leather, Furs,Down and Related Products	35.61
木材加工和木、竹、藤、棕、草制品业	Timber Processing, Wood, Bamboo, Cane, Palm and Sraw Products	72.30
家具制造业	Furniture Manufacturing	36.55
造纸和纸制品业	Papermaking and Paper Products	166.90
印刷和记录媒介复制业	Printing and Record Processing	88.46
文教、工美、体育和娱乐用品制造业	Stationery, Education and Sports Goods	24.41
石油加工、炼焦和核燃料加工业	Petroleum Processing, Coking Products and Nuclear Fuel Processing	203.82
化学原料和化学制品制造业	Raw Chemical Material and Chemical Products	2041.02
医药制造业	Medical and pharmaceutical Products	566.64
化学纤维制造业	Chemical Fibers	37.70
橡胶和塑料制品业	Rubber and plastic products	252.86
非金属矿物制品业	Nonmetal Material Products	913.96
黑色金属冶炼和压延加工业	Smelting and Pressing of Ferrous Metals	2736.61
有色金属冶炼和压延加工业	Smelting and Pressing of Nonferrous Metals	450.09
金属制品业	Metal Products	583.29
通用设备制造业	Ordinary Machinery Manufacturing	984.09
专用设备制造业	Special Purpose Equipment Manufacturing	575.39
汽车制造业	Motor manufacturing	3899.75
铁路、船舶、航空航天和其他运输设备制造业	Railway,Watercraft,Aviation and other Transporlation Equipment manufacturing	643.28
电气机械和器材制造业	Electric Machinery and Equipment	740.94
计算机、通信和其他电子设备制造业	Telecommunication Computer,Equipment and Other Electronic Equipment Manufacturing	1263.26
仪器仪表制造业	Instruments and Meters, Manufacturing	92.51
其他制造业	Other Manufacturing	125.38
废弃资源综合利用业	Waste Comprehensive Vtilization of Resources Industry	14.70
金属制品、机械和设备修理业	Metal products,Machinery and Equipment Repairing	13.42
电力、燃气及水的生产和供应业	**Electric Power, Gas and Water Production and Supply**	
电力、热力生产和供应业	Electric Power, Steam and Hot Water Production and Supply	3037.28
燃气生产和供应业	Gas Production and Supply	65.15
水的生产和供应业	Tap Water Production and Supply	210.47

(100 million yuan)

流动资产合计 Circulating Funds	固定资产合计 Total Fined Assets	固定资产原价 Original Value of Fixed Assets	主营业务收入 Revenue of Major Business	全部从业人员年平均人数(万人) Average Number of Empolyment of the Curreat Year (10 000 Bersons)
8.92	5.99	8.29	32.13	1.23
5.78	103.43	299.39	75.97	1.82
27.94	30.89	56.69	181.56	1.38
5.73	3.47	10.43	13.70	0.29
27.68	15.81	191.19	83.78	1.17
32.99	35.13	52.88	72.48	1.82
295.39	334.82	1175.93	1698.41	10.30
110.66	110.62	309.30	510.73	5.86
537.35	165.11	287.58	1047.08	7.97
304.73	29.01	81.12	547.28	0.78
255.01	222.22	447.53	1250.02	18.37
226.16	90.42	162.97	501.51	11.64
15.25	15.90	18.34	50.22	2.59
26.31	29.98	71.87	127.75	1.59
16.27	11.13	17.55	42.83	0.63
83.59	64.84	225.34	254.04	2.04
53.86	21.46	46.02	117.07	1.59
13.63	6.50	24.53	47.55	0.89
80.05	117.40	190.34	827.65	0.94
745.75	955.07	1537.77	2321.66	14.01
262.05	200.06	249.56	548.45	7.85
14.25	10.48	27.53	46.70	0.72
146.36	83.12	182.11	454.92	5.33
319.10	426.17	639.08	936.60	10.89
823.16	1180.54	2187.26	2221.88	15.26
245.47	126.93	197.00	1275.93	3.72
370.29	152.62	237.25	539.05	5.70
491.66	231.80	300.68	520.87	6.15
363.65	167.27	334.82	401.88	5.39
2142.61	718.42	1263.77	3894.26	29.40
379.87	160.74	207.03	425.34	6.28
448.94	231.98	323.57	1010.41	10.26
925.47	214.35	388.74	1326.38	12.00
40.24	37.48	42.45	57.52	1.59
70.65	29.18	44.18	101.79	1.52
5.89	4.14	5.21	16.22	0.37
8.63	3.91	6.96	18.17	0.65
202.95	2553.17	3869.93	1358.34	11.06
19.45	33.20	44.20	58.77	0.49
62.89	53.65	82.70	23.01	1.27

13—9 规模以上工业企业生产能力（2014）
OUTPUT OF MAJOR PRODUCTS OF INDUSTRY ABOVE DESIGNATED SIZE (2014)

产品名称		Item		年初生产能力 Capacity at the Beginning of the Year	年末生产能力 Capacity at the End of the Year
原煤	吨	Coal	ton	18273522	33220051
天然原油	吨	Crude Petroleum Oil	ton	991410	1076234
卷烟	万支	Cigarettes	10000 pieces	19880730	19950381
棉纺锭/纺纱量	锭/吨	Knitting Spindle/Capacity	spindle/ton	10267626	10911925
气流纺锭/纺纱量	头/吨	Air Spindle/Capacity	spindle/ton	424843	452770
棉布织机/布	台/万米	Cotton Loom/Cloth	piece/10000 meters	24873365	30745075
原油加工能力/原油加工量	吨/吨	Crude Oil Processing Capacity	ton/ton	13794549	14151500
焦炭	吨	Coke	ton	10546000	4366000
烧碱（折100%）	吨	Caustic Soda (100%)	ton	1057872	1308000
碳化钙（电石，折 300升/千克）	吨	Calcium Carbide (300 L/kg)	ton	834017	792711
农用氮、磷、钾化学肥料总计（折纯）	吨	Chemical Fertilizers	ton	16007591	15751011
初级形态塑料	吨	Primary Plastic	ton	2296476	2445583
化学纤维	吨	Chemical Fiber	ton	297828	320666
硅酸盐水泥熟料	吨	Portland Cement Clinker	ton	64154003	62205536
水泥	吨	Cement	ton	135233595	134468545
平板玻璃	重量箱	Plain Glass	weight case	398492013	335762408
生铁	吨	Pig Ion	ton	28400000	28470000
粗钢	吨	Crude Steel	ton	39397264	38408345
钢材	吨	Rolled Steel	ton	41976033	41986400
铁合金	吨	Ferroalloy	ton	613198	453831
原铝（电解铝）	吨	Electrolyzed Aluminum	ton	297000	267460
金属切削机床	台	Metal-cutting Machine Tools	piece	15065	5148
汽车	辆	Automobile	unit	1987150	2277950
其中：基本型乘用车（轿车）	辆	Cars	unit	840000	1180000
家用电冰箱	台	Home Refrigerators	piece	4800000	4800000
房间空气调节器	台	Air Conditioners	piece	13900000	15300000
移动通信手持机（手机）	台	Mobile Phones	piece	34000000	39000000
彩色电视机	台	Color Television Sets	piece	215000	628760
发电设备容量总计/发电量	万千瓦/万千瓦小时	Generating Capacity	10000 kwh	63681.50	63842.60
其中：火电设备容量/发电量		Thermal Power	10000 kwh	23111.80	23274.10
水电设备容量/发电量		Hydropower	10000 kwh	3398.80	3401.00
核电设备容量/发电量		Nuclear Power	10000 kwh		
风电设备容量/发电量		Wind Power	10000 kwh	22.10	27.80

13—10 规模以上工业主要产品产量(2014)
SCALE INDUSTRIAL OUTPUT OF MAIN ProduCTS (2014)

名 称	计量单位	name		产品产量
原煤	吨	Original Coal	ton	8904004.4
1.无烟煤	吨	1.Anthracite	ton	3256195.0
2.烟煤	吨	2.Bituminous Coal	ton	3128729.6
其中:一般烟煤	吨	General Bituminous Coal	ton	3128729.6
洗煤	吨	Washed Coal	ton	459525.0
其中:洗精煤	吨	Cleaned Coal	ton	459525.0
天然原油	吨	Natural Oil	ton	790006.0
天然气	万立方米	Natural Gas	10000 cu.m	14502.0
铁矿石原矿	吨	Iron Ore	ton	35009337.5
铜金属含量	吨	Copper	ton	64926.9
锌金属含量	吨	Zinc	ton	12571.7
锑金属含量	吨	Antimony	ton	564.0
钨精矿折合量(折三氧化钨65%)	吨	Tungsten Concentrate Equivalent Amount (65% of Tungsten Trioxide)	ton	429.8
钼精矿折合量(折纯钼45%)	吨	Molybdenum Concentrate Equivalent Amoun (45% of Pure Mo)	ton	1426.8
硫铁矿石(折含硫35%)	吨	Pyrite Stone (35% of Sulfur)	ton	164791.0
磷矿石(折含五氧化二磷30%)	吨	Phosphate Rock (30% of Phosphorus Pentoxide)	ton	46638291.2
原盐	吨	Crude Salt	ton	4657320.0
小麦粉	吨	Wheat Flour	ton	5775371.3
大米	吨	Rice	ton	26316690.3
饲料	吨	Feed	ton	15275435.1
其中:配合饲料	吨	Compoud Feed	ton	8915328.8
混合饲料	吨	Mixed feed	ton	3242528.1
精制食用植物油	吨	Refined Edible Vegetable oil	ton	6865365.5
成品糖	吨	Sugar	ton	79902.7
鲜、冷藏肉	吨	Fresh and Chilled Meat	ton	1899838.3
冷冻水产品	吨	Frozen Seafood	ton	478266.5
糖果	吨	Candy	ton	246969.4
速冻米面食品	吨	Frozen Rice\Flour Food	ton	62555.7
方便面	吨	Instant Noodles	ton	222019.7
乳制品	吨	Dairy Products	ton	870960.6
其中:液体乳	吨	Liquid Dairies	ton	859629.0
乳粉	吨	Milk Powder	ton	1431.0
罐头	吨	Can	ton	1284103.1
酱油	吨	Soy Sauce	ton	147279.0
冷冻饮品	吨	Frozen Drinks	ton	264792.8
食品添加剂	吨	Food Additives	ton	266448.8
发酵酒精(折96度,商品量)	千升	Fermentation of Alcohol (of 96 degrees, the amount of goods)	kl	32098.0

13-10 续表1 continued

名 称	计量单位	name		产品产量
饮料酒	千升	Alcoholic Beverage	kl	3424194.0
其中:白酒(折65度,商品量)	千升	Liquor (of 65 degrees, the amount of goods)	kl	849354.5
啤酒	千升	Beer	kl	2238846.4
葡萄酒	千升	Wine	kl	1576.8
软饮料	吨	Soft Drinks	ton	7849264.7
其中:碳酸饮料类(汽水)	吨	Carbonated Beverages (soft drinks)	ton	771139.0
包装饮用水类	吨	Packaging of Drinking Water	ton	2316658.9
果汁和蔬菜汁饮料类	吨	Fruit Juice and Vegetable Juice	ton	1023603.5
精制茶	吨	Refined Tea	ton	335113.6
卷烟	万支	Cigarette	10000 pieces	14076587.0
纱	吨	Yarn	ton	3351539.3
1、棉纱	吨	Cotton Yarn	ton	2112575.9
2、棉混纺纱	吨	Cotton Blended Yarn	ton	468144.2
3、化学纤维纱	吨	Chemical Fiber Yarn	ton	770819.3
布	万米	Fabric	10000 meters	824034.1
其中:色织布(含牛仔布)	万米	Dyed Fabric (including jean)	10000 meters	1644.6
其中:1.棉布	万米	1.Cotton	10000 meters	679161.0
2.棉混纺布	万米	2.Cotton Blended Cloth	10000 meters	117764.5
3.化学纤维布	万米	3.Chemical-Fiber Cloth	10000 meters	27108.6
印染布	万米	Dyed Cloth	10000 meters	39438.3
亚麻布(含亚麻≥55%)	万米	Linen Fabric (containing linen≥ 55%)	10000 meters	235.0
苎麻布(含苎麻≥55%)	万米	Ramie fabric (containing linen ≥ 55%)	10000 meters	853.7
蚕丝	吨	Silk	ton	1682.6
蚕丝被	万条	Silk Quilt	10000 pieces	389.1
无纺布(无纺织物)	吨	Non-woven Fabric	ton	362298.5
服装	万件	Clothing	10000 pieces	106302.1
1.梭织服装	万件	Tated Garments	10000 pieces	82397.6
其中:羽绒服	万件	Down Jacket	10000 pieces	690.1
西服套装	万件	Western-style	10000 pieces	1765.0
衬衫	万件	Shirt	10000 pieces	1607.3
2.针织服装	万件	Knitted Garments	10000 pieces	23904.5
轻革	平方米	Light Leather	sq.m	2945268.0
天然毛皮服装	万件	Leather Clothes	piece	30.0
皮革鞋靴	万双	Leather Footwear	10000 pairs	2311.1
人造板	立方米	Artificial Board	cu.m	9312022.4
其中:胶合板	立方米	Plywood	cu.m	3670927.8
纤维板	立方米	FibreBoard	cu.m	3076509.2
刨花板	立方米	Shaving Board	cu.m	328928.7
人造板表面装饰板	立方米	Artificial Board for Surface Decoration	cu.m	65557826.0

13—10 续表2 continued

名 称	计量单位	name		产品产量
复合木地板	平方米	Composite Wood Flooring	cu.m	42824718.8
家具	件	Furniture	piece	5847754.0
其中:木质家具	件	Wood Furniture	piece	2533719.0
金属家具	件	Metal Furniture	piece	433300.0
软体家具	件	Upholstered Furniture	piece	301884.0
纸浆(原生浆及废纸浆)	吨	Pulp (original pulp and waste paper pulp)	ton	87099.0
机制纸及纸板(外购原纸加工除外)	吨	Machine Made Paper and PaperBoard (excludingprocessing outsourcing base paper)	ton	2363926.9
其中:未涂布印刷书写用纸	吨	Uncoating Writing Paper	ton	579083.6
其中:新闻纸	吨	Newsprint	ton	19819.0
卫生用纸原纸	吨	Toilet Paper	ton	196154.2
箱纸板	吨	Case Board	ton	39822.7
纸制品	吨	Paper Products	ton	3131037.6
其中：瓦楞纸箱	吨	Corrugated Case	ton	1624117.4
单色印刷品	令	Monochrome Print	ream	8170866.6
多色印刷品	对开色令	Multi-color Print	lio color ream	17556304.4
原油加工量	吨	Crude Oil Processing Capacity	ton	12825515.8
汽油	吨	Gasoline	ton	2788777.2
煤油	吨	Kerosene	ton	848392.1
柴油	吨	Diesel Fuel	ton	4596534.8
润滑油	吨	Lubricating Oil	ton	53282.5
燃料油	吨	Fuel Oil	ton	103053.3
石脑油	吨	Naphtha	ton	1353014.0
溶剂油	吨	Megilp	ton	1281.0
液化石油气	吨	LPG	ton	566601.6
石油焦	吨	Petroleum Coke	ton	1151691.7
石油沥青	吨	Petroleum Pitch	ton	106526.2
焦炭	吨	Coke	ton	9317263.9
其中:机焦	吨	Organic	ton	9317263.9
硫酸(折100%)	吨	Sulfuric Acid (100% discount)	ton	6913081.9
盐酸(氯化氢,含量31%)	吨	Hydrochloric Acid (hydrogen chloride, 31%)	ton	723387.2
浓硝酸(折100%)	吨	Concentrated Nitric Acid (100% discount)	ton	11643.0
烧碱(折100%)	吨	Caustic Soda (100% discount)	ton	1033400.6
其中：离子膜法烧碱(折100%)	吨	Ionic Membrane Method(100% discount)	ton	843988.7
纯碱(碳酸钠)	吨	Soda Ash (sodium carbonate)	ton	1409466.6
精甲醇	吨	Refined Methanol	ton	387093.0
合成氨(无水氨)	吨	Anhydrous Amonia	ton	4713065.0
农用氮、磷、钾化学肥料总计(折纯)	吨	Agricultural Nitrogen, Phosphorus and Potass	ton	12090186.9
1、氮肥(折含N100%)	吨	1.N (of N 100%)	ton	6293352.5
其中：尿素(折含N100%)	吨	Urea (of N 100%)	ton	1931631.4

13-10 续表3 continued

名　称	计量单位	name		产品产量
2、磷肥(折五氧化二磷100 %)	吨	2.P (of 100% phosphorus pentoxide)	ton	5620143.4
3、钾肥(折氧化钾100%)	吨	3.K (of 100% potassium hydroxide)	ton	176691.0
磷酸一铵(实物量)	吨	MAP (physical quantity)	ton	7571473.8
磷酸二铵(实物量)	吨	DAP (physical quantity)	ton	4319183.0
化学农药原药(折有效成分100%)	吨	Chemical Pesticide Active Compound	ton	243628.5
其中:杀虫剂原药	吨	Pesticide Active Compound	ton	44535.0
除草剂原药	吨	Herbicide Active Compound	ton	139318.0
涂料	吨	Paint	ton	402370.6
初级形态的塑料	吨	Primary Form Plastic	ton	2086595.3
聚丙烯树脂	吨	Polypropylene Resin	ton	694369.6
聚氯乙烯树脂	吨	PVC Resin	ton	562155.0
聚苯乙烯树脂	吨	Polystyrene Resin	ton	27377.0
ABS树脂	吨	ABS Resin	ton	20990.0
合成橡胶	吨	Synthetic Rubber	ton	164816.5
合成纤维聚合物	吨	Synthetic Fiber Polymer	ton	16980.0
化学试剂	吨	Chemical Reagent	ton	471687.7
单晶硅	千克	Single Crystal Silion	kg	
多晶硅	千克	Polycrystalline Silion	kg	4542137.3
合成洗涤剂	吨	Synthetic Detergent	ton	228367.0
其中:合成洗衣粉	吨	Synthetic Washing Powder	ton	1212.0
化学药品原药	吨	Original Drug Chemicals	ton	250264.6
中成药	吨	Chinese Patent Medicine	ton	868459.9
化学纤维用浆粕	吨	Chemical Fiber Pulp	ton	62584.0
化学纤维	吨	Chemical Fiber	ton	261536.1
其中：人造纤维(纤维素纤维)	吨	Artificid Fiber	ton	109002.1
其中:粘胶短纤维	吨	Fibranne	ton	93595.1
粘胶纤维长丝	吨	Viscose Filament	ton	15407.0
合成纤维	吨	Synthetic Fiber	ton	152534.1
其中:锦纶纤维	吨	Polyamide Fiber	ton	
涤纶纤维	吨	Polyester Fiber	ton	56907.1
丙纶纤维	吨	Polypropylene Fiber	ton	75770.0
橡胶轮胎外胎	条	Rubber Cover Tyre	piece	9672755.0
其中：子午线轮胎外胎	条	Radial Tire	piece	8463141.0
塑料制品	吨	Plastic Products	ton	5515692.4
其中:塑料薄膜	吨	Plastic Film	ton	218014.3
其中：农用薄膜	吨	Agricultural Film	ton	44680.0
泡沫塑料	吨	Foam	ton	83391.4
塑料人造革、合成革	吨	Plastic Leather and Synthetic Leather	ton	50058.0
日用塑料制品	吨	Household Plastic Products	ton	475988.5
硅酸盐水泥熟料	吨	Cement Clinker	ton	54309677.4
其中:窑外分解窑水泥熟料	吨	Cement Kiln Clinker	ton	49899021.9

13-10 续表4 continued

名 称	计量单位	name		产品产量
水泥	吨	Cement	ton	116699256.1
其中:强度等级42.5水泥(含R型)	吨	Strength Grade 42.5 Cement (including R-ty	ton	15776389.2
强度等级52.5水泥(含R型)	吨	Strength Grade 52.5 Cement (including R-ty	ton	206194.0
商品混凝土	立方米	Concrete	cu.m	58648507.7
水泥混凝土排水管	千米	Concrete Drainage Pipe	km	7267.4
水泥混凝土压力管	千米	Concrete Pressure Pipe	km	5803.5
水泥混凝土电杆	根	Cement Concrete Pole	piece	833529.0
预应力混凝土桩	米	Prestressed Concrete Pile	meter	13154722.0
石膏板	万平方米	Gypsum Board	10000 sq.m	56357.3
砖	万块	Brick	10000 pieces	6401999.9
瓦	万片	Tile	10000 pieces	328661.6
瓷质砖	平方米	Porcelain Tile	sq.m	275035820.5
陶质砖	平方米	Ceramic Tile	sq.m	111874881.0
天然大理石建筑板材	平方米	Natural Marble Building Boards	sq.m	39974235.6
天然花岗石建筑板材	平方米	Natural Granite Building Boards	sq.m	20992018.3
沥青和改性沥青防水卷材	平方米	Asphalt and Modified Bitumen Sheet	sq.m	55070214.4
平板玻璃	重量箱	Plate Glass	weight case	90511321.6
钢化玻璃	平方米	Tempered Glass	sq.m	12550214.4
夹层玻璃	平方米	Laminated Glass	sq.m	1220197.0
中空玻璃	平方米	Insulating Glass	sq.m	30932171.5
日用玻璃制品	吨	Daily Glass Products	ton	695605.0
玻璃包装容器	吨	Glass Containers	ton	1598731.7
玻璃纤维纱	吨	Glass Fiber Yarn	ton	19212.7
纤维增强塑料制品	吨	Fiber Reinforced Plastic Products	ton	11652.0
卫生陶瓷制品	件	Sanitary Ceramic Products	piece	17619018.0
耐火材料制品	吨	Refractory Products	ton	1661034.1
石墨及炭素制品	吨	Graphite and Carbon Products	ton	374238.0
生铁	吨	Pig Iron	ton	24375840.1
粗钢	吨	Crude Steel	ton	30564341.1
铸铁件	吨	Iron Casting	ton	2702182.5
铸钢件	吨	Steel Casting	ton	762416.4
钢材	吨	Steel	ton	34290109.5
1.铁道用钢材	吨	1. Railway Steel	ton	749112.0
重轨	吨	Heavy Rail	ton	746556.0
2.大型型钢	吨	2. Large-scale Steel	ton	10463.0
3.中小型型钢	吨	3. Small and Medium Scale Steel	ton	1210429.0
4.棒材	吨	4. Bar	ton	2065684.3
5.钢筋	吨	5. Steel Bar	ton	6706007.8
6.线材(盘条)	吨	6. Wire (coil)	ton	2454845.5
7.特厚板	吨	7. Special Plate	ton	275286.0

13-10 续表5 continued

名　称	计量单位	name		产品产量
8.厚钢板	吨	8. Thick Steel Plate	ton	608575.0
9.中板	吨	9. Middle Plate	ton	1750594.0
10.热轧薄板	吨	10. Hot-rolled Sheet	ton	52235.0
11.冷轧薄板	吨	11. Cold-rolled Sheet	ton	2059512.2
12.中厚宽钢带	吨	12. Thick Wide Strip	ton	4364150.0
13.热轧薄宽钢带	吨	13. Hot-rolled Thin Wide Strip	ton	1708520.0
14.冷轧薄宽钢带	吨	14. Cold-rolled Wide Strip	ton	2530459.3
15.热轧窄钢带	吨	15. Hot-rolled Narrow Strip	ton	205849.0
16.冷轧窄钢带	吨	16. Cold-rolled Narrow Strip	ton	87871.0
17.镀层板(带)	吨	17. Coated Plate	ton	3003052.5
18.涂层板(带)	吨	18. Coated Plate	ton	229726.9
铁合金	吨	Ferroallory	ton	319248.0
十种有色金属	吨	10 Kinds of Nonferrous Metals	ton	1062913.5
精炼铜(电解铜)	吨	Refined Copper (electrolytic copper)	ton	523023.0
铅	吨	Lead	ton	337045.0
锌	吨	Zinc	ton	2610.0
氧化铝	吨	Alumina	ton	
原铝(电解铝)	吨	Electrolytic Aluminum	ton	197828.6
黄金	千克	Gold	kg	23747.9
白银(银锭)	千克	Silver (silver bullion)	kg	884790.6
铝合金	吨	Aluminum Alloy	ton	157938.7
铜材	吨	Copper	ton	176679.0
铝材	吨	Aluminum	ton	1090541.6
金属切削工具	万件	Metal Cutting Tools	10000 pieces	36891.3
钢丝	吨	Wire	ton	264815.0
钢丝绳	吨	Wire Rope	ton	31847.0
钢绞线	吨	Strand	ton	217957.0
锻件	吨	Forge Piece	ton	543224.3
粉末冶金零件	吨	Powder Metallurgy	ton	115851.0
工业锅炉	蒸发量吨	Industrial Boiler	ton	3865.7
发动机	千瓦	Engine	kw	106811159.0
其中：汽车用发动机	千瓦	Automotive Engine	kw	105004837.0
电站用汽轮机	千瓦	Power Plant Steam Turbine	kw	1594900.0
电站水轮机	千瓦	Turbine	kw	6250.0
金属切削机床	台	Metal Cutting Machine	piece	4048.0
其中:数控金属切削机床	台	CNC Metal Cutting Machine	piece	944.0
金属成形机床	台	Metal Forming Machine	piece	41699.0
其中：数控金属成形机床(数控锻压设备	台	CNC Metal Forming Machine	piece	202.0

13-10 续表6 continued

名　称	计量单位	name		产品产量
铸造机械	台	Foundry Machine	piece	84292.0
电焊机	台	Electric Welding Machine	piece	
机床数控装置	套	Machine Digital Control Device	piece	14315.0
起重机	吨	Crane	piece	37150.0
电动车辆(电动叉车)	台	Electric Vehicles (electric forklift)	piece	39284.0
内燃叉车	台	Internal Combustion Forklift	piece	243.0
输送机械(输送机和提升机)	吨	Transportation Machinery (conveyors and ele	ton	153639.0
泵	台	Pump	piece	285722.0
其中:真空泵	台	Vacuum Pump	piece	4070.0
气体压缩机	台	Gas Compressor	piece	27203535.0
其中:制冷设备用压缩机	台	Refrigeration Equipment with Compressor	piece	27192960.0
阀门	吨	Valve	ton	67678.8
液压元件	件	Hydraulic Components	piece	703886.0
气动元件	件	Pneumatic components	piece	1802887.0
滚动轴承	万套	Roller	10000 pieces	6483.0
齿轮	吨	Gear	ton	304286.0
风机	台	Fans	piece	30501.0
包装专用设备	台	Special Equipment Package	piece	11462.0
金属密封件	万件	Metal Sealing Element	10000 pieces	2198.4
金属紧固件	吨	Metal Fastenings	ton	51445.0
弹簧	吨	Spring	ton	54555.8
减速机	台	Reducer	piece	289429.0
矿山专用设备	台	Mining Special Equipment	ton	125088.7
挖掘、铲土运输机械	台	Digging and Scraper Transport Machinery	piece	3058.0
其中:挖掘机	台	Excavator	piece	197.0
水泥专用设备	吨	Cement Special Equipment	ton	23200.0
混凝土机械	台	Concrete Machinery	piece	1233.0
金属冶炼设备	吨	Metal Smelting Equipment	ton	13201.7
金属轧制设备	吨	Metal Rolling Equipment	ton	9012.5
炼油、化工生产专用设备	吨	Oil Refining and Chemical Production Specia	ton	721378.4
塑料加工专用设备	台	Plastics Processing Special Equipment	piece	249.0
模具	套	Mold	piece	155307.0
农产品初加工机械	台	Equipment for Agricultural Products Pretreati	piece	901472.0
饲料生产专用设备	台	Equipment for Feed Production	piece	12280.0
印刷专用设备	吨	Printing Special Equipment	ton	
中型拖拉机	台	Medium-size Tractors	piece	28.0
小型拖拉机	台	Small Tractor	piece	59973.0
收获机械	台	Harvesting Machinery	piece	4172.0
其中:谷物收获机械	台	Cereal Harvesting Machinery	piece	4172.0

13-10 续表7 continued

名　称	计量单位	name		产品产量
收获后处理机械	台	Post-harvesting Processing Machinery	piece	51437.0
环境污染防治专用设备	台(套)	Equipment for Environmental Pollution Conti	piece	77854.0
其中:大气污染防治设备	台	Air Pollution Control Equipment	piece	73132.0
水质污染防治设备	台(套)	Water Pollution Control Equipment	piece	4202.0
固体废弃物处理设备	台	Solid Waste Handling Equipment	piece	520.0
汽车	辆	Car	piece	1744588.0
其中：基本型乘用车(轿车)	辆	Passenger Vehicles	piece	761231.0
1升<排量≤1.6升	辆	(1) 1.0 Liter < Displacement ≤ 1.6 Liter	piece	529453.0
1.6升<排量≤2.0升	辆	(2) 1.6 Liter < Displacement ≤ 2.0 Liter	piece	217010.0
2.0升<排量≤2.5升	辆	(3) 2.0 Liter < Displacement ≤ 2.5 Liter	piece	14767.0
2.5升<排量≤3.0升	辆	(4) 2.5 Liter < Displacement ≤ 3.0 Liter	piece	
多功能乘用车(MPV)	辆	MPV	piece	154401.0
运动型多用途乘用车(SUV)	辆	SUV	piece	298422.0
客车	辆	Bus	piece	163303.0
(1)大型客车(车长>10米)	辆	(1) Large Passenger Bus (car length>10 m)	piece	740.0
(2)中型客车(7米<车长≤10米)	辆	(2) Medium Passenger Bus(7 m<car length	piece	4908.0
(3)轻型客车(车长≤7米)	辆	(3) light buses (car length≤ 7 m)	piece	157655.0
载货汽车	辆	Lorry	piece	360618.0
改装汽车	辆	Modified Cars	piece	234597.0
低速载货汽车	辆	Low Speed Truck	piece	6551.0
铁路货车	辆	Railway Wagon	piece	4352.0
民用钢质船舶	载重吨	Civil Steel Ships	ton	1900807.7
电动自行车	辆	Electric Bicycle	piece	835150.0
发电机组(发电设备)	千瓦	Generating Units (power equipment)	kw	879000.0
其中：水轮发电机组	千瓦	Generator Group	kw	15000.0
汽轮发电机	千瓦	Turbonator	kw	864000.0
交流电动机	千瓦	AC Motors	kw	2023132.0
变压器	千伏安	Transformer	kva	14818872.0
其中：电力变压器(额定容量≥8000kVA，电压≥500kV)	千伏安	Power Transformer	kva	262500.0
互感器	台	Mutual Inductor	kva	90264.0
高压开关板	面	High-voltage Switch Board	piece	123874.0
低压开关板	面	Low-voltage Switch Board	piece	202516.0
高压开关设备(11万伏以上)	台	High Voltage Switchgear (11 KV and above)	piece	68910.0
通信及电子网络用电缆	对千米	Communication and Electronic Networks Cal	km	1311185.8
电力电缆	千米	Power Cable	km	633648.3
光缆	芯千米	Optical Cable	km	49990430.8
绝缘制品	吨	Insulation Products	ton	56042.3

13-10 续表8 continued

名 称	计量单位	name		产品产量
锂离子电池	只(自然只)	Li-ion Battery	piece	137973367.0
铅酸蓄电池	千伏安时	Lead-acid Battery	kvah	22449994.0
碱性蓄电池	只(自然只)	Alkaline Battery	piece	7956000.0
原电池及原电池组(折R20标准只)	万只	Primary Cells and Primary Batteries (of R20 standard only)	10000 pieces	15288.2
太阳能电池	千瓦	Solar Battery	kw	801429.0
家用电冰箱	台	Household Refrigerator	piece	2435483.0
家用冷柜(家用冷冻箱)	台	Household Refrigerator (household freezers)	piece	1356269.0
房间空气调节器	台	Room Air Conditioners	piece	14415033.0
家用吸排油烟机	台	Home Ventilator	piece	12421.0
家用洗衣机	台	Household Washing Machines	piece	248455.0
家用电热水器	台	Water Heater	piece	2119585.0
家用吸尘器	台	Household Vacuum Cleaner	piece	
家用燃气灶具	台	Kitchen Range	piece	1738616.0
太阳能热水器	平方米	Solar Water Heater	sq.m	126961.0
电光源	万只	Light Sources	10000 pieces	161211.8
其中：白炽灯泡	万只	Incandescent Bulb	10000 pieces	52629.0
荧光灯	万只	Fluorescent Lamp	10000 pieces	11439.3
灯具及照明装置	套(台、个)	Lamps and Lighting Fittings	pieces	18408856.0
电子计算机整机	台	Computers	pieces	1206868.0
微型计算机设备	台	Micro-computer Equipment	pieces	1206868.0
显示器	台	Monitor	pieces	16375268.0
程控交换机	线	SPC Exchange	line	519198.0
移动通信手持机(手机)	台	Mobile Handset (cell phone)	pieces	28883514.0
组合音响	台	Music Center	pieces	
半导体分立器件	万只	Semiconductor Discrete Devices	10000 pieces	1343430.3
集成电路	万块	IC	10000 pieces	
集成电路圆片	万片	IC Wafer	10000 pieces	15.5
光电子器件	万只(片、套)	Optoelectronic Devices	10000 pieces	2496646.7
其中：发光二极管(LED)	万只	Light-emitting Diode (LED)	10000 pieces	1909210.1
电子元件	万只	Electronic Component	10000 pieces	1584623.8
其中：射频元器件	万只	RF Components	10000 pieces	2547.0
印制电路板	平方米	Printed Board	sq.m	1238558.5
工业自动调节仪表与控制系统	台(套)	Automatic Adjustment and Control System of Industrial Instrumentation	piece	73575.0
电工仪器仪表	台	Electric Instrument	piece	35547.0
分析仪器及装置	台(套)	Analytical Instrument	piece	891.0
汽车仪器仪表	台	Car Instrument	piece	4073832.0
光学仪器	台(个)	Optical Instrument	piece	10367177.0
船舶修理	载重吨	Ship Repair	ton	105.0
发电量	万千瓦小时	Power Generation	10000 kwh	23448116.8
其中：火力发电量	万千瓦小时	Thermal Capacity	10000 kwh	9333396.0
水力发电量	万千瓦小时	Hydroelectricity	10000 kwh	9333396.0
风力发电量	万千瓦小时	Wind Power Capacity	10000 kwh	65785.4
煤气生产量	万立方米	Coal Gas	10000 cu.m	3256195.0
自来水生产量	万立方米	Water Production	10000 cu.m	222968.4

13-11 规模以上工业企业主要经济效益指标（2014）

项 目	Item	企业亏损面（%） Enterprises deficit (%)
总 计	**Total**	**7.98**
一、按登记注册类型分组：	**Grouped by Type of Registration**	
内资企业	Inner Funded Enterprises	7.43
国有企业	State Owned Enterprises	19.38
中央企业	Central Enterprises	19.51
地方企业	Local Enterprises	19.33
集体企业	Collective-owned Enterprise	11.21
股份合作企业	Share Holding Cooperative Enterprises	5.26
联营企业	Joint Owned Enterprise	0.00
国有联营企业	State Joint Ownership	0.00
集体联营企业	Collective Joint Ownership	0.00
国有与集体联营企业	Joint State- Collective Ownership	0.00
其他联营企业	Other Joint Owned Enterprise	0.00
有限责任公司	Responsibility Co. Ltd	10.41
国有独资公司	State Solely Funded Co.	21.24
其他有限责任公司	Others	10.18
股份有限公司	Share Holding Co.Ltd.	10.95
私营企业	Private - owned enterprises	5.04
私营独资企业	Solely Private - owned enterprises	0.97
私营合作企业	Private Joint Venture	3.17
私营有限责任公司	Private Responsibility Co. Ltd	5.20
私营股份有限公司	Private Share Holding Co.Ltd.	5.43
其他企业	Others	4.44
港、澳、台商投资企业	Hongkong, Macao and Taiwan Funded Enterprises	16.75
合资经营企业(港或澳、台资)	Joint Venture with Hongkong, Macao and Taiwan	18.50
合作经营企业(港或澳、台资)	Cooperate with Hongkong, Macao and Taiwan Funded	25.00
港澳台商独资经营企业	Enterprises Solely Funded by Hongkong, Macao and Taiwan Businessmen	14.40
港澳台商投资股份有限公司	Share Holding Co.Ltd. With Hongkong, Macao and Taiwan Investment	20.00
外商投资企业	Foreign Funded Enterprises	18.22
中外合资经营企业	Sino - Foreign Joint Funded Enterprises	15.33
中外合作经营企业	Sino - Foreign Cooperative Funded Enterprises	10.00
外资企业	Foreign Solely Funded Enterprises	23.35
外商投资股份有限公司	Foreign Funded Share Holding Co.Ltd.	8.33
二、在总计中：亏损企业	**Of the Total: enterprises running under deficit**	100.00
在总计中：国有控股企业	Of the Total: State-Owned Share Holding Enterprises	**19.54**
在总计中：农村工业	Of the Total: Rural Industry	7.02
在总计中：轻工业	Of the Total: Light Industry	6.60
重工业	Heavy Industry	8.92
在总计中：大型企业	Of the Total: Large Scale Enterprises	11.46
中型企业	Medium Scale Enterprises	10.86
小型企业	Small Enterprises	7.49

MAJOR ECONOMIC INDICATORS OF INDUSTRIAL ENTERPRISES ABOVE DESIGNATED SIZE (2014)

总资产贡献率（%） Contributing Ratie of Tatal Assets(%)	资产负债率（%） Assets Liability Ratio(%)	流动资产周转率（次/年） Current Asset Tuinover (Times/year)	成本费用利润率（%） Ratio of Riofits to Industrial Cost(%)	产品销售率（%） Propovtion of Produts Sold(%)
14.93	**55.23**	**2.85**	**6.14**	**96.82**
14.48	54.42	2.90	6.01	97.04
7.88	58.45	2.43	6.70	99.12
7.91	58.28	2.53	6.72	99.21
7.25	62.08	1.51	6.38	97.77
22.89	58.67	4.21	4.68	97.82
16.76	58.42	3.15	4.65	92.01
22.17	66.12	10.59	2.47	97.78
10.56	85.43	3.83	6.74	93.37
6.93	70.90	1.05	1.60	102.86
47.28	49.61	26.02	2.47	98.20
15.96	60.60	2.67	5.33	96.39
30.47	61.56	2.13	5.56	96.65
12.56	60.38	2.80	5.30	96.34
9.95	50.08	1.68	7.18	97.48
21.41	43.90	4.43	6.19	97.06
37.37	36.34	8.76	6.47	97.89
29.36	40.08	8.01	5.38	97.91
20.64	43.83	4.32	6.03	97.13
27.13	46.60	4.82	8.07	95.87
32.63	38.54	7.24	6.49	98.38
12.80	53.45	3.23	5.39	93.54
11.35	57.07	3.15	4.69	91.41
4.36	27.11	2.89	1.55	74.43
15.55	48.38	3.58	6.44	97.11
13.13	45.70	1.92	9.17	98.07
19.14	62.03	2.40	7.59	96.56
21.62	63.53	2.49	7.41	96.17
28.32	64.92	5.48	15.21	98.83
11.51	55.16	1.95	6.98	97.12
14.39	64.89	2.74	11.03	100.38
1.14	72.05	1.76	-6.04	95.93
13.42	59.30	2.20	6.31	97.43
18.47	52.83	3.93	5.39	96.89
23.35	48.16	3.55	6.57	96.34
12.26	57.47	2.58	5.92	97.08
13.64	58.00	2.38	5.80	97.14
16.29	55.89	2.81	7.28	96.20
16.27	49.96	3.59	5.85	96.86

13-11 续表 continued

项 目	Item	企业亏损面（%） Enterprises Deficit(%)
按行业分	Grouped by Sector	
采矿业	**Mining and Qarrying**	
煤炭开采和洗选业	Coal Mining and Processing	8.84
石油和天然气开采业	Petroleum and Natural Gas Extraction	100.00
黑色金属矿采选业	Ferrous Metals Mining and Processing	12.50
有色金属矿采选业	Non-ferrous Metals Mining and Processing	9.30
非金属矿采选业	Non-metal Minerals Mining and Processing	5.67
开采辅助活动	Mining Auxiliary Activities	40.00
其他采矿业	Other Minerals Mining and Processing	
制造业	**Manufacturing**	
农副食品加工业	Food Processing	3.32
食品制造业	Food Production	5.45
酒、饮料和精制茶制造业	Wine,Beverage and Refined Tea Production	5.96
烟草制品业	Tobacco Processing	
纺织业	Textile Industry	8.17
纺织服装、服饰业	Textile,Garments, and Fashion Industry	5.46
皮革、毛皮、羽毛及其制品和制鞋业	Leather, Furs,Down and Related Products	4.97
木材加工和木、竹、藤、棕、草制品业	Timber Processing, Wood, Bamboo, Cane, Palm and Sraw Products	4.51
家具制造业	Furniture Manufacturing	9.68
造纸和纸制品业	Papermaking and Paper Products	11.76
印刷和记录媒介复制业	Printing and Record Processing	12.67
文教、工美、体育和娱乐用品制造业	Stationery, Education and Sports Goods	4.81
石油加工、炼焦和核燃料加工业	Petroleum Processing, Coking Products and Nuclear Fuel Processing	20.41
化学原料和化学制品制造业	Raw Chemical Material and Chemical Products	7.29
医药制造业	Medical and pharmaceutical Products	10.94
化学纤维制造业	Chemical Fibers	4.55
橡胶和塑料制品业	Rubber and plastic products	6.63
非金属矿物制品业	Nonmetal Material Products	5.16
黑色金属冶炼和压延加工业	Smelting and Pressing of Ferrous Metals	11.33
有色金属冶炼和压延加工业	Smelting and Pressing of Nonferrous Metals	13.10
金属制品业	Metal Products	7.97
通用设备制造业	Ordinary Machinery Manufacturing	10.37
专用设备制造业	Special Purpose Equipment Manufacturing	6.66
汽车制造业	Motor manufacturing	11.17
铁路、船舶、航空航天和其他运输设备制造业	Railway,Watercraft,Aviation and other Transporlation Equipment manufacturing	11.45
电气机械和器材制造业	Electric Machinery and Equipment	11.21
计算机、通信和其他电子设备制造业	Telecommunication Computer,Equipment and Other Electronic Equipment Manufacturing Other Electronic Equipment Manufacturing	12.66
仪器仪表制造业	Instruments and Meters, Manufacturing	8.94
其他制造业	Other Manufacturing	6.90
废弃资源综合利用业	Waste Comprehensive Vtilization of Resources Industry	19.61
金属制品、机械和设备修理业	Metal products,Machinery and Equipment Repairing	14.29
电力、燃气及水的生产和供应业	**Electric Power, Gas and Water Production and Supply**	
电力、热力生产和供应业	Electric Power, Steam and Hot Water Production and Supply	23.75
燃气生产和供应业	Gas Production and Supply	9.52
水的生产和供应业	Tap Water Production and Supply	21.18

总资产贡献率（%） Contributing Ratie of Tatal Assets(%)	资产负债率（%） Assets Liability Ratio(%)	流动资产周转率（次/年） Current Asset Tuinover (Times/year)	成本费用利润率（%） Ratio of Riofits to Industrial Cost(%)	产品销售率（%） Propovtion of Produts Sold(%)
26.50	46.01	4.18	10.10	98.99
1.32	17.51	17.00	-25.09	100.10
23.73	56.00	6.22	4.92	97.00
31.35	52.40	2.83	21.16	96.87
23.11	52.91	3.03	8.86	97.38
9.06	77.72	2.25	1.02	100.09
14.02	56.67	1.75	8.73	100.00
21.24	42.59	5.55	5.65	96.58
21.61	42.94	4.55	6.70	96.64
18.42	58.62	2.29	8.07	96.63
117.82	36.60	2.06	26.84	93.59
22.43	46.44	5.19	5.25	97.14
16.79	42.68	3.08	5.37	96.81
14.57	53.90	3.89	4.28	97.83
18.34	37.54	3.84	6.44	95.49
15.22	43.59	3.72	5.93	96.00
13.01	54.37	3.23	4.22	95.26
18.06	49.52	2.91	7.47	94.44
16.11	54.31	3.34	5.87	97.08
47.57	54.48	9.71	-1.09	98.10
12.54	62.07	3.46	5.42	97.48
15.71	49.49	2.46	8.27	94.68
16.46	49.29	4.00	6.41	98.30
21.87	46.01	3.80	7.08	97.52
20.02	49.30	3.77	8.20	97.25
5.12	63.41	2.78	1.29	98.73
6.23	67.76	5.20	0.94	98.68
11.98	58.50	2.41	4.64	96.53
9.37	64.85	1.67	6.89	96.97
8.75	48.57	1.46	5.38	95.78
16.85	52.76	2.03	9.19	97.76
4.67	68.49	1.29	2.43	95.30
12.45	56.04	2.39	5.65	96.41
5.25	59.51	1.52	2.60	90.15
11.52	58.61	1.67	9.33	95.25
9.98	64.68	1.92	6.40	94.25
7.59	68.68	2.66	0.71	97.72
15.84	54.18	2.34	3.59	90.81
11.79	56.67	5.47	17.15	99.38
10.56	67.71	2.45	12.04	99.06
3.31	51.97	0.67	8.08	96.08

13-12 规模以上工业企业产销总值及主要经济指标(分地区)(2014)

单位:亿元

地区	Region	企业单位数(个) Number of Enterprises(unit)	亏损企业 Enterprises Running under Deficit
全省	**Province**	**15957**	**1274**
武汉	Wuhan	2454	352
黄石	Huangshi	731	90
十堰	Shiyan	973	128
宜昌	Yichang	1476	89
襄阳	Xiangyang	1779	100
鄂州	Ezhou	541	25
荆门	Jingmen	1097	63
孝感	Xiaogan	1251	88
荆州	Jingzhou	1151	81
黄冈	Huanggang	1413	97
咸宁	Xianning	896	70
随州	Suizhou	710	28
恩施	Enshi	505	31
仙桃	Xiantao	396	11
潜江	Qianjiang	273	14
天门	Tianmen	300	2
神农架	Shennongjia	11	5

13-12 续表 1 continued

单位:亿元

地区	Region	资产总计 Total Assets	流动资产合计 Circulating Funds	应收帐款净额 Net Account Received
全省	**Province**	**32940.84**	**14798.24**	**3443.76**
武汉	Wuhan	11594.70	5750.41	1528.12
黄石	Huangshi	1857.71	931.30	148.58
十堰	Shiyan	2393.90	1105.74	238.78
宜昌	Yichang	5035.33	1525.96	271.24
襄阳	Xiangyang	2965.14	1457.51	412.22
鄂州	Ezhou	565.69	203.92	45.56
荆门	Jingmen	1176.94	476.72	82.56
孝感	Xiaogan	1300.94	582.64	135.86
荆州	Jingzhou	1369.96	661.73	172.83
黄冈	Huanggang	966.08	419.42	106.34
咸宁	Xianning	863.86	374.98	78.44
随州	Suizhou	592.37	261.90	68.77
恩施	Enshi	474.27	142.07	28.49
仙桃	Xiantao	443.61	191.63	51.57
潜江	Qianjiang	771.97	456.99	43.12
天门	Tianmen	502.15	212.64	27.09
神农架	Shennongjia	66.24	42.67	4.21

TOTAL VALUE OF PRODUCTION AND SALES AND MAJOR ECONOMIC INDICATORS OF INDUSTRIAL ENTERPRISES ABOVE DESIGNATED SIZE (BY REGIONS) (2014)

(100 million yuan)

工业总产值(当年价格) Total Output Value(current price)	工业销售产值(当年价格) Output Value of Industrial Products(current price)	出口交货值 Delivery Value for Export
43393.87	**42012.20**	**1456.40**
12224.03	11762.60	389.86
2196.72	2136.33	94.09
1871.07	1803.97	38.12
5165.19	5017.58	164.37
5195.18	5023.66	81.29
1359.24	1321.02	21.08
2925.13	2861.05	54.14
2482.09	2422.27	72.48
2188.06	2102.84	82.83
1757.46	1665.85	33.16
1700.79	1655.80	57.62
1219.80	1203.56	106.62
372.19	364.94	7.73
964.00	937.15	125.59
1032.28	1010.80	81.06
731.08	713.62	46.36
9.56	9.13	0.01

(100 million yuan)

固定资产合计 Total Value of Fixed Assets	固定资产原价 Original Price of Fixed Assets	资产总计 Total Assets	
		累计折旧 Accumulated	在建工程 Construction in Process
12605.10	**22424.03**	**10751.20**	**1637.17**
3815.88	6217.11	2721.96	697.64
681.19	947.82	309.27	90.32
488.85	676.82	274.74	76.63
2558.84	3683.20	1187.45	205.26
1049.06	1384.23	416.82	213.79
296.77	438.88	156.00	15.55
547.65	1599.22	1093.96	53.66
562.06	2416.50	1879.16	74.17
583.49	2150.61	1691.20	48.44
386.42	485.15	135.88	69.93
359.27	458.59	140.07	23.59
235.88	272.04	58.43	17.49
271.28	328.56	95.05	21.70
214.59	341.72	137.38	9.99
272.42	518.25	228.78	12.06
266.08	483.87	218.12	5.56
15.39	21.46	6.93	1.39

13-12 续表 2 continued

单位:亿元

地区	Region	负债合计 Total Liability	流动负债合计 Total Circulating Liability	应付账款 Account	非流动负债合计 Tatal Non-current Liability	所有者权益合计 Total Rights of Owners
全省	**Province**	**18193.00**	**13668.54**	**3679.72**	**3077.12**	**14624.35**
武汉	Wuhan	7102.11	5735.84	1867.13	950.92	4486.76
黄石	Huangshi	1167.13	919.19	186.81	223.65	685.01
十堰	Shiyan	1155.23	962.48	291.60	136.72	1229.81
宜昌	Yichang	2928.08	1834.53	290.66	854.33	2061.88
襄阳	Xiangyang	1545.03	1098.69	329.56	239.69	1462.42
鄂州	Ezhou	330.52	260.10	65.17	54.45	230.92
荆门	Jingmen	569.79	417.60	75.55	91.82	603.32
孝感	Xiaogan	657.08	358.93	84.32	77.32	626.75
荆州	Jingzhou	638.92	527.83	137.63	74.61	715.77
黄冈	Huanggang	488.67	349.44	85.04	71.69	456.91
咸宁	Xianning	383.19	271.57	63.57	75.98	463.52
随州	Suizhou	265.10	208.03	47.69	27.22	314.74
恩施	Enshi	273.35	171.03	21.09	88.64	194.60
仙桃	Xiantao	177.75	146.54	47.33	17.63	263.82
潜江	Qianjiang	216.74	173.46	51.40	35.35	554.71
天门	Tianmen	246.24	193.98	33.56	48.32	255.22
神农架	Shennongjia	48.06	39.30	1.61	8.76	18.17

13-12 续表 3 continued

单位:亿元

地区	Region	所有者权益合计 Total Rights of the Owners	主营业务收入 Revenue of Major Business	主营业务成本 Cost of Major Business
		外商资本 Foreign Assets		
全省	**Province**	**406.46**	**41401.49**	**34843.30**
武汉	Wuhan	234.71	11483.17	9379.94
黄石	Huangshi	59.39	2613.64	2363.38
十堰	Shiyan	5.20	1703.76	1466.07
宜昌	Yichang	11.16	4926.25	3975.41
襄阳	Xiangyang	30.95	4775.69	4070.02
鄂州	Ezhou		1287.67	1133.57
荆门	Jingmen	4.14	2851.63	2464.61
孝感	Xiaogan	10.97	2392.24	2034.69
荆州	Jingzhou	32.10	2053.80	1774.41
黄冈	Huanggang	8.11	1525.63	1325.24
咸宁	Xianning	3.10	1576.79	1357.76
随州	Suizhou	1.22	1189.28	982.05
恩施	Enshi	0.26	359.51	286.51
仙桃	Xiantao	2.77	929.92	743.29
潜江	Qianjiang	2.20	1004.14	885.09
天门	Tianmen	0.17	720.75	595.25
神农架	Shennongjia		7.62	6.02

(100 million Yuan)

实收资本 Assets Recevied	国家资本 National Assets	所有者权益合计 Total Rights of Owners			
		集体资本 Collective Assets	法人资本 Corperative Assets	个人资本 Individual Assets	港澳台资本 Assets from Hongkong,Maco and Taiwan
7327.76	**1607.76**	**111.04**	**2367.96**	**2655.51**	**149.76**
1781.06	739.43	29.50	501.58	208.64	60.94
1280.10	79.02	5.21	78.88	1050.36	7.03
414.81	236.92	10.74	72.83	87.15	1.30
653.78	190.45	15.88	217.41	200.27	17.37
608.62	112.47	12.65	295.71	150.47	5.36
272.74	65.83	0.66	80.62	125.02	0.99
278.27	64.52	2.70	81.26	120.43	2.00
371.81	39.77	4.65	135.17	173.63	7.12
292.36	15.93	12.78	75.23	152.31	0.98
240.56	11.21	7.19	88.68	106.15	18.84
249.37	6.24	2.59	163.08	67.01	6.80
146.00	9.43	1.87	40.99	88.18	3.30
125.93	27.47	2.98	48.34	44.77	0.16
100.29	1.97	0.50	50.22	29.22	15.60
397.85	5.00	1.06	366.69	12.32	0.97
109.27	1.57	0.06	69.47	37.00	1.00
4.94	0.54	0.00	1.80	2.59	0.00

(100 million Yuan)

主营业务税金及附加 Tax of Major Business	其他业务收入 Revenue of Other Business	其他业务利润 Profit from Other Business	销售费用 Selling Expenses	管理费用 Management Expense	税金 Tax
829.79	**780.57**	**86.13**	**1269.28**	**1704.51**	**99.66**
531.39	300.45	34.10	403.78	516.86	19.73
15.23	133.02	12.56	56.27	73.40	4.66
12.63	106.33	6.81	63.65	106.32	2.87
45.69	54.92	7.39	174.63	191.53	12.30
34.84	48.44	5.08	101.88	208.54	8.38
8.13	35.63	0.52	34.31	62.43	1.92
58.17	7.99	1.13	75.88	89.06	4.99
33.03	14.70	1.29	74.84	91.53	3.49
11.96	26.60	13.97	60.24	90.22	21.23
12.38	7.23	0.96	35.16	57.91	2.58
13.63	4.07	0.33	40.11	41.06	1.83
7.17	3.80	1.48	41.03	42.76	1.78
4.89	1.59	0.15	15.10	16.19	0.81
5.18	1.90	0.12	54.73	56.31	10.14
27.78	33.72	0.21	12.49	27.48	0.98
7.18	0.15	0.01	25.05	32.44	1.86
0.52	0.01	0.00	0.11	0.47	0.11

13-12 续表 4 continued

单位:亿元

地区	Region	财务费用 Financial Expense	利息支出 Interest Expense	营业利润 Operating Profit	补贴收入 Income from Subsidy
全省	**Province**	**522.40**	**37.45**	**2357.20**	**85.16**
武汉	Wuhan	116.70	9.38	473.16	24.73
黄石	Huangshi	30.07	4.12	88.90	5.83
十堰	Shiyan	13.24	10.91	152.71	2.04
宜昌	Yichang	117.86	4.80	430.91	28.71
襄阳	Xiangyang	46.55	2.52	350.65	6.61
鄂州	Ezhou	13.60	0.71	40.24	3.24
荆门	Jingmen	25.91	0.48	137.81	1.19
孝感	Xiaogan	37.40	0.73	112.47	2.89
荆州	Jingzhou	21.91	0.89	118.83	3.13
黄冈	Huanggang	19.16	0.76	83.61	1.55
咸宁	Xianning	15.84	1.02	105.92	1.67
随州	Suizhou	17.54	0.42	120.17	1.93
恩施	Enshi	11.54	0.16	25.33	0.55
仙桃	Xiantao	10.15	0.10	60.73	0.13
潜江	Qianjiang	9.46	0.38	7.57	0.88
天门	Tianmen	14.29	0.05	48.74	0.07
神农架	Shennongjia	1.19	0.04	-0.57	0.02

13-12 续表 5 continued

单位:亿元

地区	Region	应交税金及附加 Tax alafor Business	本年应付工资薪酬 Wases Welfarism Payable This Year
全省	**Province**	**2498.08**	**1916.98**
武汉	Wuhan	1087.94	672.63
黄石	Huangshi	90.98	93.11
十堰	Shiyan	73.10	138.26
宜昌	Yichang	305.06	214.52
襄阳	Xiangyang	198.45	167.39
鄂州	Ezhou	61.13	35.64
荆门	Jingmen	128.54	68.33
孝感	Xiaogan	96.34	93.62
荆州	Jingzhou	102.07	81.30
黄冈	Huanggang	60.61	70.21
咸宁	Xianning	70.92	52.47
随州	Suizhou	51.02	40.66
恩施	Enshi	19.82	18.44
仙桃	Xiantao	60.43	56.38
潜江	Qianjiang	48.86	56.00
天门	Tianmen	41.13	57.50
神农架	Shennongjia	1.68	0.52

(100 million Yuan)

营业外收入 Non-operating Income	营业外支出 Non-operating Expense	利润总额 Total Profit	应交所得税 Income Tax	亏损企业亏损总额 Total Loss of Enterprises Running under Deficit	利税总额 Total Profit
180.08	**59.97**	**2402.63**	**335.33**	**195.53**	**4465.72**
70.25	12.65	483.24	99.75	83.53	1451.69
9.43	2.84	95.83	20.31	6.79	161.85
6.82	2.45	157.39	12.54	10.99	215.08
35.97	21.89	445.19	70.57	19.30	667.37
13.45	4.84	343.28	48.80	7.54	484.56
3.57	1.10	41.83	7.41	2.89	93.64
4.36	3.92	138.23	8.12	9.16	253.66
12.16	1.37	116.23	9.75	8.52	199.32
10.08	1.54	127.37	14.05	4.70	194.16
4.42	2.46	83.68	7.10	3.66	134.61
3.36	1.69	106.31	16.49	7.89	158.92
2.07	1.16	121.07	3.99	2.26	166.32
1.09	0.95	25.55	2.91	1.73	41.66
0.56	0.17	61.12	6.82	2.59	104.58
2.33	0.77	8.14	0.71	22.86	55.32
0.11	0.14	48.70	5.91	0.05	82.07
0.06	0.03	-0.54	0.11	1.09	0.93

(100 million Yuan)

本年应交增值税 Value Added Payable of the Current Year	全部从业人员年平均人数(万人) Average Number of Empolyment of the Current Year (10000 persons)
1217.24	**359.45**
429.53	87.67
50.53	19.05
44.41	20.96
173.90	37.30
103.30	37.27
43.60	8.59
57.19	17.21
49.97	23.84
54.74	19.31
37.93	19.86
38.38	13.36
38.03	11.16
11.05	5.08
38.22	13.94
19.35	11.74
26.19	12.97
0.94	0.13

13−13 分市州规模以上工业企业主要经济效益指标（2014）

单位：%

地 区	Item	企业亏损面 Loss Making Rate of Enterprises	总资产贡献率 Contributing Rate of Total Assets
全省	**Province**	**7.98**	**14.93**
武汉市	Wuhan	14.34	13.57
黄石市	Huangshi	12.31	10.04
十堰市	Shiyan	13.16	9.39
宜昌市	Yichang	6.03	15.44
襄阳市	Xiangyang	5.62	17.82
鄂州市	Ezhou	4.62	18.42
荆门市	Jingmen	5.74	23.43
孝感市	Xiaogan	7.03	16.69
荆州市	Jingzhou	7.04	15.27
黄冈市	Huanggang	6.86	15.33
咸宁市	Xianning	7.81	19.74
随州市	Suizhou	3.94	30.25
恩施市	Enshi	6.14	11.04
仙桃市	Xiantao	2.78	25.66
潜江市	Qianjiang	5.13	7.91
天门市	Tianmen	0.67	19.00
神农架林区	Shennongjia	45.45	2.69

MAJOR INDICATORS OF ECONOMIC BENEFITS OF ABOVE DESIGNATEDSIZE INDUSTRIAL ENTERPRISES BY REGION(2014)

资产负债率 Assets Liability Ratio	流动资产周转率（次/年） Current Asset Turnover(Times/Year)	成本费用利润率 Ratio of Profits to Industrial Cost	产品销售率 Proportion of Products Sold
55.23	**2.85**	**6.14**	**96.82**
61.25	2.05	4.50	96.23
62.83	2.95	3.62	97.25
48.26	1.64	8.95	96.41
58.15	3.26	9.89	97.14
52.11	3.31	7.69	96.70
58.43	6.49	3.25	97.19
48.41	6.00	5.20	97.81
50.51	4.13	5.15	97.59
46.64	3.14	6.50	96.11
50.58	3.65	5.78	94.79
44.36	4.22	7.29	97.36
44.75	4.56	11.15	98.67
57.64	2.54	7.72	98.05
40.07	4.86	7.06	97.21
28.08	2.27	0.84	97.92
49.04	3.39	7.30	97.61
72.56	0.18	0.00	95.51

主要统计指标解释

工业 指从事自然资源的开采，对采掘品和农产品进行加工和再加工的物质生产部门。具体包括：(1)对自然资源的开采，如采矿、晒盐等(但不包括禽兽捕猎和水产捕捞)；(2)对农副产品的加工、再加工，如粮油加工、食品加工、缫丝、纺织、制革等；(3)对采掘品的加工、再加工，如炼铁、炼钢、化工生产、石油加工、机器制造、木材加工等，以及电力、自来水、煤气的生产和供应等；(4)对工业品的修理、翻新，如机器设备的修理、交通运输工具(如汽车)的修理等。

工业统计调查单位为独立核算法人工业企业。

独立核算法人工业企业指从事工业生产经营活动的单位。独立核算法人工业企业应同时具备以下条件：①依法成立，有自己的名称、组织机构和场所，能够承担民事责任；②独立拥有和使用资产，承担负债，有权与其他单位签订合同；③独立核算盈亏，并能够编制资产负债表。

本年鉴中涉及的企业登记注册类型：

国有及国有控股企业 指国有企业加上国有控股企业。国有企业(即原全民所有制工业或国营工业)指企业全部资产归国家所有，并按《中华人民共和国企业法人登记管理条例》规定登记注册的非公司制的经济组织。包括国有企业、国有独资公司和国有联营企业。1957年以前的公私合营和私营工业，后均改造为国营工业，1992年改为国有工业，这部分工业的资料不单独分列时，均包括在国有企业内。国有控股企业是对混合所有制经济的企业进行的“国有控股”分类。它是指这些企业的全部资产中国有资产(股份)相对其他所有者中的任何一个所有者占资(股)最多的企业。该分组反映了国有经济控股情况。

集体企业 指企业资产归集体所有，并按《中华人民共和国企业法人登记管理条例》规定登记注册的经济组织。是社会主义公有制经济的组成部分。包括城乡所有使用集体投资举办的企业，以及部分个人通过集资自愿放弃所有权并依法经工商行政管理机关认定为集体所有制的企业。

股份合作企业 指以合作制为基础，由企业职工共同出资入股，吸收一定比例的社会资产投资组建，实行自主经营，自负盈亏，共同劳动，民主管理，按劳分配与按股分红相结合的一种集体经济组织。

联营企业 指两个及两个以上相同或不同所有制性质的企业法人或事业单位法人，按自愿、平等、互利的原则，共同投资组成的经济组织。联营企业包括：

国有联营企业指国有企业与国有企业间的联营；

集体联营企业指集体企业与集体企业间的联营；

国有与集体联营企业指国有企业与集体企业间的联营。

有限责任公司 指根据《中华人民共和国公司登记管理条例》规定登记注册，由两个以上，五十个以下的股东共同出资，每个股东以其所认缴的出资额对公司承担有限责任，公司以其全部资产对其债务承担责任的经济组织。

有限责任公司包括国有独资公司以及其他有限责任公司。

股份有限公司 指根据《中华人民共和国企业法人登记管理条例》规定登记注册，其全部注册资本由等额股份构成并通过发行股票筹集资本，股东以其认购的股份对公司承担有限责任，公司以其全部资产对其债务承担责任的经济组织。

私营企业 指由自然人投资设立或由自然人控股，以雇佣劳动为基础的营利性经济组织。包括按照《公司法》、《合伙企业法》、《私营企业暂行条例》规定登记注册的私营有限责任公司、私营股份有限公司、私营合伙企业和私营独资企业。

港、澳、台商投资企业 指企业注册登记类型中的港、澳、台资合资、合作、独资经营企业和股份有限公司之和。

外商投资企业 指企业注册登记类型中的中外合资、合作经营企业、外资企业和外商投资股份有限公司之和。

“三资”企业系指港、澳、台商投资企业和外资企业的简称。

轻工业 指主要提供生活消费品和制作手工工具的工业。按其所使用的原料不同，可分为两大类：(1)以农产品为原料的轻工业，是指直接或间接以农产品为基本原料的轻工业。主要包括食品制造、饮料制造、烟草加工、纺织、缝纫、皮革和毛皮制作、造纸以及印刷等工业；(2)以非农产品为原料的轻工业，是指以工业品为原料的轻工业。主要包括文教体育用品、化学药品制造、合成纤维制造、日用化学制品、日用玻璃制品、日用金属制品、手工工具制造、医疗器械制造、文化和办公用机械制造等工业。

重工业　指为国民经济各部门提供物质技术基础的主要生产资料的工业。按其生产性质和产品用途，可以分为下列三类：(1)采掘(伐)工业，是指对自然资源的开采，包括石油开采、煤炭开采、金属矿开采、非金属矿开采等工业；(2)原材料工业，指向国民经济各部门提供基本材料、动力和燃料的工业。包括金属冶炼及加工、炼焦及焦炭、化学、化工原料、水泥、人造板以及电力、石油和煤炭加工等工业；(3)加工工业，是指对工业原材料进行再加工制造的工业。包括装备国民经济各部门的机械设备制造工业、金属结构、水泥制品等工业，以及为农业提供的生产资料如化肥、农药等工业。

根据上述划分原则，修理业中以重工业产品为修理作业对象的划为重工业，反之划为轻工业。

工业总产值

(1)定义：

工业总产值是以货币形式表现的，工业企业在一定时期内生产的工业最终产品或提供工业性劳务活动的总价值量。它反映一定时间内工业生产的总规模和总水平。

(2)计算原则：

工业生产的原则，即凡是企业在报告期生产的经检验合格的产品，不管是否在报告期销售，均包括在内。

最终产品的原则，即凡是计入工业总产值的产品，必须是本企业生产的经检验合格的，不需要再进行任何加工的最终产品。如果企业有中间产品(半成品)对外销售，则对外销售的中间产品应视为企业的最终产品。

工厂法原则，即工业总产值是以工业企业作为基本计算(核算)单位，即按企业的最终产品计算工业总产值。按这种方法计算的工业总产值，不允许同一产品价值在企业内部重复计算，不能把企业内部各个车间(分厂)生产的成果相加，但允许企业间的重复计算。

(3)内容及计算方法：

1995 年全国工业普查对工业总产值(原规定)的内容及计算原则和方法做了某些修订，修订后的工业总产值(新规定)包括三项内容：即本期生产成品价值、对外加工费收入、在制品半成品期末期初差额价值三部分。

本期生产成品价值：指企业本期生产，并在报告期内不再进行加工，经检验、包装入库的全部工业成品(半成品)价值合计，包括企业生产的自制设备及提供给本企业在建工程、其他非工业部门和福利部门等单位使用的成品价值。本期生产成品价值为按自备原材料生产的产品的数量乘以本期不含增值税(销项税额)的产品实际销售平均单价计算；会计核算中按成本价格转帐的自制设备和自产自用的成品，按成本价格计算生产成品价值。生产成品价值中不包括用定货者来料加工的成品(半成品)价值。

对外加工费收入：指企业在报告期内完成的对外承接的工业品加工(包括用定货者来料加工产品)的加工费收入和对外工业修理作业所取得的加工费收入。对外加工费收入按不含增值税(销项税额)的价格计算，可根据会计“产品销售收入”科目的有关资料取得。

对于本企业对内非工业部门提供的加工修理、设备安装的劳务收入，如果企业会计核算基础较好，能取得这部分资料，而且这部分价值所占比重较大，应包括在对外加工费收入中。

自制半成品在制品期末期初差额价值：指企业报告期在制品期末减期初的差额价值，本指标一般可以从会计核算资料中取得。如果会计产品成本核算中不计算半成品、在制品的成本，则总产值中也不包括这部分价值，反之则包括。

(4)工业总产值统计范围变化和计算方法修订情况：

1984 年以前工业总产值不包括村办工业，村办工业总产值划归农业。1984 年以后工业总产值包括村办工业。

1995 年工业普查对工业总产值计算方法做了修订，即从 1995 年始按新修订(新规定)方法计算工业总产值。新规定与原规定的区别如下：

全价与加工费的计算原则不同：新规定为凡自备原材料，不论其生产繁简程度如何，一律按全价计算工业总产值；凡来料加工，允许按加工费计算工业总产值。原规定则视生产加工的繁简程度不同，规定哪些行业按全价，哪些行业按加工费计算工业总产值。

自制半成品、在产品期末期初差额价值的计算原则不同：新规定要求，凡会计产品成本核算时计算了成本的差额价值，总产值中就应包括，否则可不包括；原规定则按生产周期六个月的界限区分，凡生产周期六个月以上的企业，总产值计算中应包括这部分差额价值，否则可不包括。

计算价格不同：新规定按不含增值税(销项税额)的价格计算；原规定则按含增值税(销项税额)的价格计算。

工业增加值 指工业企业在报告期内以货币表现的工业生产活动的最终成果。

工业增加值有两种计算方法：一是生产法，即工业总产出减去工业中间投入加上应交增值税；二是收入法，即从收入的角度出发，根据生产要素在生产过程中应得到的收入份额计算，具体构成项目有固定资产折旧、劳动者报酬、生产税净额、营业盈余，这种方法也称要素分配法。本年鉴中的工业增加值是以生产法计算的。

生产法工业增加值的计算方法为：

工业增加值=工业总产出－工业中间投入+应交增值税

(1)工业总产出：指工业企业在一定时期内工业生产活动的总成果。工业总产出包括：成品生产价值，对外加工费收入，自制半成品、在产品期末期初差额价值。1995年后用新规定计算的工业总产值代替。

(2)工业中间投入：指工业企业在工业生产活动中消耗的外购物质产品和对外支付的服务费用。服务费用包括支付给物质生产部门(工业、农业、批发零售贸易业、建筑业、运输邮电业)的服务费用和支付给非物质生产部门(如保险、金融、文化教育、科学研究、医疗卫生、行政管理等)的服务费用。工业中间投入的确定须遵循以下原则：必须从外部购入的，并已计入工业总产出的产品和服务价值；必须是本期投入生产，并一次性消耗掉(包括本期摊销的低值易耗品等)的产品和服务价值。

工业中间投入包括直接材料费用、制造费用中的工业中间投入、管理费用中的工业中间投入、销售费用中的工业中间投入和利息支出五部分。

资产总计 指企业拥有或控制的能以货币计量的经济资源，包括各种财产、债权和其他权利。资产按流动性分为流动资产、长期投资、固定资产、无形资产、递延资产和其他资产。该指标根据企业会计“资产负债表”中“资产总计”项目的期末数增列。

流动资产 指企业可以在一年内或者超过一年的一个生产周期内变现或者耗用的资产，包括现金及各种存款、短期投资，应收及预付款项、存货等。

流动资产平均余额 指企业在报告期内全部流动资产的平均余额。

固定资产原价 指企业在建造、购置、安装、改建、扩建、技术改造某项固定资产时所支出的全部货币总额。它一般包括买价、包装费、运杂费和安装费等。

固定资产净值年平均余额 指固定资产净值在报告期内余额的平均数。计算公式为：

$$\text{固定资产净值年平均余额}=\frac{\text{1至12月各月月初、月末固定资产净值之和}}{24}$$

该指标根据“资产负债表”中“固定资产原价”、“累计折旧”指标的期初、期末数计算填列。

固定资产净值指固定资产原价减去历年已提折旧额后的净额。计算公式为：

固定资产净值=固定资产原价－累计折旧

负债合计 指企业所承担的能以货币计量，将以资产或劳务偿付的债务，偿还形式包括货币、资产或提供劳务。负债一般按偿还期长短分为流动负债和长期负债。根据会计“资产负债表”中“负债合计”的年末数填列。

所有者权益 指企业投资人对企业净资产的所有权。企业净资产等于企业全部资产减去全部负债后的余额，包括企业投资人对企业的最初投入的实际到位的资产及资本公积金、盈余公积金和未分配利润。所有者权益合计数小于零，表示企业资不抵债。

主营业务收入 指会计“利润表”中对应指标的本年累计数。未执行2001年《企业会计制度》的企业，用“产品销售收入”的本期累计数代替。

主营业务成本 指会计“利润表”中对应指标的本年累计数。未执行2001年《企业会计制度》的企业，用“产品销售成本”的本期累计数代替。

主营业务税金及附加　指会计“利润表”中对应指标的本年累计数。未执行 2001 年《企业会计制度》的企业，用“产品销售税金及附加”的本期累计数代替。

利润总额　指企业生产经营活动的最终成果，是企业在一定时期内实现的盈亏相抵后的利润总额(亏损以“–”号表示)，它等于营业利润加上补贴收入加上投资收益加上营业外净收入再加上以前年度损益调整。

本年应交增值税　指企业在报告期内应交纳的增值税额。它等于本年销项税额加上出口退税加上进项税额转出数减去本年进项税额。小规模纳税企业直接按全年计税销售额乘以征收率计算取得。

从业人员平均人数　是指报告期内每天拥有的从业人员人数。其计算公式为：

$$季平均人数=\frac{季内各月平均人数之和}{3}$$

$$月平均人数=\frac{报告月内每天实有人数之和}{报告月日历日数}$$

$$年平均人数=\frac{年内各月平均人数之和}{12}$$

总资产贡献率　反映企业全部资产的获利能力，是企业经营业绩和管理水平的集中体现，是评价和考核企业盈利能力的核心指标。计算公式为：

$$总资产贡献率（\%）=\frac{利润总额+税金总额+利息支出}{平均资金总额}\times 100\%$$

公式中：税金总额为产品销售税金及附加与应交增值税之和；平均资产总额为期初期末资产之和的算术平均值。

资产负债率　该指标既反映企业经营风险的大小，也反映企业利用债权人提供的资金从事经营活动的能力。计算公式为：

$$资产负债率（\%）=\frac{负债总额}{资产总额}\times 100\%$$

资产与负债均为报告期期末数。

流动资产周转次数　指一定时期内流动资产完成的周转次数，反映投入工业企业流动资金的周转速度。计算公式为：

$$流动资产周转资转次数=\frac{产品销售收入}{全部流动资产平均余额}$$

公式中：全部流动资产平均余额为期初和期末的流动资产之和的算术平均值。

成本费用利润率 反映企业投入的生产成本及费用的经济效益，同时也反映企业降低成本所取得的经济效益。计算公式为：

$$成本费用利润率（\%）=\frac{利润总额}{成本费用总额}\times 100\%$$

公式中：成本费用总额为产品销售成本、销售费用、管理费用、财务费用之和。

全员劳动生产率 该指标反映企业的生产效率和劳动投入的经济效益。计算公式为：

$$全员劳动生产率（元/人）=\frac{工业增加值}{全部从业人员平均人数}$$

产品销售率 该指标反映工业产品已实现销售的程度，是分析工业产销衔接情况，研究工业产品满足社会需求的指标。计算公式为：

$$产品销售率（\%）=\frac{工业销售产值}{工业总产值（现价）}\times 100\%$$

Explanatory Notes on Main Statistical Indicators

Industry refers to the material production sector which is engaged in extraction of natural resources and processing and reprocessing of minerals and agricultural products, including (1) extraction of natural resources, such as mining, salt production (but not including hunting and fishing); (2) processing and reprocessing of farm and sideline produces, such as rice husking, flour milling, wine making, oil pressing, silk reeling, spinning and weaving, and leather making; (3) manufacture of industrial products, such as steel making, iron smelting, chemicals manufacturing, petroleum processing, machine building, timber processing; water and gas production and electricity generation and supply; (4)repairing of industrial products such as the repairing of machinery and means of transport (including cars).

Units of industrial statistics survey corporate industrial enterprises with independent accounting system.

Corporate industrial enterprises with independent accounting system refer to enterprises engaging in industrial production activities, which meet the following requirements: (1)They are established legally, having their own names, organizations, location, able to take civil liability; (2)They possess and use their assets independently, assume liabilities, and are entitled to sign contracts with other units; (3)They are financially independent and compile their own balance sheets.

Enterprises covered in the industrial statistics in the Yearbook include following categories by their registration:

State-owned and State-holding Enterprises refer to state-owned enterprises plus state-holding enterprises. State-owned enterprises (originally known as state-run enterprises with ownership by the whole society) are non-corporate economic entities registered in accordance with the Regulation of the People's Republic of China on the Management of Registration of Legal Enterprises, where all assets are owned by the state. Included in this category are state-owned enterprises, state-funded corporations and state-owned joint-operation enterprises. Joint state-private industries and private industries, which existed before 1957, were transformed into state-run industries since 1957, and into state-owned industries after 1992. Statistics on those enterprises are included in the state-owned industries instead of grouping them separately. State-holding enterprises is a sub-classification of enterprises with mixed ownership, referring to enterprises where the percentage of state assets (or shares by the state) is larger than any other single share holder of the same enterprise. This sub-classification illustrates the control of the state over a particular industry.

Collective-owned Enterprises refer to economic entities registered in accordance with the Regulation of the People's Republic of China on the Management of Registration of Legal Enterprises, where assets are owned by collectively. Collective enterprises constitute an integral part of the socialist economy with public ownership. They include urban and rural enterprises invested by collectives, and some enterprises registered in industrial and commercial administration agency as collective units where funds are pulled together by individuals who voluntarily give up their right of ownership.

Share-holding Cooperative Enterprises refer to economic units set up on cooperative basis, with funding partly from members of the enterprise and partly from outside investment, where the operation and management is decided by the members who also participate in the production, and the distribution of income is based both on work (labour input) and on shares (capital input).

Joint-operation enterprises refer to economic units that are established by joint investment by two or more corporate enterprises or institutions of the same or different types of ownership on voluntary, equal and mutual-beneficial basis. They include:

a) state-owned joint-operation enterprises (joint operation between state-owned enterprises);

b) collective joint-operation enterprises (joint operation between collective enterprises; and

c) state-collective joint-operation enterprises (joint operation between state and collective enterprises).

Limited Liability Corporations refer to economic units registered in accordance with the Regulation of the People's Republic of China on the Management of Registration of Corporations, with capitals from 2 to 49 investors, each investor bears limited liability to the corporation depending on his/her holding of shares, and the corporation bears liability to its debt to the maximum of its total assets.

Share-holding Corporations Ltd. refer to economic units registered in accordance with the Regulation of the People's Republic of China on the Management of Registration of Corporate Enterprises, with total registered capitals divided into equal shares and raised through issuing stocks. Each investor bears limited liability to the corporation depending on the holding of shares, and the corporation bears liability to its debt to the maximum of its total assets.

Private Enterprises refer to economic units invested or controlled (by holding the majority of the shares) by natural persons who hire labours for profit-making activities. Included in this category are private limited liability corporations, private share-holding corporations Ltd., private partnership enterprises and private sole investment enterprises registered in accordance with the Corporation Law, Partnership Enterprise Law and Tentative Regulation on Private Enterprises.

Enterprises with Funds from Hong Kong, Macao and Taiwan refers to all industrial enterprises registered as the joint-venture, cooperative, sole (exclusive) investment industrial enterprises and limited liability corporations with funds from Hong Kong, Macao and Taiwan.

Foreign Funded Enterprises refers to all industrial enterprises registered as the joint-venture, cooperative, sole (exclusive) investment industrial enterprises and limited liability corporations with foreign funds.

Enterprise with Hong Kong, Macao, Taiwan and foreign fund refer to all the enterpries with funds from Hong Kong Macao and Taiwan and foreign funded enterprises.

Light Industry refers to the industry that produces consumer goods and hand tools. It consists of two categories, depending on the materials used:

(1) Industries using farm products as raw materials. These are branches of light industry which directly or indirectly use farm

products as basic raw materials, including the manufacture of food and beverages, tobacco processing, textile, clothing, fur and leather manufacturing, paper making, printing, etc.

(2) Industries using non farm products as raw materials. These are branches of light industry which use manufactured goods as raw materials, including the manufacture of cultural, educational articles and sports goods, chemicals, synthetic fiber, chemical products for daily use, glass products for daily use, metal products for daily use, hand tools, medical apparatus and instruments, and the manufacture of cultural and clerical machinery.

Heavy Industry refers to the industry which produces capital goods, and provides various sectors of the national economy with necessary material and technical basis. It consists of the following three branches according to the purpose of production or the use of products:

(1) Mining, quarrying and logging industry refers to the industry that extracts natural resources, including extraction of petroleum, coal, metal and non-metal ores.

(2) Raw materials industry refers to the industry that provides various sectors of the national economy with raw materials, fuels and power. It includes smelting and processing of metals, coking and coke chemistry, chemical materials and building materials such as cement, plywood, and power, petroleum refining and coal dressing.

(3) Manufacturing industry refers to the industry that processes raw materials. It includes machine-building industry which equips sectors of the national economy, industries of metal structure and cement products, industries producing means of agricultural production, such as chemical fertilizers and pesticides.

According to the above principle of classification, the repairing trades, which are engaged primarily in repairing products of heavy industry are classified into heavy industry while these engaged in repairing products of light industry are classified into light industry.

Gross Industrial Output Value

(1) Definition: Gross industrial output value is the total volume of final industrial products produced and industrial services provided during a given period. It reflects the total achievements and overall scale of industrial production during a given period.

(2) Principles for calculation:

Statistics on industrial production follow the principle that all products produced by the enterprises and accepted during the reference period are to be included no matter whether they are sold or not during the reference period.

Determination of final products follow the principle that all products that are included in the calculation of grow industrial output value are the final products of the enterprise which have been accepted through quality check and require no further processing. If an enterprise has intermediate (semi-finished) products to sell, these intermediate products are considered as the final products of the enterprise.

Gross industrial output value is calculated following the principle of factory approach, i.e. industrial enterprise is used as the basic accounting unit in calculating the gross industrial output value. By this approach, value of the same product is not to be double counted, and the output value of different workshops (branch factories) should not be added. However, this approach does not exclude the possibility of double counting between enterprises.

(3) Content and calculation method: The old definition of gross industrial output value was modified during the national industrial census in 1995. The revised (new) definition of gross industrial output value consists of 3 components: value of the finished products during the reference period, income from external processing, and value of change in semi-finished products at the end and at the beginning of the reference period.

Value of the finished products during the reference period: refers to the value of all finished (semi-finished) industrial products that are produced during the reference period without the need for further processing, checked for acceptance, packed and put into the warehouse of the enterprise, including the value of own-produced equipment and the value of products provided to the projects under construction of the enterprise, and to other non-industrial or welfare units. Value of finished products during the reference period is calculated by the quantity of products produced using own materials multiplied by the average unit prices at which products are sold (excluding value-added tax). Own-produced equipment and products produced for own use are value at cost prices as in the case of enterprise accounting. Value of finished products does not include the value of finished products (semi-finished products) that are produced using the materials from the clients who make the orders.

Income from external processing: refers to income from contracted external processing of industrial products (including processing of industrial products using materials from the clients), and the income from industrial repairing work provided to other units. Income from external processing is calculated using information from the item "products sales income" in the enterprise accounting at the prices excluding value-added tax.

For income from services such as processing, repairing and installation of equipment provided to non-industrial units within the enterprise, if the accounting work of the enterprise is good enough to separate it from other records, and the share of such services is significant, it should also be included in the income from external processing.

Value of change in semi-finished products at the end and at the beginning of the reference period: refers to the value of change in semi-finished products at the end and at the beginning of the reference period, which generally can be obtained from accounting records of enterprises. If the enterprise accounting excludes the cost of semi-finished products, then it should not be included in the gross industrial output value, and vice versa.

(4) Changes in the coverage and method of calculation of gross industrial output value

Prior to 1984, the value of rural industry run by villages was classified into agriculture instead of industry. Since 1984, it has been included in the gross industrial output value. Method of calculation for the gross industrial output value was modified in the industrial census in 1995. The difference in the new method as compared with the old one is outlined below:

Principle in using full value vs. processing fee: The new method stipulates that all products produced using own materials are to be calculated with full value in reporting the gross industrial output value irrespective of sophistication of production, and for external processing, it allows calculation using processing fee. In the old method, however, the use of full value or processing fee was determined by the degree of sophistication of production in different branches of industries.

Principle in determining the value of change in semi-finished products: The new method requires that value of the change in semi-finished products should be included in the gross industrial output value if it is included in the accounting record of the enterprise, otherwise it should not be included. By the old method, it is determined by the type of enterprises in terms of production cycle. If the production cycle is over 6 months, the value of change in semi-finished products is included in the gross industrial output value, otherwise it is excluded.

Difference in prices: The new method uses prices excluding value-added tax in the calculation of gross industrial output value, while the old method used prices including value-added tax.

Value-added of Industry refers to the final results of industrial production of industrial enterprises in money terms during the reference period.

Industrial value-added can be calculated by two approaches: the production approach, i.e. gross industrial output value minus intermediate input plus value-added tax, and the income approach, i.e. income for various factors used in the course of production, including depreciation of fixed assets, remuneration of labourers, net of production tax, and operating surplus. Value-added of industry in the Yearbook is calculated by production approach as following:

Value-added of industry = gross industrial output industrial intermediate input + value-added tax

(1) Gross industrial output: refers to the total achievements of industrial production during a given period. Gross industrial output includes value of finished products, income from external processing, and value of change in semi-finished products at the end and at the beginning of the reference period. Since 1995, it was substituted by the gross industrial output value by new method.

(2) Industrial intermediate input: refers to purchased goods and paid services consumed during the industrial production of enterprises. Fees paid for services include fees paid for the services provided by material production sectors (industry, agriculture,

wholesale and retail trade, construction, transport, post and telecommunications) and by non-material production sectors (insurance, banking, culture, education, scientific research, health and medical care, public administration, etc.). The determination of industrial intermediate input follows the principle that the goods and services must be purchased from outside and included in the gross industrial output, and that the goods and services are inputted into production and consumed (include low-value consumables) during the reference period.

Industrial intermediate input includes 5 components, namely direct consumption of materials, industrial intermediate input in manufacturing cost, industrial intermediate input in management cost, industrial intermediate input in marketing cost and expenditure on interest.

Total Assets refer to all economic resources, in monetary terms, that is owned or controlled by enterprises, including properties, creditors equity and other economic rights of all forms. Classified by the degree of equitability, total assets include circulating assets, long-term investment, fixed assets, intangible assets and deferred assets, and other assets. Data on this indicator can be obtained by the year-end figures of total assets in the Assets and Liability Table of accounting records of enterprises.

Working Capitals refer to capitals that an enterprise can cash or use during one year or one production cycle that may exceeds one year, including cash and savings deposits of various forms, short-term investment, money receivable and prepaid money, inventories, etc.

Annual Average Value of Working Capitals refers to the average value of all working capitals of the enterprise during the reference period.

Original Value of Fixed Assets refers to the total value, in monetary terms, that an enterprise spent on fixed assets, through construction, purchase, installation, transformation, expansion or technical upgrading. Generally, it covers cost of purchase, packing, transportation and installation, etc.

Annual Average of Net Value of Fixed Assets refer to average of the net value of fixed assets during the reference period, calculated with the following formula:

Annual Average of Net Value of Fixed Assets = sum of net value of fixed assets at the beginning and at the end of each month from January to December / 24.

Information on this indicator can be obtained from the beginning and ending figures of the original value of fixed assets and cumulative depreciation from the Assets and Liability Table of enterprises.

Net value of fixed assets refers to the original value of fixed assets minus depreciation over the years, i.e.:

Net value of fixed assets = original value of fixed assets cumulative depreciation

Total Liabilities refer to payable liabilities of enterprises that have to repay in terms of money, assets or labour services. In terms of payment, it can be divided into liquid liabilities and long-term liabilities. Data on this item is obtained from the ending figures on total liabilities from the Assets and Liability Table from the enterprises.

Owner's Equity refers to the ownership of net assets of enterprise by its investors. The net assets equal the total assets minus total liabilities of the enterprise, including the actual assets invested into the enterprise by investors, accumulation of capitals and operating surplus and non-distributed profits. The enterprise's assets is less than its liabilities if the sum of owner's equity is smaller than zero.

Revenue from Principal Business refers to the annual accumulation of corresponding item in the "profit table" of the accountant. For enterprises that do not follow the 2001 Enterprise Accounting Standards, the year-end accumulation of revenue from the sales of products is used as a substitute.

Cost of Principal Business refers to the annual accumulation of corresponding item in the "profit table" of the accountant. For enterprises that do not follow the 2001 Enterprise Accounting Standards, the year-end accumulation of cost for the sales of products is used as a substitute.

Tax and Extra Charges from Principal Business refer to the annual accumulation of corresponding item in the "profit table"

of the accountant. For enterprises that do not follow the 2001 Enterprise Accounting Standards, the year-end accumulation of tax and extra charges from the sales of products is used as a substitute.

Total Profits refer to the final achievements of production and operation of the enterprises, represented by the total profits after deducting losses (loss is expressed by the negative figure). It is the sum of profits from operation, income from subsidies, investment earnings, net income from activities other than operation, and adjustment of profits and losses of previous years.

Value-added Tax Payable refers to the amount of the value-added tax which should be paid by the enterprises during the reference period. It is the sum of tax on sales, export rebate, and transferred tax on purchases of the current year, minus the tax on purchases of the current year. Value-added tax payable of small-size enterprises is determined by the taxable sales of the year multiplied by the tax rate.

Average Annual Number of Employed Persons Employed persons refer to all those who are employed in enterprises and receive remunerations therefrom, including currently working employees, retirees who are re-employed, teachers of local-run schools, as well as foreigners, staff from Hong Kong, Macao and Taiwan, part-time employees and persons with second job who are employed by the enterprise, and employees of other units temporarily working in the enterprises, but excluding former employees who left the enterprise with their employment records still kept by the enterprises.

Average number of employed persons refers to the number of employees everyday during the reference period, calculated with the following formula:

Monthly average number = sum of actual employees everyday in reference month/number of calendar dates in reference month

Quarterly average number = sum of monthly average number in reference quarter/3

Annual average number = sum of monthly average number in reference year/12

Ratio of Profits, Taxes and Interests to Average Assets reflects the profit-making capability of all assets of the enterprise and is a key indicator manifesting the performance and management and evaluating the profit-making potential of the enterprise. It is calculated as follows:

Ratio of Profits, Taxes and Interests to Average Assets (%) = [(total profits + total taxes + interest payment) / average assets]×100%

In the above formula, total taxes is the sum of tax and extra charges on the sales of products and value-added tax payable; and average assets is the arithmetic mean of the sum of beginning assets and ending assets.

Ratio of Debts to Assets reflect both the operation risk and the capability of the enterprise in making use of the capital from the creditors. It is calculated as follows:

Ratio of Debts to Assets (%) = (total debts / total assets)×100%

Both assets and debts are figures at the end of the reference period.

Turnover of Working Capitals refers to the number of times of turnover of working capital in a given period of time, which reflects the speed of the turnover of working capital of industrial enterprises, and is calculated as follows:

Turnover of Working Capital=(sales revenue of products) / (average balance of total working capital)

In the above formula, average balance of total working capital refers to the arithmetic mean of the sum of working capital at the beginning and at the end of the reference period.

Ratio of Profits to Total Industrial Costs refers to the ratio of profits realized in a given period to the total costs in the same period, which reflects the economic efficiency of input cost and is calculated as follows:

Ratio of Profits to Total Industrial Cost (%)=(total profits/ total costs)×100%

Total costs in the above formula is the sum of cost of products sold, marketing cost, management cost and financial cost.

Overall Labour Productivity is an indicator reflecting the production efficiency of an enterprise and the economic efficiency of its labour input, calculated by the formula:

Overall Labour Productivity (yuan/person) = industrial value-added / average of all persons engaged

Sales Ratio of Products is an indicator reflecting the actual sale of industrial products, analyzing the production-selling and supply-demand relations. It is calculated as:

Sales Ratio of Products (%) = value of industrial sales / gross industrial output value (current prices) * 100%

14 建筑业

Construction

资料整理：樊喜珍

建　　筑　　业
Construction
2014

建筑施工企业个数	Number of Construction Enterprises	3217	（个）
建筑施工企业职工平均人数	Average Number of Staff and Workers in Construction Enterprises	206.37	（万人）
建筑业总产值	Total Output Value of Construction Industry	10059.59	（亿元）
房屋建筑竣工面积	Floor Space of Building Completed	24867.25	（万平方米）
建筑业全员劳动生产率	Overall Labor Productivity of Construction Industry	48.75	（万元/人）

建筑业总产值(亿元)
Gross Output Value of Construction Enterprises (100 million yuan)

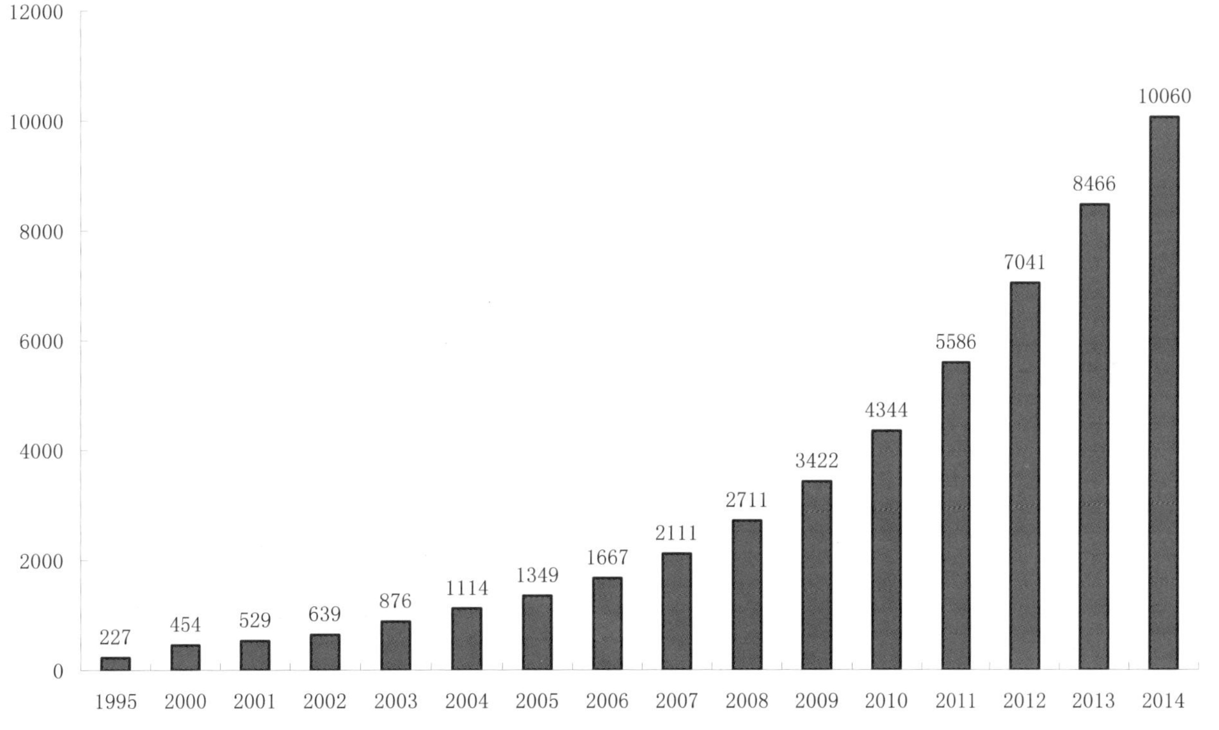

附：建筑业产值构成(%)

	2006	2007	2008	2009	2010	2011	2012	2013	2014
国有经济	32.7	50.5	49.2	47.4	52.6	52.5	48.7	46.5	47.3
城镇集体经济	4.3	3.2	2.1	2.3	1.4	1.5	1.9	0.8	0.7
乡镇企业及其他经济	63.0	46.3	51.3	50.3	45.9	45.9	49.4	52.7	52.0

14-1 建筑企业概况

BASIC STATISTICS ON CONSTRUCTION ENTERPRISES

项 目 Item	总 计 Total	国有经济 State-Owned	地 方 Local - Owned	中 央 Central- Owned	城镇集体经济 Urban Collective- Owned	其他经济 Others
企业单位个数(个) Number of Enterprises (unit)						
1991	575	179	137	42	396	
1992	603	184	142	42	419	
1993	898	241	208	40	642	15
1994	823	307	268	39	492	24
1995	912	323	277	46	539	50
1996	1696	403	250	53	1198	95
1997	1761	429	378	51	1207	125
1998	1838	433	379	54	1206	199
1999	2120	491	432	59	1297	332
2000	2070	488	440	48	1175	409
2001	1661	393	350	43	809	459
2002	1625	363	327	36	480	782
2003	1808	558	488	70	344	906
2004	2357	433	378	55	358	2566
2005	2114	524	448	76	268	1322
2006	2238	320	279	41	223	1695
2007	2516	449	383	66	191	1876
2008	2975	440	374	66	161	2374
2009	2878	396	331	65	152	2330
2010	2845	388	334	54	142	2315
2011	2640	376	330	46	130	2134
2012	2952	390	335	55	122	2440
2013	3376	399	334	66	98	2879
2014	3217	386	324	62	90	2741
职工平均人数(万人) Average Staff and Workers (10000 persons)						
1991	43.08	30.34	14.52	15.82	12.74	
1992	46.13	30.92	14.89	16.03	15.21	
1993	55.75	36.41	19.65	16.76	19.15	0.19
1994	52.66	36.83	19.07	17.76	15.43	0.40
1995	57.28	38.05	18.86	19.19	16.62	2.61
1996	76.51	36.83	18.58	18.25	36.20	3.48
1997	76.09	36.36	18.60	17.76	35.96	3.77
1998	82.63	38.22	19.22	19.00	38.82	5.59
1999	85.72	39.57	22.57	17.00	36.69	9.46
2000	82.76	36.58	21.73	14.83	35.36	10.82
2001	83.11	36.16	19.99	16.44	29.30	17.65
2002	93.50	34.20	21.25	12.95	23.50	35.80
2003	108.82	50.20	30.72	19.48	16.98	41.64
2004	105.30	44.40	28.10	16.30	12.20	48.70
2005	110.09	41.70	22.85	18.85	11.60	56.79
2006	114.25	27.26	15.18	12.08	10.28	76.71
2007	136.14	39.73	19.52	20.21	9.44	86.97
2008	137.61	38.51	18.40	20.11	6.61	92.49
2009	146.02	41.68	18.76	22.92	7.22	97.12
2010	170.71	54.40	22.31	32.09	5.57	110.74
2011	141.88	42.61	15.06	27.55	4.78	94.49
2012	169.33	50.83	15.10	35.73	4.21	114.29
2013	174.18	40.50	14.83	25.67	3.04	130.64
2014	206.37	49.04	19.48	29.56	3.35	153.98

14-1 续表 1 continued

项 目 Item	总 计 Total	国有经济 State-Owned	地 方 Local - Owned	中 央 Central- Owned	城镇集体经济 Urban Collective- Owned	其他经济 Others
建筑业总产值(亿元) Gross Output Value of Construction Enterprises (100 million yuan)						
1991	57.56	44.19	19.16	25.03	13.37	
1992	78.44	59.51	25.03	34.47	18.93	
1993	119.90	90.27	36.17	54.10	29.10	0.53
1994	169.28	140.29	56.95	83.34	27.75	1.24
1995	227.41	178.51	58.96	119.55	33.70	15.19
1996	284.43	187.00	60.83	126.17	79.14	18.29
1997	305.97	199.53	63.59	135.94	84.70	21.75
1998	343.65	223.80	73.98	149.82	93.15	26.70
1999	399.02	246.58	88.07	158.51	107.32	45.13
2000	454.35	266.03	106.76	159.27	123.46	64.86
2001	529.02	279.39	112.32	167.07	117.70	131.93
2002	639.11	301.93	143.90	158.03	98.90	238.29
2003	876.26	535.71	227.72	307.99	82.99	257.56
2004	1114.33	676.45	285.29	391.16	67.25	370.63
2005	1349.32	776.70	268.77	507.92	69.92	502.71
2006	1667.00	545.64	184.87	360.77	72.44	1048.92
2007	2110.80	1065.26	234.03	831.23	68.69	976.85
2008	2710.80	1333.87	241.63	1092.24	57.52	1319.41
2009	3421.89	1621.66	191.86	1429.80	77.86	1722.37
2010	4344.39	2287.08	414.78	1872.30	61.21	1996.10
2011	5586.45	2934.99	501.47	2433.52	85.04	2566.42
2012	7040.65	3428.40	627.89	2800.51	133.55	3478.70
2013	8465.50	3933.36	757.54	3175.82	66.75	4465.39
2014	10059.59	4755.30	921.65	3833.65	71.54	5232.75
施工房屋面积(万平方米) Floor Space of Buildings Under Construction (10000 sq.m)						
1991	1839.90	1103.30	758.10	345.20	736.60	
1992	2128.40	1190.40	829.90	360.50	938.10	
1993	2579.10	1439.30	989.10	450.20	1131.20	8.60
1994	2843.50	1894.50	1319.10	575.40	922.30	26.70
1995	3284.30	2122.80	1185.20	937.60	867.60	293.90
1996	4548.80	2224.60	1203.30	1021.30	2008.40	315.80
1997	4604.20	2330.60	1226.90	1103.70	1885.30	388.30
1998	5310.00	2488.80	1288.80	1200.00	2247.50	573.70
1999	5797.00	2703.40	1578.40	1125.00	2329.40	764.20
2000	6256.50	2889.10	1564.50	1324.60	2448.20	919.20
2001	6662.59	2792.50	1480.20	1312.30	2053.00	1817.10
2002	7215.88	2836.00	1452.00	1384.00	1742.00	2637.90
2003	8933.44	3817.50	2102.60	1714.90	1574.80	3541.10
2004	11772.31	5089.10	2522.60	2566.50	1348.90	5334.30
2005	12091.16	4568.90	1993.30	2575.60	1264.80	6257.50
2006	14478.24	3811.18	1016.18	2795.00	1021.60	9545.40
2007	16679.70	5503.80	1666.40	3837.40	1036.10	10139.80
2008	18376.50	5703.90	1060.40	4643.50	752.00	11920.60
2009	20499.30	5672.40	522.50	5149.90	799.40	14027.50
2010	25046.70	6752.80	968.80	5784.00	633.70	17660.30
2011	31023.80	9209.70	1549.00	7660.70	782.30	21031.70
2012	39112.20	10747.20	1661.70	9085.50	905.90	27459.10
2013	48937.96	14424.51	1734.33	12690.18	599.26	33914.19
2014	62227.88	22903.06	2137.75	20765.31	561.49	38763.33

14-1 续表 2 continued

项 目 Item	总 计 Total	国有经济 State-Owned	地 方 Local - Owned	中 央 Central- Owned	城镇集体经济 Urban Collective- Owned	其他经济 Others
竣工房屋面积(万平方米) Floor Space of Buildings Completed (10000 sq.m)						
1991	852.4	474.9	338.7	136.2	377.5	
1992	1002.8	508.4	378.5	129.9	494.4	
1993	1114.9	481.0	384.4	96.1	632.9	1.0
1994	1070.9	577.5	485.2	92.3	481.6	11.8
1995	1175.9	622.2	466.9	155.3	484.3	69.4
1996	1880.7	653.3	501.3	152.0	1123.5	103.9
1997	1982.3	765.3	522.1	243.2	1124.5	92.5
1998	2374.0	836.0	624.0	212.0	1298.6	239.4
1999	2873.0	1023.1	776.1	247.0	1484.3	365.6
2000	3150.1	1096.3	836.1	260.2	1572.0	481.8
2001	3673.4	1237.0	828.3	408.7	1334.1	1102.3
2002	4146.6	1261.8	889.3	372.5	1146.0	1738.8
2003	4840.8	1578.8	1143.4	435.4	993.7	2268.3
2004	6647.1	2561.3	1563.2	998.1	820.5	3265.3
2005	6896.9	2125.6	923.7	1201.9	791.5	3979.8
2006	7376.2	1137.1	450.4	686.7	678.8	5560.3
2007	8425.0	1620.9	858.6	762.3	608.8	5895.3
2008	9256.1	1386.0	537.9	848.1	476.1	7394.0
2009	10280.7	1587.1	255.9	1331.2	494.7	8198.9
2010	12813.4	2185.7	364.5	1821.2	452.8	10174.9
2011	16468.1	2593.0	600.0	1993.0	600.9	13274.2
2012	20395.2	1938.0	649.8	1288.3	705.2	17751.9
2013	22773.7	2278.0	571.7	1706.3	418.6	20077.1
2014	24867.3	2393.0	1105.0	1288.0	309.2	22165.1
房屋建筑面积竣工率(%) Rate of Floor Space of Buildings Completed (%)						
1991	46.3	43.0	44.7	39.5	51.2	
1992	47.1	42.7	45.6	36.0	52.7	
1993	43.2	33.9	38.9	21.3	56.0	11.6
1994	37.7	30.5	36.8	16.0	52.2	44.2
1995	35.8	41.2	39.4	16.6	55.8	23.6
1996	41.3	29.4	41.7	14.9	55.9	32.9
1997	43.1	32.7	42.6	22.0	59.6	23.8
1998	44.7	33.6	48.4	17.7	57.8	41.7
1999	49.6	37.8	49.2	22.0	63.7	47.8
2000	50.3	37.9	53.4	19.6	64.2	52.4
2001	55.1	44.3	56.0	31.1	65.0	60.7
2002	57.5	44.5	61.2	26.9	65.8	65.9
2003	54.2	41.3	51.1	25.4	63.1	64.1
2004	56.5	50.3	62.0	38.9	60.8	61.2
2005	57.0	46.5	46.3	46.7	60.8	63.6
2006	50.9	29.8	44.3	24.6	66.4	58.3
2007	50.5	29.5	51.5	19.9	58.8	58.1
2008	50.4	24.3	50.7	18.3	63.3	62.0
2009	50.2	28.0	49.0	25.8	61.9	58.4
2010	51.2	32.4	37.6	31.5	71.5	57.6
2011	53.1	28.2	38.7	26.0	76.8	63.1
2012	52.1	18.0	39.1	14.2	77.8	64.6
2013	46.5	15.8	33.0	13.4	69.9	59.2
2014	40.0	10.4	51.7	6.2	55.1	57.2

注：本表资料包括施工总承包和专业承包企业，不含劳务分包企业(下同)。
Note: In this table, the data including general contract and specilized contract enterprises under construction, excluding labor divided contract (the same as the following tables)

14-2 分市州建筑业企业生产情况(2014)
STATISTICS ON PRODUCTION OF CONSTRUCTION ENTERPRISES OF CITIES AND PREFECTURE(2014)

单位：亿元 (100 million yuan)

项目	Item	建筑业总产值 Total Output Value of Construction Industry	建筑工程产值 Output Value of Construction Projects	安装工程产值 Output Value of Installation Projects	其他产值 Output Value of Other Projects	竣工产值 Output Value of Projects Completed
湖北省	**Hubei Province**	**10059.59**	**8991.16**	**760.88**	**307.54**	**4875.17**
武汉市	Wuhan	5956.79	5293.31	461.45	202.03	2290.42
黄石市	Huangshi	300.05	281.05	14.64	4.36	179.87
十堰市	Shiyan	360.63	344.85	11.36	4.42	133.40
宜昌市	Yichang	694.76	616.45	57.95	20.35	263.24
襄阳市	Xiangyang	672.94	604.64	54.25	14.05	402.13
鄂州市	Ezhou	126.69	96.36	21.04	9.29	57.98
荆门市	Jingmen	114.83	98.63	10.33	5.87	81.41
孝感市	Xiaogan	394.39	350.62	33.21	10.56	291.83
荆州市	Jingzhou	227.00	205.12	15.91	5.96	185.24
黄冈市	Huanggang	695.63	637.92	46.36	11.35	639.20
咸宁市	Xianning	119.77	109.91	6.31	3.55	96.40
随州市	Suizhou	83.42	75.82	5.23	2.37	60.30
恩施自治州	Enshi	105.05	98.36	4.10	2.59	74.86
仙桃市	Xiantao	35.95	33.58	1.16	1.21	25.21
潜江市	Qianjiang	110.65	95.65	11.75	3.25	54.48
天门市	Tianmen	53.40	42.58	5.00	5.82	33.69
神农架林区	Shennongjia	7.66	6.33	0.83	0.51	5.50

14-3 按登记注册类型分的企业数及合同情况

单位：亿元

指标名称	Item	企业个数 Number of Enterprises	
		建筑业企业个数(个) Number of Construction Enterprises (unit)	有工作量的建筑业企业个数(个) Number of Construction Enterprises with Work (unit)
总计	**Total**	**3364**	**3217**
其中：国有及国有控股企业	State-owned and State-holding Enterprises	392	386
一、按登记注册类型分组	Grouped by Status of Registration		
内资企业	**Domestic Funded Enterprises**	**3344**	**3199**
国有企业	State-owned Enterprises	190	187
集体企业	Collective-owned Enterprises	92	89
股份合作企业	Cooperative Enterprises	5	5
联营企业	Joint Ownership Enterprises	2	2
国有联营企业	State Joint Ownership Enterprises		
集体联营企业	Collective Joint Ownership Enterprises	1	1
国有与集体联营企业	Joint State-collective Enterprises	1	1
其他联营企业	Other Joint Ownership Enterprises		
有限责任公司	Limited Liability Corporations	1427	1367
国有独资公司	State Sole Funded Corporations	42	41
其他有限责任公司	Other Limited Liability Corporations	1385	1326
股份有限公司	Share-holding Corporations Ltd.	149	148
私营企业	Private Enterprises	1478	1401
私营独资企业	Private-funded Enterprises	17	16
私营合伙企业	Private Partnership Enterprises	3	3
私营有限责任公司	Private Limited Liability Corporations	1375	1304
私营股份有限公司	Private Share-holding Corporations Ltd.	83	78
其他企业	Other Enterprises	1	
港、澳、台商投资企业	**Enterprises with Funds from Hong Kong,Macao and Taiw**	**16**	**14**
合资经营企业(港或澳、台资)	Joint-venture Enterprises	9	9
合作经营企业(港或澳、台资)	Cooperative Enterprises		
港、澳、台商独资经营企业	Enterprises with Sole Fund	6	4
港、澳、台商投资股份有限公司	Share-holding Corporations Ltd.	1	1
其他港澳台投资	Other Enterprises with Funds from Hong Kong,Macao and T:		
外商投资企业	**Foreign Funded Enterprises**	**4**	**4**
中外合资经营企业	Joint-venture Enterprises	4	4
中外合作经营企业	Cooperative Enterprises		
外资企业	Enterprises with Sole Fund		
外商投资股份有限公司	Share-holding Corporations Ltd.		
其他外商投资	Other Foreign Funded Enterprises		

Basic Statistics on Number of Enterprises and Contracts by Status of Registration

(100 million yuan)

合同情况（亿元） Condition on Contracts (100 million yuan)		
签订的合同额 Total Value of Contracts	1.上年结转合同额 Value from Contracts Signed in Last Year	2.本年新签合同额 Value from New Contracts Signed in This Year
18492.59	**7822.34**	**10670.24**
10784.53	5494.93	5289.59
18424.79	**7803.65**	**10621.15**
472.07	189.43	282.64
78.13	17.26	60.87
8.08	1.52	6.56
1.31	0.01	1.30
0.30	0.01	0.29
1.01	0.00	1.01
14050.71	6411.84	7638.87
3107.41	1649.09	1458.31
10943.30	4762.75	6180.55
933.85	372.00	561.85
2880.65	811.59	2069.06
21.89	2.24	19.64
0.18	0.00	0.18
2503.47	733.15	1770.32
355.11	76.19	278.92
0.00	0.00	0.00
8.59	**0.84**	**7.75**
7.94	0.56	7.38
0.30	0.06	0.25
0.35	0.22	0.13
59.20	**17.85**	**41.35**
59.20	17.85	41.35

14-4 按登记注册类型分的建筑业总产值

单位：亿元

指标名称	Item	建筑业总产值 Total Output Value
总计	**Total**	**10059.59**
其中：国有及国有控股企业	State-owned and State-holding Enterprises	4755.38
一、按登记注册类型分组	Grouped by Status of Registration	
内资企业	**Domestic Funded Enterprises**	10006.54
国有企业	State-owned Enterprises	313.56
集体企业	Collective-owned Enterprises	71.27
股份合作企业	Cooperative Enterprises	9.07
联营企业	Joint Ownership Enterprises	1.27
国有联营企业	State Joint Ownership Enterprises	
集体联营企业	Collective Joint Ownership Enterprises	0.27
国有与集体联营企业	Joint State-collective Enterprises	1.01
其他联营企业	Other Joint Ownership Enterprises	
有限责任公司	Limited Liability Corporations	7098.80
国有独资公司	State Sole Funded Corporations	1546.82
其他有限责任公司	Other Limited Liability Corporations	5551.98
股份有限公司	Share-holding Corporations Ltd.	585.54
私营企业	Private Enterprises	1927.02
私营独资企业	Private-funded Enterprises	13.22
私营合伙企业	Private Partnership Enterprises	0.18
私营有限责任公司	Private Limited Liability Corporations	1670.16
私营股份有限公司	Private Share-holding Corporations Ltd.	243.45
其他企业	Other Enterprises	
港、澳、台商投资企业	**Enterprises with Funds from Hong Kong,Macao and Taiwan**	**7.87**
合资经营企业(港或澳、台资)	Joint-venture Enterprises	7.51
合作经营企业(港或澳、台资)	Cooperative Enterprises	
港、澳、台商独资经营企业	Enterprises with Sole Fund	0.25
港、澳、台商投资股份有限公司	Share-holding Corporations Ltd.	0.11
其他港澳台投资	Other Enterprises with Funds from Hong Kong,Macao and Taiwan	
外商投资企业	**Foreign Funded Enterprises**	**45.18**
中外合资经营企业	Joint-venture Enterprises	45.18
中外合作经营企业	Cooperative Enterprises	
外资企业	Enterprises with Sole Fund	
外商投资股份有限公司	Share-holding Corporations Ltd.	
其他外商投资	Other Foreign Funded Enterprises	

Total Output Vaule of Construction by Status of Registration

(100 million yuan)

其中：装饰装修产值 Output Value of Decoration	其中：在外省完成的产值 Output Value Completed in Other Provinces	建筑工程产值 Output Value of Construction	安装工程产值 Output Vaule of Installation	其他产值 Others
450.05	**3882.04**	**8991.16**	**760.88**	**307.54**
61.75	3047.26	4300.89	313.19	141.31
443.29	3872.12	8938.63	760.45	307.45
2.87	40.37	224.34	36.20	53.03
1.51	1.04	62.65	8.12	0.50
		7.80	1.27	
0.04		1.25	0.02	
0.04		0.24	0.02	
		1.01		
222.83	3413.05	6380.26	569.02	149.52
2.83	1182.42	1449.51	91.74	5.58
220.00	2230.63	4930.74	477.29	143.94
14.42	90.33	525.88	34.47	25.19
201.62	327.32	1736.45	111.35	79.21
4.22	0.39	12.98	0.16	0.08
0.02		0.10		0.08
189.56	311.68	1492.21	102.36	75.59
7.82	15.26	231.17	8.83	3.46
6.51	**2.67**	**7.35**	**0.43**	**0.09**
6.28	2.59	7.13	0.31	0.08
0.13	0.08	0.12	0.11	0.01
0.10		0.10	0.01	
0.26	**7.25**	**45.18**		
0.26	7.25	45.18		

14-5 按隶属关系和资质等级分的建筑业总产值的构成

单位：亿元

指标名称	Item	建筑业总产值 Total Output Value
总计	**Total**	**10059.59**
一、按隶属关系分组	**Grouped by Jurisdiction of Management**	
中央	Centre	3833.65
省(自治区、直辖市)	Province (Autonomous Region、Municipality)	480.77
地区(州、盟、省辖市)	Region (State、League、Provincial Municipality)	1139.58
县(区、市、旗)	County (District、City、Banner)	906.20
街道	Street	177.92
镇	Town	122.90
乡	Countryside	27.76
居委会	Residents' Committee	10.70
村委会	Village Committee	3.67
其他	Others	3356.45
二、按企业资质等级分组	**Grouped by Qualification Criteria**	
企业资质等级(施工总承包)	General Contracting	9422.98
特级	Special Grade	2681.72
一级	First Grade	4175.19
二级	Second Grade	1858.06
三级及以下	Third Grade and Below	708.01
企业资质等级(专业总承包)	Professional Contraction Construction	636.61
一级	First Grade	346.72
二级	Second Grade	165.88
三级及以下	Third Grade and Below	124.01

Composition of Total Output Value of Construction Enterprises by Jurisdiction of Management and Qualification Criteria

(100 million yuan)

其中：装饰装修产值 Output Value of Decoration	其中：在外省完成的产值 Output Value Completed in Other Provinces	建筑工程产值 Output Value of Construction	安装工程产值 Output Vaule of Installation	其他产值 Others
450.05	**3882.04**	**8991.16**	**760.88**	**307.54**
40.22	2906.70	3502.43	246.21	85.01
8.46	41.26	417.55	47.97	15.24
44.76	177.15	967.61	115.23	56.74
24.94	106.53	814.73	67.90	23.58
13.70	45.55	145.97	29.50	2.46
1.13	11.57	115.90	5.89	1.11
0.04		27.64	0.11	0.02
0.94		8.57	1.55	0.58
0.20		3.29	0.18	0.20
315.66	593.28	2987.48	246.36	122.60
277.04	3721.51	8585.07	627.30	210.61
36.44	2092.62	2542.91	85.24	53.57
148.63	1487.46	3728.27	362.20	84.72
71.39	131.37	1688.27	129.58	40.21
20.58	10.07	625.62	50.27	32.11
173.01	160.53	406.10	133.58	96.94
122.29	112.52	225.50	45.45	75.77
41.16	40.57	105.30	46.93	13.66
9.56	7.43	75.29	41.21	7.51

14-6 按登记注册类型分的建筑业企业完成房屋建筑竣工面积

单位：万平方米

指标名称	Item	合 计 Total
总计	**Total**	**24867.26**
其中：国有及国有控股企业	State-owned and State-holding Enterprises	2392.95
按登记注册类型分组	Grouped by Status of Registration	
内资企业	**Domestic Funded Enterprises**	**24783.97**
国有企业	State-owned Enterprises	281.11
集体企业	Collective-owned Enterprises	429.31
股份合作企业	Cooperative Enterprises	8.38
联营企业	Joint Ownership Enterprises	3.13
国有联营企业	State Joint Ownership Enterprises	
集体联营企业	Collective Joint Ownership Enterprises	3.13
国有与集体联营企业	Joint State-collective Enterprises	
其他联营企业	Other Joint Ownership Enterprises	
有限责任公司	Limited Liability Corporations	14264.08
国有独资公司	State Sole Funded Corporations	181.74
其他有限责任公司	Other Limited Liability Corporations	14082.33
股份有限公司	Share-holding Corporations Ltd.	1821.12
私营企业	Private Enterprises	7976.85
私营独资企业	Private-funded Enterprises	71.92
私营合伙企业	Private Partnership Enterprises	0.39
私营有限责任公司	Private Limited Liability Corporations	7210.27
私营股份有限公司	Private Share-holding Corporations Ltd.	694.27
其他企业	Other Enterprises	
港、澳、台商投资企业	**Enterprises with Funds from Hong Kong,Macao and Taiwan**	**3.12**
合资经营企业(港或澳、台资)	Joint-venture Enterprises	3.12
合作经营企业(港或澳、台资)	Cooperative Enterprises	
港、澳、台商独资经营企业	Enterprises with Sole Fund	
港、澳、台商投资股份有限公司	Share-holding Corporations Ltd.	
其他港澳台投资	Other Enterprises with Funds from Hong Kong,Macao and Taiwan	
外商投资企业	**Foreign Funded Enterprises**	**80.17**
中外合资经营企业	Joint-venture Enterprises	80.17
中外合作经营企业	Cooperative Enterprises	
外资企业	Enterprises with Sole Fund	
外商投资股份有限公司	Share-holding Corporations Ltd.	
其他外商投资	Other Foreign Funded Enterprises	

Completed Floor Space of Buildings Constructed by Construction Enterprises by Status of Registration

(10 000sq.m)

住宅房屋 Residential Buildings	商业及服务用房屋 Houses for Business and Service	办公用房屋 Office Buildings	科研、教育、医疗用房屋 Houses for Scientific Research、Education and Medical Treatment	文化、体育、娱乐用房屋 Houses for Culture、Sports and Entertainment	厂房及建筑物 Workshop and Buildings	仓库 Storage	其他未列明的房屋建筑物* Others
17171.17	**1646.28**	**1522.23**	**930.77**	**395.72**	**2615.29**	**189.76**	**396.04**
1641.21	152.26	188.07	74.34	19.17	273.67	12.22	32.01
17118.90	**1635.96**	**1518.52**	**930.77**	**389.86**	**2604.17**	**189.76**	**396.04**
160.19	19.29	28.30	11.86	2.70	47.48	2.70	8.60
307.79	38.80	36.21	9.33	0.81	31.45	0.35	4.59
7.69					0.68		
1.38	0.20	0.42	0.54		0.47		0.12
1.38	0.20	0.42	0.54		0.47		0.12
10013.77	978.58	796.19	578.06	176.31	1427.34	39.28	254.53
52.17	2.54	0.00			127.03		
9961.60	976.04	796.19	578.06	176.31	1300.31	39.28	254.53
1047.20	219.39	129.26	118.15	29.06	226.99	26.08	25.00
5580.87	379.71	528.14	212.83	180.98	869.75	121.36	103.21
57.46		6.27	0.64		7.43	0.13	
		0.39					
4997.33	365.93	425.55	207.07	180.18	821.84	120.95	91.41
526.08	13.78	95.93	5.12	0.80	40.48	0.28	11.80
	0.36				**2.76**		
	0.36				2.76		
52.28	**9.96**	**3.71**		**5.86**	**8.35**		
52.28	9.96	3.71		5.86	8.35		

14-7 按隶属关系和资质等级分的建筑业企业工程完成情况

单位：万平方米

指标名称	Item	房屋建筑施工面积 Floor Space of Buildings under Construcion
一、按隶属关系分组	**Grouped by Jurisdiction of Management**	
中央	Centre	20765.31
省(自治区、直辖市)	Province (Autonomous Region、Municipality)	2022.37
地区(州、盟、省辖市)	Region (State、League、Provincial Municipality)	6844.30
县(区、市、旗)	County (District、City、Banner)	6412.95
街道	Street	1153.38
镇	Town	757.49
乡	Countryside	178.70
居委会	Residents' Committee	68.12
村委会	Village Committee	37.22
其他	Others	23988.04
四、按企业资质等级分组	**Grouped by Qualification Criteria**	
企业资质等级(施工总承包)	Enterprises Qualification Criteria (General Contracting)	61482.62
特级	Special Grade	17422.19
一级	First Grade	24808.08
二级	Second Grade	13630.37
三级及以下	Third Grade and Below	5621.97
企业资质等级(专业总承包)	Enterprises Qualification Criteria (Professional Contraction Construction)	745.26
一级	First Grade	176.46
二级	Second Grade	287.26
三级及以下	Third Grade and Below	281.54

Project Completion Situation on Construction Enterprises by Jurisdiction of Management and Qualification Criteria

(10 000 sq.m)

本年新开工面积 Floor Space of New Construction This Year	实行投标承包面积 Contracting Space of Bidding	房屋建筑竣工面积 Floor Space of Buildings Completed	住宅房屋 Residential Buildings	商业及服务用房屋 Houses for Business Use
4329.79	15376.70	1764.31	1288.01	99.04
900.31	1756.78	578.69	371.77	23.78
4438.28	5204.95	3245.27	2020.80	178.77
4249.64	5194.57	3909.68	2523.71	471.30
679.77	892.05	849.70	553.01	60.19
602.26	587.60	537.97	348.22	14.98
107.72	178.23	156.01	123.48	1.13
55.93	57.12	59.66	36.73	16.37
20.45	18.49	28.17	25.61	
14663.69	17357.16	13737.78	9879.83	780.72
29581.17	46180.10	24448.57	16926.96	1622.42
5877.51	12352.59	3723.50	2416.26	225.10
11805.18	20456.72	9445.29	6390.56	786.24
8637.21	9724.36	7930.14	5842.24	433.47
3261.28	3646.44	3349.65	2277.90	177.61
466.66	443.55	418.69	244.21	23.86
156.15	140.12	103.02	43.53	
121.27	115.85	118.99	81.34	5.05
189.24	187.58	196.68	119.34	18.81

14-8 分市州建筑业企业工程完成情况(2014)
STATISTICS ON PROJECTS COMPLETION OF CONSTRUCTION ENTERPRISES BY CITIES AND PREFECTURES (2014)

单位：万平方米 (10 000 sq.m)

项 目	Item	房屋建筑施工面积 Floor Space of Housing Construction	本年新开工面积 Beginning projects in This Year	实行投标承包面积 Actual Floor Space by Contracts and Bids	房屋建筑竣工面积 Floor Space of Housing Projects Completed	#住 宅 Residential Buildings	#办公用房 Office Buildings
湖北省	**Hubei Province**	**62227.88**	**30047.83**	**46623.65**	**24867.26**	**17171.17**	**1522.23**
武汉市	Wuhan	35352.18	13199.77	26447.99	10223.95	7139.92	658.39
黄石市	Huangshi	2058.19	1190.14	1493.62	1102.76	786.26	44.67
十堰市	Shiyan	1488.72	761.90	837.25	635.76	465.70	31.22
宜昌市	Yichang	3126.68	1350.40	2522.46	1157.17	831.75	48.93
襄阳市	Xiangyang	4061.51	2264.64	3187.70	1835.19	1326.55	49.53
鄂州市	Ezhou	1160.95	559.33	967.29	435.39	301.50	12.98
荆门市	Jingmen	908.01	601.32	856.66	497.39	377.01	27.69
孝感市	Xiaogan	3308.86	2455.34	2123.38	1905.51	1418.49	110.13
荆州市	Jingzhou	1638.70	958.16	1083.72	906.54	549.39	30.94
黄冈市	Huanggang	5374.12	4406.17	4444.14	4025.89	2499.79	352.48
咸宁市	Xianning	790.66	547.43	468.41	609.82	495.40	34.56
随州市	Suizhou	797.12	538.29	642.57	496.21	338.65	45.98
恩施自治州	Enshi	753.44	392.29	434.13	382.28	244.05	33.71
仙桃市	Xiantao	246.82	155.86	206.44	148.18	112.07	15.57
潜江市	Qianjiang	697.02	396.71	626.48	282.13	160.91	6.58
天门市	Tianmen	382.49	239.46	250.39	198.37	101.34	17.78
神农架林区	Shennongjia	82.41	30.62	31.01	24.71	22.40	1.08

主要统计指标解释

建筑业统计单位 指从事房屋、构筑物建造和设备安装活动的法人企业。建筑业法人企业应具有建筑业资质并能够独立核算，同时其应具备以下条件：①依法成立，有自己的名称、组织机构和场所，能够承担民事责任；②独立拥有和使用资产，承担负债，有权与其他单位签订合同；③独立核算盈亏，能够编制资产负债表。

建筑业总产值 是以货币形式表现的建筑业企业在一定时期内生产的建筑业产品和提供的服务的总和。建筑业总产值包括：

⑴建筑工程产值：指列入建筑工程预算内的各种工程价值。

⑵安装工程产值：指设备安装工程价值，不包括被安装设备本身的价值。

⑶其他产值：建筑业总产值中除建筑工程、安装工程以外的产值。包括房屋构筑物修理产值、非标准设备制造产值、总包企业向分包企业收取的管理费以及不能明确划分的施工活动所完成的产值。

a.房屋构筑物修理产值：指房屋和构筑物修理所完成的产值，但不包括被修理房屋、构筑物本身价值和生产设备的修理产值。

b.非标准设备制造产值：指加工制造没有定型的非标准生产设备的加工费和原材料价值(如化工厂、炼油厂用的各种罐、槽，矿井生产统一使用的各种漏斗、三角槽、阀门等)以及附属加工厂为本企业承建工程制作的非标准设备的价值。

建筑业增加值 指建筑业企业在报告期内以货币形式表现的建筑业生产经营活动的最终成果。

从 2004 年第一次全国经济普查开始，建筑业现价增加值按生产法和分配法(收入法)两种方法计算，以收入法的计算结果为准，即从收入的角度出发，根据生产要素在生产过程中应得的收入份额计算。具体计算方法：经济普查年度建筑业增加值按照《经济普查年度 GDP 核算方案》计算，非经济普查年度建筑业增加值按照《非经济普查年度 GDP 核算方案》计算。

房屋建筑施工面积 指在报告期内施过工的全部房屋建筑面积，包括本期新开工的房屋面积、上期施工跨入本期继续施工的房屋面积、上期停缓建在本期恢复施工的房屋面积、本期竣工的房屋面积及本期施工后又停缓建的房屋面积。

房屋建筑竣工面积 指在报告期内房屋建筑按照设计要求全部完工，达到了使用条件，经验收鉴定合格，正式移交使用单位的房屋建筑面积。

Explanatory Notes on Main Statistical Indicators

Statistical Unit in Construction refers to corporate enterprise engaged in the construction of buildings and structures and in the installation of equipment. A corporate construction enterprise should have qualification certificates with independent accounting system, and should meet the following 3 requirements: a) being set up in line with relevant legal basis, having its full name, organization and location, and capable of taking civil liabilities; b) independently possessing and using its assets and assuming its liabilities, and entitled to sign contracts with other institutions; and c) making independent accounts of its profits and losses, and capable of compiling its own balance sheet.

Gross Output Value of Construction refers to total of construction products and services, expressed in money terms, produced or rendered by construction and installation enterprises during a given period of time. It includes:

(1) Output value of construction projects, that is the value of projects covered by the project budgets;

(2) Output value of installation projects, that is the value of the installation of equipment, (excluding the value of the equipment

to be installed);

(3) Output value of others, that is the output value of construction industry excluding that of construction projects and installation projects. It includes: output value of repair of buildings and structures; output value of non-standard equipment manufacturing; overhead expenses received by contracted enterprises to the sub-contracted enterprises and the completed output value of construction activities that have no clear definition.

a. Output value of repair of buildings and structures, that is the value created through the repairs of buildings or structures, but does not include the value of buildings or structures being repaired and the value of the repair of production equipment;

b. Output value of manufactured non-standard equipment, that is the value of non-standard production equipment including raw materials and manufacturing cost made for the construction project (i.e., chemical plant; kettles or tanks used by refineries; various fillers, triangle tanks, valves used by mines), and the output value of equipment manufactured by subsidiary workshops.

Value-added of Construction refers to the final result of the activities of production and management of construction industry in monetary terms in the reference period.

Starting from the 2004 economic census, value-added of construction is calculated by both production approach and income approach, with the income approach as the final approach, where the calculation is based on the share of production factor in the production process. Specifically, value-added of construction for census years is calculated in accordance with the Programme of Compilation of GDP and National Accounts for the Year of Economic Census, and value-added of construction for other years is calculated in accordance with the Programme of Compilation of GDP and National Accounts for the Non Economic Census Years.

Floor Space of Buildings Under Construction refers to floor space of buildings under construction during the reference period, including newly started buildings, buildings started earlier and continued during the reference period, and buildings suspended earlier but restarted during the reference period, buildings completed during the reference period, and buildings under construction and then suspended during the reference period.

Floor Space of Buildings Completed refers to the floor space of buildings that are completed in the reference period in accordance with the requirements of the design, up to the standard for putting them into use, and have been checked and accepted by concerned departments as qualified ones.

15 交通运输、邮电

Transportation, Post and Telecommunications Services

资料整理：朱　焰　夏　述

交通运输、邮电

Transportation,Post and Telecommunication Service

2014

全社会客运量	Passenger Capacity of The Whole Society	103672.00	(万人)
#公路	Public Road	87804.00	(万人)
全社会货运量	Volume of Freight Traffic	154736.00	(万吨)
#公路	Public Road	116280.00	(万吨)
邮电业务总量	Postal Service Portfolio	720.35	(亿元)
#函件	Letters	0.67	(亿件)
年末固定电话用户	Local Telephone Subscriber End of Year	907.40	(万户)
年末移动电话用户	Mobile Phone Subscriber End of Year	4606.80	(万户)

全 社 会 客 货 运 量
Passenger Capactity of The Whole Society

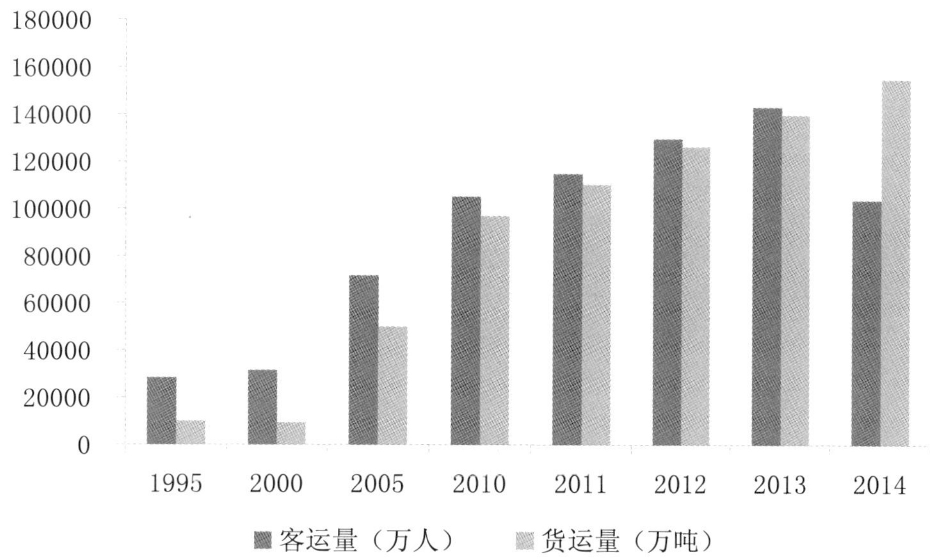

附：全社会客货运量

Passenger Capacity of The Whole Society

年份 Year	客运量（万人） Passenger Capacity (10 000 persons)	货运量（万吨） volume of freight traffic (10 000 tons)
1995	28508	10174
2000	31593	9345
2005	71892	49924
2010	105132	96938
2011	114737	110168
2012	129511	126195
2013	143100	139740
2014	103672	154736

说明：2014年因公路运输调整统计方法，与前期数据不可比（下同）。

Note:In 2014,the statistics method of transportation has been changed, the data can not be compared by the previous(the same below).

15-1 交通运输业基本情况

指　　标	Item	1995	2000
运输线路长度　(公里)	Length of Transportation Routes　(km)		
铁路营业里程	Total Railway's Length in Operation	1940	2025
公路通车里程	Total Highway in Operation	48728	57850
#等级公路里程	Length of Expressway and Class I to IV Highway	30910	48062
#高速公路	Expressway		569
一级公路	Class I Highway	641	611
二级公路	Class II Highway	4967	7911
内河航道里程	Navigable Inland Waterways	8969	8309
客运量总计　(万人)	Total Passenger Traffic　(10 000 persons)	28508.20	31593.00
铁路	Railway	2300.00	3469.00
公路	Highway	24315.00	27184.00
水运	Waterway	1745.00	679.00
民用航空	Civil Aviation	150.00	261.00
旅客周转量　(亿人公里)	Turnover Volume of Passenger Traffic　(100 million persons-km)	285.29	398.32
货物运输量总计　(万吨)	Total Freight Traffic　(10 000 tons)	10173.62	9345.19
铁路	Railway	3986.00	3857.00
公路	Highway	2600.00	2228.00
水运	Waterway	3585.00	3255.00
货物周转量　(亿吨公里)	Turnover Volume of FreightTraffic　(100 million tons-km)	776.44	831.64
民用车辆拥有量　(万辆)	Civil Moto Vehicles		
#民用汽车拥有量	Civil Vehicles	34.89	47.55
#载客汽车	Passenger Vehicles	14.96	24.69
载货汽车	Trucks	18.61	21.72
#营运汽车	Moto Vehicles in Operation		
#私人汽车	Private Vehicles		41.72
民用运输船舶拥有量　(艘)	Civil Transpot Vessels　(units)		5905
机动船	Moto Vessels		4188
驳船	Barges		1717
港口货物吞吐量　(万吨)	Cargo Handled at Ports　(10 000 tons)		4113.46

注：2014年因公路运输统计方法调整，数据与前期不可比。

Note:From 2014, due to the statistics method of road transport has been adjusted, the data can not be compared with the previous period .

TRANSPORTATION

2005	2009	2010	2011	2012	2013	2014
2758	3662	3032	3340	3463	4794	4926
91131	197196	206212	212746	218151	226912	236932
76075	168834	187812	196452	203145	212893	224184
1649	3283	3674	4006	4006	4333	5096
1092	1725	2210	2395	2515	2789	3344
15225	16261	16159	16852	17233	17576	18033
8988	8988	8988	8988	8988	8988	9055
71892.00	96219.00	105415.50	114736.92	129510.90	143100.28	103671.80
4615.00	6440.00	7281.30	8503.80	9177.40	12101.80	14302.70
66183.00	88703.00	96873.00	104971.00	118369.00	129533.75	87804.00
601.00	371.00	375.80	347.60	443.50	528.00	533.80
494.00	705.00	885.40	914.52	933.50	936.73	1031.30
803.90	1096.30	1262.26	1444.66	1576.97	1761.10	1458.24
49923.52	82714.00	97006.94	110167.83	126194.64	139740.26	154735.73
8491.00	9839.00	10145.60	10059.40	9177.40	9010.40	7681.30
33481.00	59563.00	71020.00	82741.00	97136.00	108824.21	116280.00
7944.00	13305.00	15832.00	17358.00	19070.00	24408.00	30765.00
1682.48	2808.46	3370.37	4044.45	4351.80	5036.80	5798.12
393.90	760.97	761.11	822.68	879.01	967.23	1042.36
103.04	187.02	224.60	264.82	305.07	363.68	439.39
53.40	119.81	151.51	186.72	277.76	282.29	345.84
30.96	46.07	53.29	59.72	62.69	68.62	72.73
20.33	32.20	36.60	40.28	40.37	42.04	42.95
59.66	131.56	165.39	200.38	238.64	292.00	300.61
5362	5460	5502	5505	4895	4938	4744
4158	4175	4634	4884	4531	4794	4500
1204	1285	868	621	364	232	244
13992.51	16671.77	18782.67	21662.91	23518.12	26219.00	28969.15

15-2 客 运 量
PASSENGER TRAFFIC

单位：万人 (10 000 persons)

年份 Year	总计 Total	铁路 Railway	公路 Highway	水运 Waterway	民用航空 Civil Aviation
1978	12009.20	2854.00	7429.00	1722.00	4.20
1980	16629.26	3217.00	11282.00	2123.00	7.26
1985	28178.22	3353.00	22378.00	2433.00	14.22
1990	32145.93	2107.00	27333.00	2693.00	12.93
1991	33982.62	2016.00	29279.00	2654.00	33.62
1992	34726.00	2077.00	29635.00	2894.00	120.00
1993	30152.00	2265.00	25116.00	2665.00	106.00
1994	29607.00	2358.00	24819.00	2210.00	120.00
1995	28508.20	2300.00	24315.00	1743.00	150.00
1996	29045.40	2248.00	25180.00	1449.00	168.00
1997	29503.08	2127.00	25684.00	1538.00	154.08
1998	28208.00	2218.00	24540.00	1306.00	144.00
1999	29360.14	2545.00	25596.00	1080.00	139.14
2000	63306.00	3469.00	58897.00	679.00	261.00
2001	62696.00	3632.00	58018.00	767.00	279.00
2002	63382.00	3813.00	58623.00	638.00	308.00
2003	62880.00	3602.00	58371.00	573.00	334.42
2004	68167.00	4072.00	63127.00	522.00	446.11
2005	71892.00	4615.00	66183.00	601.00	494.00
2006	75440.00	4850.00	69335.00	706.00	549.00
2007	84088.00	5125.00	77514.00	736.00	712.70
2008	89720.00	6027.00	82532.00	388.00	774.00
2009	96219.00	6440.00	88703.00	371.00	705.00
2010	105415.50	7281.30	96873.00	375.80	885.40
2011	114736.92	8503.80	104971.00	347.60	914.52
2012	129510.90	9764.90	118369.00	443.50	933.50
2013	143100.28	12101.80	129533.75	528.00	936.73
2014	103671.40	14302.70	87804.00	533.80	1031.30

注：2014年因公路运输统计方法调整，数据与前期不可比。
Note:From 2014, due to the statistics method of road transport has been adjusted, the data can not be compared with the previous period .

15-3 旅客周转量
TURNOVER VOLUME OF PASSENGER TRAFFIC

单位：亿人公里 (100 million person-kms)

年份 Year	总计 Total	铁路 Railway	公路 Highway	水运 Waterway	民用航空 Civil Aviation
1978	69.38	30.72	24.85	13.54	0.17
1980	95.88	41.79	36.20	17.52	0.37
1985	185.25	84.00	81.33	19.40	0.52
1990	225.85	82.83	112.83	29.28	0.91
1991	257.68	98.09	126.70	30.19	2.70
1992	286.35	104.89	135.61	34.72	11.13
1993	281.28	113.60	123.64	33.50	10.54
1994	283.98	121.91	121.40	28.71	11.96
1995	285.29	129.47	117.76	22.71	15.35
1996	285.04	121.17	124.97	21.09	17.81
1997	282.53	118.62	123.39	24.14	16.38
1998	278.66	126.68	118.51	18.79	14.68
1999	300.38	146.54	124.46	14.09	15.29
2000	563.78	232.00	297.46	8.84	25.48
2001	574.24	248.00	293.35	5.87	27.02
2002	633.6.9	283.00	317.02	3.60	30.07
2003	617.68	271.00	309.00	4.00	33.68
2004	703.95	322.80	334.00	3.20	43.95
2005	803.90	389.40	358.00	4.20	52.30
2006	847.42	408.10	374.80	5.10	59.42
2007	947.71	440.80	423.80	5.30	77.81
2008	1077.68	474.01	522.57	2.30	78.80
2009	1096.31	466.70	562.34	2.49	64.78
2010	1262.26	528.90	631.39	2.92	99.05
2011	1444.66	639.15	700.06	2.49	102.97
2012	1576.00	663.60	804.07	2.94	106.36
2013	1761.10	756.40	892.25	3.14	109.31
2014	1458.24	854.40	483.89	2.85	120.10

15-4 货　运　量

FREIGHT TRAFFIC

单位：万吨　　(10 000 tons)

年份 Year	总计 Total	铁路 Railway	公路 Highway	水运 Waterway	#内河 Inland Waterway	#海运 Seashipping
1978	10199	3513	3556	3130		
1980	8420	3211	2199	3110		
1985	11059	2659	3852	3463		
1990	10916	3901	2941	3784		
1991	11217	3957	2999	3996		
1992	11565	4018	2828	4364		
1993	11184	4029	2734	4248		
1994	10663	3964	2666	3641		
1995	10174	3986	2600	3585		
1996	9928	3779	2537	3268		
1997	9389	3882	2280	3119		
1998	10154	3999	2009	4040		
1999	10517	3964	2141	4313		
2000	40949	6558	27863	6270	6202	68
2001	41476	7094	29851	4275	4198	77
2002	42064	7400	28777	5630	5390	240
2003	44661	7825	30348	6195	5830	365
2004	47073	7872	31584	7259	6823	436
2005	50317	8491	33481	7944	7466	478
2006	52885	8990	35361	8242	7679	536
2007	58523	9728	39568	9027	7765	1262
2008	75778	10202	52759	12681	8182	4499
2009	82714	9839	59563	13305	8108	5197
2010	97007	10145	71020	15832	9916	6082
2011	110168	10059	82741	17358	10817	6536
2012	125392	9177	97136	19070	11836	7275
2013	139740	9010	108824	21897	13575	8042
2014	154736	7681	116280	30765	21152	8476

15-5 货物周转量

TURNOVER VOLUME OF FREIGHT TRAFFIC

单位：亿吨公里 (100 million ton-km)

年份 Year	总计 Total	铁路 Railway	公路 Highway	水运 Waterway	#内河 Inland Waterway	#沿海 Seashipping
1978	281.09	191.72	9.22	80.15		
1980	326.85	206.14	9.85	110.85		
1985	507.57	320.37	16.59	169.94		
1990	670.53	415.17	14.72	235.04		
1991	720.23	455.00	14.67	245.41		
1992	757.00	461.81	13.89	272.70		
1993	753.52	477.64	11.99	259.90		
1994	743.21	505.57	10.23	222.32		
1995	776.44	544.40	9.62	222.20		
1996	775.79	552.32	9.93	208.05		
1997	725.34	501.77	8.72	212.21		
1998	696.62	465.81	7.59	220.63		
1999	696.27	457.70	8.25	227.76		
2000	1156.57	618.37	227.16	305.29	295.07	10.22
2001	1097.60	634.90	218.97	237.31	226.15	11.16
2002	1212.82	680.00	211.49	313.60	271.30	42.29
2003	1313.13	703.80	224.00	377.00	315.38	61.61
2004	1485.76	781.83	235.60	461.08	395.75	65.33
2005	1689.86	987.60	251.00	443.20	391.05	105.00
2006	1730.93	1021.40	266.10	437.90	379.81	58.10
2007	1902.17	1138.20	302.09	458.00	361.93	95.83
2008	2699.97	1096.90	789.37	810.46	416.17	394.29
2009	2808.46	1032.40	930.10	845.18	402.82	442.36
2010	3370.37	1144.60	1079.13	1145.52	547.77	470.00
2011	4044.45	1226.80	1277.71	1538.83	625.26	609.61
2012	4693.61	1194.10	1565.45	1590.65	740.76	683.36
2013	4883.01	1195.70	1818.18	1868.08	946.02	756.69
2014	5798.12	1109.10	2340.56	2347.32	1347.07	891.82

15-6 全省民用车辆拥有量(2014)
NUMBER OF CIVIL MOTOR VEHICLES OWNED BY WHOLE PROVINCE(2014)

单位：辆 (unit)

指标	Item	总计 Total	营运 Working	非营运 Non-Working
合计	**Total**	**10423557**	**741638**	**9675074**
汽车	Civil Vehicles	4293922	603737	3683340
载客汽车	Passenger Vehicles	3458420	122271	3329304
#大型	Lage Scale	51855	36327	11822
中型	Medium Scale	40208	13529	23571
小型	Small Scale	3331852	72386	3259436
#轿车	Cars	2198633	67232	2131401
载货汽车	Trucks	727330	429542	297788
#重型	Heavy Scale	153960	141369	12591
中型	Medium Scale	82555	73606	8949
轻型	Light Scale	488322	213504	274818
#普通载货	Ordinary Trucks	330866	108573	222293
其他汽车	Other Vehicles	108172	51924	56248
#三轮汽车	Tricycle Motocars	14262	6466	7796
低速汽车	Low Speed Vehicles	53386	37136	20250
摩托车	Motorear	4804000	102091	4701909
#普通	Ordinary Motor	4740488	102065	4638423
轻便	Light Motor	63512	26	63486
拖拉机	Tractors	12882833		1288288
大中型	Large	158533		158533
小型方向盘式	Small Scale	1129755		1129755
挂车	Freight Trailers	36768	35593	1175
其他类型车	Other Motor Vehicles	577	215	362

注:本表“其他汽车”中，包括三轮和四轮农用运输车。
Note:Tricycles and four-wheel farming vehicles are inclued in "Other Vehicles".

15-7 私人车辆拥有量
NUMBER OF PRIVATE - OWNED VEHICLES

单位：辆 (unit)

指 标	Item	2000	2005	2010	2011	2012	2013	2014
民用汽车	Civil Vehicles	475500	596601	1653948	2003831	2386393	2919992	3566489
载客汽车	Passenger Vehicles	245500	297095	1153728	1473193	1861548	2366962	3006050
#大型	#Lage Scale	29200	3312	2939	2840	1258	1011	951
轿车	Cars		177650	773727	982237	1234812	1556798	1953696
载货汽车	Ordinary Trucks	211400	135352	327509	373852	405060	452886	478775
#重型	#Heavy Scale		8766	33281	40982	45874	51217	59171
其它汽车	Others		164154	172711	156786	119785	100144	81664
摩托车	Motors	1241000	2853113	4971619	5182441	4946723	4793599	4792901
载货挂车	Freight Trailers	4400	1714	6467	7866	8927	10255	10893

15-8 水路运输工具拥有量(2014)
NUMBER OF WATER TRANSPORT TOOLS(2014)

指 标		Item		机动船 Power Boat	客船 Passenger Ship	货船 Cargo Ship	拖船 Tugboat
数量	(艘)	Quantity	(ship)	4500	899	3466	135
总载重量	(吨位)	Total Carrying Capacity	(tonage)	7491749		7491749	
净载重量	(吨位)	Net Load	(tonage)	7283609		7283609	
载客量	(客位)	Passenger Carrying Capacity	(person)	45671	45671		
标准箱		TEU		23368		23368	
功率	(千瓦)	Power	(kw)	1865489	101871	1707785	55833

15-9 分市、州公路旅客运输完成情况(2014)
STATISTICS ON HIGHWAY PASSFNGER TRANSPORTATION OF CITIES AND PREFECTURES(2014)

地区	Region	旅客运输量(万人) Passenger Traffic (10,000 person)	旅客周转量(亿人公里) Turnover Volume of Passenger Traffic (100 million person-km)	货物运输量(万吨) Freight Traffic (10 000 ton)	货物周转量(亿吨公里) Turnover Volume of Freight Traffic (100 million ton-km)
武汉市	Wuhan	11648.50	741215.77	27287.42	568.41
黄石市	Huangshi	3187.50	198130.50	5364.55	107.87
十堰市	Shiyan	3523.56	300388.50	5306.38	106.70
宜昌市	Yichang	9535.57	487224.29	8465.28	164.49
襄阳市	Xiangyang	9602.39	475685.94	24841.85	483.19
鄂州市	Ezhou	2403.71	97660.79	1613.18	33.49
荆门市	Jingmen	3886.90	263269.93	6814.00	13.72
孝感市	Xiaogan	6472.71	350356.03	3058.12	60.79
荆州市	Jingzhou	9158.84	442621.40	7046.59	141.84
黄冈市	Huanggang	9592.91	482690.31	6853.90	140.30
咸宁市	Xianning	6132.39	361536.61	4188.88	84.46
随州市	Suizhou	3396.21	178085.41	6093.08	122.65
恩施自治州	Enshi	3282.32	202388.51	3861.43	77.73
仙桃市	Xiantao	1751.21	71149.26	1304.39	26.87
潜江市	Qianjiang	1804.10	79247.21	2139.61	43.07
天门市	Tianmen	1929.26	88142.02	1591.29	32.46
神农架林区	Shennongjia	495.99	19101.89	450.50	9.10

15-10 邮电业务基本情况
BASIC CONDITIONS OF THE POST AND TELECOMMUNICATION SERVICES

指　　标		Item	2005	2010	2012	2013	2014
邮电业务总量	**（亿元）**	**Total Volume of Post and Telecommunication Services (100 million yuan)**	**373.63**	**1028.09**	**491.46**	**603.67**	**720.35**
邮政业务总量		Postal Services	23.40	55.71	52.55	74.12	98.66
电信业务总量		Telecommunication Services	350.20	972.38	438.91	529.55	621.69
函件	（亿件）	Letters (100 million pcs)	1.30	1.00	1.31	1.05	0.67
包件	（万件）	Parcels (10 000 pcs)	320.00	210.10	174.70	170.20	141.70
快递业务量	（万件）	Special Express (10 000 pcs)	685.30	5476.60	11629.80	21991.00	72570.70
报刊期发数	（万份）	Newspaper and Magzines Circulation (10 000 pcs)	643.00	55102.50	67384.00	72770.50	72570.40
固定电话用户	（万户）	Fixed telephone subscribers (10 000 subscribers)	1236.00	1026.40	1003.60	984.00	907.40
年末城市电话	（万户）	Urban Telephone Subscribers at Year-end (10 000 subscribers)	900.00	670.70	666.20	662.90	613.00
年末农村电话	（万户）	Rural Telephones (10 000 subscribers)	336.00	355.70	337.40	321.10	294.40
年末移动电话用户	（万户）	Mobile Telephone Subscribers at Year-end (10 000 subscribers)	1401.00	3454.70	4554.10	4416.80	4606.80
互联网宽带接入用户	（万户）	Internet Users (10 000 subscribers)	128.00	459.40	708.00	813.30	869.70
邮路总长度(单程)	（公里）	Length of Postal Routes and Rural Delivery (One Way) (km)		57483	57125	57223	161205
邮路线路总条数	（条）	Routes		411	577	578	718
农村投递线路条数	（条）	Highway Routes		4198	3747	3747	3567
农村投递线路长度(单程)	（公里）	Railway Routes(One Way) (km)		194656	211898	206154	207494
邮电通信工具拥有量		Telecommunication Facilities					
固定电话局用交换机容量	（万门）	City Swicthboard Capacity (10 000 units)	1587.00	1690.80	1560.20	1482.60	1197.30
移动电话交换机容量	（万户）	Mobile Telephone Swicthboard Capacity (10 000 units)		5862.70	6805.70	7245.20	8450.70
固定长途电话交换机容量	（万路端）	Capacity of Long Distance Telephone Switchborad (circuit)	46.60	49.00	49.10	49.10	17.30
长途光缆线路长度	（万公里）	Length of Long Distance Optical Cable (km)		2.70	2.77	2.81	3.03

注：邮电业务总量统计口径2011年发生变化，与以前各年份不可比。

Note:The statistic on total volume of post and telecommunication have been reconfigured from 2011.Datas of other year can not compare with the data of 2011.

15-11 邮电通信水平

LEVEL OF POST AND TELECOMMUNICATION SERVICES

指 标	Item	2005	2010	2011	2012	2013	2014
每百人平均函件量 (件/百人)	Average Number of Letters Mailed Per 100 Persons (unit/100 person)	228.0	174.7	182.4	226.6	181.1	114.8
每百人平均订阅报刊量 (份/百人)	Average Number of Newspaper and Periodicals Subscribed Per 100 Persons (unit/100 person)	977.9	962.7	971.2	1166.0	1254.9	1247.8
每百人平均包件 (件/百人)	Average Number of Parcels Per 100 Persons (unit/100 person)	5.6	3.4	3.4	3.0	2.9	2.4
电话普及率 (部/百人)	Rate of Popularization of Telephone (unit/100 person)	43.9	78.3	86.9	96.2	93.1	94.8
移动电话普及率 (部/百人)	Rate of Popularization of Mobile Phones (unit/100 person)	23.3	60.4	68.7	78.8	76.2	79.2

主要统计指标解释

铁路营业里程 又称营业长度(包括正式营业和临时营业里程)，指办理客货运输业务的铁路正线总长度。凡是全线或部分建成双线及以上的线路，以第一线的实际长度计算；复线、站线、段管线、岔线和特殊用途线以及不计算运费的联络线都不计算营业里程。该指标可以反映铁路运输业基础设施的发展水平，也是计算客货周转量、运输密度和机车车辆运用效率等指标的基础资料。

公路里程 指在一定时期内实际达到《公路工程[WTBZ]技术标准 JTJ01-88》规定的等级公路，并经公路主管部门正式验收交付使用的公路里程数。包括大中城市的郊区公路以及通过小城镇街道部分的公路里程和桥梁、渡口的长度，不包括大中城市的街道、厂矿、林区生产用道和农业生产用道的里程。两条或多条公路共同经由同一路段，只计算一次，不得重复计算里程长度。该指标可以反映公路建设的发展规模，也是计算运输网密度等指标的基础资料。

内河航道里程 也称内河通航里程，指在一定时期内，能通航运输船舶及排筏的天然河流、湖泊水库、运河及通航渠道的长度。包括全年季节性通航累计三个月以上的航道，不包括仅供零散流放竹、木排的河道。该指标可以反映内河水运网的规模、水平和发展情况。

民用航空航线里程 指民航运输定期班机飞行的航线长度的总和。航线长度按机场之间的距离计算，通常有两种计算方法：一是将每条航线长度相加称为重复计算航线里程；一是将两线或两条以上航线经过同一区段里程，只计算一次航线长度称为不重复计算航线里程。一般常用的是后者，该指标可以确切反映民航运输网的规模，是表明民航事业为国民经济服务和方便人民生活程度的主要指标。

货(客)运量 指在一定时期内，各种运输工具实际运送的货物(旅客)数量。该指标是反映运输业为国民经济和人民生活服务的数量指标，也是制定和检查运输生产计划、研究运输发展规模和速度的重要指标。货运按吨计算，客运按人计算。货物不论运输距离长短、货物类别，均按实际重量统计。旅客不论行程远近或票价多少，均按一人一次客运量统计；半价票、小孩票也按一人统计。

货物(旅客)周转量 指在一定时期内，由各种运输工具运送的货物(旅客)数量与其相应运输距离的乘积之总和。该指标可以反映运输业生产的总成果，也是编制和检查运输生产计划，计算运输效率、劳动生产率以及核算运输单位成本的主要基础资料。计算货物周转量通常按发出站与到达站之间的最短距离，也就是计费距离计算。计算公式为：

货物（旅客）周转量=Σ（货物（旅客）运输量×运输距离）

民用汽车拥有量 指报告期末，在公安交通管理部门按照《机动车注册登记工作规范》，已注册登记领有民用车辆牌照的全部汽车数量。汽车拥有量统计的主要分类：根据汽车结构分为载客汽车、载货汽车及其他汽车；根据汽车所有者不同分为个人(私人)汽车、单位汽车；根据汽车的使用性质分为营运汽车、非营运汽车；根据汽车大小规格不同载客汽车分为大型、中型、小型和微型，载货汽车分为重型、中型、轻型和微型。

邮电业务总量 指以价值量形式表现的邮电通信企业为社会提供各类邮电通信服务的总数量。邮电业务量按专业分类包括函件、包件、汇票、报刊发行、邮政快件、特快专递、邮政储蓄、集邮、公众电报、用户电报、传真、长途电话、出租电路、无线寻呼、移动电话、分组交换数据通信、出租代维等。计算方法为各类产品乘以相应的平均单价(不变价)之和，再加上出租电路和设备、代用户维护电话交换机和线路等的服务收入。该指标综合反映了一定时期邮电业务发展的总成果，是研究邮电业务量构成和发展趋势的重要指标。计算公式为：

邮电业务总量=Σ（各类邮电业务量×不变单价）+出租代维及其他业务收入

=邮政业务总量+电信业务总量

移动电话用户 指通过移动电话交换机进入移动电话网、占用移动电话号码的各类电话用户。包括签约用户和智能网预付费用户。一个移动电话号码统计为一户。

互联网上网人数 指平均每周使用互联网至少1小时的中国公民人数。

本地电话用户 指接入本地电信运营商固定电话网上的电话用户。包括：住宅用户、单位用户、公用电话用户等。按电话用户位置又分为市内电话用户和农村电话用户。1997 年以前，“市内电话用户”是指接入县城及县以上城市的电话网上的电话用户；“农村电话用户”是指接入县邮电局农话台及县以下农村电话交换点，以县城为中心(除市话用户外)联通县、乡(镇)、行政村、村民小组的用户。从 1997 年起，电话用户数分组调整为以用户所在区域划分为“城市电话用户”和“乡村电话用户”，与过去的按市内电话和农村电话划分方法不同。而电话用户总数、电话机总部数统计范围不变。

城市电话用户 指直辖市、省辖市、地级市、县级市的市区、市郊区及县城(包括县人民政府所在地的县城关区或行政建制相当于县人民政府所在地的镇)范围内接入局用交换机的电话用户数，包括分布在农村地区的独立工矿区、林区、驻军等电话用户数。

农村电话用户 指按行政区划属于城市范围以外的乡(镇)、村的电话用户数。

住宅电话用户 指安装在居民住宅或农民家里并按照住宅电话用户登记注册和收费的电话用户。包括私人付费、单位付费和按规定免费安装的住宅电话用户。

长途电话交换机容量 指用于接入长途电话网的电话交换机设备的额定容量，包括国际电话交换机容量。

局用交换机容量 指安装在电信运营企业内用于接续本地固定电话的电话交换机容量，包括现用和备用的人工或自动交换机的全部容量。不包括用户交换机容量。

移动电话交换机容量 指移动电话交换机根据一定话务模型和交换机处理能力计算出来的最大同时服务用户的数量。

Explanatory Notes on Main Statistical Indicators

Length of Railways in Operation refers to the total length of the trunk line under passenger and freight transportation (including both full operation and temporary operation). The calculation is based on the actual length of the first line even if this line has a full or partial double track or more tracks, excluding double tracks, station sidings, tracks under the charge of stations, branch lines, special-purpose lines and the non-payable connecting lines. The length of railways in operation is an important indicator to show the development of the infrastructure for the railway transport, and also the essential data to calculate volume of passenger freight transport, traffic density and utilization efficiency of the locomotives and carriages.

Length of Electrified Railways refers to the length of the section of railways in operation in which the power supply lines and other equipment are installed for the running of electrified locomotives. The proportion of the length of electrified railways to the total length of railways in operation is an important indicator to show the modernization of railways.

Automatic-blocking and Semi-automatic-blocking Length of Railways refer to length of railways installed with equipment to perform automatic or manual blocking of trains. Blocking is a spacing technique by which a section of the railway only allows one train to pass at a time in the aim of ensuring the traffic safety. the proportion of automatic/semi-automatic blocking length to the total length of railways in operation is an important indicator to show the modernization of railways.

Length of Highways refers to the length of highways which are built in conformity with the grades specified by the highway engineering standard formulated by the Ministry of Communications, and have been formally checked and accepted by the departments of highways and put into use. The length of highways includes that of the suburb highways at large and medium-sized cities, highways passing through streets at small cities and towns, and also the length of bridges and ferries. It does not include the length of streets in big and medium-sized cities and highways built for the production purpose at factories, mines, forest areas and agricultural areas. If two or more highways go the same section of the way, the length of the section is only calculated for once and no duplication is allowed. The length of highways is an important indicator to show the development of the highway construction and to provide essential information to calculate the transport network density.

Length of Navigable Inland Waterways it is an indicator reflecting the size and development of inland water network, it refers to the length of the natural rivers, lakes, reservoirs, canals, and ditches open to navigation during a given period, which enables the transport by ships and rafts. It includes the channels open to navigation for over an accumulative 3 months in a year, yet this does not include the river courses, which are only used to float odd logs and bamboo rafts. This indicator can reflect the scale, level and development situation of the inland waterway network.

Length of Civil Aviation Routes refers to the length of all routes for regular civil aviation flights. There are usually two ways to calculate the distance between airports connected by the route length: One is to put the length of all air routes together, called duplicated calculation of the length of the routes; the other is not to allow the duplication in calculation when two or more routes passing the same section of aviation routes. The latter is usually used, as it can precisely show the size of the civil aviation network and indicate the extent of civil aviation serving the national economy and the people.

Length of Oil (Gas) Pipelines used as an indicator to show the development, scale and level of the pipeline transportation, it refers to the actual transport distance of oil (or gas) products, and is in general calculated in the length of single pipeline. If the length of the double pipelines and alternate pipeline are included, it is called the extension length of the oil (gas) pipelines, which indicates the actual length of the pipelines built, excluding double pipelines.

Freight (Passenger) Traffic refers to the volume of freight (passenger) transported with various means. Freight transport is calculated in tons and passenger traffic is calculated in the number of persons. Despite the type of freight and traveling distance, the freight transport is calculated in the actual weight of the goods: and despite the traveling distance and ticket price, the passenger traffic is calculated by the principle that one person can be counted only once in one travel. The passengers who travel with a half price ticket or a child ticket is also calculated as one person. The freight (passenger) traffic provides a quantitative measure to show how the transport industry serves the national economy and people, and is also an important indicator for planning the transport industry and for studying the development scale and speed of the transport industry.

Freight (Passenger) Traffic Density refers to the freight (passenger) traffic volume carried by a particular means of transportation during a given period through one kilometer of a specific section of transportation route. The formula is as follows:

Freight (Passenger) traffic density=[freight ton-kilometers (passenger-kilometers)] / (length of route in operation)

Freight (passenger) traffic density reflects the degree of business of freight (passenger) traffic on transportation routes, and therefore provides important information for balancing transport capability, planning construction and upgrading of transport routes and studying the distribution of transport network.

Freight Ton-kilometers (Passenger-kilometers) refer to the sum of the products of the volume of transported cargo (passengers) multiplying by the transport distance. It is an important indicator to reflect the achievement of transportation industry. Normally, the shortest distance between the departure station and the destination station (i.e., the payable distance) is the basis to calculate the freight ton-kilometers. This is an important indicator to show the total results of the transport industry, to prepare and examine the transport plan and to measure the efficiency, the labour productivity and the unit cost of transport.

The formula is as follows:

Freight ton-kilometers (passenger-kilometers) $=\Sigma$ {freight (passenger) traffic × distance of transportation}

Possession of Civil Motor Vehicles refer to the total numbers of vehicles that are registered and received vehicles license tags according to the Work Standard for Motor Vehicles Registration formulated by transport management office under department of public security at the end of reference period. They are divided into following categories according to the structure of motor vehicles: passenger vehicles, trucks and others; and private vehicles and vehicles for units use according to ownerships; working vehicles and non-working vehicles according to kind of usage; large passenger vehicles, medium passenger vehicles, small passenger vehicles and mini passenger vehicle, heavy trucks, light-heavy trucks, light trucks and mini trucks according to sizes of vehicles.

Business Volume of Post and Telecommunications refers to the total amount of post and telecommunication services, expressed in value terms, provided by the post and telecommunications departments for the society. Post and telecommunication services can be classified as letters, parcels, remittance, issue of newspapers and magazines, fast mail service, express mail service, savings deposits, stamps for collection, public and individual telegraph service, facsimiles, long-distance telephone service, leasing of telephone lines, urban paging service, mobile telephone service, data transfer and transmission, etc. The accounting approach is to multiply the service products of all types with their average unit price (constant price) to get sum of business value, plus income from other services such as leasing of telephone lines and equipment, maintenance of telephone switchboards and lines on behalf of customers. This indicator reflects the overall results of post and telecommunications service during a given period, and is important to study the composition of business service and the development of post and telecommunications service.

The formula is as follows:

Business volume of post and telecommunications= Σ (Transaction of post and telecommunication service x constant price) + Income from leasing, maintenance and other services = business volume of postal service + business volume of telecommunications service

Subscribers of Wireless Paging Services Wireless paging service refers the service by which telephone users send audio, digital or character signals to persons carrying small-size pagers within the designated areas through wireless paging centers. The page carriers who have registered in paging centers are counted as paging subscribers.

Mobile Telephone Subscribers refer to the persons who own mobile telephone numbers and are connected with the mobile telephone communication network through the mobile telephone switchboards, including contracted subscribers and pre-paid subscribers for intelligent network. One mobile telephone is taken as a subscriber.

Internet Users refer to the number of Chinese citizens who use Internet at least for one hour each week.

Local Telephone Subscribers refer to subscribers that are connected to the local telecommunication service provider through fix line network, including household subscribers, institutional subscribers and public telephones. They are also classified as city subscribers and rural subscribers according to locations. Before 1997, city subscribers referred to those connected to city telephone networks in county towns and cities, while village subscribers referred to those connected to village telephone stations at and below counties. Since 1997, the classification of telephone subscribers was modified on the basis of physical location of the subscribers as urban telephone subscribers and rural telephone subscribers, which is different from the previous classification of categorizing local telephones and rural telephones, while the definition of total subscribers and total number of telephones remain unchanged.

Urban Telephone Subscribers refer to number of telephone subscribers, located at municipalities, cities under the jurisdiction of province, cities at prefecture level, downtown and suburb of city at county level town and county towns (including country towns where county government located, and towns of county level according to the administrative organizational system), that are connected to the public line telephone network, including rural mineral area, forest area, military area.

Rural Telephone Subscribers refer to telephone subscribers, located at counties (towns) and villages outside the range of cities according to administrative jurisdiction.

Household Telephone Subscribers refer to telephone sets installed in the dwelling units of urban or rural residents, and registered as residence subscribers for payment, including 3 types of payment for the service: private payment, public payment and free service.

Capacity of Long Distance Telephone Exchanges refers to the rated capacity of telephone exchanges to connect long distance telephone network, including capacity of international telephone exchanges.

Capacity of Office Telephone Exchanges refers to the capacity (measured in gate) of telephone exchanges installed in the offices of telecommunication service providers for communication between fixed telephones. It includes the capacity of both manual and automatic exchanges in use and for stand-by purpose, excluding the capacity of subscribers exchanges.

Capacity of Mobile Telephone Exchanges refers to the capacity of the maximum services provided to subscribers at one time basing on a certain model and transacting capacity of the mobile telephone exchanges.

16 国内贸易

Domestic Trade

资料整理：朱　莉　陈彬彬

国　内　贸　易

Domestic Trade

2014

社会消费品零售总额	Total Retail Sales of Consumption Goods	12449.27	(亿元)
商品零售额	Retail Sales	11236.85	(亿元)
餐饮收入额	Amount of Food and beverage revenue	1212.42	(亿元)

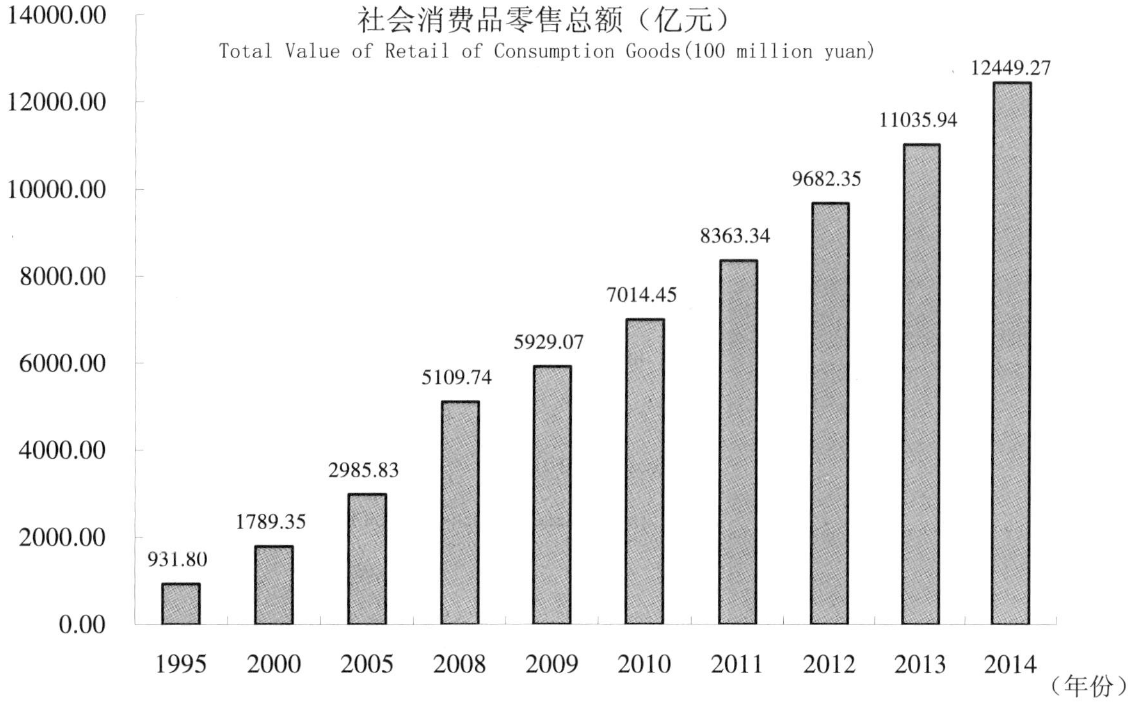

社会消费品零售总额（亿元）
Total Value of Retail Sales of Consumption Goods(100 million yuan)

年份 year	1995	2000	2005	2008	2009	2010	2011	2012	2013	2014
社会消费品零售总额 Total Value of Retail of Consumption Goods	931.80	1789.35	2985.83	5109.74	5929.07	7014.45	8363.34	9682.35	11035.94	12449.27

16-1 按地区分社会消费品零售总额

TOTAL RETAIL SALES OF CONSUMER GOODS BY REGION

单位：亿元 (100 million yuan)

年份 Year	零售额 Total Retail Sales of Consumer Goods	市 City	县 County	县以下 Below County Level
1978	59.84	19.24	16.56	24.04
1980	81.91	28.98	17.01	35.92
1983	112.44			
1984	137.34			
1985	181.17	75.26	31.64	74.17
1986	200.20	81.83	35.54	82.83
1987	234.06	103.21	38.23	92.62
1988	295.80	142.49	42.08	111.23
1989	320.68	159.89	43.78	117.01
1990	326.36	166.44	45.62	114.30
1991	362.26	190.65	50.04	121.57
1992	411.52	221.59	55.04	134.89
1993	521.35	293.82	68.88	158.65
1994	723.75	411.63	101.74	210.38
1995	931.80	539.79	127.76	264.25
1996	1145.73	688.40	130.28	327.05
1997	1345.34	802.37	146.61	396.36
1998	1481.38	896.08	156.07	429.23
1999	1617.14	1019.58	150.95	446.61
2000	1789.35	1128.47	177.65	483.23
2001	1975.16	1267.09	194.21	513.86
2002	2129.38	1429.83	200.69	498.86
2003	2358.69	1603.34	222.86	587.66
2004	2619.47	1819.80	246.21	277.44
2005	2985.83	2081.31	279.43	625.09
2006	3461.09	2430.05	325.66	705.38
2007	4115.78	2889.08	393.38	833.33
2008	5109.74	3587.49	491.44	1030.80
2009	5929.07	4128.16	586.81	1213.45
2010	7014.45	(城镇)5937.80	(城区)5030.80	(乡村)1076.10
2011	8363.34	(城镇)7003.70	(城区)5954.80	(乡村)1271.50
2012	9682.35	(城镇)8112.60	(城区)6873.80	(乡村)1449.90
2013	11035.94	(城镇)9163.80	(城区)7682.40	(乡村)1722.10
2014	12449.27	(城镇)10494.82	(城区)8396.70	(乡村)1954.45

注：1.1996年及以后社会消费品零售总额及各分组指标中不含售给城乡居民生活用住房的零售额。
2.2004、2008年为经普数据，2005-2007年为按国家统计局制定的修订方法修订数据，1993-2003年原则根据原各年环比发展速度和2004年经济普查数据调整。
3.2010年起采用国家新制定的城乡划分标准：城镇(其中:城区)、乡村

Notes:a) Since 1996, the residential house was exclued in the total retail sales of consumer goods and all the targets by groups.
b)The figures of 2004 and 2008 were from general economic Survey, that of the 2005-2007 were from statistics according to the reqirment of general economic survey; while the figures of 1993-2003 were from each year's indices (previous year =100) and readjusted according to the data of general economic survey.
c)Since 2010, a new towm and country division national standard is applied:town(including urban area), country.

16-2 分市、州社会消费品零售总额

TOTAL RETAIL SALES OF CONSUMER GOODS BY DISTRICT

单位：亿元 (100 million yuan)

地区	Region	2007	2008	2009	2010	2011	2012	2013	2014
全省	**Province**	**4115.78**	**5109.74**	**5929.07**	**7014.45**	**8363.34**	**9682.35**	**11035.94**	**12449.27**
武汉	Wuhan	1518.30	1895.89	2164.09	2570.40	3031.79	3467.37	3916.60	4369.32
黄石	Huangshi	174.97	221.60	256.09	301.63	355.05	413.50	468.86	519.71
十堰	Shiyan	170.19	217.17	254.25	308.88	364.18	424.80	491.51	548.65
宜昌	Yichang	311.34	399.41	470.41	552.72	656.00	766.19	881.93	964.53
襄阳	Xiangyang	328.87	425.01	500.56	613.34	721.51	839.51	966.31	1030.57
鄂州	Ezhou	84.58	107.89	126.68	135.55	159.68	182.20	208.68	230.28
荆门	Jingmen	151.57	194.26	228.82	263.08	311.25	362.85	414.68	451.78
孝感	Xiaogan	218.19	278.18	326.90	388.77	459.70	535.50	608.68	689.33
荆州	Jingzhou	299.59	381.19	445.42	505.34	595.66	688.36	781.36	831.44
黄冈	Huanggang	223.66	292.33	340.07	408.71	482.10	559.37	635.02	715.65
咸宁	Xianning	105.86	140.72	165.88	209.63	247.89	289.54	330.58	361.77
随州	Suizhou	122.76	156.67	182.05	215.21	254.09	293.51	333.86	354.37
恩施	Enshi	75.94	97.49	114.04	136.76	161.65	188.82	218.28	243.55
仙桃	Xiantao	82.52	108.87	127.87	146.79	172.64	200.81	229.00	233.58
潜江	Qianjiang	58.05	74.40	86.36	101.13	117.83	137.36	156.31	150.19
天门	Tianmen	90.57	115.42	135.21	151.57	179.04	206.91	237.50	231.05
林区	Shennongjia	2.57	3.25	3.72	4.38	5.14	5.92	6.75	7.52

注：1.本表各市、州数据包含了“其他”部分的全口径数据；
2.2008年以前的全省的数据根据经济普查的结果进行了调整。

Notes:a)"Others " was included in the total retail sales of consumer goods in the form.
b)Before 2008,Total was adjusted accoding to the economic census data.

16-3 批发和零售业连锁经营情况
BASIC CONDITIONS OF WHOLESALES, RETAIL SALES, CATERING CHAIN STORES INDUSTRIES

指标名称	Item	合计 Total 2013	2014	直营店 Direct Sales Store 2013	2014	加盟店 League Store 2013	2014
一、门店总数 (个)	Number of Stores (unit)	6248	7357	5643	6542	605	815
其中:批发业 (个)	Number of Stores (unit)	327	500	327	500		
零售业 (个)	Number of Stores (unit)	5921	6857	5316	6042	605	815
二、营业面积 (百平方米)	Floor Space of Business (100 sq.m)	65264	72481	64832	71968	432	513
其中:批发业 (百平方米)	Floor Space of Business (100 sq.m)	1466	2367	1466	2367		
零售业 (百平方米)	Floor Space of Business (100 sq.m)	63797	70114	63365	69601	432	513
三、从业人员 (人)	Person Engaged (person)	151591	145454	148950	142109	2641	3345
其中:批发业 (人)	Person Engaged (person)	7736	11177	7736	11177		
零售业 (人)	Person Engaged (person)	143855	134277	141214	130932	2641	3345
四、商品购进总额 (亿元)	Total Value of Commodities Purchaesd (100 000 000 yuan)	1495.00	1667.79	1492.82	1664.52	2.18	3.27
#统一配送商品购进额	#Total Purchasing Value	1095.82	1224.73	1094.04	1221.91	1.79	2.83
#自有配送中心配送商品购进额	#Commodities Purchased From Dispatching Center	824.89	884.17	823.56	881.82	1.33	2.35
#非自有配送中心配送商品购进额	#Commodities Purchased From Nondispatching Center	83.13	84.65	82.73	84.38	0.40	0.27
五、商品销售额 (亿元)	Sales Amount (100 000 000 yuan)	1714.72	1871.64	1711.84	1867.41	2.88	4.23
#零售额	#Retail Sales	1459.10	1572.98	1456.38	1569.12	2.72	3.85

16-4 住宿和餐饮业连锁经营情况

BASIC CONDITIONS OF HOTELS AND CATERING SERVICES

指标名称	Item	合计 Total 2013	合计 Total 2014	直营店 Direct Sales Store 2013	直营店 Direct Sales Store 2014	加盟店 League Store 2013	加盟店 League Store 2014
一、门店总数 (个)	Number of Stores (unit)	605	692	603	690	2	2
二、营业面积 (百平方米)	Floor Space of Business (100 sq.m)	4610	4745	4600	4735	10	10
三、从业人员 (人)	Person Engaged (person)	34493	37620	34363	37485	130	135
四、客房数 (间)	Number of Hotel Rooms (unit)	6684	6629	6622	6567	62	62
五、床位数 (个)	Number of Beds (unit)	8791	8462	8693	8364	98	98
六、餐位数 (位)	Restaurant Seating Capacity (unit)	152110	153215	151052	152157	1058	1058
七、商品购进总额 (万元)	Total Value of Commodities Purchaesd (10 000 yuan)	213758	113160	213399	112836	359	324
#统一配送商品购进额	#Total Purchasing Value	197633	102107	197274	101783	359	324
#自有配送中心配送商品购进额	#Commodities Purchased From Dispatching Center	132478	31429	359	324	132119	31106
#非自有配送中心配送商品购进额	#Commodities Purchased From Nondispatching Center	36855	41757	36855	41757		
八、连锁门店销售额 (万元)	Sales of the Chain Stores (10 000 yuan)	534276	559874	533141	558946	1135	928
#餐费收入	Meals Revenue	512910	539983	512118	539310	792	673
#商品销售额	Merchandise Sales	1819	1704	1816	1701	3	3

16-5 限额以上批发零售业基本情况(2014)
BASIC CONDITIONS OF ENTERPRISES ABOVE DESIGNATED SIZE IN WHOLESALES AND RETAILSALES TRADE (2014)

(按登记注册类型分)

(Grouped by Registration Type)

登记注册类型	Type of Registration	法人企业数(个) Number of Corperations (unit)	年末从业人数(人) Person Engaged at Year-end (person)	零售营业面积(万平方米) Floor Space of Retail Business (10 000 sq.m)
总　计	**Total**	**8835**	**563111**	**2413.37**
一、批发业	**Wholesales**	**3328**	**209089**	**652.55**
按登记注册类型分组	Grouped by Registration Type			
内资	**Domestic Funded Enterprises**	**3289**	**194544**	**579.79**
国有	State-owned Enterprises	103	15647	25.01
集体	Collective-owned Enterprises	15	785	1.94
股份合作	Cooperative Enterprises	6	287	1.07
联营企业	Joint Ownership Enterprises	1	21	
国有联营	State Joint Ownership Enterprises			
集体联营	Collective Joint Ownership Enterprises			
国有与集体联营	Joint State-collective Enterprises			
其他联营	Other Joint Ownership Enterprises	1	21	
有限责任公司	Limited Liability Corporations	1278	67308	195.97
国有独资公司	State Sole Funded Corporations	29	8552	12.22
其他有限责任公司	Other Limited Liability Corporations	1249	58756	183.75
股份有限公司	Share-holding Corporations Ltd.	75	49544	69.11
私营企业	Private Enterprises	1658	52569	247.34
私营独资	Private-funded Enterprises	77	1314	9.52
私营合伙	Private Partnership Enterprises			
私营有限责任公司	Private Limited Liability Corporations	1554	50105	231.70
私营股份有限公司	Private Share-holding Corporations Ltd.	27	1150	6.12
其他	Other Enterprises	153	8383	39.35
港澳台商投资企业	**Enterprises with Funds from Hongkong, Macao and Taiwan**	**18**	**4432**	**2.26**
合资经营	Joint-venture Enterprises	5	521	0.06
合作经营	Cooperative Enterprises			
独资经营	Enterprises with Sole Investment	13	3911	2.19
独资股份有限公司	Sole Investment Co. Ltd. With Investment			
外商投资企业	**Foreign Funded Enterprises**	**21**	**10113**	**70.51**
中外合资经营	Sino-foreign Joint-venture Enterprises	8	703	0.23
外资企业	Enterprises with Sole Foreign Investment	9	6305	0.28
外商投资股份有限公司	Share-holding Co. Ltd. with Foreign Investment	1	14	
其他外资企业	Other Enterprises with Sole Foreign Investment	3	3091	70.00

16-5 续表 continued

登记注册类型	Type of Registration	法人企业数（个）Number of Corperations (unit)	年末从业人数(人) Person Engaged at Year-end (person)	零售营业面积（万平方米）Floor Space of Retail Business (10 000 sq.m)
二、零售业	**Retail Trade**	**5507**	**354022**	**1760.82**
按登记注册类型分组	Grouped by Registration Type			
内资	**Domestic Funded Enterprises**	**5451**	**328522**	**1671.31**
国有	State-owned Enterprises	119	8714	17.48
集体	Collective-owned Enterprises	104	12197	52.31
股份合作	Cooperative Enterprises	8	304	2.61
联营企业	Joint Ownership Enterprises	4	176	0.42
国有联营	State Joint Ownership Enterprises			
集体联营	Collective Joint Ownership Enterprises	1	18	0.20
国有与集体联营	Joint State-collective Enterprises	2	144	0.16
其他联营	Other Joint Ownership Enterprises	1	14	0.06
有限责任公司	Limited Liability Corporations	1935	133870	658.02
国有独资公司	State Sole Funded Corporations	20	5112	25.66
其他有限责任公司	Other Limited Liability Corporations	1915	128758	632.36
股份有限公司	Share-holding Corporations Ltd.	127	57562	470.36
私营企业	Private Enterprises	3050	112032	461.47
私营独资	Private-funded Enterprises	577	10376	53.89
私营合伙	Private Partnership Enterprises	28	689	2.38
私营有限责任公司	Private Limited Liability Corporations	2386	97704	389.10
私营股份有限公司	Private Share-holding Corporations Ltd.	59	3263	16.10
其他	Other Enterprises	104	3667	8.64
港澳台商投资企业	**Enterprises with Funds from Hongkong, Macao and Taiwan**	**31**	**9036**	**24.1013**
合资经营	Joint-venture Enterprises	9	883	1.75
合作经营	Cooperative Enterprises			
独资经营	Enterprises with Sole Investment	22	8153	22.35
独资股份有限公司	Sole Investment Co. Ltd. With Investment			
外商投资企业	**Foreign Funded Enterprises**	**25**	**16464**	**65.41**
中外合资经营	Sino-foreign Joint-venture Enterprises	11	5663	15.51
外资企业	Enterprises with Sole Foreign Investment	12	10533	48.40
外商投资股份有限公司	Share-holding Co. Ltd. with Foreign Investment	1	207	1.30
其他外资企业	Other Enterprises with Sole Foreign Investment	1	61	0.20

16-6 限额以上批发零售业基本情况(2014) BASIC CONDITIONS OF ENTERPRISES ABOVE DESIGNATED SIZE IN WHOLESALES AND RETAILSALES TRADE (2014)

(按国民经济行业分)

(Grouped by Sector)

项　目	Item	法人企业数(个) Number of Corperations (unit)	年末从业人数(人) Person Engaged at Year-end (person)	零售营业面积(万平方米) Floor Space of Retail Business (10 000 sq.m)
总　计	**Total**	**8835**	**563111**	**2413.37**
一、批发业	**Wholesales**	**3328**	**209089**	**652.55**
农、林、牧产品批发业	Wholesales of Agriculture, Forestry and Animal Husbandry Products	350	16072	129.00
食品、饮料及烟草制品批发业	Wholesales of Foods, Beverage and Tobacco	611	58407	135.00
米、面制品及食用油批发业	Wholesales of Rice, Noodles and Edible Oil	109	5105	21.80
烟草制品批发业	Wholesales of Tobacco	42	12439	2.23
纺织、服装及日用品批发业	Wholesales of Textile Products, Garments and Daily Used Articles	198	12285	80.18
服装批发业	Wholesales of Garments	59	4065	74.05
家用电器批发业	Wholesales of Home Appliances	39	3550	1.17
文化、体育用品及器材批发业	Wholesales of Cultural and Sports Goods and Equipments	47	7246	8.12
医药及医疗器材批发业	Wholesales of Medicnes and Medical Appliances	285	31421	31.68
矿产品、建材及化工产品批发业	Wholesales of Mineral Products, Building Materials and Chemical Products	1184	64098	207.65
煤炭及制品批发业	Wholesales of Coal and Coal-made Products	190	5181	25.19
石油及制品批发业	Wholesales of Petroleum Products	105	37140	74.87
非金属矿及制品批发	Wholesales of Non-metal and Non-metal Mines	37	896	4.28
金属及金属矿批发业	Wholesales of Metal and Metal Mines	377	7317	22.81
建材批发业	Wholesales of Construction Materials	181	4238	26.94
化肥批发业	Wholesales of Chemical Fertilizers	119	5531	11.89
机械设备、五金交电及电子产品批发	Wholesales of Machinery Equipment, Hardware, Transport and Electronic Products	546	15391	37.18
汽车批发业	Wholesales of Cars	96	3300	9.55
计算机、软件及辅助设备批发业	Wholesales of Computers, Softwares and Assisted Equipments	29	901	0.26
贸易经纪与代理	Trade Agent	12	1452	0.36
其他批发业	Other Wholesales	95	2717	23.38
二、零售业	**Retail Sales**	**5507**	**354022**	**1760.82**
综合零售业	Retail Sales of Department	970	165310	965.67
百货零售业	Department Stores	459	65105	584.19
超级市场零售业	Supermarkets	371	90884	348.03
食品、饮料及烟草制品专门零售业	Monopoly Retail of Foods, Beverage and Tobacco	676	28368	73.15
纺织、服装及日用品专门零售业	Monopoly Retail of Textile, Garments,and Daily Used Articles	385	22509	66.38
服装零售业	Retail Sales of Garments	230	14617	47.14
文化、体育用品及器材专门零售业	Monopoly Retail of Cultural, Sports Products and Equipments	248	8715	20.58
体育用品零售业	Retail Sales of Sports Products	8	131	1.70
图书报刊零售业	Retail Sales of Books, Newspapers and Periodicals	82	4236	9.50
医药及医疗器材专门零售业	Monopoly Retail of Medicine and Medical Appliances	309	21897	47.72
药品零售业	Retail Sales of Medicine	267	20734	46.20
汽车、摩托车、燃料及零配件专门	Monopoly Retail of Cars, and Motorcars Parts	1342	61875	296.70
汽车零售业	Retail Sales of Cars	983	46639	225.24
机动车燃料零售业	Retail Sales of Motor Vehicles Fuels	139	11097	45.31
家用电器及电子产品专门零售业	Monopoly Retail of Home Appliances and Electronic Products	863	24982	138.86
家用电器零售业	Retail Sales of Home Appliances	431	14560	107.22
计算机、软件及辅助设备零售业	Retail Sales of Computers, Softwares and Assisted Equipments	194	3939	8.35
通讯设备零售业	Retail Sales of Communication Equipments	49	1326	3.34
五金、家具及室内装修材料专门零售业	Monopoly Retail of Hardware, Furnitures and Decorative Materials	520	13646	120.56
无店铺及其他零售业	Retail Sales of Storeless and Others	194	6720	31.18
互联网零售	Retail Sales of Internet	12	2075	0.29

16-7 限额以上住宿和餐饮业基本情况(2014)
BASIC CONDITIONS OF ENTERPRISES ABOVE DESIGNATED SIZE IN HOTELS AND CATERING SERVICES (2014)

(按登记注册类型分)

(Grouped by Registeration Type)

项　目	Item	法人企业数(个) Number of Corperations (unit)	年末从业人数(人) Person Engaged at Year-end (person)	餐饮营业面积(万平方米) Floor Space of Catering Business (10 000 sq.m)
总　计	**Total**	**2726**	**177068**	**533.26**
一、住宿业	**Hotel Trade**	**843**	**66578**	**169.35**
按登记注册类型分组	**Grouped by Registration Type**			
内资	**Domestic Funded Enterprises**	**820**	**61640**	**164.19**
国有	State-owned Enterprises	60	6730	15.69
集体	Collective-owned Enterprises	11	1142	1.95
股份合作	Cooperative Enterprises	3	147	0.43
联营企业	Joint Ownership Enterprises			
国有联营	State Joint Ownership Enterprises			
集体联营	Collective Joint Ownership Enterprises			
国有与集体联营	Joint State-collective Enterprises			
其他联营	Other Joint Ownership Enterprises			
有限责任公司	Limited Liability Corporations	305	27685	64.72
国有独资公司	State Sole Funded Corporations	10	1294	2.31
其他有限责任公司	Other Limited Liability Corporations	295	26391	62.42
股份有限公司	Share-holding Corporations Ltd.	22	2736	6.36
私营企业	Private Enterprises	397	22558	72.60
私营独资	Private-funded Enterprises	47	1446	5.19
私营合伙	Private Partnership Enterprises	14	501	3.31
私营有限责任公司	Private Limited Liability Corporations	316	19202	60.92
私营股份有限公司	Private Share-holding Corporations Ltd.	20	1409	3.17
其他	Other Enterprises	22	642	2.43
港澳台商投资企业	**Enterprises with Funds from Hongkong, Macao and Taiwan**	**18**	**4338**	**4.13**
合资经营	Joint-venture Enterprises	3	904	0.56
合作经营	Cooperative Enterprises	2	783	0.32
独资经营	Enterprises with Sole Investment	10	2079	2.64
投资股份有限公司	Share-holding Co. Ltd. With Investment	3	572	0.61
外商投资企业	**Foreign Funded Enterprises**	**5**	**600**	**1.04**
中外合资经营	Sino-foreign Joint-venture Enterprises	1	235	0.20
中外合作经营	Sino-foreign Cooperative Enterprises			
外资企业	Enterprises with Sole Foreign Investment	3	290	0.54
外商投资股份有限公司	Share-holding Co. Ltd. with Foreign Investment	1	75	0.30
二、餐饮业	**Catering Trade**	**1883**	**110490**	**363.91**
按登记注册类型分组	**Grouped by Registration Type**			
内资	**Domestic Funded Enterprises**	**1854**	**97584**	**345.07**
国有	State-owned Enterprises	20	996	3.16
集体	Collective-owned Enterprises	7	318	1.43
股份合作	Cooperative Enterprises	2	228	0.24
联营企业	Joint Ownership Enterprises	1	238	0.50
国有联营	State Joint Ownership Enterprises			
集体联营	Collective Joint Ownership Enterprises	1	238	0.50
国有与集体联营	Joint State-collective Enterprises			
其他联营	Other Joint Ownership Enterprises			
有限责任公司	Limited Liability Corporations	590	44300	134.62
国有独资公司	State Sole Funded Corporations	8	1491	1.22
其他有限责任公司	Other Limited Liability Corporations	582	42809	133.40
股份有限公司	Share-holding Corporations Ltd.	18	1154	3.38
私营企业	Private Enterprises	1142	48325	191.27
私营独资	Private-funded Enterprises	378	9272	46.17
私营合伙	Private Partnership Enterprises	11	344	1.54
私营有限责任公司	Private Limited Liability Corporations	730	36971	138.18
私营股份有限公司	Private Share-holding Corporations Ltd.	23	1738	5.39
其他	Other Enterprises	74	2025	10.47
港澳台商投资企业	**Enterprises with Funds from Hongkong, Macao and Taiwan**	**16**	**3412**	**4.17**
合资经营	Joint-venture Enterprises	3	306	0.61
合作经营	Cooperative Enterprises			
独资经营	Enterprises with Sole Investment	12	3079	3.41
投资股份有限公司	Share-holding Co. Ltd. With Investment	1	27	0.15
外商投资企业	**Foreign Funded Enterprises**	**13**	**9494**	**14.67**
中外合资经营	Sino-foreign Joint-venture Enterprises	2	584	1.60
外资企业	Enterprises with Sole Foreign Investment	11	8910	13.07
外商投资股份有限公司	Share-holding Co. Ltd. with Foreign Investment			
其他外商投资企业	Other Enterprises with Sole Foreign Investment			

16-8 限额以上住宿和餐饮业基本情况(2014)
BASIC CONDITIONS OF ENTERPRISES ABOVE DESIGNATED SIZE IN HOTELS AND CATERING SERVICES (2014)

(按国民经济行业分)
(Grouped by Sector)

行业	Item	法人企业数(个) Number of Corperations (unit)	年末从业人数(人) Person Engaged at Year-end (person)	餐饮营业面积(万平方米) Floor Space of Catering Business (10 000 sq.m)
总计	**Total**	**2726**	**177068**	**533.26**
一、住宿业	**Hotel**	**843**	**66578**	**169.35**
按国民经济行业分组	Grouped by Sector			
旅游饭店	Tourist Hotel	436	48165	110.53
一般旅馆	Regular Hotel	390	17443	54.37
其他住宿服务	Other Accomodation Service	17	970	4.46
二、餐饮业	**Catering**	**1883**	**110490**	**363.91**
按国民经济行业分组	Grouped by Sector			
正餐服务业	Dinner	1836	97526	345.60
快餐服务业	Fast Food	29	9813	14.49
饮料及冷饮服务业	Beverage and Cold Drink Services	10	2136	2.01
其他餐饮服务业	Others	8	1015	1.81

16-9 限额以上住宿和餐饮业经营情况(2014)
BUSINESS OF ENTERPRISES ABOVE DESIGNATED SIZE OF HOTELS AND CATERING SERVICES (2014)

(按国民经济行业分)
(Grouped by Sector)

行业	Item	营业额(亿元) Turn-over (100 million yuan)	客房收入 Revnue from Guest Rooms	餐费收入 Revenue from Catering Bills	商品销售收入 Revenue from Commo-dity Sales	其他收入 Revenue from Others	年末住宿和餐饮企业拥有床位数(万个) Number of Beds owned by Hotels and Catering Enterprises at Year-end (10 000 units)	年末住宿和餐饮企业拥有餐位数(万位) Number of Seats owned by Hotels and Catering Enterprises at Year-end (10 000 units)
总计	**Total**	**363.53**	**81.06**	**256.85**	**16.31**	**9.31**	**36.05**	**106.65**
一、住宿业	**Hotel**	**120.60**	**60.01**	**48.22**	**5.50**	**6.86**	**28.55**	**26.07**
按国民经济行业分组	Grouped by Sector							
旅游饭店	Tourist Hotel	81.03	39.19	33.41	2.73	5.70	22.00	18.38
一般旅馆	Regular Hotel	36.46	19.78	14.15	1.53	1.00	6.24	7.22
其他住宿服务	Other Accomodation Service	3.11	1.04	0.66	1.24	0.16	0.31	0.48
二、餐饮业	**Catering**	**242.93**	**21.05**	**208.63**	**10.80**	**2.45**	**7.50**	**80.58**
按国民经济行业分组	Grouped by Sector							
正餐服务业	Dinner	198.85	20.91	164.87	10.64	2.44	7.44	74.46
快餐服务业	Fast Food	34.48	0.03	34.37	0.08		0.02	4.99
饮料及冷饮服务业	Beverage and Cold Drink Services	4.36	0.01	4.27	0.07		0.01	0.95
其他餐饮服务业	Others	5.24	0.10	5.12	0.01	0.01	0.03	0.19

16-10 限额以上住宿和餐饮业经营情况(2014)

(按登记注册类型分)

单位：亿元

项 目	Item	营业额 Turnover	客房收入 Revnue from Guest Rooms
总 计	**Total**	**363.53**	**81.06**
一、住宿业	**Hotels**	**120.60**	**60.01**
按登记注册类型分组	**Grouped by Registration Type**		
内资	**Domestic Funded Enterprises**	**111.07**	**55.05**
国有	State-Owned Enterprises	9.63	4.47
集体	Collective-owned Enterprises	2.97	1.03
股份合作	Cooperative Enterprises	0.16	0.08
联营企业	Joint Ownership Enterprises		
国有联营	State Joint Ownership Enterprises		
集体联营	Collective Joint Ownership Enterprises		
国有与集体联营	Joint State-collective Enterprises		
其他联营	Other Joint Ownership Enterprises		
有限责任公司	Limited Liability Corporations	46.00	24.57
国有独资公司	State Sole Funded Corporations	3.30	1.05
其他有限责任公司	Other Limited Liability Corporations	42.70	23.52
股份有限公司	Share-holding Corporations Ltd.	4.08	1.89
私营企业	Private Enterprises	45.92	21.98
私营独资	Private-funded Enterprises	5.66	3.08
私营合伙	Private Partnership Enterprises	1.16	0.33
私营有限责任公司	Private Limited Liability Corporations	36.44	17.56
私营股份有限公司	Private Share-holding Corporations Ltd.	2.66	1.01
其他	Other Enterprises	2.32	1.03
港澳台商投资企业	**Enterprises with Funds from Hongkong, Macao and Taiwan**	**8.86**	**4.57**
合资经营	Joint-venture Enterprises	2.17	1.02
合作经营	Cooperative Enterprises	1.43	0.75
独资经营	Enterprises with Sole Investment	4.06	2.04
投资股份有限公司	Share-holding Co. Ltd. With Investment	1.20	0.77
外商投资企业	**Foreign Funded Enterprises**	**0.67**	**0.38**
中外合资经营	Sino-Foreign Joint-venture Enterprises	0.31	0.17
外资企业	Enterprises with Sole Foreign Investment	0.33	0.19
外商投资股份有限公司	Share-holding Co. Ltd. with Foreign Investment	0.03	0.02
其他外商投资企业	Other Foreign Founded Enterprises		
二、餐饮业	**Catering Trade**	**242.93**	**21.05**
按登记注册类型分组	**Grouped by Registration Type**		
内资	**Domestic Funded Enterprises**	**202.60**	**20.78**
国有	State-Owned Enterprises	3.12	0.87
集体	Collective-owned Enterprises	1.08	0.11
股份合作	Cooperative Enterprises	0.30	0.05
联营企业	Joint Ownership Enterprises	5.24	
国有联营	State Joint Ownership Enterprises		
集体联营	Collective Joint Ownership Enterprises	5.24	
国有与集体联营	Joint State-collective Enterprises		
其他联营	Other Joint Ownership Enterprises		
有限责任公司	Limited Liability Corporations	79.55	8.95
国有独资公司	State Sole Funded Corporations	1.74	0.16
其他有限责任公司	Other Limited Liability Corporations	77.80	8.79
股份有限公司	Share-holding Corporations Ltd.	2.18	0.30
私营企业	Private Enterprises	105.05	10.16
私营独资	Private-funded Enterprises	29.01	2.27
私营合伙	Private Partnership Enterprises	0.46	0.09
私营有限责任公司	Private Limited Liability Corporations	72.10	7.48
私营股份有限公司	Private Share-holding Corporations Ltd.	3.48	0.32
其他	Other Enterprises	6.08	0.35
港澳台商投资企业	**Enterprises with Funds from Hongkong, Macao and Taiwan**	**7.17**	**0.11**
合资经营	Joint-venture Enterprises	0.53	0.04
合作经营	Cooperative Enterprises		
独资经营	Enterprises with Sole Investment	6.61	0.07
投资股份有限公司	Share-holding Co. Ltd. With Investment	0.03	
外商投资企业	**Foreign Funded Enterprises**	**33.16**	**0.17**
中外合资经营	Sino-Foreign Joint-venture Enterprises	0.73	0.06
外资企业	Enterprises with Sole Foreign Investment	32.42	0.11
外商投资股份有限公司	Share-holding Co. Ltd. with Foreign Investment		
其他外商投资企业	Other Foreign Funded Enterprises		

BUSINESS OF ENTERPRISES ABOVE DESIGNATED SIZE OF HOTELS AND CATERING SERVICES (2014)

(Grouped by Registeration Type)

(100 million yuan)

餐费收入 Revenue from Catering Bills	商品销售收入 Revenue from Commodity Sales	其他收入 Revenue from Others	年末床位数 (万个) Number of Beds at Year-end (10 000 units)	年末餐位数 (万位) Number of Seats at Year-end (10 000 units)
256.85	**16.31**	**9.31**	**36.05**	**106.65**
48.22	**5.50**	**6.86**	**28.55**	**26.07**
44.61	**5.37**	**6.04**	**27.76**	**25.05**
4.19	0.54	0.43	1.38	2.72
1.68	0.06	0.20	0.18	0.52
0.07		0.01	0.03	0.07
16.53	1.44	3.45	18.19	10.17
1.25	0.27	0.72	0.38	0.54
15.28	1.17	2.73	17.81	9.64
1.64	0.24	0.31	0.56	1.03
19.27	3.04	1.63	7.21	10.10
2.13	0.43	0.02	0.50	0.69
0.78	0.05		0.14	0.32
14.83	2.48	1.57	6.14	8.37
1.53	0.07	0.05	0.44	0.73
1.23	0.04	0.01	0.21	0.43
3.38	**0.12**	**0.79**	**0.67**	**0.82**
0.93	0.06	0.16	0.14	0.18
0.63	0.01	0.05	0.07	0.13
1.41	0.04	0.56	0.33	0.38
0.41		0.02	0.12	0.13
0.24	**0.01**	**0.04**	**0.12**	**0.21**
0.10		0.03	0.03	0.08
0.13	0.01	0.01	0.07	0.13
			0.02	
208.63	**10.80**	**2.45**	**7.50**	**80.58**
168.90	**10.75**	**2.16**	**7.36**	**74.76**
2.11	0.07	0.08	0.21	0.79
0.96	0.01		0.06	0.59
0.25			0.02	0.09
3.26	1.98			0.40
3.26	1.98			0.40
66.72	2.69	1.19	3.15	33.16
1.56	0.02		0.07	0.68
65.16	2.67	1.19	3.08	32.48
1.37	0.30	0.21	0.13	0.49
89.06	5.21	0.63	3.64	36.92
24.84	1.76	0.14	0.74	9.41
0.37			0.03	0.36
61.00	3.18	0.44	2.75	26.09
2.85	0.26	0.04	0.12	1.06
5.18	0.50	0.05	0.15	2.32
6.78	**0.04**	**0.25**	**0.06**	**1.59**
0.25	0.01	0.23	0.04	0.15
6.50	0.03	0.01	0.02	1.43
0.03				0.02
32.94	**0.01**	**0.03**	**0.08**	**4.23**
0.67			0.04	0.31
32.27	0.01	0.03	0.05	3.92

16-11 限额以上批发和零售业商品购、销、存总额(2014)
TOTAL PURCHASES, SALES AND STOCK OF ENTERPRISES ABOVE DESIGNATED SIZE OF WHOLESALE AND RETAIL TRADES(2014)

(按登记注册类型分)

(Grouped by Registeration Type)

单位：亿元 (100 million yuan)

项　目	Item	购进总额 Total Purchasing Value	销售总额 Total Sales Value	批　发 Whole-sales	零　售 Retail Sales	年末库存总额 Total Value of Inventory at Year-end
总　计	**Total**	**15420.93**	**16338.05**	**10221.36**	**6116.70**	**1590.18**
一、批发业	**Wholesales**	**10188.14**	**10774.08**	**9752.30**	**1021.78**	**607.92**
按登记注册类型分组	**Grouped by Registration Type**					
内资	**Domestic Funded Enterprises**	**9651.58**	**10147.85**	**9218.96**	**928.89**	**580.62**
国有	State-owned Enterprises	646.91	774.45	744.98	29.47	113.45
集体	Collective-owned Enterprises	16.20	16.79	15.86	0.92	1.23
股份合作	Cooperative Enterprises	3.83	3.94	3.43	0.50	0.16
联营企业	Joint Ownership Enterprises	0.10	0.11	0.11		
国有联营	State Joint Ownership Enterprises					
集体联营	Collective Joint Ownership Enterprises					
国有与集体联营	Joint State-collective Enterprises					
其他联营	Other Joint Ownership Enterprises	0.10	0.11	0.11		
有限责任公司	Limited Liability Corporations	4731.30	4941.70	4550.42	391.29	228.22
国有独资公司	State Sole Funded Corporations	2034.31	2109.47	2027.57	81.90	17.77
其他有限责任公司	Other Limited Liability Corporations	2697.00	2832.23	2522.85	309.39	210.45
股份有限公司	Share-holding Corporations Ltd.	2587.87	2640.52	2337.47	303.05	117.55
私营企业	Private Enterprises	1545.05	1642.61	1472.34	170.28	112.61
私营独资	Private-funded Enterprises	35.86	39.04	29.61	9.43	1.62
私营合伙	Private Partnership Enterprises					
私营有限责任公司	Private Limited Liability Corporations	1473.98	1566.62	1409.77	156.86	106.96
私营股份有限公司	Private Share-holding Corporations Ltd.	35.21	36.95	32.96	3.99	4.03
其他	Other Enterprises	120.32	127.73	94.35	33.38	7.39
港澳台商投资企业	**Enterprises with Funds from Hongkong, Macao and Taiwan**	**243.38**	**254.25**	**194.65**	**59.60**	**16.13**
合资经营	Joint-venture Enterprises	12.41	13.85	11.68	2.17	2.18
合作经营	Cooperative Enterprises					
独资经营	Enterprises with Sole Investment	230.97	240.40	182.97	57.44	13.95
投资股份有限公司	Share-holding Co. Ltd. With Investment					
外商投资企业	**Foreign Funded Enterprises**	**293.18**	**371.97**	**338.69**	**33.28**	**11.17**
中外合资经营	Sino-foreign Joint-venture Enterprises	86.05	100.87	98.81	2.05	7.55
外资企业	Enterprises with Sole Foreign Investment	167.13	230.39	229.73	0.65	3.39
外商投资股份有限公司	Share-holding Co. Ltd. with Foreign Investment	0.83	1.11	1.11		
其它外商投资企业	Other Foreign Funded Enterprises	39.17	39.61	9.03	30.57	0.24
二、零售业	**Retail Trade**	**5232.79**	**5563.98**	**469.06**	**5094.92**	**982.26**
按登记注册类型分组	**Grouped by Registration Type**					
内资	**Domestic Funded Enterprises**	**4815.25**	**5193.07**	**464.26**	**4728.81**	**950.96**
国有	State-owned Enterprises	222.81	239.48	14.70	224.78	41.49
集体	Collective-owned Enterprises	156.93	171.39	11.15	160.23	12.11
股份合作	Cooperative Enterprises	3.74	3.75	0.13	3.63	0.12
联营企业	Joint Ownership Enterprises	3.50	3.50		3.50	0.04
国有联营	State Joint Ownership Enterprises					
集体联营	Collective Joint Ownership Enterprises	0.76	0.77		0.77	0.01
国有与集体联营	Joint State-collective Enterprises	2.60	2.60		2.60	0.02
其他联营	Other Joint Ownership Enterprises	0.13	0.13		0.13	
有限责任公司	Limited Liability Corporations	1949.71	2141.88	206.45	1935.44	236.68
国有独资公司	State Sole Funded Corporations	219.87	240.53	63.82	176.71	2.15
其他有限责任公司	Other Limited Liability Corporations	1729.84	1901.36	142.63	1758.72	234.52
股份有限公司	Share-holding Corporations Ltd.	1097.54	1111.62	72.90	1038.72	183.10
私营企业	Private Enterprises	1340.37	1468.51	148.40	1320.11	474.95
私营独资	Private-funded Enterprises	142.90	175.74	41.65	134.09	10.73
私营合伙	Private Partnership Enterprises	5.85	7.02	0.78	6.23	0.30
私营有限责任公司	Private Limited Liability Corporations	1108.59	1198.71	94.81	1103.90	452.16
私营股份有限公司	Private Share-holding Corporations Ltd.	83.03	87.05	11.16	75.88	11.75
其他	Other Enterprises	40.65	52.94	10.52	42.42	2.47
港澳台商投资企业	**Enterprises with Funds from Hongkong, Macao and Taiwan**	**116.07**	**150.72**	**1.27**	**149.45**	**13.46**
合资经营	Joint-venture Enterprises	5.12	7.62		7.62	1.48
合作经营	Cooperative Enterprises					
独资经营	Enterprises with Sole Investment	110.95	143.09	1.27	141.83	11.99
投资股份有限公司	Share-holding Co. Ltd. With Investment					
外商投资企业	**Foreign Funded Enterprises**	**301.48**	**220.19**	**3.53**	**216.66**	**17.83**
中外合资经营	Sino-foreign Joint-venture Enterprises	27.62	31.97	3.36	28.61	1.27
外资企业	Enterprises with Sole Foreign Investment	270.85	184.97	0.17	184.80	16.25
外商投资股份有限公司	Share-holding Co. Ltd. with Foreign Investment	1.36	1.33		1.33	0.06
其它外商投资企业	Other Foreign Funded Enterprises	1.65	1.92		1.92	0.25

16-12 限额以上批发和零售业商品购、销、存总额(2014)
TOTAL PURCHASES, SALES AND STOCK OF ENTERPRISES ABOVE DESIGNATED SIZE OF WHOLESALE AND RETAIL TRADES (2014)

(按国民经济行业分)

(Grouped by Sector)

单位：亿元 (100 million yuan)

行业	Item	购进总额 Total Purchasing Value	销售总额 Total Sales Value	批发 Whole-sales	零售 Retail Sales	年末库存总额 Total Value of Inventory at Year-end
总计	**Total**	**15420.93**	**16338.05**	**10221.36**	**6116.70**	**1590.18**
一、批发业	**Wholesales**	**10188.14**	**10774.08**	**9752.30**	**1021.78**	**607.92**
农、林、牧产品批发业	Wholesales of Agriculture, Forestry and Animal Husbandry Products	379.71	367.54	320.85	46.69	109.57
食品、饮料及烟草制品批发业	Wholesales of Foods, Beverage and Tobacco	1552.76	1857.82	1577.73	280.09	89.93
米、面制品及食用油批发业	Wholesales of Rice, Noodles and Edible Oil	143.32	143.51	123.97	19.54	16.35
烟草制品批发业	Wholesales of Tobacco	513.07	679.00	665.57	13.43	33.59
纺织、服装及日用品批发业	Wholesales of Textile Products, Garments and Daily Used Articles	390.45	388.17	308.80	79.37	51.84
服装批发业	Wholesales of Garments	132.89	144.63	83.97	60.66	3.97
家用电器批发业	Wholesales of Home Appliances	178.70	155.37	151.42	3.95	39.23
文化、体育用品及器材批发业	Wholesales of Cultural and Sports Goods and Equipments	115.11	123.04	108.15	14.89	24.14
医药及医疗器材批发业	Wholesales of Medicnes and Medical Appliances	941.65	926.86	792.86	134.00	100.41
矿产品、建材及化工产品批发业	Wholesales of Mineral Products, Building Materials and Chemical Products	5606.66	5834.47	5430.68	403.79	169.13
煤炭及制品批发业	Wholesales of Coal and Coal-made Products	236.89	251.51	222.40	29.11	10.32
石油及制品批发业	Wholesales of Petroleum Products	3580.12	3745.73	3425.38	320.35	59.27
非金属及金属矿批发业	Wholesales of Non-metellic Mineral and Metal Industry	23.44	25.74	22.71	3.03	1.10
金属及金属矿批发业	Wholesales of Metal and Metal Mines	1250.76	1272.69	1256.54	16.15	63.11
建材批发业	Wholesales of Construction Materials	115.36	124.49	106.32	18.17	5.40
化肥批发业	Wholesales of Chemical Fertilizers	202.21	206.07	201.76	4.31	20.25
机械设备、五金交电及电子产品批发	Wholesales of Machinery Equipment, Hardware, Transport and Electronic Products	598.38	660.51	605.17	55.34	47.37
汽车批发业	Wholesales of Cars	137.49	145.76	130.10	15.66	11.74
计算机、软件及辅助设备批发业	Wholesales of Computers, Softwares and Assisted Equipments	140.70	157.72	146.92	10.80	6.38
贸易经纪与代理	Trade Agent	533.59	538.99	538.87	0.12	11.98
其他批发业	Other Wholesales	69.83	76.69	69.19	7.50	3.56
二、零售业	**Retail Sales**	**5232.79**	**5563.98**	**469.06**	**5094.92**	**982.26**
综合零售业	Retail Sales of Department	1614.01	1814.14	65.79	1748.35	191.06
百货零售业	Department Stores	886.30	989.40	48.86	940.54	96.38
超级市场零售业	Supermarkets	633.09	723.99	13.79	710.20	88.33
食品、饮料及烟草制品专门零售业	Monopoly Retail of Foods, Beverage and Tobacco	386.36	450.82	83.00	367.82	35.24
纺织、服装及日用品专门零售业	Monopoly Retail of Textile, Garments,and Daily Used Articles	176.71	223.62	49.14	174.48	29.09
服装零售业	Retail Sales of Garments	118.83	153.96	45.39	108.58	19.22
文化、体育用品及器材专门零售业	Monopoly Retail of Cultural, Sports Products and Equipments	89.12	95.74	6.51	89.22	13.84
体育用品零售业	Retail Sales of Sports Products	2.14	3.10	0.02	3.09	0.13
图书报刊零售业	Retail Sales of Books, Newspapers and Periodicals	29.87	31.24	3.37	27.87	5.82
医药及医疗器材专门零售业	Monopoly Retail of Medicine and Medical Appliances	274.96	301.76	43.11	258.65	31.03
药品零售业	Retail Sales of Medicine	262.86	287.82	40.53	247.29	30.07
汽车、摩托车、燃料及零配件专门零售	Monopoly Retail of Cars, and Motorcars Parts	1853.50	1862.30	161.78	1700.53	617.83
汽车零售业	Retail Sales of Cars	1207.33	1264.15	44.66	1219.49	478.48
机动车燃料零售业	Retail Sales of Motor Vehicles Fuels	588.04	529.87	109.82	420.05	134.77
家用电器及电子产品专门零售业	Monopoly Retail of Home Appliances and Electronic Products	395.64	449.52	34.15	415.36	40.66
家用电器零售业	Retail Sales of Home Appliances	248.51	292.92	21.60	271.32	27.77
计算机、软件及辅助设备零售业	Retail Sales of Computers, Softwares and Assisted Equipments	40.71	45.06	3.97	41.09	3.58
通讯设备零售业	Retail Sales of Communication Equipments	11.18	11.36	2.33	9.03	1.10
五金、家具及室内装修材料专门零售业	Monopoly Retail of Hardware, Furnitures and Decorative Materials	182.80	199.73	19.23	180.50	9.89
无店铺及其他零售业	Retail Sales of Storeless and Others	259.69	166.35	6.35	160.00	13.61
互联网零售	Retail Sales of Internet	200.69	102.27	0.13	102.14	10.68

16-13 限额以上批发和零售业企业资产及负债(2014)
ASSETS AND LIABILITIES OF ENTERPRISES ABOVE DESIGNATED SIZE OF WHOLESALE AND RETAIL TRADES (2014)

单位：亿元 (100 million yuan)

项 目	Item	流动资产合计 Total Circulating Funds	固定资产原价 Original Price of Fixed Assets	资产总计 Total Assets	负债合计 Total Liabilities	所有者权益合计 Total Creditor's Equity
总 计	**Total**	**4132.39**	**1301.29**	**5949.90**	**4138.37**	**1811.47**
一、批发业	**Wholesales**	**2704.65**	**590.72**	**3603.66**	**2540.45**	**1063.21**
1.按登记注册类型分组	**Grouped by Registration Type**					
内资	**Domestic Funded Enterprises**	**2561.01**	**572.56**	**3437.14**	**2380.68**	**1056.46**
国有	State-owned Enterprises	261.03	70.80	342.90	177.41	165.49
集体	Collective-owned Enterprises	7.66	1.42	9.03	8.24	0.79
股份合作	Cooperative Enterprises	0.74	0.17	0.87	0.61	0.26
联营企业	Joint Ownership Enterprises	0.23	0.01	0.24	0.14	0.10
国有联营	State Joint Ownership Enterprises					
集体联营	Collective Joint Ownership Enterprises					
国有与集体联营	Joint State-collective Enterprises					
其他联营	Other Joint Ownership Enterprises	0.23	0.01	0.24	0.14	0.10
有限责任公司	Limited Liability Corporations	1245.83	180.42	1524.63	1133.32	391.32
国有独资公司	State Sole Funded Corporations	83.26	56.29	159.64	119.15	40.49
其他有限责任公司	Other Limited Liability Corporations	1162.56	124.13	1365.00	1014.17	350.83
股份有限公司	Share-holding Corporations Ltd.	435.97	203.85	790.71	506.05	284.67
私营企业	Private Enterprises	596.37	104.32	741.91	541.59	200.32
私营独资	Private-funded Enterprises	3.34	4.05	8.15	2.55	5.59
私营合伙	Private Partnership Enterprises					
私营有限责任公司	Private Limited Liability Corporations	582.90	97.03	720.19	530.52	189.67
私营股份有限公司	Private Share-holding Corporations Ltd.	10.13	3.24	13.57	8.51	5.06
其他	Other Enterprises	13.17	11.58	26.84	13.32	13.52
港澳台商投资企业	**Enterprises with Funds from Hongkong, Macao and Taiwan**	**40.91**	**15.25**	**58.37**	**43.95**	**14.42**
合资经营	Joint-venture Enterprises	8.65	0.28	8.87	6.32	2.55
合作经营	Cooperative Enterprises					
独资经营	Enterprises with Sole Investment	32.26	14.97	49.50	37.63	11.87
投资股份有限公司	Share-holding Co. Ltd. With Investment					
外商投资企业	**Foreign Funded Enterprises**	**102.73**	**2.90**	**108.15**	**115.83**	**-7.67**
中外合资经营	Sino-foreign Joint-venture Enterprises	27.63	1.60	29.00	22.75	6.25
外资企业	Enterprises with Sole Foreign Investment	65.95	0.89	68.92	84.14	-15.21
外商投资股份有限公司	Share-holding Co. Ltd. with Foreign Investment	0.44	0.01	0.45	0.15	0.29
其他外资企业	Other Enterprises with Sole Foreign Investment	8.71	0.40	9.79	8.79	0.99
2.按国民经济行业分组	**Grouped by Sector**					
农、林、牧产品批发业	Wholesales of Agriculture, Forestry and Animal Husbandry Products	182.27	44.31	252.71	176.93	75.78
食品、饮料及烟草制品批发业	Wholesales of Foods, Beverage and Tobacco	605.09	148.02	770.63	444.21	326.42
米、面制品及食用油批发业	Wholesales of Rice, Noodles and Edible Oil	95.69	13.35	119.26	86.32	32.94
烟草制品批发业	Wholesales of Tobacco	165.91	61.16	216.47	72.22	144.25
纺织、服装及日用品批发业	Wholesales of Textile Products, Garments and Daily Used Articles	133.09	11.04	150.01	132.08	17.94
服装批发业	Wholesales of Garments	25.41	3.36	32.33	30.22	2.11
家用电器批发业	Wholesales of Home Appliances	83.12	1.59	86.81	81.44	5.37
文化、体育用品及器材批发业	Wholesales of Cultural and Sports Goods and Equipments	63.53	12.79	78.54	52.02	26.52
医药及医疗器材批发业	Wholesales of Medicnes and Medical Appliances	383.34	48.48	492.05	358.29	133.76
矿产品、建材及化工产品批发业	Wholesales of Mineral Products, Building Materials and Chemical Products	869.53	289.11	1278.82	919.11	359.70
煤炭及制品批发业	Wholesales of Coal and Coal-made Products	92.56	10.01	113.79	80.96	32.83
石油及制品批发业	Wholesales of Petroleum Products	145.35	227.65	432.05	249.19	182.86
非金属及金属矿批发业	Wholesales of Non-metellic Mineral and Metal Industry	10.21	2.19	14.78	11.24	3.54
金属及金属矿批发业	Wholesales of Metal and Metal Mines	489.09	23.63	542.17	457.05	85.11
建材批发业	Wholesales of Construction Materials	28.63	10.60	40.60	26.16	14.44
化肥批发业	Wholesales of Chemical Fertilizers	45.94	7.05	56.71	39.07	17.64
机械设备、五金交电及电子产品批发	Wholesales of Machinery Equipment, Hardware, Transport and Electronic Products	263.68	25.38	308.36	241.50	66.86
汽车批发业	Wholesales of Cars	56.21	5.86	67.96	51.59	16.37
计算机、软件及辅助设备批发业	Wholesales of Computers, Softwares and Assisted Equipments	57.45	0.20	58.72	52.20	6.52
贸易经纪与代理	Trade Agent	184.90	3.70	242.85	198.44	44.41
其他批发业	Other Wholesales	19.22	7.89	29.70	17.88	11.81

16-13 续表 continued

单位：亿元 (100 million yuan)

项　目	Item	流动资产合计 Total Circulating Funds	固定资产原价 Original Price of Fixed Assets	资产总计 Total Assets	负债合计 Total Liabilities	所有者权益合计 Total Creditor's Equity
二、零售业	**Retail Trade**	**1427.75**	**710.57**	**2346.24**	**1597.92**	**748.25**
1.按登记注册类型分组	**Grouped by Registration Type**					
内资	**Domestic Funded Enterprises**	**1315.71**	**670.27**	**2188.04**	**1484.90**	**703.08**
国有	State-owned Enterprises	60.54	16.25	82.22	63.74	18.48
集体	Collective-owned Enterprises	15.99	18.71	32.47	25.02	7.45
股份合作	Cooperative Enterprises	0.53	0.72	1.00	0.47	0.54
联营企业	Joint Ownership Enterprises	0.48	0.20	0.68	0.15	0.53
国有联营	State Joint Ownership Enterprises					
集体联营	Collective Joint Ownership Enterprises	0.07	0.08	0.15	0.06	0.09
国有与集体联营	Joint State-collective Enterprises	0.39	0.11	0.50	0.09	0.42
其他联营	Other Joint Ownership Enterprises	0.03		0.03		0.03
有限责任公司	Limited Liability Corporations	671.17	286.18	1085.09	749.22	335.81
国有独资公司	State Sole Funded Corporations	8.52	30.43	51.76	31.30	20.46
其他有限责任公司	Other Limited Liability Corporations	662.65	255.75	1033.32	717.91	315.35
股份有限公司	Share-holding Corporations Ltd.	157.11	193.73	395.87	276.36	119.51
私营企业	Private Enterprises	402.67	144.74	573.45	363.33	210.12
私营独资	Private-funded Enterprises	17.40	21.82	39.40	13.22	26.18
私营合伙	Private Partnership Enterprises	0.92	1.10	1.95	0.82	1.14
私营有限责任公司	Private Limited Liability Corporations	357.96	117.51	497.37	323.60	173.77
私营股份有限公司	Private Share-holding Corporations Ltd.	26.39	4.31	34.73	25.70	9.04
其他	Other Enterprises	7.22	9.75	17.25	6.62	10.63
港澳台商投资企业	**Enterprises with Funds from Hongkong, Macao and Taiwan**	**71.69**	**11.45**	**83.14**	**59.46**	**23.68**
合资经营	Joint-venture Enterprises	2.18	0.82	3.86	3.25	0.61
合作经营	Cooperative Enterprises					
独资经营	Enterprises with Sole Investment	69.50	10.64	79.28	56.21	23.07
投资股份有限公司	Share-holding Co. Ltd. With Investment					
外商投资企业	**Foreign Funded Enterprises**	**40.35**	**28.85**	**75.05**	**53.56**	**21.49**
中外合资经营	Sino-foreign Joint-venture Enterprises	9.73	4.08	19.45	13.13	6.33
外资企业	Enterprises with Sole Foreign Investment	30.06	23.13	53.39	38.34	15.05
外商投资股份有限公司	Share-holding Co. Ltd. with Foreign Investment	0.20	0.87	1.02	0.86	0.16
其他外资企业	Other Enterprises with Sole Foreign Investment	0.36	0.76	1.19	1.24	-0.05
2.按国民经济行业分组	**Grouped by Sector**					
综合零售业	Retail Sales of Department	341.05	309.55	714.26	506.50	207.77
百货零售业	Department Stores	185.41	182.24	416.18	293.51	122.68
超级市场零售业	Supermarkets	145.41	118.80	279.85	202.07	77.78
食品、饮料及烟草制品专门零售业	Monopoly Retail of Foods, Beverage and Tobacco	76.80	38.50	119.93	50.45	69.49
纺织、服装及日用品专门零售业	Monopoly Retail of Textile, Garments,and Daily Used Articles	75.62	23.29	105.81	70.77	35.03
服装零售业	Retail Sales of Garments	56.23	17.04	79.81	58.14	21.67
文化、体育用品及器材专门零售业	Monopoly Retail of Cultural, Sports Products and Equipments	39.63	19.54	62.49	32.54	29.95
体育用品零售业	Retail Sales of Sports Products	0.46	0.23	1.08	1.05	0.02
图书报刊零售业	Retail Sales of Books, Newspapers and Periodical	22.18	9.41	31.63	14.64	17.00
医药及医疗器材专门零售业	Monopoly Retail of Medicine and Medical Appliances	168.11	17.06	196.52	161.45	35.07
药品零售业	Retail Sales of Medicine	161.04	16.58	188.58	156.63	31.95
汽车、摩托车、燃料及零配件专门零售业	Monopoly Retail of Cars, and Motorcars Parts	513.77	212.30	817.99	582.17	235.75
汽车零售业	Retail Sales of Cars	484.91	144.15	682.69	491.52	191.11
机动车燃料零售业	Retail Sales of Motor Vehicles Fuels	16.76	61.16	99.01	63.35	35.66
家用电器及电子产品专门零售业	Monopoly Retail of Home Appliances and Electronic Products	153.01	50.89	212.66	120.59	92.07
家用电器零售业	Retail Sales of Home Appliances	100.91	37.54	145.67	91.38	54.29
计算机、软件及辅助设备零售业	Retail Sales of Computers, Softwares and Assisted Equipments	32.83	2.40	35.64	12.26	23.38
通讯设备零售业	Retail Sales of Communication Equipments	2.59	1.69	4.14	2.46	1.69
五金、家具及室内装修材料专门零售业	Monopoly Retail of Hardware, Furnitures and Decorative Materials	41.39	25.80	83.62	52.39	31.23
无店铺及其他零售业	Retail Sales of Storeless and Others	18.36	13.64	32.97	21.07	11.90
互联网零售	Retail Sales of Internet	2.01	0.66	2.66	2.48	0.18

16-14 限额以上批发和零售业企业主要财务指标(2014)

MAIN FINANCIAL INDICATORS OF ENTERPRISES ABOVE DESIGNATED SIZE OF WHOLESALE AND RETAIL TRADES (2014)

单位：亿元 (100 million yuan)

项目	Item	主营业务收入 Revenue of Major Business	主营业务成本 Cost of Major Business	其他业务利润 Profits of Other Business	利润总额 Total Profits
总计	**Total**	**14118.79**	**12714.15**	**145.67**	**427.67**
一、批发业	**Wholesales**	**9251.64**	**8499.93**	**24.73**	**249.03**
1.按登记注册类型分组	**Grouped by Registration Type**				
内资	**Domestic Funded Enterprises**	**8854.28**	**8179.78**	**23.87**	**245.79**
国有	State-owned Enterprises	682.06	530.09	0.65	75.87
集体	Collective-owned Enterprises	13.19	12.31		0.12
股份合作	Cooperative Enterprises	3.59	3.18	-0.02	0.16
联营企业	Joint Ownership Enterprises	0.10	0.09		
国有联营	State Joint Ownership Enterprises				
集体联营	Collective Joint Ownership Enterprises				
国有与集体联营	Joint State-collective Enterprises				
其他联营	Other Joint Ownership Enterprises	0.10	0.09		
有限责任公司	Limited Liability Corporations	4328.46	4070.71	9.93	91.86
国有独资公司	State Sole Funded Corporations	1775.92	1740.67	-0.04	21.55
其他有限责任公司	Other Limited Liability Corporations	2552.54	2330.03	9.97	70.31
股份有限公司	Share-holding Corporations Ltd.	2207.34	2101.52	8.27	26.60
私营企业	Private Enterprises	1497.73	1353.18	5.01	46.22
私营独资	Private-funded Enterprises	36.05	27.41	0.03	4.39
私营合伙	Private Partnership Enterprises				
私营有限责任公司	Private Limited Liability Corporations	1427.33	1293.10	4.97	41.36
私营股份有限公司	Private Share-holding Corporations Ltd.	34.35	32.67	0.01	0.47
其他	Other Enterprises	121.82	108.69	0.02	4.97
港澳台商投资企业	**Enterprises with Funds from Hongkong, Macao and Taiwan**	**72.42**	**60.19**	**0.86**	**-1.81**
合资经营	Joint-venture Enterprises	11.92	10.71	0.01	0.12
合作经营	Cooperative Enterprises				
独资经营	Enterprises with Sole Investment	60.49	49.48	0.85	-1.93
投资股份有限公司	Share-holding Co. Ltd. With Investment				
外商投资企业	**Foreign Funded Enterprises**	**324.94**	**259.97**	**0.01**	**5.05**
中外合资经营	Sino-foreign Joint-venture Enterprises	87.61	82.29		2.42
外资企业	Enterprises with Sole Foreign Investment	197.34	143.20	0.01	2.27
外商投资股份有限公司	Share-holding Co. Ltd. with Foreign Investment	0.95	0.71		0.14
其他外资企业	Other Enterprises with Sole Foreign Investment	39.05	33.77		0.21
2.按国民经济行业分组	**Grouped by Sector**				
农、林、牧产品批发业	Wholesales of Agriculture, Forestry and Animal Husbandry Products	340.15	305.37	0.59	13.58
食品、饮料及烟草制品批发业	Wholesales of Foods, Beverage and Tobacco	1496.69	1155.22	2.09	128.12
米、面制品及食用油批发业	Wholesales of Rice, Noodles and Edible Oil	138.95	127.73	0.24	4.40
烟草制品批发业	Wholesales of Tobacco	593.16	446.45	0.31	75.32
纺织、服装及日用品批发业	Wholesales of Textile Products, Garments and Daily Used Articles	350.21	321.79	4.71	-0.09
服装批发业	Wholesales of Garments	137.90	126.42	0.15	-2.44
家用电器批发业	Wholesales of Home Appliances	131.61	124.47	4.01	0.80
文化、体育用品及器材批发业	Wholesales of Cultural and Sports Goods and Equipments	116.85	101.34	7.13	3.13
医药及医疗器材批发业	Wholesales of Medicnes and Medical Appliances	801.53	735.13	0.52	25.35
矿产品、建材及化工产品批发业	Wholesales of Mineral Products, Building Materials and Chemical Products	5016.36	4819.83	2.03	62.07
煤炭及制品批发业	Wholesales of Coal and Coal-made Products	223.56	202.58	0.11	6.82
石油及制品批发业	Wholesales of Petroleum Products	3112.87	3011.32	1.53	32.95
非金属及金属矿批发业	Wholesales of Non-metellic Mineral and Metal Industry	23.82	19.68		1.65
金属及金属矿批发业	Wholesales of Metal and Metal Mines	1134.88	1106.00	0.31	5.50
建材批发业	Wholesales of Construction Materials	113.31	99.89	0.01	5.68
化肥批发业	Wholesales of Chemical Fertilizers	216.96	203.19	0.05	5.00
机械设备、五金交电及电子产品批发	Wholesales of Machinery Equipment, Hardware, Transport and Electronic Products	595.57	545.28	0.88	13.77
汽车批发业	Wholesales of Cars	129.81	118.66	0.12	3.61
计算机、软件及辅助设备批发业	Wholesales of Computers, Softwares and Assisted Equipments	140.24	134.66	0.02	2.77
贸易经纪与代理	Trade Agent	460.86	453.47	6.75	0.77
其他批发业	Other Wholesales	73.43	62.52	0.04	2.32

16-14 续表 continued

单位：亿元 (100 million yuan)

项　目	Item	主营业务收入 Revenue of Major Business	主营业务成本 Cost of Major Business	其他业务利润 Profits of Other Business	利润总额 Total Profits
二、零售业	**Retail Trade**	**4867.15**	**4214.21**	**120.94**	**178.65**
1.按登记注册类型分组	**Grouped by Registration Type**				
内资	**Domestic Funded Enterprises**	**4549.28**	**3937.85**	**105.54**	**165.12**
国有	State-owned Enterprises	213.26	189.11	0.29	10.56
集体	Collective-owned Enterprises	150.27	133.25	0.87	2.06
股份合作	Cooperative Enterprises	3.80	2.41	0.07	0.99
联营企业	Joint Ownership Enterprises	3.10	2.83		0.06
国有联营	State Joint Ownership Enterprises				
集体联营	Collective Joint Ownership Enterprises	0.42	0.40		
国有与集体联营	Joint State-collective Enterprises	2.56	2.31		0.06
其他联营	Other Joint Ownership Enterprises	0.13	0.12		
有限责任公司	Limited Liability Corporations	2153.08	1895.86	84.54	63.57
国有独资公司	State Sole Funded Corporations	205.06	195.03	0.13	2.59
其他有限责任公司	Other Limited Liability Corporations	1948.02	1700.83	84.40	60.97
股份有限公司	Share-holding Corporations Ltd.	653.63	559.63	15.73	20.42
私营企业	Private Enterprises	1323.32	1115.28	4.02	62.82
私营独资	Private-funded Enterprises	121.56	94.33	0.10	10.77
私营合伙	Private Partnership Enterprises	6.91	5.45	0.02	0.23
私营有限责任公司	Private Limited Liability Corporations	1113.27	946.61	3.50	48.39
私营股份有限公司	Private Share-holding Corporations Ltd.	81.58	68.89	0.39	3.43
其他	Other Enterprises	48.82	39.49	0.03	4.64
港澳台商投资企业	**Enterprises with Funds from Hongkong, Macao and Taiwan**	**134.33**	**119.19**	**11.87**	**9.41**
合资经营	Joint-venture Enterprises	7.30	5.58	0.06	0.60
合作经营	Cooperative Enterprises				
独资经营	Enterprises with Sole Investment	127.03	113.61	11.81	8.81
投资股份有限公司	Share-holding Co. Ltd. With Investment				
外商投资企业	**Foreign Funded Enterprises**	**183.54**	**157.18**	**3.53**	**4.12**
中外合资经营	Sino-foreign Joint-venture Enterprises	26.60	20.31	0.03	0.90
外资企业	Enterprises with Sole Foreign Investment	154.02	134.23	3.47	3.36
外商投资股份有限公司	Share-holding Co. Ltd. with Foreign Investment	1.31	1.04		
其他外资企业	Other Enterprises with Sole Foreign Investment	1.61	1.60	0.02	-0.15
2.按国民经济行业分组	**Grouped by Sector**				
综合零售业	Retail Sales of Department	1250.52	1040.93	38.09	52.19
百货零售业	Department Stores	648.44	543.42	22.42	31.71
超级市场零售业	Supermarkets	505.88	416.52	15.13	14.02
食品、饮料及烟草制品专门零售业	Monopoly Retail of Foods, Beverage and Tobacco	425.06	345.12	0.69	29.17
纺织、服装及日用品专门零售业	Monopoly Retail of Textile, Garments,and Daily Used Articles	149.38	111.51	1.61	7.80
服装零售业	Retail Sales of Garments	89.08	65.23	0.28	4.51
文化、体育用品及器材专门零售业	Monopoly Retail of Cultural, Sports Products and Equipments	89.30	69.38	0.26	7.54
体育用品零售业	Retail Sales of Sports Products	2.96	2.60		0.06
图书报刊零售业	Retail Sales of Books, Newspapers and Periodicals	29.13	22.08	0.22	1.98
医药及医疗器材专门零售业	Monopoly Retail of Medicine and Medical Appliances	264.10	234.87	1.14	6.16
药品零售业	Retail Sales of Medicine	250.68	224.78	1.01	5.33
汽车、摩托车、燃料及零配件专门零售业	Monopoly Retail of Cars, and Motorcars Parts	1771.53	1625.23	76.29	31.82
汽车零售业	Retail Sales of Cars	1237.81	1136.02	75.98	16.52
机动车燃料零售业	Retail Sales of Motor Vehicles Fuels	465.16	431.85	0.29	11.61
家用电器及电子产品专门零售业	Monopoly Retail of Home Appliances and Electronic Products	585.67	508.52	2.35	27.76
家用电器零售业	Retail Sales of Home Appliances	270.68	230.24	2.09	12.96
计算机、软件及辅助设备零售业	Retail Sales of Computers, Softwares and Assisted Equipments	211.16	191.70	0.04	8.23
通讯设备零售业	Retail Sales of Communication Equipments	10.63	8.86	0.03	0.49
五金、家具及室内装修材料专门零售业	Monopoly Retail of Hardware, Furnitures and Decorative Materials	180.42	146.37	0.16	12.18
无店铺及其他零售业	Retail Sales of Storeless and Others	151.15	132.30	0.35	4.02
互联网零售	Retail Sales of Internet	87.57	80.65		

16-15 限额以上餐饮业企业资产及负债(2014)

ASSETS AND LIABILITIES OF ENTERPRISES ABOVE DESIGNATED SIZE OF CATERING SERVICES (2014)

单位：亿元　　(100 million yuan)

项　目	Item	流动资产合计 Total Circulating Funds	固定资产原价 Original Price of Fixed Assets	资产总计 Total Assets	负债合计 Total Liabilities	所有者权益合计 Total Creditor's Equity
总　计	**Total**	**86.05**	**135.01**	**255.16**	**165.56**	**89.60**
1.按国民经济行业分组	**Grouped by Sector**					
正餐服务业	Dinner	81.73	127.32	235.70	150.75	84.95
快餐服务业	Fast Food	2.75	5.97	15.52	12.89	2.63
饮料及冷饮服务业	Beverage and Cold Drink Services	0.53	1.01	2.37	1.17	1.20
其他餐饮服务业	Others	1.05	0.71	1.57	0.76	0.81
2.按登记注册类型分组	**Grouped by Registration Type**					
内资	**Domestic Funded Enterprises**	**81.40**	**122.34**	**229.85**	**143.36**	**86.49**
国有	State-Owned Enterprises	0.59	2.59	2.71	1.50	1.21
集体	Collective-owned Enterprises	0.13	0.61	0.60	0.51	0.09
股份合作	Cooperative Enterprises	0.02	0.08	0.10	0.01	0.09
联营企业	Joint Ownership Enterprises	0.42	0.81	1.11	0.21	0.90
国有联营	State Joint Ownership Enterprises					
集体联营	Collective Joint Ownership Enterprises	0.42	0.81	1.11	0.21	0.90
国有与集体联营	Joint State-collective Enterprises					
其他联营	Other Joint Ownership Enterprises					
有限责任公司	Limited Liability Corporations	41.69	54.74	109.13	81.42	27.71
国有独资公司	State Sole Funded Corporations	2.54	4.86	9.05	5.54	3.51
其他有限责任公司	Other Limited Liability Corporations	39.16	49.88	100.08	75.89	24.19
股份有限公司	Share-holding Corporations Ltd.	0.96	2.44	3.07	2.36	0.71
私营企业	Private Enterprises	36.52	58.71	109.51	56.51	53.00
私营独资	Private-funded Enterprises	4.46	11.71	15.88	4.95	10.92
私营合伙	Private Partnership Enterprises	0.15	0.45	0.57	0.20	0.37
私营有限责任公司	Private Limited Liability Corporations	30.72	45.06	86.04	45.98	40.06
私营股份有限公司	Private Share-holding Corporations Ltd.	1.19	1.49	7.03	5.38	1.64
其他	Other Enterprises	1.07	2.37	3.62	0.83	2.79
港澳台商投资企业	**Enterprises with Funds from Hongkong, Macao and Taiwan**	**1.51**	**4.27**	**6.45**	**5.51**	**0.94**
合资经营	Joint-venture Enterprises	0.48	2.06	2.39	2.59	-0.20
合作经营	Cooperative Enterprises					
独资经营	Enterprises with Sole Investment	1.02	2.21	4.05	2.89	1.16
投资股份有限公司	Share-holding Co. Ltd. With Investment	0.01	0.01	0.01	0.03	-0.01
外商投资企业	**Foreign Funded Enterprises**	**3.14**	**8.40**	**18.85**	**16.69**	**2.16**
中外合资经营	Sino-Foreign Joint-venture Enterprises	0.41	0.66	1.59	1.45	0.14
外资企业	Enterprises with Sole Foreign Investment	2.73	7.74	17.26	15.24	2.02
外商投资股份有限公司	Share-holding Co. Ltd. with Foreign Investment					
其他外商投资企业	Other Enterprises with Sole Foreign Investment					

16-16 限额以上餐饮业企业主要财务指标(2014)

MAIN FINANCIAL INDICATORS OF ENTERPRISES ABOVE DESIGNATED SIZE OF CATERING SERVICES (2014)

单位：亿元 (100 million yuan)

项　目	Item	主营业务收入 Revenue of Major Business	主营业务成本 Cost of Major Business	其他业务利润 Profits of Other Business	利润总额 Total Profits
总　计	**Total**	**238.08**	**136.14**	**1.88**	**11.97**
1.按国民经济行业分组	**Grouped by Sector**				
正餐服务业	Dinner	194.23	114.95	1.87	10.70
快餐服务业	Fast Food	34.23	15.97		0.76
饮料及冷饮服务业	Beverage and Cold Drink Services	4.39	1.26		0.54
其他餐饮服务业	Others	5.23	3.97		-0.02
2.按登记注册类型分组	**Grouped by Registration Type**				
内资	**Domestic Funded Enterprises**	**197.88**	**118.44**	**1.87**	**10.90**
国有	State-Owned Enterprises	3.01	1.96	0.05	-0.02
集体	Collective-owned Enterprises	1.07	0.65		0.08
股份合作	Cooperative Enterprises	0.30	0.17		0.07
联营企业	Joint Ownership Enterprises	5.24	4.44		0.31
国有联营	State Joint Ownership Enterprises				
集体联营	Collective Joint Ownership Enterprises	5.24	4.44		0.31
国有与集体联营	Joint State-collective Enterprises				
其他联营	Other Joint Ownership Enterprises				
有限责任公司	Limited Liability Corporations	78.60	43.59	1.00	0.82
国有独资公司	State Sole Funded Corporations	1.74	1.21		0.09
其他有限责任公司	Other Limited Liability Corporations	76.86	42.38	1.00	0.73
股份有限公司	Share-holding Corporations Ltd.	2.08	1.33		0.10
私营企业	Private Enterprises	101.92	62.44	0.82	8.79
私营独资	Private-funded Enterprises	27.91	18.48	0.17	3.80
私营合伙	Private Partnership Enterprises	0.45	0.28		0.03
私营有限责任公司	Private Limited Liability Corporations	70.28	41.82	0.65	4.87
私营股份有限公司	Private Share-holding Corporations Ltd.	3.28	1.85		0.08
其他	Other Enterprises	5.66	3.86		0.76
港澳台商投资企业	**Enterprises with Funds from Hongkong, Macao and Taiwan**	**7.16**	**2.32**		**0.42**
合资经营	Joint-venture Enterprises	0.53	0.15		-0.17
合作经营	Cooperative Enterprises				
独资经营	Enterprises with Sole Investment	6.60	2.15		0.61
独资股份有限公司	Sole Investment Co. Ltd. With Investment	0.03	0.02		-0.02
外商投资企业	**Foreign Funded Enterprises**	**33.04**	**15.38**		**0.65**
中外合资经营	Sino-Foreign Joint-venture Enterprises	0.73	0.55		-0.04
外资企业	Enterprises with Sole Foreign Investment	32.30	14.83		0.69
外商投资股份有限公司	Share-holding Co. Ltd. with Foreign Investment				
其他外商投资企业	Other Enterprises with Sole Foreign Investment				

主要统计指标解释

社会消费品零售总额 指批发和零售业、餐饮业、新闻出版业、邮政业和其他服务业等，售予城乡居民用于生活消费的商品和社会集团用于公共消费的商品之总量。社会消费品零售总额包括：

一、批发和零售业企业（单位）：

1.售予城乡居民的各种生活消费品；

2.售予入境旅游的外国人、华侨、港澳台同胞的各类商品；

3.售予行政事业单位、社会团体、军队和武警等机构的商品，以及以零售方式售予各类企业的商品。具体包括：用于非生产和社会交往的办公用品，如通讯设备、计算器具和设备、电讯网络设备、文印设备、音像视听器材和设备、纸张、本册、文具及装订文印材料、家具、日用电器、针纺织品、清洁卫生用品、文体用品、奖品、纪念品、礼品等；供内部人员乘坐的交通工具和燃料；用于办公设施修缮的各类配件、材料、工具等；用于取暖和防暑降温的设备、燃料、材料及食品等；专用于教学的用品和设备；非营利医疗机构的中、西药品、中药材和医疗设备器材；非专用的劳动保护用品；不对外营业的内部食堂用的餐具、炊具、设备、清洁卫生工具和食品、燃料等；军队、武警用于其人员生活的衣着品和个人用品；其他各类非生产性设备和用品。

二、餐饮业出售的主食、菜肴、烟酒饮料和其他商品。

三、新闻出版业、邮政业售予城乡居民、企事业单位、军队和武警等机构的书报杂志、音像制品、邮品等。

四、其他服务业出售的食品、烟酒饮料、服装鞋帽、日常生活用品、医药保健用品、艺术品、工艺美术品、玩具、殡葬用品以及其他消费品。

批发零售业商品购、销、存总额 指各种登记注册类型的批发、零售业企业(单位)以本企业(单位)为总体的，从国内、国外市场购进的商品总量，销售和出口的商品总量、库存商品总量等情况。该指标可以反映商品流转过程中商品的购进、销售、库存之间的比例关系和存在的问题。

商品购进总额 指从本企业(单位)以外的单位和个人购进(包括从境外直接进口)作为转卖或加工后转卖的商品总额。它反映批发零售贸易业从国内、国外市场上购进商品的总量。商品购进总额包括：(1)从工农业生产者购进的商品；(2)从出版社、报社的出版发行部门购进的图书、杂志和报纸；(3)从各种登记注册类型的批发零售贸易企业(单位)购进的商品；(4)从其他单位购进的商品，如从机关、团体、企业等单位购进的剩余物资，从餐饮业、服务业购进的商品，从海关、市场管理部门购进的缉私和没收的商品，从居民手中收购的废旧商品等；(5)从国(境)外直接进口的商品。不包括企业(单位)为自身经营用和未通过买卖行为而收入的商品以及销售退回、商品升溢等。

商品销售总额 指对本企业(单位)以外的单位和个人出售(包括对境外直接出口)的商品总额。它反映批发零售贸易业在国内市场上销售商品以及出口商品的总量。商品销售总额包括：(1)售给城乡居民和社会集团消费用的商品；(2)售给工业、农业、建筑业、运输邮电业、批发零售贸易业、餐饮业、服务业等作为生产、经营使用的商品；(3)售给批发零售贸易业作为转卖或加工后转卖的商品；(4)对国(境)外直接出口的商品。不包括出售本企业(单位)自用的废旧包装用品、未通过买卖行为付出的商品、经本单位介绍，由买卖双方直接结算，本单位只收取手续费的业务、购货退出的商品以及商品损耗和损失等。

批发零售业库存 指报告期末各种登记注册类型的批发零售贸易企业(单位)已取得所有权的商品。它反映批发零售贸易企业(单位)的商品库存情况和对市场商品供应的保证程度。期末库存包括：(1)存放在批发零售贸易业经营单位(如门市部、批发站、经营处)仓库、货场、货柜和货架中的商品；(2)挑选、整理、包装中的商品；(3)已记入购进而尚未运到本单位的商品，即发货单或银行承兑凭证已到而货未到的部分；(4)寄放他处的商品，如因购货方拒绝承付而暂时存放在购货方的商品和已办完加工成品收回手续而未提回的商品；(5)委托其他单位代销(未作销售或调出)尚未售出的商品；(6)代其他单位购进尚未交付的商品。不包括所有权不属于本单位的商品、拨付除批发零售贸易业以外的其他行业所属独立核算加工厂等加工生产尚未收回成品的商品、代国家物资储备部门保管的商品等。

库存总额采用的计算价格是：农副产品采购单位按购进价计算；批发单位按进货价计算；零售单位按核算价格计算，即按什么价格核算就按什么价格计算。

住宿餐饮业营业额 指住宿和餐饮业法人企业、产业活动单位在经营活动中因提供服务或销售商品等取得的收入，包括客房收入、餐费收入、商品销售收入和其他收入。客房收入指住宿和餐饮业法人企业、产业活动单位在经营活动中因提供住宿服务取得的客房收入。餐费收入指住宿和餐饮业法人企业、产业活动单位因为顾客提供就餐服务取得的收入，包括经烹饪、调制加工后出售的各种食品，如主食、炒菜、凉拌菜等的收入。商品销售收入指住宿和餐饮业法人企业、产业活动单位伴随服务而出售商品所取得的收入。其他收入指营业收入中除客房收入、餐费收入、商品销售收入以外的其他收入，包括娱乐、健身和商务服务等。

亿元商品交易市场成交额 指年成交额达到亿元以上，经工商部门批准、专门从事商品批发、零售业务活动的市场。其市场所有摊位成交总额称为商品交易市场成交额。

连锁企业（或称连锁店、连锁公司） 指在核心企业或总店的领导下，由分散的、经营同类商品或服务的企业或活动单位，采取共同方针，实行集中采购和分散销售的有机结合，通过规范化经营，实现规模效益的经济联合组织形式。一般连锁店应由若干个分店组成。其经营特征：(1)经营同类商品；(2)使用统一商号；(3)统一采购配送，采购与销售相分离（部分商品可根据物流合理和保质保鲜原则，由供应商直接送货到门店，其余均由总部统一配送）。

连锁门店包括下列三种形式：

直营连锁：也叫正规连锁。连锁门店均由总部独资或控股开设，在总部的直接领导下统一经营。总部采取纵深似的管理方式，直接下令掌管所有的零售门店，零售门店也必须完全接受总部指挥。他是大型垄断商业资本通过吞并、兼并或独资、控股等途径，发展壮大自身实力和规模的一种形式。

特许连锁：各连锁门店（被特许人）通过合同形式，取得使用总部（特许人）商标、商号、经营技术和销售总部开发的商品的特许权，各加盟连锁门店为独立法人，在总部指导下统一经营。

自由连锁：也称自愿连锁。连锁公司的门店均为独立法人，各自的资产所有权关系不变，在公司总部的指导下共同经营。各成员店使用共同的店名，与总部订阅有关购、销、宣传等方面的合同，并按合同开展经营活动。在合同规定的范围之外，各成员店可以自由活动。根据自愿原则，各成员店可自由加入连锁体系，也可自由退出。

特许连锁加上自由连锁等于加盟连锁。

Explanatory Notes on Main Statistical Indicators

Total Retail Sales of Consumer Goods refer to the sum of retail sales of commodities sold by wholesale, retail, catering, publishing, post and telecommunications and other service industries to urban and rural households for private consumption and to social institutions for public consumption. Retail sales of consumer goods include:

1) Sales by wholesale and retail units:

a) of consumer goods sold to urban and rural households

b) of commodities sold to foreigners, overseas Chinese and Chinese compatriots from Hong Kong, Macao and Taiwan visiting in China

c) of commodities sold to government agencies, institutions, social organizations, military and armed police units, and commodities sold to enterprises in the form of retail sales. More specifically, they include: office facilities and articles for non-production purposes such as communications equipment, computing equipment and instruments, TV and network equipment, printing and copying equipment, audio-visual equipment and instruments, paper, notebooks, stationeries, furniture, electric appliances, knitwear, sanitation and cleaning articles, cultural and sport articles, articles for prizes, souvenirs, etc.; transport vehicles and fuels for employees; materials, spare parts and tools for the maintenance of office facilities; equipment, fuels, materials and food for winter heating or summer cooling purposes; articles and equipment for teaching purpose; Chinese and western medicines and medical equipment and facilities purchased by non profit-making medical institutes; non-specialized work safety articles; cooking utensils, tableware, equipment, cleaning articles, food and fuels purchased by internal cafeterias; clothes and personal articles purchased by military or armed police units for their officials and soldiers; and other equipment and articles for non-production purposes.

2) Sales of stable food, cooked dishes, beverages, tobaccos and other articles by catering units.

3) Sales of books, newspapers, magazines, audio-visual products and post products by publishing, post and telecommunications departments to urban and rural households and to enterprises, institutions, military and armed police units.

4) Sales of food, beverages, tobaccos, clothing, hats, footwear, articles for daily use, medicines, medical and health articles, work of art, handicrafts, toys, funeral articles and other articles by other service industries.

Purchase, Sales and Stock of Commodities by Wholesale and Retail Trades refer to the total volume of commodities purchased, total volume of sales and exports, and the stock of commodities by wholesale and retail enterprises (establishments) of different status of registration from domestic and overseas markets. This indictor reflects the relationship among purchase, sales and stock of commodities in the circulation of goods and reveals the existing problems.

Total Purchases of Commodities refer to the total value of purchases of commodities by the enterprises (establishments) from other establishments or individuals (including direct import from abroad) for the purpose of re-selling, either with or without further processing of the commodities purchased. This indicator is used to show the total value of purchases of commodities by wholesale and retail establishments from domestic and overseas markets. The total purchases include: (1) agricultural and industrial products purchased from producers; (2) books, magazines and newspapers purchased from distribution departments of the publishers; (3) commodities purchased from wholesale and retail establishments of different status of registration; (4) commodities purchased from other units, such as surplus materials purchased from government agencies, enterprises or institutions, commodities purchased from catering and service establishments, confiscated goods purchased from customs authorities or market management agencies, second-hand goods and wastes purchased from residents; and (5) commodities directly imported from abroad. Excluded are commodities purchased by enterprises (establishments) for use in their own business operation, commodities obtained without buying or selling procedures, rejected commodities, etc.

Total Sales of Commodities refer to value of commodities sold by the establishments to other establishments and individuals (including direct export). This indicator is used to show the total value of sales of commodities at domestic markets and export. The total sales include: (1) commodities sold to urban and rural residents and social groups for their consumption; (2) commodities sold to establishments in industry, agriculture, construction, transportation, post and telecommunications, wholesale and retail trades, catering trade and public utility for their production and operation; (3) commodities sold to wholesale and retail establishments for re selling, with or without further processing; and (4)commodities for direct export to other countries. Excluded are selling of waste packaging materials used by the establishments (units) themselves, commodities transferred without buying or selling procedures, commission income from brokerage in transactions whose settlement is directly handled by buyers and sellers, rejected commodities in the purchase, loss in commodities, etc.

Commodity Stock of Wholesale and Retail Enterprises refers to total commodities possessed by wholesale and retail enterprises (units) of various types of registration status at the end of the reference period, which reflects the commodity stock level of various wholesale and retail enterprises and the potential for market supply. It includes: (1) commodities located in storage, garages, counters, and shelves of operating units (such as sale stores, wholesale centers, and operating offices) of wholesale and retail enterprises; (2) commodities in the process of selecting, sorting, and packing; (3) commodities not arrived but recorded as purchase in the account, i.e. commodities not arrived but payment receipts for the commodities from the sellers or the banks arrived; (4) commodities deposited in other places rather than places mentioned above, for instance: commodities in the hold of purchasers temporarily due to the refusal of payment and commodities not taken back after going through the formalities; (5) commodities entrusted to other units to sell but not sold yet; (6) commodities purchased for other units but not delivered yet. Commodities not included as stock are those not owned by the enterprises (units), those allocated to financially independent factories rather than wholesale and retail enterprises for processing but not taken back yet, and finally those put in stock by wholesale and retail enterprises on behalf of the state material reserves units.

For the calculation of the value of commodities stock, the value is calculated at purchasing prices in agricultural goods purchasing units and wholesale units, and at the accounting prices in retail units.

Business Revenue of Hotels and Catering Services refer to revenue received from providing services or selling commodities by corporate enterprises and establishments engaged in hotel and catering services, including income from hotel rooms, from catering services, from selling of commodities and from other services. Income from hotel rooms refers to income of corporate enterprises and establishments by providing lodging services. Income from catering services refers to income of corporate enterprises and establishments by providing catering services, including selling of cooked or prepared foods such as stable food, cooked dishes or cold dishes. Income from selling of commodities refers to income of corporate enterprises and establishments by selling commodities that accompany the services they provide. Income from other activities refers to income received other than income from hotel rooms, catering services or selling of commodities, such as income from providing recreation, fitness or business services.

Volume of Transaction at Large Commodity Markets (with transaction value over 100 million yuan) refers to markets approved by the industrial and commercial administration departments, which specialize in wholesale and retail of commodities with an annual transaction of over 100 million yuan. The sum of sales of all sellers in the markets makes up the transaction value of the markets.

Chain Enterprises (also called chain stores or chain corporations) refer to a form of joint economic entities under which scattered enterprises or establishments engaged in providing homogeneous commodities or services, with the central leadership of core enterprise or headquarters and guided by common policies, conduct centralized purchase and distributed selling of commodities, in order to gain better efficiency through standardized operation. Consisting of a number of branch stores, the chain stores have in general following features: 1) homogeneous commodities, 2) unique name of stores, 3) centralized purchase and delivery which is separated from distributed selling operation (most commodities are delivered from the headquarters except some items which, from logistics, quality or freshness considerations, might be delivered by the suppliers directly).

Chain stores have 3 categories:

a) Chain stores under direct management: These are formal chain stores invested or controlled by the headquarters. They operate under the direct and unified management from the headquarters. Adopting a direct management approach, the headquarters give orders and control all retail stores, which follow completely the directives from the headquarters. Large monopolized commercial companies develop and expand their business through purchasing, merging, direct investment and controlling of shares.

b) Chain stores through special permit: Through contracts, chain stores (or their owners) obtain licenses from the headquarters to use designated trade marks, names, operation know-how, and to sell the commodity developed by the headquarters. Under this arrangement, each store in the chain is an independent legal entity and operates under the guidance from the headquarters.

c) Chain stores through voluntary arrangement: Under this arrangement, all stores operate together under the guidance of the headquarters, while maintaining their status of independent legal entities with full ownership of their assets. They use the same store name, sign contracts with the headquarters concerning purchase, sale, publicity, etc. and operate under the contract. They are free to engage in other activities which are not bounded in the contract. They could join or leave the chain on voluntary basis.

Chain stores through special permit and those through voluntary arrangement make up chain stores through license arrangement.

17 科技和教育

Science，Technology and Education

资料整理：徐晓颖　谢　涛

17-1 科技活动基本情况

BASIC STATISTICS ON PERSONEL ENGAGED IN SCIENTIFIC AND TECHNICAL ACTIVITIES

项　目	Item	2009	2010	2011	2012	2013	2014
科技活动人员　(人)	Personels Engaged in Scientific and Technical Activities (person)	274963	282604	310240	339786	365502	388430
R&D人员　(人)	R & D Personels	131680	142683	166357	185703	205172	218094
R&D经费内部支出 (万元)	Inner Expenditures of R & D Funds (10 000 yuan)	2134490	2637885	3230128	3845239	4462690	5108973
基础研究	Basic Research	89327	102494	139256	203953	218994	186200
应用研究	Practical Research	335189	472497	471732	561485	679021	691267
实验发展	Experiment Development	1709975	2062893	2619140	3079800	3564675	4231507

17-2 科技活动项目、成果与机构情况

BASIC STATISTICS ON SCIENTIFIC AND TECHNICAL PROJECTS, ACHIEVEMENT AND INSTITUTIONS

项　目	Item	2010	2011	2012	2013	2014
发表科技论文　(篇)	Scientific Research Papers Published (piece)	84660	88826	89714	90209	93590
出版科技专著数　(种)	Scientific and Techincal Books Published (kind)	2679	2401	2672	2618	2900
科技项目(课题)数　(个)	Number of Scientific Projects (unit)		45457	48669	53088	55777
科技项目经费支出　(万元)	Expenses for Scientific Projects (10 000 yuan)		2440630	3208902	3433884	3768678
科学研究与开发机构数　(个)	Number of Scientific Research Institutions and Development Organizations (unit)	1557	1471	1744	1946	2002
科研机构R&D人员数　(人)	R & D Staff (person)	57274	72747	67997	74696	68151
科研机构R&D内部支出(万元)	Inner Expenditures of R & D Funds (10 000 yuan)	1235013	1237563	1464692	1938710	1901466
科研机构年末仪器设备资产原价　(万元)	Original Price of Fixed Assets of Scientific Research Institutions and Organizations at Year-end (10 000 yuan)	1738151	2037951	2293613	2553205	2591182

17-3 政府部门所属科学研究与开发机构科技活动情况

BASIC STATISTICS ON STATE-OWNED RESAEARCH AND DEVELOPMENT INSTITUTIONS

项 目	Item	机构(个) Number of Institutions (unit)	科技活动人员(人) Persons Engaged (person)	大学本科及以上学历 Bachelor's Degrees and Above	#R&D人员 Research and Development Persons	收费收入(万元) Revenue (10 000 yuan)	#政府拨款 Government Appropriations
2011年总计	**Total of 2011**	**274**	**9731**	**6307**	**4303**	**277585**	**229273**
一、自然科学和技术领域	Natural Science and Technology	253	8785	5568	4303	260274	214727
县级政府部门属	Department of County	137	1181	216		4505	2760
市、州级政府部门属	Department of Cities and Prefecture	71	1727	875	458	26759	13104
省政府部门属	Department of Province	54	3764	2750	1300	134026	87459
国务院部门属	Department of State Council	12	3059	2466	3494	169331	137807
#中科院武汉分院属	#Chinese Academy of Science Wuhan Branch	7	1631	1437	3078	94785	83664
二、社会、人文科学领域	Sosiety and Humanity	10	425	352		9057	8222
2012年总计	**Total of 2012**	**273**	**9929**	**6770**	**5423**	**317269**	**254809**
一、自然科学和技术领域	Natural Science and Technology	252	8938	5974	4933	296724	237331
县级政府部门属	Department of County	138	1177	232	103	4846	3447
市、州级政府部门属	Department of Cities and Prefecture	70	1704	940	477	30407	14551
省政府部门属	Department of Province	54	3841	2952	2027	150760	81231
国务院部门属	Department of State Council	11	3207	2646	3769	211957	174455
#中科院武汉分院属	#Chinese Academy of Science Wuhan Branch	7	1820	1590	3283	125113	113833
二、社会、人文科学领域	Sosiety and Humanity	10	437	374	267	11788	10671
2013年总计	**Total of 2013**	**268**	**9880**	**6997**	**6627**	**330002**	**262430**
一、自然科学和技术领域	Natural Science and Technology	249	8944	6240	6083	309814	244642
县级政府部门属	Department of County	135	1144	239	113	5135	3572
市、州级政府部门属	Department of Cities and Prefecture	68	1693	964	448	32952	17648
省政府部门属	Department of Province	53	3822	2958	2185	163291	98118
国务院部门属	Department of State Council	12	3221	2836	3881	210591	160783
#中科院武汉分院属	#Chinese Academy of Science Wuhan Branch	7	1876	1722	3487	112661	92969
二、社会、人文科学领域	Sosiety and Humanity	8	363	302	320	8003	7490
2014年总计	**Total of 2014**	**256**	**9938**	**7159**	**7077**	**458906**	**281806**
一、自然科学和技术领域	Natural Science and Technology	239	9038	6423	6650	433627	259948
县级政府部门属	Department of County	134	1151	234	175	14631	5443
市、州级政府部门属	Department of Cities and Prefecture	59	1617	938	717	36475	19505
省政府部门属	Department of Province	51	3800	3029	1917	171818	103203
国务院部门属	Department of State Council	12	3370	2958	4268	235982	172074
#中科院武汉分院属	#Chinese Academy of Science Wuhan Branch	6	1889	1690	3566	123589	97124
二、社会、人文科学领域	Sosiety and Humanity	7	325	274	208	10785	10601

17-3 续表 continued

项 目	Item	经费支出(万元) Expenditures (10 000 yuan)	#科技经费支出 Expenditure on Science & Technology	#R&D经费内部支出 Inner Expenditure of R & D	研究课题数(个) Number of Projects	课题经费投入(万元) Investment on Subject Study (10 000 Yuan)	参加课题组(人年) Number of Persons Engaged in Subjects Study (person/year)
2011年总计	**Total of 2011**	**321449**	**242197**	**108026**	**3179**	**104278**	**6024**
一、自然科学和技术领域	Natural Science and Technology	302879	227074	108026	3024	103074	5723
县级政府部门属	Department of County	12363	4532	0	39	568	109
市、州级政府部门属	Department of Cities and Prefecture	24342	18547	4167	240	3311	585
省政府部门属	Department of Province	128210	83563	21533	820	18640	2222
国务院部门属	Department of State Council	156534	135554	82325	2080	81757	3108
#中科院武汉分院属	#Chinese Academy of Science Wuhan Branch	85065	74178	68477	1425	51010	2277
二、社会、人文科学领域	Sosiety and Humanity	9722	7826		82	375	87
2012年总计	**Total of 2012**	**386332**	**283475**	**145490**	**3550**	**112506**	**6467**
一、自然科学和技术领域	Natural Science and Technology	364349	265746	138462	3385	110018	6067
县级政府部门属	Department of County	10957	5712	709	41	830	133
市、州级政府部门属	Department of Cities and Prefecture	27836	21223	5198	240	3871	604
省政府部门属	Department of Province	148703	82733	26417	3632	19049	2085
国务院部门属	Department of State Council	198834	173806	113165	2377	88755	3645
#中科院武汉分院属	#Chinese Academy of Science Wuhan Branch	117503	104469	99484	1544	57134	2485
二、社会、人文科学领域	Sosiety and Humanity	11522	9345	4841	84	403	100
2013年总计	**Total of 2013**	**414914**	**310410**	**158077**	**3738**	**126673**	**6523**
一、自然科学和技术领域	Natural Science and Technology	393283	292941	153014	3599	123807	6106
县级政府部门属	Department of County	15898	6576	850	49	1037	153
市、州级政府部门属	Department of Cities and Prefecture	31822	24529	5428	220	3907	542
省政府部门属	Department of Province	163291	78747	31809	936	22159	2151
国务院部门属	Department of State Council	217520	185486	119988	2533	99569	3678
#中科院武汉分院属	#Chinese Academy of Science Wuhan Branch	123903	111453	107873	1644	62085	2674
二、社会、人文科学领域	Sosiety and Humanity	8046	6545	2119	77	726	199
2014年总计	**Total of 2014**	**434547**	**326067**	**182264**	**3884**	**150800**	**7044**
一、自然科学和技术领域	Natural Science and Technology	412198	308486	174852	3817	149140	6631
县级政府部门属	Department of County	14947	7729	398	37	567	190
市、州级政府部门属	Department of Cities and Prefecture	32101	25007	7001	259	7125	702
省政府部门属	Department of Province	152770	92057	38017	881	22993	2124
国务院部门属	Department of State Council	234729	201272	136847	2707	120113	4028
#中科院武汉分院属	#Chinese Academy of Science Wuhan Branch	122286	104885	101373	1642	73891	2833
二、社会、人文科学领域	Sosiety and Humanity	10496	7896	4708	20	413	140

注：1.本表数据没有包括科技情报文献机构数据，但包括了县政府所属科技综合服务机构数。
2.科技部门的课题数包括生产性活动课题。

Notes:a)The data of intelligence literature is not included in this table.
b)The number of projects in science and technology department includes projects of production activities.

17-4 科学情报文献机构情况
STATISTICS ON SCIENTIFIC INTELLIGENCE LITERATURE ORGANIZATIONS

项 目	Item	1995	2000	2005	2010	2011	2012	2013	2014
机构 (个)	Institutions (unit)	12	14	12	11	11	11	11	10
职工总数 (人)	Total Number of Employees (person)	609	564	546	553	560	596	610	592
从事科技活动人员	Persons engaged in Scientific Activities	158	511	456	512	521	554	573	575
#大学本科及以上学历	#Bachelor's degrees and Above	329	337	306	347	387	422	455	462
经费收入总额 (万元)	Funds (10 000 yuan)	1529	2629	6677	8706	8253	11650	15472	14493
#政府拨款	#Government Appropriations	935	1679	5210	6009	6323	8476	12131	12515
经费支出总额 (万元)	Expendtitures (10 000 yuan)	1480	2340	6778	7955	7296	10460	13584	11852
#劳务费	#Service Charge	448	970	1179	2668	3255	4038	4105	4328

17-5 高等院校科技活动情况
BASIC STATISTICS ON SCIENTIFIC AND TECHNICAL ACTIVITIES OF INSTITUTIONS OF HIGHER EDUCATION

项 目	Item	2013			2014		
		合 计 Total	自然科学和技术领域 Natural Science and Technology	社会、人文科学领域 Sosiety and Humanity	合 计 Total	自然科学和技术领域 Natural Science and Technology	社会、人文科学领域 Sosiety and Humanity
科学研究与开发机构数 (个)	Institutions of Research and Development (unit)	517	339	178	542	360	182
科技活动人员数 (人)	Number of Personels in Scientific and Technical Activities (person)	73886	48586	25300	76371	49438	26933
研究与发展经费内部支出 (万元)	Inner Expenditures of Research and Development (10 000 yuan)	448844	383763	65081	470151	395848	74303
研究课题数 (个)	Number of Research Projects (unit)	38828	22306	16522	41376	23410	17966
项目(课题)经费投入 (万元)	Funds Invested in Research Projects (10 000 yuan)	389182	338504	50677	394202	339619	54583
项目(课题)参加人员折合全时当量 (人年)	Number of Persons Engaged in Projects (person-year)	15420	11343	4077	15386	11105	4281

17-6　大中型工业企业科技活动情况

STATISTICS ON SCIENTIFIC AND TECHNICAL ACTIVITIES OF LAREGE AND MEDIUM-SIZED INDUSTRIAL ENTERPRISES

单位：万元　　(10 000 yuan)

项　目	Item	2005	2010	2011	2012	2013	2014
大中型企业个数　(个)	Large and Medium Enterprises　(unit)	803	1421	1881	2022	2274	2277
有R&D活动的企业数　(个)	Number of Enterprises with Scientific Activities　(unit)	303	559	491	478	584	633
从事科技活动人员数　(人)	Number of Persons Engaged in Scientific Activities　(person)	60811	120581	136661	155116	157520	170579
#大学本科以上学历	#Bachelor's Degree and Above					49624	54203
研究与发展人员数　(人)	Persons Engaged in Research and Development　(person)	32005	64329	81444	93825	99563	107656
企业办科技开发机构数　(个)	Number of Scientific development Organizations Opened by Enterprises　(unit)	253	457	352	454	478	432
R&D项目数　(个)	Number of R&D Projects　(unit)	4306	4602	5222	5668	6095	6400
全部R&D项目经费支出 (万元)	Expenses for Development Projects　(10 000 yuan)	462619	1193793	1331576	1978154	1892653	2172256
研究与发展经费支出　(万元)	Expenditures for Research and Development　(10 000 yuan)	307880	1429050	1835717	2287148	2521324	2978369
新产品开发费支出　(万元)	Expenditures for Developing New Products　(10 000 yuan)	354130	1760964	2113832	2488079	2606672	2896732
技术改造经费支出　(万元)	Expenditures for Technical Innovation　(10 000 yuan)	1253563	1326521	891890	921059	883841	916673
技术引进经费支出　(万元)	Expenditures for Technology Introduction　(10 000 yuan)	83022	190418	81194	153336	121278	128533
消化吸收经费支出　(万元)	Expenditures for Technology Utilization　(10 000 yuan)	16312	29408	29911	42406	39464	38330
购买国内技术经费支出　(万元)	Expenditures for Purchasing Domestic Technology　(10 000 yuan)	7387	21561	26716	38037	72594	53481

17-7 有科技活动的规模以上工业企业主要分组指标

指标	Item	有R&D活动企业(个) Number of Enterprises with R & D Activities (unit)	
		2013	2014
总计	**Total**	**1714**	**1960**
一、按登记注册类型分	**Grouped by Type of Registration**		
内资企业	Domestic-funded Enterprises	1565	1794
国有企业	State-owned Enterprises	27	21
集体企业	Collective-owned Enterprises	4	2
股份合作企业	Cooperative Enterprises	3	
联营企业	Associated Enterprises		
有限责任公司	Limited Liability Companies	758	817
股份有限公司	Share Holding Co., Ltd	193	215
私营企业	Private Enterprises	575	736
其他企业	Others	5	3
港、澳、台商投资企业	Hongkong, Maco and Taiwan-invested Enterprises	59	68
合资经营企业(港或澳、台资)	Joint Ventures (Hongkong, Maco or Taiwan Invested Enterprises)	36	46
合作经营企业(港或澳、台资)	Cooperative Ventures(Hongkong, Maco or Taiwan Invested Enterprises)	1	1
港、澳、台商独资经营企业	Enterprises Solely Funded by hongkong, Maco and Taiwan Businessmen	18	18
港、澳、台商投资股份有限公司	Hongkong, Maco and Taiwan Funded Share Holding Co.Ltd.	4	2
其他港澳台投资企业	Other Hongkong, Maco and Taiwan Funded Share Holding Co., Ltd.		1
外商投资企业	Foreign-invested Enterprises	90	98
中外合资经营企业	Sino-Foreign Joint Ventures	68	70
中外合作经营企业	Sino-Foreign Contractual Joint Ventures		
外资企业	Foreign Funded Enterprises	20	25
外商投资股份有限公司	Foreign Funded Share Holding Co., Ltd.	2	2
其他外商投资企业	Other Enterprises Invested by Foreign Businessmen		1
二、按行业分	**Grouped by Sector**		
煤炭开采和洗选业	Coal Mining and Processing		
石油和天然气开采业	Petroleum and Natural Gas Extraction	1	1
黑色金属矿采选业	Ferrous Metals Mining and Processing	3	5
有色金属矿采选业	Non-ferrous Metals Mining and Processing		1
非金属矿采选业	Non-metal Minerals Mining and Processing	7	16
开采辅助活动	Mining Auxiliary	1	1
其他采矿业	Other Mining	1	1
农副食品加工业	Primary Products and Food Processing Industry	120	135

MAJOR INDIENTORS OF INDUSTRIAL ABOVE DESIGNATED ENTERPRISES WITH SCIENTIFIC AND TECHNOLOGICAL ACTIVITIES

有科技机构的企业(个) Nuber of Persons Engaged in Scientific and Technical Activities (person)		R&D人员合计(人) R & D Personels (person)		R&D经费支出(万元) Funding for R & D Expenditure (10 000 yuan)		新产品开发经费支出(万元) Funding for New Product Development Expenditures (10 000 yuan)		新产品销售收入(万元) Revenue of New Product Sales (10 000 yuan)	
2013	2014	2013	2014	2013	2014	2013	2014	2013	2014
903	**927**	**128952**	**138562**	**3117987**	**3629506**	**3317175**	**3646332**	**46544784**	**52745891**
849	874	111419	119212	2620092	3042462	2706003	2967692	32592756	37352710
19	14	15278	14487	675367	746975	576990	555910	4014581	3093272
1	1	211	39	2025	1005	1566	413	17790	6510
	1	117		1339		961	306	2325	2241
								16680	
355	359	50587	55138	994218	1195015	1028045	1202323	14123589	16652936
126	106	28206	29649	579808	640818	648701	684274	7043369	8039126
345	390	16821	19867	364711	456396	445697	521617	7361004	9545085
3	3	199	32	2624	2253	4043	2850	13419	13541
24	22	7032	6542	178303	153478	151334	146152	1988953	2446012
19	18	4606	4256	132329	113908	108631	102897	1009759	1867955
1		15	9	81	710	135		267	8363
4	4	2298	1864	42832	35606	38235	40485	966938	552314
		113	397	3062	2943	4332	2304	11989	17380
			16		311		465		
30	31	10501	12808	319591	433566	459838	532488	11963076	12947169
23	21	7049	8452	257023	370233	397234	462848	10919254	12035609
	1					513	514	3013	4657
5	8	1524	2102	30470	33961	51644	61021	690339	517971
2	1	1928	2236	32098	29158	10448	7891	350471	386782
			18		215		215		2150
1		584	1168	7650	3386	993	253	1145	
	1	74	66	254	1551	35	1020		4900
1	1		21		1457	900	7		
5	8	78	240	1345	9496	1279	1321	10758	89067
		242	52	2091	415	735	927		
1		27	53	188	191	280	111		
79	82	3167	3680	102229	114861	112952	123877	2695209	3559391

17-7 续表 continued

指　标	Item	有R&D活动企业(个) Number of Enterprises with R & D Activities (unit)	
		2013	2014
食品制造业	Food Production	28	36
酒、饮料和精制茶制造业	Beverage Production	38	37
烟草制品业	Tabacco Processing	2	3
纺织业	Textile Industry	37	43
纺织服装、服饰业	Textile Wearing Apparel and Accessaries	8	8
皮革、毛皮、羽毛及其制品和制鞋业	Leather, Fur, Feather and Related Products	1	1
木材加工及木、竹、藤、棕、草制品业	Timber Processing and Wood, Bamboo, Rattan, Palm and Sraw Products	14	22
家具制造业	Furniture Manufacturing	2	4
造纸及纸制品业	Papermaking and Paper Products	15	14
印刷和记录媒介复制业	Printing and Record Processing	14	18
文教、工美、体育和娱乐用品制造业	Stationery, Education, Art, Sport and Entertainment Products	7	10
石油加工、炼焦及核燃料加工业	Petroleum Processing, Coking Products and Nuclear Fuel Processing	5	10
化学原料及化学制品制造业	Raw Chemical Material and Chemical Products	179	204
医药制造业	Medical and pharmaceutical Products	127	138
化学纤维制造业	Chemical Fibers	6	4
橡胶和塑料制品业	Rubber Products and Plastic Products	45	56
非金属矿物制品业	Nonmetal Material Products	82	98
黑色金属冶炼及压延加工业	Smelting and Processing of ferrous Metals	34	39
有色金属冶炼及压延加工业	Smelting and Processing of Nonferrous Metals	19	28
金属制品业	Metal Products	76	89
通用设备械制造业	Ordinaryly Machinery Manufacturing	137	156
专用设备制造业	Special Purpose Equipment Manufacturing	120	142
汽车制造业	Automobile Manufacturing	226	260
铁路、船舶、航空航天和其他运输设备制造业	Realway, Ship, Aircraft and Other Transport Equipment Manufacturing	32	33
电气机械及器材制造业	Electric Machinery and Equipment	168	164
通信设备、计算机及其他电子设备制造业	Telecommunication Equipment, Computer and Other Electronic Equipment Manufacturing	105	116
仪器仪表及文化办公用机械制造业	Instruments, Meters, Cultural and Official Machinery	35	45
其他制造业	Other Manufacturing	5	6
废弃资源和废旧材料回收加工业	Waste Resources and Junk Material Recycled	2	3
金属制品、机械和设备修理业	Repairing of Metal and Mechanical Equipment	4	4
电力、热力的生产和供应业	Electric Power, Steam and Hot Water Production and Supply	8	7
煤气生产和供应业	Gas Production and Supply		2
水的生产和供应业	Tap Water Production and Supply		

有科技机构的企业(个) Number of Enterprises with R & D Units (unit)		R&D人员合计(人) R & D Personels (person)		R&D经费支出(万元) Funding for R & D Expenditure (10 000 yuan)		新产品开发经费支出(万元) Funding for New Product Development Expenditures (10 000 yuan)		新产品销售收入(万元) Revenue of New Product Sales (10 000 yuan)	
2013	2014	2013	2014	2013	2014	2013	2014	2013	2014
17	25	821	1003	29995	23015	54062	52758	428228	475412
33	39	1094	1370	28497	32524	62875	63737	762724	607711
1	1	549	414	20141	18238	21086	17692	59524	20794
23	36	2675	2264	33640	33016	40176	51219	452174	651173
9	9	856	642	12408	11133	15908	13591	158316	96428
1	3	13	11	238	44	275	44	2005	9247
8	11	428	745	8980	15471	11320	16074	174049	290118
1	2	92	153	1446	2206	1458	2536	36708	43310
7	9	437	453	12683	20137	15107	18301	121077	119305
5	8	592	722	12613	13757	9945	11408	93443	120899
3	3	326	448	3770	7174	5484	7148	52751	131240
1	6	275	383	8779	14161	8527	13458	2308	151541
107	101	10522	12530	255468	344470	183102	213064	4679115	6340257
72	70	10713	11222	160514	174454	149695	160459	1741568	2589468
1	1	390	309	8970	1916	4203	2978	36279	73495
30	33	3249	2932	38616	42282	62837	48874	1187589	1279985
47	56	5973	6278	95992	98276	79399	131652	1359357	1604730
17	18	7954	10212	550586	649274	470172	407435	4252497	3030192
16	11	1422	1830	90545	125194	41846	47292	2082482	2343105
39	39	6410	5832	103935	98378	102090	114846	1149136	1460463
59	59	7643	7192	137429	127703	148760	151769	1687972	2153194
52	45	6691	6877	124973	119318	157327	144356	1267284	1390951
113	120	15928	18683	411601	588543	622541	755655	13661280	14281540
18	15	10246	8759	166098	119242	160029	155383	1367078	1415472
64	54	11057	11550	190448	234423	214401	282361	3696835	4661855
48	33	14905	17522	440824	522336	504570	568123	2885791	2993740
14	15	1575	1346	23402	27366	29287	38487	224998	334406
3	4	460	532	11704	16728	15207	19449	93394	204248
2	4	24	93	617	1711	541	518	48539	87291
3	2	345	283	7582	6286	5324	903	12765	11803
1	2	1115	448	11735	4950	2445	7248	58762	109540
	1		244		4427				9623
1								1648	

17-8 全省高新技术产业发展情况(2014)
STATISTICS ON NEW AND HIGH TECHNIC INDUSTRY DEVELOPMENT IN THE WHOLE PROVINCE(2014)

单位:亿元　　(100 million yuan)

项目	Item	全省 the Whole Province	增幅(%) Increase(%)
高新技术产业增加值	**Added Value of High-tech Industry**	**4451.16**	**14.8**
"四上"高新技术产业增加值	"Four Up" Added Value of High-tech Industry	4407.98	14.8
其中：高新服务业增加值	Added Value of High-tech Service	467.88	19.8
高新制造业增加值	Added Value of High-tech Manufacturing	3940.10	14.6
1.电子信息	1.Electronic Information	550.75	21.5
2.先进制造	2.Advanced Manufacturing	1512.56	14.7
3.新材料	3.New Material	820.32	13.3
4.生物医药与医疗机械	4.Bio-medicine and Medical Instrument	320.10	12.7
"四下"高新技术产业增加值	"Four Up" Added Value of High-tech Industry	43.18	10.8
高新制造业产值*	Output Value of High-tech Manufacturing	14161.12	12.5
高新制造业产品出口交货值*	Export Value of High-tech Manufacturing	1169.49	16.9
高新制造业产品销售收入*	Revenue of High-tech Manufacturing	12957.93	8.6
高新制造业利税总额*	Tax on High-tech Manufacturing	989.45	11.0

注：带"*"号的指标口径为规模以上工业企业(下同)。
Note:Data with "*" cover industrial enterprises above designated size(the same below).

17–9 市州高新技术产业发展情况(2014)
STATISTICS ON THE DEVELOPMENT OF HIGH AND NEW TECHNOLOGY INDUSTRIE OF CITIES AND PREFECTURE (2014)

单位:亿元 (100 million yuan)

		增加值 Value Added	总产值* Total Output Value	产品销售收入* Sales Revenue of Products	利税总额* Total Value of Taxes
全省合计	**Total of the Province**	**4451.16**	**14161.12**	**12957.93**	**989.45**
武 汉 市	Wuhan	2030.73	5630.54	4810.12	406.50
黄 石 市	Huangshi	192.04	817.02	814.92	54.17
十 堰 市	Shiyan	156.61	534.03	501.83	42.63
宜 昌 市	Yichang	476.29	1477.03	1429.01	89.70
襄 阳 市	Xiangyang	686.56	2402.39	2203.72	148.63
鄂 州 市	Ezhou	100.14	365.68	347.68	35.05
荆 门 市	Jingmen	144.82	556.60	548.60	42.28
孝 感 市	Xiaogan	151.72	480.60	474.46	33.52
荆 州 市	Jingzhou	129.21	481.81	471.41	40.74
黄 冈 市	Huanggang	117.58	430.21	395.94	27.94
咸 宁 市	Xianning	63.93	231.86	220.18	15.23
随 州 市	Suizhou	75.86	278.07	276.93	18.33
恩 施 州	Enshi	8.92	32.46	32.22	2.05
仙 桃 市	Xiantao	54.46	200.18	194.55	15.20
潜 江 市	Qianjiang	29.60	121.52	117.40	5.67
天 门 市	Tianmen	32.61	121.13	118.96	11.82
神农架林区	Shennongjia	0.06			

17-10 申报登记省、部级以上成果分类及经济效益
CLASSIFICATION AND ECONOMIC BENEFITS OF SCIENTIFIC ACHIEVEMENTS APPLIED AND REGISTERED ABOVE PROVINCIAL AND MINISTRIAL LEVEL

单位：项 (unit)

项　目	Item	2000	2005	2009	2010	2011	2012	2013	2014
成果总类	**Total Calsses of Achievement**	**571**	**717**	**740**	**750**	**1200**	**1567**	**1621**	**1778**
一、按成果水平分类	Grouped by Level								
国际首创/领先	International Innovation/ Leading	19	28	56	52	94	101	81	100
国际先进	Internationl Advanced Technology	97	172	217	195	210	254	326	353
国内首创/领先	Domestic Innovation/ Leading	276	394	353	362	559	745	751	706
国内先进	Domestic Advanced Technology	84	72	60	69	133	176	177	270
其它	Others	18	3	7	39	154	14	31	299
二、按成果类型分类	Grouped by Type								
基础理论研究	Basic Theory Research	37	15	20	15	21	24	22	13
应用开发研究	Applicable Development	494	669	693	717	1150	1507	1570	1728
其它	Others	40	33	27	18	29	36	29	37
三、按成果产业属性分类	Grouped by Sector Property								
工业类成果	Industrial Achievements	145	225	178	226	355	532	514	560
农业类成果	Agricultural Achievements	79	129	113	124	209	197	251	371
医学类成果	Medical Achievements	199	291	214	231	385	414	441	446
其他类成果	Others	148	74	235	169	251	424	415	401
四、按成果完成单位分类	Grouped by Units								
高等院校完成	Institutions of Higher Education	149	169	144	137	168	160	246	271
研究单位完成	Scientific Research Institutions	92	92	70	64	110	86	74	116
厂矿企业完成	Industrial and Mineral Enterprises	137	176	272	303	513	1136	911	966
其他单位完成	Others	193	280	267	246	409	185	390	425
五、经济效益　（亿元）	Economic Benefits　(100 million yuan)								
总收入	Total Income	78.33	199.50				1212.78	331.33	462.80
本年度节约资金	Capital Saved in This Year	6.33	28.28		36.85	169.65	401.37	56.38	551.61

17-11 科学技术协会组织与活动
ORGANIZATIONS AND ACTIVITIES OF SCIENTIFIC AND TECHNOLOGICAL ASSOCIATION

项 目		Item		2013	2014
一、机构与人员		**Organizations and Personels**			
1.省级学会	(个)	Provincal Institute	(unit)	133	133
会员	(人)	Members	(person)	155183	152639
高级(资深)会员	(人)	Senoir Members	(person)	22736	21000
外国会员	(人)	Foreign Members	(person)	38	38
2.市、州学会数	(个)	City and Prefecture Institute	(unit)	546	543
3.省级科协	(个)	Provincal Scientific Assosiations	(unit)	1	1
市、州科协	(个)	City and Prefecture Scientific Assosiations	(unit)	13	13
县(区)科协	(个)	County (District) Scientific Assosiations	(unit)	104	104
二、学术活动		**Academic Activities**			
省级学会及县以上科协		**Provincial Institutes and Scientific Assosiations above County level**			
国内学术会议	(次)	Domestic Academic Conference	(time)	642	646
参加人数	(人次)	Number of Person Participated	(person-time)	60327	61440
论文数	(篇)	Number of Scholary Paper	(piece)	13739	15732
境内国际学术会议	(次)	Domestic International Academic Conference	(time)	36	43
参加人数	(人次)	Number of Person Participated	(person-time)	3006	5823
论文数	(篇)	Number of Scholary Paper	(piece)	1499	1394
三、科普活动		**Science and Technology Popularization Activities**			
省级学会及县以上科协		**Provincial Institutes and Scientific Assosiations above County level**			
举办科普宣讲活动	(次)	Events of Science Popularization Lectures	(time)	7608	9191
宣讲活动受众人数	(人次)	People Participated	(person-time)	7040613	6478417
举办实用技术培训	(次)	Technical Training	(time)	7536	10787
实用技术培训人数	(人次)	People Participated	(person-time)	1701324	1980877
播放科技广播、影视节目	(分钟)	Scientific Radio and Video Programs	(mimute)	644039	273963
参加活动科技人员	(人次)	People Participated	(person-time)	83466	96985
四、青少年科技教育		**Education in Science and Technology for the Adolescents**			
省级学会及县以上科协		**Provincial Institutes and Scientific Assosiations above County level**			
举办青少年科技竞赛	(项)	Adolescent Technology Competition	(unit)	487	494
参加人数	(人次)	Number of Person Participated	(person-time)	2157230	2163083
获奖人数	(人次)	Number of Person Rewarded	(person-time)	81605	79989
举办青少年科学营	(次)	Adolescent Technology Campus		129	314
参加人数	(人次)	Number of Person Participated	(person-time)	10435	18551
举办青少年科技教育培训	(次)	Adolescent Technology Education Training		807	982
培训人数	(人次)	Number of Person Participated	(person-time)	524014	583166
五、科普基础设施建设		**Infrastructure Construction of Science Popularization**			
县以上科协		**Scientific Assosiations above County Level**			
科技场馆	(个)	Science and Technology Museum	(unit)	61	64
建筑面积	(平方米)	Construction Area	(square metre)	178317	185219
展厅面积	(平方米)	Exhibition Area	(square metre)	70039	73064
全年参观人数	(人次)	Year-round Visitor	(person-time)	1912890	2033037
科普活动站	(个)	Science Popularization Station	(unit)	9879	11192
科普画廊建筑面积	(平方米)	Science Popularization Gallery Construction Area	(square metre)	107212	116617
省级科普教育基地	(个)	Provincial Education Base of Science Popularization	(unit)	80	93
农村科普示范基地	(个)	Rural Demonstration Base of Science Popularization	(unit)	1204	1359
六、为科技工作者服务		**Serve for Scientists**			
省级学会及县以上科协		**Provincial Institutes and Scientific Assosiations above County level**			
反映科技工作者建议	(条)	Reported Suggestions of Scientists		2171	2048
其中：获上级领导批示的建议	(条)	Answered by Leaders		415	420
答复人大政协代表(委员)提案	(件)	Replied Proposal of NPC and CPPCC Representatives(Con	(piece)	113	123
走访看望(慰问)科技工作者	(人次)	Visit Scientific Workers	(person-time)	2556	2936
科学道德与学风建设宣讲活动	(场次)	Preach Ethics of Science		1	24
宣讲活动受众人数	(人次)	Number of Audience	(person-time)	1500	12110
参加宣讲活动专家数	(人次)	Number of Specialists	(person-time)	1	316
技术创新方法培训班	(场次)	Technology Innovation Training Class		13	51
继续教育培训班	(场次)	Continuing Education Class		70	131
培训结业人数	(人次)	Number of People Completed Courses	(person-time)	5858	9650
宣传科技工作者人数	(人)	Propagating Scientific and Technology Workers	(person)	466	3432
表彰奖励科技工作者	(人次)	Rewarded Scientific and Technology Workers	(person-time)	3870	3924

17-12 专利受理量、批准量及分布状况

NUMBER OF PATENT APPLICATIONS EXAMINATION, APPROVAL AND DISTRITUTION

单位：项 (unit)

项 目	Item	受理量 Number of Patent Applications Examined				批准量 Number of Patent Applications Approved			
		2005	2010	2013	2014	2005	2010	2013	2014
合 计	**Total**	**11534**	**31311**	**50816**	**59050**	**3860**	**17362**	**28760**	**28290**
发 明	Creations and Inventions	2038	7410	18189	22536	733	2025	4052	4855
实用新型	Utility Models	4835	12792	26163	27829	2238	10431	19655	19801
外观设计	Designs	4661	11109	6464	8685	889	4906	5053	3634
在合计中	**Of This Total**								
个 人	Individual	7400	10844	16437	17294	2189	4990	7996	5822
大专院校	Universities and Colleges	1365	3265	6320	7972	574	1972	3008	3702
科研单位	Insitutions of Scientific Research	182	1112	1611	1537	101	532	742	719
工矿企业	Industrial and Mineral Enterprises	2305	15856	23813	28810	901	9744	16739	17746
机关团体	Government Agencies and Organizations	283	234	2635	3437	98	124	275	301

17-13 按市州分三种专利申请与授权状况(2014)

THREE KINDS OF PATENT APPICATION AND AUTHORIZATION BY MUNICIPALITIES AND PREFECTURES(2014)

单位：项 (item)

市、州	Municipalities and Prefecture	申请 当年累计 Patent Application Total of 2013	发明 Invention	实用新型 New type of practicial Utility	外观设计 Design	授权 当年累计 Authorization Total of 2013	发明 Invention	实用新型 New type of practicial Utility	外观设计 Design
全省合计	**Total of the Province**	**59050**	**22536**	**27829**	**8685**	**28290**	**4855**	**19801**	**3634**
武 汉	Wuhan	27723	11854	13747	2122	16294	3874	10855	1565
黄 石	Huangshi	2242	929	831	482	821	72	636	113
十 堰	Shiyan	2089	585	1350	154	1190	57	1012	121
荆 州	Jingzhou	1569	309	897	363	984	89	662	233
宜 昌	Yichang	7274	2258	2459	2557	2353	277	1923	153
襄 阳	Xiangfan	6448	2622	3580	246	1747	118	1410	219
鄂 州	Ezhou	854	412	244	198	237	16	181	40
荆 门	Jingmen	1287	513	642	132	751	46	582	123
孝 感	Xiaogan	1855	676	883	296	1136	115	749	272
黄 冈	Huanggang	2463	582	1301	580	913	53	666	194
咸 宁	Xianning	1210	306	543	361	502	33	307	162
随 州	Suizhou	946	263	513	170	418	14	287	117
恩施州	Enshi	720	343	203	174	287	59	144	84
仙 桃	Xiantao	780	297	330	153	285	21	186	78
潜 江	Qianjiang	728	275	166	287	117	4	91	22
天 门	Tianmen	836	290	139	407	239	6	98	135
神农架林区	Shennongjia Forest District	26	22	1	3	16	1	12	3

17-14 各类技术合同签定及执行情况

SIGNING AND IMPEMENTATION OF VARIOUS TECHNICAL CONTRACTS

项 目	Item	合同数(项) Number of Contracts (unit)	合同金额(万元) Value of Contracts (10 000 yuan)
2008	**2008**	**7147**	**628971**
技术开发合同	Technology Development Contracts	3703	379092
技术转让合同	Technology Transfer Contracts	235	45101
技术咨询合同	Technology Consultation Contracts	1237	42571
技术服务合同	Technology Service Contracts	1972	162207
2009	**2009**	**5694**	**779700**
技术开发合同	Technology Development Contracts	2391	337341
技术转让合同	Technology Transfer Contracts	216	239272
技术咨询合同	Technology Consultation Contracts	1144	42747
技术服务合同	Technology Service Contracts	1943	160339
2010	**2010**	**6641**	**909167**
技术开发合同	Technology Development Contracts	2390	502290
技术转让合同	Technology Transfer Contracts	199	126505
技术咨询合同	Technology Consultation Contracts	1321	71932
技术服务合同	Technology Service Contracts	2731	208439
2011	**2011**	**7799**	**1214103**
技术开发合同	Technology Development Contracts	4101	661014
技术转让合同	Technology Transfer Contracts	327	99063
技术咨询合同	Technology Consultation Contracts	1358	88232
技术服务合同	Technology Service Contracts	2013	365793
2012	**2012**	**12908**	**2345655**
技术开发合同	Technology Development Contracts	7698	1000226
技术转让合同	Technology Transfer Contracts	447	482601
技术咨询合同	Technology Consultation Contracts	1391	87457
技术服务合同	Technology Service Contracts	3372	775371
2013	**2013**	**14909**	**4187410**
技术开发合同	Technology Development Contracts	9473	1614052
技术转让合同	Technology Transfer Contracts	574	342631
技术咨询合同	Technology Consultation Contracts	1082	238981
技术服务合同	Technology Service Contracts	3780	1991746
2014	**2014**	**21696**	**6017367**
技术开发合同	Technology Development Contracts	11695	1398146
技术转让合同	Technology Transfer Contracts	518	279765
技术咨询合同	Technology Consultation Contracts	1496	389802
技术服务合同	Technology Service Contracts	7987	3949654

17-15 全省技术买卖情况(2014)
PURCHASE AND SELLING OF TECHNOLOGY IN THE WHOLE PROVINCE (2014)

卖方类别 Type of the Seller / 买方类别 Type of the Buyer		合计 Total		机关法人 Organ Corporations		事业法人 Institutions Corporations		社团法人 Associations Corporations	
		合同数(项) Number of Contracts	成交额(万元) Contracted Value (10 000 yuan)	合同数(项) Number of Contracts	成交额(万元) Contracted Value (10 000 yuan)	合同数(项) Number of Contracts	成交额(万元) Contracted Value (10 000 yuan)	合同数(项) Number of Contracts	成交额(万元) Contracted Value (10 000 yuan)
总计	**Total**	**21696**	**6017367**	**468**	**237106**	**12025**	**975664**	**14**	**1354**
机关法人	Departments	4950	1239065	393	201251	3180	485504		
事业法人	Institutions	3372	331986	18	9878	2723	185520	1	80
社团法人	Social Groups	60	3931	1	100	47	1359		
企业法人	Corporations	13176	4421582	56	25877	6041	301693	13	1274
自然人	Natural Person	33	10580			11	32		
其他组织	Other Organizations	105	10223			23	1556		

17-15 续表 continued

卖方类别 Type of the Seller / 买方类别 Type of the Buyer		企业法人 Corporations		自然人 Natural Person		其他组织 Other Organizations	
		合同数(项) Number of Contracts	成交额(万元) Contracted Value (10 000 yuan)	合同数(项) Number of Contracts	成交额(万元) Contracted Value (10 000 yuan)	合同数(项) Number of Contracts	成交额(万元) Contracted Value (10 000 yuan)
总计	**Total**	**9153**	**4771561**	**13**	**7016**	**23**	**24666**
机关法人	Departments	1377	552311				
事业法人	Institutions	629	136158			1	350
社团法人	Social Groups	12	2472				
企业法人	Corporations	7033	4063190	12	6712	21	22837
自然人	Natural Person	21	10244	1	304		
其他组织	Other Organizations	81	7187			1	1479

17-16　地震观测及地方地震工作情况
STATISTICS ON EARTHQUAKE OBSERVATION AND LOCAL EFFORTS ON EARTHQUAKE WORKS

项　目	Item	2013	2014
职工总数　(人)	Total Number of Staff and Workers　(person)	474	445
专业技术人员　(人)	Professtional Technical Personel　(person)	335	309
高级技术人员　(人)	Senior Technical Personel　(person)	77	75
市州级地震局　(个)	Number of Earthquake Agency　(unit)	17	17
重点县地震办公室　(个)	Number of Earthquake Offices in Key Counties　(unit)	32	32
地方地震工作人员　(人)	Local Seismologist　(person)	374	641
地震观测台(网)人员　(人)	Number of Staff in Earthquake Observation Station　(person)	67	73
#观测技术人员　(人)	#Technical Personel　(person)	46	53
地震台站　(个)	Earthquake Observation Station　(unit)	48	52
国家台	National Station	5	5
省级台	Provincial Station	43	47
GPS测量　(千米/点)	GPS Measurement　(km/point)	120000/230	120000/180
流动重力测量　(千米/点)	Flow Gravity Measurement　(km/point)	75000/465	90000/482

17-17　气象部门基本情况
BASIC CONDITIONS OF METEOROLOGICAL DEPARTMENT

项　目	tem	2000	2005	2010	2011	2012	2013	2014
一、气象观测人员总数　(人)	Total Number of Staff in Meteorological Depaartment　(person)	333	375	378	398	388	415	469
地面观测	Groud Observation	285	320	330	350	340	367	410
高空观测	Upper Air Observation	24	18	18	18	16	14	24
雷达观测	Radar Observation	24	20	30	30	32	34	35
特种观测	Special Observation							
二、气象台站总数　(个)	Total Number of Meteorological Obervatory　(unit)	85	87	87	87	87	89	89
气象台	Meteorological Obervatory	13	14	14	14	14	14	14
气象站	Weather Station	70	71	71	71	71	73	73
独立农试站	Independent Agricultural Station	2	2	2	2	2	2	2
三、卫星云图接收站点数　(个)	Number of Stations Receiving Satellite Image　(unit)	11	25	15	15	10	17	17
极轨卫星	Polar Orbiting Meteorological Satellite	2	23	5	5	3	4	4
同步卫星	Geostationary Satellite	9	7	10	10	7	13	13
接收卫星云图图片数	Number of Satellite Image Pictures Received							
使用云图单位数	Number of Pictures Used	144						
四、拥有雷达数　(部)	Number of Radar Owned　(unit)	11	12	15	14	14	17	14
701测风	701 Wind Sensing	4	4					
3厘米	3 cm	2	2	1	1	1	1	1
5厘米	5 cm	2	1	1	1		1	
10厘米	10 cm	3	5	10	9	10	7	10
l波段	1 Wave Band			3	3	3	8	3

17-18 质量技术监督检查情况

STATISTICS ON SUPERVISION AND EXAMINATION OF QUALITY TECHNOLOGY

年 份	机构	职工人数(人)		经费收入	经费支出	固定资产		计量器具检定台(万套件)		
Year	(个) Institutions (unit)	Number of Staff and Workers (person)	#专业技术人员 #Professional Technic Personel	(万元) Revenue (10 000 yuan)	(万元) Expenditures (10 000 yuan)	(万元) Fixed Assets (10 000 yuan)	#仪器设备 #Equipment and Devices	Number of Measuring Equipment Tested (10 000 units)	#衡 具 #Measuring Instrument	#强制检定 #Compulsory Test
1980	88	1211	327	308	306	1667	512	60		
1985	107	1668	356	640	515	3234	1402	146	36	
1990	105	3299	1409	3063	2610	7994	3760	136	68	118
1995	167	6275	2121	10095	10374	21213	6327	150	64	140
1996	102	2265	1252	3237	3177	6985	3261	136	61	108
1997	101	2337	1337	3491	3418	6751	3680	150	62	110
1998	106	2479	1439	4 079	4034	6314	3810	126	50	100
1999	105	2531	1446	4 515	4532	6732	3713	120	43	103
2000	104	2790	1478	4 568	4853	8829	5286	150	43	105
2001	91	1632	911	3005	2899	6537	3881	132	33	65
2002	360	9583	4059	36371	34024	39461	9806	165	40	138
2003	403	9137	3960	44450	41317	47323	12114	154	45	118
2004	376	9034	4703	50520	48383	53579	14549	128	23	114
2005	398	9046	3953	59089	56152	62607	19986	120	22	98
2006	398	9050	4094	67864	64078	72440	23840	119	22	110
2007	393	9065	4072	79698	75988	81822	26984	119	19	102
2008	392	9055	3732	93140	89653	94547	27832	109	16	96
2009	395	9077	3718	111477	110965	111627	35047	128	18	107
2010	388	9133	3815	116319	109915	129113	38963	125	17	119
2011	387	8828	3693	134901	135563	150114	44143	142	15	135
2012	385	8997	3645	153332	146310	159772	45440	175	16	155
2013	383	8981	3655	197287	180390	183786	57740	199	15	188
2014	379	8420	3160	191091	177558	234080	64785	202	20	156

17-19 标准事业基本情况
BASIC STATISTICS ON STANDARD ENTERPRISES

项　　目	Item	2000	2005	2010	2011	2012	2013	2014
质量监督机构　（个）	Quality Supervision Institution (unit)	86	99	99	99	99	99	99
固定人员　（人）	Fixed Personel (person)	1 007						
制定标准　（项）	Standard Established (unit)	29	36	81	96	101	69	77
修定标准　（项）	Standard Revised (unit)			4	18	8	4	21
废止标准　（项）	Standard Abolished (unit)							
当年采用国际标准（项）	International Standard Adopted (unit)	4	129	193	130	101	106	
受检产品质量监督（种）	Number of Products under Quality Supervision (kind)	99						
质量监督检测　（批次）	Quality Supervision Test (batch)	20093	26548	40288	34734	35117	40317	6429
标准文件馆藏　（万件）	Standard Document Collection (10 000 units)	25	22	30	46	57	121	160

17-20 档案事业基本情况
BASIC STATISTICS ON ARCHIVES

指 标	Item	2010	2012	2013	2014
各级各类档案馆数量 (个)	Number of Institutions (unit)				
国家综合档案馆	National Comprehensive Archives		116	116	116
专门档案馆	National Special Archives		14	14	14
部门档案馆	Department Archives		7	7	7
各级各类档案馆馆藏	Number of Collections				
全宗 (个)	Fonds (unit)	14444	14628	15403	15587
案卷 (万卷)	Archives (10 000 volumes)	1367.06	1527.17	1659.54	1734.76
以件为保管单位档案 (万件)	Archives (10 000 pieces)	531.26	490.98	678.24	632.00
照片 (万张)	Photos (10 000 sheets)	138.00	146.00	141.00	161.00
馆藏资料 (万册)	Files (10 000 volumes)	268.04	258.41	291.08	275.00
国家综合档案馆面积 (万平方米)	The Area of National Comprehensive Archives (10 000 square meters)				
总建筑面积	Floor Space		18.45	20.66	21.98
库房面积	The Area of Storerooms		7.95	8.76	9.21
全省档案专业技术职称人员 (人)	Full-time Personnel (person)				
研究馆员	Research Librarian		24	21	30
副研究馆员	Associate Research Librarian		274	247	250
馆员	Librarian	1173	1031	940	945
助理馆员	Associate Librarian	1092	882	776	630
全省档案馆本年度利用档案	Utilized Archives				
利用档案人数 (万人次)	Use of Material (10 000 person-times)	37.55	28.78	30.08	37.84
利用档案卷次 (万人次)	Number of Archives Used (10 000 person-times)	100.40	70.64	74.16	92.00
举办展览 (个)	Display Organized (unit)	172	566	604	550
接待参观 (万人次)	Visitors (10 000 person-times)	35.03	33.50	41.15	42.38
全省本年编研档案资料	Materials Edited This Year				
公开出版种数 (种)	Number of Materials Open Published (kind)	84	85	76	90
公开出版字数 (万字)	Number of Words Open Published (10 000 words)	1970.00	2142.70	1929.56	1942.64
内部参考种数 (种)	Number of Materials for Inner Reference (kind)	164	172	197	224
内部参考字数 (万字)	Number of Words for Inner reference (10 000 words)	1704.00	1859.50	2062.96	2170.68

17-21 各级各类学校数

NUMBER OF SCHOOLS OF VARIOUS LEVELS

单位：所 (unit)

学校分类	Type of Shool	2005	2007	2008	2009	2010	2011	2012	2013	2014
普通高等学校	Regular Institutions of Higher Education	85	86	87	120	120	122	122	123	123
#地方院校	#Local Schools	77	78	79	112	112	114	114	115	115
中等职业学校	Secondary Vocation Schools	437	478	462	402	413	341	332	310	301
#中师	#Secondary Teacher School			10	7	7	3	3	3	3
普通中学	Regular Middle School	3231	3108	3011	2897	2787	2707	2622	2576	2552
#初中	#Junior High Schools	2578	2440	2356	2275	2184	2122	2047	2013	2011
城市	Urban	465	435	431	383	362	507	507	509	535
县镇	Township	487	539	564	622	671	929	953	945	955
农村	Rural	1635	1466	1361	1270	1151	686	587	559	521
高中	Senior High School	653	668	655	622	603	585	575	563	541
城市	Urban	306	292	295	267	243	313	318	318	314
县镇	Township	235	289	271	268	278	222	220	212	201
农村	Rural	112	87	89	87	82	50	37	33	26
小学	Primary School	12631	10210	9302	8544	7749	7415	6614	5746	5513
城市	Urban	949	831	845	722	685	1015	1007	997	1061
县镇	Township	627	693	715	847	937	1636	1629	1536	1556
农村	Rural	11055	8686	7742	6975	6127	4764	3978	3213	2896
特殊教育学校	Special Education School	77	76	76	76	76	76	77	80	83
幼儿园	Kindergarten	2336	2572	2880	2995	4395	4670	5321	6011	6491
技工学校	School of Technology	208	208	208		206				

17–22 各级各类学校在校学生数
ENROLLMENT IN SCHOOLS OF VARIOUS LEVELS

单位：人 (person)

学校分类	Type of Shool	2000	2005	2009	2010	2011	2012	2013	2014
普通高等学校	Regular Institutions of Higher Education	346568	1012665	1249061	1296920	1340298	1386086	1421434	1419699
#地方院校	#Local Schools	205615	824960	1053341	1098570	1129010	1183416	1217155	1216228
中等职业学校	Secondary Vocation Schools	278602	606014	1041759	903834	720915	500540	411194	372601
普通中学	Regular Middle School	3509318	4466879	3650102	3418299	3208399	2652208	2471869	2294899
#初中	#Junior High Schools	2810909	3172392	2363351	2180937	2040702	1577701	1483710	1375940
城市	Urban	772160	494739	452518	413930	561141	543902	529708	538778
县镇	Township	232916	750903	811217	848967	994830	743679	689455	627833
农村	Rural	1805833	1926750	1099616	918040	484731	290120	264547	209329
高中	Senior High School	698409	1294487	1286751	1237362	1167697	1074507	988159	918959
城市	Urban	424406	541404	512139	427334	596728	580248	555182	529827
县镇	Township	171592	553411	608803	633319	465734	435656	386923	357324
农村	Rural	102411	199672	165809	176709	105235	58603	46054	31808
小学	Primary School	6677422	4291881	3592629	3655512	3773446	3267498	3282579	3211598
城市	Urban	1585037	787812	717749	713491	1005861	1027061	1050497	1120918
县镇	Township	457132	593090	812990	974019	1273914	1160375	1187536	1209864
农村	Rural	4635253	2910979	2061890	1968002	1493671	1080062	1044546	880816
特殊教育学校	Special Education School	9739	9444	13959	15349	12893	10557	10576	11080
幼儿园	Kindergarten	726712	594481	831399	1118360	1324714	1355395	1473371	1538200
技工学校	School of Technology	55812	136000		229000				

17-23 各级各类学校招生数
NEW ENROLLMENT IN SCHOOLS OF VARIOUS LEVELS

单位：人 (person)

学校分类	Type of Shool	2000	2005	2009	2010	2011	2012	2013	2014
普通高等学校	Regular Institutions of Higher Education	139666	315560	395929	387612	413600	406957	403860	400307
#地方院校	#Local Schools	94524	269042	346525	337621	358933	356113	352544	350391
中等职业学校	Secondary Vocation Schools	62418	273789	367161	283610	212318	143530	130995	126656
普通中学	Regular Middle School	1352592	1469777	1120047	1053418	981191	838372	804312	749560
#初中	#Junior High Schools	1075527	1011186	696261	657947	619213	510866	487841	454284
城市	Urban	281648	162324	139712	132571	179751	181591	177436	178772
县镇	Township	89106	241579	240542	251823	295975	237380	225227	206959
农村	Rural	704773	607283	316007	273553	143487	91895	85178	68553
高中	Senior High School	277065	458591	423786	395471	361978	327506	316471	295276
城市	Urban	168541	187976	169309	138260	184335	178360	179553	168688
县镇	Township	68314	197496	199571	199177	144925	131519	123402	116662
农村	Rural	40210	73119	54906	58034	32718	17627	13516	9926
小学	Primary School	904559	567411	642190	680166	692317	634766	607979	597543
城市	Urban	239984	113284	117466	126070	179176	186695	188925	203429
县镇	Township	75192	81622	144972	176073	228466	220893	211576	217982
农村	Rural	589383	372505	379752	378023	284675	227178	207478	176132
特殊教育学校	Special Education School	1655	1038	2167	2047	1622	1483	1788	2113
幼儿园	Kindergarten	523542	396082	537579	761044	807017	785848	825253	656652
技工学校	School of Technology	23052	73000		57000				

17-24 各级各类学校毕业生数
NUMBER OF GRADUATES FROM SCHOOLS OF VARIOUS LEVELS

单位：人 (person)

学校分类	Type of Shool	2000	2005	2009	2010	2011	2012	2013	2014
普通高等学校	Regular Institutions of Higher Education	51932	187920	328202	331303	362991	353014	361572	390921
#地方院校	#Local Schools	26461	144529	282718	285599	312189	305545	313748	342171
中等职业学校	Secondary Vocation Schools	125593	129436	307813	335776	307701	272883	200196	147158
普通中学	Regular Middle School	883828	1438503	1373676	1288944	1200425	988034	924920	826599
#初中	#Junior High Schools	718015	1055083	923759	854395	771362	575799	533709	477114
城市	Urban	198402	169257	161959	149922	203090	183511	176905	175225
县镇	Township	61909	239870	319137	326945	381043	277376	257033	224495
农村	Rural	457704	645956	442663	377528	187229	114912	99771	77394
高中	Senior High School	165813	383420	449917	434549	429063	412235	391211	349485
城市	Urban	98353	161281	181546	147307	219472	216107	216067	197220
县镇	Township	41382	164517	208682	228146	169153	173191	157143	138866
农村	Rural	26078	57622	59689	59096	40438	22937	18001	13399
小学	Primary School	1160203	1020710	646753	611620	583417	513818	489395	451925
城市	Urban	281706	149766	126806	120208	162925	162653	162408	162339
县镇	Township	84207	134340	143354	160359	201483	177913	180709	167271
农村	Rural	794290	736604	376593	331053	219009	173252	146278	122315
特殊教育学校	Special Education School	1310	1498	1675	2261	1535	1292	1227	1218
幼儿园	Kindergarten							572085	585677

17-25 各级各类学校教职工数

NUMBER OF FACULTIES AT SCHOOLS OF VARIOUS LEVELS

单位：人 (person)

学校分类	Type of Shool	2000	2005	2009	2010	2011	2012	2013	2014
普通高等学校	Regular Institutions of Higher Education	72265	107459	123693	123491	127363	127921	128185	128878
#地方院校	#Local Schools	35120	73079	89339	89205	92721	94170	94777	95718
中等职业学校	Secondary Vocation Schools	28816	36658	42244	40985	36980	33442	30845	29809
普通中学	Regular Middle School	237500	273146	267265	263055	270838	259884	254716	250873
教育部门和集体办	Run by Ministry of Education and the Collective	216338	253955	247068	243222	249476	238671	232762	227452
其他部门办	Run by Other Departments	15483	6585	1488	646	1024	971	734	442
社会力量办	Run by Non-Governmental Sectors	2316	12606	18709	19187				
私立	Private Owned	3363					20242	21189	22967
城市	Urban	97054	75581	74103	68468	101691	104952	105801	108068
县镇	Township	28889	78027	99653	107371	119012	115008	110983	109553
农村	Rural	111557	119538	93509	87216	50135	39924	37932	33252
小学	Primary Schools	299994	232888	213347	211247	197395	193609	198262	199033
城市	Urban	84877	47727	43738	42100	51939	54139	55015	58137
县镇	Township	23515	33532	44738	51059	64920	67003	69933	71558
农村	Rural	191602	151629	124871	118088	80536	72467	73314	69338
特殊教育学校	Special Education School	1676	1679	1708	1744	1811	1826	1921	1997
幼儿园	Kindergarten	40484	33094	46867	66202	79659	92024	110376	122017
技工学校	School of Technology	13070	9934						

17–26 各级各类学校专任教师数
NUMBER OF FULL-TIME TEACHERS AT SCHOOLS OF VARIOUS LEVELS

单位：人 (person)

学校分类	Type of Shool	2000	2005	2009	2010	2011	2012	2013	2014
普通高等学校	Regular Institutions of Higher Education	30363	59009	73159	74685	78952	80665	81784	82821
#地方院校	#Local Schools	15995	43240	56013	57264	60910	62913	64032	64908
中等职业学校	Secondary Vocation Schools	15549	24036	29148	28476	26208	23796	22555	21905
普通中学	Regular Middle School	198486	233517	231452	227962	225628	212305	205306	201758
#初中	#Junior High Schools	154543	169084	160662	156836	154295	141409	135580	133632
城市	Urban	49752	31803	31574	30409	43589	44766	44122	45998
县镇	Township	13138	39851	54203	59014	75088	69143	65457	64544
农村	Rural	91653	97430	74885	67413	35618	27500	26001	23090
高中	Senior High School	43943	64433	70790	71126	71333	70896	69726	68126
城市	Urban	27663	28330	29754	26883	38552	39579	40383	39873
县镇	Township	10336	27235	32913	35091	26573	27221	26097	25762
农村	Rural	5944	8868	8123	9152	6208	4096	3246	2491
小学	Primary School	274979	215693	198188	196078	194851	191699	196556	199172
城市	Urban	75377	42127	39274	37873	52716	55297	56547	60085
县镇	Township	21459	30351	41273	47480	63542	65828	68204	71378
农村	Rural	178143	143215	117641	110725	78593	70574	71805	67709
特殊教育学校	Special Education School	1231	1317	1444	1477	1527	1560	1647	1712
幼儿园	Kindergarten	29889	20018	27440	38494	43141	49153	57736	63006
技工学校	School of Technology	6182	7064						

17-27 各级各类学校专任教师学历分类
STATISTICS ON ACADEMIC DEGREE OF FULL-TIME TEACHERS AT SCHOOLS OF VARIOUS LEVELS

单位：人 (person)

学历分类	Type of School	2010	2011	2012	2013	2014
一、中等职业学校	Secondary Vocational School	28476	26208	23796	22555	21905
高等学校本科毕业及以上	Graduated from Universities and Above	22972	21322	19604	19172	19026
高等学校专科毕业	Graduated from Colleges	5170	4550	3861	3148	2696
高中阶段及以下	Degree Below Senior High School	334	336	331	235	183
二、普通中学	Regular Secondary Schools	227962	225628	212305	205306	201758
高等学校本科毕业及以上	Graduated from Universities and Above	150502	154668	156745	156715	158575
高等学校专科毕业	Graduated from Colleges	72490	66739	52938	47284	41857
中专、高中毕业的	Graduated from Secondary and High Schools	4877	4132	2521	1257	1266
三、小学	Primary School	196078	194851	191699	196556	199172
中师、高中毕业及以上的	Graduated from Teacher Schools and Degrees Above	194809	194079	191282	196300	199012
四、幼儿园(不包括园长)	Kindergarten (President is Excluded)	38494	43141	49153	57736	63006
中师、高中毕业及以上的	Graduate from Teacher Schools and Degrees Above	36869	41455	47040	55669	61096

17-28 高等学校分类别情况

单位：所、人

学校分类	Type of School	2000 学校数 Number of Colleges and Universities	2000 在校生数 Students Enrollment in Schools	2000 招生数 New Enroll-ment	2000 毕业生数 Graduates	2005 学校数 Number of Colleges and Universities	2005 在校生数 Students Enrollment in Schools	2005 招生数 New Enroll-ment	2005 毕业生数 Graduates
总　计	**Total**	**54**	**346568**	**139666**	**51932**	**85**	**989754**	**306775**	**184706**
综合大学	Comprehensive Universities	6	79303	28489	13871	10	196454	48591	48617
理工院校	Colleges and Universities of Science	11	124501	47724	18603	49	545277	181363	92857
农业院校	Colleges and Universities of Agriculture	2	13111	4311	1775	1	15715	3999	2763
林业院校	Colleges and Universities of Forestry	4	10770	4095	1068	1	1678	1062	121
医药院校	Colleges and Universities of Medicine	7	39694	17186	5950	3	26534	7686	5238
师范院校	Colleges and Universities of Teacher-Training	4	26218	9923	4466	5	52581	15687	12960
语文院校									
财经院校	Colleges and Universities of Finance	1	2482	974	448	6	93524	30319	12771
政法院校	Colleges and Universities of Politics and Law	1	2787	915	515	3	12389	3416	2369
体育院校	Colleges and Universities of Physical Education	2	2255	749	318	1	8837	2735	1154
艺术院校	Colleges and Universities of Art	2	12719	4298	2584	4	8834	4378	814
民族院校	Colleges and Universities of Minority Groups	14	32728	21002	2334	2	27931	7539	5042

CLASSIFICATION OF HIGHER EDUCATION INSTITUTIONS

(unit, person)

2010				2013				2014			
学校数 Number of Colleges and Universities	在校生数 Students Enrollment in Schools	招生数 New Enroll-ment	毕业生数 Graduates	学校数 Number of Colleges and Universities	在校生数 Students Enrollment in Schools	招生数 New Enroll-ment	毕业生数 Graduates	学校数 Number of Colleges and Universities	在校生数 Students Enrollment in Schools	招生数 New Enroll-ment	毕业生数 Graduates
120	**1290243**	**386984**	**327208**	**123**	**1419094**	**403226**	**361004**	**123**	**1417860**	**399771**	**389985**
8	166008	44736	39434	8	181239	45191	41403	8	180625	43613	43250
74	773095	238873	202148	76	851991	252535	224369	76	853331	252772	243807
1	18239	4600	3892	1	18625	4774	4335	1	18670	4613	4333
1	5721	2051	1461	1	8740	3629	2045	1	9752	3505	2378
4	38173	10979	10031	4	41375	11161	9682	4	41237	10231	10259
7	78905	24018	18007	8	89303	25122	22605	8	89299	24982	24325
								1	8973	1905	3089
12	123204	37315	30366	11	130324	35572	33885	11	127495	33988	35882
4	11698	2877	4157	4	12284	4105	2995	4	12788	4501	3991
2	14826	4298	2855	3	16692	4180	3787	3	16437	4101	4115
5	26179	8000	6898	5	27532	6522	7208	4	17667	5231	4736
2	34195	9237	7959	2	40989	10435	8690	2	41586	10329	9820

17-29 大学、中专专任教师职称情况

STATISTICS ON RANKS AND TITLES OF FULL-TIME TEACHERS AT SCHOOLS OF VARIOUS LEVELS

单位：人 (person)

职称	Ranks and Titles	2000	2005	2009	2010	2011	2012	2013	2014
普通高等学校专任教师数	**Number of Full-Time Teachers of Regular Higher Education Institutions**	**30363**	**59009**	**73159**	**74685**	**78952**	**80665**	**81784**	**82821**
正高级	Senoir	3253	6434	8297	8674	9378	9998	10217	10622
副高级	Associate Senoir	9448	17843	21608	22047	23013	24373	24959	25927
中　级	Junior	9847	19169	24978	26077	29013	30244	31147	31273
初　级	Primary	5741	10311	13817	13656	13475	11883	11242	10544
无职称	No Title	2074	5252	4459	4231	4073	4167	4219	4455
中等职业学校专任教师数	**Number of Full-Time Teachers of Specialized Schools**	**15549**	**24036**	**29148**	**28476**	**26208**	**23796**	**22555**	**21905**
副高级	Associate Senoir	3523	5152	6541	6441	5958	5644	5495	5507
中　级	Junior	7229	11467	13366	12935	11960	10760	10187	10040
初　级	Primary	4399	5889	7403	7229	6856	6082	5762	5289
无职称	No Title	398	1528	1838	1871	1434	1310	1111	1069

17-30 各级各类学校校舍建筑面积情况

STATISTICS ON FLOOR SPACE OF SCHOOL HOUSES UNDER CONSTRUCTION IN SCHOOLS OF VARIOUS LEVELS

单位：万平方米 (10 000 sq.m)

项　目	Item	2000	2005	2009	2010	2011	2012	2013	2014
中等职业学校	**Secondary Vocational School**	**736.78**	**833.01**	**899.28**	**952.02**	**852.4**	**862.85**	**857.84**	**874.37**
中等技术学校	Secondary School of Technology	647.55							
中等师范学校	Secondary Normal School	89.23							
普通中学	**Regular Middle School**	**3140.54**	**3745.41**	**3991.6**	**4000.87**	**4012.05**	**4102.65**	**4183.53**	**4119.37**
城市	Urban	1251.43	1121.26	1175.05	1070.06	1484.08	1569.82	1642.53	1692.87
县镇	Township	381.35	1083.29	1484.82	1633.3	1781.12	1863.59	1902.28	1874.56
农村	Rural	1507.76	1540.86	1331.73	1297.51	746.85	669.24	638.72	551.94
职业中学	**Vocational Middle School**	**235.91**	**20.51**	**6.71**					
城市	Urban	149.14	3.34	0.1					
县镇	Township	44.53	3.21	0.08					
农村	Rural	42.24	13.96	6.52					
小学	**Primary School**	**3603.03**	**2926.92**	**2648.74**	**2641.13**	**2496.01**	**2611.49**	**2749.99**	**2752.39**
城市	Urban	781.80	414.55	400.48	390.94	505.47	575.87	620.2	668.42
县镇	Township	251.07	319.56	469.32	521.74	727.75	846.45	933.77	958.58
农村	Rural	2570.17	2192.81	1778.94	1728.45	1262.79	1189.17	1196.02	1125.39

17-31 初中毕业生升入高中和小学毕业生升入初中的升学率

STATISTICS ON PROPORTION OF MIDDLE-SCHOOL STUDENTS ENTERING HIGH SCHOOL AND PROPORTION OF PRIMARY-SCHOOL STUDENTS ENTERING MIDDLE SCHOOL

年份 Year	初中毕业生升入高中升学率 Proportion of Middle-School Students Entering High-School			小学毕业生升学率 Proportion of Primary-School Students Entering Middle-School		
	初中毕业生数(万人) Number of Middle-School Graduates (10 000 persons)	高中招生数(万人) Number of High-School Graduates (10 000 persons)	升学率(%) Proportion of Students Entering Schools of Higher Level(%)	小学毕业生数(万人) Number of Primary School Graduates (10 000 persons)	初中招生数(万人) Number of Middle-School Graduates (10 000 persons)	升学率(%) Proportion of Students Entering Schools of Higher Level(%)
1965	7.60	3.75	49.4	29.60	24.95	84.3
1975	49.25	31.26	63.5	116.05	110.11	94.9
1978	98.80	43.33	43.9	132.37	119.46	90.3
1980	52.23	25.04	47.7	107.64	88.93	82.6
1985	49.92	19.13	38.3	104.89	69.21	66.0
1990	51.71	16.78	32.5	89.96	66.63	74.1
1995	57.85	19.88	34.4	90.76	80.53	88.7
1996	59.33	19.86	33.5	90.19	83.59	92.7
1997	64.70	21.29	32.9	95.35	89.30	93.7
1998	69.23	24.53	35.4	103.75	96.10	92.6
1999	69.60	27.20	39.1	111.24	101.40	91.2
2000	71.80	31.43	43.8	116.02	109.06	94.0
2001	76.34	35.31	46.3	121.00	113.49	93.8
2002	82.93	42.45	51.2	122.17	120.07	98.3
2003	91.61	39.61	43.2	118.70	117.83	99.3
2004	99.32	42.97	43.3	109.93	109.69	99.8
2005	105.51	45.86	43.5	102.07	101.85	99.8
2006	106.18	45.55	42.9	94.66	97.07	102.6
2007	99.77	43.98	44.1	83.29	87.27	104.8
2008	96.10	43.91	45.7	71.51	77.75	108.7
2009	92.38	42.38	45.9	64.68	69.63	107.7
2010	85.44	39.55	46.3	61.16	65.79	107.6
2011	77.14	36.20	46.9	58.34	61.92	106.1
2012	57.58	32.75	56.9	51.38	51.09	99.4
2013	53.37	31.65	59.3	48.94	48.78	99.7
2014	47.71	29.53	61.9	45.19	45.43	100.5

17-32 小学学龄儿童入学率

STATISTICS ON PROPORTION OF CHILDREN AT SCHOOLING AGE ENTERING PRIMARY SCHOOLS

年份 Year	学龄儿童数(万人) Number of Children at Schooling Age (10 000 person)	已入学学龄儿童数(万人) Number of Children Entering School (10 000 persons)	入学率(%) Proportion of Students Entering Schools of Higher Level (%)
1975	629.50	611.00	97.1
1978	616.86	597.73	96.9
1980	594.80	576.86	97.0
1985	496.69	489.38	98.5
1990	485.00	480.32	99.0
1991	556.39	549.35	98.7
1992	571.44	563.44	98.6
1993	574.54	566.84	98.7
1994	599.47	593.88	99.1
1995	637.12	632.34	99.2
1996	661.72	658.38	99.5
1997	681.52	678.95	99.6
1998	685.87	682.53	99.5
1999	669.16	665.88	99.5
2000	641.60	638.57	99.5
2001	585.99	583.29	99.5
2002	538.02	535.98	99.6
2003	490.29	488.68	99.7
2004	440.03	438.66	99.7
2005	397.52	396.11	99.7
2006	363.99	362.14	99.5
2007	345.49	344.77	99.8
2008	340.59	340.08	99.9
2009	343.63	342.74	99.7
2010	350.95	350.82	99.96
2011	362.77	362.74	99.96
2012	317.15	317.06	99.97
2013	320.48	320.41	99.98
2014	315.77	315.72	99.99

17-33 各级各类学校服务的人口及每万人口中在校学生数
STATISTICS ON THE NUMBER OF POPULATION SERVED BY SCHOOLS OF VARIOUS LEVELS AND THE NUMBER OF STUDENTS AT SCHOOL PER 10000 PERSONS

项 目	Item	2000	2005	2009	2010	2011	2012	2013	2014
每一学校服务的人口数（万人）	**Number of Population Served by Each School (10 000 persons)**								
普通高等学校	Regular Institutions of Higher Education	111.63	70.95	47.67	47.70	47.20	47.37	47.15	47.28
成人高等学校	Adults Higher Education	188.37	354.76	408.57	408.86	411.29	412.79	414.21	415.43
普通中等专业学校	Specialized Secondary School	29.69	13.80	14.23	13.86	16.89	17.41	18.71	19.32
普通中学	Regualr Middle School	1.85	1.87	1.97	2.05	2.13	2.20	2.25	2.28
小学	Primary School	0.26	0.48	0.67	0.74	0.78	0.87	1.01	1.05
幼儿园	Kindergarten	1.61	2.58	1.91	1.30	1.23	1.09	0.96	0.90
每万人口中的学生数（人）	**Number of Students at School per 10 000 Persons (person)**								
普通高等学校	Regular Institutions of Higher Education	57.49	167.91	218.37	226.58	232.77	239.85	245.12	244.10
成人高等学校	Adults Higher Education	35.94	37.05	48.27	45.79	46.19	47.59	48.77	47.31
普通中等专业学校	Specialized Secondary School	46.22	100.48	182.13	157.90	125.20	86.61	70.91	64.06
普通中学	Regualr Middle School	582.19	740.65	638.13	597.19	557.21	458.94	426.26	394.58
小学	Primary School	1107.77	711.64	628.08	638.63	655.34	565.41	566.06	552.20
幼儿园	Kindergarten	120.56	98.57	145.35	195.38	230.06	234.54	254.07	264.48

17–34 各级各类学校每个专任教师负担的学生数
STATISTICS ON STUDENT-TEACHER RATIO BY LEVELS OF SCHOOL

单位：人 (person)

项 目	Item	2000	2005	2007	2008	2009	2010	2011	2012	2013	2014
普通高等学校	Regular Institutions of Higher Education	11.41	15.86	15.35	15.29	15.7	17.37	16.98	17.18	17.35	17.14
中等职业学校	Secondary Vocation School	17.92	25.21	31.89	33.8	35.74	31.74	27.51	21.03	18.23	17.01
普通中学	Regular High School	17.68	19.13	17.66	16.823	15.77	15.00	14.22	12.49	12.04	11.37
#初中	#Junior Middle Schools	18.19	18.76	17.06	15.962	14.71	13.91	13.23	11.16	10.94	10.30
高中	Senior High School	15.89	20.09	19.11	18.829	18.18	17.40	16.37	15.16	14.17	13.49
职业中学	Vocational Secondary School	13.47	20.28	15.52	13.809						
#高中	#Senior School	12.41									
小学	Primary School	24.28	19.90	18.07	17.917	12.09	18.64	20.46	17.04	16.7	16.12
幼儿园	Kindergarten	24.31	29.70	29.45	29.947	18.13	29.05	30.71	27.58	25.52	24.41

17-35 各级学校女学生和女教师数

NUMBER OF FEMALE STUDENTS AND FEMALE TEACHERS AT SCHOOL OF VARIOUS LEVELS

单位：万人 (10 000 persons)

项　　目	Item	2000	2005	2009	2010	2011	2012	2013	2014
一、女学生数	Number of Female Students	506.17	473.27	436.92	426.07	416.40	360.95	350.98	337.8
普通高等学校	Regular Institutions of Higher Education	11.93	44.11	58.90	62.25	65.13	67.70	69.12	69.04
中等专业学校	Specialized Secondary School	14.33	29.14	49.73	44.22	34.96	24.58	19.84	17.90
普通中学	Regualr High School	155.66	203.98	166.26	154.98	145.44	119.94	112.14	104.22
小学	Primary School	317.45	194.85	161.82	164.62	170.87	148.73	149.88	146.64
二、女学生占学生总数 %	Percentage of Female Students in School	46.2	45.5	45.8	46.2	46.1	46.2	46.3	46.3
普通高等学校	Regular Institutions of Higher Education	34.4	43.6	47.2	48.0	48.6	48.8	48.6	48.6
中等专业学校	Specialized Secondary School	51.4	48.1	47.7	48.9	48.5	49.1	48.3	48.0
普通中学	Regualr High School	44.4	45.7	45.6	45.3	45.3	45.2	45.4	45.4
小学	Primary School	47.5	45.4	45.0	45.0	45.3	45.5	45.7	45.7
三、女教师数	Number of Female Teachers	20.33	21.58	22.35	22.43	22.61	22.4	22.81	23.43
普通高等学校	Regular Institutions of Higher Education	1.02	2.34	3.07	3.16	3.42	3.51	3.59	3.65
中等专业学校	Specialized Secondary School	0.60	0.94	1.19	1.17	1.07	0.99	0.94	0.92
普通中学	Regualr High School	6.26	7.94	8.37	8.4	8.43	8.22	8.15	8.21
小学	Primary School	12.07	10.32	9.71	9.7	9.69	9.68	10.13	10.65
四、女教师占教师总数 %	Percentage of Female Teachers in School	38.3	40.4	41.9	42.5	43.0	44.0	45.1	46.3
普通高等学校	Regular Institutions of Higher Education	33.6	39.7	42.0	42.3	43.3	43.5	43.9	44.1
中等专业学校	Specialized Secondary School	38.5	39.1	40.7	41.0	40.8	41.5	41.5	41.8
普通中学	Regualr High School	31.5	34.0	36.1	36.9	37.4	38.7	39.7	40.7
小学	Primary School	43.9	47.9	49.0	49.5	49.7	50.5	51.5	53.5

17-36 各级各类成人学校在校学生数
NUMBER OF ADULT STUDENTS ENROLLED AT SCHOOLS OF VARIOUS LEVELS

单位：万人 (10 000 persons)

各类学校	Items	2000	2005	2009	2010	2011	2012	2013	2014
成人高等学校	Adult Higher Education	21.66	22.34	27.61	26.21	26.60	27.5	28.28	27.51
广播电视大学	Radio and TV Universities	2.78	2.52	0.76	0.54	0.61	0.45	0.43	0.33
职工大学	Schools of Higher Education for Staff	1.36	0.22	0.30	0.04	0.01	0.01	0.004	
管理干部学院	Colleges for Management and Caders	0.90	0.60	0.48	0.35	0.20	0.06	0.04	0.02
教育学院	Pedagogical College	0.94	0.89	0.42	0.37	0.26	0.24	0.24	0.23
普通高等学校办函授部、夜大学	Correspondence and Evening College Run by Regualr High Education	15.16	18.11	25.64	24.91	25.52	26.74	27.57	26.93
成人中等学校	Secondary Schools for Adults	139.75	35.90	64.40	81.77	49.27	43.85	45.06	39.46
中学	Middle School	0.61	2.42	3.00	3.69	2.64	4.57	4.24	3.67
技术培训学校	Technical Training Schools	131.86	33.48	55.28	78.08	46.63	39.28	40.82	35.79
成人初等学校	Primary Schools for Adults	12.50	2.20	0.81	0.73	0.86	0.15	0.05	0.17
#扫盲班	#Class for Illiteracy	6.43	0.82	0.34	0.39	0.03	0.01	0.03	0.02

注：成人高等学校学生数是本、专科学生数。

Note:The number of students in Adults Higher Education refers to the number of students in vocational schools.

17-37 研究生基本情况
BASIC CONDTIONS ABOUT POST-GRADUATES

单位：人 (person)

项 目	Item	2011	2012	2013	2014
高等学校在校研究生数	Number of Post-graduates at School in Institutions of Higher Education	104879	108528	112707	114260
攻读博士学位研究生	Post-graduate Studying for Doctor's Degree	19905	20927	22367	21509
攻读硕士学位研究生	Post-graduate Studying for Master's Degree	84974	87601	90340	92751
招收研究生数	New Students Enrollment	36358	37371	39027	38867
攻读博士学位研究生	Post-graduate Studying for Doctor's Degree	4706	4766	5070	4891
攻读硕士学位研究生	Post-graduate Studying for Master's Degree	31652	32605	33957	33976
毕业研究生数	Number of Graduates	30510	32201	34585	31992
攻读博士学位研究生	Post-graduate Studying for Doctor's Degree	3763	3692	3948	4038
攻读硕士学位研究生	Post-graduate Studying for Master's Degree	26747	28509	30637	27954
科研单位在学研究生数	Number of Post-graduates Studying in Research Institutions	2288	2328	2362	2399
攻读博士学位研究生	Post-graduate Studying for Doctor's Degree	721	760	819	845
攻读硕士学位研究生	Post-graduate Studying for Master's Degree	1567	1568	1543	1554
招收研究生数	New Students Enrollment	760	777	779	790
攻读博士学位研究生	Post-graduate Studying for Doctor's Degree	212	220	229	246
攻读硕士学位研究生	Post-graduate Studying for Master's Degree	548	557	550	544
毕业研究生数	Number of Graduates	652	646	650	624
攻读博士学位研究生	Post-graduate Studying for Doctor's Degree	196	174	160	208
攻读硕士学位研究生	Post-graduate Studying for Master's Degree	456	472	490	416

主要统计指标解释

科技活动 指在自然科学、农业科学、医药科学、工程与技术科学、人文与社会科学领域(简称科学技术领域)中，与科技知识的产生、发展、传播和应用密切相关的有组织的活动。可分为研究与试验发展(R&D)、研究与试验发展成果应用及相关的科技服务三类活动。该定义是联合国教科文组织考虑成员国特别是发展中国家开展科技统计工作的需要，而对科技活动所作的统计界定。

科技活动人员 指直接从事科技活动、以及专门从事科技活动管理和为科技活动提供直接服务，累计的实际工作时间占全年制度工作时间 10%及以上的人员。(1)直接从事科技活动的人员包括：在独立核算的科学研究与技术开发机构、高等学校、各类企业及其他事业单位内设的研究室、实验室、技术开发中心及中试车间(基地)等机构中从事科技活动的研究人员、工程技术人员、技术工人及其它人员；虽不在上述机构工作，但编入科技活动项目(课题)组的人员；科技信息与文献机构中的专业技术人员；从事论文设计的研究生等。(2)专门从事科技活动管理和为科技活动提供直接服务的人员，包括：独立核算的科学研究与技术开发机构、科技信息与文献机构、高等学校、各类企业及其他事业单位主管科技工作的负责人，专门从事科技活动的计划、行政、人事、财务、物资供应、设备维护、图书资料管理等工作的各类人员，但不包括保卫、医疗保健人员、司机、食堂人员、茶炉工、水暖工、清洁工等为科技活动提供间接服务的人员。该指标用来反映投入科技活动人力的规模。

科学家与工程师 指科技活动人员中具有高、中级技术职称(职务)的人员和不具有高、中级技术职称(职务)的大学本科及以上学历人员。该指标用来反映投入科技活动人力的素质。

研究与试验发展(R&D) 指在科学技术领域，为增加知识总量，以及运用这些知识去创造新的应用进行的系统的创造性的活动，包括基础研究、应用研究、试验发展三类活动。国际上通常采用 R&D 活动的规模和强度指标反映一国的科技实力和核心竞争力。

专业技术人员 指从事专业技术工作和专业技术管理工作的人员，即企事业单位中已经聘任专业技术职务从事专业技术工作和专业技术管理工作的人员，以及未聘任专业技术职务，现在专业技术岗位上工作的人员。包括工程技术人员，农业技术人员，科学研究人员，卫生技术人员，教学人员，经济人员，会计人员，统计人员，翻译人员，图书资料、档案、文博人员，新闻出版人员，律师、公证人员，广播电视播音人员，工艺美术人员，体育人员，艺术人员及企业政治思想工作人员，共十七个专业技术职务类别。用来反映科技人力资源情况。

科技活动经费筹集 指从各种渠道筹集到的计划用于科技活动的经费，包括政府资金、企业资金、事业单位资金、金融机构贷款、国外资金和其他资金等。反映各社会经济主体对促进科技进步所做的努力。

新产品 指采用新技术原理、新设计构思研制、生产的全新产品，或在结构、材质、工艺等某一方面比原有产品有明显改进，从而显著提高了产品性能或扩大了使用功能的产品。既包括政府有关部门认定并在有效期内的新产品，也包括企业自行研制开发，未经政府有关部门认定，从投产之日起一年之内的新产品。用来反映科技产出及对经济增长的直接贡献。

专利 是专利权的简称，是对发明人的发明创造经审查合格后，由专利局依据专利法授予发明人和设计人对该项发明创造享有的专有权。包括发明、实用新型和外观设计。反映拥有自主知识产权的科技和设计成果情况。

发明 指对产品、方法或者其改进所提出的新的技术方案。是国际通行的反映拥有自主知识产权技术的核心指标。

普通高等学校 指按照国家规定的设置标准和审批程序批准举办的，通过全国普通高等学校统一招生考试，招收高中毕业生为主要培养对象，实施高等教育的全日制大学、独立设置的学院和高等专科学校、高等职业学校和其他机构。

大学、独立设置的学院主要实施本科层次以上教育，高等专科学校、高等职业学校实施专科层次教育，其他机构是承担国家普通招生计划任务不计校数的机构。包括普通高等学校分校和批准筹建的普通高等学校等。

成人高等学校 指按照国家规定的设置标准和审批程序批准举办的，通过全国成人高等学校统一招生考试，招收具有高中毕业或同等学历的在职从业人员为主要培养对象，利用函授、业余、脱产等多种形式对其实施高等学历教育的学校。包括职工高等学校、农民高等学校、管理干部学院、教育学院、独立函授学院、广播电视大学、其他机构等。其他机构是承担国家成人招生计划任务不计校数的机构。

小学学龄儿童净入学率 指调查范围内已入小学学习的学龄儿童占校内外学龄儿童总数(包括弱智儿童，不包括盲聋哑儿童)的比重。计算公式为:

$$小学学龄儿童净入学率=\frac{已入学的小学学龄儿童数}{校内外小学学龄儿童总数}\times 100\%$$

Explanatory Notes on Main Statistical Indicators

Scientific and Technological Activities (S&T Activities) refer to organized activities which are closely related with the creation, development, dissemination and application of the scientific and technical knowledge in the fields of natural sciences, agricultural science, medical science, engineering and technological science, humanities and social sciences (referred to as scientific and technological fields). S&T activities can be classified in to 3 categories: research and development (R&D) activities, application of R&D results, and related S&T services. This statistical definition is made by UNICHIEF for scientific and technological activities to meet the need of carrying out statistical work in this field for its member countries in particular those developing countries.

Personnel Engaged in S&T Activities refer to personnel directly engaged in S&T activities, in the management of S&T activities, and in providing direct service to S&T activities, who spend over 10% of the total working hours in a year in S&T activities. (1) Personnel directly engaged in S&T activities include researchers, engineers, technicians and other related personnel engaged in S&T activities in independent-accounting R&D institutions, institutions of higher learning, and in research institutes, laboratories, technology development centers and central experiment workshops under enterprises and institutions. Also included are people working in S&T research project teams, professional and technical personnel working in S&T information archiving institutes, and graduate students working on the design of their thesis. (2) Personnel engaged in the management of S&T activities and in providing direct service to S&T activities include senior management people responsible for S&T activities in independent-accounting R&D institutions, S&T information archiving institutes, institutions of higher learning, and in enterprises and institutions where S&T activities are undertaken. Also included are people responsible for the planning, administration, personnel management, financial management, logistics supply, equipment maintenance, information and library management that are related with S&T activities. People providing indirect services are excluded, such as security, medical service, drivers, plumbers, cleaners and those providing catering and related service. This indicator reflects the size of personnel engaged in S&T activities.

Scientists and Engineers refer to persons engaged in S&T activities who have obtained titles of senior and middle level professional positions, and those without such position but have completed university or higher education. This indicator reflects the quality of personnel engaged in S&T activities.

Research and Development (R&D) refers to systematic and creative activities in the field of science and technology aiming at increasing the knowledge and using the knowledge for new application. R&D includes 3 categories of activities: basic research, applied research and experiments and development. The scale and intensity of R&D are widely used internationally to reflect the strength of S&T and the core competitiveness of a country in the world.

Professional and Technical Personnel refer to persons engaged in professional and technical work or in the management of professional and technical activities, i.e., people with professional or technical positions who are engaged in professional and technical work or in the management of professional and technical activities, and people without professional or technical positions but are working on professional or technical posts. They include professionals and technicians working in 17 categories of technical occupations including engineering, agriculture, scientific researches, medical service, teaching, economic research and application, accounting, statistics, translation, libraries, archives, cultural and museum service, journalism and publication, lawyers, notarization service, radio and television broadcasting, handicraft and fine arts, sports, performing art, and political workers in enterprises. This indicator reflects the condition of human resources in S&T.

Funding for S&T Activities refers to funds obtained from various sources for S&T activities, including government funds, self-raised funds by enterprises, self-raised funds by institutions, loans from financial institutions, foreign funds and other funds. This indicator reflects the efforts made by various social economic entities in promoting the development of S&T.

New Products refer to new products produced with new technology and new design, or products that represent noticeable improvement in terms of structure, material, or production process so as to improve significantly the character or function of the older versions. They include new products certified by relevant government agencies within the period of certification, as well as new products designed and produced by enterprises within a year without certification by government agencies. This indictor reflects the direct contribution of S&T output to economic growth.

Patent is an abbreviation for the patent right and refers to the exclusive right of ownership by the inventors or designers for the creation or inventions, given from the patent offices after due process of assessment and approval in accordance with the Patent Law. Patents are granted for inventions, utility models and designs. This indicator reflects the achievements of S&T and design with independent intellectual property.

Inventions refer to the new technical proposals to the products or methods or their modifications. This is universal core indicator reflecting the technologies with independent intellectual property.

Regular Institutions of Higher Learning refer to educational establishments set up according to the government evaluation and approval procedures, enrolling graduates from senior secondary schools and providing higher education courses and training for senior professionals. They include full-time universities, colleges, high professional schools, high professional vocational schools and others.

Universities and colleges are mainly providing undergraduate courses; those high professional schools and high professional vocational schools are mainly providing professional trainings; and others refer to educational establishments, which are responsible for enrolling students but not covered in the total number of schools, including: branch schools of universities and colleges, and universities and colleges that have been proved and prepared to construct.

Institutions of Higher Learning for Adults refer to educational establishments, set up in line with relevant rules approved by the government, enrolling staff and workers with senior secondary school or equivalent education, and providing higher education courses in many forms of correspondence, spare time, or full time for adults. Professionals thus trained receive a qualification equivalent to graduates studying regular courses at regular universities, colleges and professional colleges. Institutions of higher learning for adults include schools of high education for staff and workers, schools of high education for peasants, colleges for management cadres, pedagogical colleges, independent correspondence colleges, Radio and TV universities and other educational establishments. Other educational establishments are responsible for enrolling adult students but not covered in the number of schools.

Enrollment Rate of Primary School Age Children refers to the proportion of school age children enrolled at schools to the total number of school age children both in and outside schools (including retarded children, but excluding blind, deaf and mute children). The formula is:

Enrollment Rate of Primary School-age Children = (Total Primary School-age Children at Schools)/(Total Primary School age Children Both at and Outside Schools) x 100%

18 卫生和社会服务

Public Health and Social Services

资料整理：谢　涛

18-1 卫生机构数
NUMBER OF HEALTH CARE INSTITUTIONS

单位：个 (unit)

年 份 Year	总 计 Total	医 院 Hospitals	村卫生室 Village Clinics	疗养院、所 Sanatoriums	门诊部、所 Clinics	专科防治所、站 Specialized Prevention and Treatment Stations or Centers
1970	7847	16003		10	1500	104
1975	5381	1834		2	3079	39
1980	6146	1827		12	3785	52
1985	9885	1853		12	7486	67
1990	10472	2024		11	7878	70
1991	10509	2111		11	7824	74
1992	10590	2115		11	7903	73
1993	10268	2139		12	7526	73
1994	9762	2147		12	7002	84
1995	9744	2119		11	7020	84
1996	9167	2105		10	6453	82
1997	11562	2078		10	8867	86
1998	11584	2082		10	8885	88
1999	11311	2077		11	8631	85
2000	11065	2041		11	8430	83
2001	10941	1924		10	8500	73
2002	9946	555		2	7687	168
2003	9983	552		3	7690	177
2004	9285	566		2	6949	166
2005	9459	574		1	7215	120
2006	10052	575			7687	116
2007	11089	580			7585	118
2008	10832	592			7397	107
2009	10362	614			6770	88
2010	10152	603			6499	85
2011	10455	608			6838	83
2012	35423	650	24976		6668	83
2013	35633	713	24953		6679	75
2014	36084	771	24918		7222	76

注：卫生事业机构数、床位数、卫生人员数从2012年起包含村卫生室数量。
Note:The statistics of health care units, hospital beds and health care professionals started to include the village clinics since 2012.

18-1 续表 continued

单位：个 (unit)

年 份 Year	卫生防疫站 Sanitation and Antiepidemic Station	妇幼保健所、站 Maternity and Child Care Centers	药品检验所、室 Institutions of Drug Control	医学科学研究机构 Institutions of Medical Science Research	其他卫生机构 Others
1970	106	54	5	2	63
1975	99	85	83	6	154
1980	110	97	88	7	168
1985	111	96	87	7	166
1990	120	96	87	9	177
1991	122	98	87	7	175
1992	119	96	86	8	179
1993	149	96	87	8	178
1994	149	97	87	8	176
1995	151	95	85	8	171
1996	156	95	84	8	174
1997	158	96	84	8	175
1998	158	96	85	8	172
1999	156	94	83	7	167
2000	155	94	81	7	163
2001	130	91	53	7	153
2002	107	12	87		1328
2003	110	32	92		1327
2004	110	39	92		1359
2005	113	63	96		1366
2006	114	72	95		1393
2007	113	100	59	1	2533
2008	111	99		1	2525
2009	111	98		1	2680
2010	115	100		1	2952
2011	112	100		1	2713
2012	111	100		1	2834
2013	113	101		1	2998
2014	112	101		1	2883

18-2 卫生机构人员数
NUMBER OF PERSONS ENGAGED IN HEALTH CARE INSTITUTIONS

单位：万人 (10 000 persom)

年 份 Year	总 计 Total	卫生技术人员 Medical Technical Personel	#医生 #Doctors	中 医 Chinese Traditional Medicine Doctors	西医师 Western Medicine Doctors	西医士 Wertern Medical Assistant	#护师、护士 #Nurses	每千人口医生数(人) Number of Doctors per 1000 Population (person)
1970	10.30	8.33	4.15	1.86	1.22	1.07	1.83	1.03
1975	15.05	11.85	4.91	1.74	1.63	1.55	2.05	1.11
1980	19.94	15.59	6.32	1.82	2.59	1.91	3.09	1.35
1985	23.58	18.48	7.27	2.22	3.09	1.95	3.77	1.47
1990	26.75	20.92	8.68	2.19	5.09	1.40	5.66	1.62
1991	27.51	21.55	8.79	2.18	5.11	1.50	5.97	1.62
1992	28.24	22.15	9.02	2.20	5.18	1.65	6.25	1.64
1993	28.91	22.46	9.16	2.12	5.48	1.57	6.49	1.64
1994	29.31	22.84	9.38	2.04	5.64	1.65	6.64	1.66
1995	29.55	23.20	9.58	1.98	5.79	1.76	6.83	1.68
1996	29.65	23.47	9.72	1.93	5.92	1.90	7.00	1.67
1997	30.38	23.90	9.96	1.84	6.09	1.90	7.21	1.70
1998	30.31	23.96	10.11	1.84	6.30	1.90	7.29	1.71
1999	30.40	24.05	10.31	1.81	6.58	1.85	7.41	1.74
2000	30.14	23.88	10.30	1.76	6.76	1.74	7.53	1.74
2001	29.48	23.41	10.21	1.63	6.91	1.63	7.51	1.72
2002	25.30	20.59	8.63	1.14			6.35	1.43
2003	25.62	20.83	8.72	0.94	1.73	0.13	6.38	1.45
2004	26.06	21.38	8.99				6.62	1.49
2005	26.22	21.50	8.98				6.94	1.49
2006	26.53	21.80	9.01				7.06	1.49
2007	27.80	22.70	9.20				7.69	1.52
2008	28.63	23.52	9.27				8.12	1.52
2009	29.45	24.30	9.43				8.69	1.54
2010	30.40	25.16	9.59				9.33	1.62
2011	31.30	26.00	9.60				10.00	1.67
2012	38.71	28.85	10.91				11.57	1.77
2013	41.45	31.16	11.94				12.80	2.06
2014	44.35	33.98	12.74				14.70	2.19

注：卫生事业机构数、床位数、卫生人员数从2012年起包含村卫生室数量。
Note:The statistics of health care units, hospital beds and health care professionals started to include the village clinics since 2012.

18-3 卫生机构床位数

NUMBER OF BEDS IN HEALTH CARE INSTITUTIONS

单位：万张 (10 000 beds)

年 份 Year	总 计 Total	医 院 Hospitals	#县及县以上医院 #Hospitals Above County Level	疗养院、所 Sanatoriums	其他卫生机构 Other Health Care Institutions	每千人口医院床位数(张) Number of Hospital Beds Per 10 000 Population (bed)
1970	6.14	5.56	2.84	0.18		1.38
1975	9.90	9.02	4.33	0.02		2.05
1980	12.59	11.22	5.41	0.20		2.40
1985	14.70	11.52	6.80	0.20	2.98	2.34
1990	16.34	13.16	8.27	0.19	2.99	2.45
1991	16.52	13.43	8.50	0.21	2.88	2.47
1992	16.62	13.46	8.58	0.22	2.84	2.44
1993	16.30	13.48	8.71	0.21	2.61	2.41
1994	16.13	13.40	8.73	0.21	2.52	2.36
1995	15.78	13.08	8.58	0.20	2.50	2.29
1996	14.42	13.08	8.63	0.15	1.19	2.24
1997	15.30	13.08	8.76	0.16	2.05	2.24
1998	15.09	13.03	8.77	0.17	1.89	2.21
1999	14.90	12.91	8.76	0.16	1.83	2.07
2000	14.96	12.99	8.80	0.16	1.81	2.18
2001	14.62	12.91	8.80	0.16	0.60	2.18
2002	12.72	8.53		0.03	4.16	2.12
2003	13.59	9.39		0.04	4.16	2.26
2004	13.78	9.52		0.02	4.24	2.29
2005	13.96	9.67		0.01	4.28	2.31
2006	14.24	9.81			4.43	2.35
2007	15.06	10.36			4.70	2.48
2008	16.73	11.32			5.41	2.75
2009	18.72	12.66			6.06	2.82
2010	20.07	13.51			6.56	3.26
2011	22.40	15.20			7.20	3.89
2012	25.30	17.38			7.92	4.10
2013	28.85	20.05			8.80	4.97
2014	31.83	22.20			9.63	5.47

18-4 各类卫生工作人员数

NUMBER OF SANITARY TECHNICAL PERSONELS OF VARIOUS TYPE

单位：人 (person)

人员分类	Type	1990	2000	2005	2010	2011	2012	2013	2014
合　计	**Total**	**267548**	**301415**	**262263**	**303980**	**365160**	**387086**	**414538**	**443512**
医院	Hospitals	182490	140720	138843	169985	179093	196263	214720	239228
中医院	Hospitals of Chinese Medicines	11386	17442	19274	22352	23773	27349	30304	32281
乡镇卫生院	Town Hospitals	58518	54500	69626	69823	67854	70143	71243	75088
村卫生室	Village Clinics						49202	51860	48494
疗养院、所	Sanatoriums	1271	1387	60					
门诊部、所	Clinics	44450	34020	17940	15479	17500	17299	17414	19504
专科防治所、站	Specialized Prevention & Treatment Stations or Centers	6218	7830	4352	3073	3038	3203	3198	3182
卫生防疫站	Sanitation and Antiepidemic Station	7602	10388	9149	8247	8534	8399	8605	8696
妇幼保健所、站	Maternity and Child Care Centers	4139	6874	8796	11209	12506	14111	15519	17876
药品检验所、室	Institutions of Drug Control	1098	1373						
其他卫生事业机构	Others	6376	4087						
医学科研机构	Medical Science Institutions	810	746						
高等医院院校	Institutions of Higher Education	6489	6154						
中等卫校	Secondary Health School	3762	6043						
个体开业	Run by Individuals	2843	4252						

18-5 医院业务工作开展情况
BASIC STATISTICS ON HOSPITAL BUSINESS

项 目	Item	2000	2005	2010	2011	2012	2013	2014
机构数 (个)	Number of Institutions (unit)	507	574	603	608	650	713	771
诊疗总人次数 (万人次)	Number of Clients (10 000 person-times)	4616.20	5452.11	7710.20	8404.63	9470.38	10056.28	11399.93
#门、急诊人次数 (万人次)	#Number of Outpacients and Emergency (10 000 person-times)	4396.10	5107.19	7533.44	8247.39	9236.70	9859.71	10976.72
出院人数 (万人)	Number of discharged Patients (10 000 persons)	158.93	219.45	423.28	481.61	578.82	647.55	735.70
死亡 (万人)	Dead (10 000 persons)	1.59	2.28	3.13	3.23	2.33	2.93	3.29
病死率 (%)	Rate of Death from Illness (%)	1.08	1.04	0.74	0.67	0.40	0.45	0.45
病床平均周转次数 (次)	Average times of Beds Usage (time)	18.66	23.99	32.50	33.80	35.00	34.90	35.40
病床平均工作日 (日)	Average Day of Beds Usage (day)	218.79	268.24	350.40	360.10	363.40	353.30	350.90
病床使用率 (%)	Utilization Rate of Beds (%)	59.94	73.49	96.01	98.66	99.30	99.52	96.14
出院者平均住院日 (日)	Average Days for Hospitalization Discharged (day)	11.12	10.71	10.50	10.40	10.10	9.90	9.70

18-6 农村村级卫生组织情况
STATISTICS ON HEALTH CARE INSTITUTIONS AT VILLAGE LEVEL

项　　目	Item	2000	2005	2010	2011	2012	2013	2014
行政村数 (个)	Number of Villages (unit)	32400	26678	26018	26025	25575	25452	25448
村设置的医疗点数 (个)	Medical care Station Set by Villages (unit)	26879	21136	24057	25146	24976	24953	24918
#村或集体办	#Set by Villages or Collective Set	14666	11207	15395	15923	15785	15410	15551
联合办	Set with Village Doctors	4640	3777	2815	2596	2576	2449	2445
医院设点	Set by Hospital	2403	2410	3348	3934	3920	4027	4085
私人办	Set by Individual	4344	2907	1833	1919	1941	2164	1998
其他	Others	826	835	666	774	754	903	839
乡村医生和卫生员人数 (人)	Number of Village Doctors and Medical Working Personel (person)	57511	34417	41473	44040	43873	43840	42304
#乡村医生	#Village Doctors	44490	33375	40425	42810	41664	40833	40502
卫生员	Medical Working Personel	13021	1042	1048	1230	2209	3007	1802

主要统计指标解释

卫生机构 包括医疗机构、疾病预防控制中心(防疫站)、采供血机构、卫生监督及监测(检验)机构、医学科研和在职培训机构、健康教育所等。

医疗机构 包括医院、社区卫生服务中心(站)、疗养院、卫生院、门诊部、诊所(卫生所、医务室)、妇幼保健院(所、站)、专科疾病防治院(所、站)、急救中心(站)和临床检验中心。医疗机构分为非赢利性医疗机构和赢利性医疗机构。

医院 包括综合医院、中医医院、中西医结合医院、民族医院、各类专科医院和护理院。

卫生技术人员 指卫生机构中医生、护理人员 、药剂人员、检验人员等卫生技术人员。

医生 指在医疗、预防保健机构工作且取得《执业医师证书》的执业医师和执业助理医师。

Explanatory Notes on Main Statistical Indicators

Health Care Institutions include medical institutions, disease prevention and control centers (epidemic prevention stations), blood gathering and supplying institutions, health supervision and inspection (check up) institutions, medicinal scientific research and on-job training institutions, health education and so on.

Medical Organizations include hospitals, health service centers (stations) of communities, nursing homes, health centers, clinics, clinics (health stations and infirmaries), maternity and child care agencies (centers and stations), special disease prevention and curing agencies (centers and stations), first aid centers (stations) and clinical inspection centers. Medical organizations are grouped by two types: profit-making and non-profit-making medical organizations.

Hospitals include polyclinics, traditional Chinese medical hospitals, hospitals integrated with traditional Chinese therapeutics and western therapeutics, ethical hospitals, various specialties hospitals and nursing hospitals.

Medical Technical Personnel refers to doctors, assistant nurses, pharmacists, and laboratory technicians working in medical institutions.

Doctors refer to certified physicians and certified assistant physicians with certifications working in medical and health care and prevention agencies.

19 文化和体育

Culture and Sports

资料整理：谢　涛

19-1　文化事业机构、人员数
NUMBER OF CULTURAL INSTITUTIONS AND PERSONEL

单位：个、人　　(unit, person)

项　目	Item	2008	2009	2010	2011	2012	2013	2014
艺术业机构	Art Performing Institution				239	295	363	328
#剧团	#Troupes				172	226	307	273
#剧场	#Theater				65	66	53	52
文物事业机构	Historical Relics Institutions	168	171	166	175	214	291	300
#博物馆	#Museums	111	114	121	125	161	170	174
图书馆事业机构	Library Institutions	104	104	107	109	111	112	112
群众文化事业机构	Public Culture Institutions	1356	1367	1378	1378	1379	1382	1390
群众艺术馆	Public Art Center	17	17	13	13	13	13	13
文化馆(站)	Art Center	1339	1350	1365	1365	1366	1369	1377
艺术业人员数	Number of People Engaged in Art Performing				5018	10976	10384	9774
#剧团人员	#Staff in Troupes				4580	9216	9005	8520
#剧场人员	#Staff in Theater				437	1750	1367	1241
文物事业人员数	Number of Historical Relics Staffs	3623	3915	3297	3596	4334	4713	4928
#博物馆人员	#Number of staff in Library	2076	2281	2298	2380	3078	3360	3380
图书馆事业人员数	Number of People Engaged in Library	2233	2178	2151	2149	2219	2226	2231
群众文化事业人员数	Number of People Engaged in Public Art	4786	4951	4943	5022	5044	4912	5045
群众艺术馆人员	Number of People in Public Art Center	594	610	481	489	448	494	479
文化馆(站)人员	Number of People in Cultural Station	4192	4341	4462	4533	4596	4418	4566
#乡镇文化站	#Township Cultural Stations	2013	2181	2175	2221	2256	2046	2234

19-2　公共图书馆发展情况
DEVELOPMENT STATISTICS ON PUBLIC LIBRARIES

项　目		Item		2000	2005	2010	2011	2012	2013	2014
机构数	(个)	Number of Library	(unit)	103	102	107	109	111	112	112
藏书数	(万册)	Total Collections	(10 000 volumes)	1678	1923	2361	2410	2521	2648	2822
书架单层总长度	(万米)	Total Length of Bookshelves	(10 000 m)	109	101	111	108	51	53	53
有效借书证数	(万个)	Valid Library card number	(10 000 units)	41	72	104	95	138	108	128
图书流通情况		Number of Circulation								
公共图书馆流通人次	(万人次)	The public library circulation	(10 000 person-times)	714	1145	1516	1342	1516	1763	1868
册次	(万册数)	Volume-time	(10 000 volume-times)	949	927	1846	1114	1386	1570	1755
为读者服务举办各种活动		Service for Readers								
次数	(次)	Times	(time)	1222	1621	1790	2258	2928	3098	3498
参加人数	(万人次)	Number of Readers Involved	(10 000 person-times)	115	176	105	120	128	178	173
当年新购图书	(万册)	New Books Purchaesd in 2012	(10 000 volume-times)	36	43	60	82	111	138	161
图书费	(万元)	Purchase Expenses	(10 000 yuan)	699	1296	1847	2138	4210	5076	5713

注：2013、2014年数据不含电子图书

Note:Data does not contain electronic books in 2013, 2014.

19-3 公共图书馆藏书及分类情况
STATISTICS ON BOOKS AND TYPE OF BOOKS IN PUBLIC LIBRARIES

单位：万册 (10 000 volumes)

年份 Year	合 计 Total	#外 文 #Foreign	#古 籍 #Ancient	#图书 #New Books	其它藏量 Other Reserves
1996	1472	82	97		
1997	1533	81	97		
1998	1599	81	96		
1999	1643	81	96		
2000	1678	82	97		
2001	1709	83	98		
2002	1759	81	99		
2003	1819	83	98		
2004	1867		94		
2005	1923		97		
2006	1981		100		
2007	2037		96		
2008	2106		97		
2009	2181		96		
2010	2361		95		
2011	2410		98	1860	453
2012	2521		98	2008	415
2013	3050		99	2156	796
2014	3941		101	2295	1546

注：其它藏量包括报刊、视听文献、缩微制品、电子图书和其它,总藏量含电子图书

Note: Other reserves include newspapers, audiovisual documents, microform, electronic books and other materials.Contains a total electronic books

19-4 图书、报纸、期刊出版情况
STATISTICS ON PUBLICATION OF BOOKS, NEWSPAPERS AND PERIODICALS

项　目	Item	1990	2000	2005	2010	2012	2013	2014
一、图书出版种数（种）	**Category of Library Books Published (kind)**	**2546**	**4529**	**6535**	**10464**	**14256**	**13900**	**16043**
新出版（种）	New Publications (kind)	1827	2443	3739	6328	8476	8445	9662
总印数（千册）	Total Prints (1 000 volume)	402517	288416	345510	275330	259720	262740	271933
总印张（千印张）	Total Number of Paper Printed (1 000 pages)	1418989	1552128	2495183	1997639	2045531	2088169	2288053
二、杂志出版种数（种）	**Category of Magazines Published (kind)**	**254**	**391**	**407**	**407**	**408**	**408**	**409**
总印数（千册）	Total Prints (1000 volume)	73456	220280	196800	300770	341410	309375	280895
总印张（千印张）	Total Number of Paper Printed (1 000 pages)	119523	746145	745526	1482345	1865793	1781708	1662398
三、报刊出版种数（种）	**Category of Newspapers and Periodicals Published (kind)**	**84**	**164**	**193**	**130**	**130**	**130**	**130**
总印数（千份）	Total Prints (1 000 copies)	623820	1342282	1956980	1816720	2060760	1982020	1910667
总印张（万印张）	Total Number of Paper Printed (10 000 pages)	44247	339434	520833	889514	931133	858508	826749

19-5 电影、艺术活动、群众文化活动、图书馆及博物馆活动情况
STATISTICS ON MOVIE, ART ACTIVITIES, PUBLIC CULTURE ACTIVITIES, LIBRARY AND MUSEUM

项目	Item	1990	2000	2005	2010	2012	2013	2014
城市电影活动	Movie of city							
放映场次数（万场）	Times Projected (10 000 times)					95.40	128.09	162.47
观众人数（千人次）	Number of the audience (1000 person-times)					24496	33168	43905
艺术活动	Art Activities							
年表演场次（场）	Annual Times of Performing (time)	13100	15000	16000	22850	35920	37230	39000
观众人数（千人次）	Number of Spectators (1000 person-times)	10620	21211	16939	28454	30144	28801	33444
年人均观看次数（次）	Annual Times of Watching Per Capita (time)	0.20	0.36	0.28	0.50	0.52	0.50	0.57
群众文化活动	Public Culture Activities							
举办展览个数（个）	Number of Expo Displayed (unit)	1166	2785	2653	4276	3427	4045	4467
举办训练班结业人数(万人次)	Number of Training Activities (10 000 person-times)	4.90	9.90	13.00	10.80	83.80	87.8	95.1
图书馆活动	Library Activities							
书刊外借人次（千人次）	Number of Circulation (1000 person-times)							10525
图书流通册次（千册）	Number of Circulation (1000 volumes)	9600	9485	9267	18462	13865	15701	17554
人均年借阅册数（册）	Number of Books Borrowed Per Capita Annually (volume)	0.18	0.16	0.15	0.32	0.24	0.27	0.30
人均年借阅人数(次)	Number of People Borrowing Annually (person)	0.10	0.12	0.19	0.27	0.15	0.16	0.18
博物馆活动	Museum Activities							
现有陈列展览个数（个）	Number of Display at Present (unit)	145	210	218	686	937	796	857
参观人数（千人次）	Visitors (1000 persons)	2089	1819	2194	19212	22297	23576	25996
人均年参观次数（次）	Number of Visit Per Capia Annually (time)	0.04	0.03	0.04	0.34	0.39	0.41	0.45

19-6 艺术表演团体、群众艺术馆、文化馆经费情况
STATISTICS ON EXPENSES OF ART TROUPES, PUBLIC ART CENTERS AND CULTURE ACTIVITIES CENTERS

单位：万元 (10 000 yuan)

项 目	Item	2010	2011	2012	2013	2014
艺术表演团体	**Art Troupes**					
补贴团体 (个)	Subsidized Troupes (unit)	4	4	1	2	2
国家经费补贴	National Subsidy	8082	8915	2868	2625	3219
业务及其他收入	Revenue from Business and From Others	5093	2154	831	462	441
#演出收入	#From Performing	559	842	243	243	149
总支出	Total Expenditure	13504	11168	3406	3239	3734
第三产业增加值	Value Added of Tertiary Industry	7352	8636	2186	2343	3074
经费自给率 (%)	Percentage of Self-supply Expenses (%)	37.0	19.2	24.0	14.0	11.8
群众艺术馆、文化馆(站)	**Mass Art Galleries and Culture Galleries**					
总支出	Total Expenditure	1392	2079	1985	2476	3068
#预算	#Budget	1071	1320	1344	1959	2110
#项目支出	#Project spending	653	759	1144	1452	1714
修缮费	Maintainace Fees	153				
第三产业增加值	Value Added of Tertiary Industry	611	732	869	1207	1416

注：本表各项指标仅指文化厅系统内的。
Note:Items in this table refer to those within culture bureau system.

19-7 文化、文物事业经费支出及基本建设情况
BASIC CONDITIONS ABOUT EXPENDITURES ON CULTURE AND HISTORICAL RELICS AND ITS CONSTRUCTION

单位：万元 (10 000 yuan)

项　　目	Item	2010	2011	2012	2013	2014
文化、文物事业经费支出总计	**Total Expenditures on Culture and Historical Relics**	**215061**	**244474**	**286344**	**333675**	**357361**
文化事业	Culture	170203	194222	218712	249298	270471
艺术表演团体	Art Performing Groups	39500	43000	43492	52952	54940
艺术表演场所	Art Performing Places	6244	12807	5245	9233	10163
图书馆	Library	31444	35003	34313	43633	45054
群众文化	Public Culture	26306	29273	36247	39667	43503
中等专业学校	Secondary Vocation School	2364	5533	3511	3276	2972
干部训练	Cadre Taining					
其他文化事业	Others	66719	74136	95833	100466	113768
文物事业	Historical Relics	42504	44719	67632	84377	86890
博物馆	Museum	30029	29256	38330	54176	56199
文物事业机构	Institutions of Historical Relics	6982	8567	19254	16912	12956
其它文物事业	Others	5492	6896	10048	13290	17735
文化、文物基本建设完成投资	Investment in Culture & Historical Relics Cause Construction	55110	83371	31446	83300	64377
文化事业	Culture Cause	24094	26533	21360	52887	39263
文物事业	Historical Relics Cause	31016	56838	10086	30413	25114

19-8 广播电视从业人员基本情况(2014)
BASIC STATISTICS ON PERSONEL ENGAGED IN BROADCASTING AND TELEVISION (2014)

单位：人 (person)

		全省合计 Total of the Province	省级 Provincial Level	市州级 Municiple and Prefecture Level	县级 County Level
从业人员	Personel	38247	19071	7331	11845
其中：长期职工	#Long-term Staff and Workers	37191	18270	7240	11681
党员	Party Members(Communists)	14824	6145	3068	5611
按岗位分:	Classified by Job Division:				
管理人员	Management Personel	7003	3389	1301	2313
专业技术人员	Professional Technical Personel	20339	9817	4623	5899
编辑、记者	Editors and Reporters	5894	1226	2289	2379
播音员、主持人	Announcers and Hosts	1194	310	408	476
按学历分:	Classified by Academic Qualifications:				
研究生及以上	#Graduate and Above	970	653	254	63
本科及大专	Undergraduate and Post-secondary	24739	12223	5782	6734
高中及以下	High School and Below	12538	6195	1295	5048
按职称分:	Classified According to Occupation:				
正高	Senior	308	223	83	2
副高	Vice-senior	1251	672	515	64
中级	Medium	7319	2937	2016	2366
初级及以下	Primary and Below	18834	10359	3434	5041
按年龄分:	Classified by Age:				
35岁以下	35 and Below	13607	8010	2534	3063
36岁至50岁	36-50	19084	8895	3584	6605
50岁以上	50 and Above	5556	2166	1213	2177

19-9 广播电视传输覆盖与经济效益
STATISTICS ON BROADCASTING AND TV COVERAGE RATING AND ECONOMIC BENEFITS

项　目	Item	2005	2010	2012	2013	2014
广播覆盖率 (%)	Broadcasting Coverage Rate (%)	95.99	98.10	98.72	98.80	98.90
电视覆盖率 (%)	TV Coverage Rate (%)	96.71	98.11	98.75	98.81	98.89
有线电视用户 (万)	Cable Television Users (10 000 household)	508.13	894.07	1048.38	1045.31	1070.89
中短波发射转播台/机 (座/部)	Medium and Short-Wave Transmitting Stations (set)	27/ 43	26/76	28/82	28/86	28/86
中短波发射转播台功率（千瓦）	Power of Medium and Short-Wave Transmitters (kw)	646.00	1256.00	1331.00	1371	1371
调频发射转播台 (座/部)	FM Transmitting Stations (set)	189/ 266	426/584	428/604	432/609	432/611
调频发射机功率 (千瓦)	Power of FM Transmitters (kw)	273.00	520.31	551.51	558.91	564.91
电视发射转播台 (座/部)	Television Transmitting Station (set)	1068/ 1399	991/1275	991/1273	908/1191	885/1170
电视发射转播台功率 (千瓦)	Power of Television Transmitters (kw)	335.62	592.22	590.43	583.88	586.70
微波线路站数/长度 (座/公里)	Length of Micro-Wave Route Per Station (set/km)	186/ 4894	121/2961.05	119/2936.05	116/2906.05	116/2906.05
创收收入 (亿元)	Revenue (100 million yuan)	21.86	48.57	63.09	73.12	89.02
固定资产原值 (亿元)	Original Price of Fixed Assets(100 million yuan)	46.91	90.43	116.90	95.31	104.43

19-10 广播电视宣传和节目制作
BROADCASTING PUBLICITY AND PROGRAM PRODUCTION

项　　目	Item	2000	2005	2010	2012	2013	2014
广播电台（座）	Broadcasting Station (unit)	13	11	11	6	7	6
电视台（座）	TV Station (unit)	14	12	12	7	8	8
广播电视台（座）	Radiated TV Station (unit)	65	71	71	76	75	76
广播节目套数（套）	Number of Radio Programs (unit)	82	81	85	86	87	87
广播平均日播音时间（小时）	Average Broadcasting Hour per Week (h)	821.70	1040.40	1225.65	1263.00	1289.00	1296.97
广播节目年制作能力（万小时）	Annual Capacity of Radio Program Production (10 000 h)	21.18	20.59	23.54	23.07	24.29	24.29
电视节目套数（套）	Number of TV Programs (unit)	70	113	114	115	117	117
电视平均周播出时间（万小时）	Average TV Hour per Week (10 000 h)	0.42	1.05	1.26	1.32	1.32	1.32
电视节目年制作能力（万小时）	Annual Capacity of TV program Production (10 000 h)	6.74	7.93	9.48	10.84	10.65	10.92
电视剧制作（部/集）	Production of TV Series (episode)	16/ 280	11/ 208	11/314	12/424	5/151	20/854

19-11 分单位类型、分人员类型体育系统从业人员数(2014)
NUMBER OF STAFF AND WORKERS IN SPORTS COMMISSIONS(2014)

单位：人 (person)

		合计 Total	公务员 Civilian	管理人员 Adminis-trator	专业技术人员 小计 Subtotal	其中：教练员 Coach	其中：科研人员 Scientific research personnel	其中：卫生技术人员 Health technical personnel	运动员 Athlete	工勤人员 Worker	其他 Others
合计	Total	5384	978	1078	1415	862	23	13	1025	441	447
体育行政机关	Sports Administrative Authority	1142	978							68	96
运动项目管理部门（优秀运动队）	Sports Management Department	1194		177	256	228		8	723	30	8
本科院校	Undergraduate School	335			43	32			292		
体育运动学校	Sports School for athelets	404		68	294	122		2		42	
少年儿童体育学校	Sports School for Kids	746		170	494	341	2	1	10	39	33
体育中学	Middle School for Athelets	45		6	35	22				4	
训练基地	Training Base	111		56	42	29		1		13	
体育场馆	Stadium	828		341	207	88				217	63
体育科研机构	Sports Science Reaserch Institution	47		8	39		21				
其他事业单位	Other Institution	481		209	5			1		26	241
其它	Others	51		43						2	6

19-12 等级裁判员、运动员情况
NUMBER OF ATHLETES AND REFEREES IN GRADES

单位：人 (person)

项　目	Item	1990	2000	2005	2009	2010	2011	2012	2013	2014
等级裁判员合计	**Number of Referees in Grades**	**843**	**1195**	**787**	**1438**	**1504**	**1870**	**1667**	**2335**	**1936**
国家级裁判	National Referees		29	25	6	24	23	15	27	
一级裁判	First Grade	357	143	115	467	352	378	403	377	402
二级裁判	Second Grade	486	1023	647	965	1128	1469	1249	1931	1534
等级运动员合计	**Number of Athletes in Grade**	**123**	**418**	**1149**	**1503**	**1639**	**1570**	**1723**	**2109**	**2005**
国际运动健将	International Master of Sports		6		1	1	5	8		4
运动健将	Master of Sports		36	36	51	21	54	54	61	41
一级运动员	First Grade	35	10	247	180	180	227	328	214	359
二级运动员	Second Grade	88	366	866	1271	1437	1284	1333	1834	1601

19-13 体育竞赛成果情况
STATISTICS ON ACHIEVEMENT IN SPORTS COMPETITION

项 目	Item	1990	2000	2005	2009	2010	2011	2012	2013	2014
世界比赛获奖牌数（枚）	**Number of Medals Won in International Games (unit)**	**10**	**13**	**5**	**34**	**12**	**80**	**64**	**51**	**86**
金牌	Gold Medal	9	4	3	12	2	48	30	25	41
银牌	Silver Medal	1	6	2	10	3	19	21	9	23
铜牌	Bronze Medal		3		12	7	13	13	17	22
亚洲比赛获奖牌数（枚）	**Number of Medals Won in Asia Games (unit)**	**51**	**5**	**7**	**23**	**13**	**17**	**24**	**11**	**26**
金牌	Gold Medal	37	4	5	5	8	13	15	5	17
银牌	Silver Medal	7		2	9	4	4	7	4	3
铜牌	Bronze Medal	7	1		9	1		2	2	6
全国比赛获前六名（人）	**Top Six Places in National Games (person)**			**155**	**315**	**134**	**524**	**461**	**356**	**356**
第一名	First Place	52	35	24	49	21	99	82	57	48
第二名	Second Place	50	22	23	53	21	71	74	72	53
第三名	Third Place	40	21	27	51	17	90	76	82	69
第四名	Fourth Place	29	35	24	44	23	92	68	48	55
第五名	Fifth Place	31	29	31	66	30	103	86	65	87
第六名	Sixth Place	38	26	26	52	22	69	75	32	44

19-14 新建健身场地设施情况(2014)
SITUATION OF NEW-BUILT FITNESS FACILITIES(2014)

	合计 Total	村级农民体育健身工程 Town-based Peasant Fitness Project	乡镇体育健身工程 County-based Fitness Project	全民健身路径工程 Citizen "Fitness Path" Project	全民健身活动中心 Citizen Fitness Center
数量 (个) Number (unit)	6255	2861	112	2743	12
器材件数 (件) Number of Instrument (piece)	18705			17892	
场地面积(平方米) Area (sq. m)	3589314	2052883	185122	346515	343542
场地长度 (米) Length (m)	117650				
投资总额 (万元) Total Invenstment (10 000 Yuan)	107375	6154	1624	6056	71237

19-14 续表

	户外健身场地设施 Outdoor Fitness Facilities					其他场地设施 Other Fitness Facilities
	体育公园 Fitness Park	全民健身广场 Citizen Fitness Square	户外体育营地 Outdoor Fitness Center	社区运动场地 Community-based Fitness Square	健身步道 Fitness Path	
数量 (个) Number (unit)	2	43	1	139	20	322
器材件数 (件) Number of Instrument (piece)						813
场地面积(平方米) Area (sq. m)	200334	93056		151703		216159
场地长度 (米) Length (m)					117650	
投资总额 (万元) Total Invenstment (10 000 Yuan)	14050	1970	80	2315	2909	980

19-15　分市州文化及相关产业“三上”法人单位数(2014)

NUMBER OF LEGAL PERSONS OF CULTURE AND RELAVANT INDUSTRY ABOVE DESIGNATED BY REGION(2014)

单位：个　　(unit)

地　区	Region	“三上”法人单位数 Legal Persons	规上文化制造业 Cultual Manufacturing	限上文化批发和零售业 Wholesale and Rerail of Culture	规上文化服务业 Services of Culture
全　省	**Province**	**1525**	**490**	**437**	**598**
武汉市	Wuhan	422	72	94	256
黄石市	Huangshi	51	17	8	26
十堰市	Shiyan	45	9	21	15
宜昌市	Yichang	245	84	40	121
襄阳市	Xiangyang	307	81	118	108
鄂州市	Ezhou	10	4	2	4
荆门市	Jingmen	47	21	21	5
孝感市	Xiaogan	95	58	28	9
荆州市	Jingzhou	66	25	32	9
黄冈市	Huanggang	60	31	22	7
咸宁市	Xianning	70	33	16	21
随州市	Suizhou	30	21	7	2
恩施州	Enshi	41	11	21	9
仙桃市	Xiantao	14	11	2	1
潜江市	Qianjiang	11	6	2	3
天门市	Tianmen	10	6	3	1
神农架	Shennongjia	1			1

19-16 分市州规模以上文化制造业企业基本情况(2014)
BASIC CONDITIONS CULTURAL MANUFACTURING ENTERPRISES ABOVE DESIGNATED SIZE BY REGION(2014)

单位：万元 (10 000 yuan)

地 区	Region	企业单位数(个) Number of Enterprises (unit)	年末从业人员(人) Engaged Person at Year-end (person)	资产总计 Total Assets	营业收入 Business Revenue	营业税金及附加 Taxes and Extra Charges on Business	营业利润 Operating Profit	应交增值税 Value-added Tax Payable
全 省	**Province**	**490**	**93252**	**5256239**	**8742000**	**61068**	**474824**	**219613**
武汉市	Wuhan	72	15106	1378134	1379369	5500	93770	28300
黄石市	Huangshi	17	3876	99622	144431	1022	9801	1013
十堰市	Shiyan	9	1218	24836	33762	1141	2492	1082
宜昌市	Yichang	84	18644	1398151	1696661	10265	87502	61072
襄阳市	Xiangyang	81	18397	837016	2152151	9766	104066	48130
鄂州市	Ezhou	4	561	28447	163137	1280	6437	8984
荆门市	Jingmen	21	2519	110751	274077	4733	25769	5258
孝感市	Xiaogan	58	8237	400371	913932	16950	52379	25252
荆州市	Jingzhou	25	6271	298847	843206	1744	17459	15057
黄冈市	Huanggang	31	4411	180033	224094	1780	10390	5091
咸宁市	Xianning	33	4635	225606	464966	3427	32163	7245
随州市	Suizhou	21	2997	87172	170409	803	10061	3472
恩施州	Enshi	11	2023	25149	35340	604	2924	398
仙桃市	Xiantao	11	1777	105254	165017	1146	14825	7429
潜江市	Qianjiang	6	976	14751	35159	257	906	389
天门市	Tianmen	6	1604	42099	46289	650	3880	1441
神农架	Shennongjia							

19-17 分市州限额以上文化批发和零售企业基本情况(2014)
BASIC CONDITIONS OF ENTERPRISES OF WHOLESALE AND RETAIL OF CULTURE ABOVE DESIGNATED SIZE BY REGION(2014)

单位：万元 (10 000 yuan)

地 区	Region	企业单位数(个) Number of Enterprises (unit)	年末从业人员(人) Engaged Person at Year-end (person)	资产总计 Total Assets	营业收入 Business Revenue	营业税金及附加 Taxes and Extra Charges on Business	营业利润 Operating Profit	应交增值税 Value-added Tax Payable
全 省	**Province**	**437**	**21348**	**1719242**	**3033825**	**24792**	**165233**	**32098**
武汉市	Wuhan	94	11610	1002964	1487547	7132	22358	11582
黄石市	Huangshi	8	245	9213	11801	238	1062	144
十堰市	Shiyan	21	651	26947	31236	779	2689	395
宜昌市	Yichang	40	938	119888	162668	1072	9495	2190
襄阳市	Xiangyang	118	2825	163770	593942	11436	69664	11604
鄂州市	Ezhou	2	85	3619	8467	16	239	44
荆门市	Jingmen	21	437	15896	28884	657	3346	741
孝感市	Xiaogan	28	1067	57885	142117	301	20402	670
荆州市	Jingzhou	32	788	46474	67528	924	3563	589
黄冈市	Huanggang	22	682	38024	51267	191	2393	272
咸宁市	Xianning	16	330	16800	49829	684	5580	287
随州市	Suizhou	7	230	16434	17948	213	1462	
恩施州	Enshi	21	518	26915	42267	179	2192	197
仙桃市	Xiantao	2	79	9016	8484	131	760	118
潜江市	Qianjiang	2	678	38934	166175	37	39	41
天门市	Tianmen	3	185	126463	163665	802	19989	3224
神农架	Shennongjia							

19–18 分市州规模以上文化服务业企业基本情况(2014)
BASIC CONDITIONS OF ENTERPRISES OF SERVICES OF CULTURE ABOVE DESIGNATED BY REGION(2014)

单位：万元 (10 000 yuan)

地 区	Region	企业单位数(个) Number of Enterprises (unit)	年末从业人员(人) Engaged Person at Year-end (person)	资产总计 Total Assets	营业收入 Business Revenue	营业税金及附加 Taxes and Extra Charges on Business	营业利润 Operating Profit	应交增值税 Value-added Tax Payable
全 省	**Province**	**598**	**89984**	**10857604**	**4484313**	**129527**	**542247**	**93364**
武汉市	Wuhan	256	64947	9373519	3833633	108573	452134	82863
黄石市	Huangshi	26	1825	60976	43982	782	2298	126
十堰市	Shiyan	15	2183	259853	52369	930	1570	1127
宜昌市	Yichang	121	8849	521450	282482	9142	53578	5973
襄阳市	Xiangyang	108	6382	275807	116893	5447	17843	1541
鄂州市	Ezhou	4	331	9871	7846	37	-531	8
荆门市	Jingmen	5	542	17810	6520	109	726	145
孝感市	Xiaogan	9	755	56443	19822	882	4989	344
荆州市	Jingzhou	9	523	32514	13031	103	586	245
黄冈市	Huanggang	7	483	30532	15733	938	2480	586
咸宁市	Xianning	21	1420	83147	58470	1266	2130	11
随州市	Suizhou	2	272	11487	3228	27	277	-86
恩施州	Enshi	9	994	102817	19948	995	3776	422
仙桃市	Xiantao	1	58	90	48	3	2	
潜江市	Qianjiang	3	353	20348	9325	285	387	
天门市	Tianmen	1	37	940	983	8	2	59
神农架	Shennongjia	1	30	8045	848	33	184	

主要统计指标解释

文化事业机构 指从事专业文化工作和为专业文化工作服务的独立建制的单位。不包括这些单位另外举办独立核算的其他机构和各部门的业余文化组织。该指标主要反映文化事业机构发展规模水平。

艺术表演团体 指从事戏曲、音乐、舞蹈、杂技等专业艺术表演，有独立帐户的单位，不包括半工半艺、半农半艺和民间职业剧团。该指标主要反映全国专业艺术表演团体发展规模水平。

艺术表演观众人数(人次) 指售票、包场演出或民族地区免费演出的艺术表演观众人次数，不包括彩排审查和内部观摩演出的观看人次数。该指标主要反映全国观看专业艺术表演团体演出的效益规模。

等级运动员 是指经考核正式批准授予运动员称号的运动员，等级称号由高到低依次为国际级运动健将、运动健将、一级运动员、二级运动员、三级运动员。

广播节目综合人口覆盖率 指根据国家广电总局制定的《广播电视人口覆盖率统计技术标准和方法》进行统计调查的，在对象区能接收到由中央、省、地区或县通过无线、有线或卫星等技术方式传播的各级广播节目的人口数占全国总人口数的百分比。

电视节目综合人口覆盖率 指根据国家广电总局制定的《广播电视人口覆盖率统计技术标准和方法》进行统计调查的，在对象区能接收到由中央、省、地区或县通过无线、有线或卫星等技术方式传播的各级电视节目的人口数占全国总人口数的百分比。

Explanatory Notes on Main Statistical Indicators

Cultural Institutions refer to units, which have their own organizational system and independent accounting system and specialize in or serve cultural development. They exclude other establishments run by these cultural institutions and amateur cultural groups established by various departments. This indicator reflects the development of cultural units.

Art Troupe refers to the troupe which is engaged in drama, opera, music, dance, acrobatics or other art performance, opens independent accounts with banks and has self-supporting accounting system; excluding the troupes which are engaged partly in industrial or agricultural activities, partly in art performance and the professional troupes organized by the people. This indicator reflects the development of national professional art troupes.

Number of Audience at Art Performance refers to the number of attendants at commercial shows, completely booked shows or free shows given in minority national areas, and does not include the number of spectators at rehearsals for examination and internal shows for study.

Certified Grade Athletes refer to those who are awarded the title of athletes through assessment. The titles rank from high to low as: international level athletes, national level athletes, first grade athletes, second grade athletes and third grade athletes.

Radio Coverage of Population refers to the percentage of population, which can receive central, provincial, city, prefecture, and county radio programs relayed by wireless, cable, satellite and other technical means, in the surveying area, to national total population, according to Statistical Standard and Method on Television and Radio Coverage of Population established by the State Administration of Broadcasting, Film and Television.

Television Coverage of Population refers to the percentage of population, which can receive central, provincial, city, prefecture, and county television programs relayed by wireless, cable, satellite and other technical means, in the surveying area, to national total population, according to Statistical Standard and Method on Television and Radio Coverage of Population established by the State Administration of Broadcasting, Film and Television.

20 公共管理及其他

Public Management and Other

资料整理：谢　涛

20-1 工会组织情况
BASIC STATISTICS ON LABOR UNION

年 份 Year	工会基层组织数(个) Number of Grassroot Labor Union Organizations (unit)	全省已建工会的基层单位职工与会员人数(万人) Number of Grassroot Staff and Workers and Members of Established Labor Union in the Province(10 000 persons)				工会专职工作人员人数(万人) Number of Full-time Workers in Labor Union (10 000 persons)
		职工人数 Number of Staff and Workers	#女职工 #Women Workers	会员人数 Number of Members	#女会员 #Women Members	
1975	18872	280.22	83.18	174.72	56.24	0.87
1980	22802	387.95	139.20	299.41	94.91	1.04
1985	25286	484.68	192.32	404.58	156.62	2.76
1990	33990	559.00	227.00	498.00	198.00	3.40
1995	28461	564.34	230.90	511.11	207.49	1.81
1996	28459	584.30	238.16	527.09	213.08	2.88
1997	20151	472.60	192.65	419.72	168.89	2.68
1998	17488	445.80	183.90	400.90	163.90	2.30
1999	18976	442.97	178.21	396.90	155.03	3.18
2000	45251	532.31	197.81	475.57	176.87	2.45
2001	111309	728.94	218.68	660.82	198.25	2.45
2004	50391	755.90	276.69	721.46	262.74	2.95
2005	54893	856.07	298.78	771.95	279.94	3.09
2006	61627	904.15	314.67	856.95	296.39	3.76
2007	69886	1004.92	358.44	972.30	345.64	3.94
2008	79048	1099.78	382.72	1073.22	377.43	4.48
2009	83436	1160.45	418.82	1127.68	411.12	4.75
2010	88647	1220.52	437.50	1184.88	429.00	5.80
2011	107995	1319.08	462.18	1267.28	453.11	6.10
2012	120561	1336.09	491.49	1292.06	481.87	6.44
2013	130513	1348.45	494.94	1312.16	487.57	6.36
2014	130326	1325.35	495.91	1285.13	487.36	6.67

注：因文革期间工会统计中断，表中1975年数据根据年平均增长值推算

Note:The data in 1975 were calculated by the average growth rate because Labor Union statistics had been suspended in the period of "The Great Cultural Revolution".

20-2 基层政权和村(居)委会情况
BASIC STATISTICS ON GRASSROOT REGIME AND VILLAGE COMMITTEES

单位：个 (unit)

年份 Year	镇 Township	乡 Villages	街道办事处 Regional Office	居委会个数 Number of Committees	村委会个数 Number of Village Committees
1986	859	3700	178	3257	32796
1987	836	1257	186	3394	32738
1988	828	1260	215	3483	32354
1989	840	1143	298	3545	32094
1990	849	1123	293	3573	32703
1991	849	1121	307	3709	32595
1992	852	1117	297	3830	32716
1993	857	1097	214	3921	32674
1994	864	1092	218	3998	32636
1995	865	1038	236	4110	32547
1996	823	567	252	4170	32486
1997	840	552	252	4287	32393
1998	847	543	253	4364	32293
1999	850	488	271	4425	32187
2000	860	466	283	3619	32001
2001	735	228	250	3468	31191
2002	738	224	272	3265	27667
2003	735	224	273	3351	27127
2004	738	224	274	3356	26470
2005	733	217	277	3465	29534
2006	737	210	277	3545	25828
2007	734	210	279	3653	25722
2008	735	207	285	3794	25551
2009	740	204	283	3882	25517
2010	741	199	290	3983	25763
2011	742	194	297	4051	25643
2012	746	188	298	4032	25575
2013	757	175	300	4208	25452
2014	761	170	302	4187	25448

20-3　社会福利事业、企业单位机构及人员数

BASIC STATISTICS ON NUMBER OF SOCIAL WELFARE ENTERPRISES AND PERSONS ENGAGED

单位：个　(unit)

项　目	Item	机构数 Number of Institutions					
		2005	2010	2011	2012	2013	2014
全省合计	**Total of the Province**	**4358**	**6149**	**6807**	**8251**	**12000**	**12453**
一、事业单位	Institution	3425	5395	6084	7545	11375	11919
(一)收养性事业单位	Adoptive Institutions	2755	2520	2528	2545	2213	2002
1.优抚休(疗)养院	Special Care Nursing Home	99	97	97	102	105	101
2.社会福利收养院	Welfare Homes	2656	2423	2431	2443	2108	1901
(二)非收养性事业单位	Non-Adoptive Institutions	670	2875	3556	5000	9162	9917
1.烈士纪念建筑物管理单位	Managing Organizations on Martyrs Memorials	45	46	51	52	55	56
2.军队离退休干部管理机构	Managing Organizations on Veterans	97	106	107	106	108	107
3.军供站	Military Supply Station	8	9	9	9	9	9
4.社区服务机构	Community Service Centre	278	2315	2887	4330	8466	9216
5.救助管理站	Home for Beggers and Vagrants		63	81	87	86	87
6.未成年人救助保护中心	Protection Centre for Street Children		13	81	78	66	65
7.殡葬事业单位	Funeral Units	131	132	136	147	172	178
#殡仪馆	#Funeral Home	81	83	82	84	88	85
8.福利彩票发行单位	Lottery Tickets Issuing Units	54	52	53	54	54	54
9.婚姻登记服务单位	Marriage Registration Service Center		97	108	93	99	97
10.救灾储备单位	Relief Unit		42	43	44	47	48
二、社会福利企业	Social Welfare Enterprises	933	754	723	706	625	534

20-3 续表 continued

单位：人 (person)

项目	Item	人员数 Number of Persons Engaged in					
		2005	2010	2011	2012	2013	2014
全省合计	**Total of the Province**	**51625**	**74891**	**76524**	**84733**	**95296**	**99577**
一、事业单位	Institution	25899	33401	37222	44100	56987	64951
(一)收养性事业单位	Adoptive Institutions	18132	18835	20017	19754	19871	23511
1.优抚休(疗)养院	Special Care Nursing Home	2999	2723	2700	2776	3088	3790
2.社会福利收养院	Welfare Homes	15133	16112	17317	16978	16783	19721
(二)非收养性事业单位	Non-Adoptive Institutions	7767	14566	17205	24346	37116	41440
1.烈士纪念建筑物管理单位	Managing Organizations on Martyrs Memorials	699	597	618	670	695	690
2.军队离退休干部管理机构	Managing Organizations on Veterans	844	871	848	882	879	859
3.军供站	Military Supply Station	283	247	246	247	236	229
4.社区服务机构	Community Service Centre	1940	7919	9851	16586	28863	33648
5.救助管理站	Home for Beggers and Vagrants		553	818	805	871	886
6.未成年人救助保护中心	Protection Centre for Street Children		183	324	547	541	335
7.殡葬事业单位	Funeral Units	3265	3152	3349	3440	3761	3695
#殡仪馆	#Funeral Home	2668	2552	2641	2575	2592	2449
8.福利彩票发行单位	Lottery Tickets Issuing Units	201	430	492	488	536	380
9.婚姻登记服务单位	Marriage Registration Service Center		487	538	549	603	591
10.救灾储备单位	Relief Unit		127	121	132	131	127
二、社会福利企业	Social Welfare Enterprises	25726	41490	39302	40633	38309	34626

20-4 社会保险基本情况

BASIC CONDITIONS ABOUT SOCIAL INSURANCE

年份 year	失业保险 Unemployment Insurance		城镇职工基本养老保险 Basic Endowment Insurance for Urban and Rural Employees		工伤保险年末参保人数（万人）Participants at Year-end (10 000 persons)	年末参加生育保险人数（万人）Number of People Participated in Maternity Insurance at Year-end (10 000 persons)
	年末参保人数（万人）Participants at Year-end (10 000 persons)	全年发放失业保险金（亿元）Unemployed Relief Released (100 million yuan)	年末参保职工人数（万人）Participants at Year-end (10 000 persons)	年末参保离退休人数（万人）Retirees (10 000 persons)		
1996	392.9	0.4	353.2		177.6	137.8
1997	381.2	0.5	355.8		188.5	165.5
1998	378.2	0.5	413.1	107.4	190.0	168.8
1999	517.6	0.6	455.3	122.4	183.8	189.0
2000	459.6	1.6	465.6	130.4	185.0	191.3
2001	420.8	3.2	474.4	136.6	182.3	182.1
2002	416.1	5.4	532.7	154.5	183.2	182.7
2003	390.1	5.6	554.5	167.5	189.2	182.1
2004	391.3	4.0	586.1	194.7	187.2	179.9
2005	391.5	4.0	597.6	206.4	230.3	175.9
2006	395.5	3.7	630.2	220.5	275.5	194.5
2007	405.4	3.8	651.4	235.3	328.0	225.0
2008	422.6	3.6	671.7	252.4	350.7	315.4
2009	437.0	3.6	701.9	273.7	396.5	350.6
2010	464.5	3.9	749.1	301.3	444.5	388.7
2011	496.0	3.7	766.0	341.4	467.3	412.9
2012	501.4	3.8	801.4	367.3	505.8	444.7
2013	511.9	4.2	822.0	396.0	541.0	457.9
2014	520.9	5.1	847.0	419.3	576.7	480.6

20-5 参加基本养老保险人数

NUMBER OF PRESONS PARTICIPATED IN BASIC ENDOEMENT INSURANCE

年份 Year	合计 Total	职工 Number of Employees	企业(含其他) Enterprises (including others)	离退休人员 Number of Retirees	企业(含其他) Enterprises (including others)
1996	353.2	353.2	353.2		
1997	355.8	355.8	355.8		
1998	520.5	413.1	413.1	107.4	107.4
1999	577.7	455.3	455.3	122.4	122.4
2000	596.0	465.6	465.6	130.4	130.4
2001	611.0	474.4	474.4	136.6	136.6
2002	687.2	532.7	481.5	154.5	147.2
2003	722.0	554.5	501.1	167.5	158.6
2004	780.8	586.1	530.6	194.7	184.5
2005	804.0	597.6	539.8	206.4	195.1
2006	850.7	630.2	570.0	220.5	207.5
2007	886.7	651.4	602.6	235.3	223.0
2008	924.1	671.7	628.7	252.4	238.7
2009	975.6	701.9	660.5	273.7	259.2
2010	1050.4	749.1	690.9	301.3	258.3
2011	1107.4	766.0	725.5	341.4	325.6
2012	1168.7	801.4	757.8	367.3	351.2
2013	1217.9	822.0	779.1	396.0	379.7
2014	1266.2	847.0	802.5	419.3	402.1

20-6　城乡各种福利院基本情况
BASIC CONDITIONS OF WELFARE HOUSES IN URBAN AND RURAL AREAS

年份 Year	单位数(个) Number of Units (unit)	职工人数(人) Number of Staff and Workers (person)	床位数(张) Number of Beds (unit)	收养人数(人) Number of People Adopted (person)
1986	3955	12373	52912	46818
1987	3655	12360	57698	49356
1988	3300	11901	57356	47448
1989	3285	11759	57022	47075
1990	3252	11854	57878	48017
1991	3130	11966	57839	47684
1992	3114	12361	61878	50885
1993	3101	12955	61389	51638
1994	3066	13280	63451	52866
1995	2977	13607	64417	53662
1996	2907	13664	65853	54987
1997	2715	14163	69970	57471
1998	2650	14392	72284	59753
1999	2603	14552	76203	63326
2000	2459	14203	77871	63901
2001	2191	14173	78119	62590
2002	2145	14414	79522	65564
2003	2123	14856	117511	103320
2004	2359	16344	156461	144042
2005	2755	18132	189486	168800
2006	2770	17705	198458	179385
2007	2616	17157	206049	188308
2008	2553	18395	210342	180286
2009	2504	18190	216211	185933
2010	2596	19571	228375	189782
2011	2690	21159	233503	190917
2012	2710	21106	240985	193466
2013	2365	21283	241671	183140
2014	2265	21970	277345	183173

20-7 婚姻登记和离婚情况

STATISTICS ON MARRIAGE REGISTERATION AND DIVORCE

年份 Year	准予登记结婚(对) Marriage Registeration Granted (couple)	初婚(人) First Marriage (person)	再婚(人) Digamist(person)	离婚(对) Divorce (couple)	离婚率(‰) Rate of Divorce (‰)
1986	402315	785319	19311	6322	0.25
1987	417552	809808	25296	6660	0.26
1988	362654	698447	26861	7389	0.29
1989	413460	801171	25749	9203	0.35
1990	408688	790477	26899	9477	0.35
1991	424708	820092	29324	9584	0.35
1992	463279	897899	28659	10793	0.39
1993	425276	822044	28508	11937	0.43
1994	457324	884817	29831	12910	0.46
1995	482063	930832	33294	13340	0.46
1996	442532	851577	33487	14590	0.50
1997	426460	820615	32305	21260	0.72
1998	399900	763163	36637	24711	0.84
1999	376961	716175	37747	19519	0.66
2000	353781	673294	34268	21255	0.71
2001	335421	632188	38654	22077	0.74
2002	321517	605055	37979	24003	0.80
2003	329256	614244	44268	29375	0.98
2004	381472	710633	52311	46369	1.54
2005	394093	717495	70691	53394	1.77
2006	445672	822294	69050	57682	1.91
2007	485278	896768	73788	65876	2.17
2008	542251	1025496	59006	76003	2.49
2009	565400	1058851	71949	81133	2.84
2010	570810	1068715	72905	89549	3.11
2011	626912	1169771	84053	98874	3.18
2012	615861	1155365	76357	109862	3.81
2013	645767	1201344	90190	127604	4.40
2014	621946	1182271	61621	133723	4.60

20-8 残疾人基本情况

BASIC STATISTICS ON THE DISABLED

单位：万人 (10 000 persons)

项目	Item	2013	2014
康复	Rehabilitation		
视力残疾康复	Rehabilitation of Persons with Visual Disability		
白内障复明手术 (万例)	Sight-restoring Surgeries for Cataract Patients (10 000 cases)	30428.00	30337.00
低视力者配用助视器 (万人)	Persons with Low-vision Fitted with Vision-aids (10 000 persons)	6074.00	5420.00
盲人定向行走训练 (万人)	Blind Persons Receiving Orientation Skill Training (10 000 persons)	6080.00	6000.00
听力语言残疾康复	Rehabilitation of Persons with Hearing and Speech Disability		
新收训聋儿 (万人)	Deaf Children Newly Trained in the year (10 000 persons)	833.00	829.00
培训聋儿家长 (万人)	Parents Trained (10 000 persons)	1178.00	1128.00
肢体残疾康复	Rehabilitation of Persons with Physical Disability		
肢体残疾(脑瘫)儿童机构康复训练 (万人)	Rehabilitation Training Institutions for Children with Mobility Impairment(Cerebral Palsy) (10 000 persons)	0.21	0.27
肢体残疾人社区、家庭康复训练 (万人)	Persons with Mobility Impairment Receiving Rehabilitation Training in Communities and Families (10 000 persons)	1.03	0.99
智力残疾康复	Rehabilitation of Persons with Intellectual Disability		
智力残疾儿童康复训练 (万人)	Children with Intellectual Disability Receiving Rehabilitation Training (10 000 persons)	0.54	0.55
成年智力残疾人社区、家庭康复 (万人)	Adults with Intellectual Disability Trained in Communities and Families (10 000 persons)	0.10	0.09
精神病防治康复	Prevention and Rehabilitation of Mental Illness(PRMI)		
监护精神病人 (万人)	Peoplw with Mental Illness under Guardianship (10 000 persons)	22.57	22.75
显好率 (%)	Significant Improvement Rate (%)	40.6	40.8
社会参与率 (%)	Social Involvement Rate (%)	30.6	31.3
孤独症儿童机构训练 (人)	Children with Autism Trained in Institutions (person)	586	820
残疾人辅助器具供应服务	Provision of Assistive Devices		
辅助器具供应 (万件)	Assistive Devices Provided (10 000 pieces)	4.31	3.20
残疾人假肢装配 (万件)	Prosthesis Installed for the Disabled (10 000 pieces)	0.13	0.16
残疾人矫形器装配 (万例)	Orthotic Devices for the Disabled (10 000 cases)	0.08	0.07
教育	Education		
未入学学龄残疾儿童少年 (万人)	School-age Disabled Children Unable to Enter School (10 000 persons)	0.25	0.20
特殊教育普通高中在校生 (人)	Students at Special Education Senior High Schools (persons)	334	420
残疾人中等职业教育在校生 (人)	Students at Secondary Vocational Schools for PWDs (persons)	160	262
高等院校录取残疾考生 (人)	Disabled Students Admitted to Higher Education Institutions (persons)	305	369
就业	Employment		
城镇残疾人新增安排就业 (万人)	Newly Employed PWDs in Urban Areas in the Year (10 000 persons)	3.33	1.09
集中就业	Employed in Collective Form	5.78	5.12
按比例就业	Employed by Quota Scheme	4.32	5.65
个体及其他形式就业	Self-employed or Employed in Other Forms	12.23	10.78
社会保障 (万人)	Social Security (10 000 persons)		
城镇残疾职工参加社会保险	Urban Worker with Disabilities Covered by Social Insurance	8.11	14.01
残疾居民参加城镇居民医疗保险	Residents with Disabilities Covered by the Medical Insurance for Urban Residents	8.44	15.13
农村残疾人参加新型农村社会养老保险	Rural PWDs Covered by New Types of Rural Social Pension Insurance	107.44	104.61
城乡残疾人纳入最低生活保障托养残疾人	PWDs Covered by the Basic Living Allowance System Fostered PWDs	18.46	17.66
扶贫	Poverty Alleviation		
扶持农村贫困残疾人 (万人次)	Impoverished PWDs Assited in Rural Areas (10 000 persons-times)	11.17	12.91
农村残疾人实用技术培训 (万人次)	Vocational Skills Training for PWDs (10 000 persons-times)	5.50	2.99
农村贫困残疾人危房改造 (万户)	Dilapidated House Renovation for Poor PWDs (10 000 households)	0.12	0.05
受益残疾人 (万人)	PWDs Benefited (10 000 persons)	0.15	0.06
维权	Rights Protection		
贫困残疾人家庭无障碍改造 (万户)	Barrier Free Home Renovation for Poor PWDs (10 000 households)	0.25	0.20
残疾人机动轮骑车燃油补贴 (万人)	Fuel Subsidy for Motor Wheelchairs of PWDs (10 000 persons)	4.57	4.40
组织建设	Organization Development		
残疾人人口库持证残疾人 (万人)	PWDs with Disability Certificate in the PWD Database (10 000 persons)	104.00	119.00

20-9 刑事案件发、破案情况
STATISTICS ON OCCURANCE AND CLEARING UP OF CRIMINAL CASES

指 标	Item	1995	2000	2005	2010	2011	2012	2013	2014
刑事案件发案总数 (件)	Number of Criminal Cases Occurred (case)	85876	114866	147004	221735	243521	335813	279638	265260
刑事案件破案总数 (件)	Number of Criminal Cases Cleared (case)	73831	72796	71455	76401	63849	139738	118092	90652
刑事案件破案率 (%)	Rate of Criminal Cases Cleared (%)	86.0	63.4	48.6	34.5	26.2	41.6	42.2	34.2

20-10 城市交通事故与火灾情况
BASIC STATISTICS ON TRAFFIC ACCIDENTS AND FIRE ACCIDENTS

指 标	Item	1995	2000	2005	2010	2011	2012	2013	2014
交通事故处理发生件数 (起)	Number of Traffic Accidents (case)	8336	20148	9585	6465	6490	6007	5798	5268
死亡人数 (人)	Deaths (person)	3401	3792	2417	1967	1909	1822	1801	1771
受伤人数 (人)	Injuries (person)	5353	16492	10555	7684	7609	6818	6353	5468
折合经济损失 (万元)	Losses Converted into Money (10 000 yuan)	4460	7041	4958	3294	4029	5391	4473	5071
火灾发生数 (起)	Number of Fire Accsidents (case)	1393	6780	9356	9333	8262	4951	2695	2322
死亡人数 (人)	Deaths (person)	64	54	56	17	38	11	22	2
受伤人数 (人)	Injuries (person)	86	106	47	7	4	10	72	10
折合经济损失 (万元)	Losses Converted into Money (10 000 yuan)	3221	1754	1945	3565	6014	4927	4791	5520

20-11 审查批捕、起诉情况
STATISTICS ON EXAMINATION, ARREST AND PROSECUTION

项 目	Item	1995	2000	2005	2010	2011	2012	2013	2014
受理批捕件数 (件)	Number of Cases (case)	18870	20378	19846	9120	23175	28905	27194	28267
受理批捕人数 (人)	Number of People Arrested (person)	31122	31245	29427	13391	33822	43040	37801	38379
批准逮捕 (人)	Number of Arrests Granted (person)	25257	25114	27063	12081	30633	38468	31813	32398
不批捕人数 (人)	Number of Non-Arrest (person)	1545	4329	1522	1001	2473	3725	5616	5305
受理审查起诉件数 (件)	Number of Cases Received (case)	21240	17660	21966	10028	28574	46382	36882	39980
受理审查起诉人数 (人)	Number of Prosecution Accepted (person)	33532	25416	33410	15280	43393	75876	52541	55410
起诉人数 (人)	Prosecutor (person)	24404	22396	26926	11600	35501	47348	44947	45740
不起诉人数 (人)	Non-prosecutor (person)	43	1019	982	329	1173	1343	1806	2115

20-12 检察机关查办职务犯罪情况
STATISTICS ON CRIMES COMMITTED BY TAKING ADVANTAGE OF DUTY BY PROCURATORIAL ORGAN

项 目	Item	1995	2000	2005	2010	2011	2012	2013	2014
受理案件件数 (件)	Number of Cases Dealt (case)	10906	8343	3125	1074	1733	1840	2168	2703
立案件数 (件)	Registered Cases (case)	3640	2034	1552	988	1525	1651	1935	2438
立案人数 (人)	Registered Offenders (person)	4290	2312	1682	1228	1877	2127	2374	2897
贪污贿赂件数 (件)	Number of Corruption and Bribe Cases (case)	3081	1821	1363	801	1232	1290	1508	1864
渎职侵权件数 (件)	Number of Malversation Cases (case)	559	213	189	187	1515	361	427	574
查办大案件数 (件)	Large Cases (case)	824	882	887	1039	1000	1120	1429	1972
#5万元以上件数	#Money Involved Above 50000 yuan	685	850	839	936	884	911	1319	1580
查办要案人数 (人)	Number of Offender Involved in Large Cases (person)	110	108	139	133	144	152	173	267
#厅局级人数	#Number of Offenders at Bureau Level	4	11	17	10	16	16	15	55
提起公诉人数 (人)	Number of People Prosecuted (person)	1738	1490	1265	1725	1535	1871	2053	2145

20-13 律师、公证、调解工作基本情况
BASIC STATISTICS ON LAWYERS, NOTARIZATION AND MEDIATION

项 目	Item	2000	2005	2010	2011	2012	2013	2014
一、律师工作	**Lawyers**							
律师事务所 (个)	Number of Lawyer Office (person)	350	387	466	490	512	549	595
专职律师	Number of Full-Time Lawyer	2383	3722	5869	6602	7300	7805	8502
兼职律师	Number of Part-Time Lawyer	472	165	252	278	306	334	351
担任法律顾问 (家)	Number of Units with Legal Advisors (unit)	9727	9565	12059	12706	14046	14339	16973
民事案件诉讼代理 (件)	Agent of Civil Cases (case)	21412	27079	45403	47831	61052	63917	64479
经济案件诉讼代理 (件)	Agent of Economic Cases (case)	18931	13799					
刑事诉讼辩护及代理 (件)	Defender and Agent of Criminal Cases (case)	10078	11341	17724	17964	17095	19043	18155
非诉讼法律事务 (件)	Agent of Non-Litigious Legal Affairs (case)	25142	34674	37521	37940	38011	24310	24928
涉外及港澳台法律事务(件)	Agent of Foreign, Hogkong, Maco and Taiwan Affairs (case)	305	5994					
解答法律咨询 (万人次)	Agent of Legal Advisory Services (10 000 (person-times)	11.37	15.23	11.01	12.70	12.58	11.12	12.12
代写法律事务文件 (万件)	Agent of Legal Document Written on Behalf of Clients (10 000 cases)	3.44	3.49	1.59	1.61	2.09	2.3	1.8
二、公证工作	**Notarization**							
公证机构 (个)	Number of Notary Offices (unit)	117	118	116	117	117	117	117
公证人员 (人)	Notarial Pesonel (person)	769	689	643	687	739	830	807
#公证员	#Notaries	506	455	353	378	367	387	397
公证员助理	Assistant Notaries	108	62	167	309	372	244	236
办理公证文件 (万件)	Number of Domestic Notarized Document (10 000 cases)	36.30	31.04	32.65	32.82	33.79	28.6	35.84
#涉外公证 (件)	#Foreign Notarized Documents (case)	63993	65498	79723	80818	88877	91467	107445
三、人民调解工作	**People's Mediation**							
司法助理员 (人)	Judicial Assistant (person)	1732	2210	1682	2623	2698	2347	2906
人民调解委员会 (万个)	Number of People's Mediation Committees (10 000 units)	4.90	3.70	3.62	3.43	3.43	3.44	3.36
调解人员 (万人)	Number of Mediators (10 000 persons)	38.53	17.20	20.43	16.20	15.81	15.87	14.51
调解纠纷总数 (万件)	Number of Disputes Mediated (10 000 cases)	26.47	21.62	22.85	27.20	28.33	30.00	32.13
调解成功总数 (万件)	Number of Successful Mediation (10 000 cases)	25.77	21.13	22.14	26.33	27.60	29.33	31.50

20-14 涉外公证文书分类情况
FOREIGN-RELATED NOTARIAL DOCUMENTS BY TYPE

单位：件 (case)

分类	Item	2000	2005	2008	2009	2010	2011	2012	2013	2014
合 计	**Total**	**63993**	**65498**	**71672**	**70482**	**79723**	**80818**	**88877**	**91467**	**107445**
出生	Births	9748	7243	8254	6874	11567	12956	14791	10812	12074
学历	Academic Degree	9134	10078	16682	9078	7181	6138	5367	6754	8555
经历	Personal Experience	1015	806	347	289	863	875	1068	294	775
生存和居住	Survival and Residence	74	102	48	61	67	54	62	88	127
死亡	Death	83	109	139	126	103	82	106	137	146
收养子女	Children Adoption	683	539	929	707	692	591	470	269	271
亲属关系	Kinship	3225	3962	7665	6598	6605	7811	8562	7247	9322
婚姻状况	Marital Status	4228	3691	5979	5274	5774	5464	6670	3072	2795
继承权	Rights of Inheritance	14	28	52	1003	94	81	35	122	788
遗嘱	Testament	18	18	35	43	82	75	38	48	19
职称	Title	438	141	231	21	172	239	131	15	7
身份	Identity	69	150	73	58	719	697	546	82	36
组织资格	Qualification of Organization	30	16	18	44	31	12	13	14	24
委托书	Trust Deed	133	293	298	31	643	948	1184	1916	3385
公司章程	Chapter of Company	22	24	21	159	39	31	38	15	5
副本与原本相符	Confirmation of Copy and Photo-offset Copies to Originals	11532	7861	4389	3954	12982	11230	16069	19897	24379
证书(执照)	Operation Document	139	186	32	202	285	264	1035	2392	6672
声明书	Declaration	384	3972	1039	33	1140	1526	1649	1255	1486
合同(协议)	Contract(Agreement)	16	372	43	37	46	36	18	28	37
受、未受刑事处分	Criminal Record & Uncriminal Record	6646	6126	7857	6470	10359	11279	12788	7770	10078
其他	Others	16362	9916	9059	14868	11943	12339	9799	24622	20528

20-15 履行法律监督情况
SUPERVISION ON LAW ENFORCEMENT

单位：人、件 (person, case)

项目		2000	2005	2009	2010	2011	2012	2013	2014
监督公安机关立案件数	Number of Cases Registered by Public Security	247	554	951	1088	1150	2218	3243	2429
监督追捕人数	Number of Criminals Hunted under Supervision	300	204	578	903	1387	2166	3063	2253
监督追诉人数	Number of People Being Prosecuted	61	78	520	1130	1309	2103	3746	2347
刑事抗诉件数	Number of Cases Against Crimnal Prosecutions	192	123	124	119	187	274	357	470
监督刑罚执行纠错人次	Person-times of Error Correction of Execution of Punishment	3546	51	345	499	319	1587	4635	4362
民事行政监督抗诉件数	Number of Counterappeal Civil Cases	894	514	409	432	404	435	303	218

20-16 调解民间纠纷分类
CIVIL DISPUTES MEDIATION BY TYPE

项目	Item	调解纠纷(件) Number of Disputes Mediated (case)				各种纠纷所占比重(%) Proportion (%)			
		2011	2012	2013	2014	2011	2012	2013	2014
合计	**Total**	**134674**	**196093**	**102052**	**63013**	**100.0**	**100.0**	**100.0**	**100.0**
婚姻	Marriage	24025	28264	22568	21441	17.8	14.4	22.1	34.0
继承	Rights of Inheritance	572	685	613	505	0.4	0.3	0.6	0.8
房地产开发	Real Estate Development	1615	3038	1229	964	1.2	1.5	1.2	1.5
运输合同	Transportation Contracts	244	261	210	293	0.2	0.1	0.2	0.5
买卖合同	Selling and Purchasing Contracts	5710	8856	6096	6416	4.2	4.5	6.0	10.2
借款合同	Loans Contracts	12452	22761	14684	15128	9.2	11.6	14.4	24.0
劳动争议	Labor Disputes	4562	5990	3337	3484	3.4	3.1	3.3	5.5
人身权	Personal Rights	25777	44355	13297	12005	19.1	22.6	13.0	19.1
所有权	Right of Ownership	5399	10302	3067	1845	4.0	5.3	3.0	2.9
其他	Others	54318	71581	36951	932	40.3	36.5	36.2	1.5

20-17 人民法院审理一审案件情况
STATISTICS ON FIRST INSTANCE CASES IN PEOPLE'S COURT

单位：件 (case)

年 份 Year	收案 Cases Received	刑事 Criminal Cases	民商事 Civil Cases	海事海商 Maritime	行政 Administration
1985	63079	12709	40660	26	
1990	227618	29086	166960		568
1995	257312	21391	174908	456	4359
1998	252403	17763	171025	606	6368
1999	238715	19598	151191	647	6247
2000	228804	19204	146838	618	6754
2001	251003	21741	222702	745	6560
2002	211464	19548	188163	525	3753
2003	193780	18943	171282	488	3555
2004	172889	18833	150682	592	3374
2005	155478	19672	132585	745	3221
2006	156885	19914	133584	606	3387
2007	161728	21719	137328	459	2681
2008	165099	22364	140072	746	2663
2009	173032	23481	147319	710	2232
2010	179631	22963	154299	781	2369
2011	280572	25074	249792	1458	5706
2012	395414	31489	354789	1501	9136
2013	422427	31621	387593	1914	3213
2014	344515	33931	306601	1951	3983

注：一审案件指人民法院按照诉讼级别管辖按第一审程序审理的案件。
Note:First instance cases refer to cases in the first instance process in People's Court.

20-18 人民法院刑事一审案件收结案情况
END OF FIRST INSTANCE CASES IN PEOPLE'S COURT OF CRIMINAL LAWSUITS

单位：件 (case)

项目	Item	收案 Cases Received				结案 Cases Closed			
		2011	2012	2013	2014	2011	2012	2013	2014
合　计	**Total**	**25074**	**31489**	**31621**	**33931**	**24698**	**30912**	**31188**	**33183**
危害公共安全罪	Crimes Harming Public Security	3602	5009	5564	6520	3566	4964	5455	6381
破坏社会主义市场经济秩序罪	Crimes Harming Socialism Market Economy Order	946	1319	1590	1415	913	1261	1566	1358
侵害公民人生权利民主权利罪	Crimes against Rights in Human Life and Democratic Rights	6237	7011	6650	6844	6140	6919	6518	6784
侵犯财产罪	Property Violation	8506	10435	9086	9453	8405	10164	9134	9271
妨害社会管理秩序罪	Crimes Harming Social Management Order	4545	6296	7233	8105	4489	6187	7097	7929
危害国防利益罪	Crimes Harimg National Defense Interests	5	10	6	19	5	9	7	17
贪污贿赂罪	Corruption and Bribe	1093	1190	1242	1305	1050	1186	1188	1194
渎职罪	Malversation	137	214	235	259	127	218	211	236
其他	Others	3	5	15	11	3	4	12	13
合计中含自诉案件	Self-Suing Cases	383	271	184	155	426	281	184	151

20-19 人民法院刑事案件中青少年犯罪情况
STATISTICS ON JUVENILE DELINQUENCY IN PEOPLE'S COURT OF CRIMINAL LAWSUITS

单位：人 (person)

年份 Year	刑事犯罪总数 Total Number of Criminal Cases	青少年犯罪 Juvenile Delinquency	不满18岁 Juvenile Age under 18	18-25岁 Age 18-25	青少年罪犯刑事罪犯率% Percentage of Juvenile Delinquency in Criminal Cases %
1999	20534	6836	1302	5534	33.3
2000	20076	5922	1279	4643	29.5
2001	22911	6597	1774	4823	28.8
2002	20868	5669	1901	3768	27.2
2003	20908	6207	2328	3879	29.7
2004	20429	5838	2633	3205	28.6
2005	21669	6283	2939	3344	29.0
2006	22876	6933	2945	3988	30.3
2007	17368	7459	3131	4328	43.0
2008	26682	6810	3030	3780	25.5
2009	28507	7700	2930	4770	27.0
2010	27928	7058	2287	4771	25.3
2011	29280	7263	2229	5034	24.8
2012	35419	7327	2050	5277	20.7
2013	33871	5398	1365	4033	15.9
2014	34599	4721	1170	3551	13.6

20-20 人民法院民事一审案件收结案情况(2014)
STATISTICS ON END OF FIRST INSTANCE CASES IN PEOPLE'S COURT OF CIVIL LAWSUITS (2014)

单位：件 (case)

项 目	Item	收案 Cases Received	结案 Cases Ended	调解 Mediated	判决 Judgement	驳回 Cases Rejected	撤诉 Cases Withdraw	其他 Others
合 计	**Total**	**306601**	**295761**	**85381**	**87791**	**3703**	**78487**	**40399**
婚姻家庭	Marriage	50664	49770	21441	16579	200	11188	362
继承	Rights of Inheritance	1227	1149	505	398	5	234	7
知识产权	Intelligence Property Rights	7682	7630	2875	2371	16	2356	12
房地产开发	Real Estate Development	3037	2792	964	903	37	860	28
运输合同	Transportation Contracts	804	805	293	322	3	179	8
买卖合同	Selling and Purchasing Contracts	18928	17969	6416	5055	95	6118	285
借款合同	Loans Contracts	49279	46230	15128	13036	319	17194	553
劳动争议	Labor Disputes	10302	10022	3484	3835	235	2283	185
海事海商	Martial Commerce	1951	1819	550	530	11	721	7
人身权	Personal Right	29141	28052	12005	10372	85	5399	191
特别程序	Special Procedure	65592	65278	927	16888	2196	7565	37702
破产	Bankruptcy	41	90		22	4	1	63
所有权及与其相关合同	Rights of Ownership and Relevant Contracts	7160	6877	1845	2262	107	2541	122
其他	Others	60793	57278	18948	15218	390	21848	874

注：结案中含上年旧存。
Note:The statistics of ended cases include statistics of last year.

20-21 人民法院行政一审案件收结案情况(2014)
STATISTICS ON END OF FIRST INSTANCE CASES IN PEOPLE'S COURT OF ADMINISTRATION (2014)

单位：件 (case)

项 目	Item	收案 Cases Received	结案 Cases Ended	维持 Cases Maintained	撤消 Cases Cancled	驳回 Cases Rejected	撤诉 Cases Withdraw	单独赔偿 Sole Compensation	其他 Others
合 计	**Total**	**3983**	**3725**	**377**	**303**	**564**	**1306**	**9**	**1166**
土 地	Land	346	334	21	58	30	103	1	121
公 安	Public Security	423	388	63	10	110	138	1	66
城 建	City Construction	856	820	25	52	112	264	3	364
交通运输	Transportation	49	51	1	1	6	32		11
工 商	Industry and Commerce	112	103	14	9	23	31		26
环 保	Environment	14	13			1	11		1
林 业	Forestry	116	116	24	21	23	39		9
税 务	Taxes	8	8			2	3		3
卫 生	Sanitary and Hygiene	28	27		1	6	9		11
其 他	Others	2031	1865	229	151	251	676	4	554

注：结案中含上年旧存。
Note:The statistics of ended cases include statistics of last year.

主要统计指标解释

社会福利事业单位 指集中收养社会孤老、残、幼的机构，包括由民政部门管理的社会福利院、儿童福利院、精神病人福利院和城镇集体举办的福利院及农村集体举办的敬老院以及优抚医院和具有收养能力的社区服务中心等。该指标主要反映我国在社会福利性单位投入的水平。

社会福利事业单位收养人数 包括民政部门管理和城镇、农村集体举办的社会福利事业单位中收养的老人、少年儿童、缺乏生活自理能力的残疾人员和精神病人。该指标主要反映收养性社会福利单位的收养能力。

社会福利企业单位 指以安置城镇有一定劳动能力的盲、聋、哑和肢体残疾人员就业为目的，享受国家减免税待遇的国有或集体企业。包括福利工厂、福利商业和服务业、假肢厂和安置农场等单位。该指标主要反映我国对残疾人照顾的特殊政策。

粗离婚率 指当年离婚对数占年平均人口的比重，计算公式为:

$$粗离婚率=\frac{当年离婚对数}{年平均人口数}\times 1000‰$$

基本养老保险

1.（参保）职工人数：指报告期末按照国家法律、法规和有关政策规定参加基本养老保险并在社保经办机构已建立缴费记录档案的职工人数，包括中断缴费但未终止养老保险关系的职工人数，不包括只登记未建立缴费记录档案的人数。

2.（参保）离退休人员人数：指报告期末参加基本养老保险的离休、退休和退职人员的人数。

3.基本养老保险基金收入：指根据国家有关规定，由纳入基本养老保险范围的缴费单位和个人按国家规定的缴费基数和缴费比例缴纳的养老保险基金，以及通过其他方式取得的形成基金来源的收入。包括单位和职工个人缴纳的基本养老保险费、基本养老保险基金利息收入、上级补助收入、下级上解收入、转移收入、财政补贴和其他收入。

4.基本养老保险基金支出：指按照国家政策规定的开支范围和开支标准从养老保险基金中支付给参加基本养老保险的离休、通休、退职人员个人的养老金、丧葬抚恤补助，以及由于保险关系转移、上下级之间调剂资金等原因而发生的支出。包括离休金、退休金、退职金、各种补贴、医疗费、死亡丧葬补助费、抚恤救济费、社会保险经办机构管理费、补助下级支出、上解上级支出、转移支出、其他支出等。

5.基本养老保险基金累计结余：指截止报告期末基本养老保险基金收支相抵后的累计余额。

离休、退休、退职人员 指正式办理了离休、退休、退职手续，并享受相应的离休、退休、退职待遇的人员。

基本医疗保险

1.参保人数：指报告期末按国家有关规定参加基本医疗保险的人数。包括参加保险的职工人数和退休人员人数。

2.基金收入：指根据国家有关规定，由纳入基本医疗保险范围的缴费单位和个人，按国家规定的缴费基数和缴费比例缴纳的基金，以及通过其他方式取得的形成基金来源的款项，包括：单位缴纳的社会统筹基金收入、个人缴纳的个人账户基金收入、财政补贴收入、利息收入、其他收入。

3.基金支出：指按照国家政策规定的开支范围和开支标准从社会统筹基金中支付给参加基本医疗保险的职工和退休人员的医疗保险待遇支出，和从个人帐户基金中支付给参加基本医疗保险的职工和退休人员的医疗费用支出，以及其他支出。包括：住院医疗费用支出、门急诊医疗费用支出、个人账户基金支出、其他支出。

4.基金累计结余：指截止报告期末基本医疗保险的社会统筹和个人帐户基金累计结余金额。包括银行存款、财政专户、债券投资和其他。

失业保险

1.参保人数：指报告期末按照国家法律、法规和有关政策规定参加了失业保险的城镇企业事业单位的职工及地方政府规定参加失业保险的其他人员的人数。

2.失业保险基金收入：指按照规定从企业、事业及其他单位筹集的失业保险费及其他并入失业保险基金收入的总额。包括单位和个人缴纳的失业保险费、失业保险基金利息收入、上级补助收入、下级上解收入、转移收入、财政补贴和其他收入。

3.失业保险基金支出：指报告期内为保障失业人员和下岗职工基本生活、促进其再就业等支出的基金总额。包括失业救济金、医疗费、死亡丧葬补助费、抚恤救济费、转业训练费支出、失业保险经办机构管理费、补助下级支出、上解上级支出、转移支出和其他支出。

4.基金累计结余：指截止报告期末失业保险基金收支相抵后的累计余额。

工伤保险

1.参加保险人数：指报告期末依据国家有关规定参加工伤保险的职工人数。

2.享受保险待遇人数：指劳动者因工负伤致残、死亡或因患职业病致残，根据有关规定享受工伤保险待遇职工或供养直系亲属人数。包括伤残人数、职业病人数、因工死亡人数、供养直系亲属人数。

3.基金收入：指根据国家有关规定，由参加工伤保险的单位按国家规定的缴费基数和缴费比例缴纳的工伤保险基金，以及通过其他形式取得的形成基金来源的款项。包括：单位缴纳的社会统筹基金收入、财政补贴收入、利息收入、其他收入。

4.基金支出：指按照国家政策规定的开支范围和开支标准从工伤保险基金中支付给参加工伤保险的人员及供养直系亲属工伤保险待遇支出及其他支出。包括工伤医疗费、伤残补助金、工亡补助金、护理费、丧葬补助费、工伤预防费用、职业康复费用和其他支出。

5.基金累计结余：指截止报告期末工伤保险基金累计结余金额。包括银行存款、财政专户、债券投资和其他。

生育保险

1.参保人数：指报告期末依据有关规定参加生育保险的职工人数。

2.基金收入：指根据国家有关规定，由参加生育保险的单位按照国家规定的缴费基数和缴费比例缴纳的生育保险基金，以及通过其他方式取得的形成基金来源的款项，包括：单位缴纳的基金收入、利息收入和其他收入。

3.基金支出：指按照国家政策规定的开支范围和开支标准，从生育保险基金中支付给参加生育保险的职工，因妊娠、分娩和计划生育手术而享受的待遇及其他支出。包括：生育津贴、医疗费用支出及其他支出。

4.基金累计结余：指截止报告期末生育保险基金累计结余金额。包括银行存款、财政专户、债券投资和其他。

离休、退休、退职人员保险福利费用　指离休、退休、退职人员实际得到的生活费用总额，包括从社会保险经办机构和单位得到的费用。

1.离休金：指按规定支付给离休人员的生活费用。

2.退休金：指按规定支付给退休人员的生活费用。

3.退职生活费：指按规定支付给退职人员的生活费用。

4.医疗卫生费：指单位直接支付给离休、退休、退职人员的医疗费、住院费以及住院伙食补助等费用。

5.其他：指离休金、退休金、退职生活费和医疗卫生费以外的其他保险福利费用，如丧葬抚恤救济费、生活补贴、物价补贴、冬季取暖补贴等。

律师　指依法取得律师执业证书，担任法律顾问，民事(刑事、行政)案件代理人、刑事案件辩护人、办理非诉讼业务，解答法律询问，代写法律事务文书等，为社会提供法律服务的人员。

公证人员　指在公证处工作的人员总称，包括公证处主任、副主任、公证员、公证员助理(助理公证员)和其他从事辅助性工作的人员。

公证文书　指公证处根据当事人申请，依照事实和法律，按照法定程序制作的，具有法律效力的司法证明文书。根据公证书用途和使用地，公证书分为国内公证书、国内经济公证书、涉外民事公证书、涉外经济公证书四类。

调解员　指在人民调解委员会担负调解民间纠纷工作的人员，包括调解委员会的委员和调解小组的调解员。该指标主要反映从事人民调解工作的人员数量。

调解民间纠纷　指调解委员会按照法律规定，根据自愿原则，用说服教育的方法调解民间发生的有关民事权利和义务争执的件数，包括调解成功数和调解未成功数。该指标主要反映人民调解委员会的工作量。

立案　指人民检察院对受理的报案、控告、举报或自首及自行发现的犯罪线索、犯罪嫌疑人进行初步调查后，认为存在职务犯罪事实和应追究刑事责任，并决定作为刑事案件进行侦查的诉讼活动，是追究犯罪的开始。该指标主要反映人民检察院依法将职务犯罪线索作为刑事案件进行侦查的诉讼活动。

大案 指贪污、贿赂案数额在5万元以上，挪用公款案数额在10万元以上，集体私分、巨额财产来源不明、隐瞒境外存款案数额在50万元以上以及按照《人民检察院直接受理的渎职、侵权重、特大案件标准(试行)》认定的案件。该指标主要反映人民检察院立案查办的职务犯罪案件中经济损失大、社会危害严重的案件。

要案 指县、处级以上干部的犯罪案件。该指标主要反映国家工作人员中县、处级以上干部因职务犯罪被人民检察院依法立案侦查的情况。

决定逮捕 指人民检察院对直接受理、自行侦查的案件，认为需要逮捕犯罪嫌疑人时，依据法律做出的逮捕决定。该指标主要反映人民检察院对直接受理的案件行使决定逮捕权的情况。

批准逮捕 指人民检察院对公安机关、国家安全机关、监狱管理机关提出逮捕的犯罪嫌疑人进行审查，根据事实，依法做出逮捕决定。该指标主要反映人民检察院对提请逮捕机关提请逮捕犯罪嫌疑人进行审查后依法做出批准逮捕决定的情况。

决定起诉 指人民检察院对公安机关、国家安全机关、监狱管理机关和检察机关内设机构反贪污贿赂部门等移送起诉的案件进行审查，根据事实，做出提起公诉的案件。该指标主要反映人民检察院对各种刑事案件向人民法院提起公诉的情况。

申诉 指经检察机关信访部门审查处理后，移送到检察机关申诉部门的申诉案件，包括不服检察机关处理决定和不服法院刑事判决和裁定的申诉的案件。

受理劳动争议案件数 指劳动争议仲裁委员会根据国家有关规定，对劳动争议当事人的申请予以审查，符合受理条件而正式立案、准备处理的劳动争议案件数。

Explanatory Notes on Main Statistical Indicators

Social Welfare Institutions refer to institutions taking care of old people without children, handicapped people and orphans. They include social welfare institutions run by civil affairs departments, children welfare institutions, social welfare institutions for mental patients, collective-owned old people's homes in rural areas, convalescent homes and community service centers with the capacity of receiving those people. This indicator reflects the input in social welfare institutions.

Number of People Taken in by Social Welfare Institutions refers to the number of old people, children, totally dependent handicapped people and mental patients taken in by social welfare institutions run by civil affairs departments and those run by collective units in urban and rural areas. This indicator reflects the capacity of social welfare institutions.

Social Welfare Enterprises are collective owned enterprises which employ the blind, deaf-mute, and other handicapped people who are able to work in cities and towns and enjoy exemption from state taxes, including welfare plants, welfare commercial services, artificial limb plants and farms, etc. This indicator reflects the preferential policies toward disabled persons.

Crude Divorce Rate refers to proportion of divorced people to the annual average population for the reference year, the formula is:

Crude Divorce rate= number of couples divorced for the reference year/annual average population x 1000 per thousand

Basic Medical Care Insurance:

1. Number of people participating in the insurance programme refers to people participating in the basic medical care insurance programme according to related regulations by the end of reference period, including number of staff and workers and retirees participating in this insurance programme.

2. Revenue of insurance programme refer to payments made by employers and individuals participating in medical care insurance programs in accordance with the basis and proportion stipulated in state regulations, and income from other sources that become source of medical insurance fund, including income of social comprehensive funds paid by employers, income from individual accounts, government financial subsidies, interest income and other income.

3. Expenses of insurance programme refer to payment made from social comprehensive funds to those retired and resigned people covered in basic medical care insurance within the scope and standards of expenditure according to related national policies, and medical care payment made from individual accounts to staff and workers and retirees, and other expenses, including medical expenses of hospital inpatients, medical expenses for outpatients and emergency patients, payment from individual accounts and other

expenditure.

4. Balance of basic medical care insurance refer to the balance of medical care insurance of social comprehensive funds and individual accounts at the end of the reference period, including bank savings, special fiscal accounts, investment in bonds and others.

Unemployment Insurance

1. Number of people covered refers to staff and workers in urban enterprises or institutions who have participated in unemployment insurance programme in line relevant policies and regulations, and other people who have participated according to local government regulations, by the end of reference period.

2. Revenue of unemployment insurance refer to payments made by employers and individuals participating in unemployment insurance programme in accordance with relevant regulations and other income contributed to this programme, including unemployment insurance premium made by employers and individuals, interest income, subsidies from higher level agencies, income as transfer from subordinate agencies, transferred income, government financial subsidies and other income.

3. Expenses of unemployment insurance refer to total expenses during the reference period to guarantee the basic livelihood of unemployed people and laid-off staff and workers and to encourage their re-employment. Included are unemployment relief, medical fees, funeral subsidies, compensation pension, training expenses, management fees for unemployment insurance agencies, subsidies to lower level agencies, expenses as transfer to higher level agencies, transferred expenditure and other expenditure.

4. Balance of unemployment insurance refer to the balance of unemployment revenue deducting unemployment expenses at the end of the reference period.

Work Injury Insurance

1. Number of people covered refers to staff and workers who have participated in work injury insurance programme in line with relevant national regulations.

2. Number of beneficiaries refers to staff and workers and their direct dependents who can, in line with relevant regulations, benefit from work injury insurance, as a result of work injury leading to disability or death of the staff/worker, or occupational disease leading to disability. Included in this category are number of injured and disabled people, number of people with occupational diseases, number of deaths at work places, and number of direct dependents.

3. Revenue of work injury insurance refer to payments made by employers participating in work injury insurance programs in accordance with the basis and proportion stipulated in state regulations, and income from other sources that become source of work injury insurance fund, including income of social comprehensive funds paid by employers, government financial subsidies, interest income and other income.

4. Expenses of work injury insurance refer to payments made from work injury insurance funds to those who participated in the work injury insurance programme and their direct dependents within the scope and standards of expenditure according to related national policies, and other expenditure, including medical fees for work injury, injury and disability subsidies, death subsidies, nursing fees, funeral subsidies, injury prevention fees, rehabilitation fees for occupational diseases and other expenditure.

5. Balance of work injury insurance refer to the balance of the work injury funds at the end of the reference period, including bank savings, special fiscal account, investment in bonds and others.

Maternity Insurance

1. Number of people covered refers to staff and workers who have participated in maternity insurance programme according to relevant regulation at the end of the reporting period.

2. Revenue of maternity insurance refers to payments made by employers participating in maternity insurance programs in accordance with the basis and proportion stipulated in state regulations, and income from other sources that become source of maternity insurance fund, including income of funds paid by employers, interest income and other income.

3. Expenses of maternity insurance refer to payments made from maternity insurance funds to staff and workers who participated in maternity insurance programme within the scope and standards of expenditure according to related national policies, expenses paid for pregnancy, child delivery or surgeries related to family planning, and other expenditure, including allowance for child bearing, medical fees and other expenditure.

4. Balance of the maternity insurance refers to the balance of the maternity insurance funds at the end of reference period, including bank savings, special fiscal account, investment in funds and others.

Insurance and Welfare Funds for Retirees refer to the total payment for living expenses actually received by retirees, including payment received from social insurance management agencies and units.

1. Pensions for retired veteran cadres refer to living expenses paid to retired veteran cadres according to related regulations.

2. Pensions for retirement refer to living expenses paid to retired staff and workers according to related regulations.

3. Living allowances for resigned staff and workers refer to living expenses paid to resigned staff and workers according to related regulation.

4. Medical care expenses refer to medical fees, hospitalization cost and per diem subsidies during hospitalizations paid by employers directly to retirees.

5. Others refer to insurance and welfare payments other than the above-mentioned payments, including funeral subsidies, living allowances, price subsidies and heating subsidies during winter.

Lawyers are certified legal workers according to law, and who are employed by legal counseling firms to act as legal advisers, agents in criminal or civil lawsuits, or defenders in criminal lawsuits, or to handle non-litigious legal affairs, to advise on matters of law or to write legal papers for others, and provide service to the public.

Notary Personnel refers to people working for notary offices including: directors, deputy director, notaries, assistant notaries, and other people providing assistance.

Notary Documents refer to the judicatory notary documents drawn up by the request of the party and are in accordance with facts and laws and following certain legal proceedings. According to usage and locality, the notary documents are divided into following 4 types: domestic notary documents, domestic economic notary documents, foreign-related civil notary documents and foreign-related economic notary documents.

Mediators refer to workers on peoples mediation committees responsible for mediating in civil disputes and cases of slight infraction of the law. They include members of the mediation committees and mediators of mediation groups. This indicator reflects the number of people engaged in meditation.

Mediation of Civil Disputes refers to number of cases made by mediation committees in mediating in civil disputes concerning civil rights and duties through persuasion and education in accordance with the provisions of law on a voluntary basis, so as to solve disputes by helping the parties involved come to an agreement and understanding, including those unsuccessful ones. This indicator reflects the workload of the mediation committees.

Acceptance of Case refers to the decision made by the people's procuratorate office on reported cases, prosecution, impeachment, surrender, self-found criminal clues or suspects after initial investigation to confirm the act of crime and to start legal proceedings of the case as criminal case.

Large Cases refer to cases involving a corruption or bribery of over 50,000 yuan, or a misappropriation of over 100,000 yuan. Cases of collectively illegal possession of public funds, unstated sources of large properties, or disguised overseas savings deposits involving 500,000 yuan, or a case that has been defined by the "Standard on Serious and Large Cases of Misconduct and Tortious that Directly Accepted by People's Procurators Office (trial)". This indicator mainly reflects number of accepted cases of job-related criminals that caused serious economic losses or extremely harmful to the society.

Key Cases refer to cases committed by government officials with a ranking of division director or county administrator. This indicator mainly reflects the recorded and spied on cases by the people's procurators offices toward government official with a ranking of division director or county administrator.

Decision on Arrest refers to decision made by people's procurators office, in accordance with laws, to arrest the suspect(s) in the cases that are accepted and to be investigated by procurators office. This indicator mainly reflects the implementation of the decision on arrest by people's procurators office.

Approval for Arrest refers to the decision made by people's procurators office, in accordance with laws and relevant facts, to approve the arrest of the suspect(s) that is proposed by the public security departments, state security departments or authority of prisons. This indicator reflects approved arrests made by people's procurators office that are proposed by related departments.

Decision on Prosecution refers to the decision made by people's procurators office, in accordance with laws and relevant facts, to institute proceedings to the people's court against the suspect(s) of criminal cases handed over by the public security departments, state security departments or authority of prisons, or by the anti-corruption departments within the procurators office. This indicator reflects the condition of the prosecutions made by people's procurators office toward the people's court.

Appeals refer to cases transferred to the appeal departments of procurator's offices after initial review by departments dealing with complaint letters and calls of the public. Included are appeals against decisions made by procurator's offices and appeals against court rules and verdicts.

Number of Labor Dispute Cases Accepted refers to the number of cases of labor dispute submitted that, after being reviewed by the labor dispute arbitration committees in line with the relevant national regulations, are accepted and registered for treatment.

Basic Pension Insurance

1.Number of staff and workers covered refer to staff and workers participating in basic pension insurance programme in line with national laws, regulations and related policies by the end of reference period, who have already had payment records in social security management agencies, including those who interrupt payment without terminating the insurance programme. Those who have registered in the programme with no payment records are not included.

2. Number of retirees participating in basic pension insurance programme refer to number of retirees participating in basic pension insurance programme by the end of reference period.

3. Revenue of basic pension insurance refer to payments made by employers and individuals participating in pension insurance programs in accordance with the basis and proportion stipulated in state regulations, and income from other sources that become source of pension insurance fund, including the premium paid by employers and staff and works, interest income, subsidies from higher level agencies, income as transfer from subordinate agencies, transferred income, government financial subsidies and other income.

4. Expenses of basic pension insurance refer to payment made to those retired and resigned people covered in pension insurance program in terms of pension or compensation within the scope and standards of expenditure according to related national policies, and expenditure occurred due to shift of the insurance relationship or adjustment of funds among agencies, including pension for resigned people, pension for retired people, pension for people quitting jobs, various subsidies, medical fees, funeral subsidies, compensation pension, management fees for social security agencies, expenses on subsidies to lower subordinates, expenses as transfer to agencies at higher level, transferred expenditure and other expenditure.

5. Balance of basic pension insurance refers to the balance of basic pension insurance at the end of the reference period after deducting expenses from revenue.

Retired or Resigned Personnel refers to people who have formally completed formalities for their retirement or quitting work and enjoy the corresponding retirement treatments.

21 开发区主要经济指标

Major Economic Indicators of Development Zone

资料整理：陶　禹

21-1 湖北省开发区经济发展基本情况(2014)

BASIC INDICATORS OF ECONOMIC DEVELOPMENT OF DEVELOPMAENT ZONE IN HUBEI PROVINCE(2014)

指 标		Item		2013	2014	增幅(%) Percentage of Increase (%)
基本情况		**Basic condition**				
开发区批准规划面积	(平方公里)	Floor Areas Approved in Development Zone	(sq.km.)	5129.18	5723.63	11.6
开发区实际占地面积	(平方公里)	Actual Land Areas of Development Zone	(sq.km.)	1995.43	2236.45	12.1
企业个数	(个)	Number of Enterprises	(unit)	86838	116489	34.1
其中：工业企业	(个)	#Those Belong to Industrial Enterprises	(unit)	30271	33420	10.4
其中：规模以上	(个)	#Enterprises above Designated Scale	(unit)	9022	10279	13.9
高新技术企业	(个)	High and New Technological Enterprises	(unit)	2257	2820	24.9
外商投资企业	(个)	Foreign Invested Enterprises	(unit)	1676	1738	3.7
从业人员	(万人)	Population of Employment	(10 000 persons)	415.41	452.32	8.9
其中：工业企业	(万人)	#Those Belong to Industrial Enterprises	(10 000 persons)	306.82	329.40	7.4
其中：规模以上	(万人)	#Those Engaged in Enterprises above Designated Scale	(10 000 persons)	235.04	255.51	8.7
主要经济指标		**Major Economic Indicators**				
规模以上工业总产值	(亿元)	Total Output Value of Enterprises above Designated Scale	(100 million Yuan)	29853.85	33951.99	13.7
规模以上工业增加值	(亿元)	Value-added of Enterprises above Designated Scale	(100 million Yuan)	8779.36	9946.15	13.3
其中：高新技术产业	(亿元)	#Value-added of High and New Technological Enterprises	(100 million Yuan)	3201.78	3637.38	13.6
规模以上工业主营业务收入	(亿元)	Total Income From Major Business of Enterprises above Designated Scale	(100 million Yuan)	28675.71	32525.21	13.4
固定资产投资总额	(亿元)	Total Value of Investment in Fixed Assets	(100 million Yuan)	9918.68	12019.52	21.2
其中：基础设施建设投资	(亿元)	#Infrastructure Investment	(100 million Yuan)	2012.94	2251.68	11.9
施工项目个数	(个)	Number of Projects under Construction	(unit)	10247	10922	6.6
其中:亿元以上项目	(个)	#the Value of the Projects is Worth More Than 100 million Yuan	(unit)	4010	4764	18.8
新开工项目	(个)	Newly Opened Projects	(unit)	5911	6082	2.9
外商投资项目	(个)	Foreign Invested Projects	(unit)	472	480	1.7
省外内资项目	(个)	Foreign-funded Projects	(unit)	3567	3747	5.0
开发区税收总额	(亿元)	Total Tax Revenue of Development Zone	(100 million Yuan)	1382.78	1587.02	14.8
招商引资总额	(亿元)	The Total Investment	(100 million yuan)	8286.03	9585.53	15.7
其中：外商投资金额	(亿美元)	#Total Value of Foreign Investment	(100 million dollars)	58.72	57.59	-1.9
出口总额	(亿美元)	Total Value of Export	(100 million dollars)	180.45	212.08	17.5

21-2 湖北省130家开发区主要指标(2014)

开发区名称	Name of Development Zone	实际开发面积(平方公里) Actual Land Areas of Development Zone (sq. km)	
		2013	2014
湖北省	**Hubei Province**	**1995.43**	**2236.45**
武汉市	**Wuhan**	**449.73**	**475.14**
武汉江岸经济开发区	Wuhan Jiang'an Economic Development Zone	3.31	3.31
武汉江汉经济开发区	Wuhan Jianghan Economic Development Zone	0.70	1.56
武汉硚口经济开发区	Wuhan Qiaokou Economic Development Zone	1.14	1.14
武汉汉阳经济开发区	Wuhan Hanyang Economic Development Zone	8.00	12
武汉武昌经济开发区	Wuhan Wuchang Economic Development Zone	2.34	2.34
武汉青山经济开发区	Wuhan Qingshan Economic Development Zone	6.70	10
武汉洪山经济开发区	Wuhan Hongshan Economic Development Zone	0.27	0.7
武汉临空港经济技术开发区	Wuhan Linkonggang Economic and Technology Development Zone	116.86	121
武汉汉南经济开发区	Wuhan Hannan Economic Development Zone	12.50	15.13
武汉蔡甸经济开发区	Wuhan Caidian Economic Development Zone	23.90	23.9
武汉江夏经济开发区	Wuhan Jiangxia Economic Development Zone	100.43	105
武汉盘龙城经济开发区	Wuhan Panlongcheng Economic Development Zone	20.00	20
武汉阳逻经济开发区	Wuhan Yangluo Economic Development Zone	30.88	30.88
武汉经济技术开发区	Wuhan Economic and Technology Development Zone	81.70	79.5
武汉东湖新技术产业开发区	Wuhan East Lake New Technology Industrial Development Zone	48.40	60.24
黄石市	**Huangshi**	**139.66**	**142.59**
湖北黄石港工业园区	Hubei Huangshi Port Industrial Park	1.60	2.2
湖北黄石新港工业园区	Hubei Huangshi New Port Industrial Park	11.70	12.2
湖北西塞山工业园区	Hubei Xisaishan Industrial Park	10.20	11
湖北下陆长乐山工业园区	Hubei Xialu Changleshan Industrial Park	11.60	12
黄石经济技术开发区	Huangshi Economic and Technology Development Zone	55.00	55
湖北阳新经济开发区	Hubei Yangxin Economic Development Zone	12.00	12
湖北大冶经济开发区	Hubei Daye Economic Development Zone	31.26	31.89
大冶灵成工业园	Daye Lingcheng Industrial Park	6.30	6.3
十堰市	**Shiyan**	**58.84**	**87.59**
十堰经济技术开发区	Shiyan Economic and Technology Development Zone	15.00	40
湖北郧阳区经济开发区	Hubei Yunyang County Economic Development Zone	17.38	18.76
湖北郧西工业园区	Hubei West Yun Industrial Park	1.53	1.53
湖北竹山经济开发区	Hubei Zhushan Economic Development Zone	10.00	10
湖北竹溪工业园区	Hubei Zhuxi Industrial Park	1.80	2.1
湖北房县工业园区	Hubei Fang County Industrial Park	3.53	4.2
湖北丹江口经济开发区	Hubei Danjiangkou Economic Development Zone	9.60	11
宜昌市	**Yichang**	**160.19**	**206.05**
湖北西陵经济开发区	Hubei Xiling Economic Development Zone	4.00	4
湖北伍家岗工业园区	Hubei Wujiagang Industrial Park	4.00	4
湖北点军工业园区	Hubei Dianjun Industrial Park	1.50	5.4
湖北夷陵经济开发区	Hubei Yiling Economic Development Zone	25.00	28
湖北远安工业园区	Hubei Yuan'an Industrial Park	12.30	15
湖北兴山经济开发区	Hubei Xingshan Economic Development Zone	2.20	2.6
湖北秭归经济开发区	Hubei Zigui Economic Development Zone	6.00	6
湖北长阳经济开发区	Hubei Changyang Economic Development Zone	2.76	2.8
湖北五峰工业园区	Hubei Wufeng Industrial Park	2.30	2.3
湖北五峰民族工业园	Hubei Wufeng National Industrial Park	0.71	0.79
宜昌高新技术产开发区	Yichang High-tech Industrial Development Zone	69.10	71.2
湖北宜都工业园区	Hubei Yidu Industrial Park	8.00	10.6
湖北当阳经济开发区	Hubei Dangyang Economic Development Zone	24.00	26
湖北枝江经济开发区	Hubei Zhijiang Economic Development Zone	20.60	25.52
枝江安福寺工业园	Zhijiang Anfu Temple Industrial Park	1.82	1.84

MAIN INDICATORS OF 130 DEVELOPMENT ZONE IN HUBEI(2014)

企业个数(个) Number of Enterprises (unit)		其中：规模以上工业企业(个) Among which, Industrial Enterprises above Designated Size (unit)		高新技术企业(个) Number of High and New Technological Enterprises (unit)		从业人员(万人) Population of Employment (10 000 persons)	
2013	2014	2013	2014	2013	2014	2013	2014
86838	**116489**	**9022**	**10279**	**2257**	**2820**	**415.41**	**452.32**
36911	**58266**	**1564**	**1772**	**864**	**1146**	**111.66**	**120.91**
227	183	33	28	12	11	1.16	1.08
394	399	15	15	3	3	1.62	2.36
288	344	45	29	7	9	4.41	4.46
930	921	64	61	24	24	3.35	3.77
275	293	29	29	15	15	1.99	2.04
310	321	95	98	11	15	3.63	3.67
168	151	16	15	23	24	0.85	0.84
8198	8305	61	262	55	61	22.58	25.82
473	489	126	131	11	12	3.41	3.59
295	326	85	79	8	12	3.10	3.15
675	717	168	168	45	45	6.09	6.05
562	629	40	39			3.98	4.71
123	136	57	66	11	12	2.49	2.75
3650	19037	202	203	71	89	17.32	18.80
21047	26735	638	662	582	832	40.93	43.85
6214	**7050**	**386**	**485**	**170**	**138**	**24.72**	**25.58**
39	43	7	11	8	12	0.48	0.49
24	30	13	13		2	0.19	0.20
303	310	62	71	10	10	3.50	3.60
155	158	22	26	8	8	2.01	2.02
3701	4487	137	145	49	53	7.86	8.46
374	392	46	54	6	12	3.40	3.41
1525	1569	138	180	31	35	5.93	6.24
93	61	83	26	58	6	1.35	1.16
4136	**4740**	**529**	**610**	**87**	**110**	**16.85**	**18.97**
2977	3423	232	254	51	67	8.14	9.49
197	235	73	82	14	12	2.38	2.76
29	52	26	30		3	0.28	0.36
191	198	26	28	5	5	0.58	0.62
77	103	38	39	2	3	1.70	1.80
139	186	61	71	7	11	0.98	1.10
526	543	73	106	8	9	2.79	2.84
8690	**9994**	**980**	**1099**	**154**	**224**	**36.61**	**38.28**
390	476	12	11	6	6	0.88	0.90
92	92	20	27	9	10	1.55	1.55
15	18	13	16	7	7	0.58	0.48
782	835	119	143	16	23	4.53	4.81
152	166	85	90	14	16	2.85	2.91
31	46	13	17	3	3	0.62	0.74
199	208	65	70	5	8	1.93	2.01
77	82	47	49	7	9	1.07	1.14
280	285	20	20	2	5	1.10	1.20
7	10	3	4			0.38	0.40
2435	2765	253	330	82	120	11.70	12.10
306	347	151	172	22	41	3.19	3.24
699	851	147	171	28	37	5.16	5.53
4076	4293	165	173	12	16	6.25	6.65
49	51	29	30	1	1	1.22	1.22

21-2 续表 1 continued

开发区名称	Name of Development Zone	实际开发面积(平方公里) Actual Land Areas of Development Zone (sq. km)	
		2013	2014
襄阳市	**Xianyang**	**171.3**	**196.5**
襄阳高新技术产业开发区	Xiangyang High-tech Industrial Development Zone	33.2	37.8
襄阳鱼梁州经济开发区	Xiangyang Yuliangzhou Economic Development Zone	2.0	2.0
襄阳经济技术开发区	Xiangyang Economic Development Zone	60.0	70.0
湖北襄城经济开发区	Hubei Xiangcheng Economic Development Zone	15.0	16.0
湖北樊城经济开发区	Hubei Fancheng Economic Development Zone	6.2	7.4
湖北襄州经济开发区	Hubei Xiangzhou Economic Development Zone	18.0	22.0
襄阳工业园	Xiangyang Industrial Park	3.0	3.0
湖北南漳经济开发区	Hubei Nanzhang Economic Development Zone	16.2	19.2
湖北谷城经济开发区	Hubei Gucheng Economic Development Zone	13.0	20.0
谷城石花经济开发区	Gucheng Shihua Economic Development Zone	8.0	10.0
湖北保康经济开发区	Hubei Baokang Economic Development Zone	9.0	10.0
湖北老河口经济开发区	Hubei Laohekou Economic Development Zone	27.0	27.0
湖北枣阳经济开发区	Hubei Zaoyang Economic Development Zone	6.5	6.5
枣阳吴店工业园	Zaoyang Wudian Industrial Park	3.0	3.5
湖北宜城经济开发区	Hubei Yicheng Economic Development Zone	11.2	12.1
鄂州市	**E'zhou**	**55.8**	**61.7**
湖北鄂州花湖经济开发区	Hubei E'Zhou Huahu Economic Development Zone	10.5	12.8
鄂州葛店经济技术开发区	E'Zhou Gedian Economic and Technology Development Zone	27.3	28.9
湖北鄂州经济开发区	Hubei E'Zhou Economic Development Zone	18.0	20.0
荆门市	**Jingmen**	**85.8**	**95.7**
湖北东宝工业园区	Hubei Dongbao Industrial Park	12.0	13.6
荆门高新技术产业开发区	Hubei Jingmen High-tech Industrial Development Zone	23.2	24.0
湖北荆门化工循环产业园	Hubei Jingmen Chemical Recycling Development Zone	8.0	10.4
湖北京山经济开发区	Hubei Jingshan Economic Development Zone	14.0	14.0
湖北屈家岭经济开发区	Hubei Qujialing Economic Development Zone	3.0	7.0
湖北沙洋经济开发区	Hubei Shayang Economic Development Zone	28.5	30.5
湖北钟祥经济开发区	Hubei Zhongxiang Economic Development Zone	18.0	20.0
钟祥胡集经济开发区	Zhongxiang Huji Economic Development Zone	8.5	9.0
孝感市	**Xiaogan**	**165.3**	**171.2**
孝感高新技术产业开发区	Xiaogan high-tech Industrial Development Zone	13.0	13.0
湖北孝南经济开发区	Hubei Xiaonan Economic Development Zone	30.0	30.5
湖北孝昌经济开发区	Hubei Xiaochang Economic Development Zone	10.0	12.0
湖北大悟经济开发区	Hubei Dawu Economic Development Zone	17.3	17.3
湖北云梦经济开发区	Hubei Yunmeng Economic Development Zone	20.1	21.3
湖北应城经济开发区	Hubei Yingcheng Economic Development Zone	19.0	20.0
湖北安陆经济开发区	Hubei Anlu Economic Development Zone	36.6	36.6
湖北汉川经济开发区	Hubei Hanchuan Economic Development Zone	19.2	20.5
荆州市	**Jingzhou**	**221.4**	**251.9**
湖北沙市经济开发区	Hubei Shashi Economic Development Zone	35.0	38.0
湖北荆州城南经济开发区	Jingzhou Chengnan Economic Development Zone	14.0	14.1
荆州经济技术开发区	Jingzhou Economic and Technology Development Zone	54.0	55.7
湖北公安经济开发区	Hubei Gong'an Economic Development Zone	13.8	17.6
湖北监利经济开发区	Hubei Jianli Economic Development Zone	38.4	49.2
湖北江陵经济开发区	Hubei Jiangling Economic Development Zone	14.8	14.8
湖北石首经济开发区	Hubei Shishou Economic Development Zone	22.0	28.4
湖北洪湖经济开发区	Hubei Honghu Economic Development Zone	11.4	13.1
洪湖府场经济开发区	Honghu Fuchang Economic Development Zone	12.0	15.0
湖北松滋经济开发区	Hubei Songzi Economic Development Zone	6.0	6.0
黄冈市	**Huanggang**	**224.6**	**250.7**
湖北黄冈经济开发区	Hubei Huanggang Economic Development Zone	20.3	27.3

企业个数(个) Number of Enterprises (unit)		其中：规模以上工业企业(个) Among which, Industrial Enterprises above Designated Size (unit)		高新技术企业(个) Number of High and New Technological Enterprises (unit)		从业人员(万人) Population of Employment (10 000 persons)	
2013	2014	2013	2014	2013	2014	2013	2014
9834	**12120**	**1247**	**1390**	**257**	**330**	**54.22**	**58.08**
5909	7546	262	330	117	147	13.50	14.20
38	67					0.10	0.12
653	785	120	155	27	33	10.23	10.52
212	250	42	56	6	7	2.50	2.60
326	345	108	113	23	24	3.78	4.09
465	546	118	121	25	27	7.35	7.52
218	273	23	18	2	2	2.60	2.90
101	112	79	82	3	5	1.60	1.67
1152	1358	95	100	10	22	6.30	6.94
255	280	57	52	7	12	2.70	2.90
40	49	27	32	6	8	1.11	1.21
298	358	170	192	13	24	3.84	3.98
446	489	141	151	37	42	3.87	4.25
262	302	66	66	4	4	2.64	2.87
112	145	59	77	4	6	2.33	2.83
3408	**3580**	**385**	**386**	**42**	**64**	**10.03**	**11.15**
316	327	55	54	5	15	1.50	1.45
2852	2945	255	261	28	28	7.52	8.58
240	308	75	71	9	21	1.01	1.12
1209	**1434**	**548**	**667**	**72**	**78**	**20.07**	**21.50**
126	148	88	94	10	13	3.00	3.20
434	482	254	292	45	52	6.92	7.72
43	50	25	27	3	5	0.40	0.63
347	381	59	88	14	18	2.52	2.69
32	42	9	17	1	1	0.13	0.20
133	159	52	73	11	15	2.50	2.70
238	328	108	122	12	16	5.60	6.30
46	69	27	34	3	5	1.69	1.85
2856	**3310**	**657**	**799**	**127**	**150**	**24.78**	**25.74**
1631	1924	339	394	81	95	10.58	10.62
291	362	84	131	14	17	4.50	5.10
213	236	35	35	2	5	2.35	2.22
66	60	27	28	3	3	1.50	1.50
259	285	100	113	15	17	7.90	8.13
160	160	127	134	12	18	3.40	3.41
283	352	52	61	24	28	4.12	4.26
663	738	204	281	17	19	6.23	7.14
2966	**3473**	**708**	**809**	**83**	**95**	**32.83**	**36.64**
168	184	73	89	4	5	2.70	3.30
702	712	120	132	6	6	6.15	6.51
926	1213	134	157	41	34	7.50	7.88
251	378	33	42	5	7	2.65	3.15
77	85	77	85	2	4	1.50	1.70
88	99	26	35		7	1.15	1.13
74	78	73	76	5	7	1.35	1.52
201	208	40	43	5	6	2.54	2.71
347	352	46	48	5	6	3.46	3.53
132	164	86	102	10	13	3.83	5.21
3222	**3647**	**768**	**828**	**236**	**263**	**30.64**	**35.79**
1297	1336	177	182	67	73	8.12	10.68

21-2 续表 2 continued

开发区名称	Name of Development Zone	实际开发面积(平方公里) Actual Land Areas of Development Zone (sq. km)	
		2013	2014
湖北黄州火车站经济开发区	Hubei Huangzhou Railway Station Economic Development Zone	8.0	8.5
黄州工业园	Huangzhou Industrial Park	19.0	20.0
湖北龙感湖工业园区	Hubei Longganhu Industrial Park	7.5	8.2
湖北团风经济开发区	Hubei Tuanfeng Economic Development Zone	7.8	8.0
湖北红安经济开发区	Hubei Hong'an Economic Development Zone	30.0	30.0
湖北罗田经济开发区	Hubei Luotian Economic Development Zone	8.7	9.0
湖北英山经济开发区	Hubei Yingshan Economic Development Zone	10.8	14.6
湖北浠水经济开发区	Hubei Xishui Economic Development Zone	13.0	16.0
湖北蕲春李时珍医药工业园区	Hubei Qichun Li Shizhen Pharmaceutical Industrial Park	14.0	18.0
蕲春经济开发区	Qichun Economic Development Zone	17.0	17.0
湖北黄梅经济开发区	Hubei Huangmei Economic Development Zone	20.8	24.6
湖北麻城经济开发区	Hubei Macheng Economic Development Zone	35.0	35.0
湖北武穴经济开发区	Hubei Wuxue Economic Development Zone	12.7	14.5
咸宁市	**Xianning**	**84.3**	**99.4**
湖北咸安经济开发区	Hubei Xian'an Economic Development Zone	8.6	9.9
湖北嘉鱼经济开发区	Hubei Jiayu Economic Development Zone	11.5	14.5
湖北通城经济开发区	Hubei Tongcheng Economic Development Zone	5.0	6.0
湖北崇阳工业园区	Hubei Chongyang Industrial Park	7.6	8.4
湖北通山经济开发区	Hubei Tongshan Economic Development Zone	15.0	18.0
湖北咸宁经济开发区	Hubei Xianning Economic Development Zone	16.6	16.6
湖北赤壁经济开发区	Hubei Chibi Economic Development Zone	12.0	18.0
湖北赤壁蒲纺工业园区	Hubei Chibi Puqi Textile Industrial Park	8.0	8.0
随州市	**Suizhou**	**50.4**	**58.9**
湖北随州经济开发区	Hubei Suizhou Economic Development Zone	19.0	25.0
湖北曾都经济开发区	Hubei Zengdu Economic Development Zone	18.0	20.0
湖北随县经济开发区	Hubei Sui County Economic Development Zone	4.8	4.8
湖北广水经济开发区	Hubei Guangshui Economic Development Zone	8.6	9.1
恩施自治州	**Enshi Autonomous Prefecture**	**48.1**	**52.6**
湖北恩施经济开发区	Hubei Enshi Economic Development Zone	14.7	14.7
湖北恩施州经济开发区	Hubei Enshi Prefecture Economic Development Zone	4.3	5.1
湖北利川经济开发区	Hubei Lichuan Economic Development Zone	4.1	5.0
湖北建始工业园区	Hubei Jianshi Industrial Park	2.0	4.2
湖北巴东经济开发区	Hubei Badong Economic Development Zone	8.0	8.0
湖北宣恩工业园区	Hubei Xuan'en Industrial Park	1.7	2.1
湖北咸丰工业园区	Hubei Xianfeng Industrial Park	5.8	6.1
湖北来凤经济开发区	Hubei Laifeng Economic Development Zone	5.5	5.5
湖北鹤峰经济开发区	Hubei Hefeng Economic Development Zone	2.0	2.0
仙桃市	**Xiantao**	**25.9**	**27.5**
湖北仙桃经济开发区	Hubei Xiantao Economic Development Zone	25.9	27.5
仙桃彭场工业园	Xiantao Pengchang Industrial Park	3.0	6.0
潜江市	**Qianjiang**	**22.4**	**23.9**
湖北潜江经济开发区	Hubei Qianjiang Economic Development Zone	5.0	6.5
潜江张金经济开发区	Qianjiang Zhangjin Economic Development Zone	2.4	2.4
潜江园林经济开发区	Qianjiang Yuanlin Economic Development Zone	15.0	15.0
天门市	**Tianmen**	**30.8**	**33.3**
湖北天门经济开发区	Hubei Tianmen Economic Development Zone	30.8	33.3
神农架盘水生态产业园区		1	1.8

企业个数(个) Number of Enterprises (unit)		其中：规模以上工业企业(个) Among which, Industrial Enterprises above Designated Size (unit)		高新技术企业(个) Number of High and New Technological Enterprises (unit)		从业人员(万人) Population of Employment (10 000 persons)	
2013	2014	2013	2014	2013	2014	2013	2014
45	47	12	12	4	4	0.28	0.29
55	58	25	26	10	10	0.81	0.91
106	111	24	24	3	4	0.95	1.07
78	81	22	28	10	10	1.25	1.21
250	381	127	130	40	40	5.10	5.20
69	73	32	33	12	15	0.60	0.69
79	88	26	30	18	20	1.23	1.52
420	500	56	63	24	28	3.00	3.40
102	138	27	30	5	5	1.30	1.63
63	97	23	25	2	2	1.38	1.56
381	396	78	84	10	12	2.51	2.85
97	128	51	57	22	28	1.90	2.34
180	213	88	104	9	11	2.21	2.44
963	**1037**	**435**	**514**	**60**	**84**	**11.42**	**12.36**
138	151	70	79	10	11	1.51	1.63
142	143	104	115	6	9	1.73	1.80
78	87	45	54	6	6	2.93	3.25
112	128	54	65	12	17	1.30	1.45
53	60	17	33	5	5	0.77	0.81
280	290	42	59	9	18	2.00	2.20
98	120	74	84	12	18	0.55	0.62
62	58	29	25			0.63	0.60
938	**1503**	**188**	**220**	**43**	**57**	**6.75**	**9.44**
454	958	61	70	12	20	2.90	4.93
221	265	73	78	18	21	2.50	2.80
31	39	13	25	3	5	0.19	0.43
232	241	41	45	10	11	1.16	1.28
775	**875**	**204**	**237**	**13**	**19**	**9.78**	**10.75**
336	338	34	39	1	7	2.18	2.20
27	39	3	4	1	1	1.20	1.21
44	60	20	21	1	1	0.41	0.52
26	32	18	24	3	3	0.52	0.58
120	150	11	16	2	2	0.90	1.20
58	69	16	23			1.15	1.45
68	86	41	48	3	3	1.12	1.28
72	76	43	43	1	1	1.65	1.68
24	25	18	19	1	1	0.65	0.63
2523	**3235**	**268**	**287**	**26**	**33**	**11.96**	**13.30**
2523	3235	268	287	26	33	11.96	13.30
230	230	50	55	2	2	3.85	4.85
1865	**1871**	**47**	**54**	**13**	**14**	**5.83**	**5.77**
93	88	18	21	6	6	1.58	1.46
117	122	14	15	4	4	2.11	2.12
1655	1661	15	18	3	4	2.14	2.19
306	**331**	**106**	**117**	**9**	**13**	**7.24**	**8.01**
306	331	106	117	9	13	7.24	8.01
22	23	2	5	1	2	0.02	0.05

21-2 续表 3 continued

开发区名称	Name of Development Zone	其中：规模以上工业企业(万人) Among which, Industrial Enterprises above Designated Size (10 000 persons) 2013	2014
湖北省	**Hubei Province**	**235.04**	**255.51**
武汉市	**Wuhan**	**62.04**	**63.18**
武汉江岸经济开发区	Wuhan Jiang'an Economic Development Zone	0.56	0.60
武汉江汉经济开发区	Wuhan Jianghan Economic Development Zone	0.27	0.27
武汉硚口经济开发区	Wuhan Qiaokou Economic Development Zone	1.50	1.34
武汉汉阳经济开发区	Wuhan Hanyang Economic Development Zone	1.64	1.58
武汉武昌经济开发区	Wuhan Wuchang Economic Development Zone	1.07	1.09
武汉青山经济开发区	Wuhan Qingshan Economic Development Zone	3.05	3.06
武汉洪山经济开发区	Wuhan Hongshan Economic Development Zone	0.29	0.28
武汉临空港经济技术开发区	Wuhan Linkonggang Economic and Technology Development Zone	5.51	5.76
武汉汉南经济开发区	Wuhan Hannan Economic Development Zone	1.47	1.56
武汉蔡甸经济开发区	Wuhan Caidian Economic Development Zone	2.30	1.78
武汉江夏经济开发区	Wuhan Jiangxia Economic Development Zone	4.02	4.00
武汉盘龙城经济开发区	Wuhan Panlongcheng Economic Development Zone	0.74	0.82
武汉阳逻经济开发区	Wuhan Yangluo Economic Development Zone	1.91	2.15
武汉经济技术开发区	Wuhan Economic and Technology Development Zone	10.32	11.20
武汉东湖新技术产业开发区	Wuhan East Lake New Technology Industrial Development Zone	30.71	31.02
黄石市	**Huangshi**	**13.40**	**13.75**
湖北黄石港工业园区	Hubei Huangshi Port Industrial Park	0.22	0.26
湖北黄石新港工业园区	Hubei Huangshi New Port Industrial Park	0.16	0.17
湖北西塞山工业园区	Hubei Xisaishan Industrial Park	1.48	1.52
湖北下陆长乐山工业园区	Hubei Xialu Changleshan Industrial Park	1.93	1.93
黄石经济技术开发区	Huangshi Economic and Technology Development Zone	2.37	2.58
湖北阳新经济开发区	Hubei Yangxin Economic Development Zone	2.80	2.81
湖北大冶经济开发区	Hubei Daye Economic Development Zone	4.60	4.72
大冶灵成工业园	Daye Lingcheng Industrial Park	1.16	0.75
十堰市	**Shiyan**	**8.85**	**10.65**
十堰经济技术开发区	Shiyan Economic and Technology Development Zone	4.16	5.37
湖北郧阳区经济开发区	Hubei Yun County Economic Development Zone	1.84	2.38
湖北郧西工业园区	Hubei West Yun Industrial Park	0.28	
湖北竹山经济开发区	Hubei Zhushan Economic Development Zone	0.26	0.28
湖北竹溪工业园区	Hubei Zhuxi Industrial Park	0.38	0.40
湖北房县工业园区	Hubei Fang County Industrial Park	0.51	0.76
湖北丹江口经济开发区	Hubei Danjiangkou Economic Development Zone	1.42	1.46
宜昌市	**Yichang**	**25.10**	**26.96**
湖北西陵经济开发区	Hubei Xiling Economic Development Zone	0.18	0.20
湖北伍家岗工业园区	Hubei Wujiagang Industrial Park	0.50	1.00
湖北点军工业园区	Hubei Dianjun Industrial Park	0.46	0.36
湖北夷陵经济开发区	Hubei Yiling Economic Development Zone	2.82	2.90
湖北远安工业园区	Hubei Yuan'an Industrial Park	2.21	2.32
湖北兴山经济开发区	Hubei Xingshan Economic Development Zone	0.46	0.51
湖北秭归经济开发区	Hubei Zigui Economic Development Zone	1.22	1.29
湖北长阳经济开发区	Hubei Changyang Economic Development Zone	0.75	0.79
湖北五峰工业园区	Hubei Wufeng Industrial Park	0.50	0.40
湖北五峰民族工业园	Hubei Wufeng National Industrial Park	0.30	0.31
宜昌高新技术产开发区	Yichang High-tech Industrial Development Zone	9.60	11.00
湖北宜都工业园区	Hubei Yidu Industrial Park	2.36	2.89
湖北当阳经济开发区	Hubei Dangyang Economic Development Zone	4.05	4.25
湖北枝江经济开发区	Hubei Zhijiang Economic Development Zone	4.05	4.30
枝江安福寺工业园	Zhijiang Anfu Temple Industrial Park	1.14	1.14

规模以上工业增加值(亿元) Above-scale Industrial Added Value (100 million Yuan)		规模以上工业主营业务收入(亿元) Scale Industrial Core Business Revenue (100 million Yuan)		固定资产投资总额(亿元) Total Investment In Fixed Assets (100 million Yuan)		施工项目个数(个) Number of Construction Project (unit)	
2013	2014	2013	2014	2013	2014	2013	2014
8779.36	**9946.15**	**28675.71**	**32525.21**	**9918.68**	**12019.52**	**10247**	**10922**
2830.37	**3199.06**	**9288.65**	**10510.54**	**1996.52**	**2341.14**	**1344**	**1381**
9.00	9.60	49.00	51.70	12.76	12.23	5	3
12.44	11.08	41.00	35.73	6.60	5.52	6	6
30.60	24.70	95.00	90.00	18.00	15	9	10
61.82	67.45	208.12	221.01	80.80	71.9	20	25
44.28	44.52	182.55	189.46	5.60	1.22	2	1
33.30	36.73	120.19	135.78	24.75	29.31	33	36
6.07	7.21	23.45	27.05	4.53	4.5	5	5
284.04	330.90	559.74	599.63	345.61	418.22	240	213
31.77	32.72	109.13	114.03	43.17	30.53	21	25
139.30	187.00	447.00	531.00	138.00	212	57	68
136.90	81.05	466.20	273.40	353.63	335.06	107	127
30.33	36.13	101.62	122.41	36.73	49.67	62	36
109.86	136.18	383.94	418.65	172.70	220.2	63	122
683.40	755.60	2027.90	2310.20	350.00	461.7	287	292
1173.00	1486.00	4485.00	5562.00	534.33	626.13	466	451
398.70	**445.90**	**1936.27**	**2148.31**	**717.05**	**851.08**	**602**	**570**
1.84	2.26	5.08	5.86	2.50	4.85	20	24
6.69	6.31	19.35	19.47	29.35	21.06	17	18
68.00	74.00	260.00	248.00	36.91	43	82	52
124.54	123.00	916.79	1067.00	39.01	41	27	20
242.54	282.80	754.86	909.26	345.59	442.36	212	221
26.75	32.35	72.53	93.18	54.20	62.4	58	45
126.78	162.08	379.53	468.68	154.89	178.22	165	171
28.80	34.42	86.64	107.32	54.60	58.19	21	19
345.28	**394.89**	**1124.81**	**1253.65**	**427.92**	**566.79**	**597**	**686**
221.39	268.02	710.31	858.17	208.56	312.03	203	232
36.66	39.32	99.52	127.82	46.71	58.91	96	107
4.82	5.50	10.68	17.33	12.66	13.23	11	13
11.83	12.81	32.20	35.93	31.71	35.81	43	40
10.08	10.50	26.50	27.30	15.00	19	13	16
13.80	16.30	39.10	41.60	75.13	78.57	146	189
31.70	42.44	107.50	145.50	38.15	49.24	85	89
1065.76	**1181.93**	**3295.54**	**3645.92**	**1310.42**	**1544.31**	**1247**	**1348**
5.69	6.70	14.32	18.30	25.00	26.6	47	52
13.01	14.02	13.49	4.50	29.60	30	8	5
14.19	15.52	60.26	64.48	2.20	4.02	4	5
202.25	200.11	624.95	706.16	163.14	201.4	111	140
74.32	84.93	195.90	225.69	72.36	90.35	90	93
11.10	12.54	52.20	59.51	9.07	11.7	26	34
26.43	30.35	67.53	77.58	31.75	33.01	49	60
20.57	23.28	62.34	62.93	43.63	49.95	106	74
4.53	4.88	14.20	16.43	12.23	21.36	29	44
0.91	2.53	3.17	9.54	10.29	10.51	6	7
495.18	505.00	1662.00	1950.00	476.00	582	387	396
237.66	275.61	691.82	798.32	221.15	273.69	234	315
131.01	148.77	397.37	457.22	183.11	208.37	151	170
151.70	172.66	475.50	529.18	182.00	205.6	146	129
16.65	18.73	54.19	60.98	23.69	34.72	16	16

21-2 续表 4 continued

开发区名称	Name of Development Zone	其中：规模以上工业企业(万人) Among which, Industrial Enterprises above Designated Size (10 000 persons)	
		2013	2014
襄阳市	**Xianyang**	**30.20**	**35.01**
襄阳高新技术产业开发区	Xiangyang High-tech Industrial Development Zone	10.10	12.50
襄阳鱼梁州经济开发区	Xiangyang Yuliangzhou Economic Development Zone		
襄阳经济技术开发区	Xiangyang Economic Development Zone	5.96	6.03
湖北襄城经济开发区	Hubei Xiangcheng Economic Development Zone	1.30	1.40
湖北樊城经济开发区	Hubei Fancheng Economic Development Zone	2.57	2.80
湖北襄州经济开发区	Hubei Xiangzhou Economic Development Zone	4.12	4.32
襄阳工业园	Xiangyang Industrial Park	0.41	0.63
湖北南漳经济开发区	Hubei Nanzhang Economic Development Zone	1.48	1.52
湖北谷城经济开发区	Hubei Gucheng Economic Development Zone	2.00	2.20
谷城石花经济开发区	Gucheng Shihua Economic Development Zone	1.50	1.70
湖北保康经济开发区	Hubei Baokang Economic Development Zone	0.48	0.55
湖北老河口经济开发区	Hubei Laohekou Economic Development Zone	1.82	2.13
湖北枣阳经济开发区	Hubei Zaoyang Economic Development Zone	2.03	2.41
枣阳吴店工业园	Zaoyang Wudian Industrial Park	1.02	1.11
湖北宜城经济开发区	Hubei Yicheng Economic Development Zone	1.37	1.74
鄂州市	**E'zhou**	**4.42**	**4.64**
湖北鄂州花湖经济开发区	Hubei E'Zhou Huahu Economic Development Zone	0.65	0.59
鄂州葛店经济技术开发区	E'Zhou Gedian Economic and Technology Development Zone	3.16	3.34
湖北鄂州经济开发区	Hubei E'Zhou Economic Development Zone	0.61	0.71
荆门市	**Jingmen**	**13.88**	**14.78**
湖北东宝工业园区	Hubei Dongbao Industrial Park	2.18	2.41
荆门高新技术产业开发区	Hubei Jingmen High-tech Industrial Development Zone	5.54	7.41
湖北荆门化工循环产业园	Hubei Jingmen Chemical Recycling Development Zone	0.31	0.44
湖北京山经济开发区	Hubei Jingshan Economic Development Zone	1.60	1.71
湖北屈家岭经济开发区	Hubei Qujialing Economic Development Zone	0.12	0.18
湖北沙洋经济开发区	Hubei Shayang Economic Development Zone	1.60	1.70
湖北钟祥经济开发区	Hubei Zhongxiang Economic Development Zone	3.40	3.85
钟祥胡集经济开发区	Zhongxiang Huji Economic Development Zone	1.26	1.35
孝感市	**Xiaogan**	**15.13**	**16.49**
孝感高新技术产业开发区	Xiaogan high-tech Industrial Development Zone	7.59	8.21
湖北孝南经济开发区	Hubei Xiaonan Economic Development Zone	1.25	1.40
湖北孝昌经济开发区	Hubei Xiaochang Economic Development Zone	1.28	1.31
湖北大悟经济开发区	Hubei Dawu Economic Development Zone	1.00	1.00
湖北云梦经济开发区	Hubei Yunmeng Economic Development Zone	2.54	3.02
湖北应城经济开发区	Hubei Yingcheng Economic Development Zone	2.51	2.51
湖北安陆经济开发区	Hubei Anlu Economic Development Zone	1.12	1.29
湖北汉川经济开发区	Hubei Hanchuan Economic Development Zone	4.14	4.68
荆州市	**Jingzhou**	**12.39**	**15.28**
湖北沙市经济开发区	Hubei Shashi Economic Development Zone	1.60	2.20
湖北荆州城南经济开发区	Jingzhou Chengnan Economic Development Zone	1.38	1.91
荆州经济技术开发区	Jingzhou Economic and Technology Development Zone	2.90	3.28
湖北公安经济开发区	Hubei Gong'an Economic Development Zone	0.78	1.17
湖北监利经济开发区	Hubei Jianli Economic Development Zone	1.50	1.70
湖北江陵经济开发区	Hubei Jiangling Economic Development Zone	0.45	0.58
湖北石首经济开发区	Hubei Shishou Economic Development Zone	1.34	1.51
湖北洪湖经济开发区	Hubei Honghu Economic Development Zone	0.66	0.67
洪湖府场经济开发区	Honghu Fuchang Economic Development Zone	0.44	0.47
湖北松滋经济开发区	Hubei Songzi Economic Development Zone	1.34	1.79
黄冈市	**Huanggang**	**16.76**	**18.25**
湖北黄冈经济开发区	Hubei Huanggang Economic Development Zone	3.46	3.81

规模以上工业增加值(亿元) Above-scale Industrial Added Value (100 million Yuan)		规模以上工业主营业务收入(亿元) Scale Industrial Core Business Revenue (100 million Yuan)		固定资产投资总额(亿元) Total Investment In Fixed Assets (100 million Yuan)		施工项目个数(个) Number of Construction Project (unit)	
2013	2014	2013	2014	2013	2014	2013	2014
1407.58	**1605.18**	**4205.93**	**4772.09**	**1570.86**	**1794.29**	**1174**	**1136**
569.10	661.20	1636.20	1850.30	550.00	680.5	278	305
					0.18		1
283.90	285.56	787.78	878.91	203.12	229.2	94	101
51.20	52.20	116.00	119.00	20.50	21.4	19	21
62.00	68.00	193.00	213.00	64.00	86	72	77
117.56	133.15	357.47	407.77	203.12	229.2	94	101
16.30	25.80	93.75	101.36	42.27	48.65	18	14
45.10	51.86	118.90	146.92	70.80	90.03	51	64
74.20	87.79	158.99	243.89	94.32	105.21	115	118
76.00	86.90	259.98	277.60	51.00	57	51	56
20.55	23.12	40.29	43.71	30.58	37.56	31	35
122.90	155.43	371.40	487.35	143.67	178.67	135	148
112.20	116.00	376.90	428.00	186.30	199.4	207	110
43.20	53.11	136.25	162.51	58.00		43	
67.27	90.62	216.80	290.68	56.30	60.49	60	86
205.40	**229.82**	**728.13**	**842.92**	**363.42**	**441.3**	**293**	**303**
22.70	26.79	79.30	98.22	52.30	66.9	49	34
162.02	179.90	575.50	653.30	273.00	333	223	245
20.68	23.13	73.33	91.40	38.12	41.4	21	24
440.27	**498.90**	**1756.00**	**1990.00**	**524.00**	**711**	**1050**	**1183**
63.37	71.05	229.04	257.11	141.76	153.22	397	223
210.93	255.20	717.20	906.50	261.80	305.83	367	382
8.88	13.68	37.10	47.92	9.98	26.6	32	48
63.40	89.75	225.72	301.14	61.38	62	103	177
3.75	4.84	14.70	18.05	0.80	12.53	15	24
36.20	47.46	133.65	165.32	56.17	94.19	61	78
117.00	138.00	392.00	469.00	96.83	124.77	124	184
38.83	48.58	144.14	172.54	33.57	44.86	51	67
419.70	**499.64**	**1464.81**	**1727.95**	**683.45**	**787.02**	**538**	**595**
242.10	277.30	794.61	882.62	412.89	428	287	311
33.18	48.60	118.70	162.00	130.00	227	336	342
12.40	10.32	37.80	38.60	23.08	35	55	52
7.57	9.34	23.40	26.30	20.48	32.4	13	20
69.99	78.92	274.55	289.88	132.94	162.2	113	118
90.70	114.42	365.30	422.76	37.84	42.3	282	291
39.00	46.10	131.90	138.00	69.20	85.6	86	93
118.63	156.58	477.10	642.43	157.80	206.02	97	119
430.68	**462.98**	**1365.86**	**1566.54**	**622.67**	**774.68**	**857**	**983**
41.42	45.32	122.47	137.16	97.28	127.51	58	55
75.75	84.38	232.32	292.67	78.47	84.18	58	42
80.00	76.10	210.00	255.70	170.00	204.48	320	385
33.61	36.75	105.10	118.33	75.32	90.61	48	43
55.63	61.26	186.48	197.19	35.00	32	37	45
14.89	16.68	51.13	59.60	32.00	40.06	49	53
43.14	47.97	154.75	179.33	34.46	42.11	31	43
32.84	35.38	136.38	141.61	30.00	39.44	69	90
14.21	15.24	47.86	50.06	21.32	36.73	95	110
39.19	43.90	119.37	134.89	48.82	77.56	92	117
371.98	**413.86**	**820.94**	**973.30**	**548.93**	**744.28**	**1040**	**1102**
95.40	109.81	162.43	191.96	124.37	150.06	256	270

21-2 续表 5 continued

开发区名称	Name of Development Zone	其中：规模以上工业企业(万人) Among which, Industrial Enterprises above Designated Size (10 000 persons)	
		2013	2014
湖北黄州火车站经济开发区	Hubei Huangzhou Railway Station Economic Development Zone	0.07	0.08
黄州工业园	Huangzhou Industrial Park	0.68	0.70
湖北龙感湖工业园区	Hubei Longganhu Industrial Park	0.51	0.55
湖北团风经济开发区	Hubei Tuanfeng Economic Development Zone	0.91	0.75
湖北红安经济开发区	Hubei Hong'an Economic Development Zone	2.20	2.25
湖北罗田经济开发区	Hubei Luotian Economic Development Zone	0.55	0.63
湖北英山经济开发区	Hubei Yingshan Economic Development Zone	0.76	0.91
湖北浠水经济开发区	Hubei Xishui Economic Development Zone	1.10	1.30
湖北蕲春李时珍医药工业园区	Hubei Qichun Li Shizhen Pharmaceutical Industrial Park	1.10	1.18
蕲春经济开发区	Qichun Economic Development Zone	0.84	1.08
湖北黄梅经济开发区	Hubei Huangmei Economic Development Zone	2.05	2.30
湖北麻城经济开发区	Hubei Macheng Economic Development Zone	0.90	1.03
湖北武穴经济开发区	Hubei Wuxue Economic Development Zone	1.63	1.68
咸宁市	**Xianning**	**10.00**	**11.03**
湖北咸安经济开发区	Hubei Xian'an Economic Development Zone	1.33	1.43
湖北嘉鱼经济开发区	Hubei Jiayu Economic Development Zone	1.55	1.64
湖北通城经济开发区	Hubei Tongcheng Economic Development Zone	2.50	3.12
湖北崇阳工业园区	Hubei Chongyang Industrial Park	1.06	1.13
湖北通山经济开发区	Hubei Tongshan Economic Development Zone	0.73	0.77
湖北咸宁经济开发区	Hubei Xianning Economic Development Zone	1.70	1.80
湖北赤壁经济开发区	Hubei Chibi Economic Development Zone	0.54	0.56
湖北赤壁蒲纺工业园区	Hubei Chibi Puqi Textile Industrial Park	0.59	0.58
随州市	**Suizhou**	**4.40**	**4.99**
湖北随州经济开发区	Hubei Suizhou Economic Development Zone	1.65	1.66
湖北曾都经济开发区	Hubei Zengdu Economic Development Zone	1.80	2.10
湖北随县经济开发区	Hubei Sui County Economic Development Zone	0.18	0.37
湖北广水经济开发区	Hubei Guangshui Economic Development Zone	0.77	0.86
恩施自治州	**Enshi Autonomous Prefecture**	**4.98**	**5.74**
湖北恩施经济开发区	Hubei Enshi Economic Development Zone	0.80	1.00
湖北恩施州经济开发区	Hubei Enshi Prefecture Economic Development Zone	0.10	0.11
湖北利川经济开发区	Hubei Lichuan Economic Development Zone	0.31	0.33
湖北建始工业园区	Hubei Jianshi Industrial Park	0.50	0.55
湖北巴东经济开发区	Hubei Badong Economic Development Zone	0.10	0.12
湖北宣恩工业园区	Hubei Xuan'en Industrial Park	0.52	0.86
湖北咸丰工业园区	Hubei Xianfeng Industrial Park	0.68	0.81
湖北来凤经济开发区	Hubei Laifeng Economic Development Zone	1.42	1.43
湖北鹤峰经济开发区	Hubei Hefeng Economic Development Zone	0.55	0.53
仙桃市	**Xiantao**	**5.54**	**5.91**
仙桃高新技术产业园区	Hubei Xiantao Economic Development Zone	5.54	5.91
仙桃彭场工业园	Xiantao Pengchang Industrial Park	2.86	3.19
潜江市	**Qianjiang**	**2.52**	**2.79**
湖北潜江经济开发区	Hubei Qianjiang Economic Development Zone	0.65	0.78
潜江张金经济开发区	Qianjiang Zhangjin Economic Development Zone	1.04	1.10
潜江园林经济开发区	Qianjiang Yuanlin Economic Development Zone	0.83	0.91
天门市	**Tianmen**	**5.43**	**6.04**
湖北天门经济开发区	Hubei Tianmen Economic Development Zone	5.43	6.04
神农架盘水生态产业园区			0.02

规模以上工业增加值(亿元) Above-scale Industrial Added Value(100 million Yuan)		规模以上工业主营业务收入(亿元) Scale Industrial Core Business Revenue (100 million Yuan)		固定资产投资总额(亿元) Total Investment In Fixed Assets(100 million Yuan)		施工项目个数(个) Number of Construction Project (unit)	
2013	2014	2013	2014	2013	2014	2013	2014
2.20	2.25	5.60	5.70	26.80	16.6	27	27
12.31	13.60	33.52	35.63	21.84	12.6	18	12
10.40	10.60	34.00	34.20	20.00	22.3	34	38
16.60	17.78	53.79	58.65	15.41	20.51	17	23
55.20	57.00	85.00	87.00	102.60	120	175	200
12.57	14.30	28.95	34.32	10.50	11.6	53	36
6.68	7.74	9.65	11.24	15.35	15.62	61	68
12.50	14.20	37.00	45.00	30.50	45	125	138
20.54	26.92	64.90	86.18	11.50	57.22	33	53
13.84	17.86	44.26	59.10	17.10	46.23	51	56
22.10	26.90	74.10	95.10	52.80	86.9	95	108
26.31	32.47	80.11	81.56	53.47	77.74	16	18
55.33	62.43	125.28	145.11	46.69	57.02	79	55
270.71	**326.19**	**819.11**	**895.80**	**408.11**	**537.5**	**440**	**424**
31.54	40.06	98.23	122.08	48.98	61.11	54	60
73.42	79.67	254.45	267.38	105.62	102.48	150	127
33.90	37.90	76.60	85.20	26.50	28.6	29	30
19.10	23.80	58.10	72.00	20.80	30.4	46	50
12.75	15.60	42.00	49.80	11.70	12.8	28	26
24.82	28.00	90.00	88.19	116.40	145.86	75	58
62.28	91.88	160.80	180.43	74.00	151.11	46	60
12.90	9.28	38.93	30.72	4.11	5.14	12	13
128.68	**158.15**	**409.67**	**482.64**	**185.89**	**214.12**	**257**	**306**
32.40	41.06	133.29	148.43	48.14	61.1	95	135
64.80	71.00	180.90	208.00	92.00		125	123
11.81	21.27	29.29	53.63	28.47	39.67	15	20
20.27	24.82	66.19	72.58	17.28	18.35	22	28
80.78	**95.72**	**185.87**	**238.90**	**147.99**	**204.18**	**336**	**432**
33.10	37.58	68.00	73.50	66.02	97.27	140	150
0.80	0.89	2.95	3.78	11.65	10.54	18	25
7.25	9.00	18.43	22.61	7.44	11.53	14	14
6.97	8.78	15.25	22.66	7.24	17.23	12	44
4.13	4.72	10.40	13.38	15.10	25.35	32	48
3.76	4.56	10.39	12.78	13.00	10.32	46	48
11.41	14.05	23.53	45.56	8.67	11.11	35	51
6.25	9.26	17.26	25.60	13.98	16.8	30	42
7.11	6.88	19.66	19.03	4.89	4.03	9	10
196.72	**215.98**	**616.84**	**713.11**	**170.34**	**208.64**	**140**	**151**
196.72	215.98	616.84	713.11	170.34	208.64	140	151
30.04	33.45	107.93	125.35	24.45	28.16	16	24
90.28	**99.52**	**331.33**	**369.43**	**113.12**	**142.65**	**163**	**143**
32.36	34.95	120.67	148.19	39.80	55.54	64	44
44.00	49.00	163.60	168.50	16.00	19	29	18
13.92	15.57	47.06	52.74	57.32	68.11	70	81
96.47	**117.63**	**325.95**	**393.61**	**125.69**	**153.34**	**148**	**157**
96.47	117.63	325.95	393.61	125.69	153.34	148	157
	0.8		0.5	2.3	3.2	21	22

21-2 续表 6 continued

开发区名称	Name of Development Zone	其中:亿元以上项目(个) Number of Projects above 100 million yuan (unit)	
		2013	2014
湖北省	**Hubei Province**	**4010**	**4764**
武汉市	**Wuhan**	**556**	**596**
武汉江岸经济开发区	Wuhan Jiang'an Economic Development Zone	4	3
武汉江汉经济开发区	Wuhan Jianghan Economic Development Zone		
武汉硚口经济开发区	Wuhan Qiaokou Economic Development Zone	7	7
武汉汉阳经济开发区	Wuhan Hanyang Economic Development Zone	12	18
武汉武昌经济开发区	Wuhan Wuchang Economic Development Zone	1	1
武汉青山经济开发区	Wuhan Qingshan Economic Development Zone	19	15
武汉洪山经济开发区	Wuhan Hongshan Economic Development Zone	2	2
武汉临空港经济技术开发区	Wuhan Linkonggang Economic and Technology Development Zone	157	171
武汉汉南经济开发区	Wuhan Hannan Economic Development Zone	16	15
武汉蔡甸经济开发区	Wuhan Caidian Economic Development Zone	45	59
武汉江夏经济开发区	Wuhan Jiangxia Economic Development Zone	84	101
武汉盘龙城经济开发区	Wuhan Panlongcheng Economic Development Zone	6	6
武汉阳逻经济开发区	Wuhan Yangluo Economic Development Zone	39	51
武汉经济技术开发区	Wuhan Economic and Technology Development Zone	47	48
武汉东湖新技术产业开发区	Wuhan East Lake New Technology Industrial Development Zone	136	113
黄石市	**Huangshi**	**267**	**243**
湖北黄石港工业园区	Hubei Huangshi Port Industrial Park	3	4
湖北黄石新港工业园区	Hubei Huangshi New Port Industrial Park	13	12
湖北西塞山工业园区	Hubei Xisaishan Industrial Park	57	22
湖北下陆长乐山工业园区	Hubei Xialu Changleshan Industrial Park	11	9
黄石经济技术开发区	Huangshi Economic and Technology Development Zone	95	100
湖北阳新经济开发区	Hubei Yangxin Economic Development Zone	28	36
湖北大冶经济开发区	Hubei Daye Economic Development Zone	46	51
大冶灵成工业园	Daye Lingcheng Industrial Park	14	9
十堰市	**Shiyan**	**210**	**281**
十堰经济技术开发区	Shiyan Economic and Technology Development Zone	86	112
湖北郧阳区经济开发区	Hubei Yun County Economic Development Zone	37	43
湖北郧西工业园区	Hubei West Yun Industrial Park	4	5
湖北竹山经济开发区	Hubei Zhushan Economic Development Zone	23	28
湖北竹溪工业园区	Hubei Zhuxi Industrial Park	5	7
湖北房县工业园区	Hubei Fang County Industrial Park	27	49
湖北丹江口经济开发区	Hubei Danjiangkou Economic Development Zone	28	37
宜昌市	**Yichang**	**556**	**741**
湖北西陵经济开发区	Hubei Xiling Economic Development Zone	13	16
湖北伍家岗工业园区	Hubei Wujiagang Industrial Park	6	2
湖北点军工业园区	Hubei Dianjun Industrial Park	3	3
湖北夷陵经济开发区	Hubei Yiling Economic Development Zone	84	111
湖北远安工业园区	Hubei Yuan'an Industrial Park	52	53
湖北兴山经济开发区	Hubei Xingshan Economic Development Zone	10	6
湖北秭归经济开发区	Hubei Zigui Economic Development Zone	17	15
湖北长阳经济开发区	Hubei Changyang Economic Development Zone	31	26
湖北五峰工业园区	Hubei Wufeng Industrial Park	7	10
湖北五峰民族工业园	Hubei Wufeng National Industrial Park	2	3
宜昌高新技术产开发区	Yichang High-tech Industrial Development Zone	219	250
湖北宜都工业园区	Hubei Yidu Industrial Park	23	140
湖北当阳经济开发区	Hubei Dangyang Economic Development Zone	103	143
湖北枝江经济开发区	Hubei Zhijiang Economic Development Zone	77	92
枝江安福寺工业园	Zhijiang Anfu Temple Industrial Park	11	10

新开工项目(个) Number of Newly Opened Projects (unit)		开发区税收总额(万元) Total Tax Revenue of Development (10 000 yuan)		外商投资金额(万美元) Total Value of Foreign Investment (10 000 US dollors)		出口总额(万美元) Total Value of Export (10 000 US dollors)	
2013	2014	2013	2014	2013	2014	2013	2014
5911	**6082**	**13827772.91**	**15870171.90**	**587159.23**	**575931.08**	**1804453.02**	**2120811.37**
581	**541**	**7595335.42**	**8732630.10**	**230694.36**	**230276.00**	**797097.60**	**912474.70**
3	1	46283.00	32398.10		751.00		2931.84
	4	112600.00	129500.00	240.00		4352.00	7090.00
2	3	113224.00	119911.00	650.00		18408.00	17514.00
5	12	265900.00	300467.00	1.36		3000.00	3750.00
2		50005.00	51390.00	320.00	120.00	2400.00	1600.00
23	26	95697.00	99196.00	1280.00	1397.00	7797.00	8532.00
3	3	34200.00	35750.00			420.00	500.00
163	118	1040836.00	1228198.00	24120.00	28944.00	27985.00	36731.00
16	20	65301.00	60849.00	3125.00	3238.00	10535.00	10137.00
39	37	108447.00	132441.00	9600.00	13000.00	42000.00	44126.00
56	58	379377.00	291100.00	12000.00	15100.00	14072.60	14336.86
45	5	173787.00	157285.00			2740.00	3450.00
26	96	90047.00	104540.00	10252.00	13327.00	10900.00	13080.00
72	75	2442512.00	2689997.00	59600.00	26892.00	154132.00	156544.00
149	113	3208591.00	3944510.00	111026.00	128904.00	556694.00	656898.00
359	**335**	**790941.00**	**847616.00**	**30481.00**	**27788.00**	**162972.00**	**180365.00**
15	12	2720.00	3150.00			380.00	400.00
10	8	13785.00	15858.00			200.00	200.00
37	29	87252.19	87364.00	1000.00	20.00	40896.00	48423.00
19	15	65758.10	52356.00			41221.00	39489.00
102	110	315825.00	338514.00	20022.00	22044.00	53117.00	56894.00
35	20	31000.00	31459.00	4959.00	724.00	20148.00	25914.00
129	131	255356.00	303115.00	4500.00	5000.00	6543.00	7485.00
12	10	19245.00	15800.00			467.00	1560.00
338	**292**	**431775.00**	**520145.00**	**20536.00**	**25639.00**	**51144.50**	**56747.30**
82	107	331462.00	398749.00	9955.00	13982.00	38973.00	45164.00
58	61	27160.00	33175.00	1930.00	3417.00	2610.00	2874.00
3	6	2752.00	3801.00	1000.00	1000.00	211.50	229.30
17	7	12101.00	13558.00	510.00		1310.00	1350.00
5	9	6800.00	7500.00	600.00	800.00	700.00	800.00
131	59	14483.00	15871.00	1767.00	1615.00	6220.00	4300.00
42	43	37017.00	47491.00	4774.00	4825.00	1120.00	2030.00
769	**824**	**984529.82**	**1119727.94**	**23441.00**	**25365.00**	**146926.50**	**193263.44**
35	40	26648.00	28000.00	4220.00		3634.00	6744.00
2	3	10756.00	11957.00			1933.00	13936.40
3	3	2665.00	6745.00		1800.00		4780.00
57	86	133450.00	155387.00	10609.00	11058.00	1532.00	1597.00
55	56	78783.00	85247.00	410.00	400.00	10260.00	11636.00
17	7	32800.00	37080.00			19500.00	20700.00
29	40	38897.00	47710.00	420.00	400.00	3820.00	5988.00
74	51	17738.00	15078.00	100.00		5480.00	6258.00
24	35	10577.00	12404.00			168.00	748.20
3	6	1997.42	2750.00			280.00	612.50
213	220	338662.00	470886.00	42359.00	30270.00	48343.00	54926.00
120	207	211638.40	248082.54	2137.00	3400.00	22492.80	25939.34
111	86	58714.00	61543.00	3510.00	4100.00	2877.00	5952.00
103	70	188847.00	221651.40	2035.00	3712.00	18194.70	22099.00
9	13	5996.00	6295.00		495.00	14365.00	11347.00

21-2 续表 7 continued

开发区名称	Name of Development Zone	其中:亿元以上项目(个) Number of Projects above 100 million yuan (unit)	
		2013	2014
襄阳市	**Xianyang**	**743**	**860**
襄阳高新技术产业开发区	Xiangyang High-tech Industrial Development Zone	224	252
襄阳鱼梁州经济开发区	Xiangyang Yuliangzhou Economic Development Zone		
襄阳经济技术开发区	Xiangyang Economic Development Zone	60	85
湖北襄城经济开发区	Hubei Xiangcheng Economic Development Zone	11	12
湖北樊城经济开发区	Hubei Fancheng Economic Development Zone	41	46
湖北襄州经济开发区	Hubei Xiangzhou Economic Development Zone	60	85
襄阳工业园	Xiangyang Industrial Park	14	14
湖北南漳经济开发区	Hubei Nanzhang Economic Development Zone	20	36
湖北谷城经济开发区	Hubei Gucheng Economic Development Zone	57	98
谷城石花经济开发区	Gucheng Shihua Economic Development Zone	25	22
湖北保康经济开发区	Hubei Baokang Economic Development Zone	31	35
湖北老河口经济开发区	Hubei Laohekou Economic Development Zone	119	127
湖北枣阳经济开发区	Hubei Zaoyang Economic Development Zone	75	92
枣阳吴店工业园	Zaoyang Wudian Industrial Park	26	
湖北宜城经济开发区	Hubei Yicheng Economic Development Zone	40	41
鄂州市	**E'zhou**	**155**	**169**
湖北鄂州花湖经济开发区	Hubei E'Zhou Huahu Economic Development Zone	24	19
鄂州葛店经济技术开发区	E'Zhou Gedian Economic and Technology Development Zone	115	129
湖北鄂州经济开发区	Hubei E'Zhou Economic Development Zone	16	21
荆门市	**Jingmen**	**323**	**437**
湖北东宝工业园区	Hubei Dongbao Industrial Park	60	68
荆门高新技术产业开发区	Hubei Jingmen High-tech Industrial Development Zone	73	95
湖北荆门化工循环产业园	Hubei Jingmen Chemical Recycling Development Zone	15	30
湖北京山经济开发区	Hubei Jingshan Economic Development Zone	54	82
湖北屈家岭经济开发区	Hubei Qujialing Economic Development Zone	8	12
湖北沙洋经济开发区	Hubei Shayang Economic Development Zone	37	43
湖北钟祥经济开发区	Hubei Zhongxiang Economic Development Zone	65	78
钟祥胡集经济开发区	Zhongxiang Huji Economic Development Zone	18	29
孝感市	**Xiaogan**	**238**	**276**
孝感高新技术产业开发区	Xiaogan high-tech Industrial Development Zone	108	123
湖北孝南经济开发区	Hubei Xiaonan Economic Development Zone	47	61
湖北孝昌经济开发区	Hubei Xiaochang Economic Development Zone	30	30
湖北大悟经济开发区	Hubei Dawu Economic Development Zone	9	15
湖北云梦经济开发区	Hubei Yunmeng Economic Development Zone	57	73
湖北应城经济开发区	Hubei Yingcheng Economic Development Zone	27	31
湖北安陆经济开发区	Hubei Anlu Economic Development Zone	53	63
湖北汉川经济开发区	Hubei Hanchuan Economic Development Zone	38	45
荆州市	**Jingzhou**	**215**	**304**
湖北沙市经济开发区	Hubei Shashi Economic Development Zone	29	37
湖北荆州城南经济开发区	Jingzhou Chengnan Economic Development Zone	15	11
荆州经济技术开发区	Jingzhou Economic and Technology Development Zone	30	46
湖北公安经济开发区	Hubei Gong'an Economic Development Zone	44	43
湖北监利经济开发区	Hubei Jianli Economic Development Zone	17	21
湖北江陵经济开发区	Hubei Jiangling Economic Development Zone	14	35
湖北石首经济开发区	Hubei Shishou Economic Development Zone	20	34
湖北洪湖经济开发区	Hubei Honghu Economic Development Zone	15	37
洪湖府场经济开发区	Honghu Fuchang Economic Development Zone	9	12
湖北松滋经济开发区	Hubei Songzi Economic Development Zone	22	28
黄冈市	**Huanggang**	**302**	**337**
湖北黄冈经济开发区	Hubei Huanggang Economic Development Zone	58	66

新开工项目(个) Number of Newly Opened Projects (unit)		开发区税收总额(万元) Total Tax Revenue of Development (10 000 yuan)		外商投资金额(万美元) Total Value of Foreign Investment (10 000 US dollors)		出口总额(万美元) Total Value of Export (10 000 US dollors)	
2013	2014	2013	2014	2013	2014	2013	2014
685	**640**	**1248378.52**	**1391737.75**	**80266.00**	**84977.00**	**156948.00**	**180686.80**
168	182	619821.00	671050.00	21530.00	25844.00	80021.00	81020.00
	1	3793.00	980.00				
31	62	396287.00	415987.00	7152.00	7159.00	19157.00	19531.00
8	12	79821.00	80858.00	1830.00	1853.00	1183.00	1289.00
49	41	72835.00	81575.00	1326.00	1524.00	3251.00	3738.00
31	61	153545.00	189958.00	7152.00	7159.00	9512.00	12900.00
17	8	2101.23	4269.25	35000.00	27000.00	1845.00	2436.00
16	29	15973.00	16228.00	1460.00		2132.00	2205.80
92	114	57092.00	68559.00	1250.00	1450.00	3260.00	7862.00
19	20	35896.00	48168.00	61.00	67.00	2354.00	3143.00
5	8	17229.57	8444.00	1418.00	1520.00	3920.00	4657.00
45	56	49326.00	59879.00	6387.00	9887.00	19700.00	28675.00
142	49	59200.00	65472.00	2852.00	3673.00	14580.00	16178.00
39		29905.72	37382.50			790.00	983.00
54	59	51840.00	58915.00		5000.00	14400.00	15600.00
155	**184**	**191318.30**	**238999.60**	**11070.00**	**8186.00**	**10195.00**	**11835.40**
20	25	25803.00	30262.00			1905.00	2697.40
121	138	145097.30	182170.60	9220.00	5900.00	6590.00	7213.00
14	21	20418.00	26567.00	1850.00	2286.00	1700.00	1925.00
705	**763**	**305259.00**	**387035.00**	**24961.00**	**28156.00**	**56658.00**	**76794.00**
269	194	34954.00	43439.00			1898.00	1699.00
249	267	210410.00	270113.00	11560.00	12622.00	25684.00	40206.00
14	24	5106.00	7400.00			223.00	3060.00
84	101	57703.00	73869.00	5350.00	6164.00	9180.00	13248.00
4	6	813.16	828.26	296.00	328.00	1156.00	1764.00
39	46	25368.00	27786.00	3000.00	3455.00	8600.00	11395.00
57	107	36993.00	47738.00	6970.00	7890.00	8038.00	9570.00
11	18	24096.00	29676.00			6500.00	11083.00
250	**273**	**434370.20**	**496106.20**	**24871.00**	**29882.00**	**79904.20**	**89633.00**
90	110	253150.00	291125.00	17209.00	22371.00	28302.00	33113.00
293	301	106000.00	186382.00	1700.00	3000.00	4200.00	12038.00
29	15	11384.20	11572.20	1312.00		3780.00	3310.00
6	7	26000.00	27500.00			982.00	1280.00
91	84	66154.00	83100.00	3959.00	4359.00	3500.00	12000.00
23	25	69020.00	91002.00	10009.00	10012.00	998.00	1008.00
52	58	26560.00	28963.00	1000.00	1100.00	7963.20	9232.00
73	83	117276.00	136946.00	5350.00	6411.00	38877.00	42698.00
566	**675**	**407626.36**	**473643.30**	**46597.40**	**32659.00**	**106729.60**	**121408.41**
40	42	24788.00	30416.00	5.40		15217.00	15446.00
18	8	39976.00	42557.00			13031.00	14557.00
295	370	128537.00	174599.00	18668.00	2811.00	47834.00	56804.00
27	24	55722.90	38573.30			7054.60	7374.92
8	16	16100.00	16800.00	27000.00	28600.00	4217.00	5500.00
21	24	8194.00	5617.00			1610.00	662.49
18	23	30776.00	35663.00			14891.00	17041.00
40	48	19818.00	21098.00	924.00	1248.00	2875.00	4023.00
44	50	15191.46	16558.00				
55	70	68523.00	91762.00				
578	**666**	**490665.10**	**568901.15**	**65121.27**	**60346.00**	**67887.60**	**76622.70**
87	96	152301.00	171104.00	13971.00	17075.00	21376.00	26003.00

21-2 续表 8 continued

开发区名称	Name of Development Zone	其中:亿元以上项目(个) Number of Projects above 100 million yuan (unit) 2013	2014
湖北黄州火车站经济开发区	Hubei Huangzhou Railway Station Economic Development Zone	10	7
黄州工业园	Huangzhou Industrial Park	15	10
湖北龙感湖工业园区	Hubei Longganhu Industrial Park	17	18
湖北团风经济开发区	Hubei Tuanfeng Economic Development Zone	10	10
湖北红安经济开发区	Hubei Hong'an Economic Development Zone	75	90
湖北罗田经济开发区	Hubei Luotian Economic Development Zone	10	13
湖北英山经济开发区	Hubei Yingshan Economic Development Zone	8	11
湖北浠水经济开发区	Hubei Xishui Economic Development Zone	15	17
湖北蕲春李时珍医药工业园区	Hubei Qichun Li Shizhen Pharmaceutical Industrial Park	14	14
蕲春经济开发区	Qichun Economic Development Zone	15	16
湖北黄梅经济开发区	Hubei Huangmei Economic Development Zone	23	25
湖北麻城经济开发区	Hubei Macheng Economic Development Zone	9	12
湖北武穴经济开发区	Hubei Wuxue Economic Development Zone	23	28
咸宁市	**Xianning**	**154**	**160**
湖北咸安经济开发区	Hubei Xian'an Economic Development Zone	15	17
湖北嘉鱼经济开发区	Hubei Jiayu Economic Development Zone	44	37
湖北通城经济开发区	Hubei Tongcheng Economic Development Zone	13	13
湖北崇阳工业园区	Hubei Chongyang Industrial Park	12	18
湖北通山经济开发区	Hubei Tongshan Economic Development Zone	5	5
湖北咸宁经济开发区	Hubei Xianning Economic Development Zone	46	47
湖北赤壁经济开发区	Hubei Chibi Economic Development Zone	19	21
湖北赤壁蒲纺工业园区	Hubei Chibi Puqi Textile Industrial Park		2
随州市	**Suizhou**	**70**	**92**
湖北随州经济开发区	Hubei Suizhou Economic Development Zone	30	41
湖北曾都经济开发区	Hubei Zengdu Economic Development Zone	30	36
湖北随县经济开发区	Hubei Sui County Economic Development Zone	7	10
湖北广水经济开发区	Hubei Guangshui Economic Development Zone	3	5
恩施自治州	**Enshi Autonomous Prefecture**	**70**	**89**
湖北恩施经济开发区	Hubei Enshi Economic Development Zone	30	30
湖北恩施州经济开发区	Hubei Enshi Prefecture Economic Development Zone	9	13
湖北利川经济开发区	Hubei Lichuan Economic Development Zone	4	7
湖北建始工业园区	Hubei Jianshi Industrial Park	1	5
湖北巴东经济开发区	Hubei Badong Economic Development Zone	11	12
湖北宣恩工业园区	Hubei Xuan'en Industrial Park	5	6
湖北咸丰工业园区	Hubei Xianfeng Industrial Park	3	6
湖北来凤经济开发区	Hubei Laifeng Economic Development Zone	5	9
湖北鹤峰经济开发区	Hubei Hefeng Economic Development Zone	2	1
仙桃市	**Xiantao**	**75**	**88**
仙桃高新技术产业园区	Hubei Xiantao Economic Development Zone	75	88
仙桃彭场工业园	Xiantao Pengchang Industrial Park	6	8
潜江市	**Qianjiang**	**39**	**50**
湖北潜江经济开发区	Hubei Qianjiang Economic Development Zone	11	17
潜江张金经济开发区	Qianjiang Zhangjin Economic Development Zone	4	7
潜江园林经济开发区	Qianjiang Yuanlin Economic Development Zone	24	26
天门市	**Tianmen**	**35**	**39**
湖北天门经济开发区	Hubei Tianmen Economic Development Zone	35	39
神农架盘水生态产业园区		2	2

新开工项目(个) Number of Newly Opened Projects (unit)		开发区税收总额(万元) Total Tax Revenue of Development (10 000 yuan)		外商投资金额(万美元) Total Value of Foreign Investment (10 000 US dollors)		出口总额(万美元) Total Value of Export (10 000 US dollors)	
2013	2014	2013	2014	2013	2014	2013	2014
14	23	4322.00	3132.00	100.00		4355.00	4421.00
8	4	6596.90	5285.60	16470.00	21200.00	4279.00	3169.00
18	20	7501.00	7792.85	448.00	10.00	1059.00	498.00
10	5	8947.00	12500.00			742.00	1235.00
117	142	130000.00	135000.00	4822.00	5100.00	1800.00	2005.00
29	32	7678.00	9123.00			3727.00	4126.00
45	49	12185.20	14500.30	4235.00		142.60	212.70
67	80	15000.00	18000.00	15000.00	2000.00	12000.00	12100.00
18	36	23937.00	27541.00	7060.00	8630.00	4808.00	6020.00
12	34	20641.00	24753.00		131.00	2618.00	3317.00
90	95	21601.00	28100.00	269.00	300.00	1508.00	3739.00
9	12	36950.00	56919.00	746.27	3400.00	979.00	1077.00
54	38	43005.00	52348.00	2000.00	2500.00	8494.00	8700.00
288	**255**	**303090.00**	**355559.00**	**12741.20**	**2859.08**	**28999.28**	**34707.89**
40	46	23001.00	28519.00			4015.00	4328.00
95	62	16719.00	18826.00	134.00	518.00	7027.00	7886.00
15	15	22464.00	25995.00			4511.00	5211.00
32	36	14230.00	16800.00	760.00	529.00	1800.00	2100.00
10	12	13700.00	14815.00			110.00	560.00
40	29	174788.00	194200.00	147.00	18.85	3154.00	7359.50
45	46	36798.00	55172.00	9200.20	1148.23	2652.28	4780.39
11	9	1390.00	1232.00	2500.00	645.00	5730.00	2483.00
165	**150**	**97857.50**	**130541.00**	**4020.00**	**6851.00**	**61609.50**	**86808.42**
56	69	50110.00	76927.00	2100.00	4171.00	23389.50	36570.62
85	58	35876.50	38127.00			28072.00	29449.00
9	11	3111.00	5887.00			6248.00	16588.80
15	12	8760.00	9600.00	1920.00	2680.00	3900.00	4200.00
207	**240**	**238429.30**	**255247.00**	**225.00**	**200.00**	**7565.38**	**17571.21**
80	82	147090.00	155682.00			2400.00	2600.00
7	10	4000.00	6000.00				
2	9	52301.00	45549.00			54.00	202.00
10	34	2980.90	6067.00			754.11	2775.00
15	34	9230.00	10840.00			465.80	6800.00
34	15	3482.00	3896.00	100.00		282.47	367.21
27	29	8025.40	12600.00	125.00	200.00	2180.00	2912.00
23	26	8096.00	10783.00			320.00	425.00
9	1	3224.00	3830.00			1109.00	1490.00
69	**71**	**152205.00**	**172400.00**	**7406.00**	**8303.00**	**36999.00**	**38948.00**
69	71	152205.00	172400.00	7406.00	8303.00	36999.00	38948.00
6	23	15322.00	18765.00			19554.00	21700.00
115	**100**	**111008.00**	**120037.60**	**4025.00**	**3520.00**	**28181.32**	**35946.43**
54	22	20008.00	22806.00			5870.32	5914.43
21	17	8600.00	10090.00	4025.00	3520.00	11377.00	11502.00
40	61	82400.00	87141.60			10934.00	18530.00
64	**68**	**44984.39**	**57845.26**	**703.00**	**924.00**	**4635.54**	**6998.67**
64	68	44984.39	57845.26	703.00	924.00	4635.54	6998.67
17	5		2000				

主要统计指标解释

规划面积：指国土部门核定的开发区规划面积。

实际开发面积：指开发区实际开发并已完成基础设施建设的面积。

企业个数：指报告期末已在工商行政管理机关登记注册、并在开发区管理机构进行统计登记的法人单位数，包括内资企业、港澳台投资企业和外商投资企业。不含个体企业。

工业企业：包括采矿业、制造业、电力、燃气及水的生产和供应业。

规模以上工业企业：是指企业所在地在开发区内的全部年主营收入 2000 万元及以上的法人工业企业。即无论企业是否在开发区注册，也无论企业隶属何行政级别或部门，只要所在地在开发区的所有规模以上企业都在本制度规定的统计范围以内。反之，所在地不在开发区，尽管其在开发区注册的规模以上企业也不在本制度规定的统计范围之内。

高新技术企业：指生产高新技术产品经省科学技术厅授牌的企业。

外商投资企业：指企业注册登记类型中的中外合资、合作经营企业、外资企业和外商投资股份有限公司之和。（含港、澳、台商投资企业 ： 指企业注册登记类型中的港、澳、台资合资、合作、独资经营企业和股份有限公司之和。）

第三产业：除第一、第二产业以外的其他各业。由于第三产业包括的行业多、范围广，根据我国的实际情况，第三产业可分为两大部分：一是流通部门，二是服务部门。具体又可分为四个层次：

第一层次：流通部门，包括交通运输、仓储及邮电通信业，批发和零售贸易、餐饮业。

第二层次：为生产和生活服务的部门，包括金融、保险业，地质勘查业、水利管理业，房地产业，社会服务业，农、林、牧、渔服务业，交通运输辅助业，综合技术服务业等。

第三层次：为提高科学文化水平和居民素质服务的部门，包括教育、文化艺术及广播电影电视业，卫生、体育和社会福利业，科学研究业等。

第四层次：为社会公共需要服务的部门，包括国家机关、政党机关和社会团体以及军队、警察等。

从业人员：指报告期末在开发区企业、行政和事业单位中工作，取得工资或其他形式的劳动报酬的全部人员数。包括在岗职工，再就业的离退休人员、民办教师及在企业工作的外方人员和港澳台方人员、兼职人员、借用的外单位人员和第二职业者。不包括离开本单位但仍保留劳动关系的职工。

开发区生产总值： 即按市场价格计算的国内生产总值的简称。指开发区内所有常住单位在一定时期内生产活动的最终成果。国内生产总值有三种表现形态，即价值形态、收入形态和产品形态。

从价值形态看，它是所有常住单位在一定时期内生产的全部货物和服务价值超过同期投入的全部非固定资产货物和服务价值的差额，即所有常住单位的增加值之和；从收入形态看，它是所有常住单位在一定时期内创造并分配给常住单位和非常住单位的初次分配收入之和；从产品形态看它是最终使用的货物和服务减去进口货物和服务。在实际核算中，国内生产总值的三种表现形态表现为三种计算方法，即生产法、收入法和支出法。三种方法分别从不同的方面反映国内生产总值及其构成。

（1）生产法是从生产的角度衡量常住单位在一定时期新创造价值的方法。即从生产的全部货物和服务总产品价值中，扣除生产过程中投入的中间货物和服务价值得到增加价值。国民经济各产业部门生产法增加值计算公式如下：

增加值＝总产出－中间投入 将国民经济各产业部门生产法增加值相加，得到生产法 GDP。

总产出：指常住单位在一定时期内生产的所有货物和服务的价值，既包括新增价值，也包括转移价值。它反映常住单位生产活动的总规模。总产出按生产者价格计算。

中间投入：指常住单位在一定时期内生产过程中消耗和使用的非固定资产货物和服务的价值。中间投入也称为中间消耗，反映用于生产过程中的转移价值，一般按购买者价格计算。计入中间投入的货物和服务必须具备两个条件，一是与总产出的计算范围保持一致；二是本期一次性使用的。

⑵收入法也称为分配法。按收入法计算国内生产总值是从生产过程创造收入的角度，对常住单位的生产活动成果进行核算。按照这种计算方法，增加值由劳动者报酬、生产税净额、固定资产折旧和营业盈余四个部分组成。计算公式为：增加值=劳动者报酬+生产税净额+固定资产折旧+营业盈余。国民经济各部门的增加值之和等于国内生产总值。

⑶支出法是从最终使用的角度反映国内生产总值最终使用去向的一种方法。最终使用包括货物和服务的最终消费支出、资本形成总额、货物和服务净出口三部分，计算公式为：国内生产总值=最终消费支出+资本形成总额+货物和服务净出口。

按三种方法计算的国内生产总值反映的是同一经济总体在同一时期的生产活动成果，因此，从理论上讲，三种计算方法所得到的结果应该是一致的。但是，在实践中，由于受资料来源的口径范围的限制和计算方法的影响，要保证这三种计算方法所得的结果完全相等几乎是不可能的。

工业总产值(现价)：是以货币形式表现的，工业企业在一定时期内生产的工业最终产品或提供工业性劳务活动的总价值量。

工业总产值包括本期生产成品价值、对外加工费收入，在制品半成品期末期初差额价值三部分。

①本期生产成品价值：是指企业本期生产，并在报告期内不再进行加工，经检验、包装入库的全部工业成品(半成品)价值合计，包括企业生产的自制设备及提供给本企业在建工程、其他非工业部门和生活福利部门等单位使用的成品价值，本期生产成品价值按自备原材料生产的产品的数量乘以本期不含增值税(销项税额)的产品实际销售平均单价计算；会计核算中按成本价格转帐的自制设备和自产自用的成品，按成本价格计算生产成品价值。生产成品价值中不包括用定货者来料加工的成品(半成品)价值。

②对外加工费收入：是指企业在报告期内完成的对外承接的工业品加工(包括用定货者来料加工产品)的加工费收入和对外工业修理作业所取得的加工费收入。对外加工费收入按不含增值税(销项税额)的价格计算，可根据会计“产品销售收入”科目的有关资料取得。

对于本企业对内非工业部门提供的加工修理、设备安装的劳务收入，如果企业会计核算基础比较好，能取得这部分资料，而且这部分价值所占比重较大，应包括在对外加工费收入中。

③自制半成品在制品期末期初差额价值：是指企业报告期自制半成品、在制品期末减期初的差额价值，本指标一般可从会计核算资料中取得。如果会计产品成本核算中不计算半成品、在制品的成本，则总产值中也不包括这部分价值，反之则包括。

工业增加值：指工业企业在报告期内以货币形式表现的工业生产活动的最终成果，是企业全部生产活动的总成果扣除了在生产过程中消耗或转移的物质产品和劳务价值后的余额，是企业生产过程中新增加的价值。

计算工业增加值通常采用两种方法。一是“生产法”，二是“收入法”，目前工业统计主要采用“生产法”计算工业增加值。

“生产法”，即从工业生产过程中产品和劳务价值形成的角度入手，剔除生产环节中间投入的价值，从而得到新增价值的方法。公式为：

工业增加值=工业总产值—工业中间投入+本期应交增值税

上述公式中，本期应交增值税的企业为负数时，综合部门汇总时按零处理。

“收入法”，即从工业生产过程中创造的原始收入初次分配的角度，对工业生产活动最终成果进行核算的一种方法，其计算公式为：

工业增加值=固定资产折旧+劳动者报酬+生产税净额+营业盈余

工业中间投入：1. 定义：指企业在报告期内用于工业生产活动所一次性消耗的外购原材料、燃料、动力及其他实物产品和对外支付的服务费用。

2. 计算原则：计算工业中间投入须遵循以下三条原则：(1) 必须是从企业外部购入的产品和服务的价值，不包括生产过程中回收的废料以及自制品的价值。(2) 必须是本期投入生产，并一次性消耗的产品和服务的价值，不包括固定资产转移价值：（3）中间投入的计算口径必须与总产值的计算口径相一致：即计入工业中间投入的产品和服务价值必须已经计入了工业总产值中。

3．分类：工业中间投入按企业支付对象可以分为中间物质投入和中间劳务投入。中间物质投入是指生产过程中所消耗的外购原材料、燃料、动力以及其它实物产品和支付给物质生产部门(工业、农业、批发零售贸易业、建筑业、货物运输及邮电业)的服务费用，中间劳务投入指支付给非物质生产部门(如金融、保险、文化教育、科学研究、医疗卫生、行政管理)的服务费用。

工业中间投入按照具体内容分为直接材料、制造费用中的中间投入、管理费用中的中间投入、销售费用中的中间投入和利息支出五大项。

日常统计中计算中间投入是按第二种分类计算的。

4．计算方法：计算工业中间投入的具体方法可以分为二种。一是正算法，即将制造费用、管理费用、销售费用中属于中间投入的部分分别相加，再加上直接材料和利息支出，得出工业中间投入合计。二是倒算法，即分别用制造费用、管理费用、销售费用合计减去其中属于增加值的项目(大体包括工资、福利费、折旧、劳动保险费、职工待业保险费等)，倒算出三项费用中的中间投入，再加上直接材料和利息支出，得出工业中间投入合计。在实算操作过程中，采用倒算法计算比较简便易行。

5．资料来源：计算中间投入的资料来源，可分别根据企业“产品成本表”、“管理费用”、“财务费用”、“销售费用”明细表归纳整理填报。

高新技术增加值：增加值是指报告期内企业在生产活动中新创造的价值。

高新技术增加值指报告期省科技厅认定的高新技术企业的增加值和非高新技术企业中的高新技术产品的增加值两部分。高新技术产品指高新技术领域的产品。即满足下列条件之一的产品：①首次应用新科学原理生产的最新产品；②首次应用最新工艺生产并使产品质量、成本和劳动效率有显著改进的产品；③技术水平达到90年代国际先进水平的产品。

有两种计算方法：一是“生产法”；二是“收入法”，亦称要素分配法。计算方法为：

（1）按生产法计算的工业增加值=工业总产值—工业中间投入+本期应交增值税；（2）按分配法计算的工业增加值=固定资产折旧+劳动者报酬+生产税净额+营业盈余。

主营业务收入：指企业经常性的、主要业务所产生的收入。不同行业的企业主营业务收入包括的内容不同。工业企业的主营业务收入主要包括销售产品、自制半成品、提供工业性劳务等收入；商品流通企业的主营业务收入主要包括销售商品取得的收入。主营业务收入一般占企业收入的比重较大，对企业的经济效益产生较大的影响。在会计核算中单独设置“主营业务收入”科目核算经常性的、主要业务所产生的收入。

固定资产投资总额：指开发区各单位报告期内500万元以上(含500万元)项目完成的投资额（包括实际完成的建筑安装工程价值，设备、工具、器具的购置费，以及实际发生的其他费用），是以货币表示的建造和购置固定资产活动的工作量以及与此有关的费用总称。

基础设施建设投资：指报告期内开发区基础公用设施：包括供水排水、供气、供热、供电、环卫设施、排污系统、固体废弃物收集和处理系统、电信及道路、桥梁、平整土地等施工建设投资。

施工项目个数：指报告期内曾进行建筑或安装工程施工活动的建设项目个数，包括报告期内新开工项目、报告期以前开工跨入报告期继续施工的项目以及报告期施过工并在报告期内全部建成投产或停缓建的项目个数。

税收总额：指开发区全口径税收收入。包含国税收入、地税收入。主要有增值税、营业税、所得税、城市维护建设税、城镇土地使用税、房产税、印花税、资源税、土地增值税等。

招商引资总额：指报告期内除本行政区划以外的国内外投资者在开发区的投资金额之和。

外商投资金额：指外国企业和经济组织或个人(包括华侨、港澳台胞以及我国在境外注册的企业)按我国有关政策、法规，用现汇、实物、技术等在我国境内开办外商独资企业、与我国境内的企业或经济组织共同举办中外合资经营企业、合作经营企业或合作开发资源的投资(包括外商投资收益的再投资)，以及经政府有关部门批准的项目投资总额内企业从境外借入的资金。

省外境内投资额：指报告期内除湖北省以外的国内投资者（不包括港、澳、台）在开发区的投资金额。

出口总额：指实际出口的货物总金额。我国规定出口货物按离岸价格统计。

高新产品出口交货值：指企业生产的交给外贸部门或自营(委托)出口(包括销往香港、澳门、台湾)，用外汇价格结算的批量销售，在国内或在边境批量出口等的高新产品价值，还包括外商来样、来料加工、来件装配和补偿贸易等生产的产品价值。

Explanatory Notes on Main Statistical Indicators

Land Area Approved for Development Zone refers to the land area of development zone ratified for program by the state department of territory.

Floor Area of Development Zone refers to the land area of development zone that is practically exploited and occupied.

The Number of Enterprise refers to the number of impersonal entity that has registered at industrial organs and commerce administration at the end of report period and that has been counted and registered. Included in this catogary are domestic—funded enterprises, enterprises with funds from Hong kong,Macao,Taiwan and foreign—funded enterprises. Private enterprises are excluded.

Enterprises of High and New Technology refer to enterprises verified by provincial office of science and technology that produce hi-tech products.

Industrial Enterprises include mining, manufacturing, and manufacturing and supply of power, gas and water.

Industrial enterprises above designated size refer to entity industrial enterprises whose main annual turnover exceeds 5 million in the circle of development zone where enterpriese are located. That is to say,no matter enterprises has registered or not, what department enterprises belong to, all the enterprises whose location are in the development zone are counted which are above designated size. Otherwise, enterprises above designated size whose location is not in the development zone are not counted although they have registered at development zone.

Employees refer to all the workers working in enterprises in development zone,administrative unit and public institution who have got their income or payment of labour in other forms at the end of report period. Included in this category are workers on guard, re—employed laid—off workers and retirees, citizen-managed teachers; foreign workers in enterprises,workers of Hong Kong, Macao and Taiwan, part—time workers, borrowed workers from external enterprises and second—job workers. Workers having left enterprises who reserve labour relations are excluded.

Total turnover of technology, industry and trade refers to the total sum of product sales proceeds, technological gain and goods sales proceeds that are related to our products,other business gain,external—business gain in one year,and the like.

Technological turnover refers to the gain of technology transferrance, technology contract, technology advisory and service, technology share,products of pilotscale experiment and the gain of external-entrusted scientific research.

Technology contract turnover refers to the gain from contract of technology program design,design and contract of technology project.

Technology advisory and service turnover refers to the income from technical intellegence, technilcal information,technical advisory and test analysis provided availing enterprises themselves of human resources,physical resources and data system, and other kinds of technical service.

Revenue of entrusted reserch and development refers to the revenue from reserch and development of new products contracted provided to various social units.

Gross Industrial Output Value (at current price) refers to the total volum of final industrial products produced and industrial services provided in money terms during a given period .

Gross Industrial Output Value consists of 3 components: value of the finished products during the reference period, income from external processing, and value of change in semi-finished products at the end of and at the beginning of the reference period.

①value of the finished products during the reference period refers to the value of all finished(semi-finished) industrial products that are produced during the reference period without the need for further processing, checked for accepatance, packed and put into the warehouse of the enterprise, including the value of own-produced equipment and the value of products provided to the projects under construction of the enterprise, and to other non-industrial or welfare units. Value of finished products during the reference period is calculated by the quantity of products produced using own materials multiplied by the average unit prices at which products are sold(exculding value-added tax). Own-produced equipment and products for own use are value at cost prices as in the case of enterprise accounting. Value of finished products does not include the value of finished products(semi-finished products) that are produced using the materials from the clients who make the ordres.

②Income from external processing refers to income from contracted external processing of industrial products(including processing of industrial products using materials from the clients), and the income from industrial repairing work provided to other units. Income from external processing is calculated using information from the item “products sales income” in the enterprise accounting at the prices excluding value-added tax.For income from external services such as processing, repairing and installation of equipment provided to non-industrial units within the enterprise, if the accounting work of the enterprise is good enough to separate it from other records, and the share of such services is significant, it should also be included in the income from external processing.

③value of change in semi-finished products at the end of and at the beginning of the reference period refers to the value of change in semi-finished products at the end and at the beginning of the reference period, which generally can be obtained from accounting records of enterprises. If the enterprise accounting excludes the cost of semi-finished products, then it should not be inculded in the gross industrial output value,and vice versa.

High and new technology value High and new technology products refer to products in the area of high and new technology, namely any kind of products meeting following standars: ① the latest products using latest scientific principles the first time; ②the products that are produced by the latest technology and have noticeably improved the quality, cost and work efficiency; ③ products whose technical merit has reached advanced international standards of 1990s. High and new technology value refers to 2 components: the value of high and new technology enterprises designated by provincial Science and Technology Office in reference period, and value of high and new technology products of non-high-and-new technology enterprises.

Industrial value added refers to the final results of industrial production enterprises in money terms during the the reference period.

Industrial value added can be usually calculated by two approaches:the production approach,and the income approach.Industrial stastics mainly adopts the production approach to calculate the industrial value added at present.

The production approach is the approach that newly-increased value is gained by eliminating the value indulged in the production link in terms of value formation of products and labor in the process of industrial prodution. The formula is: Industrial value added= total industrial value-industrial intermediate input

+ current value added tax receivable

In this formula,when current value added tax receivale is minus, the Integration Department will treat it as zero.

The income approach is an approach that final results of industrial production activities are checked in terms of the primary distribution of original income created in the indusrial production. Here is its formula: Industrial value added= depreciation of fixed assets+remuneration of labourers+net of produce tax+ operating surplus

Industrial intermediate input:

1.Definition: It refers to the service cost for purchased raw material,gas,power and other physical products,and external-paid services consumed during the reference period for the industrial production of enterprises.

2.Calculating principles:Calculating industrial intermediate input must follow the three principles:(1)The value must be the value of goods and services that are purchased from outside,exculding the value of reclaimed waste materials in the production and that of own products.(2) The value must be the value of goods and services that are inputted into production consumed during the reference period,excluding transfer value of fixed assets.(3)The calculating units of the intermediate input must be in correspondence with that of total value, namely the value of products and service reckoned in industrial intermediate input has been reckoned in industrial value.

3.Category: Industrial intermediate input in terms of pay objectcan be classified as intermediate material input and intermediate labor input . Intermediate material input refers to the the purchased raw material, gas,power and other physical products consumed in the production, and the cost of service paid to departments of material production(industry,agriculcuture, wholesales and retail trade,construction goods transportation and post). Intermediate labor input refers to cost of service paid to departments of nonmaterial production(finance,insurance,cultural education,scientific research,medical health and administration)

Industrial intermediate input in terms of concrete content can be classified into 5 components , namely direct consumption of materials,industrial intermediate input in manufacturing cost, industrial intermediate input in management cost, industrial intermediate input in marketing cost and expenditure on interest.

Intermediate input in common calculating is calculated by the second category.

4.Calculating approaches:the calculating approaches to industrial intermediate input have two approaches. Positive calculating, namely add respectively the manufacuring cost, management cost,sales cost that belong to intermediate input, then add direct material and interest expense.The final result is reconed into the total. Negative calculating, namely manufacturing cost, management cost, sale cost that belong to value-added items(generally included are sallary, welfarism, depreciation,labor insurance, employee's job-waiting insurance,ect)is substracted respectively from the total.The result is the its intermediate input respectively. Then direct material and interest expense are added. The final result is reconed into the total. Negative calculating is easier to carry out in pratical calculating.

5.Information source: The information source in calculating intermediate input can be obtained from product Cost Table, tables of Management Cost, Financial Expense and Sales Cost.

Value added of high and new technology value added refers to the newly created value in the production in the reference period. There are two approaches to calculting, the production approach, and the income approach,also factor distribution approach. The calculation methods are: (1)industrial value added by the production approach=total industrial value-industrial intermediate input+ current value added tax receivable; (2) industrial value added by distribution approach=depreciation of fixed assets+ remuneration of labourers+net of produce tax+ operating surplus

Value added of high and new technology refers to the value added of high and new technology enterprises designated by provincial Science and Technology Office in reference period, and value added of high and new technology products of non-high-and-new technology enterprises.

Income from major business refers to the income of regular and major bussiness of enterprises. The content of the income from major business differs from enterprise to enterprise. The income from major business of industrial enterprises mainly includes the income from product sales,own semi-finished products,industrial labor; the income from major business of commodity circulation enterprises mainly includes the incoome from commodity sales.Income from major business generally takes a big share in the income of enterprise,and has a great influence on the economic benefit.The "income from major business" item is set individually to check income from regular and major business in accounting.

Total investment in fixed assets refers to the generic term for operation capacity of building up and purchasing fixed assets in money terms during the reference period and related cost. Total investment in fixed assets in reference period is calculated by actual investment(including value of actual finish constructive installation engineering,purchasing cost of equipment,tools and devices,and other actual cost)

The number of projects under construction:refers to number of projects that has carried out construction or installation engineering in reference period, including the number of newly-opened projects during reference period,projects opened before reference period and constructed over reference period,and projects that have been constructed in reference period and completed or delayed within reference period.

Total tax revenue refers to tax revenue in all units of development zone.Included in this category are national and local tax revenue.They are mainly value added tax, turnover tax, income tax, city maintenance construction tax, use tax of town land, house tax, stamp tax, resource tax, land value increment tax, ect.

Value of foreign investment refers to the investment made by the soley foreign-owned enterprises opened according to the relevant policies and regulations and by means of convertible foreign exchange, physical goods,and technology,ect ; sino-foreign joint venture run by foreign enterprises,ecnomic organizations or individuals(including overseas Chinese,fellow citizens of Hongkong,Macao and Taiwan and Sino-enterprises registered in foreign countries) with Chinese enterprises or Chinese ecnomic organizations. And capital borrow from abroad and within the total value of investment in projects approved by the relevant department of Government.

Total value of export refers to total value of pratical outward cargoes. Our country stipulates that outward cargoes are calculated on FOB basis.

22 “两圈”主要经济指标

Major Economic Indicators of “Twice”

资料整理：李现厂　程文懿

22-1 武汉城市圈主要经济指标(2014)

MAIN ECONOMIC INDICATORS OF WUHAN URBAN CIRCLE(2014)

指标	Item	土地面积(平方公里) Land Area (sq.km)	常住人口(万人) Total Population (year-end) (10 000 persons)	地区生产总值(亿元) Gross Regional Product(100 million yuan)	第一产业(亿元) Primary Industry (100 million million yuan)	第二产业(亿元) Secondary Industry (100 million yuan)	#工业(亿元) #Industry (100 million yuan)	第三产业(亿元) Tertiary Industry (100 million yuan)	人均地区生产总值(元) Per Capita Gross Regional Prduct (yuan/person)
合计	**Total**	**58052**	**3088.99**	**17265.15**	**1565.69**	**8465.89**	**7175.37**	**7233.57**	**56047**
武汉市	Wuhan Municipality	8494	1033.80	10069.48	350.06	4785.66	3942.75	4933.76	97962
黄石市	Huangshi Municipality	4583	244.92	1218.56	105.03	723.45	648.45	390.08	49796
鄂州市	Ezhou Municipality	1594	105.88	686.64	81.15	407.19	370.19	198.30	64906
孝感市	Xiaogan Municipality	8910	486.13	1354.72	252.17	664.36	583.73	438.19	27891
黄冈市	Huanggang Municipality	17446	626.25	1477.15	375.12	586.10	454.02	515.93	23607
咸宁市	Xianning Municipality	9861	248.92	964.25	172.03	476.59	427.66	315.63	38770
仙桃市	Xiantiao Municipality	2538	118.49	552.27	83.96	295.99	272.38	172.32	46984
潜江市	Qianjiang Municipality	2004	95.44	540.22	68.07	316.86	285.96	155.29	56662
天门市	Tianmen Municipality	2622	129.16	401.86	78.10	209.69	190.23	114.07	31145

22-1 续表 1 continued

指标	Item	全社会固定资产投资(亿元) Investment in Fixed Assets (100 million yuan)	地方公共财政预算收入(亿元) Revenue of Local Governments (100 million yuan)	#各项税收(亿元) #Taxes (100 million yuan)	地方财政支出(亿元) Expenditures of Local Governments (100 million yuan)	农村居民人均可支配收入(元) Annual Per Capita Disposable Income of Rural Households (yuan)	城镇居民人均可支配收入(元) Annual Per Capita Disposable Income of Urban Households (yuan)
合计	**Total**	**14149.22**	**1571.46**	**1229.90**	**2343.72**	**10093**	**27264**
武汉市	Wuhan Municipality	6962.53	1101.02	906.76	1175.10	16160	33270
黄石市	Huangshi Municipality	1149.50	89.38	63.75	152.97	10957	25208
鄂州市	Ezhou Municipality	687.08	42.74	28.41	75.65	12692	22763
孝感市	Xiaogan Municipality	1482.93	107.32	69.15	253.18	11597	23491
黄冈市	Huanggang Municipality	1657.59	96.04	64.70	344.66	9388	20729
咸宁市	Xianning Municipality	1148.75	70.76	48.99	176.97	10891	21591
仙桃市	Xiantiao Municipality	374.73	24.16	19.41	59.56	13193	22503
潜江市	Qianjiang Municipality	369.34	22.69	16.63	51.27	12862	22609
天门市	Tianmen Municipality	316.78	17.35	12.10	54.36	12086	20622

22-1 续表 2 continued

指标	Item	农林牧渔业总产值(亿元) Gross Output Value of Agriculture (100 million yuan)	粮食产量(万吨) Output of Grain (10 000 tons)	棉花产量(万吨) Output of Cotton (tons)	油料产量(万吨) Output of Oil-bearing Crops (10 000 tons)	工业企业单位数(个) Number of Enterprises (unit)	房屋建筑竣工面积(万平方米) Floor Space Completed of Buildings (10 000 sq.m)	社会消费品零售总额(亿元) Total Retail Sales(100 million yuan)
合计	**Total**	**2530.60**	**1098.16**	**19.00**	**160.30**	**8255**	**1907.74**	**7456.62**
武汉市	Wuhan Municipality	559.44	127.13	2.05	18.55	2454	765.42	4369.32
黄石市	Huangshi Municipality	147.01	64.98	0.55	9.46	731	86.32	514.08
鄂州市	Ezhou Municipality	143.13	36.39	0.48	6.16	541	20.38	227.84
孝感市	Xiaogan Municipality	470.53	227.41	3.13	23.93	1251	276.92	678.16
黄冈市	Huanggang Municipality	559.63	325.75	5.00	55.61	1413	426.67	701.26
咸宁市	Xianning Municipality	280.29	107.22	0.36	10.45	896	184.40	356.05
仙桃市	Xiantiao Municipality	142.59	82.58	2.29	13.46	396	68.63	230.85
潜江市	Qianjiang Municipality	113.73	73.42	3.05	11.74	273	24.51	148.00
天门市	Tianmen Municipality	114.24	53.27	2.09	10.96	300	54.48	228.08

22-1 续表 3 continued

指标	Item	实际外商直接投资(万美元) Actually Foreign Direct Investments (USD 10 000)	入境旅游者人数(万人次) Number of International Tourists (10 000 person-times)	国际旅游外汇收入(万美元) Foreign Exchange Earnings (USD 10 000)	金融机构人民币存款(亿元) State Bank Deposits (100 million yuan)	金融机构人民币贷款(亿元) State Bank Loans(100 million yuan)	卫生机构床位数(张) Number of Beds in Health Care Institutions (bed)	卫生技术人员(人) Medical and Technical Personnel (person)
合计	**Total**	**625652**	**174.42**	**94824.48**	**23745.24**	**18210.65**	**167694**	**186807**
武汉市	Wuhan Municipality	485755	170.57	93402.53	16268.71	14463.40	72827	81926
黄石市	Huangshi Municipality	55000	0.10	69.00	1273.96	875.25	14183	16123
鄂州市	Ezhou Municipality	31061	0.24	77.71	449.20	303.51	5133	5288
孝感市	Xiaogan Municipality	21094	0.14	59.08	1618.30	786.14	18750	21307
黄冈市	Huanggang Municipality	8689	1.32	385.69	1995.95	811.33	30827	30327
咸宁市	Xianning Municipality	5880	1.71	619.75	893.01	534.21	12351	15667
仙桃市	Xiantiao Municipality	8971	0.23	155.11	429.81	159.05	4609	4770
潜江市	Qianjiang Municipality	5390	0.05	16.74	425.22	150.76	3999	5970
天门市	Tianmen Municipality	3812	0.07	38.87	391.08	127.02	5015	5429

22-2 鄂西生态文化旅游圈主要经济指标(2014)
MAIN ECONOMIC INDICATORS OF WUHAN URBAN CIRCLE(2014)

指标	Item	土地面积(平方公里) Land Area (sq.km)	常住人口(万人) Total Population (year-end) (10 000 persons)	地区生产总值(亿元) Gross Regional Product(100 million yuan)	第一产业 Primary Industry	第二产业 Secondary Industry	#工业 #Industry	第三产业 Tertiary Industry	人均地区生产总值(元) Per Capita Gross Regional Prduct (yuan/person)
合计	**Total**	**127909**	**2728.89**	**11609.07**	**1720.48**	**6221.03**	**5633.80**	**3667.57**	**42570**
宜昌市	Yichang Municipality	21084	410.45	3132.21	351.56	1859.78	1694.80	920.87	76369
荆州市	Jingzhou Municipality	14067	574.42	1480.49	347.00	659.58	594.54	473.91	25784
襄阳市	Xiangyang Municipality	19724	560.02	3129.26	401.60	1804.65	1641.45	923.01	55923
荆门市	Jingmen Municipality	12404	288.91	1310.59	198.11	706.52	658.52	405.96	45378
十堰市	Shiyan Municipality	23680	337.27	1200.82	151.19	610.13	551.53	439.50	35634
随州市	Suizhou Municipality	9636	218.38	723.45	130.09	350.56	307.12	242.80	33156
恩施州	Enshi Prefecture	24061	331.77	612.01	139.03	221.64	180.86	251.34	18463
神龙架	Shennongjia Forest Region	3253	7.67	20.24	1.90	8.17	4.98	10.18	26400

22-2 续表 1 continued

指标	Item	固定资产投资总额(亿元) Investment in Fixed Assets (100 million yuan)	地方公共财政预算收入(亿元) Revenue of Local Governments (100 million yuan)	#地方税收(亿元) #Taxes (100 million yuan)	地方财政支出(亿元) Expenditures of Local Governments (100 million yuan)
合计	**Total**	**10087.96**	**862.38**	**614.96**	**1928.83**
宜昌市	Yichang Municipality	2471.04	271.51	181.51	439.91
荆州市	Jingzhou Municipality	1571.09	88.17	65.56	276.29
襄阳市	Xiangyang Municipality	2448.29	249.23	177.55	437.93
荆门市	Jingmen Municipality	1190.15	69.83	49.76	178.96
十堰市	Shiyan Municipality	1040.32	85.77	65.03	258.87
随州市	Suizhou Municipality	768.81	36.68	27.02	103.71
恩施州	Enshi Prefecture	568.02	57.82	46.44	216.32
神龙架	Shennongjia Forest Region	30.24	3.37	2.09	16.84

农村居民人均可支配收入(元) Annual Per Capita Disposable Income of Rural Households (yuan)	城镇居民人均可支配收入(元) Annual Per Capita Disposable Income of Urban Households (yuan)	农林牧渔业产值(现价)(亿元) Gross Output Value of Agriculture (100 million yuan)	粮食产量(万吨) Output of Grain (10 000 tons)	棉花产量(万吨) Output of Cotton (10 000 tons)	油料产量(万吨) Output of Oil-bearing Crops (10 000 tons)	工业企业单位数(个) Number of Enterprises (unit)
11011	**23274**	**2993.55**	**1790.32**	**18.78**	**181.22**	**7702**
11837	25025	581.45	167.77	2.04	23.82	1476
12625	23128	616.16	400.02	9.64	62.33	1151
12534	24113	704.46	503.72	3.01	24.87	1779
13481	24627	351.67	272.93	3.05	39.56	1097
7046	22143	273.11	117.89	0.01	13.37	973
11984	20959	225.93	160.92	1.04	6.97	710
7194	20245	237.01	164.85	0.00	10.26	505
6920	19810	3.77	2.21	0.00	0.04	11

22-2 续表 2 continued

指标	Item	房地产企业房屋竣工面积合计(万平方米) Floor Space of Building Completed of the Real Enterprises Estate (10 000 sq.m)	房地产企业房屋竣工价值(亿元) Value of Building Completed of the Real Enterprises Estate (100 million yuan)	社会消费品零售总额(亿元) Total Retail Sales(100 million yuan)
合计	**Total**	**1423.44**	**361.56**	**4432.41**
宜昌市	Yichang Municipality	177.63	40.87	964.53
荆州市	Jingzhou Municipality	76.49	17.48	831.44
襄阳市	Xiangyang Municipality	576.96	160.10	1030.57
荆门市	Jingmen Municipality	303.86	53.42	451.78
十堰市	Shiyan Municipality	211.73	47.75	548.65
随州市	Suizhou Municipality	69.84	21.27	354.37
恩施州	Enshi Prefecture	106.92	20.67	243.55
神农架	Shennongjia Forest Region			7.52

实际使用外资(万美元) Actually Foreign Direct Investments (USD 10 000)	入境旅游者人数(万人次) Number of International Tourists (10 000 person-times)	国际旅游外汇收入(万美元) Foreign Exchange Earnings (USD 10 000)	金融机构(含外资)本外币贷款余额(亿元) Financial Institutions Local & Foreign Currency Balance of Loans (100 million yuan)	卫生机构床位数(张) Number of Beds in Health Care Institutions (bed)	卫生技术人员(人) Medical and Technical Personnel (person)
167140.00	**102.65**	**29026.81**	**6932.06**	**150612**	**152977**
31151.00	35.58	8455.89	1967.51	24082	27126
12200.00	1.98	482.60	956.96	25035	26776
63145.00	4.86	3685.49	1507.60	30218	29936
29559.00	1.92	801.53	654.14	15779	16303
18046.00	17.67	5899.63	883.64	24745	24585
9958.00	1.82	904.90	396.58	9379	9760
3081.00	35.64	8097.59	554.92	20950	18156
	3.18	699.18	10.71	424	335

23 县域经济主要指标

Economy of Cities and Counties

资料整理：王　道

23-1 县市主要经济指标
MAIN ECONOMIC INDICATORS OF COUNTIES

指标名称	Item	土地面积(平方公里) Land Area(Sq. km)	常住人口(万人) The Resident (10 000 persons)		#城镇人口(万人) #Urban Population (10 000 persons)		#乡村人口(万人) #Rural Population (10 000 persons)	
		2014	2013	2014	2013	2014	2013	2014
蔡甸区	Caidian District	1108	43.42	43.90	23.71	24.00	19.71	19.90
江夏区	Jiangxia District	2010	83.40	84.65	43.00	43.72	40.40	40.93
黄陂区	Huangpi District	2261	89.78	91.10	37.00	38.55	52.78	52.55
新洲区	Xinzhou District	1500	85.57	86.00	42.79	43.05	42.78	42.95
汉南区	Hannan District	288	12.68	12.90	7.41	7.54	5.27	5.36
阳新县	Yangxin County	2783	82.17	82.34	27.19	28.07	54.98	54.27
大冶市	Daye City	1566	89.96	90.13	48.11	48.59	41.85	41.54
郧阳区	Yun County	3863	56.17	56.31	19.91	20.78	36.26	35.53
郧西县	Yunxi County	3509	45.06	45.11	15.00	15.56	30.06	29.55
竹山县	Zhushan County	3299	41.26	41.29	14.23	14.79	27.03	26.50
竹溪县	Zhuxi County	3585	31.02	31.08	10.27	10.64	20.75	20.44
房县	Fang County	5110	39.39	39.44	13.74	14.22	25.65	25.22
丹江口市	Danjiangkou City	3121	39.07	39.65	18.30	19.21	20.77	20.44
夷陵区	Yiling District	3425	52.24	52.29	24.13	24.93	28.11	27.36
远安县	Yuanan County	1752	18.64	18.67	8.15	8.46	10.49	10.21
兴山县	Xingshan County	2328	17.05	17.07	7.22	7.42	9.83	9.65
秭归县	Zigui County	2427	36.11	36.13	12.67	13.20	23.44	22.93
长阳县	Changyang Tujia A.C.	3430	38.58	38.60	11.02	11.59	27.56	27.01
五峰县	Wufeng Tujia A.C.	2072	18.74	18.77	6.45	6.65	12.29	12.12
宜都市	Yidu City	1357	38.85	38.90	20.12	20.63	18.73	18.27
当阳市	Dangyang City	2159	46.76	46.77	21.45	22.27	25.31	24.50
枝江市	Zhijiang City	1310	50.06	50.05	25.45	26.26	24.61	23.79
襄州区	Xiangzhou District	2306	82.89	83.00	41.87	43.58	41.02	39.42
南漳县	Nanzhang County	3859	53.99	53.92	20.13	20.97	33.86	32.95
谷城县	Gucheng County	2553	50.01	50.21	21.44	22.08	28.57	28.13
保康县	Baokang County	3225	22.28	22.30	8.31	8.78	13.97	13.52
老河口市	Laohekou City	1032	48.36	48.47	23.86	24.52	24.50	23.95
枣阳市	Zaoyang City	3277	98.68	98.95	49.25	50.72	49.43	48.23
宜城市	Yicheng City	2115	51.82	52.02	22.95	23.51	28.87	28.51
梁子湖区	Liangzihu District	500	14.39	14.42	5.47	5.49	8.92	8.93
华容区	Huarong District	493	23.94	23.98	11.51	11.62	12.43	12.36
鄂城区	Echeng District	600	67.37	67.48	49.42	50.21	17.95	17.27
东宝区	Dongbao District	1645	37.12	37.13	24.25	24.74	12.87	12.39
京山县	Jingshan County	3520	54.67	54.70	27.07	28.08	27.60	26.62
沙洋县	Shayang County	2044	57.38	57.41	20.17	20.75	37.21	36.66
钟祥市	Zhongxiang City	4488	90.57	91.22	44.92	46.89	45.65	44.33
孝南区	Xiaonan District	1020	91.61	91.77	63.36	64.48	28.25	27.29
孝昌县	Xiaochang County	1217	59.35	59.45	21.50	22.16	37.85	37.29
大悟县	Dawu County	1979	61.80	61.90	25.15	25.88	36.65	36.02
云梦县	Yunmeng County	604	52.75	52.84	24.88	25.54	27.87	27.30
应城市	Yingcheng City	1103	59.71	59.81	33.33	34.12	26.38	25.69
安陆市	Anlu City	1355	57.62	57.72	26.94	27.82	30.68	29.90
汉川市	Hanchuan City	1632	102.46	102.64	52.48	54.00	49.98	48.64
荆州区	Jingzhou District	1046	56.92	57.27	42.43	42.78	14.49	14.49
江陵县	Jiangling County	981	33.97	33.25	11.35	11.44	22.62	21.81
公安县	Gongan County	2258	89.62	89.99	35.87	37.62	53.75	52.37
监利县	Jianli County	3460	109.84	107.93	42.18	43.42	67.66	64.51
石首市	Shishou City	1424	56.56	57.64	24.00	25.42	32.56	32.22
洪湖市	Honghu City	2221	84.89	85.90	33.36	35.13	51.53	50.77
松滋市	Songci City	2235	77.35	77.36	33.66	35.12	43.70	42.24
黄州区	Huangzhou District	353	36.91	37.22	27.69	28.14	9.22	9.08
团风县	Tuanfeng County	833	34.15	34.06	11.80	12.14	22.35	21.92
红安县	Hongan County	1789	60.38	60.19	22.60	23.29	37.78	36.90
罗田县	Luotian County	2129	54.68	54.69	20.47	21.14	34.21	33.55
英山县	Yingshan County	1449	35.91	35.92	13.09	13.55	22.82	22.37
浠水县	Xishui County	1949	87.65	87.76	31.16	32.28	56.49	55.48
蕲春县	Qichun County	2398	77.02	77.36	28.58	29.83	48.44	47.53
黄梅县	Huangmei County	1246	86.35	86.37	33.30	34.23	53.05	52.14
麻城市	Macheng City	1701	82.02	82.54	33.41	34.83	48.61	47.71
武穴市	Wuxue City	3599	65.12	65.14	31.26	32.11	33.86	33.03
咸安区	Xian'an District	1504	51.65	51.95	35.15	35.42	16.50	16.53
嘉鱼县	Jiayu County	1017	31.62	31.67	13.45	14.08	18.17	17.59
通城县	Tongcheng County	1141	40.85	40.72	15.30	15.98	25.55	24.74
崇阳县	Chongyang County	1968	39.74	39.80	16.70	16.95	23.04	22.85
通山县	Tongshan County	2680	36.34	36.38	13.31	13.97	23.03	22.41
赤壁市	Chibi City	1723	48.30	48.40	23.88	24.78	24.42	23.62
曾都区	Zengdu District	1425	62.37	62.67	40.66	41.75	21.71	20.92
随县	Sui Country	5673	71.42	71.56	21.06	22.59	50.36	48.97
广水市	Guangshui City	2641	76.22	76.37	32.97	34.75	43.25	41.62
恩施市	Enshi City	3972	76.45	76.58	36.76	38.37	39.69	38.21
利川市	Lichuan City	4603	65.84	65.95	23.38	24.84	42.46	41.11
建始县	Jianshi County	2666	41.47	41.54	13.04	14.22	28.43	27.32
巴东县	Badong County	3354	42.37	42.44	13.25	14.12	29.12	28.32
宣恩县	Xuanen County	2730	30.14	30.19	8.77	9.40	21.37	20.79
咸丰县	Xianfeng County	2520	30.37	30.42	10.45	11.24	19.92	19.18
来凤县	Laifeng County	1344	24.45	24.50	7.98	8.78	16.47	15.72
鹤峰县	Hefeng County	2872	20.12	20.15	5.93	6.36	14.19	13.79
仙桃市	Xiantiao City	2520	116.49	116.60	60.28	62.09	56.21	54.51
潜江市	Qianjiang City	1930	95.24	95.44	48.40	49.82	46.84	45.62
天门市	Tianmen City	2528	128.90	129.16	61.85	63.59	67.05	65.57

23-1 续表 1 continued

指标名称	Item	地区生产总值(亿元) Gross Regional Product(100 million yuan)		人均地区生产总值(元) Per Capita GDP (yuan)		固定资产投资(亿元) Investment in Fixed Assets (100 million yuan)		社会消费品零售总额(亿元) Total Retail Sales (100 million yuan)	
		2013	2014	2013	2014	2013	2014	2013	2014
蔡甸区	Caidian District	305.70	345.27	71325	79082	345.44	398.12	72.22	82.18
江夏区	Jiangxia District	550.44	583.37	66483	69429	500.94	487.85	119.60	135.74
黄陂区	Huangpi District	454.31	506.51	50826	56005	477.82	545.97	179.17	204.89
新洲区	Xinzhou District	444.54	501.57	51996	58468	346.89	400.64	155.97	177.03
汉南区	Hannan District	101.88	112.05	81149	87607	135.70	128.39	18.45	21.07
阳新县	Yangxin County	169.02	184.10	20842	22381	191.32	229.78	84.15	93.37
大冶市	Daye City	455.92	500.12	50723	55541	433.37	528.71	157.19	179.13
郧阳区	Yun County	73.62	82.82	13115	14727	109.39	135.92	49.29	56.24
郧西县	Yunxi County	53.19	59.04	13127	13095	50.61	62.30	33.26	37.79
竹山县	Zhushan County	67.13	74.19	16286	17974	95.32	117.77	32.71	36.93
竹溪县	Zhuxi County	56.18	62.02	18133	19975	52.57	64.95	23.77	26.81
房县	Fang County	60.68	66.08	16033	16766	107.12	112.28	36.15	41.18
丹江口市	Danjiangkou City	150.72	165.81	38011	42127	128.48	159.51	57.17	65.28
夷陵区	Yiling District	389.84	441.24	74730	84424	327.49	392.72	86.22	98.37
远安县	Yuanan County	152.09	172.02	81769	92211	147.95	184.50	30.89	35.06
兴山县	Xingshan County	78.08	86.47	45834	50687	27.36	33.77	21.78	24.66
秭归县	Zigui County	91.24	100.53	25289	27831	74.83	92.26	29.48	33.34
长阳县	Changyang Tujia A.C.	100.51	109.88	26087	28473	57.65	71.04	33.72	38.71
五峰县	Wufeng Tujia A.C.	50.59	55.28	27008	29477	34.95	43.01	14.88	16.75
宜都市	Yidu City	402.82	454.93	103823	117023	352.94	439.68	76.26	87.40
当阳市	Dangyang City	352.17	395.48	75398	84568	272.64	339.75	92.83	106.46
枝江市	Zhijiang City	341.95	389.63	71981	77839	290.13	335.62	92.43	103.52
襄州区	Xiangzhou District	456.05	501.53	53082	60465	300.56	447.90	124.59	142.67
南漳县	Nanzhang County	171.23	192.86	31772	35745	156.46	172.11	71.13	79.45
谷城县	Gucheng County	238.75	265.58	47530	53000	154.25	210.43	70.63	80.38
保康县	Baokang County	81.55	92.15	35742	41342	100.56	126.63	33.61	38.71
老河口市	Laohekou City	240.18	268.46	49918	55450	155.02	217.87	84.10	95.62
枣阳市	Zaoyang City	425.43	479.57	44198	48532	261.24	211.00	133.26	121.38
宜城市	Yicheng City	232.46	259.90	44951	50058	169.33	209.97	73.09	83.37
梁子湖区	Liangzihu District	52.14	56.36	36279	39125	33.41	46.11	14.68	16.67
华容区	Huarong District	191.60	217.23	85459	90664	250.01	299.60	36.50	42.15
鄂城区	Echeng District	387.20	416.38	57568	61755	283.77	340.50	156.05	174.39
东宝区	Dongbao District	234.44	262.91	68440	70818	226.46	274.55	119.52	137.15
京山县	Jingshan County	268.99	291.02	49864	53218	235.99	297.58	101.01	116.82
沙洋县	Shayang County	198.21	213.96	35566	37279	111.20	139.66	58.55	66.92
钟祥市	Zhongxiang City	332.37	361.83	37165	39807	276.72	330.13	115.97	133.64
孝南区	Xiaonan District	226.38	248.70	27999	27124	264.61	296.42	109.57	123.38
孝昌县	Xiaochang County	92.65	97.31	15777	16383	95.72	110.53	40.83	45.47
大悟县	Dawu County	104.99	110.25	17015	17825	131.90	161.64	54.40	61.15
云梦县	Yunmeng County	173.13	185.19	32875	35077	161.51	198.32	78.09	88.55
应城市	Yingcheng City	202.35	220.60	33962	36914	174.89	214.94	98.69	112.80
安陆市	Anlu City	144.79	157.26	25196	27269	154.39	163.19	78.37	89.50
汉川市	Hanchuan City	344.71	386.15	37184	37655	232.33	294.59	149.82	171.71
荆州区	Jingzhou District	195.48	216.72	34568	37958	217.61	261.58	112.35	128.19
江陵县	Jiangling County	54.96	62.21	16316	18511	43.18	57.68	27.50	31.16
公安县	Gongan County	176.37	194.89	19678	21701	168.59	206.18	98.02	112.24
监利县	Jianli County	194.87	214.78	18215	19726	126.48	154.72	95.28	108.81
石首市	Shishou City	121.91	136.29	21471	23868	117.07	143.06	76.81	87.72
洪湖市	Honghu City	163.48	182.42	19526	21362	105.15	120.00	82.04	93.52
松滋市	Songci City	179.29	200.81	23548	25960	166.98	203.89	93.00	106.39
黄州区	Huangzhou District	157.61	173.97	42713	46936	179.83	220.12	82.90	94.09
团风县	Tuanfeng County	64.35	71.76	18884	21042	56.64	68.46	20.28	22.61
红安县	Hongan County	107.67	120.76	17835	20031	117.66	143.23	44.88	51.50
罗田县	Luotian County	95.75	105.66	17838	19321	116.24	139.79	44.17	49.23
英山县	Yingshan County	71.26	78.55	19847	21870	60.82	73.79	22.72	25.67
浠水县	Xishui County	165.24	183.18	18861	20886	131.91	163.20	85.45	97.08
蕲春县	Qichun County	162.36	180.44	21215	23376	174.75	210.90	78.46	88.07
黄梅县	Huangmei County	148.83	163.43	17670	18924	150.79	172.50	83.16	94.52
麻城市	Macheng City	203.40	226.21	24577	27492	211.18	267.15	90.16	103.63
武穴市	Wuxue City	202.86	224.59	34495	34484	170.54	207.24	84.12	96.44
咸安区	Xian'an District	208.33	225.15	40406	43465	261.57	307.11	81.97	92.24
嘉鱼县	Jiayu County	174.27	189.03	55210	59735	155.44	198.03	41.54	47.69
通城县	Tongcheng County	95.09	103.84	23312	25460	96.27	116.54	41.95	47.75
崇阳县	Chongyang County	88.08	96.95	22225	24378	96.94	119.35	39.51	44.71
通山县	Tongshan County	81.21	90.10	22409	24780	110.96	133.40	36.84	41.29
赤壁市	Chibi City	284.76	316.39	65140	65437	231.82	309.18	97.04	111.95
曾都区	Zengdu District	307.28	334.15	51350	53447	252.30	314.98	142.11	162.43
随县	Sui Country	152.45	164.82	21207	23055	181.24	217.95	90.64	103.45
广水市	Guangshui City	210.98	228.01	28730	29885	195.05	235.89	81.72	91.70
恩施市	Enshi City	141.50	157.28	18524	20453	105.23	128.81	68.49	78.25
利川市	Lichuan City	82.01	90.97	12467	13729	67.83	82.89	31.48	35.64
建始县	Jianshi County	64.11	71.30	15473	17105	53.91	66.11	20.30	22.98
巴东县	Badong County	74.00	81.45	17483	19208	61.07	74.52	23.75	26.86
宣恩县	Xuanen County	45.28	50.26	15038	16596	27.52	33.21	13.37	15.08
咸丰县	Xianfeng County	54.49	60.66	17961	19866	37.87	46.54	19.75	22.54
来凤县	Laifeng County	47.09	53.01	19279	21584	40.33	50.12	17.24	19.67
鹤峰县	Hefeng County	39.51	43.62	19656	21630	31.51	37.35	16.62	18.87
仙桃市	Xiantiao City	504.28	552.27	42921	47387	306.78	374.73	202.50	233.58
潜江市	Qianjiang City	492.70	540.22	53470	56662	303.26	369.34	131.56	150.19
天门市	Tianmen City	365.19	401.86	30231	31145	260.75	316.78	202.40	231.05

23-1 续表 2 continued

指标名称	Item	财政总收入(亿元) Total Fiscal Revenue (100 million yuan) 2013	2014	地方公共财政预算收入(亿元) Revenue of Local Governments (100 million yuan) 2013	2014	#税收(亿元) Taxes (100 million yuan) 2013	2014
蔡甸区	Caidian District	38.13	41.33	25.55	26.79	14.70	16.83
江夏区	Jiangxia District	77.22	87.23	53.96	62.82	39.80	47.03
黄陂区	Huangpi District	58.28	64.35	40.71	46.74	32.52	32.82
新洲区	Xinzhou District	36.76	43.08	24.66	28.60	16.45	19.04
汉南区	Hannan District	19.71	22.58	11.42	13.11	10.22	11.69
阳新县	Yangxin County	12.60	15.10	8.45	10.24	5.61	6.80
大冶市	Daye City	60.12	67.34	35.12	40.48	23.13	28.30
郧阳区	Yun County	8.55	9.85	4.98	6.00	3.49	4.42
郧西县	Yunxi County	3.50	4.13	2.50	3.00	1.76	2.14
竹山县	Zhushan County	5.28	6.08	3.97	4.56	2.90	3.28
竹溪县	Zhuxi County	4.26	5.14	3.21	3.80	2.27	2.77
房县	Fang County	5.42	5.49	3.99	4.02	2.89	2.89
丹江口市	Danjiangkou City	14.34	17.22	9.76	11.53	6.85	8.02
夷陵区	Yiling District	42.73	48.62	27.08	33.89	19.39	22.01
远安县	Yuanan County	12.17	14.72	9.38	11.74	6.34	8.00
兴山县	Xingshan County	9.25	10.62	6.01	7.57	4.16	4.81
秭归县	Zigui County	8.07	9.67	6.20	7.84	4.55	5.39
长阳县	Changyang Tujia A.C.	7.74	9.03	5.77	7.28	3.71	4.43
五峰县	Wufeng Tujia A.C.	3.11	3.82	2.33	2.91	1.72	2.13
宜都市	Yidu City	37.13	41.50	30.00	36.62	22.61	24.14
当阳市	Dangyang City	27.94	32.78	20.02	25.03	14.10	16.87
枝江市	Zhijiang City	27.58	32.37	20.22	25.32	15.22	18.45
襄州区	Xiangzhou District	22.62	28.99	18.32	23.81	13.55	17.22
南漳县	Nanzhang County	10.07	12.24	7.97	10.37	6.21	7.83
谷城县	Gucheng County	15.65	20.02	12.19	15.98	8.39	10.71
保康县	Baokang County	9.61	11.44	7.30	9.13	4.48	5.52
老河口市	Laohekou City	19.62	24.12	16.50	21.00	10.89	13.85
枣阳市	Zaoyang City	24.34	29.43	21.02	26.25	13.85	17.34
宜城市	Yicheng City	17.75	21.37	15.26	19.08	9.22	11.56
梁子湖区	Liangzihu District	3.01	3.05	2.40	2.45	1.85	1.79
华容区	Huarong District	6.63	6.66	4.86	4.97	3.68	3.53
鄂城区	Echeng District	18.02	17.64	13.38	13.09	10.51	9.42
东宝区	Dongbao District	19.61	23.14	13.70	17.19	12.34	15.67
京山县	Jingshan County	14.28	16.99	10.74	12.75	7.64	9.06
沙洋县	Shayang County	6.34	7.52	4.92	5.81	3.54	3.99
钟祥市	Zhongxiang City	15.51	19.56	11.91	15.15	7.97	9.46
孝南区	Xiaonan District	19.16	23.78	13.52	16.56	9.40	11.07
孝昌县	Xiaochang County	9.01	10.19	7.08	8.01	4.25	4.86
大悟县	Dawu County	10.14	11.83	6.82	7.93	4.15	4.77
云梦县	Yunmeng County	12.02	14.41	9.00	10.98	5.90	7.04
应城市	Yingcheng City	17.29	20.08	12.00	14.17	7.53	9.08
安陆市	Anlu City	10.16	12.13	7.29	8.75	5.14	6.25
汉川市	Hanchuan City	22.72	26.90	14.34	17.50	9.70	12.18
荆州区	Jingzhou District	14.50	19.90	10.75	13.20	8.28	11.11
江陵县	Jiangling County	2.81	3.54	1.87	2.44	1.20	1.60
公安县	Gongan County	11.99	12.33	7.59	9.20	5.73	6.22
监利县	Jianli County	5.67	7.49	3.69	5.42	3.21	4.58
石首市	Shishou City	7.30	9.64	4.85	6.19	3.27	4.31
洪湖市	Honghu City	7.27	8.94	5.21	6.62	3.66	4.77
松滋市	Songci City	15.08	18.81	8.50	10.80	5.99	7.27
黄州区	Huangzhou District	11.99	14.18	8.54	10.58	6.24	7.83
团风县	Tuanfeng County	4.89	5.80	3.68	4.32	2.45	2.90
红安县	Hongan County	16.12	20.47	7.88	10.37	5.34	7.27
罗田县	Luotian County	6.39	7.33	4.48	5.37	2.79	3.55
英山县	Yingshan County	3.80	4.54	2.83	3.34	1.93	2.34
浠水县	Xishui County	8.88	10.18	6.32	7.52	3.98	4.93
蕲春县	Qichun County	11.67	13.66	8.31	10.02	5.13	6.36
黄梅县	Huangmei County	9.96	11.72	7.51	8.84	4.74	5.62
麻城市	Macheng City	14.99	17.62	11.17	13.03	7.35	8.51
武穴市	Wuxue City	14.59	16.79	10.68	12.82	7.05	8.52
咸安区	Xian'an District	11.40	15.41	8.41	11.51	6.63	9.09
嘉鱼县	Jiayu County	9.41	11.18	7.28	8.80	5.18	6.27
通城县	Tongcheng County	6.41	8.11	4.70	5.83	2.95	3.72
崇阳县	Chongyang County	5.47	6.81	4.22	5.30	2.80	3.52
通山县	Tongshan County	6.36	7.32	4.82	5.81	3.31	4.01
赤壁市	Chibi City	17.11	20.63	13.12	15.75	8.96	10.48
曾都区	Zengdu District	16.57	19.97	11.86	14.91	9.32	11.93
随县	Sui Country	4.65	6.42	3.06	4.11	2.19	2.90
广水市	Guangshui City	16.60	17.80	7.41	8.73	5.41	6.26
恩施市	Enshi City	20.93	23.50	15.54	18.33	13.61	15.94
利川市	Lichuan City	13.70	15.18	7.72	8.76	5.87	6.63
建始县	Jianshi County	7.77	8.48	4.08	4.62	3.18	3.57
巴东县	Badong County	7.64	7.72	5.21	5.42	4.18	4.05
宣恩县	Xuanen County	3.14	3.69	2.19	2.59	1.84	2.21
咸丰县	Xianfeng County	5.18	5.77	3.01	3.41	2.14	2.45
来凤县	Laifeng County	6.09	6.86	2.51	3.14	2.10	2.56
鹤峰县	Hefeng County	3.10	3.57	2.02	2.36	1.70	2.01
仙桃市	Xiantiao City	32.46	36.51	21.00	24.16	16.73	19.41
潜江市	Qianjiang City	29.93	34.05	20.00	22.69	14.96	16.63
天门市	Tianmen City	19.37	22.25	15.02	17.35	10.52	12.10

23-1 续表 3 continued

指标名称	Item	外贸出口（万美元） Total Exports (USD 10 000)		城镇居民人均可支配收入(元) Annual Per Capita Disposable Income of Urban (yuan)		农村居民人均可支配收入(元) Annual Per Capita Disposable Income of Rural Households(yuan)	
		2013	2014	2013	2014	2013	2014
蔡甸区	Caidian District	4035	47271	22344	24735	13328	15021
江夏区	Jiangxia District	14205	16933	21969	24309	13453	15101
黄陂区	Huangpi District	7883	9073	21754	24103	13055	14713
新洲区	Xinzhou District	16552	18382	20364	22503	12764	14410
汉南区	Hannan District	11478	13016	22249	24496	13623	15292
阳新县	Yangxin County	24129	25129	16298	17900	7451	8379
大冶市	Daye City	26826	32826	25920	28473	13013	14523
郧阳区	Yun County	5003	6516	18273	20247	6203	7038
郧西县	Yunxi County	1008	1654	17380	19193	5992	6805
竹山县	Zhushan County	1310	1928	17075	18894	6090	6900
竹溪县	Zhuxi County	1394	1603	16996	18507	6031	6818
房县	Fang County	8279	3889	18001	19888	6080	6878
丹江口市	Danjiangkou City	2638	3008	18962	21002	6778	7728
夷陵区	Yiling District	7634	8651	23476	25778	12625	14389
远安县	Yuanan County	10390	11639	21496	23587	11779	13401
兴山县	Xingshan County	27711	28517	18722	20552	7700	8757
秭归县	Zigui County	3827	5971	18180	19937	6467	7336
长阳县	Changyang Tujia A.C.	5489	5552	18771	20580	6571	7448
五峰县	Wufeng Tujia A.C.	402	926	17112	18761	6313	7164
宜都市	Yidu City	32139	37006	23843	26213	13206	15035
当阳市	Dangyang City	9164	10384	22495	24716	13347	15114
枝江市	Zhijiang City	20294	25158	21542	23675	13503	15285
襄州区	Xiangzhou District	26759	30726	20390	22354	12108	13585
南漳县	Nanzhang County	5747	9475	20215	22160	10126	11351
谷城县	Gucheng County	10884	13646	20412	22484	10358	11620
保康县	Baokang County	3927	4690	18022	19817	7445	8376
老河口市	Laohekou City	21853	26489	21780	23975	11946	13401
枣阳市	Zaoyang City	16640	21649	22382	24665	11676	13100
宜城市	Yicheng City	15000	18734	20228	22243	11831	13263
梁子湖区	Liangzihu District	120	172	15873	17380	8632	9704
华容区	Huarong District	6542	6505	18675	20428	11825	13273
鄂城区	Echeng District	10962	13705	21796	23836	12274	13766
东宝区	Dongbao District	6277	7399	24235	26498	12201	13622
京山县	Jingshan County	14163	17183	21554	23649	12087	13495
沙洋县	Shayang County	8559	11395	21371	23465	11896	13255
钟祥市	Zhongxiang City	16088	21903	21567	23681	12398	13839
孝南区	Xiaonan District	17120	16769	22912	25155	11735	13153
孝昌县	Xiaochang County	3401	4207	18898	20620	7092	7774
大悟县	Dawu County	1693	1880	19100	20846	7261	7957
云梦县	Yunmeng County	3927	13385	21549	23710	12071	13605
应城市	Yingcheng City	7706	8505	21891	24047	12352	13923
安陆市	Anlu City	5256	6111	20953	23050	10405	11731
汉川市	Hanchuan City	38877	43039	21621	23760	11780	13308
荆州区	Jingzhou District	7940	10629	23529	25846	12618	14158
江陵县	Jiangling County	1623	974	18856	20644	10026	11258
公安县	Gongan County	7101	7645	20011	21991	11793	13182
监利县	Jianli County	4777	6525	18802	20609	11021	12308
石首市	Shishou City	14891	17041	19689	21621	11140	12476
洪湖市	Honghu City	2951	6836	19502	21414	11045	12364
松滋市	Songci City	12312	10745	20022	21995	11295	12678
黄州区	Huangzhou District	8244	9714	21110	23242	10292	11566
团风县	Tuanfeng County	987	1160	17262	18988	7707	8635
红安县	Hongan County	1167	1523	17865	19516	7177	8057
罗田县	Luotian County	4374	4878	17538	19206	7029	7790
英山县	Yingshan County	1044	1418	17173	18840	7536	8364
浠水县	Xishui County	4315	5317	18437	20284	8903	9965
蕲春县	Qichun County	6526	8462	18190	20013	8372	9424
黄梅县	Huangmei County	2895	3739	18757	20738	9322	10453
麻城市	Macheng City	3910	4496	19272	21209	8088	9038
武穴市	Wuxue City	10612	12705	19934	22005	9692	10927
咸安区	Xian'an District	6869	10962	21636	23758	10769	12080
嘉鱼县	Jiayu County	7027	7888	19395	21286	11181	12551
通城县	Tongcheng County	5355	5238	18701	20547	9520	10661
崇阳县	Chongyang County	1825	2139	17690	19422	9140	10253
通山县	Tongshan County	1016	1079	16484	18073	7149	8050
赤壁市	Chibi City	7016	8551	20288	22273	11055	12400
曾都区	Zengdu District	56824	71026	20896	22939	11108	12535
随县	Sui Country	48907	48447	17207	18897	10803	12067
广水市	Guangshui City	6940	7976	18965	20769	10470	11743
恩施市	Enshi City	10940	12601	20071	22142	6585	7453
利川市	Lichuan City	6295	7201	18231	20092	6299	7091
建始县	Jianshi County	2888	3992	17182	19018	6271	7145
巴东县	Badong County	5786	6819	17301	19123	6317	7140
宣恩县	Xuanen County	2184	2779	17094	18870	6269	7048
咸丰县	Xianfeng County	4088	4797	17009	18919	6230	7077
来凤县	Laifeng County	1710	2220	17583	19398	6263	7050
鹤峰县	Hefeng County	4583	5265	17375	19231	6677	7546
仙桃市	Xiantiao City	42384	52134	20429	22503	11809	13193
潜江市	Qianjiang City	38123	43778	20541	22609	11448	12862
天门市	Tianmen City	5499	7054	18703	20622	10809	12086

23-1 续表 4 continued

指标名称	Item	农业总产值(亿元) Total Value of Agricultural Output (100 million yuan)		农产品加工业产值(亿元) Value of Agricultural Product Processing (100 million yuan)		常用耕地面积(千公顷) Area of Cultivated Land (1000 hectare)		粮食产量(万吨) Output of Grain (10 000 tons)	
		2013	2014	2013	2014	2013	2014	2013	2014
蔡甸区	Caidian District	57.53	61.19	194.40	199.60	24.53	24.35	13.28	13.34
江夏区	Jiangxia District	130.18	138.68	76.60	100.56	34.63	35.69	29.15	29.24
黄陂区	Huangpi District	160.49	170.97	152.30	187.47	52.54	52.44	46.06	46.11
新洲区	Xinzhou District	119.56	127.18	95.13	106.28	50.04	50.47	32.43	32.51
汉南区	Hannan District	21.52	22.28	28.57	26.77	9.85	10.05	3.40	3.41
阳新县	Yangxin County	67.07	73.92	29.47	41.44	51.74	51.64	35.33	35.37
大冶市	Daye City	60.00	65.69	139.29	162.44	35.70	35.67	28.01	28.51
郧阳区	Yun County	39.72	43.41	25.53	41.33	35.45	35.25	23.00	23.73
郧西县	Yunxi County	38.11	41.32	4.33	7.10	26.84	26.84	18.50	19.05
竹山县	Zhushan County	37.78	41.40	18.10	20.40	33.76	32.71	23.52	23.53
竹溪县	Zhuxi County	39.53	43.11	13.68	15.35	29.51	29.53	24.07	24.11
房县	Fang County	42.66	46.57	26.48	27.44	28.49	28.14	14.50	14.90
丹江口市	Danjiangkou City	45.52	49.71	49.11	60.75	21.11	21.19	11.90	12.01
夷陵区	Yiling District	83.42	87.37	391.74	531.25	33.66	33.65	21.62	21.73
远安县	Yuanan County	27.25	28.53	43.94	61.04	11.94	11.98	10.30	10.38
兴山县	Xingshan County	17.81	18.90	18.41	19.50	16.21	16.21	5.95	5.99
秭归县	Zigui County	32.88	34.43	44.75	50.45	23.80	23.70	8.95	9.19
长阳县	Changyang Tujia A.C.	53.49	56.00	42.41	51.17	39.65	40.65	10.61	11.03
五峰县	Wufeng Tujia A.C.	30.80	32.22	22.35	23.49	20.43	20.43	8.30	8.44
宜都市	Yidu City	64.87	67.92	220.40	258.17	15.84	15.84	11.30	11.43
当阳市	Dangyang City	115.85	121.26	214.57	262.01	54.13	54.64	52.48	53.74
枝江市	Zhijiang City	112.17	117.42	296.99	341.26	45.52	45.52	33.97	34.82
襄州区	Xiangzhou District	160.07	164.46	263.25	255.19	109.59	110.35	135.97	136.14
南漳县	Nanzhang County	68.17	72.51	97.67	107.79	41.19	40.90	44.93	45.04
谷城县	Gucheng County	54.21	56.79	103.79	222.57	28.52	28.53	27.80	27.88
保康县	Baokang County	34.69	35.36	31.35	37.39	22.93	22.80	14.10	14.30
老河口市	Laohekou City	69.13	72.34	248.53	263.82	40.45	40.46	37.18	37.23
枣阳市	Zaoyang City	156.70	161.00	327.98	352.54	111.11	111.00	136.31	136.49
宜城市	Yicheng City	84.78	87.09	264.43	306.72	62.32	62.32	69.50	69.59
梁子湖区	Liangzihu District	36.40	41.55	6.61	7.10	13.50	14.61	11.63	10.99
华容区	Huarong District	34.00	43.93	119.68	138.90	13.00	14.11	10.40	11.67
鄂城区	Echeng District	66.70	57.64	32.17	40.69	14.00	12.15	11.70	13.72
东宝区	Dongbao District	26.12	27.14	67.60	73.08	20.21	20.26	17.23	17.32
京山县	Jingshan County	87.49	91.04	367.90	430.88	69.29	69.64	71.70	73.40
沙洋县	Shayang County	94.29	97.98	182.29	220.09	78.45	78.44	81.90	83.80
钟祥市	Zhongxiang City	110.03	114.50	355.48	319.92	82.99	83.01	87.43	89.03
孝南区	Xiaonan District	52.05	54.11	130.19	142.18	34.10	34.10	21.62	21.87
孝昌县	Xiaochang County	52.20	54.15	23.95	15.06	32.63	32.71	26.67	26.92
大悟县	Dawu County	52.24	55.24	23.19	24.64	36.68	36.68	28.55	28.95
云梦县	Yunmeng County	58.64	60.88	158.33	153.86	25.42	25.52	21.73	22.05
应城市	Yingcheng City	76.70	79.28	127.05	131.61	38.19	38.56	36.20	36.90
安陆市	Anlu City	59.16	61.19	126.26	143.91	33.32	33.32	33.82	34.60
汉川市	Hanchuan City	100.16	104.40	494.99	582.44	65.16	65.98	54.62	55.69
荆州区	Jingzhou District	60.87	64.98	152.13	173.23	34.98	34.98	21.86	22.77
江陵县	Jiangling County	32.79	35.34	38.80	51.38	37.99	37.99	27.10	28.63
公安县	Gongan County	96.77	102.33	119.73	138.28	80.38	80.38	64.20	67.12
监利县	Jianli County	147.31	155.88	182.22	210.77	137.70	137.69	140.50	143.59
石首市	Shishou City	54.56	59.07	62.39	87.31	40.92	41.47	21.80	23.22
洪湖市	Honghu City	100.83	109.03	123.72	152.90	64.20	64.19	68.98	71.33
松滋市	Songci City	61.19	63.68	145.48	173.01	59.63	59.63	34.20	35.65
黄州区	Huangzhou District	19.95	20.98	71.28	68.41	10.82	10.75	5.50	5.70
团风县	Tuanfeng County	21.85	23.00	19.21	26.84	17.85	17.63	12.81	13.03
红安县	Hongan County	34.34	36.09	49.51	47.07	38.22	37.78	23.02	23.22
罗田县	Luotian County	36.80	38.71	18.41	23.60	26.25	26.35	25.47	25.60
英山县	Yingshan County	44.07	46.10	25.45	33.25	17.27	17.28	13.55	14.01
浠水县	Xishui County	85.71	90.16	71.19	89.53	44.47	44.63	50.48	51.07
蕲春县	Qichun County	64.36	68.05	100.00	117.82	40.67	40.96	51.50	52.96
黄梅县	Huangmei County	64.48	67.89	124.83	142.71	54.63	54.63	49.15	50.01
麻城市	Macheng City	82.13	86.33	45.89	73.57	53.05	53.05	54.20	55.36
武穴市	Wuxue City	70.19	73.77	91.88	80.35	36.02	36.77	31.15	32.38
咸安区	Xian'an District	42.89	44.25	191.22	205.04	35.54	35.16	18.75	19.38
嘉鱼县	Jiayu County	64.24	69.63	171.98	195.29	30.72	31.75	17.98	18.37
通城县	Tongcheng County	32.21	35.49	25.79	30.64	21.29	21.29	18.70	18.72
崇阳县	Chongyang County	38.09	39.25	18.81	19.27	23.29	23.21	19.70	20.26
通山县	Tongshan County	21.71	25.86	20.99	30.15	14.84	23.52	8.48	8.75
赤壁市	Chibi City	65.57	65.81	202.64	198.44	32.97	32.97	21.03	21.72
曾都区	Zengdu District	41.01	42.75	133.04	164.41	25.93	25.99	25.75	26.28
随县	Sui Country	100.68	105.01	128.55	158.22	78.28	78.30	91.07	92.62
广水市	Guangshui City	75.03	78.17	128.31	179.02	39.14	39.10	41.35	42.01
恩施市	Enshi City	40.80	42.56	57.95	66.40	47.14	47.08	23.10	23.39
利川市	Lichuan City	48.88	50.98	31.88	33.42	58.16	58.33	36.70	36.96
建始县	Jianshi County	29.14	30.39	11.78	13.98	34.31	34.35	23.16	23.40
巴东县	Badong County	27.34	28.52	19.19	19.89	36.32	36.32	22.21	22.59
宣恩县	Xuanen County	23.69	24.71	16.77	19.00	24.75	24.73	12.90	13.20
咸丰县	Xianfeng County	22.48	23.45	21.44	22.87	26.24	27.23	23.08	23.38
来凤县	Laifeng County	18.40	19.19	12.86	12.32	17.15	17.01	12.60	12.79
鹤峰县	Hefeng County	16.50	17.21	28.67	35.55	16.22	16.28	9.10	9.14
仙桃市	Xiantiao City	136.29	142.59	637.65	493.10	90.54	90.54	80.99	82.58
潜江市	Qianjiang City	109.28	114.24	398.69	473.80	72.10	72.18	52.00	53.27
天门市	Tianmen City	108.58	113.73	309.76	353.70	109.66	110.16	71.50	73.42

23-1 续表 5 continued

指标名称	Item	棉花产量(吨) Output of Cotton Cotton (ton)		油料产量(万吨) Output of Oil-bearing Crops(10 000 tons)		肉类产量(万吨) Output of Meat (10 000 tons)	
		2013	2014	2013	2014	2013	2014
蔡甸区	Caidian District	6418	4278	1.34	1.53	1.50	1.45
江夏区	Jiangxia District	138	196	4.14	4.27	7.81	8.09
黄陂区	Huangpi District	3510	2450	6.35	6.41	7.61	8.32
新洲区	Xinzhou District	14502	9672	5.79	5.47	3.31	3.72
汉南区	Hannan District	5615	2794	0.17	0.14	1.99	1.91
阳新县	Yangxin County	3650	2646	4.81	4.84	3.91	4.26
大冶市	Daye City	3520	2552	4.32	4.36	4.40	4.62
郧阳区	Yun County	88	56	1.98	2.04	4.58	5.45
郧西县	Yunxi County	22	14	1.61	1.63	2.00	2.63
竹山县	Zhushan County			4.23	4.27	1.86	2.22
竹溪县	Zhuxi County			2.54	2.57	2.07	2.67
房县	Fang County	44	28	1.70	1.72	2.04	2.90
丹江口市	Danjiangkou City	34	22	1.06	1.08	1.91	2.54
夷陵区	Yiling District	9		2.80	2.86	7.97	8.44
远安县	Yuanan County			1.37	1.36	2.44	2.57
兴山县	Xingshan County			0.82	0.82	2.72	3.07
秭归县	Zigui County			1.55	1.40	4.60	4.80
长阳县	Changyang Tujia A.C.			1.43	1.35	5.82	7.55
五峰县	Wufeng Tujia A.C.			0.57	0.54	2.91	3.09
宜都市	Yidu City	34	25	2.10	2.13	5.69	6.83
当阳市	Dangyang City	8100	5207	7.52	7.54	8.81	9.22
枝江市	Zhijiang City	24473	15126	5.42	5.51	8.56	9.03
襄州区	Xiangzhou District	14282	10283	8.16	8.14	10.65	15.37
南漳县	Nanzhang County	552	343	0.94	0.94	7.52	10.37
谷城县	Gucheng County			1.44	1.45	4.90	6.59
保康县	Baokang County			1.05	1.06	2.42	3.17
老河口市	Laohekou City	6034	4345	2.58	2.17	5.08	6.76
枣阳市	Zaoyang City	8922	6425	1.28	1.47	8.02	12.07
宜城市	Yicheng City	9783	6850	7.35	7.35	6.23	8.57
梁子湖区	Liangzihu District	657	1281	1.77	1.68	2.38	2.56
华容区	Huarong District	2412	2450	1.80	2.31	2.65	2.42
鄂城区	Echeng District	3881	1101	2.51	2.16	4.19	9.71
东宝区	Dongbao District	1024	850	2.84	3.20	3.65	5.27
京山县	Jingshan County	13590	7927	5.08	5.14	8.97	9.64
沙洋县	Shayang County	10762	7017	13.56	13.84	7.04	9.36
钟祥市	Zhongxiang City	20238	13621	13.19	12.92	9.56	10.56
孝南区	Xiaonan District	6698	5044	3.07	2.98	2.30	2.56
孝昌县	Xiaochang County	1681	1276	3.89	3.73	3.45	4.38
大悟县	Dawu County	337	256	5.61	5.92	3.46	4.17
云梦县	Yunmeng County	3537	2686	2.12	2.10	3.47	3.74
应城市	Yingcheng City	4470	3363	3.37	3.23	3.61	3.84
安陆市	Anlu City	1065	890	2.02	2.00	7.91	8.83
汉川市	Hanchuan City	23444	17669	3.99	3.82	5.25	5.57
荆州区	Jingzhou District	14549	7130	5.86	5.63	2.82	2.94
江陵县	Jiangling County	10382	7068	7.37	7.49	2.65	2.85
公安县	Gongan County	40273	29815	12.67	12.56	6.57	6.47
监利县	Jianli County	25004	16787	12.63	12.15	7.98	8.35
石首市	Shishou City	18426	13841	7.05	7.13	4.59	5.10
洪湖市	Honghu City	9957	6798	8.60	9.01	3.07	3.58
松滋市	Songci City	15581	11200	7.62	7.41	9.62	10.14
黄州区	Huangzhou District	9818	5800	0.61	0.60	0.63	1.02
团风县	Tuanfeng County	6046	3532	2.36	2.38	0.72	1.97
红安县	Hongan County	1772	1062	10.08	10.06	3.75	4.92
罗田县	Luotian County	348	368	2.85	2.98	1.73	3.08
英山县	Yingshan County	181	506	1.63	1.74	1.57	1.88
浠水县	Xishui County	12225	8046	7.64	7.84	6.39	8.16
蕲春县	Qichun County	8003	5008	5.37	5.39	4.03	7.64
黄梅县	Huangmei County	21420	9580	6.47	6.64	4.82	5.48
麻城市	Macheng City	12320	7500	10.42	9.84	6.73	11.90
武穴市	Wuxue City	13041	7703	7.91	8.06	6.60	7.68
咸安区	Xian'an District	228	150	4.38	4.44	3.83	4.59
嘉鱼县	Jiayu County	1844	1177	1.05	1.08	1.53	1.70
通城县	Tongcheng County	284	200	0.49	0.54	5.79	6.09
崇阳县	Chongyang County	806	560	1.11	1.16	4.84	5.47
通山县	Tongshan County			0.51	0.53	1.52	2.03
赤壁市	Chibi City	2332	1500	2.66	2.70	2.35	2.66
曾都区	Zengdu District	3785	2000	0.82	0.79	5.23	5.92
随县	Sui Country	8519	5356	2.40	2.42	7.66	9.56
广水市	Guangshui City	7094	3000	4.14	3.76	5.11	6.65
恩施市	Enshi City	25	7	1.77	1.81	8.16	9.29
利川市	Lichuan City			1.38	1.29	6.46	7.17
建始县	Jianshi County			1.62	1.58	5.96	6.57
巴东县	Badong County	11	8	2.06	2.09	6.59	7.10
宣恩县	Xuanen County			0.61	0.55	4.48	5.29
咸丰县	Xianfeng County			1.47	1.71	5.44	5.90
来凤县	Laifeng County			0.71	0.72	2.38	2.59
鹤峰县	Hefeng County			0.54	0.50	1.98	2.24
仙桃市	Xiantiao City	29259	22858	13.05	13.46	8.85	9.12
潜江市	Qianjiang City	39733	20874	11.42	10.96	8.33	9.03
天门市	Tianmen City	49266	30548	11.46	11.74	7.80	8.44

附录

全国分省主要指标

Major Indicators by Region

资料整理：王　道

附录1-1　各地区年末常住人口

THE END OF THE TOTAL POPULATION OF ALL REGIONS

单位：万人　　(10 000 persons)

地　区	Region	2008	2009	2010	2011	2012	2013	2014
全　国	**National Total**	**132802**	**133450**	**134091**	**134735**	**135404**	**136072**	**136782**
北　京	Beijing	1695	1755	1962	2019	2069	2115	2152
天　津	Tianjin	1176	1228	1299	1355	1413	1472	1517
河　北	Hebei	6989	7034	7194	7241	7288	7333	7384
山　西	Shanxi	3411	3427	3574	3593	3611	3630	3648
内蒙古	Inner Mongolia	2444	2458	2472	2482	2490	2498	2505
辽　宁	Liaoning	4315	4341	4375	4383	4389	4390	4391
吉　林	Jilin	2734	2740	2747	2749	2750	2751	2752
黑龙江	Heilongjiang	3825	3826	3833	3834	3834	3835	3833
上　海	Shanghai	2141	2210	2303	2347	2380	2415	2426
江　苏	Jiangsu	7762	7810	7869	7899	7920	7939	7960
浙　江	Zhejiang	5212	5276	5447	5463	5477	5498	5508
安　徽	Anhui	6135	6131	5957	5968	5988	6030	6083
福　建	Fujian	3639	3666	3693	3720	3748	3774	3806
江　西	Jiangxi	4400	4432	4462	4488	4504	4522	4542
山　东	Shangdong	9417	9470	9588	9637	9685	9733	9789
河　南	Henan	9429	9487	9405	9388	9406	9413	9436
湖　北	**Hubei**	**5711**	**5720**	**5728**	**5758**	**5779**	**5799**	**5816**
湖　南	Hunan	6380	6406	6570	6596	6639	6691	6737
广　东	Guangdong	9893	10130	10441	10505	10594	10644	10724
广　西	Guangxi	4816	4856	4610	4645	4682	4719	4754
海　南	Hainan	854	864	869	877	887	895	903
重　庆	Chongqing	2839	2859	2885	2919	2945	2970	2991
四　川	Sichuan	8138	8185	8045	8050	8076	8107	8140
贵　州	Guizhou	3596	3537	3479	3469	3484	3502	3508
云　南	Yunnan	4543	4571	4602	4631	4659	4687	4714
西　藏	Tibet	292	297	301	303	308	312	318
陕　西	Shaanxi	3718	3727	3735	3743	3753	3764	3775
甘　肃	Gansu	2551	2555	2560	2564	2578	2582	2591
青　海	Qinghai	554	557	563	568	573	578	583
宁　夏	Ningxia	618	625	633	639	647	654	662
新　疆	Xinjiang	2131	2159	2185	2209	2233	2264	2298

注：1.全国数据包括中国人民解放军现役军人数，但不包括香港、澳门特别行政区和台湾省数据；分省数据中未包括中国人民解放军现役军人数。
2.分地区数据均为常住人口。
3.2010年数据为第六次全国人口普查初步汇总数。

Notes:a)The number of national data including military personnel, but not including Hong Kong and Macao Special Administrative Region and Taiwan Province; provincial data does not include active duty PLA.
b)The regional data are permanent population.
c)2010 years of data for the sixth national census preliminary summary number.

附录1-2 各地区按三次产业分法人单位数(2013)
REGIONS BY THE NUMBER OF UNITS THREE INDUSTRIES CORPORATE UNITS(2013)

单位：个 (unit)

地 区	Region	法人单位数 Corporate Units	第一产业 Primary Industry	第二产业 Secondary Industry	#工业 #Industry	第三产业 Tertiary Industry
全 国	**National Total**	**10825611**	**1815**	**2743347**	**2395828**	**8080449**
北 京	Beijing	627051	60	51740	33314	575251
天 津	Tianjin	211404	1	53924	44683	157479
河 北	Hebei	434833	38	115349	101325	319446
山 西	Shanxi	205135	34	34163	27971	170938
内蒙古	Inner Mongolia	157864	70	25614	21376	132180
辽 宁	Liaoning	415421	48	108790	89063	306583
吉 林	Jilin	130301	34	26435	21494	103832
黑龙江	Heilongjiang	173343	183	33483	27335	139677
上 海	Shanghai	409125	10	95065	78902	314050
江 苏	Jiangsu	1047033	28	391733	348449	655272
浙 江	Zhejiang	962213	152	393069	369653	568992
安 徽	Anhui	350360	86	91946	75873	258328
福 建	Fujian	373792	72	104108	93986	269612
江 西	Jiangxi	241367	28	58424	51314	182915
山 东	Shangdong	823846	27	218082	188123	605737
河 南	Henan	510502	13	120655	107811	389834
湖 北	**Hubei**	**424368**	**79**	**82924**	**66485**	**341365**
湖 南	Hunan	403026	43	80298	72066	322685
广 东	Guangdong	1070306	87	334528	310589	735691
广 西	Guangxi	236831	129	34375	29645	202327
海 南	Hainan	45679	68	6373	3199	39238
重 庆	Chongqing	254834	89	53576	46457	201169
四 川	Sichuan	373424	47	68083	58275	305294
贵 州	Guizhou	146514	17	32330	28713	114167
云 南	Yunnan	190607	89	32809	25049	157709
西 藏	Tibet	21162	1	3302	1235	17859
陕 西	Shaanxi	243170	17	42776	32297	200377
甘 肃	Gansu	130203	33	18458	15621	111712
青 海	Qinghai	34202	20	5321	4114	28861
宁 夏	Ningxia	43029	20	7220	5951	35789
新 疆	Xinjiang	134666	192	18394	15460	116080

附录1-3 各地区按行业分法人单位数(2013)

REGION NUMBER OF CORPORATE UNITS BY SECTOR(2013)

单位：个 (unit)

地 区	Region	法人单位数 Corporate Units	#农、林、牧、渔业 Agriculture, Forestry, Animal husbandry, Fishery	#采矿业 Mining Industry	#制造业 Manufacturing	#电力、煤气及水的生产和供应业 Electricity, Gas and Water Production and Supply	#建筑业 Construction	#交通运输、仓储及邮政业 Traffic, Transport, Storage and Postal Industry
全国总计	**National Total**	**10825611**	**161824**	**89112**	**2252225**	**70409**	**347519**	**262048**
北 京	Beijing	627051	561	127	33023	638	18426	14150
天 津	Tianjin	211404	481	93	44653	528	9241	10440
河 北	Hebei	434833	9590	6588	93568	1839	14024	9582
山 西	Shanxi	205135	5022	5567	21612	1211	6192	5205
内蒙古	Inner Mongolia	157864	7416	4657	15438	1587	4238	4492
辽 宁	Liaoning	415421	9607	5444	82972	1895	19727	12109
吉 林	Jilin	130301	7610	1182	19348	1149	4941	3146
黑龙江	Heilongjiang	173343	10946	1866	24466	1367	6148	4305
上 海	Shanghai	409125	368	2	79599	165	16163	15013
江 苏	Jiangsu	1047033	12971	643	346771	2471	43284	25948
浙 江	Zhejiang	962213	4118	1279	365388	4338	23416	16851
安 徽	Anhui	350360	11993	2405	71494	2426	16073	10242
福 建	Fujian	373792	2468	2157	86140	6096	10122	8976
江 西	Jiangxi	241367	4108	3635	44179	3758	7110	8097
山 东	Shangdong	823846	12933	3733	183231	2399	29959	21632
河 南	Henan	510502	10713	5741	100313	2181	12844	9392
湖 北	**Hubei**	**424368**	**7819**	**3749**	**60233**	**2969**	**16439**	**10062**
湖 南	Hunan	403026	7023	7122	59905	5339	8232	6398
广 东	Guangdong	1070306	8613	2794	300938	8431	23939	26662
广 西	Guangxi	236831	3420	2988	24216	2587	4730	5092
海 南	Hainan	45679	784	240	2661	345	3174	1127
重 庆	Chongqing	254834	2982	2206	42594	1929	7119	5035
四 川	Sichuan	373424	4505	4660	48284	5701	9808	7846
贵 州	Guizhou	146514	1084	5575	21692	1606	3617	2648
云 南	Yunnan	190607	4541	5739	17148	2291	7760	4006
西 藏	Tibet	21162	44	160	981	119	2067	254
陕 西	Shaanxi	243170	1958	3314	28282	1831	10479	4885
甘 肃	Gansu	130203	1872	1779	12677	1374	2837	2514
青 海	Qinghai	34202	465	715	2997	443	1207	710
宁 夏	Ningxia	43029	1117	676	5040	282	1269	979
新 疆	Xinjiang	134666	4692	2276	12382	1114	2934	4250

附录1−3　续表1 continued

单位：个 (unit)

地　区	Region	#信息传输、计算机服务和软件业 Information Transmission, Computer Services and Software	#批发和零售业 Wholesale and Retail Trade	#住宿和餐饮业 Accommodation and Catering Services	#房地产业 Real Estate	#租赁和商务服务业 Leasing and Business Services
全国总计	**National Total**	**226107**	**2810531**	**199592**	**343924**	**916953**
北　京	Beijing	47608	190705	16323	17806	134953
天　津	Tianjin	7844	66138	2981	5842	23441
河　北	Hebei	4211	111227	4458	13782	24379
山　西	Shanxi	1744	45404	3411	6747	12053
内蒙古	Inner Mongolia	1869	39002	2773	6041	10390
辽　宁	Liaoning	8724	115758	6474	15314	32694
吉　林	Jilin	2399	28095	1594	4384	8223
黑龙江	Heilongjiang	2703	39955	2693	6024	9757
上　海	Shanghai	14045	145683	12514	15129	51181
江　苏	Jiangsu	21460	299067	11328	29144	77822
浙　江	Zhejiang	16505	253594	13887	23807	73675
安　徽	Anhui	6130	82267	5874	12522	28508
福　建	Fujian	6636	97491	6430	10048	29040
江　西	Jiangxi	2506	44458	3291	7337	15567
山　东	Shangdong	10079	236206	12168	21817	49917
河　南	Henan	4809	99916	11136	14387	22923
湖　北	**Hubei**	**7728**	**119635**	**10214**	**15705**	**30386**
湖　南	Hunan	5672	91397	9228	11361	24175
广　东	Guangdong	27126	291131	18606	41719	131863
广　西	Guangxi	2546	64262	3472	8447	18610
海　南	Hainan	855	10880	1362	4165	4543
重　庆	Chongqing	5775	80603	12436	8709	20506
四　川	Sichuan	5120	56653	7794	10927	25165
贵　州	Guizhou	1410	28382	4060	5550	9129
云　南	Yunnan	3433	41751	3572	7488	14332
西　藏	Tibet	144	1913	461	158	1004
陕　西	Shaanxi	3694	55337	5933	8226	13100
甘　肃	Gansu	1047	25811	2483	3845	6033
青　海	Qinghai	373	5312	734	1139	2094
宁　夏	Ningxia	422	10963	702	1371	2643
新　疆	Xinjiang	1490	31535	1200	4983	8847

附录1-3 续表2 continued

单位：个 (unit)

地区	Region	#科学研究、技术服务和地质勘查业 Research, Technical Service and Geological Prospecting	#水利、环境和公共设施管理业 Water, Environment and Public Facilities Management	#居民服务和其他服务业 Resident Services and Other Services	#教育 Education	#卫生、社会保障和社会福利业 Health, Social Security and Social Welfare	#文化、体育和娱乐业 Culture, Sports and Entertainment	#公共管理和社会组织 Public Management and Social Organization
全国总计	**National Total**	**455778**	**84803**	**190692**	**413908**	**249567**	**230544**	**1520075**
北京	Beijing	71148	3964	18734	11145	3811	26787	17142
天津	Tianjin	14491	1416	5798	3803	1500	2544	10170
河北	Hebei	13650	3243	6292	19794	9432	7388	81786
山西	Shanxi	6911	2583	2801	10068	5321	5601	57682
内蒙古	Inner Mongolia	5512	2129	2621	6488	4775	3104	35332
辽宁	Liaoning	17888	3745	7471	13308	11978	7967	42346
吉林	Jilin	4556	1335	2942	5572	3483	2736	27606
黑龙江	Heilongjiang	5916	1708	2748	7719	5573	3988	35461
上海	Shanghai	17386	2035	12073	5708	3118	6266	12677
江苏	Jiangsu	40130	7501	14760	17858	14231	15410	66234
浙江	Zhejiang	25323	5542	12375	21049	7375	14697	78994
安徽	Anhui	12606	3043	5473	14217	8574	8852	47661
福建	Fujian	12126	3028	5993	13974	7483	7234	58350
江西	Jiangxi	6936	2414	3892	13457	9845	5098	55679
山东	Shangdong	40568	5025	11901	24364	18572	11541	127801
河南	Henan	24110	4033	6898	40079	34020	13048	93959
湖北	**Hubei**	**20212**	**4821**	**9419**	**17774**	**11427**	**10128**	**65648**
湖南	Hunan	13489	3866	7827	21741	16035	14474	89742
广东	Guangdong	35982	5549	17589	36113	10362	14695	68194
广西	Guangxi	10361	2762	3541	18301	5387	6665	49444
海南	Hainan	1525	384	847	3110	1054	1343	7280
重庆	Chongqing	6947	1710	7613	10133	5337	5682	27518
四川	Sichuan	15817	3537	5285	23458	17582	12806	108476
贵州	Guizhou	3919	1224	3418	9880	3998	2853	36469
云南	Yunnan	7507	2347	3122	9890	5171	5432	45077
西藏	Tibet	445	72	125	791	318	363	11743
陕西	Shaanxi	9181	2661	4236	14851	14694	5611	54897
甘肃	Gansu	3713	1156	1805	9421	3941	3331	44564
青海	Qinghai	1266	445	477	1677	1050	888	12210
宁夏	Ningxia	1209	395	691	1855	914	1087	11414
新疆	Xinjiang	4948	1130	1925	6310	3206	2925	38519

附录1-4 地区生产总值

GROSS DOMESTIC PRODUCT

单位：亿元 (100 million yuan)

地 区	Region	2008	2009	2010	2011	2012	2013	2014
北 京	Beijing	11115.0	12153.0	14113.6	16251.9	17879.4	19800.8	21330.8
天 津	Tianjin	6719.0	7521.9	9224.5	11307.3	12893.9	14442.0	15722.5
河 北	Hebei	16012.0	17235.5	20394.3	24515.8	26575.0	28443.0	29421.2
山 西	Shanxi	7315.4	7358.3	9200.9	11237.6	12112.8	12665.3	12759.4
内蒙古	Inner Mongolia	8496.2	9740.3	11672.0	14359.9	15880.6	16916.5	17769.5
辽 宁	Liaoning	13668.6	15212.5	18457.3	22226.7	24846.4	27213.2	28626.6
吉 林	Jilin	6426.1	7278.8	8667.6	10568.8	11939.2	13046.4	13803.8
黑龙江	Heilongjiang	8314.4	8587.0	10368.6	12582.0	13691.6	14454.9	15039.4
上 海	Shanghai	14069.9	15046.5	17166.0	19195.7	20181.7	21818.2	23560.9
江 苏	Jiangsu	30982.0	34457.3	41425.5	49110.3	54058.2	59753.4	65088.3
浙 江	Zhejiang	21462.7	22990.4	27722.3	32318.9	34665.3	37756.6	40153.5
安 徽	Anhui	8851.7	10062.8	12359.3	15300.6	17212.1	19229.3	20848.8
福 建	Fujian	10823.0	12236.5	14737.1	17560.2	19701.8	21868.5	24055.8
江 西	Jiangxi	6971.1	7655.2	9451.3	11702.8	12948.9	14410.2	15708.6
山 东	Shangdong	30933.3	33896.7	39169.9	45361.9	50013.2	55230.3	59426.6
河 南	Henan	18018.5	19480.5	23092.4	26931.0	29599.3	32191.3	34939.4
湖 北	**Hubei**	**11328.9**	**12961.1**	**15967.6**	**19632.3**	**22250.5**	**24791.8**	**27367.0**
湖 南	Hunan	11555.0	13059.7	16038.0	19669.6	22154.2	24621.7	27048.5
广 东	Guangdong	36796.7	39482.6	46013.1	53210.3	57067.9	62474.8	67792.2
广 西	Guangxi	7021.0	7759.2	9569.9	11720.9	13035.1	14449.9	15673.0
海 南	Hainan	1503.1	1654.2	2064.5	2522.7	2855.5	3177.6	3500.7
重 庆	Chongqing	5793.7	6530.0	7925.6	10011.4	11409.6	12783.3	14265.4
四 川	Sichuan	12601.2	14151.3	17185.5	21026.7	23872.8	26392.1	28536.7
贵 州	Guizhou	3561.6	3912.7	4602.2	5701.8	6852.2	8086.9	9251.0
云 南	Yunnan	5692.1	6169.8	7224.2	8893.1	10309.5	11832.3	12814.6
西 藏	Tibet	394.9	441.4	507.5	605.8	701.0	815.7	920.8
陕 西	Shaanxi	7314.6	8169.8	10123.5	12512.3	14453.7	16205.5	17689.9
甘 肃	Gansu	3166.8	3387.6	4120.8	5020.4	5650.2	6330.7	6835.3
青 海	Qinghai	1018.6	1081.3	1350.4	1670.4	1893.5	2122.1	2301.1
宁 夏	Ningxia	1203.9	1353.3	1689.7	2102.2	2341.3	2577.6	2752.1
新 疆	Xinjiang	4183.2	4277.1	5437.5	6610.1	7505.3	8443.8	9264.1

注：本表按当年价格计算。本表数据为国家统计局最终核实数。

Note:The table at current prices.National Bureau of Statistics data for this table is to verify the final number.

附录1-5　地区生产总值指数

INDICES OF GROSS DOMESTIC PRODUCT

(上年=100)　(last year=100)

地　区	Region	2008	2009	2010	2011	2012	2013	2014
北　京	Beijing	109.1	110.2	110.3	108.1	107.7	107.7	107.3
天　津	Tianjin	116.5	116.5	117.4	116.4	113.8	112.5	110.0
河　北	Hebei	110.1	110.0	112.2	111.3	109.6	108.2	106.5
山　西	Shanxi	108.5	105.4	113.9	113.0	110.1	108.9	104.9
内蒙古	Inner Mongolia	117.8	116.9	115.0	114.3	111.5	109.0	107.8
辽　宁	Liaoning	113.4	113.1	114.2	112.1	109.5	108.7	105.8
吉　林	Jilin	116.0	113.6	113.8	113.7	112.0	108.3	106.5
黑龙江	Heilongjiang	111.8	111.4	112.7	112.2	110.0	108.0	105.6
上　海	Shanghai	109.7	108.2	110.3	108.2	107.5	107.7	107.0
江　苏	Jiangsu	112.7	112.4	112.7	111.0	110.1	109.6	108.7
浙　江	Zhejiang	110.1	108.9	111.9	109.0	108.0	108.2	107.6
安　徽	Anhui	112.7	112.9	114.6	113.5	112.1	110.4	109.2
福　建	Fujian	113.0	112.3	113.9	112.2	111.4	111.0	109.9
江　西	Jiangxi	113.2	113.1	114.0	112.5	111.0	110.1	109.7
山　东	Shangdong	112.0	112.2	112.3	110.9	109.8	109.6	108.7
河　南	Henan	112.1	110.9	112.5	111.6	110.1	109.0	108.9
湖　北	**Hubei**	**113.4**	**113.5**	**114.8**	**113.8**	**111.3**	**110.1**	**109.7**
湖　南	Hunan	113.9	113.7	114.6	112.8	111.3	110.1	109.5
广　东	Guangdong	110.4	109.7	112.4	110.0	108.2	108.5	107.8
广　西	Guangxi	112.8	113.9	114.2	112.3	111.3	110.2	108.5
海　南	Hainan	110.3	111.7	116.0	112.0	109.1	109.9	108.5
重　庆	Chongqing	114.5	114.9	117.1	116.4	113.6	112.3	110.9
四　川	Sichuan	111.0	114.5	115.1	115.0	112.6	110.0	108.5
贵　州	Guizhou	111.3	111.4	112.8	115.0	113.6	112.5	110.8
云　南	Yunnan	110.6	112.1	112.3	113.7	113.0	112.1	108.1
西　藏	Tibet	110.1	112.4	112.3	112.7	111.8	112.1	110.8
陕　西	Shaanxi	116.4	113.6	114.6	113.9	112.9	111.0	109.7
甘　肃	Gansu	110.1	110.3	111.8	112.5	112.6	110.8	108.9
青　海	Qinghai	113.5	110.1	115.3	113.5	112.3	110.8	109.2
宁　夏	Ningxia	112.6	111.9	113.5	112.0	111.5	109.8	108.0
新　疆	Xinjiang	111.0	108.1	110.6	112.0	112.0	111.0	110.0

注：本表按不变价格计算。本表数据为国家统计局最终核实数。

Note:At constant prices, this table.National Bureau of Statistics data for this table is to verify the final number.

附录1-6　地区生产总值构成(2014)

COMPOSITION OF GROSS DOMESTIC PRODUCT(2014)

(地区生产总值=100)

(GDP=100)

地 区	Region	第一产业 Primary Industry	第二产业 Secondary Industry	工业 Industry	建筑业 Contruction	第三产业 Tertiary Industry
北 京	Beijing	0.8	21.3	17.6	3.7	78.0
天 津	Tianjin	1.3	49.2	45.1	4.1	49.6
河 北	Hebei	11.7	51.1	45.3	5.7	37.2
山 西	Shanxi	6.2	49.7	43.3	6.4	44.1
内蒙古	Inner Mongolia	9.2	51.3	44.5	6.8	39.5
辽 宁	Liaoning	8.0	50.3	44.2	6.0	41.8
吉 林	Jilin	11.0	52.8	46.5	6.3	36.2
黑龙江	Heilongjiang	17.4	36.6	31.5	5.1	46.0
上 海	Shanghai	0.5	34.7	31.3	3.4	64.8
江 苏	Jiangsu	5.6	47.7	41.7	6.0	46.7
浙 江	Zhejiang	4.4	47.7	41.7	6.0	47.9
安 徽	Anhui	11.5	53.7	46.0	7.8	34.8
福 建	Fujian	8.4	52.0	43.3	8.7	39.6
江 西	Jiangxi	10.7	53.4	44.5	8.9	35.9
山 东	Shangdong	8.1	48.4	42.6	5.8	43.5
河 南	Henan	11.9	51.2	45.5	5.7	36.9
湖 北	**Hubei**	**11.6**	**46.9**	**40.2**	**6.8**	**41.5**
湖 南	Hunan	11.6	46.2	39.7	6.4	42.2
广 东	Guangdong	4.7	46.2	42.9	3.3	49.1
广 西	Guangxi	15.4	46.8	38.7	8.1	37.8
海 南	Hainan	23.1	25.0	14.7	10.3	51.9
重 庆	Chongqing	7.4	45.8	36.3	9.5	46.8
四 川	Sichuan	12.4	50.9	43.5	7.4	36.8
贵 州	Guizhou	13.8	41.6	34.0	7.6	44.6
云 南	Yunnan	15.5	41.2	30.4	10.8	43.2
西 藏	Tibet	9.9	36.6	7.2	29.4	53.5
陕 西	Shaanxi	8.9	54.8	45.7	9.0	36.4
甘 肃	Gansu	13.2	42.8	33.1	9.7	44.0
青 海	Qinghai	9.4	53.5	41.5	12.1	37.1
宁 夏	Ningxia	7.9	48.8	35.4	13.4	43.3
新 疆	Xinjiang	16.6	42.4	34.3	8.1	41.0

注：本表按当年价格计算。本表数据为国家统计局最终核实数。

Note:At present year price,this table.National Bureau of Statistics data for this table is to verify the final number.

附录1-7 人均地区生产总值

PER CAPITA GROSS DOMESTIC PRODUCT

单位：元　　本表按当年价格计算（At current price）　　（yuan）

地区	Region	2008	2009	2010	2011	2012	2013	2014
北 京	Beijing	66797	70452	75943	80394	87091	94648	99985
天 津	Tianjin	58656	62574	72994	84337	93110	100105	105195
河 北	Hebei	22986	24581	28668	33571	36584	38909	39984
山 西	Shanxi	21506	21522	26283	30974	33628	34984	35064
内蒙古	Inner Mongolia	34869	39735	47347	57515	64319	67836	71041
辽 宁	Liaoning	31739	35149	42355	50299	56547	61996	65201
吉 林	Jilin	23521	26595	31599	38321	43412	47427	50166
黑龙江	Heilongjiang	21740	22447	27076	32615	35711	37697	39226
上 海	Shanghai	66932	69164	76074	82560	85033	90993	97336
江 苏	Jiangsu	40014	44253	52840	61649	68347	75354	81875
浙 江	Zhejiang	41405	43842	51711	58665	63266	68805	72967
安 徽	Anhui	14448	16408	20888	25340	28792	32001	34424
福 建	Fujian	29755	33437	40025	46972	52763	58145	63472
江 西	Jiangxi	15900	17335	21253	25884	28799	31930	34661
山 东	Shangdong	32936	35894	41106	47260	51768	56885	60880
河 南	Henan	19181	20597	24446	28981	31723	34211	37072
湖 北	**Hubei**	**19858**	**22677**	**27906**	**34131**	**38572**	**42826**	**47124**
湖 南	Hunan	18147	20428	24719	29828	33480	36943	40288
广 东	Guangdong	37638	39436	44736	50295	54095	58833	63452
广 西	Guangxi	14652	16045	20219	25315	27943	30741	33090
海 南	Hainan	17691	19254	23831	28797	32374	35667	38934
重 庆	Chongqing	20490	22920	27596	34500	39083	43223	47862
四 川	Sichuan	15495	17339	21182	26133	29579	32617	35129
贵 州	Guizhou	9855	10971	13119	16413	19566	23151	26393
云 南	Yunnan	12570	13539	15752	18957	22195	25322	27263
西 藏	Tibet	13588	15008	17027	20077	22757	26327	29230
陕 西	Shaanxi	19700	21947	27133	33142	38557	43116	46929
甘 肃	Gansu	12421	13269	16113	19517	21978	24539	26426
青 海	Qinghai	18421	19454	24115	28891	33023	36875	39647
宁 夏	Ningxia	19609	21777	26860	32392	36166	39613	41819
新 疆	Xinjiang	19797	19942	25034	29496	33621	37552	40612

附录1-8 各地区全社会固定资产投资

REGIONAL TOTAL INVESTMENT IN FIXED ASSETS

单位：亿元 (100 million yuan)

地 区	Region	2008	2009	2010	2011	2012	2013	2014
全国总计	**National Total**	**172828.4**	**224598.8**	**278121.9**	**311485.1**	**374694.7**	**447074.4**	**512760.7**
北 京	Beijing	3814.7	4616.9	5403.0	5578.9	6112.4	6847.1	6924.2
天 津	Tianjin	3389.8	4738.2	6278.1	7067.7	7934.8	9130.3	10518.2
河 北	Hebei	8866.6	12269.8	15083.4	16389.3	19661.3	23194.2	26671.9
山 西	Shanxi	3531.2	4943.2	6063.2	7073.1	8863.3	11031.9	12296.1
内蒙古	Inner Mongolia	5475.4	7336.8	8926.5	10365.2	11875.7	14215.5	17585.0
辽 宁	Liaoning	10019.1	12292.5	16043.0	17726.3	21836.3	25107.7	24730.8
吉 林	Jilin	5038.9	6411.6	7870.4	7441.7	9511.5	10133.5	11486.5
黑龙江	Heilongjiang	3656.0	5028.8	6812.6	7475.4	9694.7	12126.0	9878.2
上 海	Shanghai	4823.1	5043.8	5108.9	4962.1	5117.6	5647.8	6016.5
江 苏	Jiangsu	15300.6	18949.9	23184.3	26692.6	30854.2	36373.8	41938.7
浙 江	Zhejiang	9323.0	10742.3	12376.0	14185.3	17649.4	20777.1	24262.8
安 徽	Anhui	6747.0	8990.7	11542.9	12455.7	15425.8	18621.6	21688.5
福 建	Fujian	5207.7	6231.2	8199.1	9910.9	12439.9	15327.4	18219.8
江 西	Jiangxi	4745.4	6643.1	8772.3	9087.6	10774.2	12866.1	15109.9
山 东	Shangdong	15435.9	19034.5	23280.5	26749.7	31256.0	36789.1	42495.5
河 南	Henan	10490.6	13704.5	16585.9	17769.0	21450.0	26220.9	30782.2
湖 北	**Hubei**	**5647.0**	**7866.9**	**10262.7**	**12557.3**	**15578.3**	**19307.3**	**22965.3**
湖 南	Hunan	5534.0	7703.4	9663.6	11880.9	14523.2	17846.3	21269.7
广 东	Guangdong	10868.7	12933.1	15623.7	17069.2	18751.5	22307.8	26294.0
广 西	Guangxi	3756.4	5237.2	7057.6	7990.7	9808.6	11907.7	13843.2
海 南	Hainan	705.4	988.3	1317.0	1657.2	2145.4	2697.4	3112.3
重 庆	Chongqing	3979.6	5214.3	6688.9	7473.4	8736.2	10429.6	12281.1
四 川	Sichuan	7127.8	11371.9	13116.7	14222.2	17040.0	20325.2	23318.7
贵 州	Guizhou	1864.5	2412.0	3104.9	4235.9	5717.8	7373.6	9025.7
云 南	Yunnan	3435.9	4526.4	5528.7	6191.0	7831.1	9968.3	11498.6
西 藏	Tibet	309.9	378.3	462.7	516.3	670.5	876.0	1069.2
陕 西	Shaanxi	4614.4	6246.9	7963.7	9431.1	12044.5	14867.3	17192.1
甘 肃	Gansu	1712.8	2363.0	3158.3	3965.8	5145.0	6527.9	7884.1
青 海	Qinghai	583.2	798.2	1016.9	1435.6	1883.4	2361.1	2861.2
宁 夏	Ningxia	828.9	1075.9	1444.2	1644.7	2096.9	2651.1	3173.8
新 疆	Xinjiang	2260.0	2725.5	3423.2	4632.1	6158.8	7724.5	9438.3
不分地区	**Irrespective of region**	**3734.9**	**5779.7**	**6759.1**	**5651.3**	**6106.4**	**5493.3**	**6928.7**

附录1–9　各地区固定资产投资
REGIONAL INVESTMENT IN FIXED ASSET

单位：亿元　　(100 million yuan)

地　区	Region	2008	2009	2010	2011	2012	2013	2014
全国总计	**National Total**	**148738.30**	**193920.39**	**241430.89**	**302396.06**	**364854.15**	**436527.70**	**502004.90**
北　京	Beijing	3520.95	4149.63	4916.53	5519.84	6064.86	6797.54	6873.44
天　津	Tianjin	3175.14	4446.57	5896.52	7040.68	7913.26	9103.01	10490.37
河　北	Hebei	7463.77	10476.50	12922.66	15780.26	19104.63	22629.77	26147.20
山　西	Shanxi	3194.57	4509.56	5526.60	6837.69	8584.85	10745.35	11976.96
内蒙古	Inner Mongolia	5327.04	7143.84	8687.99	10252.97	11749.77	14070.50	17431.05
辽　宁	Liaoning	8881.95	11605.12	15106.33	17431.46	21535.37	24791.40	24426.83
吉　林	Jilin	4592.71	5958.95	7395.23	7226.65	9262.23	9880.00	11254.84
黑龙江	Heilongjiang	3354.82	4695.74	6292.67	7157.92	9375.44	11794.17	9587.09
上　海	Shanghai	4404.95	4618.91	4630.47	4959.93	5114.64	5644.13	6012.97
江　苏	Jiangsu	11609.71	14266.80	17416.47	26313.46	30473.74	35983.00	41552.75
浙　江	Zhejiang	6551.10	7454.33	8438.08	13651.65	17095.96	20189.07	23554.76
安　徽	Anhui	5948.61	7945.50	10281.29	12007.87	14943.81	18090.89	21069.24
福　建	Fujian	4601.50	5548.61	7385.78	9677.09	12182.52	15045.81	17911.71
江　西	Jiangxi	4325.38	6008.12	7856.94	8753.93	10378.37	12450.84	14677.04
山　东	Shangdong	12528.96	15439.10	18844.41	25907.38	30319.76	35875.86	41599.13
河　南	Henan	8721.19	11454.89	13934.82	16934.32	20558.61	25321.52	30012.28
湖　北	**Hubei**	**5148.76**	**7183.67**	**9405.63**	**12195.39**	**15148.71**	**18796.85**	**22491.67**
湖　南	Hunan	4879.96	6880.00	8617.98	11407.74	13966.26	17230.14	20575.33
广　东	Guangdong	8640.87	10230.05	12599.26	16599.16	18250.13	21794.98	25843.06
广　西	Guangxi	3325.95	4689.88	6383.26	7580.90	9345.18	11383.93	13287.60
海　南	Hainan	668.02	942.68	1257.50	1599.14	2064.44	2625.02	3039.46
重　庆	Chongqing	3715.90	4855.11	6170.61	7366.95	8610.37	10285.29	12136.52
四　川	Sichuan	6362.08	9090.09	11061.38	13687.75	16530.31	19754.36	22662.26
贵　州	Guizhou	1609.34	2049.83	2609.36	4026.47	5504.95	7102.78	8778.40
云　南	Yunnan	3106.33	4117.51	5052.61	5932.75	7553.51	9621.83	11073.86
西　藏	Tibet	271.25	327.64	404.98	516.31	670.52	876.00	1069.23
陕　西	Shaanxi	4286.42	5888.37	7569.90	9108.98	11705.83	14516.71	16840.44
甘　肃	Gansu	1510.75	2076.36	2808.55	3870.08	5040.03	6407.20	7759.62
青　海	Qinghai	514.05	689.09	840.01	1365.91	1808.67	2285.30	2788.91
宁　夏	Ningxia	735.71	964.16	1292.80	1589.14	2033.03	2577.79	3093.92
新　疆	Xinjiang	2025.64	2434.15	3065.13	4444.99	5857.98	7363.39	9058.31
不分地区	**Irrespective of region**	**3734.93**	**5779.66**	**6759.14**	**5651.29**	**6106.38**	**5493.28**	**6928.66**

注：2010年前为城镇固定资产投资口径；2011年起为固定资产投资（不含农户）。

Note: Datas of the table are urban fixed asset investment before 2011, and are investment in fixed assets in 2011.

附录1-10　各地区房地产开发企业(单位)房屋施工、竣工面积和商品房销售面积

REGIONAL REAL ESTATE DEVELOPMENT ENTERPRISES(UNITS) HOUSING CONSTRUCTION, COMPLETION AND SALES OF COMMERCIAL SPACE AREA

单位：万平方米　　(10 000 sqm)

地　区	Region	房屋施工面积 Housing Construction Area		房屋竣工面积 Housing Completed Area		商品房销售面积 Sales of Commercial Area	
		2013	2014	2013	2014	2013	2014
全国总计	**National Total**	**665572**	**726482**	**101435**	**107459**	**130551**	**120649**
北　京	Beijing	13887	13588	2666	3054	1903	1454
天　津	Tianjin	10892	10652	2805	2925	1847	1613
河　北	Hebei	29949	31628	4437	4038	5676	5706
山　西	Shanxi	14040	15477	2285	2182	1643	1576
内蒙古	Inner Mongolia	18624	18474	2638	2012	2738	2457
辽　宁	Liaoning	41626	38617	6152	6147	9292	5755
吉　林	Jilin	12181	12268	2254	1574	2215	1582
黑龙江	Heilongjiang	13567	14218	2933	3001	3340	2476
上　海	Shanghai	13517	14690	2254	2313	2382	2085
江　苏	Jiangsu	52574	57638	9712	9620	11455	9847
浙　江	Zhejiang	37647	42144	4692	6390	4887	4677
安　徽	Anhui	30235	33479	5180	5196	6265	6202
福　建	Fujian	26287	30052	3370	3584	4676	4119
江　西	Jiangxi	11996	13333	1790	1872	3167	3067
山　东	Shangdong	50549	54508	7509	7787	10330	9180
河　南	Henan	35979	38858	5966	7324	7310	7880
湖　北	**Hubei**	**21866**	**26322**	**3041**	**3431**	**5299**	**5602**
湖　南	Hunan	25400	27748	4594	4023	5952	5440
广　东	Guangdong	46480	53977	6273	7328	9836	9316
广　西	Guangxi	16040	17472	1713	1866	2996	3157
海　南	Hainan	6173	7557	609	1204	1191	1004
重　庆	Chongqing	26252	28624	3804	3718	4818	5100
四　川	Sichuan	32165	36499	5109	5334	7313	7142
贵　州	Guizhou	17357	20369	1765	2842	2972	3178
云　南	Yunnan	18261	20035	2019	1789	3309	3194
西　藏	Tibet	58	273	18	52	25	59
陕　西	Shaanxi	17241	19466	1512	2189	3046	3094
甘　肃	Gansu	6848	7660	916	813	1220	1326
青　海	Qinghai	2377	2546	593	559	382	416
宁　夏	Ningxia	6043	7019	1104	1204	1048	1129
新　疆	Xinjiang	9460	11289	1722	2086	2017	1816

注：商品房销售面积包括期房。
Note:Sales of Commercial, including Forward House.

附录1-11 各地区房地产开发企业(单位)投资和商品房销售额

REGIONAL REAL ESTATE DEVELOPMENT COMPANY(UNITS) OF INVESTMENT AND COMMERCIAL HOUSING SALES

单位：亿元 (100 million yuan)

地 区	Region	房地产开发投资额 Real Estate Development Investment		商品房销售额 Commercial Housing Sales		#住 宅 #Residential	
		2013	2014	2013	2014	2013	2014
全国总计	**National Total**	**86013.4**	**95035.6**	**81428.3**	**76292.4**	**67694.9**	**62395.6**
北 京	Beijing	3483.4	3715.3	3530.8	2738.7	2434.7	2102.5
天 津	Tianjin	1480.8	1699.6	1615.5	1486.9	1443.3	1294.3
河 北	Hebei	3445.4	4059.7	2779.7	2928.0	2329.1	2501.6
山 西	Shanxi	1308.6	1403.6	728.3	746.1	625.1	639.8
内蒙古	Inner Mongolia	1479.0	1370.9	1177.4	1064.8	874.4	765.0
辽 宁	Liaoning	6450.8	5301.3	4759.2	3092.1	3941.9	2518.9
吉 林	Jilin	1252.4	1030.1	993.0	808.6	839.7	667.6
黑龙江	Heilongjiang	1604.8	1324.1	1582.3	1208.5	1305.9	962.7
上 海	Shanghai	2819.6	3206.5	3911.6	3499.5	3264.0	2923.4
江 苏	Jiangsu	7241.5	8240.2	7913.7	6898.4	6777.7	5969.6
浙 江	Zhejiang	6216.2	7262.4	5396.0	4923.0	4513.9	4172.6
安 徽	Anhui	3946.2	4339.0	3182.9	3345.2	2662.0	2691.8
福 建	Fujian	3703.0	4567.4	4232.1	3763.5	3410.6	2939.6
江 西	Jiangxi	1174.6	1322.5	1647.9	1621.8	1396.1	1379.5
山 东	Shangdong	5444.5	5818.0	5215.1	4879.7	4461.1	4009.5
河 南	Henan	3843.8	4375.7	3074.1	3440.6	2516.3	2739.7
湖 北	**Hubei**	**3286.0**	**3983.8**	**2790.3**	**3088.3**	**2310.0**	**2543.8**
湖 南	Hunan	2628.3	2883.6	2525.6	2299.1	2115.0	1858.6
广 东	Guangdong	6489.6	7638.5	8941.1	8461.8	7476.1	6960.3
广 西	Guangxi	1614.6	1838.5	1375.8	1532.1	1166.7	1274.6
海 南	Hainan	1196.8	1431.7	1032.7	935.2	997.0	873.2
重 庆	Chongqing	3012.8	3630.2	2682.8	2815.0	2283.6	2253.3
四 川	Sichuan	3853.0	4380.1	4020.3	3997.4	3308.6	3145.0
贵 州	Guizhou	1942.5	2187.7	1276.7	1370.3	988.8	1000.0
云 南	Yunnan	2488.3	2846.7	1487.2	1596.4	1192.6	1165.4
西 藏	Tibet	9.7	52.9	10.6	34.3	8.8	28.6
陕 西	Shaanxi	2240.2	2426.5	1608.1	1598.0	1413.2	1368.1
甘 肃	Gansu	724.6	721.5	474.1	602.3	418.1	513.5
青 海	Qinghai	247.6	308.3	158.8	211.3	146.3	155.8
宁 夏	Ningxia	559.0	654.8	443.7	465.0	363.6	352.0
新 疆	Xinjiang	825.7	1014.8	861.0	840.5	710.7	625.3

附录1-12 各地区货物进出口总额
TOTAL IMPORT AND EXPORT REGIONS

(按经营单位所在地分)

(Location of Points by Business Units)

单位：亿美元 (100 million US dollors)

地 区	Region	2008	2009	2010	2011	2012	2013	2014
全国总计	**National Total**	**25632.6**	**22075.4**	**29740.0**	**36418.6**	**38671.2**	**41589.9**	**43030.4**
北 京	Beijing	2716.9	2147.3	3017.2	3895.6	4081.1	4290.0	4156.5
天 津	Tianjin	804.0	638.3	821.0	1033.8	1156.3	1285.0	1339.1
河 北	Hebei	384.2	296.3	420.6	536.0	505.6	549.1	598.8
山 西	Shanxi	144.0	85.7	125.8	147.4	150.4	157.9	162.5
内蒙古	Inner Mongolia	89.2	67.7	87.3	119.3	112.6	119.9	145.5
辽 宁	Liaoning	724.3	629.3	807.1	960.4	1040.9	1144.8	1139.6
吉 林	Jilin	133.3	117.4	168.5	220.6	245.6	258.3	263.8
黑龙江	Heilongjiang	231.3	162.3	255.2	385.2	375.9	388.8	389.0
上 海	Shanghai	3220.6	2777.1	3689.5	4375.5	4365.9	4412.7	4664.1
江 苏	Jiangsu	3922.7	3387.4	4658.0	5395.8	5479.6	5508.0	5637.6
浙 江	Zhejiang	2111.3	1877.3	2535.3	3093.8	3124.0	3357.9	3551.5
安 徽	Anhui	201.8	156.8	242.7	313.1	392.8	455.2	492.7
福 建	Fujian	848.2	796.5	1087.8	1435.2	1559.4	1693.2	1775.0
江 西	Jiangxi	136.2	127.8	216.2	314.7	334.1	367.5	427.8
山 东	Shangdong	1584.1	1390.5	1891.6	2358.9	2455.4	2665.3	2771.2
河 南	Henan	174.8	134.8	178.3	326.2	517.4	599.6	650.3
湖 北	**Hubei**	**207.1**	**172.5**	**259.3**	**335.9**	**319.6**	**363.8**	**430.6**
湖 南	Hunan	125.5	101.5	146.6	189.4	219.5	251.8	310.3
广 东	Guangdong	6849.7	6110.9	7849.0	9134.7	9840.2	10915.8	10767.3
广 西	Guangxi	132.4	142.5	177.4	233.6	294.8	328.3	405.5
海 南	Hainan	45.3	48.8	86.5	127.6	143.2	149.9	158.7
重 庆	Chongqing	95.2	77.1	124.3	292.1	532.0	686.9	954.5
四 川	Sichuan	221.1	241.7	326.9	477.2	591.4	645.7	702.5
贵 州	Guizhou	33.7	23.0	31.5	48.9	66.3	82.9	108.1
云 南	Yunnan	96.0	80.5	134.3	160.3	210.1	253.0	296.2
西 藏	Tibet	7.7	4.0	8.4	13.6	34.2	33.2	22.5
陕 西	Shaanxi	83.3	84.1	121.0	146.5	148.0	201.3	274.1
甘 肃	Gansu	61.0	38.7	74.0	87.3	89.0	102.4	86.5
青 海	Qinghai	6.9	5.9	7.9	9.2	11.6	14.0	17.2
宁 夏	Ningxia	18.8	12.0	19.6	22.9	22.2	32.2	54.4
新 疆	Xinjiang	222.2	139.5	171.3	228.2	251.7	275.6	276.7

附录1-13 各地区货物出口、进口额(2014)

TOTAL IMPORT AND EXPORT REGIONS(2014)

单位：亿美元 (100 million yuan)

地 区	Region	按经营单位所在地分 Location of Points by Business Units	
		出口额 Exports	进口额 Imports
全国总计	**National Total**	**23427.5**	**19602.9**
北 京	Beijing	623.5	3533.1
天 津	Tianjin	526.0	813.2
河 北	Hebei	357.1	241.7
山 西	Shanxi	89.4	73.1
内蒙古	Inner Mongolia	63.9	81.6
辽 宁	Liaoning	587.6	552.0
吉 林	Jilin	57.8	206.0
黑龙江	Heilongjiang	173.4	215.6
上 海	Shanghai	2101.6	2562.5
江 苏	Jiangsu	3418.7	2218.9
浙 江	Zhejiang	2733.5	817.9
安 徽	Anhui	314.9	177.8
福 建	Fujian	1134.6	640.4
江 西	Jiangxi	320.4	107.4
山 东	Shangdong	1447.5	1323.7
河 南	Henan	393.8	256.5
湖 北	**Hubei**	**266.5**	**164.2**
湖 南	Hunan	200.2	110.0
广 东	Guangdong	6462.2	4305.1
广 西	Guangxi	243.3	162.2
海 南	Hainan	44.2	114.6
重 庆	Chongqing	634.1	320.4
四 川	Sichuan	448.5	254.0
贵 州	Guizhou	94.0	14.2
云 南	Yunnan	188.0	108.2
西 藏	Tibet	21.0	1.5
陕 西	Shaanxi	139.3	134.8
甘 肃	Gansu	53.3	33.2
青 海	Qinghai	11.3	5.9
宁 夏	Ningxia	43.0	11.3
新 疆	Xinjiang	234.8	41.9

附录1－14 各地区居民消费价格指数
REGIONAL CONSUMER PRICE INDEX

(上年=100) (Previous Year = 100)

地 区	Region	2008	2009	2010	2011	2012	2013	2014
全 国	**National Total**	**105.9**	**99.3**	**103.3**	**105.4**	**102.6**	**102.6**	**102.0**
北 京	Beijing	105.1	98.5	102.4	105.6	103.3	103.3	101.6
天 津	Tianjin	105.4	99.0	103.5	104.9	102.7	103.1	101.9
河 北	Hebei	106.2	99.3	103.1	105.7	102.6	103.0	101.7
山 西	Shanxi	107.2	99.6	103.0	105.2	102.5	103.1	101.7
内蒙古	Inner Mongolia	105.7	99.7	103.2	105.6	103.1	103.2	101.6
辽 宁	Liaoning	104.6	100.0	103.0	105.2	102.8	102.4	101.7
吉 林	Jilin	105.1	100.1	103.7	105.2	102.5	102.9	102.0
黑龙江	Heilongjiang	105.6	100.2	103.9	105.8	103.2	102.2	101.5
上 海	Shanghai	105.8	99.6	103.1	105.2	102.8	102.3	102.7
江 苏	Jiangsu	105.4	99.6	103.8	105.3	102.6	102.3	102.2
浙 江	Zhejiang	105.0	98.5	103.8	105.4	102.2	102.3	102.1
安 徽	Anhui	106.2	99.1	103.1	105.6	102.3	102.4	101.6
福 建	Fujian	104.6	98.2	103.2	105.3	102.4	102.5	102.0
江 西	Jiangxi	106.0	99.3	103.0	105.2	102.7	102.5	102.3
山 东	Shangdong	105.3	100.0	102.9	105.0	102.1	102.2	101.9
河 南	Henan	107.0	99.4	103.5	105.6	102.5	102.9	101.9
湖 北	**Hubei**	**106.3**	**99.6**	**102.9**	**105.8**	**102.9**	**102.8**	**102.0**
湖 南	Hunan	106.0	99.6	103.1	105.5	102.0	102.5	101.9
广 东	Guangdong	105.6	97.7	103.1	105.3	102.8	102.5	102.3
广 西	Guangxi	107.8	97.9	103.0	105.9	103.2	102.2	102.1
海 南	Hainan	106.9	99.3	104.8	106.1	103.2	102.8	102.4
重 庆	Chongqing	105.6	98.4	103.2	105.3	102.6	102.7	101.8
四 川	Sichuan	105.1	100.8	103.2	105.3	102.5	102.8	101.6
贵 州	Guizhou	107.6	98.7	102.9	105.1	102.7	102.5	102.4
云 南	Yunnan	105.7	100.4	103.7	104.9	102.7	103.1	102.4
西 藏	Tibet	105.7	101.4	102.2	105.0	103.5	103.6	102.9
陕 西	Shaanxi	106.4	100.5	104.0	105.7	102.8	103.0	101.6
甘 肃	Gansu	108.2	101.3	104.1	105.9	102.7	103.2	102.1
青 海	Qinghai	110.1	102.6	105.4	106.1	103.1	103.9	102.8
宁 夏	Ningxia	108.5	100.7	104.1	106.3	102.0	103.4	101.9
新 疆	Xinjiang	108.1	100.7	104.3	105.9	103.8	103.9	102.1

附录1－15　各地区全体居民人均收入与支出

REGIONAL PER CAPITA INCOME AND CONSUMPTION EXPENDITURE OF URBAN AND RURAL HOUSEHOLDS

单位：元 (yuan)

地　区	Region	可支配收入 Disposable Income		消费支出 Expenses on Consumption	
		2013	2014	2013	2014
全国总计	**National Total**	**18310.8**	**20167.1**	**13220.4**	**14491.4**
北　京	Beijing	40830.0	44488.6	29175.6	31102.9
天　津	Tianjin	26359.2	28832.3	20418.7	22343.0
河　北	Hebei	15189.6	16647.4	10872.2	11931.5
山　西	Shanxi	15119.7	16538.3	10118.3	10863.8
内蒙古	Inner Mongolia	18692.9	20559.3	14877.7	16258.1
辽　宁	Liaoning	20817.8	22820.2	14950.2	16068.0
吉　林	Jilin	15998.1	17520.4	12054.3	13026.0
黑龙江	Heilongjiang	15903.4	17404.4	12037.2	12768.8
上　海	Shanghai	42173.6	45965.8	30399.9	33064.8
江　苏	Jiangsu	24775.5	27172.8	17925.8	19163.6
浙　江	Zhejiang	29775.0	32657.6	20610.1	22552.0
安　徽	Anhui	15154.3	16795.5	10544.1	11727.0
福　建	Fujian	21217.9	23330.9	16176.6	17644.5
江　西	Jiangxi	15099.7	16734.2	10052.8	11088.9
山　东	Shangdong	19008.3	20864.2	11896.8	13328.9
河　南	Henan	14203.7	15695.2	10002.5	11000.4
湖　北	**Hubei**	**16472.5**	**18283.2**	**11760.8**	**12928.3**
湖　南	Hunan	16004.9	17621.7	11945.9	13288.7
广　东	Guangdong	23420.7	25685.0	17421.0	19205.5
广　西	Guangxi	14082.3	15557.1	9596.5	10274.3
海　南	Hainan	15733.3	17476.5	11192.9	12470.6
重　庆	Chongqing	16568.7	18351.9	12600.2	13810.6
四　川	Sichuan	14231.0	15749.0	11054.7	12368.4
贵　州	Guizhou	11083.1	12371.1	8288.0	9303.4
云　南	Yunnan	12577.9	13772.2	8823.8	9869.5
西　藏	Tibet	9740.4	10730.2	6306.8	7317.0
陕　西	Shaanxi	14371.5	15836.7	11217.3	12203.6
甘　肃	Gansu	10954.4	12184.7	8943.4	9874.6
青　海	Qinghai	12947.8	14374.0	11576.5	12604.8
宁　夏	Ningxia	14565.8	15906.8	11292.0	12484.5
新　疆	Xinjiang	13669.6	15096.6	11391.8	11903.7

注：本表按当年价格计算。
Note:The table at current prices.

附录1-16 各地区城镇居民人均可支配收入与支出
REGIONAL PER CAPITA INCOME AND CONSUMPTION EXPENDITURE OF URBAN HOUSEHOLDS

单位：元 (yuan)

地 区	Region	可支配收入 Disposable Income		消费支出 Expenses on Consumption	
		2013	2014	2013	2014
全国总计	**National Total**	**26467.0**	**28843.9**	**18487.5**	**19968.1**
北 京	Beijing	44563.9	48531.8	31632.2	33717.5
天 津	Tianjin	28979.8	31506.0	22306.2	24289.6
河 北	Hebei	22226.7	24141.3	14970.0	16203.8
山 西	Shanxi	22258.2	24069.4	13762.7	14636.9
内蒙古	Inner Mongolia	26003.6	28349.6	19244.0	20885.2
辽 宁	Liaoning	26697.0	29081.7	19318.4	20519.6
吉 林	Jilin	21331.1	23217.8	15940.7	17156.1
黑龙江	Heilongjiang	20848.4	22609.0	15704.1	16466.6
上 海	Shanghai	44878.3	48841.4	32447.2	35182.4
江 苏	Jiangsu	31585.5	34346.3	22262.3	23476.3
浙 江	Zhejiang	37079.7	40392.7	25253.5	27241.7
安 徽	Anhui	22789.3	24838.5	14593.6	16107.1
福 建	Fujian	28173.9	30722.4	20564.7	22204.1
江 西	Jiangxi	22119.7	24309.2	13843.0	15141.8
山 东	Shangdong	26882.4	29221.9	16646.5	18322.6
河 南	Henan	21740.7	23672.1	15248.8	16184.5
湖 北	**Hubei**	**22667.9**	**24852.3**	**15334.5**	**16681.4**
湖 南	Hunan	24352.0	26570.2	16867.3	18334.7
广 东	Guangdong	29537.3	32148.1	21621.5	23611.7
广 西	Guangxi	22689.4	24669.0	14470.1	15045.4
海 南	Hainan	22411.4	24486.5	15833.5	17513.8
重 庆	Chongqing	23058.2	25147.2	17123.8	18279.5
四 川	Sichuan	22227.5	24234.4	16098.2	17759.9
贵 州	Guizhou	20564.9	22548.2	13768.2	15254.6
云 南	Yunnan	22460.0	24299.0	14862.3	16268.3
西 藏	Tibet	20394.5	22015.8	13678.6	15669.4
陕 西	Shaanxi	22345.9	24365.8	16398.6	17546.0
甘 肃	Gansu	19873.4	21803.9	14411.3	15942.3
青 海	Qinghai	20352.4	22306.6	16223.4	17492.9
宁 夏	Ningxia	21475.7	23284.6	15806.9	17216.2
新 疆	Xinjiang	21091.5	23214.0	16858.1	17684.5

注：本表按当年价格计算。
Note:The table at current prices.

附录1-17 各地区农村居民人均可支配收入与支出
REGIONAL PER CAPITA INCOME AND CONSUMPTION EXPENDITURE OF RURAL HOUSEHOLDS

单位：元 (yuan)

地 区	Region	可支配收入 Disposable Income		消费支出 Expenses on Consumption	
		2013	2014	2013	2014
全国总计	**National Total**	**9429.6**	**10488.9**	**7485.1**	**8382.6**
北 京	Beijing	17101.2	18867.3	13563.9	14535.1
天 津	Tianjin	15352.6	17014.2	12491.1	13738.6
河 北	Hebei	9187.7	10186.1	7377.1	8248.0
山 西	Shanxi	7949.5	8809.4	6457.7	6991.7
内蒙古	Inner Mongolia	8984.9	9976.3	9079.6	9972.2
辽 宁	Liaoning	10161.2	11191.5	7032.1	7800.7
吉 林	Jilin	9780.7	10780.1	7523.4	8139.8
黑龙江	Heilongjiang	9369.0	10453.2	7191.7	7830.0
上 海	Shanghai	19208.3	21191.6	13016.2	14820.1
江 苏	Jiangsu	13521.3	14958.4	10759.0	11820.3
浙 江	Zhejiang	17493.9	19373.3	12803.3	14497.8
安 徽	Anhui	8850.0	9916.4	7200.3	7980.8
福 建	Fujian	11404.8	12650.2	9986.2	11055.9
江 西	Jiangxi	9088.8	10116.6	6807.4	7548.3
山 东	Shangdong	10686.9	11882.3	6877.3	7962.2
河 南	Henan	8969.1	9966.1	6358.7	7277.2
湖 北	**Hubei**	**9691.8**	**10849.1**	**7849.5**	**8680.9**
湖 南	Hunan	9028.6	10060.2	7832.6	9024.8
广 东	Guangdong	11067.8	12245.6	8937.8	10043.2
广 西	Guangxi	7793.1	8683.2	6035.3	6675.1
海 南	Hainan	8801.7	9912.6	6376.2	7029.0
重 庆	Chongqing	8492.5	9489.8	6970.7	7982.6
四 川	Sichuan	8380.7	9347.7	7364.8	8301.1
贵 州	Guizhou	5897.8	6671.2	5291.1	5970.3
云 南	Yunnan	6723.6	7456.1	5246.6	6030.3
西 藏	Tibet	6553.4	7359.2	4101.6	4822.1
陕 西	Shaanxi	7092.2	7932.2	6487.6	7252.4
甘 肃	Gansu	5588.8	6276.6	5653.9	6147.8
青 海	Qinghai	6461.6	7282.7	7505.9	8235.1
宁 夏	Ningxia	7598.7	8410.0	6739.8	7676.5
新 疆	Xinjiang	7846.6	8723.8	7103.1	7365.3

注：本表按当年价格计算。
Note:The table at current prices.

附录1－18 各地区农林牧渔业总产值及增长速度(2014)
REGIONAL FORESTYR,ANIMAL HUSBANDDRY AND FISHERY OUTPUT VALUE GROWTH RATE(2014)

地区	Region	农林牧渔业总产值(亿元) Forestry, Animal Husbandry Fishery (million)	#农业 #Agriculture	#林业 #Forestry	#牧业 #Livestock	#渔业 #Fishing	农林牧渔业总产值比上年增长(%) Previous Year (%)
全国总计	**National Total**	**102226.1**	**54771.5**	**4256.0**	**28956.3**	**10334.3**	**4.2**
北　京	Beijing	420.1	155.1	90.7	152.7	13.2	
天　津	Tianjin	441.7	230.7	3.2	117.6	79.5	3.0
河　北	Hebei	5994.8	3453.4	108.1	1952.0	191.0	4.0
山　西	Shanxi	1530.5	984.0	98.5	354.6	9.8	4.0
内蒙古	Inner Mongolia	2779.8	1408.4	96.4	1205.7	29.1	3.1
辽　宁	Liaoning	4498.4	1734.1	152.4	1717.5	699.8	2.4
吉　林	Jilin	2763.0	1342.5	104.4	1195.0	40.1	4.1
黑龙江	Heilongjiang	4894.8	3015.6	195.7	1486.1	102.7	5.5
上　海	Shanghai	322.2	169.5	8.8	69.9	62.5	1.0
江　苏	Jiangsu	6443.4	3362.8	118.2	1182.7	1426.7	3.1
浙　江	Zhejiang	2844.6	1386.0	147.0	472.2	779.4	1.0
安　徽	Anhui	4223.7	2119.2	283.1	1182.1	459.7	4.6
福　建	Fujian	3522.3	1529.6	323.3	522.9	1025.2	4.5
江　西	Jiangxi	2726.5	1144.1	274.2	814.9	400.7	4.8
山　东	Shangdong	9198.3	4765.8	131.5	2418.3	1481.7	4.0
河　南	Henan	7549.1	4492.0	152.4	2505.2	105.1	4.2
湖　北	**Hubei**	**5452.8**	**2761.7**	**157.0**	**1427.7**	**844.2**	**5.6**
湖　南	Hunan	5304.8	2884.7	304.8	1503.2	338.9	4.7
广　东	Guangdong	5234.2	2613.2	279.8	1077.4	1080.3	3.0
广　西	Guangxi	3947.7	1994.0	303.2	1087.2	413.1	3.7
海　南	Hainan	1252.2	568.2	103.2	228.0	310.2	4.9
重　庆	Chongqing	1595.0	967.9	53.6	486.4	64.9	4.3
四　川	Sichuan	5888.1	3078.6	196.0	2318.8	192.4	4.0
贵　州	Guizhou	2118.5	1321.9	99.6	569.3	47.0	6.6
云　南	Yunnan	3263.3	1806.3	303.1	975.8	78.1	6.2
西　藏	Tibet	138.7	63.3	2.6	69.3	0.2	4.2
陕　西	Shaanxi	2741.8	1870.8	73.6	648.3	19.9	5.1
甘　肃	Gansu	1618.8	1174.9	25.5	268.4	2.1	5.4
青　海	Qinghai	327.5	144.2	6.6	169.1	2.2	5.4
宁　夏	Ningxia	445.5	274.0	10.0	126.8	14.9	6.1
新　疆	Xinjiang	2744.0	1955.1	49.4	651.2	19.6	6.8

注：本表绝对数按当年价格计算，增长速度按可比价格计算。
Note:In this table are at current prices, growth rates at constant prices.

附录1-19 各地区主要农产品产量(2014)
MAJOR AGRICULTURAL PRODUCTION REGIONS(2014)

单位：万吨 (10 000 tons)

地 区	Region	粮 食 Food	油 料 Oil feed	棉 花 Cotton	糖 料 Sugar	蔬 菜 Vegetables	水 果 Fruit
全国总计	**National Total**	**60702.6**	**3507.4**	**617.8**	**13361.2**	**76005.5**	**26142.2**
北 京	Beijing	63.9	0.7	0.01		236.2	96.5
天 津	Tianjin	176.0	0.5	3.8		460.2	62.7
河 北	Hebei	3360.2	150.2	43.1	75.6	8125.7	2019.0
山 西	Shanxi	1330.8	17.3	2.4	8.0	1271.4	770.8
内蒙古	Inner Mongolia	2753.0	170.3	0.2	160.2	1472.7	322.3
辽 宁	Liaoning	1753.9	63.7		10.1	3090.1	870.6
吉 林	Jilin	3532.8	85.7	0.1	6.4	876.0	229.7
黑龙江	Heilongjiang	6242.2	17.1		41.1	985.6	258.7
上 海	Shanghai	112.5	1.3	0.1	0.6	393.2	86.2
江 苏	Jiangsu	3490.6	146.6	16.0	10.1	5417.0	861.6
浙 江	Zhejiang	757.4	30.7	2.5	62.7	1762.8	714.8
安 徽	Anhui	3415.8	228.8	26.3	19.7	2551.0	965.3
福 建	Fujian	667.0	29.8	0.01	53.1	1801.4	790.8
江 西	Jiangxi	2143.5	121.7	13.4	64.5	1312.4	627.1
山 东	Shangdong	4596.6	335.9	66.5	0.01	9973.7	3134.0
河 南	Henan	5772.3	584.3	14.7	27.3	7272.5	2560.2
湖 北	**Hubei**	**2584.2**	**341.7**	**36.0**	**30.4**	**3671.5**	**972.3**
湖 南	Hunan	3001.3	233.8	12.9	65.9	3763.5	920.0
广 东	Guangdong	1357.3	105.5		1504.7	3274.7	1560.7
广 西	Guangxi	1534.4	61.3	0.3	7952.6	2610.1	1560.6
海 南	Hainan	186.6	11.6		424.9	551.5	413.0
重 庆	Chongqing	1144.5	56.9		10.3	1689.1	347.6
四 川	Sichuan	3374.9	300.8	1.2	55.8	4069.3	884.5
贵 州	Guizhou	1138.5	98.0	0.1	168.3	1625.6	196.4
云 南	Yunnan	1860.7	64.7	0.03	2110.4	1735.5	669.0
西 藏	Tibet	98.0	6.4			68.2	1.4
陕 西	Shaanxi	1197.8	62.3	4.2	0.1	1724.7	1849.9
甘 肃	Gansu	1158.7	72.4	6.4	26.4	1705.2	636.6
青 海	Qinghai	104.8	31.5		0.10	158.6	2.6
宁 夏	Ningxia	377.9	16.5			540.8	290.2
新 疆	Xinjiang	1414.5	59.3	367.7	471.9	1815.4	1466.9

注：水果产量含果用瓜。
Note:Fruit production with fruit with a melon.

附录1−19 续表 continued

单位：万吨 (10 000 tons)

地 区	Region	肉 类 Meat	#猪 肉 #Pork	#牛 肉 #Beef	#羊 肉 #Sheep Meat	奶 类 Dairy
全国总计	**National Total**	**8706.7**	**5671.4**	**689.2**	**428.2**	**3841.2**
北 京	Beijing	39.3	24.0	1.7	1.2	59.5
天 津	Tianjin	46.4	29.9	3.4	1.6	68.9
河 北	Hebei	468.1	281.2	52.4	30.4	496.1
山 西	Shanxi	87.5	64.2	5.8	6.7	97.2
内蒙古	Inner Mongolia	252.3	73.3	54.5	93.3	797.1
辽 宁	Liaoning	429.2	240.3	42.8	8.9	134.5
吉 林	Jilin	262.0	140.4	46.0	4.5	49.8
黑龙江	Heilongjiang	230.2	142.6	40.6	11.9	560.1
上 海	Shanghai	23.4	18.8	0.10	0.5	27.1
江 苏	Jiangsu	379.5	232.4	3.3	8.0	60.7
浙 江	Zhejiang	157.1	127.0	1.2	1.7	15.9
安 徽	Anhui	414.0	264.8	17.9	15.5	27.9
福 建	Fujian	213.7	151.1	2.9	2.2	15.4
江 西	Jiangxi	339.8	259.8	13.1	1.1	12.9
山 东	Shangdong	770.2	406.8	66.6	36.0	289.6
河 南	Henan	719.0	478.0	82.1	25.4	342.4
湖 北	**Hubei**	**440.4**	**339.6**	**21.9**	**8.6**	**16.4**
湖 南	Hunan	546.5	458.1	18.9	11.1	9.3
广 东	Guangdong	429.4	282.6	7.0	0.9	13.8
广 西	Guangxi	420.0	266.3	14.4	3.2	9.7
海 南	Hainan	79.5	48.6	2.6	1.1	0.2
重 庆	Chongqing	214.2	158.5	8.4	3.4	5.7
四 川	Sichuan	714.7	527.2	33.4	25.3	71.3
贵 州	Guizhou	201.8	165.6	14.7	3.8	5.7
云 南	Yunnan	378.5	292.4	33.6	14.6	64.6
西 藏	Tibet	26.4	1.5	16.0	7.9	34.3
陕 西	Shaanxi	116.7	91.8	7.7	7.5	192.3
甘 肃	Gansu	95.5	52.7	18.1	17.9	40.3
青 海	Qinghai	33.4	10.5	10.6	10.9	31.3
宁 夏	Ningxia	28.5	7.7	8.8	9.5	135.7
新 疆	Xinjiang	149.3	33.9	39.2	53.6	155.6

附录1－20 各地区规模以上工业企业主要经济指标(2014)

REGIONAL-SCALE INDUSTRIAL ENTERPRISES MAIN ECONOMIC INDICATORS (2014)

单位：亿元 (100 million yuan)

地 区	Region	主营业务收入 Main Business Income	主营业务成本 Main Business Costs	主营业务税金及附加 Business Tax And Additional	销售费用 Selling expenses	利润总额 Total Profit	税金总额 Total Tax
全国总计	**National Total**	**1094646.5**	**937493.4**	**16894.0**	**27476.8**	**64715.3**	**48401.7**
北 京	Beijing	19439.6	16422.3	303.7	862.3	1493.2	847.7
天 津	Tianjin	28275.9	24405.0	322.2	630.1	2042.8	1125.8
河 北	Hebei	46532.2	40846.9	463.8	784.9	2421.7	1540.8
山 西	Shanxi	17119.9	14820.7	151.2	560.2	210.6	762.8
内蒙古	Inner Mongolia	19064.0	15615.7	265.2	440.7	1294.4	967.8
辽 宁	Liaoning	49686.1	43541.6	898.0	1052.3	2011.7	2058.7
吉 林	Jilin	23220.0	19352.5	537.1	884.7	1397.7	1165.4
黑龙江	Heilongjiang	13086.0	10485.5	601.6	306.7	985.0	1144.2
上 海	Shanghai	34725.0	28507.8	965.1	1277.4	2646.5	1856.3
江 苏	Jiangsu	142387.9	123159.7	1242.9	3280.5	8839.7	5789.5
浙 江	Zhejiang	63237.0	54099.3	721.1	1601.8	3543.7	2425.2
安 徽	Anhui	36653.6	31968.3	474.9	870.0	1775.2	1394.4
福 建	Fujian	36300.1	31424.0	417.1	914.1	2081.7	1395.0
江 西	Jiangxi	30597.1	26866.2	318.6	505.7	2043.9	1314.8
山 东	Shangdong	143488.1	125581.8	1573.1	2647.5	8763.4	5499.7
河 南	Henan	66787.5	58022.7	677.5	1217.9	4771.4	2180.4
湖 北	**Hubei**	**40708.0**	**34531.1**	**801.9**	**1251.2**	**2174.6**	**1811.8**
湖 南	Hunan	33303.2	27987.8	903.5	904.8	1523.2	2066.1
广 东	Guangdong	113827.8	96949.1	1199.3	3899.3	6611.9	3991.2
广 西	Guangxi	18455.1	15886.6	346.3	437.2	963.8	911.1
海 南	Hainan	1742.3	1436.1	76.2	61.0	88.5	135.0
重 庆	Chongqing	18057.1	15361.3	262.8	509.0	1160.5	937.6
四 川	Sichuan	37559.7	31674.6	614.2	1073.6	2046.3	1851.0
贵 州	Guizhou	8108.0	6432.6	313.6	265.8	530.5	658.3
云 南	Yunnan	10041.6	7823.9	830.6	259.5	478.9	1283.4
西 藏	Tibet	113.5	86.2	1.7	8.4	12.4	11.7
陕 西	Shaanxi	18313.6	14313.1	721.0	471.0	1706.5	1600.9
甘 肃	Gansu	9092.6	7983.7	310.2	138.5	233.2	543.8
青 海	Qinghai	2249.8	1848.1	61.0	77.0	98.9	144.6
宁 夏	Ningxia	3468.9	2985.1	72.3	67.6	102.5	163.5
新 疆	Xinjiang	9005.0	7074.1	446.4	216.0	661.2	823.2

注：本表为2014年1－11月快报数据(下表同)。
Note:This table is from January to November 2014, Express Data (the same).

附录1-20　续表 continued

单位：亿元 (100 million yuan)

地　区	Region	亏损企业亏损总额 Total Loss of Enterprises Running under Deficit	应收账款 Account Received	存货 Inventory	产成品 Finished Products	资产总计 Total Assets	负债合计 Total Liability
全国总计	**National Total**	**6917.8**	**105168.0**	**99565.7**	**37109.6**	**925244.9**	**525865.5**
北　京	Beijing	138.4	3574.6	2199.3	750.8	33018.7	16737.8
天　津	Tianjin	193.7	3213.8	2912.8	958.9	23246.3	14411.5
河　北	Hebei	390.8	3073.8	3907.0	1426.8	39177.3	22683.5
山　西	Shanxi	471.7	2234.4	1991.6	792.5	29184.9	21192.5
内蒙古	Inner Mongolia	346.7	1741.2	1585.9	635.7	25751.5	15839.7
辽　宁	Liaoning	409.4	3577.5	4096.1	1429.7	38035.9	21674.1
吉　林	Jilin	179.0	1249.0	1824.6	605.2	16453.7	8876.3
黑龙江	Heilongjiang	238.4	1227.1	1561.4	508.6	14449.7	8181.1
上　海	Shanghai	284.1	5901.3	4423.3	1436.9	34349.7	16951.5
江　苏	Jiangsu	584.2	16325.1	11734.0	4412.1	100150.4	54997.3
浙　江	Zhejiang	282.8	9577.3	8030.7	3294.1	63198.6	37188.7
安　徽	Anhui	212.2	3492.4	3005.0	1191.8	28283.3	16590.5
福　建	Fujian	150.6	3543.1	3439.2	1370.0	27435.1	14953.8
江　西	Jiangxi	44.1	1485.4	1630.1	671.1	15535.7	8042.0
山　东	Shangdong	344.6	7615.8	9897.4	3987.0	91367.5	49660.9
河　南	Henan	257.2	4262.4	3798.1	1339.1	48528.8	22716.7
湖　北	**Hubei**	**161.8**	**3280.2**	**3696.6**	**1521.4**	**31490.4**	**17109.7**
湖　南	Hunan	112.8	2525.4	2474.3	847.0	20843.5	11049.9
广　东	Guangdong	449.8	15118.8	11765.8	4348.8	86745.5	50131.7
广　西	Guangxi	152.6	1277.4	1726.1	721.4	13915.5	8696.6
海　南	Hainan	23.5	154.3	236.5	103.8	2423.0	1257.8
重　庆	Chongqing	96.6	1765.2	1394.4	550.7	14563.1	9033.0
四　川	Sichuan	404.6	3514.1	3480.8	1240.0	36172.9	21797.5
贵　州	Guizhou	139.0	713.5	996.6	290.7	11041.6	7013.3
云　南	Yunnan	218.3	806.4	2145.7	544.9	16595.5	10697.6
西　藏	Tibet	12.2	17.0	22.4	7.8	656.9	258.4
陕　西	Shaanxi	136.7	1690.4	1826.5	762.4	23897.3	13334.7
甘　肃	Gansu	119.5	670.3	1522.7	467.2	10730.6	6759.7
青　海	Qinghai	68.7	230.9	315.6	117.4	5300.9	3585.1
宁　夏	Ningxia	62.1	409.4	711.4	281.2	6769.1	4493.1
新　疆	Xinjiang	231.8	900.4	1213.7	494.7	15932.0	9949.5

附录1-21 各地区主要工业产品产量(2014)
MAJOR INDUSTRIAL PRODUCTS BY REGION(2014)

地 区	Region	原油(万吨) Crude Oil (10 000 tons)	天然气(万立方米 Natural gas (10 000 cu.m)	布(亿米) Cloth (100 million meters)	农用化肥(万吨) Agricultural Fertilizers (10 000 Tons)	水泥(万吨) Cement (10 000 tons)	生铁(万吨) Pig Iron (10 000 tons)	粗钢(万吨) Crude steel (10 000 tons)
全国总计	**National Total**	**21142.9**	**1301.6**	**893.7**	**6887.2**	**247613.5**	**71159.9**	**82269.8**
北 京	Beijing		12.8			703.6		2.1
天 津	Tianjin	3074.8	21.2	2.3	16.0	957.9	2182.5	2287.1
河 北	Hebei	592.3	17.5	66.1	203.1	10677.4	16932.6	18530.3
山 西	Shanxi		31.6	0.8	424.4	4700.0	4052.0	4325.4
内蒙古	Inner Mongolia	21.5	15.5		126.1	6294.0	1330.7	1661.5
辽 宁	Liaoning	1021.9	8.1	6.7	71.9	5807.6	6167.7	6511.4
吉 林	Jilin	663.9	22.3	0.4	17.9	3702.7	1132.8	1264.8
黑龙江	Heilongjiang	4000.0	35.4	0.1	48.4	3702.6	456.7	476.3
上 海	Shanghai	5.7	2.1	1.4	1.5	686.0	1643.3	1774.5
江 苏	Jiangsu	206.0	0.5	141.6	234.8	19395.8	7080.1	10195.5
浙 江	Zhejiang			250.7	35.7	12390.0	1140.3	1748.3
安 徽	Anhui			12.7	299.7	12921.0	1998.6	2451.4
福 建	Fujian			74.3	48.9	7760.9	907.7	1820.8
江 西	Jiangxi		0.4	9.9	135.8	9831.2	2075.3	2235.3
山 东	Shangdong	2713.2	4.9	128.1	555.0	16496.3	6719.1	6411.0
河 南	Henan	470.5	4.9	32.3	491.7	17080.7	2779.6	2882.2
湖 北	**Hubei**	**79.0**	**1.5**	**84.0**	**1206.0**	**11418.1**	**2437.6**	**3056.4**
湖 南	Hunan			3.9	113.6	12060.1	1780.7	1917.6
广 东	Guangdong	1245.4	83.7	43.6	58.4	14783.4	1082.4	1710.4
广 西	Guangxi	58.7	0.2	0.5	111.5	10706.5	1231.7	2084.3
海 南	Hainan	28.5	1.6		66.3	2151.6		22.4
重 庆	Chongqing		7.8	6.9	215.2	6688.8	444.6	785.6
四 川	Sichuan	19.2	253.5	20.3	453.6	14612.7	1931.4	2243.0
贵 州	Guizhou		0.4		529.2	9456.4	498.6	551.6
云 南	Yunnan				318.4	9596.9	1704.9	1689.1
西 藏	Tibet					342.2		
陕 西	Shaanxi	3767.8	410.1	6.7	179.2	9129.7	884.0	1038.3
甘 肃	Gansu	71.2	0.2		50.2	4931.5	898.8	1074.0
青 海	Qinghai	220.0	68.9		504.9	1859.6	127.0	144.3
宁 夏	Ningxia	7.9			46.5	1793.9	201.7	161.5
新 疆	Xinjiang	2875.3	296.7	0.6	323.6	4974.6	1337.5	1213.4

附录1−21 续表 continued

地 区	Region	钢材(万吨) Steel (10 000 tons)	汽车(万辆) Car (10 000)	家用电冰箱(万台) Household Refrigerators (10 000 units)	程控交换机(万线) PBX (10 000 lines)	移动通信手持机(万台) Mobile Handset (10 000 units)	微型计算机设备(万台) Micro-computer Equipment (10 000 units)	发电量(亿千瓦小时) generation (Billion kilowatt hours)
全国总计	**National Total**	**112557.2**	**2372.5**	**8796.1**	**3123.1**	**162719.8**	**35079.6**	**56495.8**
北 京	Beijing	195.0	206.3		973.0	17983.6	1015.6	364.0
天 津	Tianjin	7303.9	51.2	45.4		9754.2	1100.5	625.5
河 北	Hebei	23995.2	97.8		13.6			2499.9
山 西	Shanxi	4701.0				2255.4		2647.0
内蒙古	Inner Mongolia	1763.2	2.4					3857.8
辽 宁	Liaoning	6946.0	112.1	157.0	62.7	2895.0	0.2	1647.8
吉 林	Jilin	1412.2	237.4					771.7
黑龙江	Heilongjiang	483.5	10.8				3.5	881.3
上 海	Shanghai	2309.1	247.4	154.0	215.8	5484.8	6295.4	792.3
江 苏	Jiangsu	13255.2	121.6	969.7	1.9	2884.1	6708.0	4347.6
浙 江	Zhejiang	4171.0	30.9	757.8	179.4	3611.3	191.0	2885.3
安 徽	Anhui	3265.7	93.4	2765.8			1715.9	2033.9
福 建	Fujian	3019.6	18.1			1278.0	985.4	1873.4
江 西	Jiangxi	2611.1	46.2	109.5		5540.5		873.3
山 东	Shangdong	8939.4	103.0	610.1	10.9	6590.8	23.3	3691.1
河 南	Henan	4704.1	40.9	320.9		12065.2		2729.9
湖 北	**Hubei**	**3429.0**	**174.5**	**243.5**	**51.9**	**2888.4**	**120.7**	**2382.3**
湖 南	Hunan	1989.3	29.5	12.2	2.8	60.9	34.2	1313.7
广 东	Guangdong	3447.1	216.8	2139.9	1605.8	79562.8	2819.5	3948.4
广 西	Guangxi	3262.6	209.2				0.6	1310.0
海 南	Hainan	29.7	9.0					244.6
重 庆	Chongqing	1322.0	231.4	262.0		9418.2	6446.8	675.8
四 川	Sichuan	2935.2	32.4	80.2		411.0	7619.0	3079.4
贵 州	Guizhou	552.4		168.2		6.5		1747.7
云 南	Yunnan	1935.1	11.0		5.3			2550.0
西 藏	Tibet	1.1						32.3
陕 西	Shaanxi	1683.9	37.5			29.1		1620.8
甘 肃	Gansu	1108.1	0.7					1241.1
青 海	Qinghai	131.4						580.3
宁 夏	Ningxia	165.6						1156.6
新 疆	Xinjiang	1489.5	1.1					2090.9

附录1－22　各地区电力消费量

REGIONAL ELECTRICITY CONSUMPTION

单位：亿千瓦时　　(10 000 KW/h)

地　区	Region	2008	2009	2010	2011	2012	2013
北　京	Beijing	689.7	739.1	809.9	821.7	874.3	913.1
天　津	Tianjin	515.9	550.2	645.7	695.2	722.5	774.5
河　北	Hebei	2095.0	2343.8	2691.5	2984.9	3077.7	3251.2
山　西	Shanxi	1314.3	1267.5	1460.0	1650.4	1765.8	1832.3
内蒙古	Inner Mongolia	1220.6	1287.9	1536.8	1864.1	2016.8	2181.9
辽　宁	Liaoning	1412.0	1488.2	1715.3	1861.5	1899.9	2008.5
吉　林	Jilin	496.5	515.3	577.0	630.2	637.0	653.8
黑龙江	Heilongjiang	669.9	688.7	747.8	801.9	827.9	845.2
上　海	Shanghai	1138.2	1153.4	1295.9	1339.6	1353.4	1410.6
江　苏	Jiangsu	3118.3	3314.0	3864.4	4281.6	4580.9	4956.6
浙　江	Zhejiang	2322.9	2471.4	2820.9	3116.9	3210.6	3453.1
安　徽	Anhui	858.9	952.3	1077.9	1221.2	1361.1	1528.1
福　建	Fujian	1073.5	1134.9	1315.1	1515.9	1579.5	1700.7
江　西	Jiangxi	545.9	609.2	700.5	835.1	867.7	947.1
山　东	Shangdong	2727.0	2941.1	3298.5	3635.3	3794.6	4083.1
河　南	Henan	1970.8	2081.4	2354.0	2659.1	2747.7	2899.2
湖　北	**Hubei**	**1058.5**	**1135.1**	**1330.4**	**1450.8**	**1507.9**	**1629.8**
湖　南	Hunan	905.0	1010.6	1171.9	1293.4	1346.5	1423.1
广　东	Guangdong	3504.8	3609.6	4060.1	4399.0	4619.4	4830.1
广　西	Guangxi	753.4	856.4	993.2	1112.2	1153.9	1237.7
海　南	Hainan	121.7	133.8	159.0	185.3	210.3	232.0
重　庆	Chongqing	484.4	533.8	626.4	717.0	723.5	813.3
四　川	Sichuan	1210.1	1324.6	1549.0	1751.4	1830.7	1949.0
贵　州	Guizhou	679.2	750.3	835.4	944.1	1046.7	1126.3
云　南	Yunnan	829.4	891.2	1004.1	1204.1	1315.9	1459.8
西　藏	Tibet	16.0	17.7	20.4	23.8	27.8	30.7
陕　西	Shaanxi	708.0	740.1	859.2	982.5	1066.7	1152.2
甘　肃	Gansu	677.8	705.5	804.4	923.4	994.6	1073.2
青　海	Qinghai	313.2	337.2	465.2	560.7	602.2	676.3
宁　夏	Ningxia	439.6	463.0	546.8	724.5	741.8	811.2
新　疆	Xinjiang	479.4	547.9	662.0	839.1	1151.5	1539.8

附录1-23 各地区社会消费品零售总额
REGIONAL TOTAL RETAIL SALES OF CONSUMER GOODS

单位：亿元 (100 million yuan)

地 区	Region	2008	2009	2010	2011	2012	2013	2014
全国总计	**National Total**	**114830.1**	**132678.4**	**156998.4**	**183918.6**	**210307.0**	**242842.8**	**271896.1**
北 京	Beijing	4645.5	5309.9	6229.3	6900.3	7702.8	8872.1	9638.0
天 津	Tianjin	2078.7	2430.8	2860.2	3395.1	3921.4	4470.4	4738.7
河 北	Hebei	4991.1	5764.9	6821.8	8035.5	9254.0	10516.7	11820.5
山 西	Shanxi	2421.1	2809.0	3318.2	3903.4	4506.8	5139.3	5717.9
内蒙古	Inner Mongolia	2463.0	2855.3	3384.0	3991.7	4572.5	5114.2	5657.6
辽 宁	Liaoning	5032.4	5812.6	6887.6	8095.3	9304.2	10581.4	11857.0
吉 林	Jilin	2549.2	2957.3	3504.9	4119.8	4772.9	5426.4	6080.9
黑龙江	Heilongjiang	2928.3	3401.8	4039.2	4750.1	5491.0	6251.2	7015.3
上 海	Shanghai	4577.2	5173.2	6070.5	6814.8	7412.3	8557.0	9303.5
江 苏	Jiangsu	9905.1	11484.1	13606.8	15988.4	18331.3	20878.2	23458.1
浙 江	Zhejiang	7533.3	8622.3	10245.4	12028.0	13588.3	15970.8	17835.3
安 徽	Anhui	3045.2	3527.8	4197.7	4955.1	5736.6	7044.7	7957.0
福 建	Fujian	3866.7	4481.0	5310.0	6276.2	7256.5	8275.3	9346.7
江 西	Jiangxi	2142.0	2484.4	2956.2	3485.1	4027.2	4696.1	5292.6
山 东	Shangdong	10658.8	12363.0	14620.3	17155.5	19651.9	22294.8	25111.5
河 南	Henan	5815.4	6746.4	8004.2	9453.6	10915.6	12426.6	14005.0
湖 北	**Hubei**	**5109.7**	**5928.4**	**7013.9**	**8275.2**	**9562.5**	**11035.9**	**12449.3**
湖 南	Hunan	4222.6	4913.7	5839.5	6884.7	7921.9	9509.5	10723.5
广 东	Guangdong	12986.6	14891.8	17458.4	20297.5	22677.1	25453.9	28471.1
广 西	Guangxi	2395.8	2790.7	3312.0	3908.2	4516.6	5133.1	5772.8
海 南	Hainan	463.2	537.5	639.3	759.5	870.8	1090.9	1224.5
重 庆	Chongqing	2147.1	2479.0	2938.6	3487.8	4033.7	5055.8	5710.7
四 川	Sichuan	4944.8	5758.7	6810.1	8044.6	9268.6	11001.0	12393.0
贵 州	Guizhou	1075.2	1247.3	1482.7	1751.6	2075.9	2601.2	2936.9
云 南	Yunnan	1764.7	2051.1	2542.4	3000.1	3511.6	4112.6	4632.9
西 藏	Tibet	130.0	156.6	185.3	219.0	254.6	322.2	364.5
陕 西	Shaanxi	2317.1	2699.7	3195.7	3790.0	4383.8	5245.0	5918.7
甘 肃	Gansu	1023.6	1183.0	1394.5	1648.0	1906.5	2368.8	2668.3
青 海	Qinghai	259.7	300.5	350.8	410.5	476.0	549.6	620.8
宁 夏	Ningxia	295.4	339.3	403.6	477.6	542.9	668.5	737.2
新 疆	Xinjiang	1041.5	1177.5	1375.1	1616.3	1858.6	2179.5	2436.5

附录1−24　各地区客运量和旅客周转量(2014年)
REGIONAL PASSENGER TRAFFIC AND TURNOVER VOLUME OF PASSENGER TRAFFIC（2014）

地　区	Region	客运量（万人）Passenger Traffic (10 000 Persons)	#铁路 Railway	#公路 Highway	#水运 Waterway	旅客周转量（亿人公里）Turnover Volume of Passenger Traffic (100 million person-kms)	#铁路 Railway	#公路 Highway	#水运 Waterway
全国总计	**National Total**	**2209361**	**235704**	**1908198**	**26293**	**30096**	**11605**	**12084**	**74**
北　京	Beijing	65063	12709	52354		274.0	135.6	138.3	
天　津	Tianjin	18300	3687	14530	83	247.0	158.1	88.5	0.1
河　北	Hebei	60726	9571	51151	4	1277.0	985.9	290.5	0.3
山　西	Shanxi	34168	6949	27091	128	385.0	202.4	182.0	0.1
内蒙古	Inner Mongolia	18283	4789	13494		363.0	201.7	161.4	
辽　宁	Liaoning	94172	12841	80789	542	991.0	609.1	375.6	6.5
吉　林	Jilin	35004	6935	27866	203	424.0	251.0	173.3	0.2
黑龙江	Heilongjiang	46841	10096	36379	366	493.0	261.4	231.2	0.4
上　海	Shanghai	13317	9194	3754	369	210.0	84.5	124.3	1.1
江　苏	Jiangsu	155207	15374	137270	2563	1455.0	600.2	852.0	3.0
浙　江	Zhejiang	130144	13648	112915	3581	1077.0	513.1	558.1	5.6
安　徽	Anhui	139553	7972	131403	178	1417.0	617.6	799.4	0.3
福　建	Fujian	58719	8345	48580	1794	623.0	284.9	334.9	2.9
江　西	Jiangxi	67795	7840	59674	281	971.0	654.5	316.5	0.4
山　东	Shangdong	74378	10304	62052	2022	1144.0	620.4	511.4	11.8
河　南	Henan	140180	11647	128279	254	1746.0	900.6	844.9	0.5
湖　北	**Hubei**	**100730**	**12379**	**87803**	**548**	**1209.0**	**722.2**	**483.9**	**2.9**
湖　南	Hunan	161838	9806	150583	1449	1661.0	881.4	776.5	2.8
广　东	Guangdong	180789	20942	157234	2613	2315.0	674.9	1629.8	10.7
广　西	Guangxi	51905	4770	46623	512	653.0	237.0	413.2	2.5
海　南	Hainan	14209	1543	11042	1624	120.0	28.1	89.1	3.3
重　庆	Chongqing	68399	4057	63630	712	507.0	147.0	352.6	7.6
四　川	Sichuan	138274	8905	126691	2678	955.0	322.0	630.0	2.7
贵　州	Guizhou	86571	4409	80231	1931	635.0	217.4	412.9	5.2
云　南	Yunnan	49080	3479	44502	1099	437.0	113.9	321.1	2.4
西　藏	Tibet	1571	163	1408		45.0	12.3	32.8	
陕　西	Shaanxi	74188	7077	66720	391	804.0	464.7	339.0	0.7
甘　肃	Gansu	38985	2672	36224	89	607.0	377.9	229.0	0.2
青　海	Qinghai	5444	615	4769	60	103.0	56.3	46.5	0.1
宁　夏	Ningxia	9187	657	8311	219	114.0	48.5	65.7	0.1
新　疆	Xinjiang	37176	2329	34847		500.0	220.2	279.8	
不分地区		39166				6333.0			

注：不分地区合计为民航完成数。
Note: The total passenyer traffil not classified by region lefers to thut completed by civil aviation

附录1—25 各地区货运量和货物周转量（2014）
REGIONAL FREIGHT TRAFFIC AND TURNOVER VOLUME OF FREIGHT TRAFFIC（2014）

地区	Region	货运量（万吨）Freight Traffic (10 000 Persons)	#铁路 Railway	#公路 Highway	#水运 Waterway	货物周转量（亿吨公里）Turnover Volume of Freight Traffic (100 million person-kms)	#铁路 Railway	#公路 Highway	#水运 Waterway
全国总计	**National Total**	**4381089**	**381334**	**3332838**	**598283**	**185398.0**	**27530.2**	**61016.6**	**92774.6**
北京	Beijing	26551	1135	25416		1037.0	871.5	165.2	
天津	Tianjin	49753	8874	31130	9749	3602.0	519.3	349.0	2734.0
河北	Hebei	209946	20619	185286	4041	12684.0	4183.1	7019.6	1481.8
山西	Shanxi	164919	76411	88491	17	3711.0	2347.6	1363.2	
内蒙古	Inner Mongolia	191869	65165	126704		4471.0	2367.6	2103.5	
辽宁	Liaoning	222138	19154	189174	13810	12236.0	1181.3	3074.9	7979.5
吉林	Jilin	48311	6074	41830	407	1704.0	511.7	1190.8	1.4
黑龙江	Heilongjiang	60212	11777	47173	1262	1811.0	794.7	1008.5	7.9
上海	Shanghai	89980	549	42848	46583	18633.0	12.4	300.8	18320.1
江苏	Jiangsu	196153	6376	114449	75328	10418.0	352.3	1978.5	8087.1
浙江	Zhejiang	194250	4343	117070	72837	9540.0	223.1	1419.4	7897.2
安徽	Anhui	434298	10488	315223	108587	13501.0	810.0	7392.4	5298.2
福建	Fujian	111757	3402	82573	25782	4780.0	149.7	974.8	3655.7
江西	Jiangxi	151878	4934	137782	9162	3828.0	539.3	3073.3	215.4
山东	Shangdong	264458	20268	230018	14172	8253.0	1314.2	5711.4	1227.4
河南	Henan	200801	11770	179680	9351	7401.0	1963.2	4822.4	615.6
湖北	**Hubei**	**150762**	**4689**	**116279**	**29794**	**5504.0**	**846.8**	**2340.6**	**2316.2**
湖南	Hunan	203053	4753	172613	25687	4138.0	849.5	2578.9	709.9
广东	Guangdong	343491	9136	257136	77219	14801.0	279.4	3113.8	11407.8
广西	Guangxi	163023	6684	134330	22009	4090.0	770.4	2068.5	1250.7
海南	Hainan	23632	854	11015	11763	1488.0	12.4	81.5	1394.2
重庆	Chongqing	97377	2054	81206	14117	2595.0	165.8	797.8	1631.3
四川	Sichuan	159034	8541	142132	8361	2465.0	800.4	1510.5	154.2
贵州	Guizhou	85672	6317	78017	1338	1442.0	633.9	776.9	30.9
云南	Yunnan	108544	4823	103161	560	1446.0	430.1	1002.3	13.1
西藏	Tibet	1914	43	1871		110.0	24.4	86.0	
陕西	Shaanxi	157012	37483	119343	186	3521.0	1603.4	1917.5	0.6
甘肃	Gansu	57239	6448	50781	10	2515.0	1522.9	992.6	
青海	Qinghai	14638	3608	11030		507.0	272.6	234.4	
宁夏	Ningxia	41308	6990	34318		837.0	306.4	530.5	
新疆	Xinjiang	72168	7410	64758		1881.0	843.6	1037.3	
不分地区		84946	162		16150	20447.0	27.2		16344.1

注：不分地区合计中包括铁路行包运输、管道运输企业、民航运输企业及中远集团海外公司完成数。

Note: The freight ton-kilometers ont classified by iegion refers to raihuay baggaye freight,civil aviation,pipelines and that completed bycommpanies abroad under the China Ocan shipping(Gronp)company.

中国统计出版社最新图书简目

（仅供参考，以实际出版为准）

统计资料

中国统计年鉴　中国统计摘要　中国发展报告
中国经济普查年鉴2013　国际统计年鉴　金砖国家联合统计手册
中国-东盟国家统计手册　中国区域经济统计年鉴　中国县域统计年鉴
中国城市统计年鉴　中国农村统计年鉴　中国地区经济监测报告
中国贸易外经统计年鉴　中国对外直接投资统计公报　中国商品交易市场统计年鉴
大中型批发零售和住宿餐饮企业统计年鉴　中国零售和餐饮连锁企业统计年鉴　中国住户调查年鉴
中国价格统计年鉴　中国农产品价格调查年鉴　全国农产品成本收益资料汇编
中国环境统计年鉴　中国能源统计年鉴　国外资源、能源和环境统计资料汇编
中国工业统计年鉴　中国建筑业统计年鉴　中国房地产统计年鉴
中国城市建设统计年鉴　中国城乡建设统计年鉴　中国第三产业统计年鉴
中国证券期货统计年鉴　中国科技统计年鉴　中国高技术产业统计年鉴
工业企业科技活动资料　中国劳动统计年鉴　中国人口和就业统计年鉴
中国人才资源统计报告　中国社会统计年鉴　中国文化及相关产业统计年鉴
文化及相关产业统计概览　中国教育经费统计年鉴　中国民政统计年鉴
中国民族统计年鉴　中国工会统计年鉴　中国残疾人事业统计年鉴
中国妇女儿童状况统计资料（英）　中国乡镇街道行政区域简册

省级综合统计年鉴系列

北京 天津 河北 山西 内蒙古 辽宁 吉林 黑龙江 上海 江苏 浙江 安徽 福建 江西 山东 河南 湖北 湖南 广东 广西 海南 重庆 四川 贵州 云南 西藏 陕西 甘肃 青海 宁夏 新疆 新疆生产建设兵团

市(县)级综合统计年鉴系列

天津滨海新区 石家庄 唐山 邯郸 保定 沧州 邢台 廊坊 承德 衡水 秦皇岛 张家口 太原 大同 阳泉 长治 晋城 朔州 晋中 运城 忻州 临汾 呼和浩特 呼和浩特新城区 鄂尔多斯 包头 沈阳 大连 长春 四平 哈尔滨 齐齐哈尔 黑龙江垦区 上海浦东新区 南京 无锡 徐州 常州 苏州 南通 连云港 淮安 盐城 扬州 镇江 泰州 宿迁 江阴 丹阳 杭州 宁波 温州 嘉兴 绍兴 金华 衢州 舟山 台州 丽水 合肥 安庆 马鞍山 福州 厦门 宁德 南昌 九江 上饶 新余 抚州 济南 青岛 枣庄 滕州 郑州 洛阳 平顶山 三门峡 南阳 商丘 济源 武汉 十堰 荆州 宜昌 荆门 咸宁 长沙 广州 深圳 惠州 东莞 南宁 柳州 桂林 来宾 海口 三亚 成都 贵阳 昆明 西安 兰州 庆阳 银川 乌鲁木齐 兵团一师 兵团十师

调查年鉴系列

天津 山西 内蒙古 辽宁 吉林 上海 福建 河南 湖北 湖南 广西 重庆 四川 云南 甘肃 宁夏 新疆

“十二五”规划教材

统计学（经济管理类专业本科适用，单薇 等）　抽样调查理论与方法（冯士雍 等）
贝叶斯统计（茆诗松 等）　统计学（黄良文 等）　试验设计（茆诗松 等）
统计学：从数据到结论（吴喜之）　医学统计学（于浩）　统计学（经济、管理类专业基础教材，张小斐）
概率论与数理统计三十三讲（魏振军）　概率论与数理统计三十三：学习指导与习题解答（魏振军）
非参数统计（吴喜之 等）　统计学：经济与管理中的数据分析（李慧云 等）
卫生管理统计学（新编医学院校基础课教材，尚磊）　医院统计学（新编医学院校基础课教材，徐天和 等）
社会统计学（蒋萍 等）　现代金融投资统计分析（李腊生 等）
国民经济核算初级教程（经济类、统计类、管理类专业适用，蒋萍 等）

重点图书

图解中国经济2015　新编英汉汉英统计大词典　中华医学统计百科全书
挑大学选专业2016—考研择校指南　挑大学选专业2015—高考志愿填报指南